In the Name of the Lord

~~~

M. Jamal Haider

Kitab Bhavan
New Delhi – 1100 02 (INDIA)
~~~

Kitab Bhavan

Publishers, Distributors, Exporters & Importers
1784, Kalan Mahal, Darya Ganj
New Delhi – 1100 02 (India)

Phones : (91-11) 23277392/93, 23274686, 32906494
Fax : (91-11) 23263383

Website: www.nusratalinasri.com

Email : nasri@vsnl.com
nusrat@bol.net.in

The Andalusian poems in the chapter 'Verdant Verses' is from the site: http://www.islamicspain.tv/Arts-and-Science/andalusi_poetry.htm It has been reproduced by permission of **Unity Productions Foundation,** *P.O. Box 650458, Potomac Falls, VA 20165-0458, USA.*
The poems 'Quietness' and 'The Gift of Water' are from 'The Essential Rumi', translations by Coleman Barks with John Moyne. This material was reproduced by permission of Coleman Barks, Maypop Books, 196 Westview Drive, Athens, GA 3060, USA.
The poem 'O Lord' by Rabia Basri is from 'Perfume of the Desert', translated by Andrew Harvey and Eryk Hanut. This material was reproduced by permission of Quest Books, the imprint of The Theosophical Publishing House (www.questbooks.net).

First Published : 2014

ISBN : 81-7151-396-4

Book code No. 100360

Printed and Published in India by
Nusrat Ali Nasri for KITAB BHAVAN
1784, Kalan Mahal, Darya Ganj,

~~~

This is the path of knowledge
It is a realisation

~~~

Table of Content

Prologue

There is a direct correlation between knowledge and civilisation. In fact, civilisation can be defined, from one and probably the most important perspective, as the research, development, accumulation and application of knowledge.

Through the ages, civilisations have risen, applied themselves in changing the world, and fallen when they have strayed from the path of correct knowledge. They have left their accumulated knowledge to subsequent civilisations, which became more adept and more advanced than the previous ones and which further developed and added to the existing storehouse of knowledge. Thus, in today's civilisation, the bank of knowledge is the sum total of all that has been developed and contributed by geographically diverse people of various civilisations at different historical times starting from the very origin of humanity.

One of the chief contributors to this bank of knowledge was the people of the Islamic Civilisation. For a thousand years, before the rise of the West, the Muslims were the torchbearers of world knowledge. They ruled the most extensive and most progressive empires of their times and advanced knowledge in all its forms. Science, commerce, philosophy and arts, all flourished in their domain. But a few centuries ago this society disintegrated and degenerated due to a lack of vision among the ruling elite and was replaced by the Western Civilisation as the vanguard of knowledgeable societies. The contributions of the Islamic Civilisation were gradually erased from historical memory.

The last few centuries have seen rationalism reach incredible heights. All fields of knowledge have made phenomenal progress, with economy being the driving philosophy behind all political affairs. But exploitation has not been eradicated and that has bred restless greed on one side and reckless hatred on the other. It remains the root cause of wars, famine, fundamentalism, riots, ethnic cleansing, discrimination and all such evils that still pervade the planet.

In such a global environment Muslims, fallen from the heights of civilisation over the centuries, occupy a regressed position. Though endowed with natural and human resources, large portions of the Muslim populace are under-educated and under-privileged living a ritualistic dogmatic life and thus victims of vagaries – confounded, humiliated or coerced. The dawn of the 21st century has witnessed a troubled awakening, a tempestuous assertion, a search for a soul, and the beginning of the quintessential quest.

Is not He Who created
The heaven and the earth
Able to create the like thereof?
Yes, Indeed! For He is the Creator Supreme
Of skill and knowledge infinite.
And, when He intends a thing
He commands -
'Be!'
and it is.

Quran [36:82]

~~~

And thus it began, the universe as we know or know not of, in a flash. After six eons the spreading universe had consolidated in parts and the world was ready for life.

The weaving of events, continuous, incessant, persistent, sometimes catastrophic and dramatic while at other times subtle and uniform- but always .... History became. Just an instance ago it began when human first sowed the root of civilization, when human saw the first spark of knowledge......
~~~

Part 1 - Civilisations: Streams of Knowledge

The Creation Lore

So relate the story, perhaps they may reflect

Quran [7: 76]

The Omnipresent was present when creation was not. The Omniscient first created the Pen which recorded all the events that will eventuate till the Day of Judgement on the Tablet. He ordained the measures of creation and then He created the Heavens and Earth (Bukhari and Muslim Hadith).

The Angels were created from light and the Jinns from fire. For his righteous dedication Iblis was elevated high among the Angels.

God declared, "I shall place a Regent on earth."

It would be the responsibility of the generations of the Regents - Humans - to apply God's laws on Earth. But Jinns, who already lived on the earth, had created anarchy. So the Angels said, "Will You place there one that will make mischief and shed blood? While we celebrate your praises and glorify your holy name?"

God replied, "I know what you know not."

He created human from variegated clay, which lay as an earthen body for a long time. In due course He blew the soul into the hollow shell and Adam was created. He taught Adam the names of things and thus they developed language and the ability to learn – knowledge. This ability to learn was what the Angel did not possess. Some had vast knowledge but only which they needed to carry out their work. They were not to be the Regents.

Then God showed the things to the Angels and asked, 'Tell me the names of these if you are true?"

They said, "Glory be to you, we have no knowledge but the knowledge that you gave us. Indeed, You are the All Knower, the All Wise."

Then God said, "Adam, inform them of these names."

As Adam informed them God told the Angels that there was wisdom behind His every act. Then He asked them to prostrate to Adam. They obeyed their Lord, except for Iblis. In his arrogance, he refused to bow to Adam. He deliberately disobeyed God and rejected faith.

Iblis was stripped of his position, but he challenged that he would mislead humans to weakness and evil. He asked for reprieve till the Day of Judgement and became the Satan.

Adam and Eve lived in heaven, and had access to all of it, "Dwell with your wife in heaven and eat from its bounties whatever you want but do not approach this tree or you will run into harm and transgression."

But Satan gave them evil inspirations. He infused into their minds and whispered that the tree was the giver of eternal life and great endless kingdoms. The naïve and innocent Adam and Eve ate from the tree.

Then God said, "Get you down all, with enmity amongst yourselves. On the earth will be a dwelling place for you and enjoyment for a time." [2: 30]

On earth Adam and Eve applied themselves to give effort and learn from God's inspiration and knowledge. They prayed, "Our lord, we have wronged ourselves and harmed ourselves, if You do not have forgiveness and mercy for us we will be of the losers." [7: 23]

God pardoned them and after their life on Earth they returned to God. And the generations of their children to come became the Regents on the world to carry out their covenant with God.

The unfolding of the world, the beginning of History, civilisation gathered the sparks of knowledge

~~~

We created not the heaven and the earth and all that is in between them without a purpose! That is the consideration of those who disbelieve.
Then woe to those who disbelieve from the Fire! [38:27]

By the sun and its glorious splendour
By the Moon as it follows
By the Day as it shows the glory
By the Night as it conceals it
By the Firmament and its wonderful structure
By the Earth and its wide expanse
By the Soul, and its given proportion and order
Truly he succeeds that purifies
And he fails that corrupts [91:1-9]
~~~

The Ancient World

Surely the ruins We have left are a veritable sign for people of understanding. [29:35]

According to modern science, more than 13 billion years ago, the universe came into being in an instant, an explosion known as Big Bang, and started to expand. That was the start of the physical dimensions and time. After the explosion there was nothing except for Hydrogen and Helium spread over the much smaller but very hot and expanding universe. Huge balls of Hydrogen formed, much bigger than the sun, in which heavier elements like oxygen, carbon and iron developed. As the intense temperature started to come down Oxygen reacted explosively with Hydrogen forming vast quantities of water. Initially, the water was in gaseous or vapour form and spread over the universe. Other elements reacted with each other forming different compounds. As the universe cooled over Eons, from the primordial gaseous matter the galaxies and its solar systems were formed.

The Human World

The Earth was formed 4.5 billion years ago. The appearance of water on earth was the first stage that would see the evolution of life forms, first as micro-organisms in water bodies and then on land. Only very 'recently' Man appeared on Earth. Migration trends and fossil records so far suggest that the origin of humanoids - human like primates - started in Africa, millions of years after the dinosaurs had become extinct. Earliest tools have been found there dated from 2 million years ago, and the first evidence of fire has been dated to 1.9 million years ago. The fossil records place the appearance of Homo Sapiens at about 100,000 years ago (Fagan, M. 1998). This was the time when archaic languages also appeared, though some rudimentary guttural and sign language would have existed before this, among the archaic humanoids such as Neanderthals, Homo erectus and others. Though many scientists postulate the evolution of Man from primates, they have not been able to furnish the proof. The missing links, evidently, still remain missing.

The world climate saw fluctuations of temperature causing Ice Ages when the average temperature of the world would fall and ice covered a large part of the world. The last Ice Age had started 70,000 years ago and ended about 15,000 years ago. At its height 30 percent of the world was covered by ice and in the vast icy regions temperature plummeted to sub zero levels. The change of clime had a profound effect on the environment. Much of the fauna and flora were depleted, and food and shelter became sparse. Animals like mastodons, mammoths and sabre-toothed tigers could not adopt or migrate to favourable climes and became extinct.

But humans adapted. The Ice Age caused humans to fight back against the environment and this struggle for survival improved their cognitive skills. They acquired the knowledge of fire and use of stone tools like axes and hammers that helped them in the fight against the hostile environment. Their main activity though, other than biological ones, involved scavenging for provisions, searching for shelters and safeguarding themselves from predators. Archaeological records of about 45,000 years ago show shifts in cultural and behavioural maturation. Humans began to use larger and more specialised tools made of bones, antlers, and other materials, in addition to those of stones. They also used ornamental artefacts and constructed better shelters.

The humans spread to a variety of environments. According to evolutionist, each type of environment affected their genes differently. This genotype interaction created local variations - phenotypes - in human characteristics. Variations in skin colour and facial features slowly became perceptible. Whatever the cause, people with slight variation in feature populated various regions of the planet. Biologically, these variations were always due to the local environment and otherwise insignificant and irrelevant. But politically, these differences became important. In the human 'need to survive' it was evident that a larger group could out-survive a smaller group. In the primitive tribal world it became easier to form groups based on these superficial features. For tribal security these groups stayed together over generations, breeding and absorbing smaller groups and increasing in numbers. There was always an animal tendency between the groups to show 'we are stronger than you', which would at a much later time be refined to 'we are more intelligent than you'. Thus started the classification of humans into tribes and races.

The science of Anthropology has proven, despite what some old fashioned political manifesto may subscribe to, that there was and there is no such thing as a pure race. Migration events and population expansion have been reconstructed by research into fossil records and patterns of genetic variation. These investigations suggest that there has been large scale migration and mixing of humans and all humans actually are variations and mixtures of a number of previous groups.

They had divided into groups and then again coalesced. In the on going process, races have coalesced not from any human rationale or higher ideal but from the need for tribal self defence. As they evolved 'technology', like irrigation, these groups gradually became bigger and gathered more knowledge and ultimately formed civilisations. The Semites of Mesopotamia were the first of these civilisations. Some Archaeologists concur that since about 45,000 years ago humans suddenly developed the consciousness to that of the present level. But with current understanding of fossil records the error margin still remains too wide to arrive at any definite time.

Is an accord possible between what religion has said of human genesis but maybe in the way of parables and what science is saying but unable to prove? Where was the first appearance of the human of modern time? In this scheme when was the coming down of Adam? When was the first human to be infused with the breath of a soul? When did the body that was to be human incorporated the consciousness that is human? Darwinists have their evolution theory. Creationists hotly dispute it and maintain that the Darwinists are speaking more from a political perspective rather than a scientific one. All evolutionary changes are intra-species and not inter-species (Yahya, H., 2008). The third alternative, a modification of the creationist theory, is that creation involved the coming into existence of not only the physical universe but all the processes in it including evolution as well. That would be in accord with the 'six' days (periods) of creation revealed by religion.

The Human Civilisation

It is amazing the amount of progress that had taken place in various civilisations of the ancient world even before the Persians and the Greeks. Buildings and monuments had been constructed, schools which existed over many generations had been formed and beautiful literature had been written; science, philosophy and state administration had been developed. Even political reformist revolutions had taken place – Urukagina of Lagash in Sumeria was such a reformer.

The story of civilisation started from Mesopotamia (present day Iraq) with the agricultural revolution by the river Euphrates. All initial civilisations rose by great rivers – Euphrates, Indus, Nile or Huang He. Mesopotamia emerged as the cradle of civilisation with the first farming in 14,000 BC, animal domestication in 12,000 BC, ceramics and geometric motifs in 7,000 BC and organised irrigation in 6,000 BC. By 5,000 BC, societies were flourishing, hierarchical social organisation had developed, some form of money was in use and musical instruments had been crafted. Houses built to a similar plan were widespread in both towns and villages, and towns also had gathering places like temples.

Between 4,000 and 3,000 BC Sumeria had developed a mature society which understood aspects of architecture and engineering. There was a rapid growth of cities and towns, the larger ones being walled. Public buildings and temples became bigger. Mass production of pottery started with the introduction of mould manufacturing and wheel-throwing. Similar artefacts have been discovered over a large area including Turkey and Iran. Accounting system that had started in the previous millennia became diverse and more elaborate (Pollock, S. 1999).

One of the most significant remnants of that time is the building structure known as the ziggurat. The pyramid shaped ziggurat was built in receding tiers upon a rectangular or oval base. The whole structure would have two to seven tiers with a temple or shrine at the summit. The entire structure was made of bricks with sun baked bricks in the core, fired bricks - often with colour glazed face - on the outside. The shrine was accessed by a series of ramps on one side of the ziggurat or by a spiral ramp from base to summit. Of the 32 ziggurats four are found in Iran while the rest are in Iraq.

Religion pervaded political and economic facets of the society. Thus the ziggurat temples were also socio-political institutions and centres of national pride and power. Besides being used as a place of worship these monuments also functioned as courts of justice, academic centres and administration office for labour and goods. Though it supported a patriarchal system there are evidences of feminine participation in religion and politics. Loyalty to the king, responsibility to the family, public honour, social propriety and guidance of the priests were held in high esteem. Besides the priests, the temples also supported artists, craftsmen, couriers, accountants, scribes, teachers and other intellectuals. Grand festivals, feasts and civic processions were held in and around these buildings celebrating past and present achievements.

The Sumerians had developed a huge trade network. They imported Lapis Lazuli from what is now Northern Pakistan - a distance of 3000 kms. By this time, the Sumerians had already invented the wheel, invented writing - pictorial as well as cuneiform - developed astronomy, a calendar and sexagesimal mathematics which described the 360 degree circle and the 60 minute hour. Contracts, on clay tablets, were legal instruments in Sumeria. By studying the ziggurats it is quite evident that the Sumerians had a good understanding of geometry and measurement, brick making of different types, and architecture. This proves the existence of related sciences like mathematics and rudimentary engineering. The ziggurats also indicate that the centralisation of religion, accompanied with human fabrication, had already taken place. The appearance of centralised religion as well as science proves that this was also the birth time of the bridge between the two, philosophy, though the term philosophy itself would be applied to this discipline much later by the Greeks. This was the first scientific and philosophical age.

The Sumerians controlled the city-states of Ur, Uruk, Umma, Nippu, Lagash, and Eridu, between the lower Euphrates and Tigris rivers. Another group of people - the Akkadian - developed in northern Mesopotamia. Two of the oldest known cities, Susa and Sialk, developed approximately to the east on the Iranian Plateau. The first Persian village settlement was in Susa in 8000 BC. The painted pottery of this civilization dates back to 5000 BC.

The 'Haji Firuz Tepe Wine Jar' is the oldest archaeological evidence of wine-making in the world. By 4000 BC Susa was a full fledged city mostly allied to Sumeria but in a later period it would became the capital of the Elamite Empire.

Susa, one of the oldest cities of the world was first settled in 8th millennia BC. It would persist as an important city for thousands of years. In 586 BC, the Babylonians occupied the land of Judah. They enslaved the Jews and displaced them to the north into their empire. At that time the prophet Nehemiah and Daniel (also considered prophet by many) had lived in Susa. (The tomb Shush-Daniel, a white stone cone, is presumed to be that of Daniel. It was discovered in the 7th century CE during the reign of Caliph Umar.) In 539 BC, the Persians occupied Babylonia and set the Jews free. Susa is mentioned in the Hebrew Ketuvium and the Christian Bible stories related to Queen Esther.

Esther was a Persian Jew, descendent of those who were set free. She became the Queen of one of the Persian Emperors mentioned in the Bible as Ahasuerus (Artexerxes or Xerxes). When Vashti, the previous wife of Ahasuerus had became disobedient he had banished her. Then he chose the beautiful Esther from among a large number of virgins. Her cousin, Mordecai, had saved the king from the plot of the Palace Guards. But the Prime Minister, Haman, savoured an intense dislike for the Jews. He belonged to the Agagite people who had, a long time ago, been almost wiped out by the Jews under King Saul. There always was animosity between them and it was further aggravated when Mordecai refused to bow to Haman. Thus Haman planned to massacre the Jews living in the Persian Empire.

But the plan was discovered and Esther disclosed Haman's plan and her Jewish identity to the Emperor. He made Mordecai the Prime Minister and gave the Jews the right to protect themselves. On the day the Jews were to be massacred they counter attacked the people of Haman and killed many. Thus Esther was able to save the Jews in the Persian Empire.

The Sumerian civilisation would last for thousands of years before being attacked by enemies from all around and collapsing.

Away from Mesopotamia, during the same time period, other civilisations were developing. Out of the mire of mystery and 'magic', the people of the Nile took a concrete shape. There existed a grain grinding, hunter, fisher and gatherer society by 11,000 BC. From 8000 to 6000 BC, west of Egypt over the Sahara Desert the climate started to get increasingly wet. Well organised agriculture and buildings were constructed by 6000 BC. Various nomads with different culture and traditions came together around 4,000 BC starting the formation of a nation. Soon, they invented the sail and hieroglyphic writing. As the pre-dynastic civilisation progressed the Egyptians started measuring time by using the sundial and developed a calendar by measuring the solar and lunar periods.

By 3300 BC there were two kingdoms - Upper and Lower Egypt. In 3100 BC, King Menes joined the two Kingdoms and established a capital in Memphis to become the first Pharaoh. He ruled for a long time, for 62 years in one account, and under him the influence of Egypt spread. Then started the rule of the Pharaohs, 31 dynasties ruled Egypt up to 300 BC. After that Egypt was ruled by the Persians, then Greco-Romans and finally by the Muslims.

After unification under Menes, the Egyptians having invented the sail spread their influence into the Mediterranean leaving their mark on Islands like Crete. During the Second Dynasty, Egyptians began mining in Sinai and writing on papyrus. Poetry and music were widely popular. They built the first fortress by the Nile and the first obelisk in Cairo. The "Wall of the Prince" in the Sinai was built to protect Egypt's eastern frontier from invasions. Pyramids with straight sides were also constructed during this period.

In China, by 5000 BC, farming, animal husbandry and pottery-making had already commenced. The first settlements grew along the Yellow River. The Chinese domesticated animals and planted and harvested crops such as millet, rice and vegetables. The Niuheliang archaeological site in the Nuluerhu Mountain valley represents the last of Stone Age period (Neolithic Age) in China. It is a large burial site with a Temple, known as the Goddess Temple, and a complex of alters, burrows and life size statues (WR6, 2009: UNESCO).

The Indian Neolithic is represented by the Mehrgarh Settlement dating back to 7000 BC, west of Indus Valley near today's Quetta of Pakistan. Initially, these people were semi-nomadic who farmed and raised animals. Later, they lived in mud dwellings with four internal subdivisions. Ornaments of turquoise, lapis lazuli, sea shell, limestone, sandstone and polished copper were used. Stone axes, simple figurines of women and animals have been found there. Twenty such villages have been excavated. People were buried with goods such as faience beads, bangles, baskets, stone and bone tools and pendants. More goods were left in the graves of males than the females. At later times the burial goods in graves decreased and ornaments were discovered from female graves only. Occasionally animal sacrifices accompanied burial.

Around 3000 BC, Mehrgarh was part of a wider cultural region spreading into Iran. This region was drained by a lake-canal system which at a later period dried up due to climatic change. Ancient Sanskrit poetry mentions a 'Saraswati' river in this area (Wood, Michael, 2007).

The Arc and the Deluge

Sometime after the Sumerian Neolithic the most famous flood occurred. This event, known through religious history, is recorded as Noah's flood. An ancient Sumerian text from the 3rd millennia BC, which is older than the Old Testament, mentions this flood as well. Thus the flood must have occurred in a period before the writing of the text i.e. the 3rd millennia BC. At the same time, both the biblical and Sumerian texts mention the building of an arc - a boat - which indicates a post Neolithic period (when humans had developed the skill to build boats) most likely after 4th millennia BC. This gives evidence that the flood took place between the 4th and 3rd millennia BC. The religious history of Noah and his Arc can be conceptualised as below:

Adam was the dawning of consciousness. He was also a Prophet and thus a direction provider for his progeny – the Regent on Earth. Noah epitomises the next level of consciousness. He was a Prophet and Messenger and represents the establishment of law on earth, and a growing awareness of the physical environment and the ecology - mountain, valley, river, rain, flood, fauna and flora. It also represents the realisation of the important fact that the after-affects of human actions would affect the physical environment and ecology as well. Undue human action could lead to the destruction of all – The Deluge, or proper action could be the saviour of it all – The Arc.

A few generations after Adam, people slowly forgot the Path that God had established for humans. Satan came to them and said, "Why not make statues of all the good people so that you will remember all good things they taught." [Ibn Abbas in Bukhari: Muhsin, 1997]

It appeared to be a good idea, so they built the statues. And Satan left them alone. Over time, the people forgot what the statues were for and why they were built. Then the Satan reappeared and said, "Why not worship them?"

There is a very thin line separating veneration from worship and that was soon crossed. There is also a very thin line separating the true Path of human progression from the labyrinth of confused desires which the human find so easy and pleasurable to follow.

The Prophets came and warned their people and asked them to follow the right path. Some of the people would follow them for a while and then relapse again to confusion. In such a time Noah preached his people the correct Path but not to much avail. For years he admonished them but only a few followed him. The powerful and the elite taunted him and made fun of him. For years after years this kept on happening – rejections, insults and taunts - until it became unbearable to Noah. He realised that these people would never change and if the progeny was to be salvaged these people will have to be destroyed. So he prayed to God for their destruction and God asked him to build the Ark – the microcosm of humanity.

Only a few supported him in building the Ark. When he warned the people of the coming disaster they laughed at him, "A flood? Up here?"

They refused to heed him and found it all amusing until the day arrived. The sky darkened and poured down and all the springs burst forth and rivers overflowed till there were mountains of waves and storm all around and nothing else could be seen. All perished except those who took refuge in the Ark. For days, the storm, rain and flood continued. Then, gradually, the water started to recede with the Ark floating aimlessly with no land in sight. One day, Noah sent out the raven which found carrion to feed on and did not return. Then he sent out the dove which returned with mud on its legs. Noah realised that there was land nearby. Soon, the Ark rested on Mount Judi and all the people and animals came out. In this vicinity Noah established the enlightened society which spread out to the rest of the world.

The great city of Nineveh developed near Mount Judi. This historical city would become very important under the Assyrians. It is from this region that Abraham would embark on his mission of teaching Monotheism to Egypt and Arabia.

The deluge is mentioned in Judaic, Christian and Islamic literature. The Quran does not envisage that the deluge was global and that it submerged the entire planet but only the people of Noah [25, 37]. Despite that, under the influence of Hebrew exegeses and stories know as *Israeliyat* to the Muslims, the more apocalyptic global story found its way into some Islamic exegeses. Biblical traditions consider it a global phenomenon. Conceptually, the people of Noah were in the 'cradle of civilisation' and thus at that time the flooding of their world may be considered flooding of the whole human world.

The final resting place of the Ark in the Bible is Mount Ararat [Genesis 8:4] while in the Quran it is the much lower Mount Judi [11:44], which lies in the same mountainous region. The Quran does not claim the whole of the world including the Ararat Mount, more than 5000 meter above sea level, was totally submerged. Under the same philosophy, the Quran states the Ark landed not on the highest elevation in the region but on heights which is relatively lower. As the whole region in the past had been known as Ararat (Urartu) the location indicated in both the Bible and the Quran can be considered as the same. It is only individual interpretations that vary.

Interesting Events of Millennium 3000 BC – 2000 BC

This is the millennium of the Bronze Age. Humans left the Stone Age behind and started using tools and weapons of copper and bronze.

~~~

The Egyptians became the most advanced civilisation of this time period. They were the masters of the Mediterranean Sea and were the first to bring civilisation to the Mediterranean Islands. The society was hierarchical and much institutionalised where everyone formed part of the state apparatus. The culture of the Egyptians from Elephantine to the Mediterranean remained more or less uniform throughout the dynastic periods and their courts were visited by different people like Nubians, Libyans and various Asians (Kemp, 2006). They did not have an emotive racial identity, and anyone living in Egypt was an Egyptian (Tait, 2003).

~~~

The Indus Valley civilisation was built by the Dravidians, indigenous Indians, and flourished from 2600 BC to 1900 BC. It was a very advanced civilization of this time period spreading over half a million square miles over North West India, which was a land area bigger than ancient Egypt or Mesopotamia. No monumental buildings have been excavated but very well planned cities with the first known sanitation system, brick houses, criss-crossing roads with drainage, buildings and baths have been found. Standardised weighing measures were used. Urban planning and Municipal governance was well established. 2000 settlements extended up to Oxus River in Afghanistan. Strabo, in the 1st century BC, wrote based on Alexandrian data that this area consisted of 5000 *Polis* (cities). Gold jewelry, seals, pottery and sculpture have been found there. Terracotta figurines including those of dancing girls exhibiting well detailed anatomy were also excavated.

~~~

At about 2700 BC settlements were established in the island of Crete in the Mediterranean Island. Their rise as an island state civilisation and main phase of building would start in the next millennia.

Previous settlements called 'Cycladic' had existed in some of the Greek Cycladic Islands of which some pottery and similar artefacts have been found. They probably were a sea faring people from Asia Minor who had settled into villages and were later over run by the Cretans. These are first 'people' of Greece in record.

~~~

In the second half of this millennium, The Akkadian king Sargon the Great conquered Semuria and united it with Akkad into an empire that extended from the Persian Gulf to the Syrian Levantine.

~~~

In Persia, The Elamite civilisation started during the second half of the millennium as well. Elam was situated in Khuzestan region of modern day Iran, east of the Tigris and Euphrates rivers. The Elamite civilisation had their own style in art and architecture. They possessed a long 'written' tradition in cuneiform. They adopted Sumerian logograms in their writings (Brosius, 2006). The Jiroft civilisation thrived in the Kerman Province. Like the Elamite they were a Bronze Age civilisation with their own architectural style.

~~~

The agrarian Xia Dynasty, mentioned in ancient historical Chronicle, was established in China by the end of this millenium. Tea, ink, silk and alloys of tin and copper were in use. This was a transitional stage in Chinese history which was moving towards the urbanised Shang civilisation.

Achievements of the Millennium:

Princess Enheduanna who was the daughter of Akkadian King Sargon the Great is the first known poet. She was a high priestess dedicated to the goddess Inanna. Her writing is complex, powerful and exhibits insights into human psychology.

The temples, ziggurats, palaces and city walls of Sumeria took on Monumental proportions. The city wall of Uruk was 15 meters thick. The early rulers administrated the city states in god's name. Later this changed and the rulers, who were military heroes, based their authority to rule by right of conquest.

Significant portion of the sedentary populace left the villages to settle in urban regions. Each city developed a patron god and other minor ones.

~~~

A brilliant character of ancient times was the Egyptian Vizier Imhotep (or Immutef) which means 'The one who comes in Peace'. He was born a commoner but rose through the ranks of the temple and court to become a Vizier of Pharaoh Djoser. Imhotep was a poet, priest and the first physician and architect who is known by name. He designed the Step Pyramid at Saqqara in Egypt, during the 3rd Dynasty. He was responsible for the first known
~~~

use of columns in architecture. The Step Pyramid Complex remains today one of the most brilliant architectural wonders of the ancient world and is recognized as the first monumental stone structure. He is regarded by the Egyptians as the 'Father of Medicine' and wrote many medical and didactic texts. One of his medical documents which is still extant is known as the Edwin Smith Papyrus in which more than 90 anatomical terms and 48 types of injuries are described.

Much later, probably in later Ptolemaic time, an inscription known as Famine Stela was engraved. It contains a legend about a famine of seven years during the reign of Pharaoh Djoser. Imhotep is credited with having been instrumental in ending it. It has parallels with the biblical story of Prophet Joseph. The storyline of rise from being a commoner and the seven year famine is common in both the text.

About two thousand years after his death Imhotep was deified. Imhotep became the prototype for Asclepius, the Greek god of Medicine. Later, the Roman Emperors Claudius and Tiberius had praises of Imhotep inscribed in the temples in Egypt.

The Smith and Ebers papyrus shows some of the achievements of ancient Egyptian medical research. During that time there were many physicians as well as specialists like 'dentists', 'eye physicians' and 'bowel physicians'. The Egyptian Ebers papyrus mentions the first diabetes mellitus and contains remedies for the elimination of excessive urination: A measuring glass filled with water from the bird pond, elderberry, fibres of the Asit plant, fresh milk, beer swill, flower of cucumber and green dates.

A document of great interest is the *'Egyptian book of Dead'* which was first composed during this period. The original name was *'Reu nu pert em hru'* meaning *'The Chapters of coming forth by day'*. Over time it went through a number of versions and the final one consisted of a collection of 200 chapters giving a description of the ancient Egyptian conception of the afterlife and a collection of hymns, spells, and instructions that would allow the deceased to pass through obstacles after death. Selected parts accompanied with illustrations were copied into papyrus scrolls called vignettes which were placed with the dead in order to assist them through the dangers of the underworld and attain a blissful afterlife. Alternatively, the vignettes were also written on the walls of tombs and on coffins or on linen or vellum rather than on papyrus.

~~~

Egyptians and Indians achieved a modern urban life during this millennium. In Egypt, the Sphinx and Pyramid of Giza were built. The Giza Pyramid is the only ancient wonder of the world that is still standing. But it was the Dravidians of India who lived in the most sophisticated urban culture. Their towns had developed under advanced municipal planning with sophisticated drainage system, a hygienic environment, and public buildings made of
~~~

bricks. There existed a vast trade network which saw the first use of systematic and uniform weights and measures.

~~~

There was a good deal of trading and cultural interactions between the civilisations which lead to knowledge transfer. The gods and goddess of one area were taken to other areas and were worshiped under new names. However, China developed in relative isolation.
~~~

Development of Pantheons

Al Biruni, the 11th century scientist, was the first to postulate a theory in the development of anthropomorphic pantheons. He said that the worship of idols "was due to a kind of confusion or corruption," and also that, "The physical images are monuments in honor of certain much venerated persons, prophets, sages, angels destined to keep alive their memory when they are absent or dead, to create for them a lasting place of grateful veneration in the hearts of men." Commenting on this Emeritus Professor Montgomery Watt states that "Al Biruni goes on to maintain that in the course of generations, the origin of the veneration of the images is forgotten, and further that the ancient legislators, seeing that the veneration of images as advantageous, made it obligatory for the ordinary." (WR7, 2009)

Monotheistic religions are generally against producing relics of their omnipresent God. Thus, these religions left no artefacts that could be discovered from ruins. The single unseen God concept taught by prophets like Abraham, Noah and probably Zoroaster and Buddha had always come under the influence of pantheistic anthropomorphic culture and had adopted multiple deities over time. These religions have created and incorporated into their culture various idols represented by statues and similar artefacts. And they have left these artefacts behind to be discovered in their ruins. The remarkable exception were the Hebrews, even though they faced deviation among their people at times, in general, they clung to monotheism.

Archaeological evidence has proven the existence of religion at the very start of civilisation. Artefacts representing pantheons have been excavated from a variety of sites. Legends describe the gods and goddess as anthropomorphic but were immortals and had super-powers. The deities of the pantheons were not omniscient or omnipresent and had human follies. The Sumerians had a fully developed pantheon before the 3rd millennium BC. Initially, their deities were associated with natural phenomena most likely due to their dependence on nature for agriculture. They practised religious rituals but, at present, these are not well understood. Prayer used to be part of daily life. There appears to be a concept of divine presence behind the Sumerian religious makeup. The Akkadians adopted many of the Sumerian gods and goddesses, with names changed, into their own Pantheon. Their deities became more human-like in action and attitude, most likely due to an increase in rituals that supported the Kings and Rulers and gave them the authority to conquer and rule larger areas. The Egyptians developed their Pantheon, on the whole in isolation, probably representing a ruling royal family that reigned just before and during the first half of the 3rd millennium

BC. The Indo-Persian (Vedic-Zoroastrian) Pantheon was almost contemporary to the Egyptians, while the Greco-Roman Pantheons would develop in the subsequent millennia.

The supreme god in the Egyptian pantheon is Amon-Ra who actually represents two sun gods Amon and Ra-Herakhty. By the fifth dynasty these two were unified into one by the Egyptian priests. Various sources give slightly varying mythological origins of this Pantheon but the general story (Green, 2004) is as follows.

The Myth of Ra

The Shining Ra arose from Nun the spirit-goddess of water. He became the all powerful and creator of things. Unknown to all the secret of his great power was in his hidden name. One after another, Ra created Shu, god of air and space, and his sister Tefnut, the goddess of rain and fertility. Then he made Geb, the earth, who rose above the sea and whose laughter caused the earthquakes. Then he made Nut the sky goddess. Geb and Nut were then separated by Tefnut. Then Ra created and gave names to all things. Lastly Men and Women were created who started to dwell all over Egypt.

When his creation was complete he took the form of a man and was acknowledged as the first Pharaoh. A golden age of thousands of years began, with the Nile flooding every year to give a fertile land which yielded good crops. As time passed, the man-form of Ra started to grow old. Apophis, the Evil Dragon, that had grown in evil vapours of darkness thought that the time to devour all that is good and bright was approaching. The power of Ra had kept him at bay, but with old age Ra's bones became like silver, his flesh like gold and his hair like lapis lazuli and he was failing in his rule over Egypt and his fight against Apophis. Ra perceived Apophis was entering the souls of the Egyptians and plotting against him. He ordered his attendants to summon the high gods to the court. The asssembly was to be in secret so that the evil ones would not know that he was aware of their presence.

One by one Shu, Tefnut, Geb, Nut and Nun bowed and kissed the ground in front of Ra. Nun, the eldest of all, was the first one to speak addressing Ra as the maker of the world. Wishing him long life and strength she inquired the reason behind the summon.

Then Ra addressed Nun and the gods that he had spawned. He had created mankind with one glance of his Eye and made them flourish in the world to serve him. But behold! They now plot against him. Inspired by the evil they gather together in Upper Egypt in conspiracy. Should he destroy them with a single glance of fire of his Eye?

But Nun stopped Ra. She asked him not to turn the fire of his Eye on them. For it will destroy all, good and bad, and turn Egypt into a lifeless desert. A way had to be devised by which only the evil is punished, the good is unharmed.

Then Ra decreed that he will send Sekhmet against them, and immediately the gargantuan lioness leapt into being and sped to Upper Egypt. There Sekhmet unleashed an unprecedented massacre, feeding on all who came in front of her until the Nile and its swamps became red with blood. The wicked were all slain the good prayed to Ra for mercy. But Sekhmet had tasted blood and had become addicted to it. She could not stop devouring during the days and stalking during the nights.

Ra said that Sekhmet could not be stopped but by a scheme. He will stop her by giving her a power greater than the one she now possessed.

Then Ra ordered that seven thousand vessels of beer be mixed with the red ochre of Elephantine until it gleamed like blood. Then he ordered the mixture to be dumped in the region where Sekhmet stalked and preyed. When Sekhmet saw the thick red liquid she mistook it for blood and roared in pleasure. She drank and she drank until the beer in the mixture affected her brain and she became so incapacitated that she was unable to slay anymore.

Ra awaited her in Heliopolis where she came without slaying anymore. Ra informed that she has come to him in peace. From now on she will not be a slayer, but become Hathor, the goddess of love. All of mankind will be under her control, for love is stronger than hate. And from then on, to celebrate the day of her becoming Hathor, the priestesses in the Temple of love will, on the first day of each year, drink beer made red by the ochre of Elephantine in her honour.

Time went by. Long after Ra had thus saved mankind, Thot, the god of wisdom, articulated a prophesy that the sky goddess Nut will give birth to a son. This son after growing up will rule Egypt in place of Ra.

That made Ra furious and he said that none will take away the throne of Egypt from him! He cursed and decreed that Nut will never be a mother on *any day or night of any year!* His ruling was unchangeable.

Devastated by this fateful decree Nut felt very sad and helpless. Yet, she suspected, that there had to be some value in the prophecy of Thot for he was the wisest of the gods. She had a hidden desire that her son should rule Egypt. But she did not know how that could now eventuate as Ra has placed the unbreakable curse on her. So she visited Thot, the god who loved her, and asked for his help.

Thot said that if she loved him he will make her wish come true without breaking Ra's decree. Nut agreed to this proposal and Thot embarked on his scheme. Khonsu, the moon god, was a great gambler. Thot challenged him in a game of draughts. As the game progressed the stakes of the game rose high and Khonsu had to wager moonlight. Thot, the wise, won enough moonlight from which he was able to make five days.

Each year had three hundred and sixty days. Now Thot fitted his new five days that were made out of the moonlight. These five days and nights *did not belong to any year* that Ra had cursed Nut with. And on these five days Nut gave birth to five children – Osiris, Seth, Harmachis, Isis, and Nepthys. The moon, having lost so much light, didn't have enough to shine throughout the entire month. It would dwindle every month until it became dark for a night and then would start slowly to grow back to its full grandeur.

At the birth of Osiris, the eldest of the siblings, there were numerous signs of his greatness. People heard voices from the sky and prophecies were made that 'Osiris, the king is born'. Palmyres, a Theban who had heard such a voice coming out of Ra's temple, was assigned by Nut to bring up Osiris. Thot taught Osiris all the wisdom that he possessed. Isis, also a great learner, became the greatest magician that Egypt had ever seen. She learned wisdom from Thot and all the mysteries of the moon from Khonsu.

When the children grew up, Osiris was married to Isis and Seth to Nepthys. Taking them as models the later Pharaohs would marry their sisters. Among all the wives of the Pharaoh, the sister-bride was the queen. Soon Isis, who had been taught wisdom by Thot, decided it was time to diplomatically end the Reign of Ra so that Osiris could become the Pharaoh.

As part of the ploy, Isis planned to make the first cobra, the sacred serpent of Egypt. Ra was old and as he walked he would shake with palsy and froth at the mouth. But he was the creator and no living thing could be made without a part of him. One morning, as he surveyed Egypt, his spittle fell on the sand. Isis collected this moist sand and fashioned the cobra out of it. Next day, when Ra was out again he saw the cobra but could not understand what manner of animal it was. Taking advantage of Ra's curiosity the cobra bit him and escaped. As the venom spread through him like a burning flame Ra let out a loud cry. All the gods and goddesses came running to him and Isis asked what ailed the one who made the world and all men.

Ra replied that he has wounded by something he has never seen before, something that he has not made. So he did not know how to cure myself from this affliction. He requested the children of the gods in their wisdom to help him.

One by one the gods came to help him but in vain. The pain became more intense. Finally Isis addressing him as 'father divine' said that she knew the magic that will cure him. But for that magic to work she needed to know his hidden name which only he knew. This name was the ultimate source of all power and would make Isis formidable.

In his pain Ra gave Isis many of his names but not the name of power. The magic did not work and the pain kept of getting worse. Isis said that the magic will work with only the all powerful name.

As the pain became intolerable, Ra said he will give her the name but she must promise that no one shall know it except for Horus, the son she will bear to Osiris. For it is Horus who shall rule Egypt.

Like all men, Ra's man-form also comprised of three components- his spirit, his body and an image or apparition that is the double of the body known as the 'Ka'. His Ka whispered his secret name to the Ka of Isis so that no one else would hear it. Isis then chanted her spell and the poison dissipated and the pain subsided.

But after that, Ra stopped ruling Egypt and took his place in the sky where during the day he passed like the sun and at night he went to the twelve regions of the underworld - the Duat. It is these twelve regions of the underworld through which the spirits of the dead must pass to attain a place in Ra's kingdom.

When Osiris and Isis became the rulers of Egypt, many people in their kingdom were barbarians. But under their rule much changed and there was progress. They taught the people agriculture, crafts, law, religion and all the arts of civilisation. But an evil group, who did not agree with Osiris, was also gathering force in secret. The leader of this group was none other than Seth, the brother of Osiris and Isis. He with his followers devised a way to usurp power. By trickery he cut Osiris into fourteen parts and spread the parts all over Egypt so that the spirit of Osiris could not enter Duat. For only when the body is buried together can the spirit enter. But Isis, after a great adventure, brought the parts together and buried Osiris whole. Thus, the spirit of Osiris was able to enter Duat. There he became the King of the Underworld and started to welcome all the good spirits to his army.

But the world was ruled, for the present, by Seth. His greatest desire was to kill the child Horus, the only remaining challenge to his rule. He went to the Island where Isis lived in a hut amidst the papyrus reeds. He turned into a scorpion and crawled up to the cradle and bit Horus. Isis heard Horus cry out and rushed back to him. Though Seth had left, she knew what had happened. She nursed the child through out the night and tried all her magic. But the poison of Seth was too strong and in the morning the child lay still. Hearing her cry of despair Thot arrived. Isis said that Seth has killed Horus, like he killed the father! Now how can Horus avenge the death of his father?

The wise Thot said that Horus will rise again. His spirit is in Duat now with Osiris. He will return in the shape of a Bennu bird. As the bird will perch on the great obelisk of Heliopolis the burning heat of Ra's eye will turn it into ash. But a new Bennu bird will rise from that ash and its fame will spread worldwide. In the meantime, before the return of Horus, Thot will convene a council of the gods to decide who the ruler of Egypt should be – Horus or Seth.

In the council Isis convinced the gods that Horus was the true Pharaoh as he was the son of Osiris, the first born. And as Thot had predicted, Horus ultimately returned from Duat and there were tremendous battles between Horus and Seth but at the end Horus prevailed. Thus there came peace in Egypt.

Horus ruled for many centuries until the time of the great gods dwelling on earth ended. The Pharaohs who came after him also had the spirit of a god and were thus worshipped. Their bodies were embalmed and hidden in the mighty pyramids below the Valley of the Kings. The bodies lie in wait for the day when Osiris and Horus will return and fight the final and greatest battle against the evil Seth. The ultimate destruction of Seth would cause all the dead, who had lived a virtuous life, to return from the Duat and again inhabit their bodies. And they would dwell forever in a land where all evil had been eliminated.

~~~

It is quite evident that the Egyptian Pantheon is based on an improvised and fancied history of some royal Egyptian family of antiquity that has been later deified for political reasons. The myths, obviously, have been added to and modified over time and also represents the philosophical dichotomies of chaos versus order, good versus bad and dark versus light (Kemp, 2006).
~~~

Development of Literature

Besides the Pantheons, archaeology has also brought to light ancient literature. By the 3rd millennium before Christ the development of literature had started in earnest. The oldest known epic work of literature is the *Epic of Gilgamesh*. This epic poem is the story of a great king. The strands of the story reflect the inner desires, fears and hopes of the Mesopotamian people.

There are five episodes in the original Sumerian language in which the name of the protagonist is actually Bilgames. Only in the later versions of Akkadian language the name became Gilgamesh. One of the episodes refers to a pagan version of Noah's flood. The setting of the Epic is in post diluvian Uruk, the greatest city of its time. The pantheon is represented by three supreme gods: Anu the sky god, Enlil god of earth and Ea the god who lives in the fresh water ocean. There are many other gods and goddesses like the love goddess Inanna (Babylonian Ishtar), Erishkigal who is the Queen of the Netherworld and Namtar her gruesome minister. The period of the story depicts a mythical time when the world is being civilised and Ea had sent Seven Sages to do the job. The five episodes (George, Andrew, 1999) are:

1. **The emissaries of Akka**: The battle between Gilgamesh's city of Uruk and the city of Kish: Akka King of Kish and his army attack Uruk. But Gilgamesh and his army battle and win. Gilgamesh reveals that, long ago, Akka had unknowingly helped him. So he makes the defeated Akka an ally.
2. **The living one's mountain**: The adventurous journey of Gilgamesh and his friend, servant and general called Enkido to the Cedar Mountains where they have to battle the demigod Huwawa: But Huwawa has seven powerful 'auras', weapons, which make him invincible. Gilgamesh deceives him by giving him two of his sisters as wife and concubine and entices him with various goods and luxuries of city life for easy living and enjoyment in exchange of his auras. After he gets all the seven 'auras' he attacks and defeats Huwawa, who is slain by Enkido.
3. **Hero in battle** - The feud between Gilgamesh and goddess Inanna: Inanna tries to seduce him, but he rejects her. The infuriated Inanna unleashes the Bull of Heaven to destroy Uruk but Gilgamesh dispatches of it and pacifies Inanna with the offering of a flask of sweet oil made from the two horns of the bull.
4. **In those far off days** – The journey of Enkido to the Netherworld: Gilgamesh rids a willow tree of its evil and demonic creatures. He makes furniture out of the willow for the goddess Inana and a ball and mallet for himself. Gilgamesh and the young men play with the ball and mallet in the city square. They play through out the day and their women folk have to bring food. The next day the women complain to the

gods. When the play resumes the ball falls through a deep hole to the Netherworld. Unable to reach the ball Gilgamesh is very perturbed and weeps bitterly. Enkidu volunteers to go to the Netherworld and fetch it. Gilgamesh warns him that he must be careful not to attract attention of the 'souls' residing in the Netherworld. He must pretend that he is attending a funeral. For there he will view the awful lamentation of goddess Erishkigal, who having torn off her clothes and uses her nails like a rake and pulls out hair. But once in the Netherworld, Enkidu pays no heed to the advice and is thus taken captive. The sad Gilgamesh petitions the gods for help. At dawn, as the sun god Utu arises from the Netherworld he brings along Enkidu. Gilgamesh rejoices and curiosity makes him enquire about the Netherworld and the souls that reside there. Enkidu informs him that those who have left fewer offspring in the world are worse off in Netherworld as they have no one in the world to make offerings for them. Those who died of leprosy or by falling are still suffering. Those who were burnt did not reach there at all as their smoke went up to heaven. Those who died as a child live well in 'the bed of gods'. Those who did not respect their parents do not get adequate water. Gilgamesh also learns that his forbears are drinking 'dirty water' in the Netherworld. In filial piety he has statues of his ancestors made and institutes mourning rites. The dead are thus appeased.

5. **Never to rise again** – The death of Gilgamesh: Gilgamesh is stricken with sickness and seized by Namtar, the emissary of Death. The dilemma of the gods is whether to treat Gilgamesh as a god and give him heaven or should he go to the Netherworld like all men. They review his life, his heroic exploits. It is decided that despite his divine birth and despite being a king Gilgamesh must descend to the Netherworld like all men. But in the Netherworld he would have a special place. Like the two divine inhabitants of Netherworld, Dumuzi and Ningishzida, he would sit on judgement over the dead. In the world, his death would be commemorated in annual festivals. There was no need for him to despair as in the Netherworld he would be reunited with his family as well his friend Enkidu.

The Epic of Gilgamesh was first written by the Sumerians about five thousand years ago. This is also the first known 'text book' that was taught in schools and academic institutions of Sumeria, and later in Akkad, Hattusa and Babylon teachers and students wrote and re-wrote these episodes on clay tablets. The students graduated to professionals who recorded commercial transactions for the royal administration and wrote stories for the pleasure of the royal court. Initially written in Semitic cuneiform languages (Sumerian and Akkadian) on extensive clay tablets these were later copied to Indo-European languages like Hurrian and Hittite. Thousands of these fragments have been unearthed and more are being discovered completing the gaps in the master epic.

Poems and cuneiform writings were common during this period, the most popular being *Gilgamesh*. The Epic became widely known in ancient times, and had influenced literature from India to Europe. The Greek historian Ioannis Kordatos found verses and themes of episodes in the Greek epic *Odyssey* similar to those found in *Gilgamesh* (WR5, 2009).

Some of these epics written in the schools were preserved in libraries of great kings. King Shulgi (2090 – 2050 BC) was an intellectual, athlete and warrior. During his school life he was the most brilliant student and became a great literary and cultural patron. He founded libraries in Ur and Nippur for his scribes and minstrels. A large number of Akkadian tablets have been unearthed belonging to King Hamurabi's time, 18th century BC. In Nineveh, King Ashurbanipal's (660-630 BC) Assyrian scribes copied the Epic of Gilgamesh. In his royal library over 24,000 cuneiform documents were collected with texts varying from mathematics to royal correspondence. Ashurbanipal was also a multi-talented person trained both in scholarly and martial arts. After Nineven fell to the alliance of the Persian Medes and Babylonians, these tablets would lie buried for 2,500 years. In 1850 CE the royal libraries of Nineveh were discovered and the tablets excavated and preserved in the British Museum.

While the Epic was being copied and re-written over the three thousand years, the episodes changed. In the later Akkadian version Gilgamesh is a mighty and virile tyrant. His laws are oppressive and indulgent. Even the brides of Uruk pay him their virginal tribute before they can get married. The gods then create Enkidu, as mighty as Gilgamesh but a savage brought up by animals in a forest. The aim of the gods was that Enkidu would be powerful enough to keep Gilgamesh occupied and thus the people of Uruk would have some respite. A harlot seduces Enkidu and ultimately takes him to Gilgamesh. The two of them become great friends and embark on the cedar mountain adventure where, unlike the Sumerian version, they do not deceive Humbaba (Huwawa) but defeat him in a fair fight.

After the death of Enkidu, Gilgamesh is afflicted with the fear of death. He leaves Uruk in search of the immortal Uta-naphisti (Sumerian Ziusudra), the only man to have survived the great flood. He sails across the Waters of Death on a Ferry and meets Uta-naphisti. But ultimately, like the Sumerian version, his quest for immortality is denied.

An interesting part of the story in verses is Uta-naphisti's recount of the deluge, a pagan version of Noah's flood, as follows:

> The gods reside in the old city of Shuruppak by the river Euphrates. The great gods decides to send down the deluge. The god Ea advises Uta-naphisti, his devotee, to build a boat with a roof of which the dimensions, length and breath, should be the same. Uta-naphisti then builds a huge boat and loads aboard all that he has, including silver and gold, all the living creatures – domestic and wild, along with his kith and kin, and people of every skill and craft.
>
> First, the terrible gale winds flatten the country for a full day. After that comes the flood and the cataclysm passes over the people as a huge battle. In the destruction that follows

people cannot discern each other. Even the gods take fright and so they take leave, escaping up to the heaven of Anu.

After seven days the gale and tempest ends. The boat finally runs aground on the mountain of Nimush. After seven more days of remaining aground, Uta-naphisti sends out a dove but it returns as all the land was still flooded. He sends out a swallow, but it also returns. Finally, when he sent a raven it does not return. It has found land.

The story was written many generations after Noah. The drama of Noah's flood is clearly discernible but people had forgotten the essence of Noah's teaching. Over the many generations of oral transmission the story had been incorporated within a pantheistic setting. In the Old Testament, it is 'Yahweh' who brings down the deluge. Probably, in the version of the story adopted by the pagan writers Noah's God becomes Ea. The reference to the deluge, in one form or another, recurs in other myths as well, for example, the story of Deucalion and his wife Pyrrha in Greek myths (Littleton, 2002).

Interesting Events of Millennium 2000 – 1000 BC

The Iron Age starts towards the end of this millennium in which humans learnt the use of iron tools and weapons, bringing a gradual end to the Bronze Age. The Iron Age first came to West Asia and India and the rest of the world slowly caught up, some in the following millennium.

~~~

The fall of the Akkadian Civilisation, like the Indus Valley Civilisation, was due to climatic changes. Their economy was agrarian and the drying up of the land and drop in cultivation made the economy unsustainable. In their stead, in nearby regions, rose new kingdoms: Assyria and Babilu ("Gateway of god" - Babylon). Under King Hamurabi Babylon became the dominant power in the region. By the end of the millennia, though, the Assyrians, with their army deployed with metal armour, iron swords and lances, became dominant.

~~~

Early in this millennium Abraham had migrated to Canaan (which included regions of modern day Lebanon, Jordan, Palestine, Israel and Syria) and then to Egypt opening the doors of migration for Semitic people. Later the Hebrew people were enslaved by the Egyptians and used in various labour works including large scale construction. The Iron Age gradually caught up with Palestine in around 1300 BC. Soon after that, Moses led the Hebrews to Palestine. In the power struggle that ensued the Hebrews defeated the Canaanites and finally, at the end of the millennium, David captured Jerusalem. He made it the capital of his unified kingdom of Judah and Israel.

The pantheist philosophy of the Pharaohs could be imperial and extremely oppressive as was during the time of Moses. But at other times, like those of Abraham and Joseph's time it was more benign. It is probable that at the time of Joseph Lower Egypt was ruled by the 'Hyksos' or foreign kings who were benign to the Semites. But the inimical Pharoahs returned to power before the time of Moses.

~~~

The rise of the Hittite Empire was centred in Hattusa in Central North Anatolia (Turkey). Its army was one of the first to use chariots and became contender with the Egyptians in empire building. Ramses II of Egypt, suffering defeat in battle, was ultimately forced to sign a peace treaty with Hittite King Muwattalis. This is the first known peace accord on record. Centuries later, after 1180 BC, this empire disintegrated to form independent Neo-Hittite states (Hawkins 1982).
~~~

During the expansion of their Empire, groups of Hittites had also moved west to Greece and Italy. Large numbers settled in Italy and came to be known as the Etruscans.

~~~

During the New Kingdom era (1550 – 1070 BC), the Egyptian state had two opposing characteristics. Egypt became a more pluralistic society so the ruling style had to be practical or essentially political. At the same time, the ruler's absolute authority was to remain based on mythology (Kemp, 2006). There had to be some kind of adaptation between the two philosophies.

During the episode of Moses, which most likely took place in this period, the adaptation failed. Moses led the Hebrew opposition against the Pharaoh's authority. It is not known who the Pharaoh was during Moses' life span but there are at least ten candidates including Seti I, Ramses II, Merneptah and Setnakhte.

Egyptian resources were stretched due to battles with the Hittites and the revolt of the Hebrews. After the disintegration of the Hittite civilisation and decline of the Egyptian empire a political vacuum was created in which many kingdoms arose - Phoenicia, Philistia, Judah, Moab and Edom. The Phoenicians became an international sea faring mercantile power. They established colonies in Anatolia as well as in far away places like Italy, Spain, Cyprus and Gibraltar from where they could get raw materials to produce various goods including dyes.

~~~

In China, the Shang Dynasty ruled from 1600 BC to 1000 BC. They are the first well documented Chinese dynasty and had established an urban lifestyle with large use of bronze wares.

~~~

Well into the third Millennium BC the indigenous Europeans were still tribes of hunter-gatherers living off the land. Almost in the middle of the Mediterranean Sea between Turkey, Greece, Egypt and Libya lies the Island of Crete. Sir Arthur Evans was the main discoverer of some large ruins in Crete; he called the building structures 'Palaces' and named the Cretan civilisation Minoan after King Minos of Greek legend. The spectacular finds included marvellous frescoes, traded items that had originated in Egypt and Babylon, along with a large number of clay tablets with script writing (Murray, T. 1999). Evans used these artefacts for cross reference with Mediterranean civilisation and to date the site. Studies of the excavation proved that though the Cretan civilisation had a major impact on the initiation of
~~~

civilisation in Greece, the people who lived on the Island were not Greeks and did not speak any Greek language. They had migrated or sailed there from other regions.

The root of the Cretan Civilisation was laid around 2700 BC, at a time when the Greeks had not yet mastered sea sailing. Evans found the Minoan civilisation to be a part of a chain that related to Egypt and Asia and people from those civilisations who had sailed to the Island and established a home there. They came from large civilisations and thus had the skills to build an island state – The Minoan Civilisation. In the 2nd millennium BC communities grew up around the eastern and southern parts of the island coast with its inhabitants abruptly learning advanced practices in agriculture, pot-making, metalwork, etc. The Palaces were also built approximately at the same time. Egyptians knew Crete as 'Keftiu'. Records and paintings of Crete have been found in Egyptian documents.

The first of the Cretan Palaces were built around the start of the second millennia BC. Researchers assumed that the Palaces used to be inhabited by the rulers of the island. Each large complex had space for kitchens, metal workshops and various types of trade people giving it the appearance of a small town with interconnected rooms and houses. Other researchers have suggested that the large structures were temples or administrative centres or maybe both. So far, five such sites have been discovered in Crete. The Knossos Palace, the largest of the buildings, is far removed from any fertile area and all the palaces are completely devoid of fortifications and no weapons have ever been found in them. The access through these buildings is cumbersome. It has also been suggested, perhaps incorrectly, that these were burial sites to which only a small band of priests and embalmers had access to.

According to Hans Wunderlich the Minoans were a vassal state of Egypt. It is possible that king Minos, the founder of the Minoan state-civilisation in Greek legends, is based on the person of the Pharaoh Menes. The similarity in the names is quite apparent. But irrespective of whether that is correct or not, the Egyptian influence in Crete is abundantly clear in the archaeological artefacts that have been excavated. Egyptian style paintings and symbols – sun disks, bulls, lilies, lotuses, serpents, etc. – are quite common. Painting of reddish brown men and white women in frescos has been found from Minoan sites. The use of different skin colour was initially thought to differentiate between men and women, but now appears to represent the multicultural aspect of the Minoan civilisation. The Cretans had formed writing scripts, at first in pictorial and later in linear form. Some of the Cretan pictographic symbols are identical with Egyptian hieroglyphs but a large number seems to be indigenously formed. Another possibility is that the pictographs and linear scripts belonged to people coming to the Island from two different origins.

Around 1400 BC the Mycenaean warriors from Greek mainland invaded and took control of Crete. They destroyed the Minoan state and burnt the palaces but assimilated much of its culture including the Minoan script. The Mycenaean soon developed into very artistic builders after which the Mycenaean civilisation flourished in the Greek mainland and islands. This was the first true Greek civilisation and it was this civilisation that Homer later wrote about.

~~~

Many interesting events were taking place in the Indo-Persian region. The huge land mass that surrounded the centres of civilisations of Mesopotamia was inhabited by a vast proliferation of nomadic tribes. Quite a few hypotheses have been postulated to 'define' these Indo-European people. The hypothesis of a master Aryan race which had gone about conquering nations is no longer tenable. Most of these hypotheses are based more on nationalistic feelings or racial bias rather than on historical or archaeological evidence. In fact, the Persian Achaemenids were the only Aryans who would go about conquering the known world from Eastern Europe to North Western India.

In some of these Ancient Persian groups, for example the Samaritans, women had played dominant roles including that of warriors. These women were identified by the Greeks as the Amazons. Female warriors of these Persian societies fascinated the classical Greeks as in their society women were passive and dependent on males.

Surrounded by oceans and the Himalayas, the only land access to India was the corridor in the Iran-Afghanistan region. After the disintegration of the Indus Valley Civilisation in the beginning of this millennium, swarms of Aryan tribes, cousins to the Persian Aryans, slowly moved into northern India through this corridor over the centuries. The Aryan tribes were forced to move from their original abode due to the similar climatic changes previously experienced by the Indus Valley people. Over time they established settlements in North India called the 'Janas' which, later, coalesced to form 'Janapadas' or kingdoms.

The Persian Aryan and Indian Aryan coming from the similar stock were initially very alike. Sanskrit, the language of the Indian holy book Vedas, is very similar to Avestan, the language of the Persian Zoroastrian holy book. The tribes that had settled in India were 'Indianised' and ultimately became acrimonious toward their Persian cousins most likely when the Persians attempted to invade them. This enmity can be discerned from the religious texts of that time. In Vedic scripts *deva*s are the auspicious Gods, while the *ashura*s (Persian Ahuras) are destructive demons. By contrast, in battles depicted in Zoroastrian texts, the *Ahura*s are good and the *Daeva*s (Indian Devas) are irreconcilably evil.
~~~

Achievements of the Millennium:

In this millennium the events flew rapidly in the story of the Empires. More was achieved in this millennium than all the previous ones put together. There was a huge eruption of literature, arts and technology that led to the consolidation and spread of urbanised societies. With the domestication of the horse, a manifold increase occurred in communication between the civilisations.

In Babylon, city-state of Mesopotamia, the famous 'Code of Hamurabi' (1787 BC) was the first constitution to give rights to the state by curtailing the power of the king. Among other laws, it contained legal aspects of every day life. This code mentions the retributory law 'An eye for an eye' that is found in the biblical texts. In the prologue of the code, the King Hamurabi is praised for being so enlightened as to implement this code. During the same period the seven storied Etemenank ('House of the foundation of heaven on earth'), later known as Tower of Babylon was built.

Power and strength soon turned Babylon to arrogant imperialism. They would at one time attack and capture Jerusalem. They would enslave all Hebrew people and forcibly displace them to Babylon.

~~~

The Egyptians rose to incredible heights of development during this period. Mathematics and medical science improved further. Tumours were treated and the process documented. Surveying methods were developed and hydraulic cement was used. Natural water reservoirs were used for cultivation in lean seasons. Sun-dials were used to keep time and high quality glasses were manufactured. The first geologic and topographic maps were made.

As the centuries went by, the local temples made of mud bricks became more elaborate and the position of the chief priest was generally held by the political leader of the region and the priests were theologians as well as scholars. The temples had access to and could generate revenue from enterprises like gold mines (Kemp, 2006).

One of the wonders of the time was the colossal Egyptian Labyrinth built during this period by Pharaoh Amenemhet. According to the 5th-century BC Greek historian Herodotus (Greene, 1987) the Egyptian Labyrinth was a vast structure on the shores of a large lake 'Moeris' located seven days journey up the Nile from the Pyramids at Giza. Herodotus found the lake Moeris amazing. According to him it was man made and 397 miles in circumference with two Pyramids in the centre. Each had a giant stone statue sitting on a throne at the top. The pyramids, as well, were greater than words could express, and each of them were equivalent to many of the great works of the Greeks.
~~~

But the labyrinth surpassed the Pyramids too. Herodotus wrote that it was a wonder past words and all the Greek buildings and their most striking architecture, including the temples at Ephesus and Samos, clearly have cost less labour and money than the labyrinth.

> The labyrinth was divided into twelve enormous courts and its walls were covered with sculpture, and a large pyramid decorated with colossal figures was connected to it by a subterranean passage. It had twelve roofed courtyards with gates. Six of the gates were situated as a row facing north, the other six exactly opposite them facing south. The entire structure was surrounded by exterior enclosing wall. Inside there were two sets of 1500 chambers, one underground, the other directly over it and aboveground – 3000 chambers altogether.
>
> The complex passages through the rooms and the winding going ins and outs through the courts caused Herodotus and his group countless marvels as they went through, from the court into the rooms, and from the rooms into the pillared corridors, and then from these corridors into other rooms again, and from the rooms into other courts afterwards. The whole roof and the walls, full of engraved figures, were made of stone and each court was set round with pillars of white stone, very exactly fitted. Nearby, at the corner where the labyrinth finishes off was a pyramid 240 feet high and engraved with great animals. The passage to this pyramid was also subterranean.

The 1st century BC Greek geographer Strabo called it "a great palace composed of many palaces" and marvelled at the enormity of the stone slabs that made up its roof and walls. The Cretan palaces were similar, in idea, to this labyrinth though comparatively miniatures in dimension.

This period also witnessed the flourishing of Egyptian literature. Many genres of story had been developed such as adventure, historical, magical and mythic. Some of the famous ones of this time were:

- Ipuwer Papyrus - 1800 BC: This is a marvellous poem of lamentations describing natural disasters and social upheaval, written in a very advanced style for its time.

- The story of the Shipwrecked sailor – 1900 ~ BC. The original story of a shipwrecked sailor on an uninhabited Island with a magical serpent.

- Adventures of Sinuhe - 1800 BC: The story depicts the flight of Sinuhe from Egypt in the wake of a murder plot of the Pharaoh. His adventure leads him to what is now Syria and then to Lebanon. Nearly dead in a desert he is rescued by Bedouins. Courage and determination enables him to progress in life and marry a princess and finally become a king. But after many years he becomes nostalgic for homeland and returns to Egypt welcomed by the Pharaoh.

- Westcar Papyrus - 1600 BC: A set of stories depicting marvels performed by

Egyptian temple scholars. The stories are told to Pharaoh Khufu by his sons.

- Papyrus Harris I – 1100 BC: History of the reign of Pharaoh Ramses III and also includes a list of temple endowments written in the hieratic method – hand written in running style. This method developed in Egypt alongside the hieroglyphics.

- Story of Wenamun - 1000 BC: Wenamun is robbed on his way to buy cedar from Lebanon. Left helpless he struggles to return to Egypt.

- The Peasant and the Workman 1000 BC ~ : Story of a hardworking and talented peasant and his cruel supervisor. The peasant is ultimately rewarded and the supervisor punished.

- The Girl with the rose red slippers: Adapted by Aelian in Greek in the 3rd century CE. This is the original 'Cinderella' story in which Pharaoh Amasis searches for the girl who owns the rose red slipper.

The 'belle lettres', of Egyptian literature, emerged in the fourth millennium. Soon, trends and social reflections become noticeable in the writings. For example, Sinuhe lives in a civilised world where the Kings are benevolent and the Bedouins are kind and honourable (Kemp, 2006). In the 'Story of Wenamun' Egypt is the centre of cosmos. Apparently, the authors created cultural values that would be transmitted to the general people (Fischer-Elfert, 2003). Sometimes, the plot in stories is deliberately set without any reference to any historical period such as the 'Shipwrecked Sailor'. But generally the stories based in the past – recent, medium or distant past. The Sinuhe plot was set in the recent past (Morenz, 2003).

~~~

During this period, the Phoenicians (ancient Lebanese) manufactured dyes, brilliant textiles, transparent glass etc. But their main contribution was the first phonetic based alphabets that would be the ancestor of many languages. These inscriptions have been discovered in Lebanon, Syria, and various other areas. They spread their language and the greater Mesopotamian culture along the Aegean trade route including coastal Turkey (Anatolia), Crete and Mycenae (Greece). Cadmus, a noble of Tyre, was the founder of Thebes, which became the largest city in central Greece. According to Herodotus Cadmus is credited to having taught the alphabet to the Greeks (Jeffery, 1982). The Ionic Greeks were the first to adopt it and called it 'Phoenician Letters'. The Phoenician alphabet served as a basis for the Greek alphabet and was a key factor in the initiation of Greek literature.

~~~

In China, at this time, palaces were built in capital city of Anyang (Henan Province). Irrigation was practiced, war chariots were used and the first Chinese alphabets were written. The world's oldest known complex road network is from this time. There were five grades of roads ranging from pathways to stone surface roads which were three-wagon wide. Courier stations on the roadside supported a mail service. Peasants grew food and craftsmen made tools, weapons, clothing, ornaments and household goods using bronze, silk, jade and clay.

The first Chinese writing was done on oracle bones and bronze. Diviners wrote questions on the 'oracle' bones of turtles then scorched the bone. The marks that appeared due to scorching were supposed to be messages from the ancient spirits that were read by the diviners. When kings died they were buried with servants who would accompany them to heaven (Michaelson, 1996).

~~~

In Greek Mycenae, monumental structures and citadels were built during this time, such as the 1,100-meter long 'Lion's Gate'. From these impressive forts their kings ruled over numerous settlements and villages bound to them by feudal loyalties and trade. The bronze armour, pottery, and ivory found in the unique beehive tombs of Mycenaean nobles also suggests the Mycenaean were involved in trade in the eastern Mediterranean until the collapse of their civilization in the 12th century BC. After this period of progress ushered by the Minoans and Mycenaean, the Greeks would be lost in a dark age of unknown isolation (Pomeroy 1999). They would flourish again in the classical age starting approximately 500 years later.

~~~

During the end of this millennium, the Medes were gathering strength and would build the first powerful Persian nation.

~~~

The progressive influence of one civilisation on another, over time, can be seen by the study of the mythical creatures Griffin and Phoenix. The Griffin has the body of a lion and head and wings of an eagle. The griffin is first known from the arts of Babylon and next depicted in the artwork of ancient Persia of around 6th century BC such as the sculptor in Persipolis and Bronze Griffin in Susa. Griffin-headed gold rhytons have been excavated from Achaemenid sites (Curtis and Tallis, 2005). Finally, this artwork was to become popular in other parts of the ancient world including Scythia, Macedonia and Greece.

The Phoenix, the mythical bird, is of Egyptian origin. In the Egyptian myth the spirit of Horus returns in the shape of a Bennu bird. The burning heat of Ra's eye turns it into ash. But a new Bennu bird rises from the ashes. Thus, from the ashes of the Egyptian Bennu rose the Greek Phoenix.
~~~

The Persian Prophet

One of the important events of the 2nd millennium BC was the birth of the Prophet-Philosopher Zardusht, also known as Zarathustra or more commonly as Zoroaster. He lived in Iran (Aryavejo) in 1200 BC a few centuries after Abraham made his epochal journey. There is a debate on the time he lived in but most scholars place him in a time period older than 700 BC at least. He was the son of Pourushaspa and Dugdova. He was a professional priest cum chanter and since his youth was opposed to the prevailing religion and political philosophy which led him to start a quest for knowledge and truth. He struggled and suffered and did not have a single follower for years. Finally, after years of search Asha Vahishta, the Truth, dawned upon him - the purpose of life on earth was to strive for perfection via action and inaction.

The innovative aspect of his religion required social reforms that caused a conflict between Zoroaster and the representatives of the established cult - the priests of the god Mithra and the goddess Anahita. He found it difficult to preach his religion and was ill treated even in his mother's hometown. At about the age of thirty, facing oppression, he fled and approached Prince Vishtaspa with his religious philosophy. The Prince, after initial doubts, recommended him to his people and granted him protection. Ultimately, his religion and enlightened philosophy was to triumph.

According to the Avesta, Zoroaster was given the mission by Ahura Mazda the supreme creator. The essence of the mission can be described as follows: In the universe there are two forces locked in struggle: the *Spenta Mainyu*, the benevolent or creative spirit of Ahura Mazda, and the *Angra Mainyu,* the malevolent or destructive spirit. Ahura Mazda will be the ultimate victor and all of creation, even the banished souls, will be reunited in him. He also emanated six aspects of creation, the *Amesha Spentas* (Everlasting - Truth - Laws). The Amesha Spentas, personification of the attributes of Ahura Mazda, along with Ahura Mazda form a divine 'Heptad'. These attributes also represents virtuous qualities which people must strive for and imitate if they wish to be included in the followers of Ahura Mazda destined to enjoy the benefits of *Frashokereti* - the world's refreshment (Moulton 1917). The six stages of attaining Amesha Spentas are:

Stage 1: Bah-Man (Vohu Mana) or Good Mind

The Good Mind is the wisdom, knowledge and experience needed to make the correct decisions to establish the TRUTH. In nature this knowledge is only instinctive and learning capacity is nil or limited to 'About Itself'. Humans, on the other hand, can acquire unlimited knowledge and wisdom.

The first rule to Asha (Truth) is
All should aspire to make
Good use of wisdom in the mind
Thus bringing harmony to the universe
And also to the individual soul.

Gatha – Yasna 28.1 (FR)

The rival of Vohu Mana is Ahri Mana the Evil Mind. The same mind has two forces, the good and the evil. Zoroaster places great emphasis on these two forces, which are equal in strength. If the mind succumbs to the evil force the end result will be the undesirable.

Wisdom and Knowledge (Mazda Ashem) also brings evil

Gatha HA 28.9 (FR)

Stage 2: Ordibehest (Asha Vahista) or the Good Truth.

The good truth is obtained through the good mind. It is the knowledge about us and our environment including the physical and behavioural aspects.

Certainly I shall acquire
The Wisdom in Existence (Mazda Ahura)
Through Good use of the mind
I shall master them all
Physical and that of the mind
Gaining through knowledge
Whereby desiring and getting perfection

Gatha – Yasna - 28.2 (FR)

Stage 3: Shahrivar (Khash Atra Vairya) – Good Guidance or Harmony

The development of just human laws and rules to conduct worldly affairs based on the Ordibehest or Good Truth. Not to disrupt the harmony but instead evolve, advance and provide a righteous society.

Truly the knowledge derived
By the good mind
Never before known
(In) the Great Wisdom and in the Universe
From it bring good rule, never waning

And make righteous society
Leading us towards perfection
Gatha – Yasna 28.3 (FR)

Stage 4: Esfand (Spenta Armaita) - Lawful Desire

Good guidance leads the individual, community and thus the nation towards lawful desires, love, harmony, righteousness, peace and justice.

Truly the spiritual result is high
Good thoughts give harmony
Which results in goodness
In tune with the wisdom in creation
Gatha – Yasna 28.4 (FR)

Stage 5: Khordad (Haurvatat) - Perfection

And such a pure, wise and righteous ambience gives rise to mental, physical and spiritual Perfection

Stage 6: Amordad (Ameretat) or Immortal

Perfection leads to total freedom from fear and the material world. One is not afraid of death or the unknown and attains a level of being where one does not depend on material goods or others for happiness. In essence, one lives in a timeless zone and becomes an immortal.

Significant information about ancient Zoroastrianism comes from the Greeks. Xanthos, a contemporary of King Xerxes, wrote a book on Persian religion. Besides him, Aristotle, Plutarch, Diogenes Laertius and others wrote about Zoroastrianism.

Zoroaster was a prophet who did not belong to the Abrahamic family but preached and philosophised concepts similar to monotheism - inherent duality and conflict of good and evil, and mankind's free choice between these two alternatives. He preached that God was omniscient and loving, kind, and forgiving. He spoke of messianic redemption, resurrection, final judgment, heaven and hell (The word "paradise" is derived from Old Persian). He preached that salvation, both in this life and the afterlife, could only be achieved through Good Words, Good Thoughts, and Good Deeds. Many of these concepts are similar to those of Judaism, Christianity and Islam. Zoroaster had also warned the people of a Last Judgment similar to Islam.

Zoroaster is one of the earliest known philosophers and founded Mazda-Yasna which in Avestan language means "Worship of Wisdom" and in essence is a rational system dealing with humanity and ethics. The Greeks coming in contact with the 'Worship of Wisdom' used their own term 'philosophy' meaning "Love of Wisdom" to define the system of rational thought.

The Avesta is the holy book of the Zoroastrians or, as they are called today, the Parsees. The Avesta was codified in 600 CE, but it contains much older material, such as the *Gathas*. These hymns were probably written almost two millennia before the codification of the Avesta and most scholars think that they were composed by Zoroaster himself. The Gathas are poetic admonitions and prophecies, cast in the form of dialogues with God and the Amesha Spentas. The verses are terse and metrical in nature with a few grammatical constructs.

According to the *Book of Arda Viraf*, composed in the 3rd century CE, the Gathas and some other texts that were incorporated into the Avesta had previously existed in the palace library of the Achaemenid kings (648–330 BC) in Persepolis. The Old Persian treatise of *Shatroiha-I Airan* states that the palace library was lost in a fire caused by the troops of Alexander the Great as they conquered Persia. In this fire all the religious and scholarly enquiries of the Persians were burnt including the original Avesta. The present text was assembled in the 3rd–7th century CE from the remains of a larger body of scripture. According to Pliny the Elder the original Avesta included segments that are now lost. In his *Naturalis Historiae* he mentions one Hermippus of Smyrna of having "interpreted two million verses of Zoroaster" in the 3rd century BC.

Ahuramazda of the Gathas was in essence a single god but the Achaemenids, in their acceptance of all different gods from different lands, made him the supreme god. The Zoroastrian tradition is univocal that the Yashts were composed by Zoroaster. The Yashts or Avestan hymns mentions and are dedicated to lower deities which would make him a polytheist. Scholars have argued that the Yashts are written in the language of cuneiform texts of the Achaemenid Empire that existed between 521 and 331 BC. This indicates the Yashts were written after the Prophet Zoroaster. Irrespective of what the Prophet might have been the Achaemenid Zoroastrianism was polytheistic.

In the Gathas the Daevas (Deva of Vedic India) are not antagonised. This implies that the Gathas are of more archaic age then the time when the conflict between the Avestanic Persians and the Vedic Indians started. In the later Avesta though, the Prophet is depicted as fighting the Devaes or 'evil immortals', and is tempted by Ahriman, Ahura Mazda's evil dual, to renounce his faith. Thus it can be implied that the acrimony between the Avestanic Persians and the Vedic Indians started after the Gathas were written.

During the 5th century BC the Zurvanism concept rose from one of the passages of the

Gathas, "Truly, there are two primal Spirits, twins in conflict. In thought and speech, in act they are two – the good and the bad (Yasna 30.3)". Zurvanism represents a belief in a form of 'Holy Triad', in which Zurvan is the hypostasis, the underlying and absolute reality, of time and space and was the "father" of the twin spirits, the malevolent Angra Mainyu and the benevolent Ahura Mazda. They differed from the main form of Zoroastrianism that considered Ahura Mazda as the transcendental creator. After becoming influential the Triad Form was officially sanctioned in the Persian Sassanian era (225 – 650 CE) and existed till the 10th century CE.

The Indian Epics

Originally, three ancient Veda *Samahitas* (collections) developed out of the Indian – Aryan philosophy: The Rig-Veda, the oldest Veda, consists of a collection of 1,028 hymns in ten volumes recited by priests as invocations and litanies dedicated to the Vedic deities. Ajur-Veda consists of prose mantras and verses borrowed from Rig-Veda recited by priests during sacrifices. Sama-Veda consists of melodious hymns recited by priests during the Soma sacrifice praising the vitalising properties of *soma pavamana* - juice of the soma plant. It is a rearrangement of parts of Rig-Veda along with original mantras. The three Vedas deal to a great extent with ceremonial sacrifices. The fourth samahita, Atharva-Veda, consists mainly of spells and incantations to be used as protection against demons and disaster. It also contains spells for the healing of diseases, for attainment of long life and for the satisfaction of various desires or aims in life.

The ages of the Vedas and the later epics Ramayana and Mahabharata are hotly disputed. The western authorities claim the Vedas to be of the 2nd millennium BC while some Indian authorities claim a much earlier antiquity. The Rig Veda describes a Bronze Age world thus it is older then the Iron Age and, at the same time, it mentions ruins (Indus Valley), so it is younger than the Indus Civilization. This indicates that the oral tradition of Rig Veda started from around 1500 BC (Wood, M., 2007). The 'Mitanni Text' of 1380 BC found in Northern Syria is linguistically very similar to the Vedic language. In it Vedic-Indian gods Indra, Mitra and Varuna are mentioned in the same order as they appear in formulaic phrases of Rig Veda. It becomes apparent that the stories of the gods have traveled between India and Syria along with their worshippers. For two thousand years the oral Rig Veda was transmitted by the Brahmins and first written on palm leaves after 500 CE.

The Ramayana and Mahabharata texts are of a later age than the Vedas and are absorbing, political, moral and fascinating epics in poetic form which gives evidence to the racial and caste-divided Indian society in the pre-classical age before the Gupta Empire. In the Ramayana, the faultless Prince Rama, with support from loyal brother Laxman, sets out and rescues his chaste and indomitable wife Seeta who has been abducted by the powerful demon King Ravan of Sri Lanka. After he rescues her she has to undergo and pass a chastity test by fire. Politically, this epic represents the Aryan incursion into South India and Srilanka. There are parallels in the plot between Iliad and Ramayana. Iliad also portrays invasion, brotherly love and kidnapping of the wife by the ruler of an Island. The Ramayana text, though smaller than the Mahabharata, is four times the size of the Iliad.

The plot of Mahabharata is the power struggle between the cousins Pandavas and the Kauravas. It is the fight back of five brave Pandava Princes in pursuit of justice against their one hundred Kaurava cousins who had usurped the throne. But the plot, though very absorbing, is not the main factor in this multi-thematic epic. Military expeditions, political intrigues, philosophy, religion, great bravery, treachery, love, trust, chivalry, sacrifice, duty and a host of historical allusions form the ingredients. At that time, apparently, a woman could have more than one husband as depicted by Princess Draupadi who was the wife to all the five Pandava brothers. Even though the fight was amongst the Aryan cousins, the main political protagonist was the all powerful dark skinned avatar, Krishna, indicating a further move away from racial segregation from the time when the Ramayana was composed.

The Bhagavat Geeta, contained within the Mahabharata, is the philosophical discourse between Krishna and Arjuna, one of the Pandava brothers and leader of the Army, just before the start of a great battle against the Kauravas. The following is the gist of the eighteen chapters.

Bhagavat Geeta (The Celestial Song)

In the great Kurushetra battlefield Krishna, the avatar, is Arjuna's charioteer. He moves the chariot between the two armies facing each other. When brave Arjuna sees his relatives, teachers and friends facing him from the opposing army he loses his resolve to fight. It is Krishna who sings the Celestial Song.

Krishna indicates that death is not important, as "It is only the body that gets killed, and eternal self is indestructible. As a warrior it is your duty to fight for the righteous path (dharma)."

Arjuna asks, "If knowledge is more important than action, why should I fight?"

Krishna replies, "Perform your duties for the greater good. Do not be deluded by the result, and that is the correct course of action."

Krishna explains that he has lived through many births and has always taught Yoga meditation and discipline for the protection of the pious and the destruction of the evil. For the learner a mentor is imperative. At this Arjuna asks, "Which is better, active worldly life or renunciation of it?"

Krishna replies, "Salvation may be achieved through both. But the best course is to act on path of duty without seeking reward (Karma Yoga)." He then shows Arjuna the correct postures of transcendental meditation and how to reach higher levels of consciousness. He teaches the path of knowledge (Jana Yoga) and defines supernatural terms, and how to remember him at the time of death so as to attain the paramount paradise. "All things are from me," he ends, "And I am the ultimate source of all material and spiritual world."

Finally, Arjuna is convinced. He acknowledges Krishna as the Supreme Being and requests to see his real celestial form. Krishna displays his 'celestial appearance' (Viswarupa) – a being facing every direction and emanating the brilliance of a thousand suns, consisting of all existence. Then Krishna describes devotion, the self, consciousness, nature and its three modes.

"It is a tree," Krishna says, "with roots in heaven and foliage on the earth. It has to be felled by the axe of detachment. And only then one can reach the paramount paradise."

He explains the human traits of the divine and the demonic natures and the need to give up lust, anger and greed and to discern between right and wrong actions on the basis of the scripture. He also explains faith, thoughts, deeds and the central tendencies or qualities of existence, action and inaction. Finally, he exhorts Arjuna to abandon all cosmic laws and surrender to him as such surrender is the ultimate perfection of life.

Interesting Events of Millennium 1000 – 0 BC

The kingdom of Nubia (present day Sudan), situated south of Egypt, was a major source of gold for the Egyptian dynasties. However, by 8th century BC Egypt had become decadent, being ruled by a number of warlords. King Piye of Nubia invaded Egypt and after a year-long campaign subjugated the whole of the country. He then took all the booty and returned to Nubia and never returned to Egypt. He was the first of the Black Pharaohs, the 25th dynasty, which ruled Egypt for almost a century.

~~~

Meanwhile in Persia (modern day Iran) the first world superpower was forming. Persian King Cyrus the Great, born at the start of the 6th century BC, established the Achaemenid Empire. The Achaemenids conquered the lands of Assyria, Media, Elam, Babylon, Phoenicia, Egypt, Ionian Greece, Thessaly, Macedonia and the Indus Valley. In about 520 BC Darius the Great ruled an empire that had an area of 3 million square miles.

By 510 BC, the Ionian Greeks of Asia Minor and the Greek Islands had submitted to the Persian rule. There were pro-Persian Greeks even in Athens. But when there was an Ionian Greek revolt against the Persians, the Athenians and the Eretrians sent support to the Ionians. This was the start of the Persian wars. Darius crushed the revolt and decided to capture the rest of Greece. His army captured Thrace, Macedonia and Eretria. The Eretrians were reduced to slavery. In 491 BC, all of Greece, except for Athens and Sparta, submitted to Persia.

In 490 BC, the Persians lost an important battle in Marathon which saved Athens from falling to the Persians. Over a war of attrition the Persians retreated from some of the occupied territory.

In 480 BC Athens fell to the army of King Xerxes the Great. But soon after that the combined Greek naval fleet won a tactical battle near the Island of Salamis in which they destroyed much of the Persian fleet. The supplies for the Persian army were carried by their fleet. With much of their supplies gone the Persian had to fall back to Thessaly for its winter camp.

These victories became momentous in Greek history. The formation of the Delian League by Greek city-states become a threat but aside from that the Persian Empire continued as usual (Briant, 2005). For the time being these two defeats appeared to the Persians more as irritants in their strategy to dominate the world.

With revolts brewing in Egypt and Babylonia, the stubbornly brave and tactical Greek city-states were not lucrative enough for the Persians to venture there again. Instead their policy shifted from a military approach to diplomacy. There was constant squabbling between
~~~

the Greek city-states. The Persian kings successfully played the Athenians and the Spartans Greeks against each other for 150 years. Persia's financial and naval assistance was instrumental in Sparta's victory over Athens in the Great Peloponnesian War. The Persian influence was such that the Persian King Artaxerxes II was asked to mediate between the warring cities which led to the King's Peace of 387 BC - 'those who dwelt on this side of the sea remained Persian subjects, and those who dwelt across the sea were to be controlled by Sparta'. The Ionian and the Dorian Greeks lost all their Asian lands on the east coast of the Aegean Sea to Persia. Afterwards, when the Spartans started to become powerful Persia shifted their support to the Athenians.

~~~

In 336 BC, Phillip II became the king of Macedon. After more than two centuries of domination by the Persians he was the first person who started to forge the Greek city states to a single Greek nation with aggression against the Persian in mind. However, he was killed due to internal politics before he could do anything significant. That was left for his son to achieve. His son was Alexander, known as The Great.

In 334 BC, Alexander set out for Persia with about 40,000 soldiers, 30 days provisions, and 70 talents of gold from north eastern Greece. In a span of three years, he first took Tyre and Egypt then conquered Persia bringing the end of the Achaemenid dynasty, and then marched with his army up to the bank of the Indus River. As it marched the conquering army of Alexander swelled in rank first with Egyptians and Tyrians, and when it reached India, a large number were Persians.

But the great conqueror died at the age of thirty two before he could consolidate his rule. A long succession struggle followed between his successors. It was not before 280 BC that the bitter struggle was superficially settled with the establishment of four territorial states.

- Seleucid dynasty in Syria and Mesopotamia based at Antioch
- Ptolemaic dynasty in Egypt based at Alexandria
- Antigonid dynasty in Macedonia and central Greece
- Attalid dynasty in Anatolia based at Pergamum

The dynastic capitals became major centres of learning. Syncretisation of Greek with local gods took place in some of these localities like in Hatra which was a trading city near Palmyra (Brosius, 2006). The Hellenics, a mixed culture of Greeks and Persians in one area and Greeks and Egyptians in another, failed to unify and remained embroiled in quarrels.

Rome occupied Greek mainland in 147 BC. The resurgent Persians under the Parthian Dynasty soon started to exert their presence and took over the Seleucid lands. Finally, the
~~~

Parthians and the Romans separately overran the Hellenic Greeks from most of the conquered lands. In other regions the Greeks assimilated with the local culture.

~~~

The rise of Rome can be traced back to the beginning of the millennia. At around 800 BC, a small civilization known as Etruscan had flourished in Italy. According to Herodotus the Etruscans migrated to Italy from Lydia (Neo Hittite state in what is now Turkey). Initially, the Etruscans formed a powerful kingdom in the Northern Italy while the Greeks established a sophisticated colony in the south. The Etruscans lived in fortified cities and were more advanced then the indigenous people and soon pushed south and took over the rule of the city of Rome. Under them Rome developed from settlement to a city (Tingay and Badcock, 1989). Etruscan kings ruled Rome from 616 BC to 509 BC at which time the Roman Republic was formed. They developed public works, built road networks, and cut canals and tunnels for water to flow through. The Temple of Jupiter in Capitoline Hill which is the largest temple in central Italy was built by them. They originally started the chariot racecourse which would later become the famous Circus Maximus of Rome. They, to a large extent, introduced 'technology' to Italy. By 100 BC, as Rome rose in power all the variety of people living there including the Etruscans gradually assimilated.

Rome became a Republic with three classes of people. The Patricians - A group of powerful families who ruled over the republic. The Plebeians - The ordinary working class people who held no power and at the bottom of the rung were the slaves, the third class, who were owned by the rich Patricians. Governors were deployed by the Patricians to levy heavy tax on the general people outside of Rome. This unfair state of affairs finally led to civil wars and slave revolts.

The Roman Empire was initiated with the occupation of Carthage, the remnant of the Phoenician Empire located in North Africa, and Greece. The Roman Generals became the most powerful people in the republic. General Lucius defeated the legendary and formidable King Mithradates VI of Pontus, a region situated by the Black Sea off Turkey, in 77 BC. General Pompey conquered Syria and Jerusalem while Julius Caesar, a General and popular politician, conquered Gaul (France) and invaded Britain. He formed a triumvirate with General Crassus and General Pompey that dominated Roman politics for several years (Bringman, K 2007).

But in the first war against Persia, General Crassus was defeated and killed by the Parthians in Syria. This led to the collapse of the triumvirate and a stand-off between Pompey and the Senate. A civil war ensued in which Caesar with his legions emerged victorious in 49 BC.

After assuming control of the Roman Senate, Julius Caesar began widespread reforms of Roman society and government. He was proclaimed dictator for life and he took all
~~~

executive power into his hands. The Senate, being thus deprived of political clout, was unhappy and a group of senators led by Marcus Junius Brutus, a friend of Caesar, assassinated the dictator on the Ides of March (March 15) in 44 BC. This led to another Roman civil war. Four years later Octavian, the adopted son of Caesar, and his supporters were victorious against the assassins. Later he defeated the coalition of Roman General Mark Antony and Egyptian Queen Cleopatra. Around 30 BC he took the title of Augustus and became the first Roman emperor. He decentralized the Roman administration and ensured that talented people from all over the empire would rise to important positions. He also stationed most of his army in the frontiers to protect the empire and not indulge in politics. His able administration brought stability to the emerging Empire.

~~~

In India, the Persian and the Greek invasions were restricted to the northwest. Just a year after Alexander's death, in 322 BC, as the overextended Hellenic sphere started to decline, a king known as Chandragupta Maurya swept back through the country from Magadha (Bihar) and conquered his way well into Afghanistan. This was the beginning of one of India's great dynasties – the Maurya.

The greatest of the Maurya was Ashoka the Great (268-231 BC) under whom the Empire became one of the most advanced in the world. It collapsed one hundred years after his death. After the end of the Maurya dynasty, the empire was fragmented into a medley of kingdoms and smaller dynasties, the Sunga being the most dominant. The Greek rule of Punjab on the northwest returned briefly in 150 BC. But by this time Buddhism had become very influential and the Greek king Menander forsook the Hellenic pantheon and became a Buddhist.

~~~

China developed without being directly affected by the rest of the world. The Shang Empire was conquered by Wu, the founder of the Zhou Dynasty, in 1122 BC. The Zhou Dynasty Emperors ruled over a decentralized feudal system - a federation of city states. They ruled for 800 years and were called the "Sons of Heaven". In 256 BC the Qin deposed the last Zhou emperor. Qin Emperor Shi Huangdi united the whole of China in 221 BC. In 106 BC, by a treaty between Chinese Han Emperor Wu Di and Parthian King Mithridates II, the Silk Road was inaugurated, leading to an increase in trade.

Achievements of the Millennium:

The dominant Egyptian dynastic period came to an end after the conquest by Persians and Greeks. But they had left their mark on the civilisations of posterity. The colossal dimensions of the pyramids and temples, the intrigue of the hieroglyphs, the exotic sphinx and zoomorphic gods remained amazing to all. Their architecture, the original design, has had an incredible influence on many parts of the modern world in all the continents. Decorative features like Cavetto cornices, torus mouldings, battered walls, sphinxes, pyramids, obelisks and many others have been used in a range of buildings such as suspension bridges, reservoirs, prisons, museums, zoos, cinemas, etc., all over the world (Humbert and Price, 2003)

~~~

Persia formed the world's first religiously tolerant empire and consisted of a multitude of different languages, races, religions and cultures. It set a precedent for the importance of the rule of law, a powerful centralized army and an efficient and systematic state administration.

Earlier the Jewish people of Judah had been captured by the Babylonians, enslaved and brought to Babylon. In 539 BC Babylonia surrendered peacefully to Cyrus the Great, the first Persian Achaemenid Emperor. Cyrus freed the Jews from captivity and assisted them to migrate to their homeland and to reconstruct their temple in Jerusalem. In the Book of Isaiah of the Old Testament Cyrus is hailed as the Shepherd of the Lord.

His respect for local traditions, laws, languages, and religions set the foundation of a relatively benevolent empire. He also declared the first Charter of Human Rights known to mankind, which was written on a 23 cm long clay cylinder that was discovered in Nineveh, Iraq and is on display in the British Museum.

In 521 BC Darius, another Great Achaemenid, made Aramaic the official language of the Persian Empire. Aramaic remained the lingua franca of a great part of the civilized world till the 7th century CE Muslim opening. Banking houses were formed and the introduction of the earliest common coinage, the Daric, and the use of gold, silver and bronze coins on a very large scale revolutionised economic activities. Many roads, ports and elaborate irrigation systems were developed. The Persians also built a central road network which later would be connected by the Parthians to Europe on the west and China in the east forming the silk route. The royal palace in Persepolis built by Darius reflected the wealth and the multi-cultural dimension of the Persian Empire. The origin of the game of polo dates back from this time and was played by the Persian nobility for both sport and combat training. Excavations in Persepolis have exposed evidence of great wealth, grand architecture, and extravagant works of silver and gold that was unparalleled in the ancient world. These include beautifully crafted rhytons, cups, jars, plates, decanters, ornaments, jewelleries, earrings,
~~~

necklaces, arm plates and many other decoration pieces of gold and silver (Curtis and Tallis, 2005) that would put the artisans of current times to shame. Grand and luxurious works of decorative art were produced. There also were outstanding feats of monumental arts and architecture. Some of the great constructions include the Palace of Darius, the Palace of Xerxes, the Apadana, Gate of all Nations, Stairs of All Nations, and the Hall of Hundred Columns.

> The Apadana or Audience Hall of Persepolis belongs to the oldest building phase of Persepolis. It was superbly designed during the time of Darius the Great. People of all the nations in the Achaemenid Empire paid tribute to the King there. They presented him with gifts which were stored in the Treasury. The beautiful huge Hall and its three porticoes could hold thousands of people at the same time. The twenty five meter high roof of the Apadana was supported by seventy-two columns.
>
> The subjects of the Achaemenid as represented on the relief work of one of the walls of the Apadana included Thracians, Sagartians, Bactrians, Egyptians, Arians, Parthians, Elamites, Medes, Carians, Arabs, Sogdians, Gandarans, Sacae, Syrians, Babylonians, Armenians, Nubians, Libyans, Indians, Arachosians, Greeks, Cappadocians and Lydians. The relief is intricately engraved capturing the traditional dresses, hairstyle, headgears, and beard particular to each nation.

The monumental works of the Egyptians and the Persians had remained unequalled up to recent centuries. The greatest legacy of the Persian Empire was that it demonstrated for the first time how diverse peoples can culturally flourish and economically prosper under one central government.

When Alexander had invaded Egypt, he was received as a liberator from the Persians and was declared the son of Amon, the Egyptian supreme god, by the Egyptian priests. Alexander, henceforth, called himself the son of Amon and wore a Ram-horned helmet. But after conquering Persia he showed positive disposition towards Persian culture. He claimed to be successor to Achaemenid Kings and paid tribute to Cyrus at his tomb and praised Darius. Alexander adopted Persian culture that included Persian dress and customs of his court. He practiced the custom of *proskynesis*, a symbolic salute of raising the hand up to the face that the Persians paid to their social superiors, but previously not practiced by the Greeks. Instead of going back to Macedon he married a Bactrian (Afghan) lady, Roxana, and a Persian Princess, Stateira, and settled down in Persia. He asked his Generals and soldiers to assimilate as well and many thousands were married to Persians. His political alliances with all that he conquered indicate that he, himself, did not believe in pantheons – Greek, Egyptian or Persian. He, most likely, believed in a more universal or omnipresent deity.

~~~
~~~

When the Persians had started to build their empire, Gautama Siddhartha, a Prince of a Nepalese Kingdom in the Indian subcontinent, was born around 550 BC. He lived a 'royal' life away from the ordinary people for 29 years of his life. When he first came in contact with the poor, sick and the dispossessed and witnessed their hardship he was exceedingly moved. He left his kingdom and family in search for the cause of human suffering. After years of ascetic wandering he 'awakened' and declared that human suffering was due to ignorance, and that happiness was in enlightenment (Nirvana) towards which all souls should aim for. In the feudal caste-ridden and unequal India his philosophy was a quasi-socialist doctrine.

During the same period the ascetic Prince Mahavira founded Jainism in northern India. Jainism stresses renunciation to the extent that its followers renounces not only the world but, ultimately, life itself. It espouses spiritual independence and equality of all life forms with a particular emphasis on non-violence.

This period also saw Chanakya, advisor to Chandragupta, write 'Arthashastra' that discusses the feudal management of an efficient and effective economy. In this millennium the Indians had progressed considerably ahead in Grammar (Panini 400 BC) and Mathematics (the various Sutras).

Megasthenes, the Greek ambassador at the court of Chandragupta Maurya, in his book 'Indica' wrote of the prosperity of India and expressed his admiration for the efficient administration of the Indian Maurya empire. He further reported that water, mineral wealth and agricultural products were abundant. Speaking of the general prosperity, Megasthenes wrote, "The Indians, dressed in bright and rich colours, liberally used ornaments and gems." He also spoke of the division of society according to profession and the large number of religious sects and of foreigners in the empire.

Ashoka (304 BC - 232 BC) was one of the greatest emperors of India. While still a prince he was a fierce warrior and a feared individual. In the process of consolidating royal power he had all the vying princes executed. When he embarked on conquest he conquered nearly the entire subcontinent. In Orissa, however, his rampant army shed so much blood that the repentant king gave up warfare forever. Fascinatingly, the conquering Warrior King turned into a Philosopher King. He promoted tolerance towards all religions and also supported them financially.

The 'Ashokavandana' text states that Ashoka built 87,000 religious 'structures' and monasteries called Stupa and Vihara. Some Viharas became extremely important institutions evolving into major Buddhist Universities with thousands of students, such as the one at Nalanda, which was located in what is modern day Bihar.

~~~
~~~

Meanwhile in Greece, in 500 BC Cleisthenes established the world's first democracy, with power being held by an assembly of all male citizens. Under Pericles, the first citizen, Athens became the educational and cultural centre of ancient Greece. After the death of Pericles, in 429 BC, Athenian democracy was interrupted twice by the revolutions of the murderous oligarchy known as 'Thirty Tyrants'. But it was restored in an altered form by Euclides, the Archon of Athens, in 402 BC. The end of Athenian democracy came when it was terminated by the Macedonians in 322 BC.

The first Greeks prose was introduced by Anaximender (611 – 547) of Miletus. Others consider Pherecides of Syros or Cadmus Milesius, who became the first Greek historian, to have introduced prose work during the time of Cyrus the Great of Persia. In 525, the works of Aeschylus, Sophocles, and Euripides made tragedy the style in Greek literature probably reflecting the socio-political situation under Persian domination.

Coins became common in most of Greece after the 5th century. The major Greek art forms of the classical period were in sculpture and architecture. Like those of the Persians much of the Greek buildings have not survived. They were either pillaged in war or looted for building materials or destroyed in earthquakes. Only a few temples, such as the Parthenon and the Temple of Hephaestus in Athens, overcame the ravages of time. No sign whatsoever have survived of the four Wonders of the World created by the Greeks - the Statue of Zeus at Olympia, the Colossus of Rhodes, the Temple of Artemis at Ephesus and the Lighthouse of Alexandria.

The true greatness of the Greeks was their pursuit of philosophy and academia. The Greeks inherited science from the Egyptians, philosophy from the Persians and the polytheistic world view from all the pre-existing civilisations and set on a quest for knowledge. It was for this search of knowledge that the world remains indebted to them.

The Olympic Games had started in 776 BC, as religious celebration held in Olympus. It consisted of contests alternating with sacrifices and ceremonies in honour of both Zeus and Pelops. Held over a number of days the events consisted of racing and wrestling. Naked young men would participate in the events and winners were given a crown of olive leaves and were greatly admired.

The Parthenon was a temple built in the 5th century BC on the acropolis of Athens. It replaced an older temple of Athena that had been destroyed by the Persians in 480 BC. Like most Greek temples the Parthenon was used as a treasury, and for a time also served as the treasury of the Delian League. It is the most famous building of ancient Greece and indicates the finest achievement of Greek architecture. Its decorative sculptures are considered one of the high points of Greek art.

As its beauty was exquisite its history also remains pervasive over time. In the sixth century CE, the Parthenon was converted into a Church and dedicated to the Virgin.

After the Turkish conquest of Greece, it was converted into a mosque. In 1687 a Turkish ammunition dump inside the building was ignited by a Venetian cannonball. The resulting explosion severely damaged the Parthenon and its sculptures. In the 19th century CE, some surviving sculptures were taken to England and are now on display in the British Museum.

The Greek had institutionalised a form of homosexuality, i.e., Pederasty (Greek for boy lover). This was sexual relationship between adult men and adolescent boys by which a man could have a boy as a sexual partner. According to Plutarch and Xenophon, similar relationship existed between adult women and adolescent girls. Closely associated with the Olympic Games was the gymnasium (Greek "place to be nude") where competitors trained in the nude. It was also a place for socialization. Plato identified the states that "especially encourage the use of gymnasia" as being those notable for pederasty traditions.

The pervasion of sexuality into sports would eventually end a thousand-year old tradition. The Games gradually declined in importance as the Romans gained power in Greece. When Christianity became the official religion of the Roman Empire, the Olympic Games were seen as a pagan festival and in discord with Christian ethics, and in 393 CE the Emperor Theodosius I outlawed the Olympics.

~~~

From the ancient times the Chinese had believed in ancestral spirits and a god or creator who could see the past, present and future. Later, Buddhist belief - karma (deeds), reincarnation and nirvana - overshadowed these previous beliefs. Along with Buddhism the non-theistic moralist philosophy of Confucius and harmony-with-nature Dao philosophy became the foundation of the social, natural and spiritual aspects of Chinese life. Under the Zhou dynasty three system of thought evolved - Confucianism, Daoism and Legalism (Michaelson, 1996). Legalism imbued the ideology that it was everyone's duty to follow the king and contribute to the army and to the production of food.

Qin Emperor Shi Huangdi favoured the legalist school of thought and outlawed all other schools. He buried 346 scholars alive whom he disfavoured. When he died in around 210 BC he was buried in a colossal tomb near Xian, surrounded by thousands of terracotta soldiers. Each soldier statue was life size and made to minute individual details. Facial forms, eyes, ears, noses, clothes, everything were different for each individual.

The Chinese led a well regulated cultural life. Images of very large dance and music groups are depicted in 'tiles' from this period. The empire was unified by strict laws, taxes and a standard writing script. Roads, canals, bridges and about 5000 km of the Great Wall were built during this period.
~~~

There were scientific advances. The Halley's Comet was, in fact, first observed and recorded in China in 240 BC. An instrument called armillary sphere, used to divide the sky visually so that it could be measured and mapped, was invented by the Chinese of this period. Gun powder and paper was first invented in China in this period.

China was located on the far eastern 'end' of the world and at times developed in relative isolation. But many of its inventions and discoveries would reach other civilisations.

Ancient Tales

Many Classicists now believe that the Homeric poems, Iliad and the Odyssey, were the works of oral poets of 9th to the 7th century BC. They were later put down in written form by a poet or group of poets in the 6th century BC. Homer was the fictitious name given by the Greeks to the supposed author of the early Greek poems. No biographical information is available about Homer.

Stesichorus around 600 BC had written a version of the Helen of the Iliad story and named it 'The story of the Greek Princess' (Green, 2004). In it Prince Paris of Troy is the antagonist and quirk of the plot is that Helen never goes to Troy. This story is mentioned by Herodotus and is the basis of a play by Euripides.

The Story of the Greek Princess

When the Trojan Prince Paris went to Sparta as an Ambassador of Troy he was the honoured guest of good king Menelus. But when Menelus went away on state business, Paris took the form of Menelus and lured his beautiful wife Helen to his ship. Then he escaped taking along with him much treasure as well. But on the way to Troy a storm forced their ship to take shelter in Egypt. There, Paris and his men were brought to the presence of the Pharaoh Seti.

In the court the Pharaoh said that if Paris serves the gods and comes in peace to Egypt he was welcome. The Pharaoh was always delighted to hear the stories of distant lands and asked the Prince to speak about himself and the land from where he came.

Paris acknowledged that he indeed comes in peace and was the son of King Priam of Troy. It was the gods of the seas that had forced them to Egypt. But of Helen, the most beautiful, he lied claiming that he had won her fairly in Sparta to be his wife.

But Seti had a vast knowledge of the world of which Paris was unaware. Seti was not satisfied with the statement that the King of Sparta had given his daughter to a Prince of Troy. He knew that the Greek Achaeans of Sparta were at conflict with the Trojans. He asked Paris how was it that the Achaean King had given Paris his daughter as according to the Egyptian scribes there was hostility between them.

Paris claimed that the scribes were mistaken. There used to be hostility in the past, but now they lived in peace. The king Tyndareaus himself had given Paris his daughter from among many Achaean Princes.

Some of the sailors of Paris were Greeks. They were unhappy with Paris for what he had done and had asked for asylum in Egypt. They were present in the court and at this point made some noise of indignation which attracted the attention of the Pharaoh. He asked them to speak with no fear as due to the asylum they were now the Pharaoh's subjects and under his protection.

The leader among the Greeks then addressed the mighty king saying that they did not serve Prince Paris anymore because he lies and has done wrong. About Helen he said that she was the daughter of King Tyndareaus of Sparta and Queen Ledz, but it is said she is actually the daughter of Greek god Zeus.

Seti believed what the man said about Helen as there was a similar Egyptian example. Hatshepsut, great queen of Egypt, was said to be the daughter of Ra.

Then the leader continued with his story: When Helen was old enough to be married there were a large number of suitors, Greeks and other Princes, for her hand. She was so beautiful and the person who would marry her would become the king of Sparta. That was many years ago and Paris was not among them. The king married her to Menelus and the two of them reigned in Sparta until Paris used deception and force to sail away with her and along with a lot of treasures.

Paris shouted out loud that those were lies claiming that, in fact, Helen hated her husband and came with him on her own free will. She took only her own treasures along.

After listening to them the Pharaoh said to the Prince that he has already given two versions of his story. First he said that her father gave her to him and now he admits that he has taken her from her husband. There appeared to be some deception. Then he turned to the Vizier and ordered that the Prince be taken with due honour to the guest house and his men be kept under guard.

The Vizier followed the Pharaoh's command and also seized the treasures that Paris had brought from Sparta.

Seti then talked with Helen herself who wept and told him the truth. The Pharaoh was moved by her unhappy state of affairs and promised to protect her.

During the night the god Thot drew out from Helen her 'Ka' or her image double. This illusory double which had the exact likeness of Helen was given to Paris. He rejoiced and sailed for Troy taking the Ka with him thinking it to be the real Helen.

Helen remained in the Temple of Hathor, goddess of love, with Tausert the high priestess. Years went by and many people started to worship Helen as the avatar of Hathor.

Seti died and Set Nakhte became the new Pharaoh. But he died soon and after some political turmoil Ramses the third, son of Tausert and Pharaoh Set Nakhte, became the Pharaoh. Helen, over these years, remained as beautiful as ever. Ramses became enamoured of Helen and declared that he would marry her. Tausert tried to dissuade him but he would not listen to anything. Finally she asked what if Menelus is still alive?

That seemed to affect him and put him off, at least, temporarily.

Seventeen years passed since Helen's arrival when, one day, Tausert found a shipwrecked sailor kneeling in the Temple of Hathor. She asked him where he has come from and what was he doing there instead of going to the Temple of Herscef, the sanctuary for strangers.

The sailor said that he was Menelus, king of Sparta. He was told in a dream to come here. His wife was stolen by the Trojans, the rescue attempt had led to a war that lasted ten years. The Achaeans had finally won and he was reunited with his wife. After the war they sailed together from Troy but ill winds kept pushing them out of their course till they came to the mouth of the Nile where they were shipwrecked. He and Helen took shelter in a cave. But in the morning she was nowhere to be found. Menelus was afraid that the crocodiles may have taken her and, in despair, had wanted to give up his life. But Hermes appeared to him and asked him to go and seek Helen in the Temple of Strange Hathor.

Tausert looked up and said that the will of Amon Ra has been realised. For the last seventeen years his wife dwelled here in the Temple.

Menelus found that hard to believe because they had fought a war over her in Troy and she was with him till the day before!

She told him that it was the Ka of Helen that was with him and explained everything to Menelus. Then she turned and presented Helen to him.

As Helen emerged, the amazed Menelus put his arms around her tightly as if trying to make certain that this was not an apparition, then said to Tausert that in Greece, the Egyptians are regarded as the wisest. But their magic is stronger than they had imagined.

When, finally, Helen addressed her lord she said that the danger was not yet over for the Pharaoh Ramses wants to marry her.

Tausert assured them that she would help them to find a way out of their predicament. They sat down together to device a plan of escape. The next day the three of them went to the Pharaoh with Helen in mourning clothes and loose hair.

Ramses asked what had happened. Tausert told her son that his wish is finally coming true. Pointing at the still dishevelled Menelus she said that this was a sailor from the ship of Menelus. The ship was wrecked and Menelus was dead. Ramses was delighted as nothing now stood between him and Helen.

Helen pretended to be sad. Seti noticed her distress and said that surely she did not grieve for Menelus after such long years. Helen replied that before anything else she had to honour the memory of Menelus. She had to sacrifice a bull out in the sea accompanied by the men of Menelus. She said that the ship wrecked sailors would help her to carry out the solemn ceremony. For that she requested a ship, all of Menelus' sailors, a bull for sacrifice and the treasure that Paris had originally brought from Sparta. Lovelorn Ramses, so near to possess his object of desire, agreed to all she asked for.

Helen, Menelus and their sailors boarded the ship as if to perform the sacrifice and were soon on their way to Sparta. When Ramses realised what had happened he was so angry that he decided to have his mother, Tausert, executed. But Thot appeared to him and said that all had taken place by the will of Amon Ra. Ramses bowed to the god's will and praised his mother.

The First Super Power

The Persian Achaemenid after the 5th century BC was the first super power of the world. They ruled an empire of unprecedented extent with a very sophisticated administration. Their realm comprised of diverse ethnic groups speaking and writing in various languages. The Persians encouraged the diversity in culture and respected all religions. These events are noted in historical texts as well as the Bible.

The mingling of all the ethnic groups within the empire caused syncretisation of culture and religion. The Persian mixed with the Babylonians, Greeks, Assyrians, Egyptians, Arabs and Jews. In ethnic regions the Persians are known to have taken the names of other ethnic groups and worshipped other ethnic gods like those of Babylonians and Greeks. Significant numbers of Indians had visited their cities in search of knowledge and wealth. It is recorded that in 499 BC an Indian named Abbatama came with 20 others and again in 498 BC Karabba, another Indian, came with 180 men. An Indian woman owned an Inn in the Persian Capital (Dandamaev and Lukin, 1989).

There is a huge misunderstanding about the contributions of Persians to the development of knowledge. In the Persian philosophy of accommodating all the cultures they also encouraged and sponsored the development of technology in all the ethnic groups in their domain. Much of late Babylonian and Egyptian knowledge and early Greek knowledge developed when these nations were under their domination. Philosopher Heraclites of Ephesus, astronomers Kidimma and Naburianus of Babylon, historian Herodotus - who actually grew up in Halicarnassus of Caria which is now in Turkey - were all subjects of the Persian Achaemenids. The Temple of Artemes at Ephesus and the Halicarnassus Mausoleum was built by their subjects. A large number of calendars - Zoroastrian, Egyptian, Babylonian, Judaic, Solar, Lunar – existed within their empire. Babylonian mathematical astronomy was most creative under the Achaemenid. There were astronomical schools in a number of cities and astronomical charts with distance between stars, constellations, and their relative positions were prepared. One such chart gave observation of Jupiter from 5th century BC up to Alexander's time. Improved methods to obtain enamel by artificial means were developed, terminology to define silver purity evolved and glass making improved highly in Egypt, Phoenicia and Babylonia.

Thus good deal of what is considered as Egyptian, Babylonian, Greek and Phoenician development actually flourished under the Persians.

Since the start of civilisation knowledge had developed in different regions. The Achaemenid Empire brought a regional stability that allowed these cultures to come face to face without enmity and co-exist in mutual development of knowledge. But it was the great Greeks who actually grasped knowledge and gave concrete shape to the abstract form – Philosophy. Even before the Persians, the Greeks were in touch with various empires – The Semitic Mesopotamians, the Aryan Hittites, the Pharaonic Egyptians and the seafaring Phoenicians. They started off as tradesmen, craftsmen, performers and mercenaries and ended as writers, philosophers, statesmen and finally conquerors. In the meantime they developed a Pantheon with influences from a variety of foreign gods and goddesses. The Greeks visited foreign lands and centres of learning in the search for knowledge. At the face of Persian oppression their thirst for knowledge developed into an obsession. They become the first to truly assimilate regional knowledge which shaped the Greek nation and gave them the power to become rulers of the world.

Dandamaev and Lukin (1989) in their study on Persian history record the Achaemenid's syncretisation policy. The Achaemenids mixed with various ethnic groups and encouraged such syncretisation among the ethnic groups including the Greeks, Babylonians and Egyptians. This opened up the culture, science and philosophy of all the ethnic people leading to inter-ethnic enrichment. The authors claim that the 'Greek culture achieved its incredible flowering owing no small degree to the Babylonian and Egyptian mathematics, Phoenician writing and many other achievements and inventions of previous civilisation of the East'.

The Greeks themselves have admitted to this indebtedness. They deemed their mathematics came from Egypt when the likes of Pythagoras journeyed to Egypt and became acquainted with Egyptian mathematicians. The famous materialist Democritus spent five years in Egypt learning their science. The observations of Egyptian physicians were included in the works of Hippocrates of Cos. The works of Babylonians astronomers were translated to Greek. Around 270 BC the school established by the Babylonian Berosso (Bel-reusu) in the Island of Cos played a large part in translating the Achaemedian-Babylonian astronomical knowledge to Greek.

Initially, like other ethnic groups, the Greeks also came to Persia for various reasons ranging from political exigencies to earning a livelihood. Greek physicians, scholars and craftsmen lived in Persia. Darius, Artaxerxes I and Artaxerxes II had Greek physicians.

> When Darius I dislocated his leg during hunting of wild beasts, his Egyptian physicians were unable to heal him. Democedes, at that time an unknown slave to a Persian, was brought to the King. He had medical knowledge and was able to heal Darius. As a result

he was made the King's physician and given a huge house in Susa. He was also given expensive gifts by the wives of Darius.

The Spartan King Demaratos fled and lived in the court of Xerxes. The illustrious Athenian Themistocles lived in Persia and married a Persian woman. He became fluent in Persian language and preached the teaching of Zoroastrian Magi. The sister of Alexander (Macedonian king at the beginning of 5th century BC) was married to a Persian. Another Greek named Timocreon was a clown and 'King of Gluttons' in the Persian court. Zeno from Crete, not the philosopher, and others earned their livelihood as dancers. There were Greek mercenaries in the Persian army and Greek translators worked for the Satrap officials. A Persian named Mithradates son of Orontobates presented the Athenian Academy with the statue of Plato. According to Pliny the Elder in *Natural History* Osthanes, the chief Magus of emperor Xerses of Persia, was "chiefly responsible for stirring up among the Greeks not merely an appetite but a mad obsession for this art (of Alchemy)." Thus, it is clear that the syncretisation between the Greeks and Persians were extensive and at multiple levels.

Provenance of the Greek gods

A study of ancient Pantheons and heroes shows a definitive correlation among the Egyptian, Phoenician, Hittite, Hurrian and Greek gods, goddesses and their myths. Some of the gods had been derived out of natural phenomena like the sun, moon, ocean, and storm. While others were based on real people whose cults and stories spread over time and become deified. The myths, via multiple oral transmissions, became more colourful and fascinating taking on native hues, and survived well into the Christian era.

Over the ages, there had been continuous movement of people between the Greek mainland, Greek islands and Egypt and west Asia. Political refugees and other people driven away from the Mesopotamian and Egyptian empires due to wars would migrate to the Greek regions for safety. Wandering tribes and adventurers would settle there and add bits of there own culture which would later homogenise and form a Greek identity. The Greek cities had been formed at different times by people of different origin. Though myths and legends are fictional, they are based on some patterns of reality. Examples from Greek myths give some idea of the origin of these cities and their heroes.

Origin of the Heroes

According to Thucydides, the mythical Cecrops originally founded Athens which at that time was called Attica. There are two main source of his origin. According to Theopompus the historian, Cecrops came from Egypt. The other source, a much later one, identifies him as a Pelasgian, the ancient tribal people of Asia Minor and Greece. But the previous origin is more consistent as there is an Egyptian connection in the Greek myth itself. In the myth Cecrops is described as half human and half snake. This notion is Egyptian as Egypt also had an ancient snake god, Nehebkau, depicted as part snake and part man. According to Sir Isaac Newton, in *The Chronology of Ancient Kingdoms*, a large number of Canaanites, after being defeated by the Hebrews in Canaan, fled to and occupied Lower Egypt. There they lived for some time being ruled by their own kings. But Mephtramuthosis, Pharaoh of the 18th dynasty, made a protracted war and managed to drive them away. The Egyptian-Canaanites fled to various regions – Palestine, Idumaea and Libya. 'And under Lelux, Aezeus, Inachus, Pelasgus, Aeolus the first, Cecrops and other captains into Greece. Before that Greece and all Europe was peopled by wandering Cimmerians and Scythians'.

Both Athena and Poseidon had wanted to be the deity of Attica. It was by Cecrops' arbitration that Athena became the goddess of Athens (Hamilton, 1969). From the reign of Cecrops and the initial kings to that of Theseus, Attica was ethnically diverse and divided into small communes or tribes, having their own town halls and magistrates. They were autonomous and administered their own affairs. They fought amongst themselves and even fought against their own king. Only external danger brought them together under the king.

Theseus, a descendent of Cecrops II, united all the inhabitants of Attica under a single council and town hall. The ethnic communes continued to live on their own lands but all were citizens of the same metropolis. To enlarge the city he invited outsiders to join them and promised to give them the same rights as other residents. Multitudes, from various regions, started to flow to Attica. He named the city Athens and instituted the Metoika or Feast of Migration. This multi-ethnicity caused the sowing of the seeds of democracy.

Plutarch mentions that Theseus promised a commonwealth without monarchy to the powerful communes. The ordinary people generally accepted his advice and during wars he would become the Chief of Athens and the enforcer of law. Theseus divided the Athenian Commonwealth into three distinct ranks: the noblemen, the farmers and the artisans. The nobility had the main share of power and honour including the control over religion, the choice of magistrates, the instructions and dispensation of the laws.

The city-state of Thebes in Ancient Greece was founded by Cadmus, a Phoenician (ancient Lebanese) prince, and was ruled over by his descendents for generations. According to Greek mythology, before he founded Thebes, his sister Europa was carried away by Zeus. Cadmus started the search for his sister but in vain. The Oracle of Delphi directed him to give up his search and to follow a special cow which will 'show' him a place where he was to build a town. Cadmus and his men followed the cow and arrived at the location which was to become Thebes. There he built the town which was originally called Cadmea, after him, and later came to be known as Thebes.

Peloponnesus, meaning the 'Island of Pelops', is a peninsula at the south of Greece on which the towns like Sparta, Corinth, Petra are located. This whole region was conquered by the hero Pelops, the son of a Hittite King Tantalus of Anatolia (Turkey). He was very highly venerated in Olympia and from his cult developed the original ritual of the Olympic Games. The Hittite influence can also be seen in Greek names. The following are coupled names of which the first ones are Hittite and the second ones Greek: Ahhiyawa – Ahaiwoi, Alaksandu - Alexandro(s), Apasa - Ephesos, Attarsiya - Odysseo(s), Lukka - Lykia, Milawata – Milletos.

The Argive dynasty, rulers of the ancient Greek city of Argos, also has an Egyptian origin. According to the legends, the king of Egypt had twin sons Danaus and Aegyptus. Danaus had fifty daughters while Aegyptus had fifty sons. Aegyptus ordered his sons to marry the Danaides. But Danaus disagreed with the proposition and decided to flee in 'the first ship that was ever built' to Argos of Greece where he established his kingdom. When the sons of Aegyptus arrived there for their brides, Danaus agreed to wed his daughters because he did not want the Argives to suffer the pain of battle. But in secret he told his daughters to kill all their husbands on the wedding night. Forty nine of his daughters obeyed but Hypermnestra refused to kill her husband Lynceus as he had honoured her wish to remain a virgin on the wedding night. Danaus was angry at Hypermnestra and wanted to punish her but she was saved by the love goddess Aphrodite. Later, Lynceus killed Danaus as a revenge for the death of his brothers. Then he and Hypermnestra became the progenitors of the Danaan/Argive Dynasty that ruled Argos.

The hero Perseus, son of Argive Princess Danae and the god Zues, became the founder of Mycenae that would ultimately occupy ancient Crete. Perseus is considered to be the builder of the palace of Mycenae. The palace gateway was inscribed with the name of Amenhotep III. Plates with hieroglyphics of his name were also discovered in the same location. Cepheus was the father and **Cassiopeia** the mother of Perseus' wife Andromeda. They probably were Kheper-khepru-re Ai and his wife An-**khesenpaa**-ten who lived in the 14th century BC (WR1, 2009).

Origin of the Deities

Around 700 BC, a famous Greek oral poet named Hesoid wrote the Theogeny. It is a collection of oral myths and gives the origin and genealogy of the Greek gods and is often used as a sourcebook for Greek mythology. In recent researches, it was found that the Hurrian-Hittite 'Song of Ullikummi' is its predecessor and has parallels in content (Burkert, 1987). Scholars now claim that the Hesoid includes stories from different cultures such as the Atlas figure that carries the Heavens and Earth. The 'Castration of Uranus' story has its parallel in older Hittite text (Barnett, 1996). Besides the theory of ages - humanity passing through a good age and progressing to bad ones - which is described by Hesoid and the cyclic rotation of the ages adopted by Heraclitus and the Stoic's 'doctrine of eternal return' was a result of oriental influence (Eliot, 1990). Indian mythology has the similar concept of rotation of *Satyayug* (good age) and *Kalyug* (bad age).

The Egyptians also influenced the Greek Pantheon. According to Herodotus the rituals of many Greek Gods were exactly the same as those of the older Egyptian gods. The Greek Hermes is the adoption of Egyptian Thot. They both have similar attributes and functions. One of Thot's title 'Three times great' was translated to Greek 'Trismegistos' and thus yielding Hermes Trismegistos – a syncretisation effect. The Egyptian god Amon had a profound impact on Greeks. The Greeks identified Zeus with Amon, as the king of the gods, and his consort Hera with Mut. The Oracle of Amon in the oasis of Siwa in Libya was very famous among the Greeks. After the battle of Issus, Alexander the Great went there to be acknowledged as the son of the god. Several Greek words including ammonia and ammonite have been derived from Amon. Due to its horned appearance *Conu ammonis* (Amon's Horns) is a region in the brain.

Some Greek gods have Mesopotamian and West Asian origin. Adonis the annually rejuvenated, ever youthful god of vegetation is Semitic. He was absorbed in the Greek pantheon from the Syrian Tahmuz. The original was the Sumerian Tahmuz who was the consort of Inanna and in Akkadian version the consort of Ishtar. He later came to represent the handsome youth. His cults consisted of females like the one in Sappo of Lesbos. Aphrodite was the adoption of Inanna (Ishtar). Both are love goddesses who could be spiteful and perverse.

The Greek god Apollo was originally an Anatolian one. The name Aplu, meaning 'son of', was derived from the Babylonian plague god Nergal son of Enlil. Those who suffered the plague sought his intervention and thus Aplu became the god of medicine as well. He was brought to Delos from Anatolia at the end of the Bronze Age in the guise of Phoebus Apollo, god of the sun and surpassed the older indo-European sun god Helios.

Similarly, Poseidon can be identified with the Phoenician sea god Yah or Yam, historically who may have been Yakobaam, Hyksos' vassal, who ruled in northern Sinai in about 1650 BC. The name of Poseidon is likely to have been derived from the Greek words 'Apo Sidon' meaning 'from Sidon' or from the Phoenician 'Abi Sidon'. It may have originated from 'Baal-Sidon' meaning 'Father of Sidon' indicating the city where the worship of Yah was practiced until 1300 BC (WR1, 2009).

Hadad, the Canaanite god of storms, had many incarnations among the ancient people. Among the Hittites he was named as Tarhunt and the later Luwains, people related to the Hittites, called him Tarchon while the Etruscans called him Tarquin. Hurrians called him Teshub while the Tyrians named him Baal-Melkart who fought and killed Lawtan. The Greeks named Baal as Hercules and Lawtan as Ladon.

Among all these people there was a myth of a battle between the storm god and a serpent that lived beneath the sea. The origin of this story may have been derived from the fight of Babylonian god Marduk (the storm god who had the combined attributes of Akkadian Enlil and Ea) and Tiamat, the sea serpent personifying the sea. Many versions of this myth are found in the battles of Teshab/ Tarhunt with Ilyukanas, Baal with Lawtan, Zeus with Typhon, and Hercules with Ladons.

Taranis of Celtic mythology, Perkunas of Baltic mythology, Perun of Slav Mythology and Thor the Scandinavian god of thunder also have aspect of Tarhunt. The most popular story about Thor, the Viking god, is that he tried to catch the World Serpent. His plot was successful and the monster Jormungand was trapped by a lure. But Thor's assistant giant Humir was frightened by the serpent and he cut the rope allowing Jormungand to escape destruction. A similar plot is found in the Indian mythology in the fight between Indra and Vritra.

Development of Philosophy

In the third millennium BC, tribes roamed the regions of Asia Minor, Greece, Southern Italy, Sicily, Rhodes, Delos and other Islands of the Aegean Sea. All these different tribes have been classified under the Indo-European group to differentiate from the sedentary Semites and Egyptians.

Located on the fringe of empires for thousands of years, the Greco-Italian region had seen a continuous import of ideas and religious doctrines. The Egyptians, being the first to discover the sail, were also the first to influence the Mediterranean Greeks via Crete. The West Asian empires – Babylonian, Persian, Hittite - influenced the Ionian and Dorian Greeks of Asia Minor due to their proximity. Among the Greek tribes the Ionian and Dorian became enlightened first. This influence gradually moved inwards towards mainland Greece. The initial West Asian influence was greatest in Miletus a city of Ionia (now western Turkey) and the birthplace of Greek philosophy, mathematics and science. Before 500 BC Miletus was the greatest Greek city. After Miletus, Athens became the centre of philosophy and mathematics in the classical period between 600 – 300 BC. After Alexander the Great founded Alexandria in Egypt, the centre of mathematics moved there. Alexandria remained a mathematical centre till 700 CE when it was annexed by the Muslims, after which the scientific and philosophic centre moved to Baghdad and Cordova before dissipating to other regions.

The Greeks were the first to grasp knowledge as pure knowledge and wrest it from the domain of petty gods to that of humans. It took centuries, in the 1st millennium BC, for this process to occur. The early Greeks personified elements of nature into powerful divinities and provided them with human passion and relationships. For example sky was personified by Uranus, the world ocean by Oceanus and thunder by Zeus. 620-550 BC was the time of the Seven Sages, men notable for their wisdom. The age of the Seven Wise Men in Greece coincided with a Saitic revival in Northern Egypt and vigorous contact with Greeks. The names of these sages are as follows.

- Solon of Athens: He devised a constitution which was in between democracy and oligarchy. Solon travelled for ten years to Egypt, Cyprus and Lydia. In Egypt he studied under the Priests of temple of Neith. His visit to Egypt is mentioned in Plato's Timeaus.
- Chilons of Sparta: He was one of the five Ephors of Sparta who upheld the rule of the two kings.
- Thales of Miletus: He was the first Greek Philosopher.
- Bias of Priene: He was a wise man who is known to have paid a ransom for women prisoners and educated them before sending them home. He lived in

Priene, a city said to have been established by the mythical Egyptian king Aegyptus.

- Cleobulus of Lindos: He was a poet and tyrant and studied philosophy in Egypt.
- Pittacus of Mytilene: He was a sage as well as a Mytilene General who defeated the Athenians and their commander Phrynon.
- Periander of Corinth: He upgraded Corinth's port and also organised an annual musical contest. The increased revenue from the port gave Corinth improved security and stability. But he was also a tyrant who got rid of people who he feared may take power from him. He had young boys castrated, and stands accused of having his own wife murdered and committing necrophilia. When his son learned of his mother's murder, Periander sent him to exile.

Greece was initially inspired by the Egyptian and near Asian anthropomorphic pantheons. With the rise of Persia and the movement of the Hebrews, the idea of dualism and of an omnipotent god also entered the consciousness of Greek thought. The famous pithy maxim 'Know thyself' have been attributed to five wise men – Solon, Chilon, Thales, Socrates, Pythagoras along with the mythical poetess Phemonoe. This probably reflected the Zoroastrian 'Self Realisation' that was achieved at the final stage of the Amesha Spenta. The Persian influence is also demonstrated by other notions like Heraclitus' interest in fire and Anaximender's hypotheses of the stars being nearer than the moon.

In Plato's *Timaeus*, the Demiurge is the divine creator of the universe similar to the Semitic concept. But Plato's cosmogony differs from the Semitic one in the sense that the Demiurge is not omnipotent and cannot create out of nothing. He mentions another eternal being or necessity Ananke. This duality, Demiurge-Ananke, does not incorporate the morality, good versus evil, of the Zoroastrian duality.

The Persians were not anthropomorphic like the Greeks. Temples, statues and altar were not constructed in Persia and were considered foolish. This conflict of Semitic-Zoroastrian notion with the anthropomorphic pantheon caused the Greek cosmogony to shift swiftly resulting in political discord. Consequently, Socrates and his followers no longer agreed with the Pantheon.

From the time of the Sages to the breakdown of Alexander's Empire the Greeks produced remarkable men of science and philosophy. Some of them are listed below.

Thales

Thales (624 – 546 BC) is considered the first Greek philosopher and lived in the city of Miletus in Anatoly (Turkey).

Originally, Miletus consisted of the aboriginal Anatolian Leleges population. Over time Carians, Cretans, Phoenician, Luwains and Hittites came, settled and mixed with the local inhabitants who came to be known as Carian (Turkish Karya). They were followed by the Ionian and Dorian Greeks before the rise of Persian Achaemenid Empire.
In 547 BC, the wealthy Croesus was the king of Lydia (Izmir and Manisha, Turkey). He prepared to fight against Cyrus and aligned himself with Amasis II of Egypt and Nabonidus of Babylon. The small cities neighbouring Miletus sided with Croesus. But Miletus, under Thales counsel, did not join the coalition. When Cyrus defeated Croesus, he subjugated all the cities but gave favourable terms to Miletus (Hall 2007).

The father of Thales did not have a Greek name but a Carian one. Diogenes Laertius mentions the parents to be Examyas and Cleobulina who were a descendents of Phoenician Cadmus, who had established Thebes. According to Herodotus he was Phoenician by descent. Thales was a merchant and travelled widely and went to Egypt and Babylon which was under the Persians. He had exposure to Egyptian and Babylonian mythology, philosophy, astronomy and mathematics. He brought geometry from Egypt and predicted solstices by studying Babylonian records.

Thales was the initiator of the 'Arche' (principle) that water was the basic constituent of the universe. His cosmogony evolved probably under Egyptian and Babylonian influence (King, 2004). According to him the world was disk shaped and had water above and below it. Thus it floated on water below and was rained upon from above. He was first among the Greek intellectual and had moved away from anthropomorphic gods. His god appear to be more Judaic-Zoroastrian. One of his maxims is said to be, "Of all things, the most ancient is God, as he is uncreated." But on the other hand he is also reported to have said. "All things are full of gods".

His concept of justice included not just the law but its spirit as well. For him adultery was as bad as perjury about adultery. He maintained that people should live the best and the most just life possible and they should not succumb to innuendo, while wealth is to be made only in lawful ways. However, typical for his time, he viewed men as better than women.

Thales belonged to the Ionian school to which belonged Anaximander and Anaximenes.

Pythagoras

Pythagoras (582-507) was born in the Island of Samos.

The Island of Samos lies about a mile away from the coast of Turkey. It was a member of the Ionian League of cities, had its own dialect, and was a leading commercial centre.

Among the Greeks it was one of Islands that prospered first. It was ruled by Polycrates from 535 BC to 515 BC. Polycrates was a warrior, a tyrant but an able administrator. He built an aqueduct, a palace and a temple to Hera for which Amasis of Egypt sent him gifts. He was also a patron of poetry. He destroyed the Gymnasia to stop pederasty but kept a boy named Smerdis for his own pleasure.
According to Herodotus, the Pharaoh of Egypt Amasis considered Polycrates to be over-fortunate. So the Pharaoh asked Polycrates to sacrifice what he prized most to escape a reversal of fortune. Polycrates obeyed and threw away a jewelled ring to the sea. A few days later when his cooks were cooking a large fish they found the ring in its stomach. Polycrates told the Pharaoh of his luck. But Amasis believed this to be a bad omen and broke off all relationship with him. Then Polycrates tried to align with the Persians but was finally assassinated by one of the Satraps of the Persian Emperor Cambyses.

Pythagoras was the son of a Phoenician merchant from Tyre named Mnesarchus and a native Samos mother Pythais. According to Iamblicchus Chalcidensis, Thales advised Pythagoras to go to Egypt and learn from the famous priest-philosophers. He travelled to Egypt where he was taught mathematics. He was also taught in Tyre and Byblos (in present day Lebanon). He finally settled in Kroton, southern Italy and became influential due to his political doctrines.

Pythagoras is best known for the Pythagorean Theorem which states that in a right angled triangle, if the lengths of any two sides are known, the length of the third side can be worked out. The Berlin Papyrus, an ancient Egypt papyrus document from before 1200 BC, contains mathematical and medical knowledge including pregnancy test procedures. This document contains a mathematical problem which is almost the same as this theorem.

In Kroton, he established the mystical, religious and mathematical society known as the Pythagoreans. It was the views of this society that appears in Aristotle's works. His school worked on mathematics, and he considered Numbers as the first principle and that Numbers and their relationships were the essence of things. The Monad was his first divine being, the source without division. His school observed strict rules such as that of silence or secrecy, echemythia, because man's word is usually careless and misrepresents him. The Pythagoreans who lived in the school believed, similar to Indians, in the transmigration of base human souls into animals, were vegetarians and owned no possessions. Pythagoras introduced Jewish laws into his philosophy. Hemippus of Smyrna states that Pythagoras was familiar with and praised Judaism. No text by Pythagoras survives as his teachings were oral referred to by later philosophers.

Heraclitus

Heraclitus was the first person to create a philosophical system in the Aegean world. He was from Ephesus, Lydia (Turkey).

Ephesus or Apasa was the capital of the Kingdom of Arzawa. According to the ancient 'Amarna letters' Arzawa, during the 2nd millennium, was an Egyptian ally. The Hittite kings Suppliluliuma I and Mursili II defeated Arzawa and split it into vassal states known as Mira, Hanballa and Seha.

After the collapse of the Hittite empire in the 12th century BC Neo-Hittite Independent states emerged including Lydia. In the seventh century the first Mermanad king Gyges ruled Lydia and came to power by killing the ruler Candaules. Herodotus paints king Candaules as a pervert who forced Gyges, his minister, to hide behind the door of the royal bedroom and see the queen Tudo alone in a compromised state. But the queen saw Gyges as he was silently leaving and realised her husband's involvement in the plot and silently vowed revenge. The day after the event took place she called Gyges and told him that he will have to kill Candaules, seize the kingship and make her the queen or else he will have to die himself for carrying out the evil plot against her modesty. Gyges decided to live, and with the collaboration of the queen killed Candaules and seized powers.

Plato's rendering of this event is more fanciful. According to him Gyges found a ring that made him invisible by which he was able to seize power. According to Plutarch, Gyges was assisted by a Carian prince in seizing the power. The people of Lydia revolted against the murder of their king but were put down by Gyges' Ionian and Carian mercenaries. Some scholars of the Bible take Gyges as Gog the ruler of Magog. Creoses, mentioned earlier, was the last king of this dynasty.

The concept of Logos was advanced by Heraclitus. 'Logos' is important in Greek philosophy denoting the link between man and God. The conceptual meaning behind the word has changed with time.

The Stoics, a philosophic school started by 'Zeno the Phoenician' of Kition in the 3rd century BC, viewed ethics as the main focus of human knowledge and considered God as the immanent vitalising force. Thus to them God was Logos and anything developing from this force was *Spermaticos Logos* or the 'seeds of Logos'. In later Neo-Platonism Logos is the system of emanations. Then logos took the meaning of the Hebrew principal "the wisdom of God". Later Christian thinkers incorporated the Stoic logos doctrine particularly associating it with Christ. To Oregin, Christ - the first emanation - was the Logos. And much later, the emanation concept was taken over and explained by Al Ghazzali in his esoteric *Mishkat Al-Anwar* (The Niche of Lights) based on a single verse of the Quran.

Heraclitus wrote a book, probably outlining all his ideas, but all that remains of his work is 45 pages of poetry.

Xenophanes of Colophon

Xenophanes (570 BC – 480 BC) was born in Colophon, Ionia (Turkey). He was a religious philosopher whose work was in poetical form. When the Persian Mede Harpagus invaded Ionia in 545 BC Xenophanes went to the Greek communities in Sicily. There he ridiculed the Greek anthropomorphic pantheon in satirical verses. Then he went to Greece to continue his work. There he was a prime influence in the founding of the Eleatic School. During these wanderings his two sons died, he himself was sold to slavery and later released.

His satirical poetry criticises poets Homer and Hesoid for ascribing all kind of shameful things like theft, adultery and deceit to the gods. He believed in a "one" god over all gods and men, and rejected the birth of and the manlike form of god. He articulates:

'The Ethiops say that gods are pug-nosed and dark,
And the Thracians that theirs have blue eyes and red hair.
If cattle or horses or lions had hands and could draw and sculpture,
then the horses would draw gods like horses,
And cattle like cattle.'

His god was similar to the transcendental Judaic-Zoroastrian God that is abstract, eternal and unchanging. Xenophanes also spoke out against the adulation of athletes in similar terms. An athlete is "not as valuable as me. For my wisdom is better than strength possessed by men or horses". Only fragments of Xenophanes' works are extant.

Parmenides of Elea

Parmenides, born at the end of the 6th century BC, was a philosopher of the Greek town Elea in Southern Greece. He is believed by some to have been a disciple of Xenophanes. What was 'äo èeos' or God to Xenophanes was 'To Eov' or Being to Parmenides. His only known work is a poem called "On Nature" of which 150 lines are extant. The work originally contained three parts.

1. Proem (Preamble)
2. The way of truth
3. The way of opinion.

In the proem, Parmenides is borne in a chariot escorted by sun-maidens travelling to the palace of a goddess. They reach the locked 'gate of day and night'. The sun-maidens persuade Dike, the keeper of key, to open the gate and they enter the realm of day. When they reach the palace the goddess welcomes him. She teaches him the two ways – one of

Truth and the other of Opinion. The way of the truth is the correct way and the way of opinion is delusional and is the view held by the majority. He says that although 'opinion' is illusion, it is worth knowing for practical reasons. Aristotle stated that for Parmenides, ultimately, only one thing exists - Being.

Parmenides said that, in the way of truth, what reason (logos) can think, exists. What it cannot think is not. What is not, is not thinkable. Therefore, Being exists and Non-being does not exist. There is only one Being, if there were many Beings then it would be necessary for Non-being to exist to separate the Beings. But the basic premise is that Non-being does not exist. Therefore there is only one Being. There is no change – alteration or motion – in Being, as that would presuppose existence of Non-being. Being is a complete sphere. Being is rational and what is rational is Being. (Later Hegel said what is rational is real, and what is real is rational). This can be philosophically extended to mean Being is knowledge and knowledge is Being.

The Eleatic school

The philosophy of Parmenides, Melissos of Samos, and Zeno of Elea is known as the Eleatic school and was influenced by Xenophanes.

Melissos was also the Admiral of the Samos Navy that had defeated the Athenian Navy of Pericles. He differed from Parmenides in certain aspects. His point of view was that if Being is a sphere than it is limited or finite. Anything finite must also be finite in a temporal sense and thus have a beginning and an end. This contradicts the basic premise and thus to Melissos' Being is infinite. While Parmenides recognized the existence of 'voids', Melissos thought that along with Non-being there also cannot be any void and if there is no void there is no motion. He also believed that Being does not feel pain or pleasure as nothing can be added or subtracted from Being.

Zeno wrote a book named *Attacks* of dialectic paradoxes with which he used to confound the opponents of Parmenides. He argues that things are both finite and infinite. That things are in space. Space must be something or nothing. If space is something then space itself is in something, which again is in something else and so on. He also has paradoxes regarding motion. Four of his eight known paradoxes are as follows:

1. Being is one: If Being was many, it has to be both like and unlike at the same time. This is not possible as like cannot be unlike and nor unlike like.

2. A flying arrow is actually standing still: At any singular instance of time during its flight the arrow is still. Which means that the arrow is still at all instances of time. Thus a flying arrow is at standstill through out its flight.

3. It is never possible to go from one place to another: The distance between two places can be divided into an infinite number of points, smaller and smaller. In limited time it is not possible to travel an infinite number of points or intermediaries.

4. In a race the fastest runner cannot overtake the slowest runner: The hero Achilles is racing a tortoise that is a little distance ahead of him. To overtake the tortoise Achilles must first reach the point where the tortoise is. But by the time Achilles reaches that specific point the tortoise would have moved ahead to a second point. Now Achilles has to reach the second point that the tortoise has moved to. Again, as Achilles reaches the second point, the tortoise also has moved a little further again to a third point. This keeps on happening infinitely, every time Achilles reaches the position of the tortoise the tortoise has moved ahead a certain distance. Thus it is impossible to catch up with the tortoise.

Hippocrates of Cos

Hippocrates is the most outstanding figure in Medicine of his time. He was an inhabitant of the Island of Cos, off the coast of Western Turkey, which originally had a Carian population and where the Dorians had arrived in the 11th century BC and became dominant. He was contemporary to Pericles of Athens and claimed maternal ancestry from the legendary Hercules and paternal ancestry from Asclepius the demigod of medicine.

Hippocrates revolutionized medicine in ancient Greece and was followed by his students Galen and Aretaeus. After their death medical research became centred in Alexandria of Egypt and around the 3rd and 2nd centuries BC their work was incorporated in a collection. The collection contains textbooks, lectures, research, notes and philosophical essays on various medical subjects. The Corpus does not have any particular order or style, parts of it being written at different times. It was written for both specialists and laymen and contains significant contradictions. The Hippocratic Oath, a seminal document on the ethics of medical practice, is the most famous document of the Corpus.

The school of Hippocrates held that the human body contained four humours or fluids – blood, yellow bile, black bile and phlegm – in equal balance. All illness was the result of an imbalance in the body of the four humours. The body contains the power to rebalance the four humours and thus heal itself. Aretaeus dealt with diabetes and called it "A wondrous affliction, not very frequent among men, being a melting down of the flesh and limbs into urine."

This work by the Greeks which also included the Egyptian medical knowledge was transferred to the later day Muslim scholars via Alexandria. They worked on it in Arabic and their work, in turn, was translated to Latin by the Europeans and came to be known as the Hippocratic Corpus.

Herodotus

Herodotus (484 – 425 BC), the famous historian, spent his childhood and youth in Halicarnassus, capital of Caria in Asia Minor. The population of Caria were half Greek and half Carian and were bilingual and intermingled. Though Herodotus' father was Carian he himself wrote in the Ionic Greek dialect. Herodotus took part in the struggle against the tyrant Lygdamis and was forced to go to the Island of Samos. From there he embarked on an extensive journey of the West Asia including Persia, Babylonia, Phoenicia and Egypt, finally Athens. The main theme of his *Histories* was the Persian wars which occupied five volumes of his nine volume compendium. This included the pre war history, the history of Egypt, Lydia, Babylonia and other countries with interesting folklores and short stories of various regions. Unlike other Greeks he wrote objectively about the Persians without any rancour or malice.

The Philosophy of Athens

For over two hundred years Greek philosophy and ideas flowed freely. The flowering came mainly from three regions: The Greek settlements of Asia Minor and Islands under the Persians and the Greek settlements of Southern Italy and Sicily (Magna Graecia).

The defeat of the Persians at the hands of the Athenians in 490 and 480 BC placed Athens in the centre of the Greek world. Trade and Commerce flourished, arts bloomed. During the rule of Pericles, from 460 to 430, BC Aeschylus, Sophocles and Euripedes produced literary tragedies and Aristophanes wrote comedies, Herodotus wrote his history of the Persian wars and Thucudides wrote the History of the Peloponnesian war. Pheidias fashioned his statues. All were brilliant masterpieces. But in philosophy Athens had not produced any one of notice.

In 430 BC Athens was devastated by plague. The same year the Peloponnesian war against Sparta started. This war would end with total defeat of Athens in 404 BC. In 327 BC Philip of Macedon would conquer Athens. It was during this period of political decline that Athens produced its remarkable philosophers.

The Sophist

The Greek philosophical systems (Ionian, Eleatic, etc) that had evolved were paradoxical and contradictory to each other. Some people were not satisfied with these systems and became sceptics. The group of sceptics came to be known as the Sophist and their chief was Protagorus. According to him all the talk about gods and formation of matter, its first principles and origins, were at best hypothetical. They found in all these systems no place for 'man'. Instead of wasting time on these subjects man should occupy their thought about *themselves*. Thus, his famous saying, "Man is the measure of all things: of things that are and that they are and things that are not and they are not."

To him senses used for perception were not perfect. Reason and ethics were relative. What is good for one may not be good for another. While Protagorus doubted the existence of certain knowledge, his contemporary, Gorgias, went much further to claim that nothing actually exists and whatever that may exist cannot be known and what can be known was not communicable.

Following them the Sophists became itinerant teachers teaching worldly subjects like logic, rhetorics and grammar. These subjects were popular among the rich elite class and they were paid for their tutoring of the youth. Many people disliked them for their association with the rich and philosophers disliked them as they took money to teach. Plato had a dim view of the sophists claiming them not to be philosophers but rather tutors who taught for money. He considered them as people who used linguistic ambiguities to support fallacious ideas.

Socrates

The unexamined life is not worth living.
- Socrates

Among the Greeks the age of learning and scholarly works started in earnest at about the same time the Peace treaty of 449 BC was signed with the Persians. The most famous Greeks philosophers, historians, poets and men of learning all thrived in this period.

Socrates, born in 469 BC, was a sculptor in early life and joined the army at the age of eighteen as a Hoplite, i.e., a foot soldier with heavy armour. When, in 449, the peace treaty was signed, he lost his army job and turned his attention to philosophy. Most of what is known about Socrates comes from Plato's writings as Socrates himself wrote nothing.

Socrates discarded metaphysics, natural science and mathematics. He was passionate about righteous and virtues living. There were five virtues – courage, moderation, piety, wisdom and justice. His mission was to urge people to acquire these virtues. He stated, "I spend all my time going about trying to persuade you, young and old, to make your first and chief concern not for your bodies nor for your possessions, but for the highest welfare of your souls, proclaiming as I go, wealth does not bring goodness, but goodness brings wealth and every other blessing, both to the individual and to the state." (Raphael and Monk, 2001).

Socrates believed in God, immortal soul, and blissful life after death for the noble. He claimed that his mission was divine, "This duty I have accepted .... in obedience to God's commands given in oracles and dreams and in every other way that any other divine dispensation has ever impressed a duty upon man." (Raphael and Monk, 2001).

But his God was not the anthropomorphic Athenian gods. Many times he spoke of a God that is non-anthropomorphic and singular, and also that all wisdom belongs to God. He also mentioned a *daimonian* -- an angel, spirit or inner voice -- to which he would appeal and which had been with him since childhood.

He did not have or care for wealth and comfort, being too busy with his mission, but he did not really teach abstinence *per se*. He said that the Athenians should be ashamed of their attempts to acquire as much money as possible and seek reputation and fame, and because they spent so little time for understanding the Truth and perfection of the Soul. It appears that Socrates was not just a philosopher. Schools of philosophy flowed from Socrates but he, himself, was more a philosopher-prophet.

He taught by dialogue or conversation, known as the Socratic or Dialectic Method. He would talk to people until his querying would bring out knowledge from the subconscious depth of people's mind. He believed that people committed evil deeds due to ignorance or lack of knowledge. As knowledge was needed to keep away from evil, so, to him it was a virtue. Socrates was ugly but still people were attracted by his wisdom and inner beauty. A way to understand the character of Socrates is by understanding how he died. In 399 BC, he was charged by the state that:

- He refused to recognise the official gods.
- He introduced new gods
- He corrupted the youths.

Eventually, he was sentenced to death and required to die by drinking the poison hemlock. The irony of the matter was that during the reign of the Thirty Tyrants when he had continued the exhortations of 'Know Thyself' he was often threatened but he survived. But when Athenian democracy arrived he was put to death. It is said that he agreed to accept the majority verdict against him and drank the poison handed over to him without fear. Although the Jury offered him to deny his beliefs and get freedom, he declined and accepted death.

The four main writers on Socrates' thought were Plato, Antisthenes, Xenophon and Aristotle. In the centuries that would follow, their works on Socrates, even his name, would eventually vanish from the face of the earth only to be rediscovered and investigated, much later, by the Muslim scholars.

Plato

Plato was born in 428 BC among the Athenian aristocracy. He is said to be a descendent of Codrus the last Athenian King. He is the most famous disciple of Socrates and after the execution of Socrates he left Athens. He travelled to Egypt and Sicily and finally returned to

Athens. At the age of forty he and Theaetetus, a mathematician, co-founded 'The Academy'. It was a school of knowledge and consisted of 'a large enclosure of ground' which was once the property of a citizen at Athens named Academus. This school would exist up to 529 CE for nearly a thousand years. Its most famous student was Aristotle.

In Athens, after half a century of criticism of the previous philosophies Plato set to rebuilding it. For Plato, it was more a transformation and combination of all the previous systems – Thales, Heraclites, Eleatics, etc – into a framework of Greek Philosophy. Plato is the first Greek philosopher all of whose works are actually extant and is considered the Father of Western Philosophy. He wrote a few dozen philosophical dialogues in the form of conversations, with Socrates as a participant. The initial dialogues that he wrote were mainly about methods of acquiring knowledge. The later ones were on justice and practical ethics. His most famous works shows an abstract view of ethics, knowledge, metaphysics, reason, and human life.

He argued that knowledge was the understanding of the true being of things which cannot be known by the perception of the senses but by inquiry. Generally the Idea or Form of a thing is considered to be held in the mind of the beholder. But Plato considered that idea to be the eternal reality and the material or worldly copies to be transient Not-Being. Thus, the eternal ideas are the only pure beings and world of ideas the only real world. Everyday matters were more an affair of conviction rather than knowledge.

Put another way, as everything in the world is changing and nothing is absolute, these cannot be the objects of true knowledge. For example, different people can be beautiful, but they look dissimilar. So there has to be an ideal form of beauty, of which beautiful objects are representations of. This ideal form or idea is the real essence of things and called Forms. The senses can only perceive imperfect copies of the Forms but the philosophers can experience the world of Forms through reason. And these Forms or knowledge, at least a considerable part of it, are latent in human beings. This concept was the basis of what later came to be known as Rationalism.

Plato's cosmology considers God as the creater of the world, the orbits of the seven heavens, time, the heavenly race of gods (stars and planets), all animal species and man. The soul of the man is non-corporeal and formed prior to man. It is placed in man for purification. After death, the souls of the virtuous go to the Isles of the Blessed. The wicked are punished in Tartarus and Hades where they go through cycles of reincarnation. He said that genuine knowledge is not learned but recollected by the soul, which forgets previous knowledge due to the severe trauma of rebirth. It was the teachers' job to help the student regain knowledge.

The biggest and the most famous of Plato's dialogues is the Republic. It depicts an ideal society and justice concerning individual and the State. Plato's society consists of three tiers or classes. The pinnacle is formed by the scholar-rulers of the society called Guardians. The army and the defence forms the Auxiliaries. The mass of the society is represented by the Workers or Producers. Here is a remarkable similarity with the Hindu caste system. The Guardian is the same as the Hindu *Brahmins* – the scholar-ruler caste. The Auxiliaries are the same as the *Kshatria* or warrior caste. The Producers are equivalent to the *Vaisha* (Traders and agriculturist) and *Shudra* (service providers and artisans). In the Hindu system the Producer class is subdivided into two.

Plato's republic is an autocratic aristocracy. People do not have private property, not even wives or children. They are a one big family. The men and women are brought together by the state for reproduction. The children thus begotten are brought up by the State. A State should not be allowed to become too rich or too poor, too big or too small as both poverty and richness are social evils. In his *Laws* Plato portrays a modified and more practicable State. In the Republic, Plato writes, "The ideal society we have described can never grow into a reality or see the light of day, and there will be no end to the troubles of states, or indeed of humanity itself, till philosopher become kings in this world, or till those we now call kings and rulers really and truly become philosophers."

After the death of Socrates, Plato spent a few years in Egypt where he came in contact with Egyptian knowledge. In some of his important dialogues he operated from a world in which Egypt was omnipresent and ubiquitous. *Timaeus* is the dialogue which is famous for presenting the Forms of Plato. It also portrays the extensive and prolonged relationship between Greece and Egypt. This dialogue depicts Egyptians priests teaching history to the Greeks and also that Athena is the double of an Egyptian goddess. It also shows that the Egyptians were cordial towards the Greeks. In the text, an Egyptian priest states that Greeks are all children under the ancient eyes of Egypt. *Laws*, which is Plato's last work, portrays political and social engagements that were desirable. It also presents the excellence in the Egyptian forms of music, arts and education. The *Republic* is not entirely free of the Egyptian influence, in which Socrates twice swears, "by the dog of Egypt" referring to Anubis, the Egyptian god of funerary and judgment. By thus swearing Socrates was affecting and asserting the truth of his proposition.

Aristotle

Aristotle was born in Macedon in 384 BC. A renowned Greek philosopher, he wrote on diverse subjects like physics, metaphysics, ethics, politics, de anima (on the soul), poetics, etc. His complete work can be considered as the encyclopaedia of Greek knowledge which would much influence many later Muslim scholars. Aristotle was one of Plato's students, but unlike Plato he placed much more importance on the ability of the senses to acquire knowledge. He was more of an empiricist and set the stage for what would eventually develop into the scientific methods centuries later. The works of Aristotle that still exist today appear in treatise form.

Aristotle wrote about all the subjects existing during his time. He is the founder of Logic. According to him Logic is the process of correct reasoning. Though earlier philosophers used Logic, Aristotle studied it theoretically, clarified and organised it into a robust system. This collection on Logic is known as *Organon*. His system had a profound influence on subsequent thought of the East and the West.

The Physics of Aristotle defined the world as the centre of the universe. Around the world are concentric circles of water, air, fire and ether. The motion of the universe is not linear but circular. Space and time are the two conditions of motion. Space, that bounds a body, is limited. There is no space beyond the space of the stars. But time is infinite and the universe is eternal.

Soul is the form of the living body. Each soul develops its own body and thus there is no transmigration. There are different grades of soul – plant soul, animal soul and man soul - as there are different ranks of life. The human soul combines the function of all animate souls and thus is a microcosm. Reason is passive and active. Passive reasons have potential concepts while active reason has actualisation. Only active reason is universal and exists after the death of the body.

In Aristotalean ethics, the supreme excellence of a man is the exercise of the faculty of reason. The ultimate end is defined as Happiness which is different from Pleasure. Happiness is always good while pleasure may be good or bad depending on whether it accompanies good or bad activity.

The natural unit of the community is the patriarchal family, which includes slaves. It is the duty of the State to create not warriors but happy and virtuous individuals. But the State has to be strong enough to protect itself. The combination of courage and culture makes the Greeks superior.

Goodness and beauty are different. Goodness exists only in conduct. Beauty, that can be created by arts, can be in things that are not moved.

Aristotle went to Athens and entered Plato's Academy at the age of seventeen. Twenty years later, when Plato died, Aristotle went to Assos in Asia Minor, where he began the work on his book, *Politics*. When the Persians sacked Assos, Aristotle went to Macedon. In 342 BC King Philip of Macedon hired Aristotle as a teacher for Alexander. Alexander learned Aristotle's views on geography, biology, cosmology, and medicine and was enthralled by his politics, logic, metaphysics, and poetry. The educated and enlightened Alexander would include men of wisdom - philosophers and scientists - in his army.

When Alexander became king and prepared for his subsequent conquests, Aristotle returned to Athens. Plato's academy was being run by Xenocrates, and Platonism was the dominant philosophy of Athens. Aristotle set up his own school at Lyceum. For the next thirteen years he devoted himself towards composing and teaching his treatises. He gave two kinds of lectures, the more detailed discussions in the morning for advanced students, and the popular discourses in the evening for the general students.

When Alexander died suddenly, the pro-Macedonian government in Athens was overthrown, and a general anti-Macedonian reaction took place. A charge of impiety was brought against Aristotle. He fled to Chalcis in the Greek Island of Euboea so that, "The Athenians may not again commit the same sin against philosophy as they had already done in the person of Socrates." In 322 BC, about a year later, he died of a stomach illness.

Even Aristotle was not immune to the Egyptian pervasion of Greek culture. According to his *Metaphysics*, "Egypt was the cradle of the art of mathematics." And in his *On The Heavens* he records that the Egyptians and Babylonians were the founders of the science of astronomy. In his *Meteorology* he described the topology of the Nile.

On the more political side, Aristotle was a friend of King Philip and probably shared his vision of a unified Greek nation. He taught the Greeks that Persia was a decadent and despotic barbaric superpower. It was such assertions by people like Aristotle that they, the Greeks, were better then the Persians that finally broke the psychological barrier that had mesmerised the Greeks to a defensive attitude for centuries. This psychological turnaround, the developing knowledge of the world, and Philip's ambition of unifying the small cities into a Greek nation, inculcated in Alexander the will and wisdom to go on the offensive and take on the world. It was, in fact, the Persian invasions that unified the various Greek tribes to one nation (Hall, 2007).

The Hellenic era

The superb era of Greek philosophy and science was followed by the Hellenistic era, which signifies 'like the Greeks'. This period started with the death of Alexander and lasted up to the time when the Romans annexed the classical Greek heartland. After the Greek era different sub-schools of Greek and Roman thought developed but there was no significant innovation. The most notable schools were those of Neo-Pythagoreanism, Neo-Platonism, Cynicism and Stoicism.

About a century after the end of Hellenistic era was the birth of Jesus in Bethlehem. In the next five centuries Christianity would spread. It would affect not only the Greco-Roman regions but also the rest of Europe which had remained barbaric with competing or conflicting 'tribal' views and systems. Christianity replaced all these views after taking over the Roman Empire and started the real unification of the whole region. The 5th century CE would see the start of dormant European mediaeval period, also known as the Middle Ages, which would last up to the 16th century CE. But during this period would flourish the grand and illuminated Islamic Empires.

Interesting Events of Centuries 0 – 600 CE

Christianity rose in the first four centuries of the new millennium. It started from Jerusalem when a dozen of Jesus' disciples spread out, teaching a profound religion. The rise of Christianity was by an immense struggle of morality against severe persecution and imperialism.

Up to 50 CE, there is no document that mentions Christ. In the next fifty years the Christians themselves wrote most of the New Testament of the Bible. In the second century of the Christian era, Roman documents start to mention Christ (Gascoign, 2003). Tacitus the Historian states, "There is a group, hated for their abominations, called Christians by the people. Christus, from whom the name comes, suffered the extreme penalty during the reign of Tiberius at the hands of one of our officials, Pontius Pilate".

Pliny the Younger wrote about the Christians, "the contagion of this perverse and extravagant superstition has penetrated not the cities only, but the villages and the country. Yet it seems possible to stop it and set it right."

~~~

Rome in 113 CE under Emperor Trajan captured Armenia and Babylon. The Persian-Parthians suffered grave losses in the hands of the Romans. Seleucia, on the River Tigris, and Ctesiphone, capital of the Parthians were captured by the Romans. Trajan declared Mesopotamia part of the Roman Empire after which he captured Susa. Under him the Roman Empire pervaded furthest into the east and reached its maximum land extent ever. Trajan ruled from Mesopotamia in the east to Britain on the west, and also Syria, Jordan, Egypt and the Mediterranean fringe of North Africa.

In 70 CE after a revolt by the Jews, Jerusalem was razed to the ground. The second great Jewish revolt was in 115-117, during the time of Trajan. Jews in various regions - North Africa, Egypt, Cyprus, and what is present day Syria and Iraq - revolted and were only contained by the Roman legions after great loss of life. In 136 CE, Bar-Cochba, believed by some to be the Messiah, led the Jews to the third major revolt against Rome. But Emperor Hadrian totally suppressed the Jewish resistance and forbade the Jews from ever entering Jerusalem. He had rebuilt Jerusalem for his legions and changed the name of the city to Aelia Capitolina. Rebellions in Mesopotamia resulted in military and resource strain for the Romans. They had to hand over Mesopotamia back to the Parthians because it became indefensible and by doing so they managed to avoid a war with the Parthians. In the two centuries after Trajan, Rome was beset with wars, conspiracies and assassinations, a situation somewhat similar to that which had prevailed towards the end of the Achaemenid rule.

In 212 CE, Emperor Caracalla granted Roman citizenship to all free people who lived in the Roman Empire irrespective of ethnicity. After Trajan, the Roman Empire had consisted
~~~

of a large number of people of different cultural background and it ceased to be an Etruscan-Italian Empire. The Severan dynasty was one such 'non Italian' rulers. It was established by General Lucius Septimius Severus. His father was a Berber of indigenous Libyan-Tunisian descent. Lucius was born in Libya and became the first Roman Emperor to be born in Africa. 'Non Italian' religion also started to play major role in Rome. When Marcus Aurelius Antoninus became the Emperor he endorsed the cult of Elegabalus - a Syriac sun god. To historians he came to be known as Elegabalus or as 'Heliogabalus'.

In 224 CE, the Persian Sassanian Dynasty captured power from the Parthians and took their place as the arch-rival of Rome, and in 235 CE, the Roman army suffered a defeat at the hands of the Sassanians. This defeat along with the inefficient handling of rebels in Gaul and cost-cutting of army funds resulted in mutinous soldiers of the Roman army killing Alexander Severus, the last emperor of the Severan Dynasty. This was followed by a period of military anarchy, known as 'The Crises of the Third Century', from 235 to 284. During this time between 20 to 25 Roman Pro-Generals took control of the empire only to be dislodged, assassinated or defeated in battles.

The next successful emperor was Diocletian (285-305) who made fundamental reforms to change the prevailing situation. Diocletian ruled via a Tetrarchy, a group of four people, in which an Augusti was the senior emperor and the Caesars were the junior emperors. He made Maximian the Caesar, or ruler, of the western part of the empire. On the east, Diocletian was able to check the Sassanian invasions in Syria and Palestine. After stabilisation he issued an 'edict' against the Christians in 303 CE by which Christians were expelled from the army, Christian and church properties were confiscated and holy books destroyed. The Christians were given options to apostatise or be put to death.

In 306, when Constantine was declared a Caesar, Maxentius who was the son of former Emperor Maximian revolted and declared himself Emperor. His rule was over the western region of the Roman Empire. Constantine's advisers, generals and soothsayers had cautioned him against an attack on Maxentius. But one day, while marching in the Roman countryside he saw a sign on the sun, the monogram of letters CH and R and words, *In Hoc signo vinces*, 'With this as your standard you shall have victory'. Constantine believed this was a sign from the Christian God and ignored all the cautions of his advisors. He attacked and defeated Maxentius and captured Rome. Thus Constantine found God and the Christians found a great patron.

The persecution of Christians continued till the Edict of Milano, issued by Emperor Constantine, which proclaimed religious tolerance. He ruled from 306 to 337 CE and is also known as Constantine the Great or Saint Constantine.

He made the Eastern Roman Empire a centre of learning. He rebuilt the city of Byzantium and called it Nova Rome (New Rome) and it prospered under his reign. By his time about one fourth of the Empire's 60 million population were Christians. The figures of pagan deities were either replaced or assimilated into Christian symbolism.

In 380, Emperor Theodosius finally proclaimed Christianity as the sole religion of the Empire. The Olympics were closed due to pagan rituals and un-Christian practices. The temple of Zeus was shut down. He also formalised the political divide of the Empire into the West and the East with Milano and Constantinople the capitals, respectively.

In 450, Marcion became the first emperor to be crowned by a Christian religious leader, the Patriarch of Constantinople. Christianity that had started from Palestine against the Empire now prevailed over the Empire despite having faced incredible persecution and prosecution.

Meanwhile, the empire had been facing countless invasions from barbarians from the west and the Persians on the east. In the late 5th century, the once mighty Western Empire fell to the barbarians. Odoacer the Hun, leader of the Germanic mercenaries in the Roman army, deposed the western Roman Emperor that brought to an end the Western Roman Empire (Roberts, 1997).

In the meantime, internal changes were taking place in the remaining Eastern Roman Empire. Greek replaced the Latin way of life with the re-introduction of Greek language and new laws. Byzantium enforced anti-Jewish laws and the Jews vacated the Eastern Roman Empire.

In 533 CE, Emperor Justinian's *'Corpus Juri Civilis'*, a code of law, was published. The next year his general Belisarius destroyed the Arian kingdom of the Vandals and re-conquered southern Spain and northern Africa (Roberts, 1997). Justinian also shut down the Academia of Plato, due to its non- Christian practices.

In 542 CE, the plague again devastated the Empire. The city of Rome now had a population of only 30,000 people. Comparatively, Byzantine-Contantinople had a population in hundreds of thousands.

~~~

Meanwhile in Persia, Ardashir founded the Persian Sassanian Dynasty with his capital in Istakhr, near Persepolis. He was the descendent of the priests of Sassan. In 224 CE he seized the throne of Persia from the Parthians ending the Arsacid dynasty and was declared 'King of the Kings'. The Sassanians considered themselves as exponents of the Achaemenid and re-established the Achaemenid norms and Zoroastrian religion. As the region stabilised under the Sassanian rule, long distance trade was fostered by them causing Persia to prosper and strengthen. They sponsored trade both with the Byzantines, their arch-enemy, as well as the Chinese. Excavations in China have unearthed Sassanian gold and silver coins covering a span of several centuries.

In 244 CE Shapur I became the emperor and soon invaded the Roman Empire. In 256 CE the Persians Sassanians conquered Dura Europus in Mesopotamia and in 260 CE after defeating the Roman army they captured the Roman Emperor Valerian. By this time the Persians had emerged as the most powerful force in the region.
~~~

In one of the on-going battles, Shapur II defeated the Roman Emperor Julian and recaptured Nisibis and Armenia from the Romans. Shapur II died in 359 CE after conquering Arabia and reaching the border with China. In mid 5th century, after Armenia had revolted, King Firuz of Persia defeated Christian Armenia. He let the Christians keep their religion but he persecuted the Jews who migrated to Arabia.

In the first half of the 6th century, the political philosophy of Mazdak became very popular. Like Buddha, he was of an egalitarian bent of mind and was, probably, the first 'quasi-communist' in historical record. He advocated abolition of private property, the division of wealth, as well as non-violence and vegetarianism. His ideas brought about a major class struggle between the peasants and the nobility.

Khasru I (531-579 CE) embraced Mazdaic philosophy and became very popular. He gave audience to his ordinary subjects. His prime minister, the famous Bozorgmehr, invented the game of backgammon. This reign marked another high of the Sassanian dynasty. Khasrow promoted scholarship and by his time Gundespur library had amassed the largest collection of books in the world. He also gave refuge and financial assistance to philosophers fleeing oppression in the Byzantine Empire.

But Hormizd, son of Khosru I, led the empire less successfully. He killed his brothers after accessing the throne and continued the war with Byzantine. He was killed when his own son, Khosru II, revolted against him. Initially, Khosru II was in good terms with Emperor Maurice of Byzantine who had help him consolidate his rule. When Maurice was killed by an usurper in 602, Khosru II attacked the Byzantine Empire to avenge the death. His Generals defeated the Romans in a number of engagements and annexed considerable Byzantine territory. They also killed Noman III, the Arab King of Al Hira which was the buffer state between Persia and Arabia, and took over this Arab territory. They also started to exorbitantly tax these people to make up for the wealth spent on war efforts. The wealth and power that they yielded made them arrogant, intolerant and decadent.

~~~

Meanwhile in India, After the Maurya reign (321-180 BC), the next great empire to rise was the Gupta Empire which ruled from 240 to 550 CE. This was the most enlightened of the ancient Indian Empires. Chandra Gupta established a kingdom in Magadha of Bengal (Comprising of current Bangladesh and the West Bengal Province in India) and extended its domain over northern India moving the Capital to Patna. In 350, Samudra Gupta extended the Gupta kingdom to Assam of north-eastern India, and Deccan, Malwa of Central India. At its height it covered a large part of modern day Bangladesh, northern India and eastern Pakistan.

~~~

In China, the Han dynasty (206 BC–220 CE) formed the model of Chinese imperial order that created the nationalist political consciousness that remains to the present. China had become the most populous country in the world with a population of 57 million people. Luoyang, the second Han capital, was one of the largest cities in the ancient world and was the end point of trade routes that went via the centrally placed Sassanian Empire.

As the Han dynasty waned civil war ensued with several rulers contending for the control over the lands of China. Southern China with a developed agricultural economy remained relatively calm. The Hans were forced to the south by tribes from the North.

For the next 300 years China was divided between northern and southern dynasties. The northern dynasty was that of the Wei rulers who were Buddhist. Monks studied and taught Buddhist ideas which were compatible with Daoist philosophy. In the south, where the Han ruled, Confucian intellectuals engaged in debates on metaphysical subjects. In 600 CE, the Sui Dynasty reunited the empire which they ruled from their capital at Changan.

Achievements of 0 – 600 CE:

In 159 CE, king Eumenes II of Pergamum (a Hellenistic city on the west coast of modern Turkey) inaugurated a library which was the second best in the Hellenistic region. The library volumes were generally made of papyrus imported from Egypt. When the Ptolemys of Egypt stopped exporting papyrus, the Pergamenes began to use *pergaminus* or *pergamena* parchment made of fine calf skin and named after the city. The library at Pergamum is said to have contained 200,000 volumes. According to a legend, Mark Antony is said to have given the library to Cleopatra as a wedding gift.

~~~

Starting with Augustus, the first five emperors of Rome belongs to the Julio-Claudian Dynasty. After Augustus came Tiberius, Caligula, Claudius and finally Nero. A parallel political drama was enacted during each of their reigns. Each took power after the murder of the previous Emperor and each had an indirect or adopted relationship with the deceased. Ancient historians paint them as tyrannical, narcissist, egoist, insane and sexually perverse. Strangely though, all of them had a measure of popular support. Their popularity was disliked by the elite Roman political class and they constantly conspired to remove them and restore the Republic. The Emperors, likewise, executed or banished anyone who could be considered a threat to their power (It is probable that these Emperor were not as hideous as they have been sometimes portrayed as but rather victims of character assassination). Each of these Emperors expanded the Roman Empire and took on massive construction work in Rome.
~~~

Nero became Emperor of Rome at sixteen years of age. His mother Agrippina had considerable political clout. At one stage she wanted to sit next to the Emperor to receive envoys. When Nero severed his relationship with her she turned her attention to Brittanicus, the fifteen year old son of deceased Emperor Claudius. She hoped to make him the Emperor when he turned adult. But Brittanicus died mysteriously the very day he was to be proclaimed adult. Later, Nero had his mother executed, and even later, his friend the poet Lucan was charged with conspiracy and was executed while his advisor Seneca was ordered to commit suicide.

Nero cut taxes on the general mass and vetoed harsh regulations against the freedman and slaves. He was a great lover of art and entertainment to the extent of hedonism. He opted for peace with Parthians to manage a fiscal crisis.

He was oppressive to the Christians and dealt with Jews with an iron hand. In 64 CE, a great fire burnt four of the fourteen localities of the city of Rome. It raged for five days when initially Nero did nothing as the fire was in the area where the Christians lived. Some historians claim Nero to be the arsonist, while others claim that he used the fire as an excuse to oppress the Christians, blaming them to be the arsonists.

Finally, in 68 CE, after being out manoeuvred by the Roman politicians Nero committed suicide and was succeeded by the Flavian Dynasty- Vespasian and his two sons. In 66 CE, the Jews in Judea had revolted. Nero dispatched General Vespasian to restore order. This revolt was put down in 70 CE, after his death, in which the Romans destroyed the Temple of Jerusalem and the Jews again spread out to Armenia, Iraq, Iran, Arabia, Egypt, Italy, Spain and Greece.

There are also five other consecutive emperors (96-180CE) in Roman annals — Nerva, Trajan, Hadrian, Antoninus Pius and Marcus Aurelius – whom historians term as good emperors. The good emperors had been mentioned by Machiavelli who believed that those who became emperors by birth would be bad and those who inherited it by adoption would be good. According to Edward Gibbon, during their rule the Roman Empire though still under absolute power was guided by wisdom and virtue.

Constantine, in 325 CE, convoked a conference of the Bishops in Nicaea (in present day Turkey). More than 300 bishops attended this conference. The main agenda of the council was the resolution of the Arian controversy whether Jesus was part of the Trinity or has been created later by God as advocated by Bishop Arius of Alexandria. The council overwhelmingly decided against Arius.

The council also resolved two other major issues. Some of the Christians who had apostatised due to oppression by Diocletian wanted to return to Christianity. But, Bishop Meletius of Lycopolis (Egypt), who had suffered prison for his refusal to apostatise, declined to receive these people back into the faith. He drew a large support from various Bishops of Egypt and Palestine. But other Bishops regarded him as disturbing peace among Christians.

The council decided to let him remain the Bishop of Lycopolis, but with nominal authority. After his death, however, his follower joined the Arians. Arianism continued to spread during the remainder of the fourth century but was assimilated in the subsequent centuries. The other issue was the separation of Easter, Christian Passover, from the Jewish Passover. The 'Crucifixion' of Jesus had taken place during this festival. The council ensured that Easter would not fall on the same day as the Passover. Twenty new church canons were also promulgated during the conference.

The Romans were not just conquerors but also great builders. The coliseum was a giant amphitheatre (Stadium) in the city centre of Rome, just east of the Roman Forum. It took 10 years to construct ending in 70 CE. It was used for gladiatorial contests and could hold up to 50,000 spectators.

The Circus Maximus was a hippodrome (open chariot course) and mass entertainment venue located in Rome. The Etruscan kings of Rome had first used it for public games and entertainment. The festivities came under Greek influence in the 2nd century BC. Julius Caesar expanded the Circus to meet the public demand for entertainment. Chariot racing was the main event in the course. The track was approximately 600 m in length, 80 m in breadth and could hold up to 12 chariots. The two sides of the track were separated by a ridge termed the *spina*. Statues of various gods were set up in the central *spina* including an Egyptian obelisk. The huge open area around the Circus had space for 200,000 people.

Another great achievement of the Romans was their road network. The Romans at their peak had constructed or refurbished a road system that spanned more than 80,000 km. The roads were designed and maintained for fast military deployment in regions of resistance or uprising in the provinces. By 130 BC the distance of the main roads were marked by milestones, a mile was a 1000 paces or 1480 metres approximately.

~~~

The Gupta rulers of India (240 – 550 CE) were great conquerors and skilled administrators. There was internal stability and all external invasions and infiltrations were checked. Economic prosperity led to cultural growth and increase in long distance trade. The peace and prosperity created under leadership of the Guptas enabled the pursuit of science, arts, astronomy, religion, literature, music, architecture, and philosophy.

Chandra Gupta II inscribed on the Ashoka Pillar:

> 'Through out the country no living creature is killed, nor is intoxicating drinks taken, nor are eaten garlic, onion.... except by the Chandals who are the polluted people and live apart.'
~~~

Fa Xian, the Chinese Buddhist monk who was in India around 400 CE, wrote of beautiful cities, fine hospitals and universities, and described a content and prosperous people. Nalənda, in modern day Bihar of India, became the first residential University (Wood, M. 2007). This period was another golden age of the world.

Very advanced books on medicine, veterinary science, mathematics, astronomy and astrophysics were written in this period. Aryabhatta (born in 476 CE, Kusumpura, Bihar), a master of mathematics and astronomy, was one of the greatest scientists of the Gupta period. He gave a systematic analysis of the position of the planets in space. He gave a non-mythical explanation of the eclipses and also deduced that the moon and the planets shone due to reflected sunlight.

The Indian philosophical formulations concerning *Shunya* - emptiness, null or the void – probably assisted in the understanding of the concept of zero by the later day Arabs / Muslims. They would put into practice the method of expressing every possible number by using a set of ten symbols, with each symbol having a place value and an absolute value. This seemingly simple idea had a profound importance as it greatly facilitated calculation and placed mathematics at the root of all sciences.

~~~

In Persia, Shahpur I established the city of Gundeshapur (Jondi Shahpur) which became the major centre of learning of the Sassanian. Gundeshapur University became famous through out the world during 528-570 CE as a prestigious scientific and cultural centre of which the most famous were the astronomy and medical faculties. A hospital was also established where projects on pharmacology and alchemy were carried out. This was the world's oldest known teaching hospital that also contained a library. According to *The Cambridge History of Iran*, it was the most important medical centre of the ancient world during the 6th and 7th centuries.

~~~

In China, the first printing method was developed. Paper was in use by the third century, printing blocks were developed by carving texts in reverse on blocks of jujube or pear wood. Paint was applied on these blocks and printed on paper. Books were made by sewing the printed papers. Books on history are known to have existed. The Han supported scholarship and learning. Many philosophers, historians, poets and artists contributed during this age. There was schooling for general people both male and female with the female receiving schooling on homemaking and family affairs. A 2000 km long canal linking Yangtze and Huang He was built. Tools, silk and paper came under mass production (Michaelson, 1996).

~~~
~~~

Written political history is replete with wars, conquest, plunder, genocide, bravery, treachery and cruelty. It is very important to understand that written history only displays a much skewed view of humanity. For every bad deed committed in the political world, ordinary social beings have done a billion good deeds towards other individuals and other people that have gone unrecorded. It has gone unrecorded because it is beyond the capacity of written history and is always taken as granted. And that goodness in humanity is the reason that the human civilisation has progressed, ultimately, for the better.

Civilisations have progressed as a whole by the cooperation and coordination of the many. But there are some great individuals who have shown the path to progress. The most remarkable among them were the Prophets, who committed deeds of greatness not for their own benefit but to improve humanity in the name of the Lord. They were the founts that fed the streams of civilisation.

The path is straight.
But the journey dire, every step a lure of illusions and distractions. And humanity in strength rises and reaches arrogant heights, or in ignorant weakness, loses the path

and falls.

The heralds, the admonishers, the teachers and the messengers rise and stretch out a hand of knowledge and with the other point to the path to rise again and rise further. For every stream of knowledge has its source, its fountain.

~~~

And all that We relate to you of these stories of the Messengers
We strengthen with them your heart
Through them comes to you the truth as well as admonition
And a reminder to those who believe [11:120]

And there are, certainly, among the people of the Book (Jews and Christians), those who believe in God and in that which has been revealed to you, and in that which has been revealed to them, humbling themselves before God. They do not sell the Verses of God for a little price, for them is a reward with their Lord. Surely, God is Swift in account. [3:199]
~~~

People of the Book.

By 2000 BC the foundation of civilisation had been laid down by the ancient Mesopotamians, Egyptians, Indians and Chinese. Progress in literature, arts, philosophy and technology had led to formation of urbanised societies. There were empires, nations, tribes, races and there were heroes, kings and gods. There were kings who became emperors and emperors who declared themselves gods. Dynasties had ruled and Dynasties had fallen paving the way for new ones to rise.

Civilisations progressed. The fundamental reason of progress was the on-going quest for knowledge and its cumulative increase. Knowledge also led to social upliftment and improved material production. But there always was a need to equally uplift the humane qualities, as well, to balance the rise of materialism in society. Any disruption in the balance between materialism and morality caused disorder affecting human progress. Thus, the progress of civilisation was over a clear but thread-fine path.

Over the ages, there were times of stagnations or regressions when people moved away from this finely balanced path. The responsibility to maintain the clear direction belonged to the rulers who had the twin objective of the continuation of the quest for knowledge and the rights of people in their domain. When the rulers had given up the quest for knowledge their nation had become weak and when they had given up the rights of the people they have caused oppression, pain and conflict in the world. These derailments had been most acute when the rulers had tried to fulfil their lust for power and wealth at the cost of human values or progressive change. To force their arrogant dominance over the people they made their subjects move away from the right path to one of meaningless low life based on animal instincts or ignorance. This caused the rule by force, fear and misinformation.

But always, from among the people, arose individuals who would speak up against the corrupt or misguided establishment and show the people the clear Path. Individuals who had vision, who were humane and who were heralds of God. These people were known as prophets (peace be upon them all). Prophets had been born among all the people of the world and according to Islamic tradition there had been more than 120,000 prophets. Of these more than 300 had been messengers. Messengers were those prophets who brought a new law or a legal framework into existence like Moses and Jesus while those who were only prophets but not messengers, like Aaron, were those who taught the laws of a previous prophet. The prophets were the founts of knowledge from whose teachings civilisation had risen and progressed.

Most of these prophets have been forgotten and are unknown today. From Adam to Noah only a few of these transmitters of knowledge, law and humanity are known through the Testaments and the Quran. There are justifiable claims that individuals like Zoroaster, Buddha, Rama and Socrates were also prophets. But the best known and established prophets are the ones belonging to the Abrahamic group who came to the world after Noah and were based in the Middle East. This group include stalwarts among stalwarts such as Abraham, Moses and Jesus.

These were the men who preached Judaism and Christianity to the world. To them was revealed the book of religion. And their followers, in the powerful phraseology of the Quran, are the People of the Book.

In Babylon a powerful king, Nimrod according to the Old Testament, had become so arrogant that he declared himself god and led his people astray. In the imperial system, besides the king, numerous other deities were worshiped by various groups of people. The whole system was oppressive with strong groups dominating weaker ones and forcing them to live a slavish and ignorant life without any opportunity for improvement. Instead of questioning this unjust authority and this incorrect way of life, many accepted it as *fait accompli*, as most people do.

There have been attempts to find the historical Nimrod. A translation of a verse (Genesis 10:11) from the Torah states that Nineveh was established by Ashur the son of Shem son of Noah. Another translation of the same verse attributes Nimrod the son of Cush as the founder. According to the ancient Persians the city was established by King Nisun. Ctesias of Cnidus, the Greek physician to the Persian king Artexerxes II in 400 BC had access to the Persian royal library and wrote about King Nisun from the archives of the library. In one of his books called *Persica* he dealt with the history of Assyria, Babylonia and Persia. Some later literature claims Nisun to be Nimrod.

But among the multitude, Abraham, a strong young man in the city of Ur (in modern day Iraq) stood up against the degradation of humanity and declared a single humanity and a single God. The people, especially the powerful, were angered by his teachings which were so opposed to their traditional belief system. Abraham had an altercation with his father, an employee of the king, who refused to accept his ideas. So Abraham embarked on a more radical course. During a festival, when all the inhabitants left to partake in festivities outside the city, Abraham alone went to the main temple within the city. Using an axe he broke down all the idols. But he left the biggest idol intact. Placing the axe on its shoulder he silently went away. When the people returned after the festivity, there was mayhem. They immediately knew whose handiwork this was.

They charged Abraham, "Did you break all the idols?"

"No," he denied and pointed at the intact big idol with the axe on its shoulder saying, "Maybe the big one broke the others. Why don't you ask him? He should tell you who broke them."

The elite of the city knew what Abraham was deliberately implying: The idols were lifeless and could not help themselves then how could they be expected to be divine and help others. The elite were incensed and also feared that this man's religion had the potential to shake the very foundation of their imperial system. They wanted to make sure no one would follow Abraham and decided to make an example of him. When this news reached Nimrod, he ordered Abraham to be brought to his presence. He commanded Abraham to accept him as god. But, as recorded in the Quran, Abraham said, "My lord is one who gives life and death."

The king ordered that two prisoners be brought from the dungeons. He had one executed and let the other free and said, "I too give life and death."

Abraham did not debate with this shallow meaning of 'life giving' but countered, "My God makes the sun rise in the east, if you can then make it rise from the west." Nimrod decided that Abraham would be burnt to death in a spectacular manner. They gathered wood for days and lit a fire that bellowed wide and high over a very large area. Even birds flying over it fell dead due to the intense heat. Finally Abraham was thrown into the fire using a catapult. To every one's amazement, the fire did not burn Abraham and he emerged unscathed.

Abraham migrated to the land of Canaan which constituted of a region that now comprises parts of Lebanon, Palestine, Syria, and Jordan. He taught God's truth and universality to the people. There was no difference between the Semites and the Egyptians or any other people and all belonged to the domain of a single God. That was his covenant with God and in return God promised greatness among his progeny.

Abraham's beautiful wife Sarah and nephew Lot had accompanied him. Lot parted ways and went to Sodom to preach there while they progressed to Egypt. Sarah was barren, so she asked Abraham to take their maid Hagar as his wife in order to continue his progeny. Hagar gave birth to Ishmael. Soon, Sarah too gave birth to a son Isaac. The relationship between the two women became acrimonious. Consequently, Abraham, under divine counsel, separated them. He took Hagar and Ishmael to the desert of Arabia to resettle them there. As he was about to leave, Hagar asked why he was leaving them. When he said it was the will of God, she did not restrain him anymore.

Under the hot sun of Arabia, the infant Ishmael became thirsty and soon was very sick. Hagar looked around for water but in vain. She ran up and down the Safa and Marwa Mounts looking for water as she despaired for her son's life. Then she miraculously discovered a pool of life-giving water which emerged at the foot of the baby Ishmael. This pool came from an underground aquifer which still exists in Makkah and is called 'Zamzam'. Later, the Arab tribe of Jurham found her and Ishmael by the pool. The tribe settled down with them in the area near the pool. Ishmael grew up and married among the Jurham and lived in what came to be known as Makkah.

There was Divine design in Abraham's leaving Hagar and Ishmael in the middle of the desert. Abraham would visit them at times and he, with Ishmael, built a house of God which was destined to become the 'Kaba'.

> *Behold! We gave the site of the sacred house to Abraham (saying): Do not associate with me anything, and purify My House for those who circumambulate it, who stand to pray, and who bow and prostrate themselves. And proclaim the pilgrimage among people, and they shall come to you on foot, and on every lean camel through deep and distant mountain highways. [2:26-27]*

Forty years later another house of God was established by Isaac's son Jacob. This was the first one in Jerusalem.

Not much detail exists about Abraham's method of teaching. But it was exceptionally progressive for his time and his migration to Canaan led to the foundation of the great Abrahamic family of religions – Judaism, Christianity and Islam. Of his sons, Ishmael and Isaac were the fore bearers of the Arabs and Hebrews respectively. Even though these two groups were ethnically same and lived side by side for centuries, they drifted away philosophically. The Hebrews maintained monotheism but the Arabs, who had a short taste of Monotheism from Ishmael, reverted to paganism. Eventually, though, Abraham's covenant did materialise and both the groups of people achieved greatness over historical time. A large number of prophets were born to the progeny of Isaac, but the last great prophet belonged to the progeny of Ishmael. Besides these two groups, Abraham also left behind a devout group of followers who had existed up to the 6th century CE and were known as 'Hanifs'.

Abraham's sons Ishmael and Isaac were both prophets. Isaac's son Jacob and grandson Joseph were also prophets.

Prophet Joseph

Joseph's life story was dramatic to the extreme. He had ten step brothers and another one, Benjamin, from his own mother. His older step brothers were envious of him because they thought that their father loved him most. In a conspiracy they took him far away and threw him into a well and informed the father that he has been devoured by a wild beast. The water-drawers of a passing caravan rescued Joseph and hid him. He was bought by one of the traders at a very low price and was taken to Egypt and bonded into slavery. Joseph, fortunately, ended up in the house of the Aziz, the 'Prime Minister' of Egypt.

The man in Egypt who bought him, said to his wife: "Make his stay (among us) honourable: maybe he will bring us much good, or we shall adopt him as a son." Thus did We establish Joseph in the land that We might teach him the interpretation of stories, and God has full power over His affairs but most of people do not know. And when he attained his maturity, We gave him wisdom and knowledge. And thus We do reward those who do right [12:21]

Joseph grew up wise and knowledgeable with the ability to interpret visions and dreams. He was also irresistibly handsome. It is said that 'One half of the beauty of the entire creation was Joseph'. Julekha, the very pretty wife of the Aziz, became infatuated by him, her heart was struck by love. Ultimately, she invited him to her room, closed the door and tried to seduce him. She was beautiful as well as a woman of position and Joseph was human. The power of attraction on him was extreme, but his righteousness was stronger, "I seek refuge in God. Your husband, my master, has made my stay agreeable. I will never betray him. Wrong-doers will never succeed."

As he tried to run away she caught him by the shirt at his back and it tore. At that instance the door opened and the Aziz walked in. Immediately, she changed her stance and shouted in apparent self defence, "What is the recompense for him who intended evil against your wife?"

The Aziz was very angry. Joseph protested but was disbelieved. One of the relatives of the Aziz walked in and summing up the situation told the Aziz that if the shirt is torn from the front than Joseph was guilty as it proved that he was attacking her. But if the shirt was torn at the back then Joseph was not guilty as it meant that he was trying to run away and was held from behind. The Aziz realised what had happened and told all not to speak of this anymore and told his wife to repent.

But the elite women of the society soon came to know the story and gossiped about it, "She is violently in love with him. How can she be so infatuated by a slave?"

Julekha soon got fed up of the gossips and decided to teach them a lesson. She invited a group of the elite woman to a party. She put sharp knives and trays of fruits in front of them and requested them to slice these. Then, she made Joseph enter and walk in front of them. As the "half of the beauty of creation" walked in front of them, the women were mesmerised and with their eyes fixed on him they cut into their fingers instead of slicing the fruits. And they said, "This certainly is not a man but an angel."

After Joseph left, Julekha said, "This is the young man you blamed me for desiring. I did try to seduce him but he refused. But if he does not obey me, he will be cast to the prison."

After seeing him, the women changed their mind, and in fact thought it was natural for Julekha to be so enamoured. They encouraged Joseph to listen to his mistress. Joseph was going through turmoil as seduction and righteousness pulled him in opposing directions. He prayed, "O my lord, prison is more to my liking than what they invite me to. Unless You turn away their plot from me, I will feel inclined towards them and be one who commit the sin and one who is ignorant".

As the scandal spread the Aziz, to save face, blamed Joseph for the whole episode and put him in prison. Joseph passed years in jail where he impressed many of the inmates with his knowledge and wisdom. Two of the inmates told Joseph of their dreams and asked what was going to happen to them. He said that one will be executed and the other released. And it came to pass exactly as he had predicted. The one released was the Cup-bearer in the King's court and went back to his work.

> *And he said to the one he deemed to be saved: "mention me to your master.' But Satan made him forget to mention to his lord. And Joseph lingered in prison for a few more years [12:42]*

Egypt's economy was dependant to a large extent on agriculture by the Nile. Thus climatic instability caused economic hardship and social instability. During periods of drought lands produced no crop and Egypt would fall into famine. When the Egyptians tried to store food grains over long years it would rot. The King had a dream of seven fat cows being devoured by seven lean ones. He asked the scholars and priests to interpret the vision. But none could understand what his vision meant or how to tackle the famines and the resulting instability. Then the ex-inmate Cup-bearer of the King remembered Joseph. He told the King that he knew a man who had knowledge and wisdom and would be able to interpret the vision.

Joseph, upon being informed by the Cup-bearer, gave an interpretation of the King's vision – a period of seven years of high yield followed by a seven years of drought. He laid down a strategy for the first seven years to use only the essential amount of corns and store the rest for the alternate famine period. He also gave a plan how to store the corn along within the corn-ear so that it would not rot.

After learning of the strategy the King was amazed that such an intelligent person was languishing in a prison. He said, "Bring him forth."

But to everyone's amazement, Joseph refused to be freed. He said "First of all ask the King about what happened to the women for whom I have languished in jail for so long."

The women were brought in front of the King and they admitted that Joseph was innocent. Julekha also testified claiming his innocence. Finally, Joseph was released and became a member of the King's court.

Joseph, by virtue of his qualities and talents became the Aziz, the second most powerful person after the king. He managed the economy in a remarkable manner. During famines people from all around Egypt would come to Egypt for food aid. One day, Joseph found his ten step brothers among those who had come for aid. Initially, he kept his identity a secret and played along with them. But later, after they had relegated to begging for food, he could bear it no longer and forgave them. Through them he was finally reunited with his mother, Benjamin and father Jacob.

During those times, the Semites of Mesopotamia were relatively welcome in the Egyptian Empire and there was significant migration. But later they were enslaved by the Pharaohs and were put to hard work with little or no wages. The Israelites would endure untold hardship and torture at the hand of the ruling Egyptians.

Prophet Moses

Around the middle of the second Millennium BC, the population of the Israelites in Egypt, enslaved and subjugated, kept on increasing in numbers. Their monotheistic belief was different from the 'pharaoh-god' system on which the Egyptian society was based on. By sheer increasing numbers the Israelites were becoming a powerful political force which had come to represent a foreign cultural system with the potential to destabilise the very foundation of political Egypt. The religious texts do not clarify which Pharaoh ruled at this time but mentions that he had a vision that some day an Israelite would capture power in Egypt. The Pharaoh decided to nip this problem in the bud. It was declared that all the male children born to the Israelites would henceforth be slain; only females would be allowed to live and serve as slaves. All the Israelite women were put under surveillance and their pregnancies were supervised. It was, therefore, up to Moses to lead his people out of this brutal and appalling slavery. And he was yet to be born into a situation where at his very birth he was supposed to be put to death.

Aaron, the elder brother of Moses, was born when the decree of slaying of male children had not yet been passed. Some exegetes say that the Israelite male infants were slain in alternative years to maintain a balance, otherwise, the Israelites would become totally devoid of male members and the Pharaoh couldn't let that happen as the Israelite slaves were needed for the Egyptian work force. According to those exegetes, Aaron was born in one of the years in which the infants were allowed to live.

When Moses was conceived his mother concealed her pregnancy. But when he was delivered it became impossible to hide the infant. In fear of discovery by the pharaoh's police, she was divinely inspired to cast him adrift in the Nile. Along the bank of the Nile his sister followed the wooden box in which the infant Moses was floating. Most of Egypt had been built along the Nile, but the box found its way and was obstructed, incredibly, at the bank of the Palace of the Pharaoh – the very nemesis of the infant. The inspiration of the mother of Moses was to be vindicated. The baby was found and adopted by the Queen Aseeya, wife of the Pharaoh (According to the Old Testament, it is the Pharaoh's daughter who adopts him). And amazingly Moses' own mother was employed as the wet nurse. The mother was extremely happy at the turn of events.

Moses grew up a prince in the palace of the Pharaoh. He was a well built, strong and wise person with a disposition to be enraged at any sign of injustice. As a young man when he finally learned of his true identity from his family, his days in the Palace were numbered. Soon, he felt himself belonging to the Hebrew people and lost his favour in the royal court of Egypt. One day he got involved in a fight between two men – one was an Israelite slave and the other an Egyptian. The Israelite, who was being beaten up, implored for his help. In his anger Moses landed a blow on the Egyptian which killed him.

In the unequal Egyptian empire, the killing of an Israelite would not have made great news but the killing of any Egyptian was a capital crime. A friend warned Moses that the Pharaoh's court had agreed to have him slain for his crime. Moses escaped and embarked on a life in exile. He went to a place called Midian, between Egypt and Syria, and settled down there having married a local girl. He lived there for ten years where the secluded silence of the desert served as the physical and spiritual preparation for his approaching prophethood.

After ten years in Midian, he was on a journey with his family. Late one night, as they approached Mount Tur after passing Mount Sinai, Moses perceived God as firelight. He heard a Voice asking him to throw his staff, which was in his right hand, to the ground. As he threw the staff and it changed to a writhing snake, frightening Moses. The Voice asked him to pick up the snake, and as he did so it turned back into his staff. Then he was asked to place his hand on his bosom and bring it out. As he did so, his hand turned shining white. After these miracles, God conferred prophethood on Moses and gave him the mission to go to Egypt, acquaint the Pharaoh with the Path of the true religion, and save his suffering people.

After returning to Egypt Moses re-established his old connections with his people that, probably, allowed him to assert some political leverage. His mission was not against the Pharaoh but an attempt to convert him and get agreeable terms for the Hebrews. According to the Quran and its exegesis, the Pharaoh granted him audience and Moses, along with his brother Aaron, went to the palace to ask the Pharaoh to accept his religion. In the debate that ensued with the Pharaoh, Moses unleashed his grasp of knowledge and power, he let go of his staff and it changed to a snake. The Pharaoh was dumbfounded and afraid that the system by which he ruled was at stake due to the righteous knowledge of Moses. He assembled his greatest scholars-magicians to counter Moses. But their 'magic', based on trickery and illusion, was way too weak to withstand Moses' wisdom. His snake vanquished the small snakes that the magicians could conjure. Finally, being men of wisdom themselves, they recognised the truth in what Moses was saying and became, much to the chagrin of the Pharaoh, the followers of Moses. They were threatened with death for this treachery.

> *And certainly We seized Pharaoh's people with years of scarcity, and diminution of fruit, that they might be mindful. So when good came to them, they said, "This is our due," but if evil afflicted them, they would ascribe it to Moses and those with him. Whereas their misfortune was with God, but most of them do not know. And they said, "Whatever signs you may bring to us to enchant us, we will not believe in you." So We let loose upon them the flood and the locusts, the lice and the frogs, and the blood, clear signs, but they were arrogant and were a sinful people. [7:130-133]*

Even after clear signs, the Pharaoh, his chiefs, and even a few Israelites like Korah, who had managed to accumulate wealth, remained against Moses. The general people, afraid of the power and wrath of the Pharaoh, remained passive. But Moses did gather a following, mostly among the Israelites and few among the enlightened Egyptians of whom at least one was the Pharaoh's relative. They were among those who could foresee the destruction and damage that ultimately befalls oppression.

Moses, by now a political reality, demanded the release of the Israelites from slavery, but was denied by the Pharaoh. At the same time, Egypt was passing through a number of calamities – drought, flooding, infestation and disease. These brought great suffering to the Egyptians and they asked for Moses' help promising that his demands including the freedom of the Israelites would be met if he helped them. Moses prayed to God and helped the Egyptian in alleviating the calamities. But each time the calamity subsided the Egyptians went back on their word.

Finally, Moses realised that the Pharaoh and the Egyptians would never relent and never let them have freedom. The only course of action left was to escape - an exodus. In the darkness of the night he led his people to the Red Sea. They took much of their valuables with them. But soon the Pharaoh learnt of their departure and personally led his army to pursue and destroy the Israelites. By morning, the Israelites were trapped with the sea in front of them and the advancing army behind them. Then God inspired Moses to use the power of his staff. With this he slashed at the sea and the sea parted to form a land bridge between two mountains of rising water. The Israelites crossed to the other side. The Pharaoh and his army took the same route chasing after them. But by the time they were in the centre of the land-bridge the water-mountains collapsed and drowned the Pharaoh and his army. Thus the Israelites were delivered from the clutches of the Pharaoh.

That was the end of Egyptian chapter in the life of Moses. In the next stage of his prophethood, Moses set himself to convert his people to a nation. The Hebrews were still homeless and had long years to wander. After centuries of servitude and slavery their mentality had degraded and they did not have any code of law, governance or ability to live as an independent nation. Moses went away alone, leaving his people under his brother Aaron, to receive the 'Ten Commandments' from God that would form the foundation of Judaic laws. The commandments would be same or similar to the laws of Abraham and may have even entered Egyptian legal system via Joseph. The Bible states that God had inscribed the commandments on stone tablets:

1. I am the Lord your God, Who has brought you out of the land of Egypt, out of the house of bondage. You shall have no other gods before me.
2. You shall not take the name of the Lord your God in vain.
3. You shall not make any graven image, or any likeness of anything that is in heaven above, or that is in the earth beneath, or that is in the water under the earth. You shalt not bow down yourself to them, nor serve them.
4. Remember the Sabbath day, to keep it holy (After six days of work, the seventh would be the Sabbath).
5. Honour your father and your mother: that your days may be long.

6. You shall not kill.
7. You shall not commit adultery.
8. You shall not steal.
9. You shall not bear false witness against your neighbour.
10. You shall not covet your neighbour's house, you shall not covet your neighbour's wife, nor his manservant, nor his maidservant, nor his ox, nor his ass, nor anything that is your neighbour's.

And We gave Moses and Aaron the Criterion and a Light, and a remembrance for the pious, those who fear God in the Unseen, and who tremble in awe of the Hour. And this is a blessed Quran which We have revealed, do you then deny it? [21:48-50]

But when Moses returned he found that in his absence, the Hebrews had taken to worshipping the statue of a cow that they had carved out of their gold. He was very enraged and only after punishment the event was resolved.

The Hebrew people were living in wilderness and had a limited variety of food. According to the Quran they were provided food by God. They did not possess much agricultural knowledge and soon were dissatisfied with the food supplied to them. They asked Moses for divine intervention so that a larger variety of food is supplied to them. Moses reprimanded them that under the circumstances that would only be possible if they went back to Egypt and accepted slavery again. It took a generation, forty years, to overcome this kind of mentality. During this period, the knowledge of the Torah was revealed to Moses.

During the years of wandering, Moses had learnt of a very knowledgeable person named Khidir. (Khidir is claimed to be a prophet by some Islamic Tradition or just a wise person by others. Some unconventional sources claim that he may have been granted eternal life by God and will live till the end of days hidden among people. In essence, he is the symbol of eternal knowledge.) Moses himself was an enlightened and scholarly person famous for his wisdom. When he learnt of the wisdom of Khidir he felt a great desire to meet him. Taking Joshua, one of his employees, along Moses went in search for Khidir. After a long search he finally met Khidir in a distant land near the sea. While walking together they came to a river where a boatman took them across. After getting off on the other side of the river, Khidir struck the boat so hard with his staff that one of its planks was damaged. This made Moses angry at Khidir for his action appeared very uncivilised and ungrateful. Khidir apparently committed more irrational deeds which further aggravated Moses. For some time there was no discourse between the two but finally he asked Khidir why he had damaged the poor man's boat. Khidir told him that the king's soldiers were requisitioning all boats which were fit and worthy for war. If they had found the poor man's boat fit they would have seized it. The poor man would have lost his boat if Khidir had not done it a minor damage. Moses understood that actions and events need to be judged from the bigger context. He learned not just to look at events and their reactions but also to consider what causes lay behind the events and the consequence of actions which were not so apparent.

The prophethood of Moses comprised of two main facets. On the religious side he re-enforced monotheism and on political side he put up a fight for the rights of the minority, the rights of the disadvantaged and backward against the powerful and oppressive. Both Aaron and Moses died without setting up any permanent settlement for their nation. But the knowledge in the form of Torah that Moses left with the Israelite people allowed them to achieve greatness.

After Moses the mantle of leadership passed to Joshua. Under him the Jews consolidated into a nation in Canaan. Their prophets like, Elijah (Elias), Elisha and Samuel, had to endure suffering and exhaustion by wars, but they persevered. And by the time of David and Solomon they had built a magnificent nation.

Torah: The Torah, Tawrat or Pentateuch is also known as the Five Books of Moses. It forms the central doctrine of the Jewish faith and is the first part of the Tanakh or Old Testament. It forms an important part of the Bible and is also revered by the Christians and Muslims. The five books that comprise the Torah are Genesis, Exodus, Leviticus, Numbers, and Deuteronomy. It contains a narrative history of the beginning that resulted in Judaism. The Genesis, Number and initial part of Exodus is rich with narratives depicting the philosophy, concept and ideas of Torah. It also contains a system of laws for Jewish people, in particular the 613 Commandments. The Deuteronomy consists of the speeches to Israelites as delivered by Moses towards the end of his life.

Prophet David

After the death of Saul, Ish-bosheth, the fourth son of King Saul, became the king of Israel. But the tribe of Judah ceded from the Ish-bosheth's rule and made David their ruler. A war followed and within two years David and Judah prevailed. David, at the start of the 1st millennium BC, became the king of a unified kingdom.

And We strengthened his kingdom, and bestowed on him wisdom and sound judgement. [38:20]

His was hereditary kingship and prophethood together. He was a great warrior, a scholar and the most righteous of all the ancient kings of Israel. He was among the first to exploit the Iron Age.

We endowed David with bounties from us: "O mountains, submit with him, and you too, O birds." We softened the iron for him.
"You may make shields that fit perfectly, and work righteousness; surely, I see all that you do." [34:10-11]

The Psalm or Zabur was revealed to him and he recited it in a very beautiful voice.

And We gave David the Zabur. [4:163]

In return for his devotion, God promised David that his royal house would endure forever. According to the Jewish traditions the Jewish Messiah would be David's descendent. Muslims and Christians trace the lineage of Jesus back to him.

David first gained note, before he became the king, in the battle with the Philistines who were most likely an Indo-European people. In the battle field, Goliath, the famous warrior and leader of the Philistines challenged the Jewish warriors to a dual. Goliath was a giant of a man and no one wanted to face him. But young David armed with a slingshot accepted the challenge. He attacked Goliath and killed him with stones thrown from the slingshot.

The Biblical history attributes some faults in David – that he was enamoured of Bathsheba and committed adultery. He instructed his commander in Joab to abandon Uriah, Bathsheba's husband, in battle. After Uriah was struck down he married Bathsheba. The Jews claim that Bathsheba was already divorced so David committed no sin by taking her. The Islamic tradition rejects that David was an adulterer or murderer attributing those stories to later concoction.

Psalms or Zabur: The Psalms (Greek: "songs sung to a harp") is a book of the Tanakh i.e. the Hebrew Bible or the Old Testament. It is a collection of ancient hymns and spiritual songs. It was the holy book used in the House of God built by Solomon. The book was revealed to David. There are 150 chapters or Hymns which were originally recited as well as sung.

Prophet Solomon

The Prophet Solomon was the son of David and the next ruler of the unified kingdom. He was the third and final king of the united monarchy which would divide into the northern kingdom of Israel and southern kingdom of Judah.

Both David and Solomon were endowed with knowledge and wisdom. But the wisdom of Solomon is legendary. When David was king a complaint came to his court from a farmer that some stray sheep had destroyed part of his farm. David decided that as compensation the farmer would become the owner of the sheep. But Solomon gave a different ruling. He said that the sheep would be given to the farmer temporarily. He would make use of the sheep and take its milk while the owner of the sheep fixed the farm. Once the farm was fixed the owner would get back his sheep. This appealed to David and the verdict was altered.

Another of Solomon's famous cases was when he became the king. Two women had infant boys of the same age. Unfortunately, one of the infant was eaten by a wolf. Now both the women claimed the surviving infant as their own. In the court there was no way to prove who the actual mother was. Suddenly, Solomon passed the verdict that the child be cut into two with a sword and one half be given to each woman. At this the younger woman started to cry hysterically begging that the child be given to the other woman. Solomon then knew that the younger woman was mother as she was willing to give away the child rather than see it harmed. He then gave the child to the younger woman.

One of his famous exploits was the subjugation of the kingdom of Sheba. Solomon ruled over an army of men, jinn and animals. As the army marched it caused a lot of commotion in the countryside.

> *And for Solomon were assembled his host of jinn, men and birds, and they were ranged in order and rank. When they came to the valleys of the ants, an ant said: "O you ants! Enter your dwelling places, lest Solomon and his hosts trample you without noticing."[27:17-19]*

As Solomon inspected the army he found the Hoopoe bird missing. But the bird was not long in returning and said:

> *I have come to know something that you do not know, and I have come from Sheba with sure news for you. There I found a woman ruling over them, and she has been given abundance of every thing, and she has a magnificent throne. I found her and her people prostrating themselves to the sun, instead of God. Satan has made their deeds alluring to them, and has hindered them from the Way, so that they are not guided. [27:24]*

He marched with a large army towards Sheba which was ruled by a queen. He sent the Hoopoe with a letter to the Queen of Sheba announcing his approach. She was not sure how to deal with the approaching threat and after discussing with her counsellors she sent him substantial gifts. But Solomon refused to accept the gifts. Then the queen, with an entourage, went and met him. She was amazed by the power, wisdom and grandeur of Solomon and finally acceded to his demands.

Tanakh: The Tanakh, the sacred text of the Jews, comprises of 39 books divided into 3 sections - Torah, Nevium, and Ketuvim. Tanakh is the acronym of these sections. The Nevium narrates the rise of the Hebrew kingdom, its division into two- Israel and Judah, and mentions the Hebrew Prophets of God. This section ends with the Assyrian conquest of the Kingdom of Israel and the Babylonian conquest of the Kingdom of Judah which resulted in the destruction of the Temple in Jerusalem. The prophetic books are read by Jews on the Sabbath while the Book of Jonah is read on Yom Kippur (The holiest day for the Jews).

The Ketuvim, or 'Writings' may have been written during or after the Babylonian Exile. It is composed of lyrical songs, proverbs, and eight other books of the bible. These scriptures are less authoritative than the Torah. It ends with the Achaemenid Persian declaration allowing Jews to return to Jerusalem to rebuild the Temple. The Tanakh is the Judaic Bible and the sections of which used with certain modifications in the Christian Bible is called the 'Old Testament'. According to the Talmud the Tanakh was compiled in the 5th century BC. Modern scholars of religion believe it was canonised between 200 BC and 200 CE.

As the psalms in the book of Psalms are attributed revelations to David, the Song of Songs (read on Passover), Proverbs, Ecclesiastes (read on Sukkot) are attributed to Solomon. Lamentations (read on the Ninth of Av) is attributed to Prophet Jeremiah.

According to the Old Testament, Solomon built the Temple in Jerusalem with assistance from Phoenician king Hiram I who provided skilled men and quality building material. According to Islamic source it was Jacob who built the first house of God in Jerusalem which is now the Al Aqsa Mosque. In the historical periods following Solomon the temple was plundered a number of times. The first to pillage it is named as Shashik who may have been Shoshanq, founder of the Twelfth Dynasty of Egypt. Then several kings of Judah plundered it.

Jeremiah was one of the prophets mentioned in the Old Testament. His writings consist of the *Book of Jeremiah* and traditionally, the *Book of Lamentations* is also ascribed to him. Jeremiah under divine guidance warned the Hebrew people that they had violated the covenant with God and if they did not rectify this, punishment was due.

> *Then We granted you (Israelites) victory over them, and We increased you in wealth and children, and We made you the more numerous. "If you do good, it is for the food of your own souls, and if you do evil, you do it against yourselves." And when the latter warning came to pass (your enemies) disfigured your faces and entered the Mosque (Temple) as they had entered it before, and to destroy all that fell in their hands. It may be that your Lord show mercy upon you, but if you turn back, We shall renew Our punishment. [17:6-8]*

In the 6th century BC Nebuchadnezzar II of Babylon conquered the whole of Judah and Israel and pillaged the Temple twice taking all the treasure in it to Babylon. He also destroyed the Temple and deported the Jews of Judah to Babylon as captives and slaves after killing many, including old people. Jeremiah was imprisoned along with all the others, but was later set free by Nebuchadnezzar.

Jeremiah later met Daniel (Azami, 2003). According to the *Book of Daniel*, a part of the Hebrew Bible, Daniel was carried off along with the jews to Babylon. He was trained in the service of the Babylonian court. He became famous for interpreting dreams and rose to become an important figure in the court. After the Persians occupied Babylon he retained a high position. But some jealous nobles plotted against him and had him thrown in a pit along with two lions. But the lions did him no harm

It was during the Babylonians bondage that the Rabbi started on the written Talmud, which is Jewish equivalent to the Islamic Sharia. Before this, most of the Hebrew laws were orally transmitted. The Persian Emperor Cyrus, after occupying Babylon, released the Jews and restored the treasures and sacred vessels to the Jews.

Towards the end of the 4th century Jerusalem was under Hellenistic domination. In the second century the Seleucids sacked Jerusalem and after plundering it built an altar for Zeus. After a short recapture by the Jews the Romans under Pompey captured Jerusalem.

And nearest among them in love for the (Muslim) Believers will you find those who say, 'We are Christians': because among them are men devoted to learning and men who have renounced the world, and they are not arrogant. [5,82]

One of the post-Alexander (Hellenistic) Dynasties were the Seleucids who took over Jerusalem in 198 BC by defeating the ruling Greek-Egyptian Ptolemaic dynasty. The Seleucids carried out a brutal repressive campaign in Jerusalem, trying their best to obliterate the Judaic religion. The Jews responded with a heroic struggle against this subjugation. Under the leadership of the Maccabee family they fought a brutal guerrilla war until the Hellenistic Greeks capitulated in 129 BC. The Jews were free but, unfortunately, not for long.

About 2000 years ago when Jesus was born, Jerusalem and its inhabitants were under the imperial rule of the Roman Empire. Roman General Pompey had captured Jerusalem after a three month siege from the Hasmonean dynasty of high priests in 63 BC. For the last six hundred years the Jews had known only 66 years of freedom after the Seleucid capitulation. They had undergone harrowing and shattering experiences to annihilate them. But yet an unshakeable faith in their religion had kept them from total destruction.

In 40 BC, Herod the Great was installed as the client king of Judea by the directives of Mark Antony and Augustus (Octavius Caesar). He was king for thirty six years and ruled with utter brutality. While Herod lived in a marble palace, the ordinary Jews languished in poverty. Jesus was already born when Herod died. His kingdom was divided into four parts and inherited by his four sons. Herod Antipas, One of the sons, inherited Galilee and Parea, parts of Palestine including Jerusalem. His patron was Emperor Tiberius of Rome. Between 26 CE and 36 CE, Pontius Pilate was the Roman Governor or Prefect for the Judea province. He had little respect for Jewish sensibility. He had decided to bring effigies of Caesar, idolatrous to the Jews, to Jerusalem. He had used the money from the temple to build an aqueduct. According to Jewish philosopher Philo (40 CE), Pilate's tenure was associated with numerous executions without trails, bribes, robberies, cruelty and injustice.

During this time the governing establishment comprised of three constituents: The Prefect or regional representative of the Roman Empire, the Client-King and his regime, and the High Priest and his religious aristocracy of the Temple. The Temple was a place of prayer and sacrifice as well as a treasury for religious taxes and tithes and had a strong hold on the general mass. At times it had been the seat of labour organization, justice dispensation, goods distribution and bureaucracy as well. Thus its political control was imperative for the Romans, which was gained by liaison with the temple priests and corrupting and weakening the priestly establishment. This alliance between the Temple authority and the Romans had not gone unopposed; but whenever a High Priest had proved to be difficult, he had been removed. At least eight such cases of removal are known within a period of fifty years

(Longford, 1974). At about 5 BC, a group of youths numbering nearly fifty, tried to chop down the 'golden eagle', symbol of Roman imperialism, from the Temple roof. Those who were observed on the rooftop were burnt alive and their collaborators executed. By the year 6 BC opposition to Roman odium, pagan culture and taxation started to seethe. The subsequent uprising was met by force and about 2000 Jews were crucified and thousands enslaved. In 41 CE Roman Emperor Caligula wanted his statue, considering himself an incarnation of Zeus, to be installed in the Temple. Thousands of unarmed Jews resisted by lying prostrate in front of the temple to offer their lives to the Roman soldiers. The timely assassination of Caligula stopped the event from moving towards another tragedy. But ten years later when the Jews were celebrating Passover, the Roman soldiers deliberately insulted the event. According to *Jewish Antiquities* of historian Josephus, who wrote in 90 CE, this resulted in an uproar in which more than 30,000 Jews perished.

Though the Romans had inherited the imperial administrative style of the Persian Satrapy via the Greeks, there were differences between these systems. While the Persians and Greeks, in spite of believing in their pre-eminence, honoured and sponsored a multiracial and multicultural empire, at this juncture of history the Romans had no such inclinations. It was not until two centuries later that all the people within the Empire were accepted as citizens. The Romans, in the 1st century CE, were the 'masters' of all they ruled. Their client-kings were usurpers with little legitimacy and were, obviously, facilitators of Roman rule which caused resentment in the people they governed.

The suppressive measures of the Romans included the recruitment of soldiers from Hellenistic regions who specially hated the Jews. Besides the political suppression, the taxation system was oppressive. There were taxes paid to the Romans, taxes paid to the client rulers and taxes or fees for the priests.

The environment was stifling to people with a minimum sensitivity and the reaction was xenophobic introversion. A large section of the Jewish people, in a quest to retain their identity and sense of honour, became highly conservative and started to abide by a way of life based on a stricter code or fundamental interpretation of the Torah. This led to the categorisation of religious philosophy into two broad classes: The passive but conservative anti-Roman attitude which appealed to the general mass and the corrupt manipulative rituals which was followed by a small but powerful priestly aristocracy. Jesus' call was aimed at correcting both these conditions. He, in course of time, would stand up against the manipulative designs of the temple priests that included breaking the deceptive practices of the Sabbath.

Before Jesus appeared in the scene, there already were some socio-politically conscious intellectuals, forming a loose confederation of think-alikes, who were discontent with the yoke of subjugation and corrupt autocracy that supported the subjugation. These people provided an anti-establishment leadership and spread discontent toward the priests and the Romans. Prophet Zachariah and his son Prophet John the Baptist (Yahya) were such individuals.

After Zachariah's death, John led the movement against the Romans and their clients. His followers confessed their sins and lived an ascetic life, believing in apocalyptic intervention. Their purification ritual involved immersion in waters of River Jordan as opposed to the rituals of the Temple. According to Historian Josephus, Herod feared that the growing popularity of John would ultimately lead to a power struggle, so he made a pre-emptive strike. He had John beheaded. According to the Gospel of Matthew the event started with the John's condemnation of Herod's marriage to Herodias, who was the ex-wife of Herod's half brother. Herodias' daughter Salome enthralled Herod with a dance and he promised to give her whatever she wished for. Herodias, who spited John, asked her daughter to ask for his head. But the execution of John only managed to fan the embers of the movement.

Jesus moved to the forefront of opposition to the Roman and Temple politics and went about re-establishing and re-enforcing the practical religious views of Moses. The world of God, as opposed to the world of the Caesar, was described as filled with love, peace and happiness for all. This challenge to the status quo was totally incompatible with Roman paganism and imperial design. The Romans and their clients were well aware of his grassroots movement and even though the movement was taking place in a non-violent fashion, as far as known, the Romans deemed it dangerous as the fundamental philosophy of the movement would alienate the public from their power bases – the client kings and the Temple aristocracy - and weaken their political control over them.

Since the time of Prophet Zachariah they had been desperate to get rid of this passive, simmering and widespread movement, and had started killing the leaders on the slightest pretext. According to the apocryphal Protoevangelium (23, 1-3) Herod the Great, like the Pharaohs, ordered infant Jews around Bethlehem to be killed so that he would not lose his kingdom to a newborn King of the Jews - the event known as 'the massacre of the innocents'. According to Orthodox Christian view when Zachariah refused to reveal the whereabouts of his son, he was killed.

Hannah, the mother of Mary, was from an elite family of Jerusalem. Her cousin (by another account – her aunt) was married to Zachariah. Before Zachariah's death Hannah had dedicated her daughter, Mary, to the service of God and had handed her over to the temple elders at birth. Zachariah built a special room for Mary in the temple in which she grew up dedicated to the service of God. One night, while she was praying in the temple an angel appeared in the form of a man and informed her that she, even though a virgin, would give birth to a son. This caused Mary a great deal of consternation as she did not know how to explain the situation to the people and her family. She left the Temple with a sad heart and finally gave birth to Jesus in Bethlehem.

After his birth the infant was visited by Persian Zurvan philosophers (Magi), who were believers of a divine 'Holy Triad', gave Jesus three symbolic gifts of gold, myrrh (an expensive dried sap of Commophora tree used as ingredient in medicine and incense) and olibanum (an aromatic resin used in perfumery and aromatherapy, also known as frankincense). According to At-Tabari, the Arabian encyclopaedist and historian of the 10th

century CE, these three gifts were symbolic of the power of material world, of healing and rising to heaven. Christian traditions suggest that those Magi or 'The three wise men' were the first to 'worship' Christ.

When Mary returned to Jerusalem, people questioned her innocence. But the miraculous attributes of Jesus, he spoke as an infant, soon made them silent. He grew up to be an intelligent young man who could debate with the clerics and confound them and was a person who could think independently. This was not appreciated by the dogmatic clerics.

Jesus conversed in Aramaic as that was still the dominant language in the region among the non-Romans. He grew up in an environment where the Mosaic laws were being manipulated. By the time of Jesus the Jews had fragmented into quarrelling sects – Pharisees, Sadducees etc – who had their own interpretation of the Torah. The weekly Sabbath (Saturday) was supposed to be a day of rest and worship and refrain from work. A number of activities were unlawful on Sabbath. But the sects used tricks to circumbent these restrictions.

The small group of dissidents, now including John and Jesus, became roving reformers. They wandered away from the sight of the establishment – the Romans, their client ruling class and the degenerated priests – and reached out to the people. These reformers were very intelligent, well read, charismatic and good orators. Though they did not have large followings, the fear of the Roman establishment was definitely an inhibitor of any public display of support, they were held in high esteem by the mass and their words yielded a lot of influence. The disciples revoked the materialistic world, which made them even more idealistic and incorruptible to the people. But to the priests they were blasphemers and to the ruling class and their Roman sponsors they were revolutionaries.

As a protest against the corrupt priests Jesus violated Sabbath. One Saturday, on his way to the temple he made a fire for an old woman to keep her warm from the freezing air; he also picked two pieces of fruit to feed a hungry child. Both were violations of the Sabbath laws. In the temple he found more priest and fewer visitors. The temple had been commercialised by the priests under the pretext of sacrifice to God. They sold sheep and doves and tempted the temple visitors to spend money in various ways. The poor people unable to pay would have to stand aside. While the priests burnt offerings to God within the Temple hungry poor people crowded outside. This degeneration kept the Romans and their sponsored ruling class quite happy as the influential priests were too busy with materialistic motives to initiate any movement against the Roman imperialism. Jesus' violations, actions and words against their laws were not well taken by the establishment.

Jesus' fight against imperialism is evident in his renunciation of the temptation or the 'deal with the devil'. People can be classified into three major groups depending on their political orientation and alliance. The first group are those who fight to establish imperialism - The unequal economic, cultural, and territorial domination and subordination. The second group consists of those who actively oppose imperialism and want to establish a more equitable society. The third group consists of submissive, apprehensive, docile and silent mass that lets 'fate' decide what happens to them. The Temptation can be deemed to be the perpetual offer by all imperialist powers to people or individuals of influence among those struggling against the imperialist. It is evident in the lines from Matthew:

> *"Then leading him to a height, Satan showed him in a moment of time all the kingdoms of the world and their splendour and said to him, 'I will give you all the power and glory of all these kingdoms....worship me then and it shall be all yours.' Then Jesus replied, 'Be gone, Satan! For the scripture says: You must worship your Lord, your God and serve Him alone.' (Matthew 4:8-10)*

This event took place when Jesus was fasting alone in the desert for forty days, having been baptized by John, and is famously known as the Temptations of Christ. Jesus was offered the greatest deal – 'I will give you power and glory of all these kingdoms… worship me…" The denial by Jesus, on the one hand, portrays his infallibility while on the other hand it shows his common humanity, the fact that he is suspect to temptation.

After Herod Antipas had John killed, the mantle of Prophethood had fallen on Jesus. He had extraordinary qualities: he inspired people and showed love to all - even to his enemies. He could heal sick people and many miracles are attributed to him. He prayed to God, and God acknowledged him by bringing dead people back to life. He taught the people the political concept of a 'Kingdom of Heaven' as opposed to the imperial kingdom they were forced to endure. He instructed people in spiritual and moral truths and distinguished between right and wrong.

Like Moses, the prophethood of Jesus had a dual role: to reinforce and rectify the rule of God among the Jews, and secondly, to deliver the Jews from Roman imperialism. He was not against the Torah, as his detractors claimed, but he wanted the correct implementation of the Mosaic laws unlike the impracticable, conservative, and sometime manipulative views held by the then existing religious body. In the Sermon of the Mount he said, "Think not I have come to abolish the law and the prophets, I have come not to abolish them but to fulfil them." In this sermon, attended by a large number of people, he warned his followers against anger, desire and adultery and he spoke of Christian ethics of humility and forgiveness, "Love your neighbours and pray for those who persecute you."

Though the whole life of Jesus was a mission, he started his real movement in the last few years of his life from Galilee. His method was to go to the people and spread the good news – that would eventually become the Gospel. Galilee was a well-known centre of resistance against Romans (Gascoign, 2003), and Jesus started to attract large crowds. To accommodate them, he would stand on top of a small mount and the people would gather round him.

From Galilee he spread his movement to Tyre, Sidon and Philippi Caesarea. Everywhere he went large enthusiastic crowds gathered to hear him speak. Even non-Jews came to his gatherings. People were, in general, helpless due to the heavy taxes they were paying and the poverty they were living in. They were frustrated with the Jewish authority in the Temple, puppets of the Romans, who were involved in corrupt practices and cared little about the people. They were like lost sheep, and in Jesus they saw a shepherd who would show them a way out of this miserable life they were in. People started to talk of him as the *King of the Jews* and Jesus declared that the *Kingdom of Heaven* was at hand. In Caesarea Philippi he accepted the role of the Messiah.

In the Autumn of 29 CE he left Galilee for the last time. His plan was to spread his movement to Jerusalem itself. He had been to Jerusalem on missions previously, but this time his entry was much more politically formal. Multitudes thronged to meet Jesus of Nazareth from Galilee. There was a mood of great expectancy and revolutionary fervour. Here was the Messiah who would liberate them from yoke of subjugation and corruption.

The mission of Jesus was coming to an end. Jesus knew it, lived it and delivered the mission. He arranged for a supper that would be his last supper with his apostles. He had twelve apostles whom he had trained to take leadership when he was gone. He gave his final advice: "Let the greatest among you become the youngest, and let the leader be the one who serves."

According to Christian tradition and historians, he appeared troubled for a while, probably knowing that it would be one of his own, Judas Iscariot, who would betray him. After Judas left, he said, "Little children, yet a little while I am with you. I give you a new commandment. Love one another as I have loved you."

The apostles were unaware of what Jesus meant by having a little time with them and did not realise that his mission was at an end. His foes, the Romans and Temple authorities had realised that this man was too potent in his selfless love and too powerful in his truth to be ignored. His call for truth, piety and humanity was making people respond. The response was turning into a vast movement that would ultimately overthrow the existing establishment. So they decided to end his life. The Roman Governor, who not surprisingly had arrived in Jerusalem, and the High Priest, connived to have him arrested

Judas returned with Roman soldiers followed by a sword-wielding crowd that included priests of the Temple. Jesus was arrested by the Roman soldiers from an olive grove immediately west of Jerusalem known as the Garden of Gethsemane.

Two historians, the Jewish Flavius Josephus and the Roman Tacitus both have written that Jesus was condemned to be crucified by Pilate. But Josephus also adds that the Jewish aristocracy also 'urged' Pilate to put Jesus to the cross. The trial of Jesus was held in two stages.

Firstly, Joseph Caiaphas, Jewish high priest of the Sanhedrin - the supreme Jewish council and court - pronounced him a blasphemer. This was a political move to destroy the credibility of Christ among the ordinary Jews. Secondly, Pontius Pilate the Roman had the crucifixion carried out, albeit with a show of political 'reluctance'. The Romans convicted him and condemned him to death by crucifixion, which was a Roman sentence for ordinary criminals, agitators, and slaves. Christ's crucifixion proves he was a violator of Roman law as crucifixion was a Roman punishment for foreigners and slaves only, too painful and ignoble for a Roman. The capital punishment for violating Jewish law would be stoning to death as was the fate of James, the brother of Jesus.

Jesus was flogged by a Roman soldier just before being taken for crucifixion. Golgotha – the place of skull – where the crucifixion took place was guarded by Roman soldiers as well. A large crowd followed Jesus to his crucifixion. By now most of them were contemptuous of Jesus and even physically abusive.

According to Christian history Jesus was tortured and crucified. Then he was resurrected by God to return to the world in the future. During the last supper Jesus had promised, "I will return."

Judas Iscariot after his betrayal went to the priests, his accomplices, and there sought to redeem himself. But getting no support from them he went out and hanged himself.

When Jesus was brought to Golgotha his face was unrecognisable. Caryll Houselander, ecclesiastical artist, mystic, popular religious writer, artist, mystic and poet, describes: The eyes that could see in the secret places of men's soul were blinded, swollen from the long sleepless nights of trial and judgement, and filled with sweat and blood. The cheeks were bruised and dirty; the mouth swollen; the hair tangled by the crown of thorn, and matted with blood (Longford, 1974).

According to Islamic tradition there was a crucifixion but the person who was mistakenly crucified was someone else. Jesus ascended bodily to heaven, raised by God, to return in future.

The Romans were satisfied with their power and the Jews boasted that they had killed Jesus. But the Truth that Jesus had borne could not be extinguished. It was God's plan to save humanity as prophesied in the Old Testament. That led to the rise of Christianity.

Over generations, the Jews would persecute the early Christians. Later, when Christianity spread in Rome mainly by the Gentiles, the Christians of non-Jewish origin, the Roman complicity in the crucifixion was played down and only the Jewish authority remained the main conniver of the crucifixion. And later still, the Jews, as a whole, were held responsible for the crime, thus giving rise to the development of anti-Semitism. Only in 1974, the Vatican announced that the Jewish people were no longer held collectively responsible for the crucifixion.

The Disciples

After Jesus, his disciples took up his holy mission with zeal and spread out across the known world. This is celebrated as the Christian festival of the Pentecost. The movements of some of the disciples are vague and some traditions of where they went may be conflicting but there is no doubt that they spread out to different far flung regions with their mission. As a reaction to the persecution of Jesus and the impetus provided by the movement of his disciples, despite the Roman-Jewish aristocracy propaganda attempting to confound the people, the Jesus movement started to spread and take root. A number of Jewish uprisings and infighting also took place.

James, brother of Jesus, led the Christians in Jerusalem in the years after the crucifixion. He treated the Jesus movement as a reformed Jewish movement. He was condemned by the Sanhedrin and stoned to death. After the first great revolt, that followed a few years later, Jerusalem was recaptured by legions of Roman General Titus Flavius Vespasian who would become the Emperor in 79 CE. Jerusalem was besieged and put an effective break on James' version of Christ's mission. Simeon became the successor of James, but was executed during the reign of Emperor Trajan.

Saint Peter was a slim, almost white complexioned person of a tallish medium height. He had a short thick curled beard and thin eyebrows with black eyes. Before being recruited by Jesus, he and his brother Andrew became partners with Zebedee and his sons James and John in a fishing business. All four young men become disciples of Jesus and later were appointed Apostles. Due to Peter's unflinching faith Jesus gave him the name of Cephas, meaning a rock in Aramaic. 'Peter' is the Greek translation of Cephas.

After the crucifixion, Peter started his mission in Jerusalem but was imprisoned a number of times. So he left Jerusalem with his wife. He preached in Babylon where he wrote his first epistle, set up the church of Antioch, and eventually reached Rome. He is said to have carried out his mission there for 25 years. Saint Mark was his translator, and as Peter repeatedly spoke of his experiences regarding Jesus, Mark precisely and faithfully memorised it all and later reproduced it as 'The Gospel of Mark', the earliest Gospel. But the Romans did not take this lightly and Peter was persecuted. He was held manacled in a dark and horrible prison for nine months. The Roman Emperor Nero had Peter crucified upside down in Nero's Circus in 67 CE. Even during the final hours Peter's faith remained unshaken and when he saw his own wife led out to die, he called out to her very encouragingly and said, "O thou, remember the Lord." Before his death he had converted his jailers Martinianus Proessus and few others to Christianity. Saint Peter is considered the foremost among the Apostles and is revered as the first Pope of the Catholic Church.

Saint Andrew was the first among the Apostles to accept Jesus (John 1:35-42) and after the crucifixion went to the foothills of the Caucasus Mountains by the Caspian Sea (present day Georgia) to preach to the Scythians. He later preached in Byzantium and Greece where he was martyred by Aigeatis the Governor of Patros. Andrew hung upon the cross for three days suffering and yet continuing to tell the people the message of Jesus.

Saint James, son of Zebedee, carried on his ministry for 14 years before his martyrdom. James visited the Jewish colonies and slaves in Spain to preach the Gospel. By order of

Herod Agrippa I, James was beheaded Jerusalem by a sword in 44 CE. He was the first of the Apostles to be martyred. He was falsely accused and the false witness was standing by when James was being taken for execution. The look of joy and fearlessness on James' face convinced the false witness that the mission of James was correct. The witness declared his belief, and consequently, had to die with him.

The apostle John, son of Zebedee, rose to a position of influence as Christianity spread. In 70 CE he moved to Ephesus shortly before the destruction of Jerusalem by the Romans. He became the pastor of the church in Ephesus and established relationship with other churches in the area. In Ephesus he had with him Mary, the mother of Jesus, for a few years. Roman emperor Domitian ordered the exile of John to an island in the Aegean Sea called Patmos. There John recorded what is written in the book of Revelation of the New Testament. Besides this John is also accredited with the Gospel of John.

When he was released from exile, John returned to Ephesus and lived till the time of the Roman emperor Trajan. He built churches in Asia till he died peacefully, the last of the Apostles. In his old age he was accustomed to just say "Little children, love one another!" After some time, his followers tired at always hearing the same words inquired, "Master, why do you always say this?"

"It is the Lord's command," John said, "and if this alone be done, it is enough!"

Phillip and Bartholomew went to 'Turkey.' They healed the wife of the Roman proconsul and she became a Christian. The angry proconsul ordered Philip and Bartholomew to be put to death by crucifixion. Philip was crucified but Bartholomew was taken down from the cross and let off. From there, Bartholomew went eastward to India and then Armenia.

Apostle Jude (Thaddaeus) was among the first to leave Jerusalem on the mission and was the first to evangelize Armenia between the years of 43 to 66 CE and Bartholomew joined him in 60 CE. He probably met Thomas there as well. He is supposed to have gone to Syria and Persia where he was martyred. Bartholomew was martyred in 68 CE in Albanopolis (now Derbend in Azerbaijan).

Simon the Zealot's mission was in Egypt, North Africa. There are a number of traditions of his death but the most widespread tradition is that after evangelizing in Egypt, Simon teamed with Jude in Persia and Armenia, where both were martyred.

Thomas' ministry was in Babylon where he established a church. He then went to Persia and India making converts till he was killed in Mylapur, a suburb of Madras in India.

Matthew and James were two sons of Alphaeus. Matthew, a tax collector before being recruited by Jesus, was a gifted writer and an ardent disciple. He was the writer of The Gospel of Matthew. He remained in the Holy Land for 15 years going on several missions to Persia and was probably martyred there. His brother James, a lesser known disciple, may have been the first bishop of the Syrian church. He was, later, stoned to death in Jerusalem and buried by the Sanctuary.

There were subtle differences in the teachings of the disciples that made the political situation quite complex. The Jews were already of different shades and now added to this were the range of followers of Jesus including those who were radicals totally defying the Romans, those who were defying the religious authority of the temple establishment, those against the ruling Judaic-Roman coalition, those who considered themselves reformed Jews and those who considered themselves as a new evolution from Judaism. The involvement of the Gentiles (Greeks and other non - Jews) into the Christian movement was probably the main factor that turned the Christian from a reformed Jewish sect to a separate religious entity.

Despite the subtle differences in the manner of Apostolic preaching, the quality that made their mission indomitable was that it represented truth and enlightenment perpetuated by compassion and the genuine desire to struggle for the people, and coveted no self aggrandising, self centred or selfish motives and harboured no fear of death. The preachers were all killed by the establishment, but the idea that has been borne by them was indomitable and would not perish. Jesus and, after him, his disciples, wanted nothing in return for all the toil and pain that they faced, and had no desire to be kings or leaders. They were quite content to leave all material possessions and be beggars, beggars of probity, purity and rectitude in the realm of God.

The Gospels

Among the general people there were many different responses to the teachings of Jesus. Immediately after his death small groups or movements formed in various places starting at Galilee. These groups were similar in their political outlook but varied in the details of their religious practices. The Gospels had not yet been written and the religious literature these groups produced is no longer extant. Some of those can be derived from the Gospels of Mathew and Luke. Both of them had used two sources in the writing of their Gospels. One was the Gospel of Mark and the other an unknown 'collection' of sayings. A list of this collection can be obtained from the common elements in their Gospels which cannot be found in Mark. This hypothetical text is known as 'Q' and some of the sayings in it are as follows:

Say, "The kingdom of God has come near to you."
Love your enemies
Don't worry about your living.
Carry no money, bag, or sandals.
Give to every one who begs.
Ensure God's rule over you.
Judge not and you won't be judged.
Leave the dead to bury their dead.

Over the next three centuries a large variety of texts would be written varying from the traditional gnostic form to the radical and spirited form like that of Paul. Among the texts were a number of Gospels or 'good news' written by various persons from the teachings and life of Christ. Paul had used the term Gospel or 'good news' before any were written when he spoke to the people of Corinth. Some of those Gospels are lost, some are still extant but the names of the authors have been lost. Around 50 CE, intellectuals like Marcion of Sinope, Justin of Samara, and Valentinus of Alexandria engaged in scholarly debates to find out what the unifying views of Christianity should be. By the end of the 3rd century the growing centrist Christian majority had homogenized all these forms into a mono-linear history of the Christian Church.

Of all the Gospels written four – those by Mathew, Mark, Luke and John – were to be declared as canonical by the Roman Church and considered inspired by God and accepted by the later Churches. These would form the first four books of the New Testament. The first three are known as 'Synoptic' as they contain views which are the same or similar to each other. Those that were accepted by some but not all of the churches, in spite of being non – canonical, are called apocryphal instead of canonical. The canonization process took place gradually over several centuries.

The Holy Bible

The Holy Bible, Scriptures, or Word of God is the Christian sacred text. It comprises of the Old Testament and the New Testament. The Christian Old Testament while being common with the Jewish Tanakh varies in the order of the constituent books, and in the interpretations it gives and the emphasis it places. Some additional books are also considered as part of the Old Testament. The New Testament is a collection of 27 books, produced by Christians, with Jesus as its central figure. It relates the life and teachings of Jesus, the letters of the Apostle Paul and other disciples to the early church, and the Book of Revelation.

The Fundamental importance of the Bible in Christian thought is that it represents God's purpose for humankind. The huge cosmic plot and the history of mankind in the Bible are geared to remedy the tribulations and suffering that humanity endures. That is precisely the reason for which Jesus took up his mission against imperial Rome, and precisely the reason his Disciples spread out to different regions, including Rome, to enlighten the people with his words. This mission reached its apex when Constantine accepted Christianity. With this acceptance, the Roman Church gained importance as the most powerful Church. Eusebius, a bishop, wrote of Constantine's victory of Rome and conversion as, "Throughout the world a bright and glorious day, an unclouded brilliance, illuminated all the churches of Christ with a heavenly light."

Among the writers of the canonical Gospel, Matthew and John had been among the twelve disciples and eye-witnesses of Jesus. Mark wrote his accounts after learning and listening to Peter over a long period of time. Luke worked with Paul and interviewed eye witnesses and followers of Jesus and collated all the interviews into a single work. John lived longest among the canonical writers.

Another group of Gnostic writings about the teachings of Jesus, written from the 2nd - 4th century CE, is known as the Gnostic Gospels. The most famous of these are: Gospel of Mary, Gospel of Thomas, Gospel of Truth, Gospel of Philip and Gospel of Judas. These gospels were discovered at much later dates and are not part of the standard Biblical canon of any major Christian denomination. Another contentious Gospel is the Gospel of Barnabas, which espouses the 'Islamic' view of Jesus' ministry. Christian scholars view it as a remnant of a Gnostic Gospel which has been modified, while Muslim scholars view it as the original but suppressed account of the Jesus movement.

The original Gospels were spoken by Jesus in Aramaic or Hebrew. There are claims of different versions originally written in Aramaic, Koine Greek, Hebrew and Syriac Peshitta. The authorship of the some biblical books is also disputed by recent scholars.

Followers of Christ

Saint Paul

Among the followers of Christ, the person who had the greatest influence on Christian thought was Paul, also known as Saul of Tarsus (now in modern Turkey). Unlike most Jews his family had acquired Roman citizenship. He had never met Jesus and had been a great enemy to his followers. Paul witnessed the stoning of Stephen and was on his way to Damascus when a miracle unfolded. He saw a vision of the 'resurrected' Jesus and was struck down. When he recovered he converted to the mission of Jesus. He emphasized that he received the Gospel from the vision of Jesus not from any man. Soon he went to Jerusalem and met Peter, James and John, and some time later he went to preach with Barnabas. Details of his missionary journeys are present in the New Testament. He was imprisoned in Rome but later released. After visiting Gaul and Spain he returned to Rome. There he was imprisoned again and beheaded on Nero's order.

Paul was educated, politically adept, and of immense intellect, talent and enthusiasm. Jesus considered himself a Hebrew reformer and purifier of the laws of Moses, which is a tribal religion. But it was Paul who was instrumental in involving the Gentiles, or non-Jews, into the mission of Jesus and came to be known as the 'Apostles of the Gentiles'. He was the second most prolific writer after Luke and his inspired writings make up a large part of the New Testament. Fourteen of the Epistles are attributed to him.

The Pauline epistles, considered the oldest part of the New Testament, contain the earliest account of the Christian Doctrine and information about the early Church. The fourteen letters are expositions more on what to believe and how to live and less on historical aspects such as the commandments of Jesus on love, divorce and idolatry. Paul differentiated between the Spiritual and Animal thought and action and placed importance on the Spirit in Christian life. To him the entire Christian community was a single body of which Christ was the Spirit.

Mary Magdalene

Mary Magdalene (from the village named Magdala) was a follower of Jesus. In Luke, she appears relatively early in the Ministry of Jesus, while he was still preaching in Galilee. She is mentioned in Mark and Mathew during the crucifixion of Jesus as being among the followers of Jesus in Judea. According to tradition she was the last person at the cross and the first to see the resurrected Jesus. She was a woman of means as she and her friend, the wife of a high dignitary in Herod's court, financially supported Jesus and his disciples.

Origen

Origen (185–254 CE) of Alexandria was one of the greatest Christian theologians. He was born in an educated and devout Egyptian Christian family during the late second century and was a young man of twenty years or less when he became head teacher of the Alexandrian School of Christian Catechism. He was taught by his father Leonides, who was killed, a victim of persecution.

Later, to be independent and carry out his studies and preaching he sold the School and castrated himself following Matthew's (19:12) which states '... *and there be eunuchs, which have made themselves eunuchs for the kingdom of heaven's sake*'. He started a life of preaching in the day and studying during night. He lived a frugal life of utmost asceticism.

He became an authority not only in biblical knowledge but also of Hellenic philosophy. He wrote a number of sermons and biblical commentaries but his two great works were the seminal treatise *On First Principles,* which was a work of Christian Neo-Platonism and *Denouncing Celsus*, which was a critical answer to the attack on Christianity by the pagan philosopher Celsus.

During his time the Christian religion had not achieved any unique theology. About the Holy Spirit he wrote, "With regard to the Holy Spirit it is not yet clearly known whether He is to be thought of as begotten or not begotten, or as being himself a Son of God or not, but these are matters which we must investigate to the best of our power from holy scriptures" (Gascoigne, 2003). Different sects gave different opinions or 'truth' about the faith. Gnosticism, a loosely organized religio-philosophical movement, was flourishing. Origen was a critic of both pagan and Gnostic philosophy and the proponent of a Neo-Platonic Christianity that had inherited components from pagan Hellenic philosophy. His intellectualism was to have profound impact on Christian religious system.

In *On First Principles*, he borrowed the 'Monad, Dyad and world Soul' of Plato and named them in Christian terms Father, Christ and the Holy Ghost – The Holy Trinity. His concept was that the Father, the universal bond, is the Unique, Supreme and Perfect entity superior to all else. The Christ or Son is the first emanation from the Father and is superior to all rational beings but lesser than the Father. The Holy Spirit, emanating from Father and Son, is lesser than the Father and Son and resides only within Saints.

There is a humane quality in Origen philosophy as he believed that all, even the devil, will ultimately achieve heaven. He did not believe in eternal damnation of God-created souls. He believed in a form of soul transmigration, or reincarnation, from bad to good and ultimate salvation. The similarity to Buddhism is apparent but his metempsychosis was different from the Indian and Pythagorean which believed base souls would reincarnate as animals.

In 250 CE, persecution against the church escalated under the Roman Emperor Decius. Origen was one of the victims. For days he was tortured continuously with hands and feet tied. He did not die during the period of torture, but died over a year later of the wounds. Had he died while being tortured, which he would have preferred, he would have been declared a martyr.

His philosophy was widely used in the church, till the 5th century, when due to the excesses of his followers, the Church had to condemn him. Emperor Justinian, politically, also had to disagree with the 'salvation for all', as that would undermine the imperial system of the Roman Empire. Though controversial, he still remains a father of the Church.

Eusebius

Eusebius, Bishop of Caesarea in Palestine, is often considered as the father of the Church History. He met Constantine when the Emperor visited Palestine and, later, was an influential participant in the Council of Nicaea in 325 CE, convened by Constantine.

His two major works are his *Ecclesiastical History* and *Chronicle*. In the *Ecclesiastical history* he narrates the history of the church from the time of the apostles to his time. The history of the Christians teachers, Jews, heretics and heathens were grouped relative to the reign of the Emperors.

His doctrine is the extrapolation of Origen's. He considers God as the cause of all, including all that is good and virtuous, and from whom all life emanates. God sent Christ to earth, subject as a second God, to give His blessings. To avoid polytheism, he emphasized the difference between the Trinity and maintaining the subordination of Jesus to God. In all else he follows Origen's thought system.

Eusebius wrote passages about Hegesippus, one of the earliest Chroniclers of the Church, who lived in the second century BC. Hegesippus' writings included a list of heresies, a long account of the death of James, brother of Jesus, and the election of his successor Simeon. But, unfortunately, his work is lost.

Christianity produced many remarkable men of knowledge, sagacity and forbearance, who spread the religion through out the known world within a few centuries of Christ. In Rome its spread was from bottom to the top, where the general people were first converted leading, finally, to the acceptance of the religion by the Emperor and the ruling class. In other regions, though, the conversion would be top to bottom where the rulers and chieftains would first get converted leading to the conversion of the general mass.

Within the first few centuries, Christianity became more widespread and politically more potent than its parent religion, Judaism. At the very start of Christianity there had existed a substantial groups of followers of Jesus like the Ebionites, the Nazarenes, the Cerinthians, the Basilidians, etc., who were monothiestic and believed in the prophetic human nature of Jesus. They were akin to Jews and remained in Jerusalem. On the other hand, Paul and the Disciples spread out of Jerusalem and preached a Christianity that would deliver the concept of Trinity and Divinity of Jesus. From their mission a powerful church emerged that declared the sects in Jerusalem as heretics and subsumed them. As Christianity overcame Rome, it also absorbed certain Roman pagan culture. For example, In pagan Rome, December 25th was celeberated as the birthday of the gods Mithra and Sol. The Council of Nicea under Constantine decided that the birthday of Jesus should be the same December 25th. (Al-Ashanti and Bowes, 2005).

Over centuries, Christianity had seen significant changes. In the 7th century, it was time for the reinforcement of monotheism – Islam.

The fountains of knowledge sprouted and the streams flowed. Knowledge accumulated, becoming more and more, and enabled people increasingly. Even as a civilisation fell another fount illuminated. Then it was time for the last and best message, the enabler of eternal humanity – The Seal.

And thus the knowledge of the Path was perfected.

~~~

He has ordained for you (O' Mohammad) the same religion which He enjoined on Noah, and ….. to Abraham and Moses and Jesus: Establish the religion, and do not be divided therein. [42:13]

Whether We shall show you within your lifetime
Part of what We promised them
Or take to Ourselves your soul
Before it is all accomplished

Your duty is to make the Message reach them
It is Our part to call them to account. [13,40]
~~~

Part 2 - Light of his Countenance

Like a spiralling projection, civilisation keeps moving ahead towards a universal goal. A new idea is infused, a better way of life is established and civilisation is vitalised and moves forward. A time comes when the temporal scope of the idea is used up and there is deviation from the Path. The apex of development is reached and civilisation slows down. Then, again, it is time for another improvement and there is re-infusion and newer ideas bursts forth which revitalises civilisation and places it again on the clear Path. The cycle of progress starts all over again.

The 6th century was such a time when all the world's civilizations were suffering from a lack of momentum. A denouement had been reached, all ideas consumed with nothing further to achieve. Persia and Byzantium were constantly at war wasting the resources of the Empires. The Gupta Empires of India had disintegrated and even the indomitable Chinese had been suffering from disunity and chaos. The golden age of the Tang dynasty was yet to flourish. Most of Europe was ruled by barbarians; the great city of Rome had fallen and was populated only in thousands. The eastern part of Imperial Rome, Byzantium, continued to exist but, at times, was subject to misleading religious dogma. They had lost all the great works of the classical Greeks, while their philosophers and scholars had faced persecution. The world had lost the momentum that keeps it progressing. But all that was due for a change.

Far away from the centres of civilizations, within the ominous sands of the Arabian Desert, amidst the tough, ferocious, unlettered tribes was born a man who would make an end to all of that. His name was Mohammad (peace be upon him).

Regional and Cultural Setting of Arabia

Arabia lies in the cross road between Asia, Europe and Africa. It is the largest peninsula in the world situated in the western part of the Asian continent. On the west the encroaching Red Sea separates it from Africa. On the south is the Indian Ocean and on the east are the Gulfs of Persia and Oman. Historical Arabia proper consists of Saudi Arabia, Yemen, Oman, United Arab Emirates, Bahrain, and Kuwait. Greater Arabia also consists of Iraq, Syria, Lebanon, Israel and Jordan. The centre of Peninsular Arabia is a vast dry desert region bounded by mountain ranges. Between the ranges and the seas are coastal lowlands which are the most populous areas. Arabia is the hottest and driest region in the world.

The world's civilisations during the late 6th century included the Zoroastrian Persia and Christian Byzantium. West Europe consisted of a large number of small kingdoms, some barbaric and pagan. East of Persia was India, a melee of minor Hindu, Buddhist and Dravidian revivalist kingdoms. In the Far East, China was ruled by the northern Buddhist and southern Confucian Dynasties. There were a few minor kingdoms in Africa and far Southeast Asia. Christian kings ruled Abyssinia (Ethiopia) and Coptic Alexandria (Egypt). America and Australia were yet to be discovered, and were populated by indigenous tribes, many nomadic, with no established or extensive civilisation.

The Arabian Desert, south of Persia and Byzantine, was sparsely populated by nomadic desert-dwelling Bedouin Arabs. They lived in tents and raised camels and sheep. Dates formed part of the staple diet for the Arabs. Each tent belonged to a family, and a number of related families formed a clan. And a number of clans, related over generations, formed a tribe. There were isolated cities and oases in which lived tribes that had become sedentary.

Among the important cities, besides Jerusalem on the North, Makkah had a unique importance as it housed the Kaba – The House of God – built by Abraham. Each year people from all over Arabia visited the Kaba for pilgrimage at the time of a big fair. The Kaba was a single cubic structure and housed 360 idols of gods and goddesses. Hubal was the chief god. Female goddesses, Lat, Uzzah and Munat were called the daughters of Allah. Animals were sacrificed and sometimes even people were sacrificed on the altar of the gods. Many of the animist and polytheist supplicants circumnavigated the Kaba naked.

The other reason of Makkah's importance was that it was also a mercantile hub lying in the trading route between Byzantium and Persia on the north, Yemen on the south and Africa across the Red Sea on the southwest. The economy of Makkah was primarily centred around the trading of goods brought from afar. The traders moved in caravans of camels through the desert to their destination. Usury and 'sleeping partnerships', in which the wealthy invested money without getting involved in the venture itself and took most of the profit, were quite common. The dominant people of Makkah were the Quraish. The Bani Umayyah and Bani Hashim were the two main Quraish clans in Makkah. The Bani Hashim was the custodian of the Kaba, while the Bani Umayyah represented the major mercantile power. The city was run by a Council of Elders, of various tribes, and to some extent was like the pre Socratic Greeks state of Athens and Sparta.

Yathrib, later to be known as Madinah, was an oasis city about 300 km north of Makkah. It consisted of two main tribes, Aus and Khazraj, who had been engaged in hostilities for generations. It was also inhabited by some Jewish tribes and few Christians as well. Here the economy was more agro-based.

In the absence of a viable state framework or legal system, the tribal and clan bonds were extremely powerful. The tribe was the law, the support and the succour. The whole clan would go to war if any individual member was 'wronged'. And the whole clan would be held responsible if any of its individuals committed any wrong. There were bound to be conflicts over the meagre resources in the desert. Thus tribal bonding or clannishness was of utmost importance for the survival of the clans and its members. These people were very superstitious, and quarrels over minor issues could escalate to tribal wars fought over years. The accepted way of alliance was by inter-tribe marriage.

There existed a well established genealogy and naming convention. Everyone's proper name contained the father's name by extension. For example, the name 'Hashim bin Abd Manaf' means Hashim 'son of' Abd Manaf or the short form of the name 'Ibn Abd Manaf' means son of Abd Manaf, with 'bin' and 'ibn' both meaning son and 'binti' or 'ibniti' meaning daughter. This was important because in the tribal times it was important to know each individual's tribal affiliation and their Arab or non-Arab origin since the tribe was the only support and succor. For the tribes every individual was the tribe's liability and they would not want to provide this support to people, Arabs or non-Arabs, who did not belong to them.

Though there was an absence of learning, linguistic eloquence and poetry were well prized in the desert. A number of master poets - Imr ul Qais, Amr bin Katthum, Antarah ibn Shaddad - lived during that time. The intricate metrical odes transcended those of the poetry of previous civilisations. A poet's public recitation had great impact on the people's opinion and attitude. Thus the poets wielded considerable political clout and could socially bring down an individual or a tribe by their poems that would spread orally, and were thus accountable for their praise or profanity.

Exploitation of women was rampant; a man could have any number of wives he could afford. Women were a 'burden' to the family and cases of female infant being buried alive had been recorded. Slavery was prevalent with the masters having the right of life and death over the slaves.

In the strip between the Arabian Desert and the empires of Persia and Byzantium formed a few small and nominal Arab buffer tribal 'states' or kingdoms. Those in, what is now, the Iraqi region were Persian allies and those in Syriaic region were Byzantine allies. They paid tax and were actually under the sovereignty of the two empires. The empires had their outposts and garrisons in those states. This was resented by the Arabs in the desert who viewed the presence of the armies of both the Empires as invaders. In the buffer states a significant number of Arabs, especially near Byzantium, were Christians.

Seal of the Prophets

There are an incredibly large number of biographies of the Prophet Mohammad with many still being written today. The main sources are the Quran, the sayings and the norms of the Prophet known as Hadith or Tradition, and the earliest biographies known as the *Seeras*. The first known biography of the Prophet was written by Ibn Ishaq (704~767). It was a compilation of written and oral Traditions. He had written other books, which had been referred to by other authors, but none of these have survived. Ibn Hisham in 834 revised and edited Ibn Ishaq's work and wrote a more comprehensive biography. Ibn Saad (784-845) wrote the *Kitab Tabaqat al Kubra*, The Book of the Major Classes, a fifteen volume compendium which contained the biography of the Prophet, information of the Prophet's followers from Makkah and Madinah with a special chapter on those who fought the first Battle in the desert field of Badr against Makkah's polytheists, and also wrote about the following generation. The *Tabaqats*, like the *Seeras*, are another genre of Islamic biographical work which are chronologically arranged by centuries. These biographies were written between 100 – 200 years after the death of the Prophet. Within this time span Islam has spread incredibly fast. By Ibn Ishaq's time, in the mid 8th century, the Muslim world encompassed the whole of Arabia, and much of Middle East and Central Asia, Northern Africa and Spain.

The scholars of Hadith were very stringent and critical in analysing and compiling the books of Hadith and scrutinizing the source material. These were religious doctrines on which much jurisprudence would be based, and thus were formulaic. The writer of the biographies, on the other hand, dwelled more on producing a connected flowing history which did not affect jurisprudence or legal rulings. At a later stage, many scholars wrote biographies based on the Hadith which were stricter in its derivation of content. The *Seeras*, or biographies, dwell more on the political and military strategy of the Prophet, while his disposition and characteristics are found more in the *Hadiths*. The *Shamail-E-Tirmidhi* written by Imam Abu Isa At-Tirmidhi (824- 892 CE) is such a collection of Hadiths showing the virtues and character of the Prophet.

But, irrespective of the style or format, each of the biographies produced an astonishing personification of an individual whose parallel is found nowhere in history. Professor Michael Hart, author of *The 100: A Ranking of the Most Influential Persons in History*, places the Prophet as the most influential figure in the entire history of the world as the Prophet was the only man in history who was supremely successful in both the religious and secular levels simultaneously.

The lineage of the Prophet goes back to Abraham's son Ishmael. According to Islamic tradition, after the discovery of the Zamzam spring in the desert, Hagar and Ishmael had settled down in the region, west of the Arabian Desert. The sprouting Zamzam soon attracted the animals of the desert. The Jurham tribe that was in the vicinity saw some birds circling over an area and investigation led them to Hagar and Ishmael. The Jurham settled down in that area which would come to be known as Makkah. This tribe had been nomadic Bedouin that had originally emigrated, like many other Arab tribes, from the Kingdom of Sheba in Yemen.

Sheba had flourished in the past with their agriculture and irrigation system being centred round a dam. The population had increased dynamically. But when the dam broke down it caused a collapse of the agricultural system. Tribes were forced to move out and settle in areas all over Arabia such as the Hijaz (The western region of Arabian Peninsula including Makkah and Madinah), the Najd (central desert region of the Arabian Peninsula) and also to regions of present day Oman, Syria, Iraq. The tribes Aus and Khazraj settled in Madinah, which was then known as Yathrib.

The history of the city of Makkah started from the time of Ishmael, son of Abraham, when he settled there among the tribe of Jurham. Ishmael married among them and adopted their language, Arabic, which was different from his father's principal language of Aramaic. Hagar and Ishmael retained the token ownership of the Zamzam spring. Later, when Ishmael grew up, Abraham came to visit and both of them together built the Kaba.

As Makkah flourished over time, the Jurham became the political leaders of the region, but the descendants of Ishmael retained the religious authority from the time of building of the Kaba. Starting some time in the 2nd millennia BC, the Jurham stayed in Makkah for about 2000 years in which period the descendants of Ishmael developed into tribes. Around the same time period the descendants of Isaac escaped from Pharaonic slavery; built their kingdom and then lost it; were enslaved by the Babylonians and freed by the Persians, and then subjugated by the Greeks and imperial Rome.

The Jurham degenerated and this weakening gave the Khuja, another tribe that had emigrated from Sheba and settled in the Hijaz, the opportunity to move in and evict the Jurham in early 1st century CE. Before the Jurham escaped they covered up and the totally obliterated any trace of the Zamzam spring. They also took all the treasure of the Kaba. One tribe, the Quraish, stayed back in Makkah when the Khuja took over the political leadership.

The monotheistic religion that Ishmael had brought with him no longer existed among the tribes. Amar bin Lahi Khujahi, a Khuja leader probably during the eviction of the Jurham, had visited the region of Syria where he saw people worshipping idols. He was told that these deities were intermediaries between god and man and watched over various human needs. So Amar brought back with him the idol of Hubal, one of the famous gods. Various gods were brought into the Kaba in this manner.

Qusay bin Kilab (~400–480), the head of Quraish, unified his tribe and drove the Khuja out. He became the guardian of the Kaba. He was also entrusted with the highly revered responsibility of distributing food and water to all the Arabs who came for pilgrimage to Makkah. He was the supreme leader of the Quraish Assembly and in charge of their Banner of War. Thus the political, military and religious authority became entirely vested in the hands of the Quraish.

When Qusay bin Kilab died, all of these functions were distributed among his sons. His grandson, Amr (whose nickname was Hashim) inherited the provisioning rights of food and water to the pilgrims. Hashim was the great grandfather of the Prophet. Hashim died on a trading journey to Gaza. Al Muttalib, the brother of Hashim, brought up Hashim's son Shaiba, and thus Shaiba came to be known as Abd Al Muttalib. He and his son Harith rediscovered the well of Zamzam 300 years after it had been covered up.

The Prophet who would change the course of the world and humanity was born on April 20, 571 CE in Makkah in the clan of Bani Hashim of the Quraish. His father, Abdullah, a handsome young man of engaging qualities, died of sudden illness two months before the Prophet was born. It was the tradition of the noble families to have the infant sons brought up for the first few years in the desert under the care of a Bedouin foster mother. The great openness, fresh air and freedom were thought to breed nobility and resilience into the infant's character. Thus Aminah, the Prophet's mother, handed him over to Halimah of the Bedouin tribe Bani Saad. After living more than two years in the desert he was returned to his biological mother. While visiting Yathrib with his mother, he learned archery and played with a little girl called Anisah (Raheem, 1988). He learned to swim in a pool that belonged to his Khazraj kinsman, and their boys taught him to fly a kite (Lings, 2005). But on their return journey to Makkah his mother died. Two years later he suffered the pain of another bereavement when his grandfather Abdul Muttalib died of old age. His paternal Uncle Abu Talib became his guardian. His uncle, though not rich, was a much venerated person. Both his uncle and aunt, Fatima, loved the Prophet like their own children.

There is evidence that as he grew up he participated in horse riding, racing and wrestling (Raheem, 1988). He was involved in social welfare and was a member of the *Hilful Fudul*, a social welfare league from among the tribes for helping people in distress.

He worked as a shepherd for some time and as a young man became a merchant and is known to have joined caravans to Yemen, Bostra and Bahrain. He was a social person and loved children. As he grew in esteem, Makkans started to call him *Al-Amin* meaning the trustworthy, the truthful, and the honest. He was gentle and kind hearted, possessed sophisticated manners with unassuming simplicity and had a firm control over his emotions. He was of middle stature, of light tanned complexion, had a beard and black hair that at times almost reached his shoulders.

He was twenty five when he married Khadijah, a beautiful and sought after widow and one of the rich merchants of Makkah. She was about fifteen years older than him and had employed him to manage her trade, but was so impressed by his personality and presence that she sent a proposal of marriage to him. They lived a happy life of love and understanding till she died twenty one years later. She bore him six children of whom two were sons,

Qasim and Abdullah, and four were daughters, Zainab, Ruqayya, Umme Kulthum and Fatima. The two sons died in infancy.

He also came to be known as a very good arbitrator. One day, after the renovation of the Kaba, a dispute rose among the Quraish. The most holy object within the Kaba is the black stone placed there by Abraham. The stone had been removed from its place for the renovation work. After the renovation each clan wanted its member to carry the stone back to its resting place within the Kaba. They were not prepared to forego the honour to any other clan. When the Prophet, still a young man, arrived in the scene, he placed a sheet on the ground and placed the stone on the sheet. Then he asked one member from each clan to grab hold of the sheet border and together carry the stone to its place of rest.

The Prophet in Makkah

The hills outside Makkah resounded in quietude. In the middle of the night, a solitary figure meditated in one of the caves of Mount Hira. On and off, for the last few years, he had come to this cave in a quest, a spiritual meditation, for the ultimate knowledge. This night of the year 610 his quest was to be answered.

Gabriel, manifested in human form, approached the man and said, 'Read.'

The man, besieged with fear, said, 'I cannot read.'

'Read.' Gabriel said again.

'I cannot read,' the man said.

'Read.' Gabriel evoked.

Then through Gabriel, God revealed to Mohammad, peace and blessing of God be upon him, the first verse of the Quran:

"Read in the name of your Lord and Cherisher, Who created -
Created man out of a clot that clings.
Read! And your Lord is most bountiful
He Who taught the use of Pen.
Taught Man what he knew not." [96:1]

The Prophet was overwhelmed by the dawning of the Divine Consciousness. In fear and awe he ran back home to his wife, Khadijah, and lay down shivering saying, "Wrap me in a blanket, wrap me in a blanket". Concerned, she wrapped a blanket around him. As he disclosed the incident to her, the shivering subsided and he fell asleep.

The Prophet was perplexed and apprehensive. He did not understand what had happened. Khadijah comforted him and took him to her cousin, Waraqah bin Nowfel, for advise. Waraqah was a Christian scholar who had considerable command over religion and history. After hearing them he said, "It was the Arch-Angel." Then he turned towards the Prophet and said, "I wish I was young. Then I would be there when your people throw you out."

The Prophet was surprised. He was the most trusted and appreciated person in Makkah. He belonged to a highly respectable family. There was no reason for him to be concerned of him being thrown out of Makkah. But Waraqah's words would be vindicated.

Two year passed by without anything significant happening. Then one day, when the Prophet was resting wrapped in a cloak, the revelations restarted.

> *'O you, covered in your cloak,*
> *arise and warn,*
> *your Lord magnify,*
> *your raiment purify,*
> *pollution shun ...' [74,15]*

This time the Prophet was ready and resolved. He got up and went to his wife and said, "O' Khadijah, from today there is no rest." And, in fact, he would not rest till the day of his final rest.

Soon the revelations started to come at rapid intervals evoking the call to Prophethood. Khadijah was the first to accept the new religion. Among the earliest to accept Islam included young cousin and ward Ali and the rich merchant and friend Abu Bakr. The other early converts to the new religion also included Usman bin Affan, a young man belonging to a rich aristocratic business family.

After three years of concealed isolation the Prophet, in a revelation, was asked to take his small group of followers to openly declare the Prophethood to the people with the proclamation – There is no God but Allah and Mohammad is his messenger. The declaration caused uproar especially among the elite inhabitants of Makkah. Explicitly, this was a challenge to the existing polytheism based tribal traditions, institutions and economy. Implicitly, the Prophet's eschatological declaration and knowledge of God's mandate implied superlative social leadership. The universal equality in 'There is no God but God…' meant that all tribes and clans, illustrious or inconsequential, would become equal. The prominent leaders would be equal to ordinary people, even to slaves. Black, white, men, women, and children would all have rights. And in the final analysis even animals and trees would have rights.

The leaders of the Quraish, Makkah's dominant tribe, became extremely hostile to the new religion. They embarked on a systematic campaign of insult, intimidation and torture. One day, when the Prophet went to pray in the Kaba, Uqba bin Abi Muwaed, One of the tribal leaders, grabbed him and tried to strangle him. Abu Bakr pushed Uqba away and said, "Will you kill a man just because he says God is my lord?"

The Muslims, specially the poor ones, were reviled, abused, tortured and killed. The Prophet, however, remained resolute and people, gradually, were attracted to him. They formed a small band of activists who bowed to none but the one Creator. They embarked on a mission of justice and equality for humankind. On a number of occasions the leaders of Makkah went to Abu Talib, Prophet's uncle and guardian, who was the esteemed leader of the highly revered Hashemite clan, to work out a deal. They asked him, sometimes threatening and sometimes imploring, to withdraw his protection over his nephew, so that the Prophet could be killed without the threat of retribution from the Hashemite. To this Abu Talib would always respond negatively. On one occasion the Quraish leaders offered one of the strong and handsome youth to Abu Talib, "Take Imara Ibn Al-Walid in exchange and make him your son. Take his patronage and blood money. In return give us your nephew."

Abu Talib replied, "It's a fine transaction you seek. You give me your son to feed, and take my son to kill. It shall not be so!"

Soon they tried to tempt the Prophet, "We will give him all the wealth he desires, the most beautiful women, and even make him our king. Just ask him to stop this mission."

When Abu Talib, finally, presented the proposal to his nephew, the reply was, "If they put the sun in my right hand and the moon on the left I will not forsake my mission till my death or till God expounds it." His life was the mission and the mission was his life. It was not possible to separate one from the other.

In the year 616, as the time for annual pilgrimage to the Kaba and pagan festival approached, the Quraish became worried that pilgrims who may meet the Prophet may be attracted by the new religion. In a meeting they decided that they will approach the pilgrims outside the gates of Makkah before the Prophet does and give them a negative impression about him. Al-Walid, One of the elderly leaders, said, "Let's prepare to be unanimous on what we say to the pilgrims about him."

One of the Quraish said, "Let's say he is a priest."

"No," said Al-Walid, "He does not speak the ambiguous words which the priests are famous for."

"Then let's say he is mad."

"No, he is not confused or disoriented."

"Say he is a poet."

"No, what he speaks is not poetry."

"Then let's say he is a magician."

Al-Walid disagreed with that as well. It was difficult to discredit or accuse the Prophet of anything. Nonetheless, they agreed on the plan to portray him as mad and possessed. During the pilgrimage, the Quraish took up various positions at the major entrances to Makkah and started to spread malicious rumours about him among the pilgrims as they entered. Dunad Al Azdi, a man from Southern Arabia heard someone say that there was a man possessed by Jinn. Dunad was a healer who treated such afflictions and went to the Prophet, and in all innocence said, "I have heard of your affliction, I am offering you my service."

The Prophet realised that the man has been misguided. Without giving any reply he started to recite, "*Praise be to God, Him we praise and His help we seek, whomever He leads aright no one can lead astray whomever He leads astray no one can lead aright. I testify that there is no God but God alone and Who has no associates...*"

After listening for a while, Dunad interrupted the Prophet, "Can you repeat what you just said?"

The Prophet repeated and as he finished Dunad said, "I have never heard such words. These will reach the depth of the oceans."

The Prophet asked him to accept the religion and Dunad did, promising allegiance of his tribe. In one short meeting the healer was healed.

Gradually, more people started to join Islam. Belal, an African slave to a man named Umayyah bin Khalaf, accepted Islam. The owner was so incensed that he began torturing Belal. Belal was laid on the hot desert sand under the sun and a huge boulder was placed on his chest. Then he was asked to recant under this crushing painful pressure. As Belal was tortured he kept on saying "Unique", indicating that there is only one God. The more Belal was tortured the louder he said "Unique". This added to the frustration and anger of Umayyah. Without food or water, with the hot desert sun blazing on him and with the huge painful weight on him Belal still kept on repeating the word, "Unique" with the last bit of his strength. When Abu Bakr came to know of this he went to Umayyah and bought Belal from him and set him free. But there were others, like Sumaiya and her husband, who became martyrs due to inhuman torture.

The Migration to Abyssinia

As the oppression increased, it was decided by the Prophet that it was time to create a base outside of Makkah beyond the influence of the Quraish. Those who were socially vulnerable or simply poor and weak would go to Abyssinia. This would also ensure that a group of Muslims would still exist in case the Quraish tried to kil! all of them in Makkah. In 616, the Negus or King of Abyssinia was a very just Christian ruler who persecuted none. A group of Muslims migrated to Abyssinia in secret. The group included Jaafar bin Abu Talib, Ali's brother, as well as Umme Habiba, the daughter of Abu Sufiyan the foremost leader of Makkah.

The Quraish found out about this migration after the event had already taken place. It disturbed them considerably and they felt that they had lost a lot of esteem and standing in the Arabian society due to their own leaving under conscientious reason. They sent two well-connected Quraish representatives to the court of the Negus to force the emigrants back. One of them, Amr bin Al Aas, had business ties and friends in Abyssinia. He met the Abyssinian Generals and courtiers in private and gave them exquisite gifts.

In the king's court, Amr said, "Your Majesty, some foolish men and women from among our people have taken refuge in your kingdom. They have left their own religion, not for yours, but for an invented one. The nobles of our land, their fathers and uncles, request their return. If not, they will remain here but as thorns and will poison your very environment."

The Generals supported him with one voice. But the Negus was annoyed, "I will not betray those who have sought my protection without hearing their version of the account. Let the emigrants be produced to the court."

As the court reassembled, all bowed to the Negus except the emigrants. This was noticed by all including the Negus causing unease in the court. The Negus asked, "Don't you bow to your Prophet?"

Jaafar bin Abu Talib, a good orator and a handsome man, stepped forward and said "By command of our Prophet we bow our head only to God and no one else."

The Negus asked, "What is this religion by which you have become separate from your own people?"

"O' king," Jaafar said, "we were living a life of ignorance and superstition, burying infant females, worshipping idols which we moulded ourselves, ate unhealthy carrion, shed blood, completely ignored matters of right and wrong, the strong oppressing the weak, and permitting things immoral. God sent to us a Prophet from among ourselves, whose honesty and trustworthiness was established among us. Our Prophet brought to us a new religion of discipline, empathy and knowledge and asked us to renounce the ways of our fathers. He called on us to pray to God alone without associates. He told us to respect the rights of kinship, and to honour rights of hospitality. He ordered us to pray to God Almighty and fast for him and affirm to none else. He ordered us to be truthful and be trustworthy, and to abandon blood shedding. He forbade us to do anything immoral, to lie or misuse funds of orphans or make false accusations on women of virtue. But our leaders aggressed against us, besieged us, prosecuted us and forced us to give up our religion. So we migrated to your kingdom."

"Do you possess any revelations of your Prophet?"

"Yes, your Majesty."

"Recite it to me," commanded the Negus.

Jaafar recited the words of God from the chapter 'Mary' of the Quran :

Relate in the book the story of Mary, when she withdrew from her people to a place in the East and secluded herself. Then We sent to her our angel, and he appeared before her as a man in all respects.

She said: I seek refuge from you to God most gracious: come not near me if you fear God.

He said: No, I am only a messenger from your Lord, to announce to you the gift of a holy son.

She said: How can there be for me any son, when no man has touched me, nor am I unchaste.

He said: Even so shall it be; your Lord says 'It is easy for Me. That We may make him a sign for mankind and a mercy from Us; and it is a thing ordained.' [19,16]

The eyes of the Negus and the Bishops filled with tears. The Negus said, "We are rays from the same source. Go your ways, for you are safe in my land. Not for mountains of gold would I harm a single one of you.'

For Umme Habiba the migration to Abbyssinia was distressing. She was the daughter of Abu Sufian, the undisputed leader of Makkah, and was forced to leave the comfort of an aristocratic house. It became doubly distressing when, after reaching Abbyssinia, her husband apostatised and became a drunkard. She separated from him and remained resolute. But she had to pass through very difficult times living by herself in a foreign land. She could not go back to Makkah because there her very father was against the Muslims. But she would soon receive a communication from the Prophet that would remove the distress from her and give her the support she required.

The Ban of the Hashemite

While in Makkah, the leaders were infuriated due to the failure of their diplomacy. In their frustration, they slammed an interdiction ostracising the Prophet and the Hashemite clan. The Prophet and the Hashemites were forced to live in a mountainous enclave and all contacts with them – social, economic or cultural – were banned. The Quraish declared that the socio-economic ban would only be lifted if the clan disowned the Prophet. This ban which lasted two years caused severe economic problems of famine proportion to the clan. Families starved for food and were short of clothes. This news spread all over Arabia and seeing their plight and suffering the general mass started to feel sympathy for them. When the Quraish realised this, they were alarmed and decided to act. The ban was lifted, about two years after it was imposed, and for the time being the Muslims and the Hashemites could again breathe freely. The Quraish sent an offer to the Prophet, "We will accept your God, if you accept our gods."

The Prophet knew that this was political manipulation to revert to polytheism. He could not accept this despite the suffering they were going through. Then came the revelation asking the Prophet to:

Proclaim, "O disbelievers!"
Neither do I worship what you worship.
Nor do you worship Whom I worship.
And neither will I ever worship what you worship.
Nor will you worship Whom I worship.
For you is your religion, and for me is mine. [109,1]

This was a resolution to the situation and the Quraish agreed to it.

The ban was lifted, about two years after it was imposed, and for the time being the Muslims and the Hashemites could again breathe freely.

The Year of Sorrow

In 619, the Prophet's uncle, guardian and protector, the much respected Abu Talib died. Two months later Khadijah, the Prophet's beloved wife of over 20 years, also died. In quick succession the Prophet lost the two most important people in his life - the guardian who had offered him security and the dear wife who offered him psychological support and comfort. Both had provided him with unconditional love and affection. This was the 'year of sorrow' for him and if both the losses caused immense grief, the first death also had political ramifications. The Prophet's protector was gone and the Quraish decided to forego the deal they had agreed to when lifting the ban. There was a dramatic resurgence of oppression against the Muslims. Even eminent businessman like Abu Bakr was beaten up and left lying on the street with hands and feet tied. Passer-bys threw putrefying offal at the Prophet's house. A sheep's uterus, filthy with blood and excrement, was thrown on him. One day, as he returned from the mosque, a man threw a handful of dirt on his face. As one of his daughters cleansed him tears started to run down her cheeks. He said, "Weep not, little daughter. God will protect your father."

With every difficulty there is relief.
Indeed, with every difficulty there is relief.
So when you are free from immediate task
Still labour hard
And to your Lord turn all your attention. [94:5]

The Prophet realised that the days in Makkah for him and his followers were numbered. He needed a base somewhere away from Makkah or the Quraish will annihilate them. He went to the mountainous city of Taif and sought help and support from its inhabitant. But there he was received with spite. One of the leaders said "Couldn't God find anyone better then you to send as a Prophet?"

When his message was rejected by the Taif leaders, the Prophet requested them to keep the meeting a secret. He knew that if the people of Makkah heard of this failure the oppression on the Muslims will be increased. But, instead, the leaders of Taif insulted him and on the street made the slaves and children to yell, shout and to throw stones at him and call him a madman. Bruised and bloody, he somehow escaped from there with his life. This was a very painful day for him.

He then negotiated with some other tribes but none agreed to accept him or give him sanctuary. When all seemed lost, miracles unfolded. Yathrib, the oasis city on the north, was populated by two tribes which were in a perennial state of civil war. The pagan tribes were the Khazraj and Aus who were too filled with mutual enmity, envy and distrust to accept any member of the other tribe as king or leader. The Prophet known for his arbitration became the choice to unify and lead the tribes and thus culminate the civil war.

The Hijra

In 622, in a secret meeting at Al-Aqaba near Makkah, a Yathrib delegation met and pledged to protect the Prophet in return for his leadership and guidance. Musab bin Umair, a handsome young Companion of the Prophet, was sent by the Prophet to prepare Yathrib for the Muslims. There was a concern among the tribes of Yathrib that giving sanctuary to the Prophet would make them an enemy of the Quariash and their allies. In the meeting, as the Yathrib group prepared to give allegiance to the Prophet, Abul Hisham of Yathrib commented, "Messenger of God, this allegiance can force us to give up our existing alliances. We are concerned that after victory has been achieved, you may abandon us leaving us behind to face the enemies."

The Prophet smiled, "If your blood is sought, ours will be sought. Your destruction is mine, you are of me and I am of you, I will battle those you battle, and make peace with those with whom you make peace." In effect, this was a promise that he will be with them forever whatever the consequences.

The Muslims of Makkah started to migrate, this time to Madinah. This was a much larger migration then the one to Abyssinia. Again, there were vicious attempts by the Quraish to stop the Muslims from migrating. Umme Salamah, a Muslim woman, was restricted from accompanying her Muslim husband and her child was taken away. People were locked, chained and tortured, but despite these attempts to stop them the migration trickle developed into a hidden stream and many of the houses of Makkah gradually became empty.

Finally, the Quraish in total frustration sent a group of young men to murder the Prophet. The young men were chosen from all the clans of Quraish so that the blame would be shared and retribution of the Hashemite would not be possible. But that very night the Prophet left Makkah.

In the darkness of the desert, the Prophet and Abu Bakr escaped on camels and took refuge in a cave. Ali, the young son of Abu Talib and the Prophet's ward, slept in the Prophet's bed. Thus when the Quraish spied on his house, they thought it was the Prophet sleeping. At the break of the day when the young men attacked they found Ali in the Prophet's bed instead and realised that the Prophet had left.

Soon, armed groups on horseback were tracking and scouring the desert for the Prophet and Abu Bakr. On the third day, the silence of the mountainous cave sanctuary *of the two* Companions was broken by the appearance of armed warriors. As the group approached the cave Abu Bakr whispered. "If I die, no harm is done. But if you die, all is doomed. They are too many, we are just two."

The Prophet was calm, "Grieve not, we are not two. God's with us."

They heard someone urging the others to enter the cave. But the voice of Umayyah bin Khalaf said, "There are spider webs covering the entrance of the cave. If anyone had gone in, the webs would have broken."

There was a murmur of assent and the warriors did not enter the cave and retraced their steps. After a few days of hiding and trekking in the desert the Prophet reached Yathrib, much to the delight and celebration of his people now residing there. Yathrib was renamed Madinah – the City, the city of the Prophet.

The Prophet in Madinah

The Prophet's sojourn through the desert, called the *Hijra*, was the turning point for Islam and would have momentous affect on the history of humankind. The Prophet, immediately after reaching Madinah, embarked on setting up a modern state. He established rules and social reforms. The first thing he did was to establish a Mosque which came to be known as the 'Prophet's Mosque'. The mosque was not just a place of spiritual worship but became the political and military centre as well as the area of social confluence. All, men and women, went to the mosque. The Prophet had also established another mosque on the outskirts of Madinah, at Quba, when he had rested there at the end of the Hijra before entering Madinah proper.

As most of the Muslims had lost everything when they migrated to Madinah, the new community was in dire need for basic financial support. The *Mahajirs* (emigrants from Makkah) and *Ansars* (Aus and Khazraj helpers in Madinah) were declared brothers. As the Mahajirs did not have any possession or place to stay, the Ansars were asked to take one Mahahir brother each to their homes. The Mahajirs would stay with them till they were able to establish themselves. This arrangement turned out to be immensely successful and the generosity of Ansars was exemplary. One of the Ansars, who had two wives, queried whether he should give half his lands to his Mahajir brother and if the Mahajir wanted to marry one of his wives then he could talk with one them for a divorce. The Mahajir, of course, refused it all. Some of the Mahajirs just wanted to know where the market place was, where they could setup a business. Abu Bakr and Usman were able to establish their businesses in no time by sheer mercantile acumen.

Some Mahajirs preferred to work on fields. As the Ansars owned the agricultural lands, it was decided that the Mahajirs would give the labour and toil needed to cultivated the fields and then the crop would be shared in partnership. Eventually, it was found that whenever the Ansars got the opportunity they would also toil in the field and still gave the Mahajir-brothers their full share of the crop. The Mahajirs, in fact, complained to the Prophet that the Ansars 'are working harder than us. We do not want to lag behind in doing good.'

The Prophet, initially, set up a rudimentary constitution for Madinah. It was mandated after an agreement was reached with all the parties in Madinah including the Jewish tribes.

All had equal citizenship rights in this covenant. The Muslims and Jews were equal, to be treated as equal by each other, and were to fight as a single force against any foe. The Jews were not required to recognise him as the Prophet. The Prophet expected Muslims not just to tolerate but also respect other religions and customs within their state.

Let there be no compulsion in religion (2,256)

No one was to be forced to accept Islam. The Prophet said, "Beware! Whoever is cruel and hard on a non-Muslim minority or curtails their rights or burdens them in more then that they can bear or takes anything away from them against their free will, I will complain against that person on the Day of Judgement".

The relationship between the Jews and the Muslims started off remarkably well. At times, the Jewish scholars were condescending towards the 'new' religion and debates would ensue. But when a few of the Jewish leaders impressed by the modern and just outlook of Islam accepted it as their religion, their tribes became inimical towards the Prophet and began to conspire against him in secret.

During this time, the Muslims used to pray with Jerusalem as their *Kibla* or direction of prayer. But after more than a year had passed in Madinah, a revelation came down on the Prophet asking him to change the Kibla towards Makkah. As Makkah lay in the opposite direction from Jerusalem the Jews and Christians, to whom Jerusalem was holy as well, said that the Muslims were no longer akin to them. Makkah and Kaba was still under the pagans, and all said this was the first step of the Muslims returning to their pagan origin.

The Prophet had also started to build a militia. The migration to Madinah gave the Muslims immediate safety from the Quraish but did not allow them complacency for long. The small community was still at a constant threat of being attacked and exterminated by the hostile tribes that surrounded Madinah or by the Quraish and their many allies. The group of Muslims that had earlier migrated to Abyssinia was not summoned to Madinah due to this threat. If the Muslims in Madinah faced destruction there would still be the second base in Abyssinia. The Abyssinian Muslims would ultimately come to Madinah seven year after the Hijra when a firm foundation had been established. All the Muslim males, excluding boys and old men, and some females were part of the militia. The militia was voluntary and the individuals were not paid salary. Though encouraged to join the militia no one was forced to join. The only immediate reward for the warriors would be the movable property left by the rivals on the battlefield after the battle. This war booty was known called *Ghanimah*, one fifth of which went to the state and the rest would be divided between the warriors.

Reforms also took place in the economic sector. To raise revenue for the state a number of taxes were gradually levied. Revenue was raised by the *Zakaat* tax from the Muslims and *Jizya* tax from the non Muslims. Later on, agricultural taxes were also incorporated. The economy was based on the non-exploitative Quranic concept in which any form of economic exploitation or *Riba* was prohibited, which included interest, usury and speculative monetary dealings or pricings. Most of the laws came to the Prophet as Quranic revelations.

The Battles

Initially, in Madinah, the Muslims did not even have enough to feed themselves let alone pay taxes. Even after support from the Ansars, many of the Mahajirs remained impoverished as they had to leave all their movable and immovable property in Makkah, and which the Quraish were unwilling to return. They were forced to leave the place of their birth, were forcefully separated from the members of their families, and finally all their properties were confiscated, sold or traded by the Quraish caravans. The beleaguered Muslims needed some of their wealth or goods to survive even at subsistence level.

The continuous persecution and torture by the Quraish had driven the Muslims to the edge. The attempt on the Prophet's life had been the last straw and amounted to an open declaration of war by the Quraish. After the Hijra the Prophet had still tried his best for peace and resist violence even though his Companions wanted to fight to defend their property. But finally the revelation came down on him that changed his plans.

> *Permission to fight is given to those who fight because they have been wronged, and God is able to give them victory; those who have been driven from their homes unjustly for no other reason than for saying: Our Lord is God. (22,39)*

Thus, it was decided that those caravans of Makkah that passed by Madinah and contained goods belonging to the Mahajirs would be attacked and their goods taken forcefully– this was compensation for the Muslims properties seized in Makkah. The Quraish merchant caravans to Syria used routes that went by Madina. Attacking the caravans on this trade route would be of two fold benefit. This would act as an economic stranglehold against the Quraish and the dispossessed and destitute Mahajirs could get some of their property back.

Meanwhile, the Quraish were not just sitting idle and were in no mood to be subdued by this fledgling group and its petty attacks. They decided to attack Madinah and get rid of this problem once and for all. When they heard that the Muslims were planning to attack their caravan the preparation for war began. When the Muslims heard of the march of the Quraish militia and their allies they held a meeting to decide the next course of action. A revelation to the Prophet declared:

> *Make war on the persecutors*
> *Till persecution is no more*
> *And religion is for God alone.* [2:19]

A very non-imperialistic war was envisaged aimed only at persecutors. Along with the formal declaration of Jihad came stringent injunctions to check any untoward violence. The Prophet stated, "Go to war in adherence to the religion of God. Never touch the elderly, the women or the children. Always improve their situation and be kind to them. God loves those who are sincere."

In the next five years, three major battles were fought against the Quraish and their allies. The Muslims were numerically out numbered in all three battles. In the first battle that was fought in *Badr* in 624 only 313 Muslims fought against a thousand Quraish with incredible bravery and fortitude and earned an unprecedented victory. Many prominent Quraish were killed and many others were imprisoned. The prisoners, as was the usual practice, were ransomed. The Prophet declared, "Any one of the prisoner who can teach ten Muslims to read will be freed without ransom."

The progressiveness and social justice inherent in Islam and the success of the Muslims in the social as well as military discipline made people from different regions to go to Madinah and join Islam. To accommodate many of these people who had no place to stay, a shade was built for them behind the Mosque. These people came to be known as *Ahle Safa* meaning 'The purified people'. In days to come these people would form an austere and highly scholastic group. Some people, like Abu Hurairah, sought deliberately to be part of this group so that they could be near the Prophet and learn from him. While the Mahajirs were trying to establish their business and Ansars were cultivating their lands, Abu Hurairah always followed the Prophet and learnt all that he could even though he had to do so with an empty stomach. The Prophet gave whatever he had for these people. In doing so he even denied help to his own daughter Fatima who was relegated to menial work to subsist.

After the Battle of Badr, the Muslims and Quraish armies met again the following year, 625, by the Mount of Uhud. The Quraish were raging for revenge after their defeat in Badr. In the battlefield, the Muslim army was strategically stationed besides the Mount such that behind them was an open pass. The Prophet set a group of archer on the slope of the Mount to guard the pass and told them not to move from their position under any circumstances. The Muslims were outnumbered 1000 to 3000 but as the battle begun their ferocious charge gave them the upper hand almost immediately. As the fight progressed the Makkans ran away leaving their camps unprotected. The battle appeared to be over and the archers left their position to collect the spoils on the battle field. It was then that, a strong young Quraish cavalry commander, Khalid bin Walid, led a group of horsemen through the unguarded pass and attacked the Muslims from the rear. The sudden attack devastated the Muslims and to make things worse the fleeing Quraish infantry, aware of the change in circumstance, now turned around and attacked from the front. The assault from both the front and rear caused the Muslims to loose a large number of men. The Muslims army was on the backfoot and was soon dispersed. The Prophet in the battle was separated from the main body of the army and was violently attacked by the Quraish. He was wounded and bleeding with only a small group of Companions standing by him and fighting with incorrigible determination. Finally, the Muslims climbed up the Mount where it became dangerous for the Quraish army to follow. The Quraish were satisfied for the moment, they had avenged the defeat of Badr, and left boasting to return the next year to obliterate the Muslims.

After Uhud, though the Quraish had left, trouble brewed for the Muslims from other nearby tribes. The hostile tribes around Madinah now considered the Muslims to be in a weakened state and vulnerable to attack. Before the proposed return of the Quraish, the Quraish allies among these tribes did their utmost to destabilise the Muslims further. But the Prophet had established an effective intelligence gathering system and received reports that these tribes were on the verge of attacking the unaware Muslims. A number of campaigns were led by the Prophet against these tribes and minor battles were fought. One of the battles was with the Bani Mustaliq tribe. The Muslims won the battle and the entire tribe was imprisoned and their movable properties on the battlefield were confiscated. A beautiful female prisoner requested to see the Prophet. She said to him, "Messenger of God, I am Juwariah, daughter of the chief of Mustaliq. I request you to release me from this predicament."

The Prophet delved into the matter and then said, "I have a proposal, will you consider it."

Juwariah asked, "What do you propose?"

The Prophet said, "I shall pay the ransom for your freedom and then I would like to marry you."

"That was the intention with which I came to you," replied Juwariah.

After the marriage, the Muslims found that the Bani Mustaliq were now related to the Prophet. So they gave freedom to the entire tribe many of the adult male members of which had been condemned to execution, and also returned their properties.

Even though the Muslims were able to contain the enemy there was another enemy within. Clandestine and hostile agents who had infiltrated the Muslims tried to encourage dissension between the Muhajirs and Ansars immediately after the battle. In the Muslim camp, isolated quarrels started to flare up between Ansars and Muhajirs. An eye-witness of such a quarrel reported to the Prophet that these quarrels were the work of the infiltrators. He had heard a man named Abdullah bin Ubai deliberately provoking the Ansars to distance themselves from the Mahajirs. Umar bin Khattab, one of the Prophets lieutenants, proposed that Abdullah bin Ubai be put to death. But the Prophet never prescribed drastic actions without proof. Instead, he ordered the Muslim camp be broken earlier than usual and the army embarked on the return journey for Madinah, thus not providing the infiltrators the opportunity to foment any further unrest.

The army stopped for a short rest near Madinah. Ayesha, the wife of the Prophet who had accompanied him in this campaign, went away to relieve herself. While she was returning she realised that she had dropped her Yemeni agate necklace. She retraced her steps and after searching for a while found the necklace. But by the time she returned everyone was gone. The group that accompanied her thought that she was resting in the covered *Howda* on her camel and had simply pulled the camel along with them. Ayesha decided to wait on the spot knowing that when they find her missing they will return to the spot to investigate. But a rear scout named Safwan discovered her first sleeping in the desert. He got off his camel and let her mount it. He then steered the animal back to Madinah.

Having failed to cause dissension among the Muslims earlier, the infiltrators seized this event as an opportunity and spread a slander about Ayesha and Safwan. The circulating rumour reached the Prophet. He did not even speak a word of this to her, but she realized that his demeanour had changed. She had been sick for a few days, which restricted her social activities, and was unaware of what had happened. When she finally found out about the rumour from one of the ladies she was totally heartbroken. She cried day and night but did not utter a single word in her own support. Her attitude was that he was the Prophet and should know the truth without being told. After a month, a revelation came down to the Prophet:

"Verily! Those who brought forth the slander are a group among you. Consider it not a bad thing for you. Nay, it is good for you. Unto every man among them will be paid that which he had earned of the sin, and as for him among them who had the greater share therein, his will be a great torment..." (24:11)

Finally, there was a smile on the Prophet's face and he greeted Ayesha with the good news.

In 627, the Quraish returned with a large army of ten thousand which was a confederation of Arab polytheists and Jewish tribes. This army had a very strong cavalry. This time the Muslims decided not to go on the offensive but decided to defend from within Madinah itself. A Persian man was instrumental in the Muslim defence strategy.

At the end of the Hijra to Madinah, when the Prophet had arrived at Quba on the outskirts, a man had approached him with some food and said, "I have heard that you are a very good man and you have companions who are needy. So I have brought food for you as charity."

The Prophet accepted the food and asked his hungry companions to eat but he did not eat from it himself. The next day the same man brought more food and said, "This is a gift for you."

The Prophet accepted the food and asked his companions to eat, but this time he ate with them as well. This man was Salman Farsi, son of a Persian village head from Isfahan and was born a Magian. He had run away from his comfortable home in search of truth and knowledge. He was attracted by Christianity and had studied under a chain of Bishops, one after another. When the last of his mentors was dying he asked where to go next to further his search for truth. The Bishop had said the world was now changed and he did not know of any fitting mentor for him.

But he added that it was time for a Prophet's advent and informed him about some of the characteristics that the Prophet would have. One of the characteristics was that the Prophet would accept gifts for himself but not charity. Salman had travelled in search of the Prophet through Musol and Syria but when he arrived in Arabia he was captured and sold to slavery in Madinah. When the Prophet arrived Salman decided to test him to find out if the Prophet was authentic. When he was satisfied that this was the Prophet indeed, in his joy he prostrated in front of him. But the Prophet forbade him to prostrate and asked him to rise.

As he was a slave, Salman could not partake in the battles of Badr and Uhud. One day, after the two battles, the Prophet had called him and asked him to free himself from slavery. His bondage was paid off by the Prophet and the companions and Salman was once again a free man. As the next battle approached it was Salman who proposed that they should build a trench around Madinah to compliment its natural hilly fortification. This would make the cavalry of the invading army ineffective as well slow down the charge of the infantry. All the Muslims toiled hard to dig the trench. As the Quraish approached, the Muslims were divided into groups and placed in strategic regions guarding the trench. The Quraish laid a siege and skirmishes ensued but the trench negated an all out battle. In this critical juncture, the Muslims were horrified to uncover that the Bani Quraiza, a Jewish tribe living in a fortress within Madinah and who had signed the covenant of alliance with the Prophet, had betrayed them and were conniving with the Quraish against the Muslims. Besieged by enemies from without and betrayed from within, the Muslims faced annihilation. But miraculously the weather came to the rescue of the Muslims. After a fortnight of siege very cold, wet and windy weather totally immobilised the Quraish army and their beasts. They were forced to leave Madinah and in the process abandoned their ally, the Bani Quraiza. The Muslims then besieged and captured the Quraiza. Their treachery and guilt was judged according to the Jewish law of Deuteronomy (Raheem, 1988), the traitors were taken to the trench and beheaded and their property confiscated.

The Peace Treaty of Hudaibiah

In the three wars both the Muslims and the Quraish had suffered in men and material. For the Muslims the loss of even a single person amounted to a lot as they were a very small society. For the Quraish one of their main business route and economic lifeline was under threat. And what more, they had lost a lot of their prestige as the elite tribe of Arabia. A small society had stood up to them and, so far, had outmanoeuvered them. Prominent people had been killed on both side, kinsmen had faced each other with swords in hand. Enmity and hatred had risen to great heights.

At such a time the Prophet declared that he would go in peace for Pilgrimage to the Kaba in Makkah. It was a great surprise for all as Makkah lied in the heart of the enemy land with whom they were engaged in a life and death struggle. Even though this decision of the

Prophet was a surprise, the Companions were only glad to do what the Prophet asked. Preparations were made and soon the Prophet and his followers were on their way.

It was customary to provide sanctuary to all who came to Makkah for pilgrimage. But the Quraish decided to make the case of the Muslims an exception. While some did not want the Muslims in Makkah just out of spite others considered that once within Makkah the Muslims would become a great threat, thus advocating the Muslim had to be turned back. Fighting was not permitted during the period of Pilgrimage but as the procession of the Muslims progressed, Khaled bin Walid and his horsemen tried to provoke them near a place called Afsan. The Muslims, moving in peace, did not respond and Khaled returned to Makkah in case his cavalry came to be needed there.

After that the Muslims travelled fast and quiet through unused paths and arrived near Makkah unnoticed and camped in an open place called Hudaibiyah. The Prophet sent a deputation to Makkah informing that he has come to perform pilgrimage peacefully. But the Quraish were still bent on belligerency and sent delegations asking the Muslims to leave. Al Hulais, one of the delegates and leader of a clan, was very much impressed by the non-violent and pious intention of the Muslims. After the return of Al Hulais, another delegation led by a man named Urwah bin Masud came to confer with the Prophet. In the meeting, he sat in front of the Prophet and started to behave in a very condescending manner. He said, "You are intent on destroying traditions, have you ever heard of such a thing among Arabs? You have led a mixed people against your own people. But when you will face a disadvantageous situation, the congregation of tribes in your group will break up and flee. They will abandon you."

This incensed Abu Bakr who was generally a man of good manners and calm disposition. He rebuked Urwah with vile obscenity and said, "Flee and abandon him! Never!"

As the talks progressed, Urwah touched the beard of the Prophet to emphasize the points he was making. One of the Muslims, Mugheerah, who stood guard besides the Prophet, said, "Withdraw your hand while you still have it to withdraw!"

Mugheerah was in fact Urwah's nephew and used to be a murderous, highway robber. But when he came in touch with the Muslims, he accepted the faith and gave up the brutal life to become a new person. His face was covered with armour and thus Urwah was unable to recognise him.

Urwah was a famous negotiator who had visited a number of different kingdoms and empires on diplomatic missions. When he returned to Makkah he said, "I have visited the courts of kings, I have seen the Khasrow of Persia, I have seen Heracle of Byzantium. But I have never seen such love and obedience like the Muslims have for their Prophet. Do what you want, these people will not forsake their leader, they shall not be deterred."

The first delegate from the Muslim side to Makkah was Kharash bin Umayya. When he entered Makkah he was attacked by the Quraish, his horse was killed but he was saved by the people of Al Hulais. The Prophet considered sending Umar bin Khattab as the next delegate. Umar belonged to the Bani Adi clan which did not have any significant standing in Makkah. On the other hand, Usman bin Affan was an Umayyad aristocrat who would get protection there. Finally, the Prophet asked Usman to go to Makkah and present the case of the Muslims to them. Usman went to Makkah and met with the leaders. When he told them that the Muslims only wanted to go to the Holy house in peace, they refused to accept it. Instead they said, "If you want, you can go and visit the Kaba and we will allow it, but the Prophet and the Muslims will not be allowed." Usman refused the offer saying he could not perform the pilgrimage without the Prophet.

In the meantime, a rumour spread in the Muslim camp that Usman may have been killed. All the Muslims gathered together and the Prophet asked them to pledge that if Usman is killed they will fight to the last. All the Muslims solemnly pledged on the hands of the Prophet and he himself pledged on behalf of Usman. This is known as the 'Pledge of Ridwan'

Usman returned safely and was soon followed by a Quraish delegation led by Suhail bin Amr to negotiate a workable solution. The Prophet negotiated with him a ten years peace treaty. There were a number of clauses in the treaty which were largely in favour of the Quraish. For instance, a few Muslims and new converts that still remained in Makkah wanted to leave and join the Muslims in Medina, but were not allowed to do so by the Quraish. The treaty stipulated that if a Muslim left Makkah for Madinah he would be returned to the Quraish. But if a polytheist left Madinah for Makkah he would not be hindered. Another clause mentioned that the Muslims would not be allowed to perform the pilgrimage that year. They would have to return next year if they wanted to perform the pilgrimage.

The scribe of the treaty document was Ali bin Abu Talib. In the document he wrote that the treaty was between the 'Prophet of Allah' and Suhail son of Amr. Suhail objected and said, "If I accepted you as the Prophet I would not be opposing you. Instead of 'Prophet of Allah', write 'son of Abdullah.' "

Ali immediately objected but the Prophet, himself, struck out the text 'Prophet of Allah' from the document and asked Ali to write 'bin Abdullah' instead. The treaty was finally signed and witnessed.

Suhail had a son named Abu Jandal who had accepted Islam. He had been chained and imprisoned in Makkah to stop him from going to Madinah. But Abu Jandal broke free and still in chain took the arduous journey across the desert and reached Madinah soon after the treaty was signed. When Suhail learned this, he demanded that according to the treaty Abu Jandal be returned.

The situation was a heart-rending moment for the Prophet but he stood by his covenant. He went and said to Abu Jandal, "Be patient and wait for reward from Allah. He will provide you with a way out."

When the Quraish left, some of the Muslims were pained at this tragic situation and the signing of an unequal treaty. Umar asked the Prophet, "Are you the Messenger of Allah?"

"Yes," replied the Prophet.

"Are we Muslims?"
"Yes"
"Are they the unbelievers?"
"Yes."
"Then why are we accepting this humiliation of ourselves and of our religion."
The Prophet said, "I am the Messenger of Allah and I will not disobey Him."

"Verily, we have given you a manifest victory." [48:1]

This peace treaty turned out to be the greatest victory for the Muslims. During the next few years the Muslims stabilised themselves. They were able to tackle other groups of people around Madinah who harboured ill intent towards them. This political stability gave them the opportunity to work hard in the fields and business and their economic condition improved. They studied and educated themselves. Most importantly, this stability enabled the Muslims to approach a large number of people all around Arabia and explain to them what Islam was really about. The Muslims 'read' and the Muslims 'taught' and they turned into a more enlightened people. The name of the Prophet and the Muslims spread far and wide and people flooded to join them. As the situation evolved, powerful people came and accepted Islam. Khaled bin Walid became a Muslim. Amr bin Al As came to the Prophet and said, "O' Prophet, I want to become a Muslim. Extend your hand so I can pledge allegiance to you."

As the Prophet extended his hand Amr withdrew his. The Prophet asked, "What's wrong?"

"I want to make a condition," said Amr.

"What condition?" asked the Prophet.

"I want a pardon for my past crimes first," said Amr.

The Prophet smiled and said, "O' Amr, don't you know Islam erases everything before it, Hijra erases everything before it and Hajj erases everything before it."

Amr, who was a great plotter against the Prophet, accepted Islam and developed a great love for the Prophet in his heart.

Meanwhile, Abu Jandal escaped again, but did not go to Madinah or join the Muslims. He went to another place called Saif Al Bahr. There he joined other people like him and they started to attack the caravans from Makkah. The Quraish became so frustrated with them that they finally requested the Prophet to allow the group into Madinah so long that they do not attack the caravans.

The Opening of Makkah

In 630, the allies of the Quraish breached the Hudaibiya treaty by attacking and killing Muslim allies. With the breaking of the treaty the Prophet decided to march on to Makkah. A huge Muslim army of numerous tribes was raised and it started its march. On the way, the Prophet noticed a bitch with her litter of puppies on the ground. He posted one of his men as a guard there so that the animals would not get trampled by the marching army.

As the army swelled into Makkah, the Quraish watched with terror expecting retribution for all the cruelty they had perpetrated. Instead, the Prophet granted general amnesty and prohibited any violence or plunder. His violence was directed to one place only. He went to the Kaba and destroyed all the stone idols, gods of inequality, stationed there. After settling affairs in and around Makkah he returned to Madinah, which remained the political centre of the Muslims. The Prophet did not go back to his beloved Makkah but remained in Madinah as he had promised long years ago in Aqaba.

The Year of Deputations

In 631, the 9th year of Hijra, the Prophet came to know that the Roman Byzantines were organising the Arabs in the Syrian borders against local Muslims. The Byzantines had passed a decree that who ever became a Muslim would be executed. The Muslims in the periphery needed security. The Byzantines had also started to support and build clandestine networks in and around Madinah to overthrow the Islamic state.

Abu Amir, a notable among the Khajraj of Madinah, had embraced Christianity. After the Hijra, he refused to accept the presence of Muslims in Madinah. He went to Makkah and helped the Quriash idolators in their war efforts with the Muslims. When this did not work out as he had expected he went to Byzantium and met Emperor Heraclius. Heraclius promised him all support needed and they started to plan for the clandestine network in Madinah. Abu Amir wrote to his hypocrite followers in Madinah that he would soon lead an army to Madinah. He also asked them to build a Mosque so that it could be used as a outpost where he would be able to send his clandestine emissaries and also as stronghold during the actual attack.

Under the plan from Byzantium the hypocrites built the Dirar Mosque which was not very far from the Quba Mosque. They even invited the Prophet to go to their mosque to give it legitimacy. But a revelation came upon the Prophet.

> *And as for those who put up a Mosque by way of harm and disbelief and to disunite the believers and as an outpost for those who warred against God and His Messenger aforetime, they will indeed swear that their intention is nothing but good. God bears witness that they are certainly liars.*
> *Never stand you therein.* [9:107-108]

The Prophet led an army to Tabuk in Syria which was still a dominion of the Romans. The journey was arduous and the army turned out to be ill prepared for it. They didn't have enough animals to ride on or enough weapon and water was scarce for the fearsome long desert trek. The climate was unbearingly hot and everyone suffered. The journey came to be known as the 'Journey of Distress'. But they persevered and when they reached Syria the Byzantine army wasn't there. For one reason or another they were not prepared to engage with the Muslims at that time. In their absence the local tribes gave allegiance to the Muslims. After camping there for twenty nights the Prophet embarked on the return journey. The Prophet sent some of his Companions who demolished the Dirar Mosque. The whole episode provided much needed security to the Muslims in the Syrian border area and boosted the prestige of the Islamic state.

Throughout the year, deputations arrived in Madinah from all over Arabia to give allegiance to Islam. While few gave allegiance without converting, large number of people converted to Islam en masse.

When comes the help of God
And Victory
And you see the people enter God's religion
In crowds
Celebrate the praises of your Lord
And pray for His forgiveness;
For he is ever relenting [110:1-3]

The Farewell Pilgrimage

It was in the year 632 that the Prophet felt that his earthly mission was coming to an end. He decided to lead the Haj, annual pilgrimage, to Makkah. In due time, he set off with 30,000 men and women from Madinah. After eleven days the caravan entered Makkah. As the Kaba came within his sight the Prophet raised both his hands in supplication. With the reins of the camel still in his left hand he prayed, "O God, increase this House in honour, magnificence, bounty, reverence and piety that it receives from humanity." He went around the Kaba seven times and then prayed from the Station of Abraham.

Makkah was brimming with people - 120, 000 had come to see the Prophet. At sunset, the Prophet started the sermon of the final pilgrimage. After praising God he said, "Hear me, O people, for I know not if ever I shall meet you after this year." It was a sermon filled with guidance and instruction on many issues. He asked his followers to respect each other as the bond between them was sacred. He advised them about what was good and bad, bidden and forbidden, "I have left amongst you that which, if you hold fast to, shall preserve you from all error" - an indication to the Quran, the book of God, and Sunnah, the way of the Prophet. He emphasised on being just and good in all aspects of life. He said that there was no racial superiority, and he asked the men to treat women with respect. Then he recited the revelation in which God states:

...This day have I perfected for you your religion
and fulfilled My favour unto you,
and it had been My good pleasure to choose Islam for you as your religion. [5,3]

Finally, for certitude, The Prophet earnestly asked, "O' people, have I faithfully delivered to you my message?"

A murmur rumbled among the multitude, "O' God, yes!"

Relieved, The Prophet raised his forefinger beseeching Divine ratification of the verdict, "O' God, bear witness!"

And thus he proved that he was a Prophet and a man.

Female Emancipation

In a world of inequity Islam declared that the only criterion for judging between human beings is Taqwa or righteousness. Gender, colour, cast or wealth are not criteria at all. This profoundly affected the status of women who, at that time, were treated as lesser than human beings the world over. They obtained numerous rights some of which include:

Spiritual rights: Men and women are considered of the same nature in Islam. They are expected to carry out the same religious ritual and both are to receive the same due rewards. Paradise is not a male domain as wrongly interpreted by ignorance or deliberate misrepresentation.

If any of you do deeds of righteousness - be male or female - and have faith, they will surely enter paradise and not the least injustice shall be done with them. [4, 124]

Socio-economic-legal rights: Adult Muslim women can own or dispose any property she wants without anyone's consent irrespective whether she is married or single. This right was given 14 hundred years ago. Only in the 19th century this was allowed in England.

The women has been given rights similar to as against them, but the men has a degree higher. [2,228]

Men are a degree higher in responsibility and with that come leadership in general. But to balance that women enjoy more rights. Men are responsible to the family for all financial obligations. Women are not responsible at all in this respect. So she can do a job or not, it is her prerogative. She only has to ensure her modesty remains intact at workplace and that the family is not affected by her work hours. What she earns is hers. At marriage women receive dower from men, which is obligatory. Again her money is hers and she does not need to spend any of it on the family. Although, if she wants she can. Irrespective of how rich the wife is, the husband is obligated to feed, clothe and look after her commensurate with his income. He has to respect her and treat her properly even if he does not like her.

Live with them (wife) on a footing of kindness and equity. If you take a dislike to them, it may be you dislike a thing that God brings about through it a great deal of good. [4,19]

While the world considered women as chattel Islam declared that women have the right to inherit, be witness in a court and the right to divorce. Women cannot be married against their will. When a father married her daughter against her will she complained to the Prophet and he annulled the marriage. There is no partiality in the upbringing of the son or daughter. When a man kissed his son and placed him on his lap with his daughter by his side the Prophet objected saying he should do the same to his daughter.

While the great civilisations considered pregnancy a punishment for women for their weakness and misdeed, in Islam Motherhood and pregnancy was to be respected.

Respect the wombs that bore you. [4,1]

We have enjoined on human being to be kind to the parents. In pain did the mother bore them and in pain did she gave them birth. [46,15]

Education and knowledge became a right of women as of men. When the women asked the Prophet if he could give them a day every week to educate them and to answer their questions, he agreed. He also sent other Companions to teach knowledge to the women.

Women could take part in law making. When Caliph Umar tried to make a law to put an upper limit to the dower that women receive during their marraige, a woman objected and gave evidence from the Quran that there should be no upper limit. Umar said, "Umar is wrong and the woman is right."

Women could join the army. The Sahih Bukhari has a chapter in which women in the battlefield is discussed.

In effect, an amazing variety of rights were enjoined to woman. This was the first time that such extensive female rights were incorporated into a legal framework and was applicable to all, rich or poor, not just the nobility as in some past societies. Nothing like this has ever happened before and it proved to be a great emancipatory leap for women the magnitude of which had not been seen up to this age.

Men and women became equal, not identical, with each having important roles to play. In certain roles the women were given greater status. In the mosque, a man approached the Prophet and asked, "After God, who should I respect most?"

"Your mother," replied the Prophet.

"And then who," asked the man again.

"Your mother," replied the Prophet again.

"And then who?" asked the man again.

"Your mother," said the Prophet again.

"And then who?" insisted the man.

Finally, after the fourth time the Prophet said, "Your father".

Later, in the final pilgrimage sermon in Makkah, the Prophet had said, "Women have rights over you and you have rights over them. Be good to them. You soon may have to appear before God and answer for your deeds. So beware."

The Prophet recognised the actions of women and gave them their due credit. In the seventh year of Hijra, the Muslims of Abyssinia finally arrived in Madinah. Asma, wife of Jaafar bin Abu Talib, on arrival went to meet Hafsa, the daughter of Umar. While they were talking Umar himself appeared there and asked Hafsa, "who is this?"

Hafsa said, "This is Asma bint Umais."

Umar asked, "From Abyssinia across the sea?"

"Yes," said Hafsa.

In the conversation that ensued Umar and Asma started to debate about who deserves more credit for their migrations. Umar said, "We made Hijra to Madinah before you came here and, so, are closer to the Prophet than you."

"No, you are not," retorted Asma, "You were (fortunate to be) with him while he fed the poor and taught the ignorant. We had to languish in distant foreign lands."

When she met the Prophet she reported to him her dialogue with Umar. The Prophet said, "No, Umar and his companions do not have more rights than you, he has the reward of one Hijra and you have the reward of two."

The first Hijra was to Abyssinia and other was from there to Madinah. This was a joy to Asma and her companions who had come to Madinah from Abyssinia. Ultimately, she became a much respected scholar and later groups of people including companions like Abu Musa Al Ashari would come to listen to the Hadith from her.

The Prophet would listen to intelligent advice from women. After the treaty of Hudaibiya, which appeared to be in favour of the Quraish, the Muslims were unhappy and refrained from carrying out the usual pilgrimage rites. The Prophet was contemplating on what to do when Umme Salama asked him to carry out the rituals himself. He did what she said and after that all the Muslims followed him and completed their rites.

The Prophet did not restrict women from sharing the world with the men. Only that this sharing be accomplished with dignity, decency and the required formality by both the sexes. The Hijab was introduced as a symbol of dignity for women.

> *"Those who harass believing men and believing women unjustifiably shall bear the guilt of slander and a grievous sin. O Prophet! Enjoin your wives, your daughters, and the wives of true believers to draw their cloaks over them [when they go out]. That is more proper, so that they may be distinguished and not be harassed. God is ever forgiving and merciful." (33:58)*

Woman wore the Hijab as a matter of a universal identity, pride, cultural significance, modesty, non-availability to public lust and a denial to be looked on as a commodity. Aristocratic ladies, especially those living in extreme climes, would cover their heads and faces as protection from damage of facial skin and diseases due to exposure.

The emancipation of women is more evident during the time of the Prophet and immediately after him. The first person to accept Islam was a woman – Khadija. The first person to be martyred for Islam was a woman – Sumaiya. Among the first to migrate for Islam was the daughter of Abu Sufiyan – Umme Habiba. There were a large number of women who participated in the Hijra to Madinah. Fatimah bint Kaif was one such emancipated woman. She had a full day of discussion and debate on Jurisprudence (Fiqh) with Umar and Ayesha and they could not fault her in any of her arguments. Imam An Nawawi mentions that she had profound knowledge. During the reign of the first Caliph Abu Bakr, Khaled bin Walid, the brilliant General and cavalry commander, was leading the army against the Byzantines. As the armies faced each other, he noticed a lone warrior making sorties riding a horse into the enemy lines, engaging and striking the enemy and returning to the Muslim ranks. The warrior did this on and on. Impressed by this bravery, Khaled ordered the warrior to be brought to his presence. The warrior turned out to be a woman name Khaula.

Muslim women were responsible for supporting the development of great men. Sayeeda Nafisa, great grand daughter of the Prophet, was one of the early teachers of the Great Imam Shafii. One of Great Imam Malik's tutors was a woman named Aisha Bin Saad Ibn Abi Waqqas. The father of the famous Imam Bukhari died when he was a child. It was his mother and sister who supported and financed his studies. Mohammad bin Qasim, the famous Umayyad General was educated by his mother. She and tutors she hired supervised his education. Rabia Basri became one of the most renowned Sufi in the world. Even later, there were Muslim Queens ruling the states in Egypt and India. There are many other women who have been mentioned in Muslim annals in relation to political achievements, dedication to God or place in society. In fact, it was during the period of colonisation that Muslim women regressed.

The Prophet's wives.

Starting from the days of Makkah women, both free and slaves, were attracted to Islam. After that, in the Madinah period, the death of men due to battles increased manifolds leaving behind widows. The proportions of female population among the Muslims thus increased dramatically. And during those times, women by themselves were not safe in any part of the world. There were no jobs, no decent manner of livelihood, and no safe place to stay for single women. A woman without any family or family attachment was a prey in an unsafe world or victim to ill-repute. The state had to provide solutions for all and the only way to provide for these single women, some with small children and most without any money, was to absorb them into other families. That was a practicle reason for men to be allowed more than one wife.

Every aspect of the Prophet's life, including his marriages, was dedicated to the cause of Islam. He lived with a single woman up to the age of about fifty five years, first with

Khadija and then with Sauda. He belonged to a noble family of the Quraish and in his youth could have, along with Khadijah, the best women of Arabia for his wives. In fact that was the general tradition. In Madinah, when he was in his mid fifties, he married a number of times due to political exigencies or on humanitarian grounds. All his wives, except Ayesha, were widows – some twice widowed. He married Umme Salamah, the relatively aged widow of one of the martyrs, so that she and her children could have a home. Because of her age she did not have any suitors neither did she have any wealth to look after the children. His marriage to Juwariah of Mustaliq led to the freedom of her defeated and imprisoned tribe who were condemned to death. Umme Habiba was left alone in Abyssinia after her husband apostatised, became a drunkard and finally died. She was alone in a foreign land and was going through a very difficult period. After the first year of Hijra to Madinah the Prophet sent her a proposal of marriage. She was overjoyed by this support and they were married by proxy. She retained her dignity. She moved to Madinah only after the 7th year of Hijra. Zainab was a social worker, the support and succour to the poor masses. Safiya was an intellectual well versed in Fiqh. Umme Salama was the teacher of 32 scholars.

The Prophet's marriage to a very young Ayesha, daughter of Abu Bakr, has caused some stirring among the later detractors of Islam. But history has proven that this marriage turned out to be a blessing for the Muslims. Ayesha became the fourth greatest Hadith scholar of Islam. Laws including most of the family laws come through her. There is no book of Hadith and Tafsir which does not directly mention her. She had taught 88 scholars and the jurisprudence that was to rule nations and empires for a thousand years is significantly indebted to her. She remains probably the most influential women in the history of the world.

Social Emancipation: Opening of the World

According to Professor Sir Thomas Arnold the spread of Islam was not due to its military policies but, in fact, due to the acceptance of the Islamic ideal by the people world over. The Quran had forbidden any forced conversion ensuring acceptance of Islam was voluntary. Despite the fact that a military force had marched and taken over Makkah, its fall was not due to any battle, but due to the acceptance of Islamic ideals by the rest of Arabia, which became so overwhelming that the leaders of Makkah simply had to capitulate. The next major military actions that the Muslims would take would be the reclamation of lands occupied by the Byzantines and Persians Empires. Military engagement in the Persian front would continue as a reaction to the covert Persian attempts to destabilise the Muslims by supporting anti-Muslim elements within the Arabs. Tactically, the Muslim occupation of Persia was initiated from defence against Persian imperial policies rather than due to a policy of offence.

In later history, there would be a lot of conquest by Muslim Empires – Umayyad, Abbasid, Ottoman, Moghuls and others. This led to the usual suppression of rebellions, and fighting and squabbling between empires and kingdoms. But all these were Muslim conquests in an imperial world rather than an Islamic one. The fine line of distinction between the two is that Islam is a divine, universal and timeless system, while the Muslims, though followers of the Islamic system, also include temporal and political elements in their makeup which makes them not necessarily infallible.

Islam does not condone conquest for the sake of conquest. Historical proof to this is the fate of its greatest conquering Generals like Khaled Bin Walid in Arabia, Tariq Bin Ziyad and Musa Nusayr in Europe and Mohammad Bin Quasim in India. They were all removed from office at the heights of their conquests and exploits. Historians have given various political explanations for this, but the inherent reason is that Islam is incompatible with pure conquest. Islam only calls for *Fatah* which means opening the people living in ignorance to a world of universality, equity, knowledge and non-exploitation.

Thus, when Muslims occupied regions after military engagements they had never done that to subjugate the people or forcefully convert them or to take the resources of their lands. Wherever the Muslims went they taught the people how to develop themselves and, inevitably, the economic situation of the region improved dramatically and rapidly. When the Muslims went to Damascus, Syria developed. When they founded Baghdad it became the wonder of the world. When they went to Spain the transformation was dazzling, it turned into the jewel of Europe. When they went to India, it saw the rise of its greatest empire. This great uplifting force started off from Madinah. When the Prophet went to Madinah, the insignificant oasis became the major political centre of Arabia.

In Madinah, while the military, political and diplomatic events were taking place in a conspicuously spectacular manner, a far greater social revolution was taking place in silence.

The Prophet established the universal city of Madinah based on the Islamic tenets. It was not a political state for a religious or cultural group but a universal state for all who agreed with the universality of humanity that was Islam, or even those who agreed to just live with such an universality.

While setting up the new state the Prophet did not just establish a model of governance but also a completely new and modern way of life. He was redefining nationhood and society that would lead to a legal, economical and scientific revolution that would transform the entire planet. He employed two main sources of knowledge in his teaching and framing of the new way of life. One consisted of the revelations that came down to him from God, which is the Quran, and the other was his own judgement or personal code of life known as his *Sunnah*. He had to deal with all the incredibly varied aspect of a nation from the very small to the biggest issues. He had to manage every macro and micro aspects of society: political and military affairs, legal and diplomatic affairs, economic and social affairs, family and individual affairs. The main body of his knowledge and teachings did not deal only with rituals of a religion and legalistic commandments or cosmogeny but more with establishing a framework for all aspects of life that provided the new direction for humanity. It is a rational impossibility for a single person to have dealt with and established all of these aspects single handed, and thus the revelations or its embodiment, the Quran, is considered the true miracle of the Prophet.

One of the aspects of the State that the Prophet altered was 'war' itself. During the wars, he had encouraged his followers to take part in the Jihad promising the martyrs unconditional paradise. But at the same time he redefined war: no children, women, old people, animals or even trees were to be harmed. Even if the Muslims had to fight a tribe that had Christian members, the Christian Monks, who were the most significant proselytising force of Christianity of that time, were not to be harmed. Dead bodies of enemies were no longer mutilated as was the practice in those times. Non combatants were not to be harmed, and prisoners of war were to be well treated, which remains a historical rarity. The booty that could be legally acquired by the warriors consisted only of the movable property that the enemy warrior had left behind on the battlefield, the non-combatants could not be plundered. Though the Muslim armies fought and defeated the armies of imperialist empires and pagan nations which were dividing humanity into sectarian, unequal and fratricidal factions, the people of those empires were won not by the sword but by the rich ideas and concepts of the universal message. None were to be forced to accept Islam, and all could live their own lives and practice their own religion and rituals. But above all, Jihad itself had a greater implication as it meant struggle in the path of God, not war. The Prophet said, "The most excellent Jihad is the conquest of the self."

He made knowledge the prime and mandatory focus of every Muslim. On innumerable occasions he exhorted people to acquire knowledge. China was then considered the farthest and historically cultured country and the Prophet said, "Go even to China if you can acquire knowledge." The position of a scholar, in the scheme of the society, was set abundantly clear when the Prophet said, "The ink of the scholar is holier than the blood of the martyr".

The companions of the Prophet also strongly advocated the acquisition of knowledge. One example is Abu Darda who is known to have said that people could only be pious if they were knowledgeable, and knowledge could really be enjoyed by applying it practically. Abu Darda lauded both the student and the teacher, saying they would receive equal reward from God. He had heard the Prophet say, "If anyone travels on the road of knowledge, God will cause him to travel on one of the roads of Paradise."

The Prophet was very conscious of the environment and had said that it is a blessed act to plant a tree even if it be the day the world ends.

During the time of the Prophet, numerous superstitions and ill practices were rampant in the society. It was prevalent that once any non-biological relationship was adopted or accepted it became biologically binding. For example, if someone declared a wife as mother, that relationship was binding. Unscrupulous men took advantage of this and declared their wives as mother and thus would get an automatic divorce. The Quran was against such social ills:

> *If any men among you divorce their wives by Zihar (calling them mother), they cannot be their mothers. None can be their mothers except those who give birth to them. [58:2]*

The Prophet set about breaking other similar social ailments. He adopted a slave, Zaid bin Harith as a son, which was unheard of. He then married his distant cousin, Zainab, to Zaid which broke another social taboo. But, on the long run, this marriage was not harmonious. Both Zainab and Zaid repeatedly requested him for a divorce. The Prophet realised that for the happiness of both a divorce had become a necessity and he approved of it. Adoption was changed to foster parenting which meant that, in reality, a adopted son was not a real son. While foster parenting or gaurdianship became sanctioned in Islam, adoption was not viewed as a factual relation. The Prophet himself married Zainab, the ex-wife of his erstwhile adopted son but later considered his ward, and established that non-biological relationship was not genetically binding.

The abolition of slavery also started with the advent of Islam. The Prophet freed slaves and encouraged other's to do the same. It was declared illegal to turn any free person into a slave and only existing slaves could be bought. Only prisoners of war could be ransomed or turned into bondage. Those who were still kept as slaves found a new life - the very definition of slavery was totally re-written. In the Muslim annals a slave was no longer a helpless 'thing' confined to burdens of chores and the master's whim. A slave was an individual bonded to a family or another individual and would have to pay a certain amount of their earning to the owner. Many would earn enough to buy their freedom. A female slave could become a wife with all the basic rights of a human being. Some later slave-wives were mothers to emperors. A slave could rise to any level in professional and social heights. Historically, there were 'slaves' who became Generals and even Sultans. In the farewell sermon of his final pilgrimage the Prophet had said, 'All Muslims, free or enslaved, have the same right and same responsibilities. None is higher then the other unless higher in virtue.'

The overall influence of the Prophet on his followers was incredible. His teachings and presence among them transformed ordinary men to great ones. Among the best of his companions included Abu Bakr though respected and wealthy was an ordinary and cordial business man. Umar though literate was a hot headed youth given to drinking, Usman was a handsome young man of a rich family living the life of the young and rich, Ali was a child of no known qualities till he became the Prophet's ward. Many were simple illiterate folks, and others were vagabonds, wayfarers or brigands. And what more, they all belonged to an obscure, insignificant and almost uncivilised and illiterate corner of the world. All of them were transformed by the Prophet's influence into great men of impeccable moral aptitude and became rulers and founders of dynasties, great Generals, and brilliant scholars, administrator and judges of international stature the likes of who are rare or absent in history. Wherever they went, whatever region came under their dominion became marvels of the world. They were transformed into teachers of humanity.

They still remained humans, not angels, and were not devoid of human frailties. There would be times when the Muslims would be unable to handle the political cross currents that would accompany the incredibly rapid social and economic changes that had been initiated. Even righteous men would become helpless at the face of gigantic political upheavals, the momentum of which tended to sway every thing out of control. One such example was the *Fitna* (anarchy or civil war) that raged during the time of Caliphs Usman, Ali and Muawiah in the mid 7th century CE.

The march towards the advanced brand of civilisation was novel in experience and extremely dynamic. After the death of the Prophet there were no more revelations to guide these people, and there were bound to be trials and errors. In the making of this vast, enlightened and mighty Empire the grandest of achievements were sometimes accompanied with greatest of tragedies.

But irrespective of these upheavals and individual tragedies, which abounds in all human civilisations and more so in the contemporary world, the overall progress of the Muslim empires was remarkable and unprecedented.

In 632, after a few days of sickness the Prophet died with his head on the lap of his beloved Ayesha. But he had completed his mission - the ultimate universal message had been delivered to humanity. This message exploded with a force that was to cultivate a civilisation across the known continents ranging from Spain to the doors of India and soon beyond. It was a civilisation the likes of which had never been seen before. Its extent reached dimension greater than any previous empires, it was enlightened with knowledge that would illuminate the entire world. The Muslim empires excelled above all other civilization the world had ever witnessed. Everywhere the Muslims went, enlightened cities sprung up. Of the many examples, two such jewels were Baghdad and Cordova.

Baghdad was an accomplishment of pure architectural marvels. For miles stretched exquisite suburbs with gardens and parks, bazaars, superb mosques and beautiful promenades by the clear shining riverside. Cordova, a city that could rival Baghdad, was described by a visiting German Saxon nun named Hroswitha as 'the ornament of the world'. It was a vast mesmerising symphony of high learning and sophisticated culture, an interweaving of poetry, perfume, mathematics and philosophy, theology and science, delicacies on porcelain, glorious palaces lush with garden and flowing water, an interplay or orchestration of architectural light, paved streets with street lights and houses with running water - a way of life that was to influence and change the world forever.

The cities were not only aesthetically spectacular but were stunning marvels in spirit and mind as well. The greatest minds and scholars of the time gathered in Baghdad harnessing the knowledge of the entire world needed to run the all encompassing empire. Besides the local greats, philosophers and scientist from India, Persia, Byzantium and all over the world debated in the Hall of Wisdom of Baghdad. The best Christian and Jewish minds would go to Baghdad to become part of this enlightenment. Muslim scholars were sent out to search out and acquire all manners of knowledge from all corners of the world. The first international scientific inquiry for knowledge was thus convened.

The greatest intellectual innovations emerged from these cities. Algebra, trigonometry, chemistry, engineering, astronomy, medicine became definite and discrete sciences. The knowledge of the great masters of the past – Greek, Indian, Chinese and others – were amassed, translated, challenged and corrected. Hundreds of scribes were continuously recording the innovative works in numerous books. There were roads in the cities with its sides lined up with hundreds of books shops. In all the cities of the universal empire paper books had become commercially available which started the 'Age of Books' and that age continues even today.

As the Prophet had altered his companions into superb beings, wherever Islam went it changed the people it touched to enlightenment, progressive life, universal ideas and the pursuit of knowledge. Islam did not conquer or force conversions but 'opened' up people and the lands to a universal light without recourse to any exploitation. The local resources were used to develop the local people. That was the essential difference between the Empire of Islam and the Empires of imperialism. This was the Muslim civilisation, resplendent in its glory and prosperity while most of the world languored in squalor and its inhabitants, living in untidy shacks, could not start to imagine the kind of progressive life that the Muslims lived, till they too became illuminated by the same light.

The Pillars of Islam

The inability to comprehend God is comprehension

- Abu Bakr

The five prime tenets of Islam are:

1. *Kalama* - The unique sentence that declares faith in Islam
2. *Salah* - Prayer
3. *Zakaat* - Tax or religious obligation
4. *Siyam* - Fasting
5. *Hajj* - Pilgrimage.

The *Kalama* is the declaration of Faith in Islam. It is one single line a person has to utter to become a Muslim. The line is 'There is no god but Allah and Mohammad is his messenger'. The simple meaning of the Kalama is obvious. But a profound meaning is implied in this seemingly simple statement. It proclaims the oneness or indivisibility of God which is the absolutely most important concept in Islam. Not only are other gods unacceptable but submission, and there is a fine difference between submission and attainment of, to anything else - possessions, status, power – are prohibited as all these can become material or intellectual idols.

The first part of the statement 'There is no god but Allah…' declares a universal unity and equality of humanity. As there is one God for all of humanity, all humanity is one, equal in all senses, in the view of God. There is no racial, gender or any other kind of superiority. People may have different traits unique to them, different tasks and roles to attend to, but the difference remain in their duties, in their responsibilities and not in their beings.

People born in a non-universal environment belong only to certain discrete groups of human like races or nations, and are in servitude of, or subject to, other authoritative humans such as kings or presidents. This degrades the individual and divides humanity. Islam sees people as subject to none but to the Universal Creator alone and belonging to just one humanity.

The second part '...... and Mohammad is his messenger' declares the commonality of all human endeavours. The Prophet is a messenger and thus has a message from God for humanity. This message from God is the Quran. The very first statement of the Quran as revealed to the Prophet reads as such:

"Read in the name of your Lord and Cherisher, Who created -
Created man out of a clot that clings.
Read! And your Lord is most bountiful
He Who taught the use of Pen.
Taught Man what he knew not."

This revelation is a holistic introduction to the message of the Quran. It says 'Read', it mentions 'Pen', and it mentions teaching of 'what they knew not'. It even mentions science, more appropriately, biological science -'Who has created man from a clot that clings'. The very first verse of the Quran is simply and clearly indicating one and only thing – knowledge.

Throughout the Quran, knowledge has been mentioned innumerable times. So what knowledge does the Quran signify and advocate? Islam declares that all knowledge comes from God. Hence there cannot be any qualification in the source of knowledge. The notion that the source of only religious knowledge is God while scientific knowledge is secular implies that there is another source for the scientific knowledge besides God. This notion of equating another source to God in known as *Shirk* and is the only unpardonable sin in Islam. Thus Islam contends that humanity pursue knowledge in one and all of its forms and avenues. And that the pursuit of knowledge will lead to the understanding of where humanity stands in the grand universal design and what part it needs to play in it. That is the heart of the message of God which was revealed to the Prophet for humankind.

The Prophet has on innumerable occasions directed his followers to acquire knowledge. He had ordained 'Acquiring knowledge is mandatory for all Muslim men and women' and thus for the first time in human history erudition came into the domain of the general mass. The early Muslims had indeed done exactly that and had led the world, for hundreds of years, in the research and acquisition of various branches of knowledge – be it theological, philosophical or scientific.

The second pillar of Islam is prayer that represents the direct connection between individuals and God. There are five prayers a day during which the Muslims, wherever their geographical location may be, faces the Kaba and prays in a prescribed manner. Each mandatory prayer itself averages between ten to fifteen minutes. Ablution, washing the face and limbs in preparation for prayer adds some more time. During prayer, each individual Muslim stands right in front of God without any intermediaries.

According to Islamic tradition, God made the prayers obligatory during the journey of the Prophet through the heavens. The Prophet experienced the *Miraj*, a miraculous journey, in the year 620. One night the angel Gabriel took him first to Al Aqsa Mosque in Jerusalem and from there he was taken through the seven encompassing universes (heavens) where he met the earlier Prophets – Adam, Abraham, Moses, Jesus, and others. Then he entered Paradise and finally, he faced the *presence* of God and was given the gift of the five times prayer. In Islamic tradition, the Heavens and Paradise are different. The seven heavens are the creation of God of which the first heaven comprises of the known universe of galaxies. The second universe encompasses it and is indefinitely larger than the first one. A similitude would be a ring in a desert. The third universe encompasses the second one in a similar fashion and so forth. Before the Day of Judgment, all these universes will be destroyed but Paradise, the abode of the afterlife, will persist. Ibn Ishaq, the first author of the Prophet's biography, considers the journey of *Miraj* as a spiritual experience. Later historians like At-Tabari and Ibn Kathir present it as a physical journey.

About prayers Islam never asks anyone to 'say or do your prayers'. The Quran guides the Muslims to 'establish prayers' in their life. Performing some rituals for rituals sake, or praying for a boon from God, is vastly different from establishing prayers in life. It is establishing spirituality in a material life. But there are more facets to establishing prayer. The timing of the five mandatory prayers is spread such that it divides the day into very practical segments which leads to a highly disciplined life. The prayers had initiated, for the first time in history, a daily dusk to dawn routine for the general people establishing a disciplined society.

The prayers have spiritual, mental and physical aspects which are all dedicated to God. The spiritual aspect brings the individual in direct proximity of God. The Imam who leads the prayer is just one of the people, who is generally expected to be well read, enlightened and a pious religious scholar. Islam did not have any clergy and in the time of the Prophet, Governors and Generals were Imams (The Shia sect would, though, develop a clergy at a later stage). Muslim prayer is also the best form of meditation - it increases mental control, decreases stress and moves the heart to a restful state. Physically, it is the best light exercise applicable equally to all, young or old. Before every prayer ablution, *Wadu,* or cleansing of the limbs and face with water is performed as well as the mind is purged of any ill thoughts. No form of dirtiness, depravity or deviation is acceptable while performing the prayers. Thus, for the first time in history a daily cleanliness and hygiene regime was also established for the common people.

> *... When you rise up for prayer, wash your face, and your hands up to the elbows, and lightly rub your heads and (wash) your feet up to your anklets [74:1]*

All Muslims pray facing the Kaba - a unifying direction. There is a black stone in the Kaba which is simply treated by Muslims as a historical centre-point of reference. It is not a holy object by itself though there are fond memories associated with it. This very stone has been held by the very hands of Abraham, Ishmael, Mohammad and many of the great followers of Islam.

During the daily five prayers, parts of the Quran are recited which reinforces a greater appreciation of the Quran. Thus, all in all, 'establishing prayers' in Islam is not just utterance of poetical words or begging for boons, but an immense more. Above all, it is the worship – a complete submission, adoration and reverence - of the one God.

God is the only 'Being' worthy of worship. But it should be understood that God is not at all a being in the general sense of the word. God is beyond human comprehension and is shapeless, formless, neither singular nor plural. Nobody or nothing is like God, and God is like nobody or nothing. God is the only Creator of all creation and not confined to the physical laws of this creation. He creates out of nothing, and gives life out of nothing. God is complete and can only be realised to some extent by His attributes. The Quran refers to God with a large number of shifting pronouns or attributes. Some of the attributes are as follows:

Eternal (with no start)
Everlasting (with no end)
Omnipresent (Existing everywhere in the universe and beyond)
Different from the entire creation.
Self sufficient or self sustaining
Absolute
Possessor of complete knowledge
The all powerful
Possessor of will and purpose
Living
Possessor of the complete sense of hearing
Possessor of the complete sense of vision.
Possessor of the complete sense of speech.

When the early (8-9th Century) Muslims came in contact with concepts of foreign metaphysics, anthropomorphism and astrology, all these concepts were studied by one scholar or another but all were ultimately rejected by the main body of Islamic thought. It is only and only the omniscient God that Islam envisages worthy of worship and only Islam views God in such Unique and Superlative light.

The third pillar of Islam is the payment of *Zakaat*. It is an annual charity, as defined by the Ulemas, or a tax on savings which is mandatory for all Muslims. It is an instrument of Islamic economy which provides for revenue for the state and the poor. It causes social welfare, development and security. Islamic economy is based on social justice and one of its prominent principles is the prohibition of *Riba* or economic exploitation like interest and speculative monetary dealings. The ban on Riba can be found in the Quran, in the compiled sayings of the Prophet, in the sayings of the Prophet's companion as well as in the *Ijma* (concensus) of Muslim scholars. The reason Islam is so against Interest is because it can be used as a powerful economic tool to control others. Not only can it ruin an individual, Interest can subjugate and ruin nations.

The fourth pillar is Fasting during the month of *Ramadan*. It is obligatory for adult Muslims to fast, dawn to dusk, for this lunar month every year. Fasting is not only staying without food and drink throughout the day but is the physical and mental forbearance to curtail all immorality, in action and thought, that desires can unleash. Throughout the month Muslims pray, read the Quran and do other good deeds and refrain from bad habits. Fasting is the spiritual retraining of the self to stay on the right path for the rest of the year. It is not just an annual detoxication of the body but the cleansing and purification of the body, heart, mind and soul.

The fifth pillar is the *Hajj* or pilgrimage which takes place in Makkah once every year when Muslims from all over the world gather together at the house of God - the Kaba. During the Hajj, besides worshipping God, Muslims experiences the Universal human family to which they belong. Muslims see and meet different people from all over the world and pray, men and women together, in equality. Hajj reminds the Muslims of their traditional history from the days of Abraham, who built the Kaba, till the present. In the past all the people travelled by land from far away places to reach the Kaba. Thus, they would get to see a large section of the world. In this way Islam condoned internationalism or universalism. The Hajj also is a central point of communication where people from distant lands can exchange ideas.

It should be understood that the various benefits and aspects discussed above are incidental and not the focus or intention of Muslim worship. Each and every worship is for God alone and no one and nothing else.

The Days of Festivity

Muslims have two days of obligatory festivity every year - *Eidul Fitr* and *Eidul Adha*. Eid Al Fitr is the day for festivity and feasting after the month long Ramadan fasting. Eid Al Adha, which is celebrated after the Hajj, besides being a festive occasion also commemorates an important aspect of Muslim characteristic. On this day Muslims sacrifice animals in the name of God and divides the meat into three part giving one part to the poor, one part to friends and relatives and keeps the third part for home consumption. This gives the ability to sacrifice and share and thus extricate the tribal greed that is inherent in human psychology. The day also commemorates Abraham's readiness to sacrifice his son for the sake of God. This is, of course, only symbolic in Muslim thought and indicates the readiness to sacrifice their greatest personal love and pleasure for the sake of God.

The Scientific Dimension of Revelation

And if all the trees of earth were pens
And the ocean was ink,
With seven oceans behind it to add to its supply
Yet would not the words of God be exhausted;
For God is exalted in power, full of wisdom. [31,27]

The original source of information about the five pillars of Islam is the Quran. It is the compendium of revelations, the basic objective of which is religious guidance. It consists of a large number of verses providing legal injunctions, admonitions, inspirations and much more. It provides not only for a moral and just life but knowledge needed for a progressive and complete *code of life* and thus it also has dimensions and aspects of science, history, economics and politics.

Of these the verses which states scientific ideas and facts are quite amazing and has much influenced the Muslims from the time of the Prophet. Dr. Maurice Bucaille, a French physician-scientist, in his book *La Bible, Le Coran et la Science* writes that all the compiled citations of scientific aspects mentioned in the Quran are compatible with modern day science. Among all the religious scriptures this is a unique quality of Quran. He further states:

'In view of the level of knowledge in Muhammad's day, it is inconceivable that many of the statements in the Quran which are connected with science could have been the work of a man. It is, moreover, perfectly legitimate, not only to regard the Quran as the expression of a revelation, but also to award it a very special place, on account of the guarantee of authenticity it provides and the presence in it of scientific statement which when studied today, appear as a challenge to explanations in human terms.'

The following are examples of verses that denote the scientific dimensions in the Quran. The scientific information is followed by the verses corroborating the statements:

Astrophysics and Astronomy postulates that after the initial formation of the universe the primordial universal matter consisted of gaseous masses of hydrogen and helium formed by nucleo-synthesis of the big bang. In the hot expanding universe huge balls of Hydrogen formed, much bigger than the Sun, in which nucleo-synthesis would start creating heavier elements like oxygen, carbon and iron. As the temperature came down from that of nuclear levels chemical-synthesis became possible. Oxygen reacted explosively with Hydrogen forming vast quantity of water, one of the first constituents. Initially, the water was in gaseous form and spread over the universe.

He is the One Who created the heavens and the earth in six periods - at the time when His Throne was rested on the water - so that He may test to find out which of you is the best in deeds. [11,7]

Other compounds formed by elements reacting with each other. Initially it was all in a gaseous, smokey or cloud like form.

Moreover, He comprehended in His design the sky
And it had been smoke. [41,11]

Over a time period of billions of years these gaseous matter separated into huge fragments and coalesced. These interstellar galactic matters over time formed the nebulae in which the coalescing matter formed the stars and planets, and in the process gave rise to powerful gravity and thermonuclear reaction.

Do not the believers see that the heaven and earth were fused together
Before we clove them asunder? [21,30]

Recently, with information received from powerful telescope in orbit around the world and other scientific sources, it has been proven that the universe is expanding.

Heavens We built with power and We are expanding it. [51,47]

There are balance, equilibrium, laws and patterns in the universe. The Quran also highlights such balance and due proportion in nature, in the cosmos, in the earth and in the ecology.

God created everything in due and proper measure [25,2]

The sun and moon are subject to calculations. [55,5]

It is not permitted for the sun to catch up with the moon,
Nor the night outstrip the day
Each swims along in its own orbit. [36,40]

He draws the night as a veil over the day
Each seeking the other in rapid succession,
He created the sun, the moon and the stars ,
All governed by laws under His command. [7,54]

It has now been proven that there are many other planets even in our own galaxy.

*Praise be to God the Cherisher and Sustainer of the **Worlds**. [1,2]*

Like multiple worlds the Quran also speaks of multiple heavens which some scholars believe indicates to the existence of multiple universes.

*And God created the **heavens** and the earth in truth. [45,21]*

According to science the sun will burn out and die determined by the end of nuclear fission of hydrogen converting to helium.

And the sun runs its course for a period determined for it;
*That is the decree of the Almighty, the All-knowing. [*36, 38]

In the Earth, life first formed in water from which amphibians went on to the land and finally the land animals occupied the earth.

We made from water every living thing
Will they not then believe. [21,30]

Science now states that there was a central place from where humanity migrated and spread on the world. About migration of humanity after being created the Quran says the first to be created were Adam and Eve and then,

And of His signs is that He created you from dust; then behold, you are men scattered far and wide. [Al-Rum 30:20]

Archaeological findings show the continuous existence of several civilisation at the estimated time of Noah which indicates that Noah's deluge was not global. Had it been global all the people would have been destroyed at the same time. The deluge in the Quran is not global but rather local affecting only the people of Noah.

*And **the people of Noah** –*
When they rejected the messengers,
*We drowned **them**,*
And We made them
As a sign for mankind. [25,37]

The Quran was revealed at a time when all information of the Pharaohs and ancient Egypt was lost. Information about mummification and preservation of Pharaohs' bodies came to be known in recent times from archaeological sites. When the Pharaoh was drowned while chasing Moses and the Israelites, there is indication in the Quran of his preservation or mummification.

This day shall We save thee in your body
That you may be a sign to those who come after you. [10,95]

The world evolved through geological periods. Both the Bible and the Quran states the formation of the world in six days, i.e., six stages. Both teach in parables and metaphors. The Arabic or Hebrew for a day is *eom / yom*. But the meaning of '*eom*', can be a day or it can be an eon, an age or a period relative to the context. This relative time usage of *eom* is clarified in the Quran.

The angels and the Spirit ascend to Him in a day (eom) the measure of which is fifty thousand years. [70:4]

Similar verses indicate the relativity of time.

A day (eom) with your Lord is equivalent to a thousand years in the way you count. [22:4]

He rules all affairs from the heavens to the earth.
In the end will all the affairs go up to him
On a day whose space will be a thousand years of your reckoning. [32:5]

The Quran speaks of vegetation and water in many verses.

Don't you see that God sends down rain from the sky,
And leads it through springs in the earth?
Then he causes, therewith, products of various colours. [39,21]

Scientist has discovered that two large natural water bodies, like currents of seas and oceans, do not mix together immediately after they come together. There is a time delay till certain barrier - salinity, temperature, density - between the water bodies are over come. One example is where the Mediterranean meets the Atlantic, the two bodies of water stay separate even after they come in contact.

He has let free the two bodies of flowing water meeting together;
Between them is a barrier which they do not transgress; [55,19-20]

The 20th century concept of Plate Tectonics and the orogenic movements by which the mountains rise and then are weathered, eroded and again flattened and passes away in time is depicted in the following verse:

You see the mountains and see them firmly fixed.
But they shall pass away as the clouds pass away.
Such is the artistry of God,
Who dispossess of all things in perfect order. [27, 88]

Studies in Geology have established the fact that high mountains also have 'roots' in the earth. The crust goes deeper into the mantle under the mountains like pegs.

Have We not made the earth as a wide expanse,
And the mountains as pegs? [78,6-7]

Zoological studies have led to the understanding that not only humans but animals have communities with working and social organisation, for example, the working organisation into groups by ants and bees, the localisations whereby the tigers divide regions in the forest for preying without disturbing each other, and the migrations of birds.

There is not an animal on the earth,
Nor a being that flies on its wings,
But forms part of communities like you. [6,38]

An object, for example a rocket, to leave the earth has to pierce through the gravitational pull at a certain velocity. If that velocity is not attained the rocket falls back to the earth.

O company of jinn and human beings. If you are able to pierce through the confines of the heavens and Earth, pierce through them. You will not pierce through, except with a clear authority. [55:33]

Physiology and Chemistry shows that the nutrients from the contents of the intestine passes to the systemic circulation, i.e., the blood circulation that acts as the conduit for these nutrients, which nourishes the organs including mammary glands that produces milk.

From what is within their bodies
Coming from a conjunction of intestines and blood
We produce, for your drink, milk
Pure and agreeable for those who drink it. [16,66]

Maurice Buccaille reasons, "Our knowledge of these disciplines is such that it is impossible to explain how a text produced at the time of the Quran could have contained ideas that have only been discovered in modern times".

A good example of what he stated above is the process of human reproduction mentioned in the Quran. Human reproduction starts with fertilisation of the ovule that has detached from the ovary of a female. It is fertilised by sperm from a male formed internally due to a *mingling of fluids* originating from different glands – the testicles, the seminal vesicles, the prostrate gland, the glands annexed to the urinary tract.

Verily, we fashioned man from a small quantity of mingled liquids. [76,2]

The emitted sperm contains millions of cells or spermatozoon of which a very small amount or a single cell is needed for fertilisation.

God fashioned man from a small quantity of sperm. [16,4]

After fertilisation, the egg descends down the Fallopian tube in the female and lodges in the body of the uterus where it implants itself.

We cause whom We will to rest in the womb for an appointed term. [22,5]

The egg develops villosities, which are like roots in the soil, that clings to the uterus and draw nourishment.

Was man not a small quantity of sperm which has been poured out? After that he was something which clings; then God fashioned him in due proportions. [75,37-38]

Soon, it becomes large enough to be observed by the naked eye. It is a small mass of flesh without any features and grows in progressive stages.

God fashions you in stages. [71,14]

The foetus develops first like a clinging irregular flesh which soon grows to an intact lump. Bones develop and are covered by flesh.

Then We made the sperm into a clot that clings. Then out of the clot We made an intact lump. Then We made out of the lump bones and clothed the bones with flesh; Then We developed out of it another creature. [23,14]

As the embryo starts to take form, some parts of it appear out of proportion compared to a full grown human body.

We fashioned you .... into a lump of flesh partly in proportion and partly out of proportion... [22,5]

Then the embryo develops the senses.

There came over man a long period of time
When he was nothing – not even worth mentioning
Verily We created man from a drop of mingled sperm,
In order to try him: so we gave him the gifts of hearing and sight. [76,1-2]

A noted embryologist Professor Keith L. Moore, upon being presented with the verses of the Quran about the stages of formation of the embryo's development remarked, "It has been a pleasure for me to help clarify statements in the Quran about Human Development. It is clear to me that these statements must have come to Muhammad from God or Allah because almost all of this knowledge was not discovered until many centuries later."

Professor Moore presented his findings at several conferences and modified his own textbook on the subject. He included all the relevant passages of the Quran and authentic statements of the Prophet Mohammad into his book, *The Developing Human: Clinically oriented embryology with Islamic additions*. This book was published by WB Saunders in 1987 and was a university textbook in the United States.

Professor Tejatet Tejasen of the department of Anatomy, faculty of Medicine, Chiang Mei University in Thailand, after studying the passages of the Quran regarding embryology stated, "From my studies and what I have learnt at this conference I believe that everything that has been recorded in the Qur'an 1400 years ago must be true. That can be proved the scientific way".

Professor E. Marshal Johnson, Chairman, department of Anatomy, Daniel Bough Institute, Thomas Jefferson University, Philadelphia, USA, remarked on embryology, "The Qur'an describes not only the development of external form but emphasizes also the internal stages - the stages inside the embryo of its creation and development, emphasizing major events recognised by contemporary science... If I was to transpose myself into that era, knowing what I do today and describing things, I could not describe the things that were described... I see no evidence to refute the concept that this individual Muhammad had to be developing this information from some place... so I see nothing in conflict with the concept that divine intervention was involved..."

Professor Alfred Kroner a world famous geologist and Chairman of the Department of Geology at the Institute of Geosciences, Johannes Gutenberg University, Mainz, in Germany states, "Thinking about many of these questions and thinking where Muhammad came from, he was after all a Bedouin. I think it is almost impossible that he could have known about things like the common origin of the universe, because scientists have only found out within the last few years with very complicated and advanced technological methods that this is the case."

Professor Joe Leigh Simpson, Obstetrics and Gynaecology, North-western University Medical School, Chicago, Illinois, USA studied the Hadiths of the Prophet and said: "... these Hadeeths could not have been obtained on the basis of the scientific knowledge that was available at the time of the writer... It follows that not only is there no conflict between genetics and religion (Islam) but in fact religion (Islam) may guide science by adding revelation to some of the traditional scientific approaches... There exist statements in the Qur'an shown centuries later to be valid which support knowledge in the Qur'an having been derived from God".

Professor T.V.N. Persaud, head of the Dept. of Anatomy, Faculty of Medicine and Dentistry, University of Manitoba, Canada, stated, "Muhammad was a very ordinary man, he couldn't read, didn't know how to write, in fact he was an illiterate... about 1400 years ago, you have some illiterate person making profound statements that are amazingly accurate, of a scientific nature... I personally can't see how this could be mere chance, there are too many accuracies and like Dr. Moore I have no difficulty in my mind reconciling that this is a divine inspiration or revelation which led him to these statements".

It is only recently that the scholars are starting to see the connections between the verses of revelation and the established theories of science. In the past, when science had not uncovered much of the facts and verses like those mentioned above needed explanations, some scholars would attribute meanings to these verses which were esoteric or arbitrary. At-Tabari, in the 10th century, had noticed such ambiguities about the then-inexplicable verses and commented, 'It is our duty to keep silent when we don't know.'

Although many scholars remained silent over such verses, they were still motivated by these and numerous other verses which contain phrases like – *...don't they think, ...don't they see, ... don't they hear,* and *... don't they reflect,* which encouraged investigation. These scholars started to think, see, hear, study, analyse and, in the process, discover. If now some scholars are using these verses as proof of authenticity of the Quran, in the past, starting from the time of the Prophet and the four *Rashidun* Caliphs (Righteous Caliphs), these verses had directed the Muslims into an incredible quest for scientific knowledge that had lasted for centuries.

Do they not carefully consider the Quran
Or are there locks upon their hearts. [47:24]

Rule of the Rashidun: The Righteous Caliphs

There was unbelief and paralytic incapacity in Madinah at the death of the Prophet. He had been the source of revelations, fount of knowledge and arbitrator of one and all issues. Suddenly, this vast source of information and the point of reference and guidance was gone. Madinah was still a new nation with loose groupings of different types of people who now were unsure what to do and where they belonged. And most of all there was this feeling that pervaded the senses – how could such a man die? Even the strong, stern and staunch Omar bin Khattab, for once, was bewildered and brought out his sword threatening anyone who would dare to say that the Prophet was dead. The warrior Ali went to his house to Fatema, the aristocratic Osman was tongue tied and did not know what to do. People hallucinated and simply fell down on the ground.

But one man stood firm – Abu Bakr. As he had been firm to accept Islam, during its first days, so he accepted the death of the Prophet. Abu Bakr had incredible wisdom and the power of vision. Long time ago in Makkah, he knew that it was time for the advent of a Prophet and thus, unlike others, was able to accept Islam and the Prophet without any hesitation. And when, during the final pilgrimage of the Prophet, the verse *'This day have I perfected for you your religion...'* was revealed, Abu Bakr knew the mission of the Prophet was over and, thus, the time of his departure near.

Abu Bakr was always a soft and compassionate person and while the Prophet was alive he kept a subdued profile. But when the Prophet died and everyone was reeling from the impact, Abu Bakr emerged from his shell and exposed the giant he was, the iron will and vision that he represented. He was the man who would dare to challenge the two greatest empires of the world – the Persians and the Romans – and deal them defeat after defeat.

As Umar stood with his bare sword in the Mosque, Abu Bakr entered and looked at the gathered people and said calmly, 'Listen to me, you people. Those who worship Mohammad, know Mohammad is dead. Those who worship God, know that God lives forever."

The assembly of people fell silent. Umar slumped down to his knees as the significance of what Abu Bakr had said dawned on him – the Prophet was dead. No matter how great or how beloved the man, he was dead. But the wisdom of Abu Bakr's words slowly emerged - the profound message lived on. Abu Bakr's words re-instilled and reinforced the infinite continuity of Islam in the heart of the people.

Then came the crucial time to elect a new leader, a regent or Caliph of the Prophet. Crucial because there arose an apprehension that the new nation of Islam would disintegrate if the correct leader was not chosen soon, as apostatising by some tribes had already started. If the Prophet was buried while Madinah was disintegrating it would become a political defeat in the eyes of the rest of the world and a great disrespect to the Prophet. It was crucial that the Muslims, at least, bury him together as one people under one Imam. Crucial also because the Prophet had not specifically mentioned who would be the leader after him. Had he nominated a successor, this would have been taken as the precedence by future leaders to nominate their own successors leading to a autocratic norm.

The Ansars gathered in their meeting place called *Saqifa Bani Sadah* in Madinah. There, Saad bin Ubaidah, a prominent Ansar leader, declared that an Ansar should be the Caliph (Representative of the Prophet to rule the Muslims) as they were the ones who had protected and given shelter to the Prophet and his Mahajir Companions after the Hijra. The capital city of Islam was Madinah and Islam had, in fact, spread from there. His words appealed to the Ansars. But this resolution had the potential to isolate the Ansars from the rest of the Muslims, specially the Makkans who were now staunch Muslims as well.

When the Ansars were on the verge of electing Saad bin Ubaidah as the Caliph, Abu Bakr along with Umar and Abu Ubaidah reached Saqifah Bani Sadah. Abu Bakr initiated a negotiation with them. His main concern was that the nomination of Caliph was an issue for all the Muslims and not only the Ansars. As a majority of tribes of Arabia were allied to the Quraish, they would more easily accept a Quraish as a leader and, thus, a Quraish Caliph was more likely to keep the nation united. The choice of leader was not only a matter of political expedience but the right of one and all the Muslims. He said to the Ansars, "No one can deny the excellence of your position as regards to religion. You were chosen by God to be the *Ansars* (helpers) of God's religion and the Messenger. The Prophet undertook the Hijra to come to you and a majority of his Companions and wives come from you. In your deeds you are only second to the very few Companions of the Prophet who joined Islam the earliest. So, if one of them is taken as a candidate, while you form the Council of the Companions there should be no arguments or obstinacy from you. No decision would be taken without your counsel."

There was much wisdom in the articulation of Abu Bakr. In fact, it was the earliest Companions who had brought Islam to Madinah and to the Ansars. They were most highly regarded by Muslims due to their knowledge of Islam, dedication to it and the sacrifices they had made from the very first days. But the Ansars were not ready to forego their rights as yet. After some debate they proposed that there be two *Amirs*, one for the Ansars and one for the Mahajirs.

Umar raised an objection, "Islam stands for unity. There is one God, one Prophet and one Quran and thus there will be only one Amir of Islam."

There began a hot altercation between Habab, an Ansar, and Umar. At this Abu Ubaidah intervened and said, "Ansars, you were the first to help Islam. Do not take the first step towards its disintegration."

Abu Bakr said, "God is our witness that we are not doing this for any selfish motive. This is only for the interest and solidarity of Islam." And as a proof of his motive he declared that he did not want to be the leader. "Let the candidate be either Umar or Abu Ubaidah".

It was then that Zaid bin Thabit, a prominent Ansar, rose and said, "The Prophet himself was from the Quraish. There is considerable logic in appointing one from them as his successor. God had chosen the Ansars to be helpers, and thus they should continue in their role."

Another Ansar leader supported this and said that the Ansars have achieved a superior position and stature in order to please God and obey the Prophet, "Let's not indulge in self aggrandisement. Let our reward be in the hand of God."

As a consensus emerged among those present, Abu Bakr proposed the name of Umar and Abu Ubaidah again. At this Umar jumped up and said, "Abu Bakr, how can Abu Ubaidah or I be preferred over you? You are the best of the Muslims, you are mentioned in the Quran as the *second of the two* in the cave during Hijra, when the Prophet was sick he nominated you to lead the prayers in his stead. You are the most precious to us. Stretch out your hand that we may declare allegiance."

Umar assisted Abu Bakr to stand and held his hands to declare allegiance. He was followed by Abu Ubaidah and all the other Ansars. Only Saad bin Ubaidah refrained. The next day, a large number of people and representatives from various regions gathered at the Prophet's mosque for the afternoon prayers. Umar stood up and declared to the assembly, "I had expected the Prophet would outlive us all. But he had completed his mission and God willed his return. He came from God and to God he has returned."

Umar continued, "The Quran is now our guidance. And also amongst us is Abu Bakr, the second of the two mentioned in the Quran, the most able to run our affairs."

Then he requested all to offer allegiance to Abu Bakr, to strengthen his hands and maintain the solidarity of Islam. The nomination of Abu Bakr was complete.

Abu Bakr

573 – 634

In 632, the simple man in a cloak took his place in the pulpit, a step lower then where the Prophet used to sit. He stretched out his slender hand to all present and they, one by one, gave allegiance to him.

Finally, he rose to address the assembly and said, "I swear by God that I had not coveted this position, never prayed to God for it. I only accept this to prevent any mischief adversely affecting Islam. In fact, an enormous responsibility has been conferred on me and I am not worthy of it. I had expected a much stronger person in this position."

He continued, "No doubt, I am your leader now, but I am in no way superior to you. So help me if I am right, correct me if I am wrong. Trust is trust and falsehood treason. The weak among you will be strong with me till, with God's will, their rights are vindicated. The strong among you will be weak with me till, with God's will, I have received what is due from them. Obey me as long as I follow God and his Prophet. If I disobey God and His Prophet, obey me not. Now rise for prayer. God's mercy be on you."

And thus Abu Bakr bin Abu Qahafa became the first Caliph of the Messenger of God. Von Kremar in *The Orient under the Caliphs* states that after Abu Bakr became the Caliph, "His household remained as unpretentious as ever. He had only one slave who after finishing the domestic work, made himself useful by cleaning the swords of the faithful." There were not many chores to do in the house of Abu Bakr, the Caliph.

Abu Bakr was, by nature, of an excellent disposition. The companions would at times compete with each other in doing good deeds. Umar had tried to out do Abu Bakr a number of times. He had, to fund a military expedition, brought half of his wealth to donate to the Prophet, only to find that Abu Bakr had given his whole fortune to the Prophet. When Umar went to help an old blind woman he found Abu Bakr had already given her all the help she needed. Abu Bakr surpassed all others in good deeds without even realising that others were competing with him.

The reign of Abu Bakr constituted of two major facets: keeping Islam exactly the way the Prophet had intended, prohibiting any form of modification or corruption, and the assimilation of the universal state that the Prophet had fashioned in Arabia. Though the selection of Abu Bakr had throttled the rebellion of many tribes and the probable confrontation between Madinah and Makkah, many other tribes from all around Arabia who had declared acceptance of Islam and allegiance to Madinah now apostatised. The state that had gradually formed during the 'year of deputation' started to disintegrate. The tribes used many pretexts to revoke their allegiance to Madinah and the economy of the state was ready to collapse due to the non-payment of the Zakaat tax. Some tribes said that their treaty was with the Prophet and on his death the treaty had been nullified. Others wanted to continue allegiance but without paying the Zakaat tax to the state. Some others simply changed their ways back to that of ignorant pagan days and gave no excuse at all.

Madinah, itself, was encircled by unpredictable and unreliable tribes who could attack at this time of weakness. The situation was delicate, similar to the early days of Islam when the Muslims had first migrated to Madinah. Many of the Muslims became concerned. Abu Bakr realised that some Muslims, in this juncture of weakness, were willing to compromise due to the need of security. But he also knew that the apostate tribes all over Arabia were hatching plans to destroy Madinah. The Muslims had to face this danger from a vantage point of strength. Any compromise will be taken as a sign of weakness.

It was in such difficult times that Abu Bakr took the responsibility of running the state. He had been many things in the past. He had been the constant companion, friend and advisor to the Prophet. He had been the Prophet's shadow from the very first day the Prophet had received his call. He had betrothed his daughter Ayesha to the Prophet. He had paid for the land on which the Prophet's mosque was built in Madinah. Even though he had fought in the battles valiantly, he was a sentimental person and was known to weep. But now, in times of tribulation, he revealed the metal of his fibre. Ayesha, at a later stage, would say, 'The burden that my father had to bear would have squashed a mountain.'

The historical Byzantine encroachment into Syriaic lands was considered an invasion by the Arabs. The Prophet had sent an emissary to the Syriaic lands who was killed by the Arab Christians who lived there. Those who had become Muslims were under threat as the Byzantines gave a standing order to their Arab allies that all those who became Muslims should be killed. So, in 629, the Prophet had sent an expedition there under the command of Zaid bin Harith. This expedition was not aimed at destroying the Byzantine Empire or encroaching into Byzantine land. It was to secure the Muslims living there and send a signal to the Byzantines not to harbour any imperial design over the Muslims as any such meddling in their internal affairs would not go unchallenged. But the arrogant Byzantines were not about to change their policies and that would lead to greater battles.

The army of Zaid that the Prophet had sent was only 3000 strong. The Byzantines in the meantime had sent a huge army to the region. Zaid and the Muslim army reached their destination to find a Byzantine army of over 100,000 that filled the horizon. This was an army the likes of which they have never seen in Arabia. In the war council some of the companions proposed that they should return and report the situation to Madinah. But Abdullah bin Rawaha said that, "O' believers, we have come to fight and be martyrs. We don't fight with numbers, we fight with the help of Allah. Either we are victorious or we are martyrs. Why go back?..." He gave an inspirational speech which motivated the whole army

The battle with the huge Byzantine army, who were also supported by some local tribes, had turned out to be a bloody affair for the Muslims. As fierce fighting progressed they were slowly being swallowed up by their opponents. Zaid, who was carrying the Muslim standard, was killed in action. According to the battle plan, the standard was picked by Jaafar bin Abu Talib. He died fighting. The standard was then picked up by Abdullah bin

Rawaha. He too fell fighting. There was no more battle plan. The Muslims chose Khaled bin Walid. He took the standard with much humility and then said, "Sufficient is Allah as disposer of affairs. O' Muslims the doors of heaven has been flung open". Then he and the army attacked with such ferocity that the Byzantine were taken aback. On that day Khaled broke nine swords fighting and was on his tenth sword when it became too dark to fight. From the disadvantageous position, by sheer tactics and bravery, he tore through, incising the Byzantines ranks, and took the Muslims from a point of annihilation to one of safety and stood at par again. Khaled knew it was not possible to keep on fighting such a huge army. In the night he rearranged the army position and gave them new flags, sent a regiment back to hide till daybreak and then to join the main army so the Byzantines would think re-inforcement were arriving. He also sent horsemen further back in the desert to stir up dust. In the morning the Byzantine saw new faces and flags and then they saw what appeared further reinforcement arriving. Then they saw dust rising from the desert. This made them confused. Khaled attacked and retreated. The Byzantines had lost a large number of their warriors and were totally confused as to what was happening. They did not push anymore and Khaled took this opportunity to return. That was end of the fighting. When the army returned to Madinah, Khaled was much praised. The Prophet bestowed on him the title of Al Saifullah, The Sword of God. The next year, the Prophet himself led another expedition to Tabuk, Syria. But for unknown reasons the Byzantine army failed to appear.

Just before his death the Prophet had ordered an army to march again to confront the situation in Syria. The army was under the command of the nineteen year old Usama, son of Zaid bin Harith. If the Muslims led a successful campaign Muslims there would live in security and Madinah would stamp their authority in the Syriaic region. On hearing of the Prophet's illness, the army had delayed their march and remained encamped in a place called *Jorf* just outside Madinah. On the death of the Prophet, Usama returned to Madinah for orders.

But the situation in Madinah had now changed. Around Madinah and in other areas of Arabia the tribes had apostatised. In this critical situation if the army left, Madinah itself would be left defenceless. Byzantine was not an imminent danger. Some of the Companions advised that the expedition be abandoned. But the Caliph was adamant, "I do not bear the authority to stop an army which the Prophet had ordered to march. Come what may, if Madinah falls, so it falls. If the Caliphate is destroyed, so be it. But the command of the Prophet stands!"

No one dared to argue with this kind of resolve. But some of the Companions maintained that if the army must march then there should be a change in its command. Usama was young. An experienced General should be appointed as its commander. Umar was asked to put this proposal to the Caliph. After hearing him patiently, Abu Bakr replied, "Umar, Usama was appointed by the Prophet. You want me to contradict the pronouncement of the Prophet? Does your tongue make such a request? How can I, the Caliph of the Prophet, rescind his order? Go and tell those who have sent you, as long as Abu Bakr lives he cannot commit such a sacrilege!"

Umar was embarrassed by this rebuke. He went back to those who had sent him and vented his anger on them. Umar was learning what was required to be a Caliph from Abu Bakr.

The Caliph ordered the army to depart. He personally went up to Jorf to bid them farewell. Before the army left he gave them instructions, "Let there be no treachery. Let there be no departure from the right path. Let there be no mutilation, no woman, child or old man killed. Do not damage or burn the date palm trees. Do not cut any tree which bears food for man or animal. Do not slay the camel herds, but for sustenance. Eat of what the people may bring to you, but eat in the name of God. Do not harm the monks in the churches, let them be."

Abu Bakr showed great respect for Christianity and Judaism and its true adherents. It was imperialism and inequity practiced by the Byzantines and Persians with which he was in conflict. Finally, the Caliph gave the command, "Advance in the name of God. Fulfil your mission. May God protect you from sword and disease."

As the army marched Abu Bakr walked with it for some distance. The Prophet used to do the same when he sent out armies. Usama, who was riding a horse said, "Caliph, permit me to dismount and walk along with you, or mount a horse yourself."

Abu Bakr replied, "Neither shall you dismount, nor I mount. You ride in the service of God. Every step I take with you, God will place that as a reward in my account."

It was the end of June, 632. The army reached the Syrian border in ten days and attacked the tribes that had fought alongside the Byzantine army against Zaid's army. Riding on his father's horse *'Sabah'* Usama searched and found the man who had killed Zaid. There was no torture or vengeance, just a quick execution. The Byzantine army did not appear. They, for their own reason, preferred not to engage the Muslims at that time. The tribes were bewildered and helpless and pledged allegiance to the Muslims and agreed to pay the appropriate taxes to the state instead of paying the Byzantines.

In the meantime, the dissident tribes around Madinah sent a delegation to the Caliph for new terms of allegiance. As the Prophet was dead, they considered their treaty with Islam terminated. Their chief demand was that they would continue to give allegiance to the Caliphate but would not pay the tax of Zakaat. Due to the tribes apostatising and revolting in different areas of Arabia the Caliphate was under a precarious situation. Companions including Umar advised that the terms of the tribes be accepted. With its army far away at the Byzantines doors Madinah was vulnerable. It would not be prudent to create enemies right at their own doorsteps at such a time. But the Caliph, the second of the two, was not just a pragmatic person but a visionary as well. He declared, "Islam is not a treaty with the Prophet, but an agreement with God. Thus allegiance with Islam never expires." He added, "Zakaat is a principle of Islam, not a political consideration that can be changed. I cannot do anything that would compromise Islam in any way. If this day I compromised on one issue, tomorrow there would be demands for more compromises."

Then he went back and addressed the delegation, "If even a rope that's used to tie a camel is due to the Caliphate as Zakaat, and you withhold it, know that I will fight for it. The consequences are immaterial. I am willing to face any adversity but I cannot compromise on the principles of Islam."

The delegation left sullen and aggravated. During their stay they had witnessed, with its army gone, the vulnerability of Madinah. The tribes decided to attack Madinah at this tactically favourable moment. They planned to gather in two fields, *Zul Hissa* and *Zul Kissa*, and attack at nighttime.

Abu Bakr had anticipated the whole stratagem. After the tribes left he asked all available adult males to gather at the mosque. He formed pickets under the commands of the elders who had remained in Madinah - Ali, Talha, Zubayr, Abdur Rahman bin Auf, Abdullah bin Masud and others. Pickets were placed all around Madinah with the members keeping constant vigil based on a time roster.

The scouts from Zul Hissa brought the information that the tribes were in motion and were expected to attack that very night. After night prayers the men spread out to their respective pickets around the city. Abu Bakr, at the head of a contingent, took up position facing Zul Hissa, the direction from where the attack was anticipated.

The dissident tribes had expected Madinah to be unaware and to offer no resistance. But as they attacked, the Muslims counter attacked. The tribes were themselves surprised and fell into disarray and soon started to retreat. Though small in number the Muslims gave them chase till they reached Zul Hissa. Here the tribes, being boosted by their reserves, made a stand. As a stratagem they threw water bags on the path of the camels on which Muslims were riding. This caused the camels to panic and become disordered. In the confusion the Muslims returned to Madinah.

The tribes assuming that was the end of fighting for the night retired to their two camps. But the Muslims regrouped in Madinah and led a fierce attack on the tribes in Zul Hissa. Many of the tribesmen fell while the rest fled to the other camp in Zul Kissa. The Muslims then attacked Zul kissa. The tribesmen were totally annihilated and many just ran away in confusion. By morning, Abu Bakr had won the battle. He decided to camp his troops in Zul Kissa under the command of Nowman bin Makran and himself returned to Madinah.

As Abu Bakr exhibited his intention and proved his mettle, many tribes started to send their deputations to express solidarity with him. But others now openly rebelled. The situation was no longer ambiguous or mystifying, friends were friends and foes were foes – all in the open. A large number of these apostate tribes gathered in a place called *Abraq*. The first act they performed was to fall upon the Muslims in their own tribes and horrendously torture them. Some were cut open by the sword, some were burnt, while others were thrown off cliff tops. The torture continued till all the Muslims of Abraq were dead. When the words reached Madinah, Abu Bakr was furious. For once, the man known to weep on sentimental issues vowed vengeance.

Usama returned to Madinah in August of 632 with funds from Zakaat and Jizya taxes. But more important was the fact that Arabia realised that the Muslims were still a force to reckon with and who were not afraid to challenge even the Byzantines.

Abu Bakr now decided it was time to go on the offensive against the apostate tribes. He ordered for the preparation for an expedition that he intended to lead. His Companions were wary about having the Caliph in the battle field. One of the Companions said, "Caliph of Prophet, do not endanger your life by leading the army yourself. If something happens to you, the tribes will take advantage of it. Appoint a General for the expedition. A General in not indispensable and can be replaced."

But Abu Bakr replied, "The holy Prophet himself had led campaigns. It befits his Caliph to do the same and lead the army in the name of God."

Upon reaching Abraq, Abu Bakr found a large tribal army already in battle formation. After the battle plans were laid, the Caliph ordered the charge. But the tribal forces withstood the attack. Then they counter attacked and the Muslim forces retreated. The tribesmen continued onwards recklessly and penetrated the Muslim ranks. Then the Muslims counter charged in which, of the three tribal General, two fell and the third was captured.

With its leadership removed, the tribal army disintegrated. A great victory was won and the land in the region was confiscated and turned into state pasture. This ended the immediate threat of tribes around Madinah. Abu Bakr returned to Madinah to look after the affairs of the state and started to organise his government.

The Caliphate under Abu Bakr was a people's government in the universal sense. A theocracy was out of the question as Islam did not even have a clergy or priesthood. The rule of Abu Bakr was constitutional, with the Quran being the basis of the constitution. The Caliph ran the state for the people but remained one of them with no pretences of being a ruler. He was not anyone special and the office of Caliph was a responsibility rather than a privilege for him. The people had access to the Caliph via the Companions or by personal audiences.

In governance and legislation, Abu Bakr was supported by the group of Companions all of whom resided in Madinah and who acted as a 'Parliament' (Shura). The core group of the Companions had been trained by the Prophet himself and each possessed extraordinary calibre. They came from various tribes and ethnic groups including Persians and Abyssinians and included slaves, aristocrats, destitutes, traders, warriors, illiterates and scholars who had all become equal in Islam and were now called the Companions of the Prophet. The Mosque of the Prophet in Madinah acted as the Parliament House, where all issues were open to debate until the solution were agreed upon.

The army was divided into eleven corps under eleven commanders. Each corp was given a tribal region to control or contain. Khaled bin Walid and Amr bin Al-Aas were two such commanders who would play major roles in the future.

Rise of the False Prophets

As Abu Bakr set up the state administration, threats to the state were still looming large. One such threat was from the rise of the false Prophets. The success in the establishment of Prophethood in Madinah caused pretenders to claim to be prophets as well. Though most of these dramas pattered out with time, a person by the name of Musailama grew very strong. He was based in the Yamama valley in central Arabia.

Musailama was an attractive and charismatic man with excellent oratory skills, and had developed a large following. When the Prophet was alive in Madinah, Musailama had sent him a letter which was addressed as follows:

> *From Musailama, Prophet of Allah, to Mohammad, Prophet of Allah.*
> *Peace be on you. I am prepared to share this mission with you. I shall have (control over) half the land and you shall have the other half. Even though the Quraish are an aggressive people."*

On Musailama's part this was a diplomatic move of mutual recognition. But he had misunderstood the truth in the mission of the Prophet and was appalled to get the following reply:

> *In the name of Allah, the Beneficent, the Compassionate.*
> *From Mohammad, the Prophet of Allah, to Musailama, the liar.*
> *Peace be upon whoever follows the guidance. God will bequeath the earth to whosoever of His servants He wishes and the final triumph will be for those who are careful of their duty to God.*

This issue remained unresolved in the lifetime of the Prophet. Later, when Abu Bakr became the Caliph, Sajjah, a beautiful woman from present day southern Iraq, claimed that she was a prophetess and started to look for tribal alliances. She gathered a good support from her mother's clan. She next wanted to muster support from her father's tribe, which was the Iraq based Bani Tamim. She met Malik bin Nuwera, chief of Bani Tamim, and spoke of an alliance. Malik thought he could use this alliance to overcome sections of his tribe that were opposed to him.

Sajjah was attracted to the handsome Malik. But Malik had a gorgeous and influential wife, Laila, which negated the possibility of any personal relationship between them. The combined forces of Sajjah and Malik had some initial successes against those opposed to Malik, but they were defeated in a place called *Nibha.* Peace was only established on the condition that the alliance between Malik and Sajjah to be repudiated.

This caused Sajjah and her followers to go to Yamama, the bastion of Musailama. Musailama, a shrewd person, immediately took Sajjah in his folds. He hosted a royal reception for her in which he suggested that they join forces to fight the Muslims. Sajjah agreed and both of them recited verses which had been 'revealed' to them. Then Musailama suggested that to be real partners they should become husband and wife. Sajjah was a passionate person and under the hypnotic charm of Musailama's personality agreed to marry him immediately. As a marriage gift Musailama told their followers that they need not pray during the morning or evening anymore.

After the marriage, Sajjah started to live in Musailama's camp. But after three days Musailama began to disregard her. This caused discontent to brew among her followers and her prestige ebbed. Her tribal people were unhappy that Musailama had swept her off her feet and she had given in so easily. Sajjah realised the political suicide she had committed and how Musailama had toyed with her. Disillusioned she returned to her home and lived a life of obscurity. Later, when Iraq came under the Muslims she converted to Islam with whatever followers she had left.

In the meantime, Khaled bin Walid had been carrying out campaigns against the apostates of central Arabia. He won his battles, one after another, including one against Taleaha, another pretender to Prophethood. After defeating Taleaha and completing the military commission set for him by the Caliph, he decided to march against the apostates of the Bani Tamim. This led to a series of confusing events. First, the Ansar contingent refused to go as the Caliph had not commissioned them to fight the Bani Tamim. Khaled said they were free to go back and he would press on with the others irrespective. But, later, the Ansars decided to join him. As Khaled marched, a deputation from Bani Tamim met him and brought him the Zakaat. But since half of the clans of Bani Tamim had apostatised while the other half had remained Muslims, Khaled decided to press on to personally ensure all was well there.

The Caliph had, previously, informed all the tribes that if they see any Muslim army approaching they should in a loud voice pronounce the *Adhan*, the call to prayers, which would indicate that they have not apostatised and thus would not be harmed. But as Khaled's corp approached the Banu Tamim, neither was there an army prepared to fight them nor any Adhan could be heard. Furthermore, the chief Malik bin Nuwera was found to be absconding. That cast a doubt in Khaled's mind that Malik probably belonged to the apostate group many of whom were still at large. After foraging, Khaled's soldiers found Malik and his wife Laila and that night, after all had retired, Malik and his male companions were killed. The entire tribe surrendered after the death of Malik.

After the death of the Prophet, many tribes led by provincial leaders started to join Musailama in Yamama. To them a 'live' Prophet was of more significance than a dead one. Musailama grew strong and due to his open hostility towards Islam and aspirations of destroying it, Abu Bakr thought it prudent to actively tackle the situation. Abu Bakr sent two corps under the commands of Ikrama bin Abu Jahl and Shurahbil bin Hasanah. He commanded that the attack on Musailama be carried out by both the corps together. Ikrama reached the Yamama valley first. In his injudicious enthusiasm Ikrama decided not to wait for Shurahbil and attacked Musailama's army alone. His corp retreated after considerable loss. On receiving this news Abu Bakr was considerably distressed. He ordered Ikrama not to return to Madinah but to proceed to South Arabia and take up engagements with apostates there. There Ikrama was much more successful.

When Shurahbil arrived he too did not stop to consider the situation or wait for Ikrama's replacement. Rashly, he attacked Musailama with the same end result. With these two victories Musailama achieved super human status. His followers started to believe that he was indeed a Prophet and their numbers swelled.

The Caliph, in Madinah, decided it was time to wield the Sword of God. An army of fifteen thousand marched under Khaled's command. The army included seasoned warriors and advisors like Abu Dujana the famous warrior of the battle of Uhud, Muawiah who was destined to establish the Umayyad Dynasty, Abdur Rahman son of Abu Bakr and Abdullah son of Umar. Abu Bakr policy was against sending the veterans of the battle of Badr in military expeditions as they were all now men of great knowledge and wisdom. But he made an exception and let the veterans join this army. Women also joined the army, one of them being Umme Ammarah, who had fought in the Battle of Uhud. Musailama had killed her son for becoming a Muslim.

The Muslim army marched for Yamama. But Musailama with an army of forty thousand intercepted them in a place called *Akraba*. The two armies went into battle formation and then clashed in the desert. Waves of attack and counter attack took place. Meantime, a dust storm started to blow. The air blew towards the Muslims causing dust to fall in their eyes. Taking advantage of the situation Musailama increased the pressure on the Muslims. Fighting desperately the Muslims retreated from several fronts. Some of Musailama's warriors even reached Khaled's tent while Khaled was directing the battle at the head of a thousand strong cavalry elsewhere.

At the end of the first day of battle Musailama's army was in rejoicing mood. The day had favoured them. As the next day started, their elation put them on the offensive. With Musailama in the centre, his army started to go round like a whirlpool. As the battle raged, Khaled waited patiently with his cavalry. The centre of the battle shifted and finally the two armies came face to face in a headlong manner. This was disadvantageous for the smaller army.

Musailama's army attempted to utilise this advantage and made the final push to bring things to culmination. It was then that Khaled made his move. In a furious gallop he took his cavalry tangentially away from the battle field, then turned to outflank the desperately fighting armies and then moved in and attacked the very mound from which Musailama was directing his army. In the furious charge Khaled totally disregarded personal safety plunging right through enemy lines. The boldness and the speed of the attack left Musailama's army bewildered. Musailama's bodyguards fought desperately but in vain. All of his Generals fell under this ferocious attack. In one blinding stroke Khaled had eliminated Musailama's command staff and totally turned the battle to his favour.

With the fall of his Generals, Musailama lost his nerve and retreated with a significant part of his army to a nearby fortified garden. Some of the Muslims scaled the walls and opened a door through which the Muslim army poured in. Musailamah's demoralized army was systematically cut down. Finally Wahsi, the slave who had killed Hamza in Uhud and later became a Muslim, and Abdullah, a son of Umme Ammarah, the warrior lady who had fought in Uhud to protect the Prophet, killed Musailama.

Musailama's tribe formally surrendered. This was, so far, the bloodiest battle fought by the Muslims. Musailama army lost seven thousand men, while the Muslims lost twelve hundred of their fighters. Though the victory was great the loss of life was also painful. Everyone in Madinah was affected by the loss of relatives. Among the prominent martyrs were renowned companions like Abu Hudaifa and Abu Dujana.

Having won the most important battle in Arabia, Khaled celebrated it in his own eccentric style. He married the daughter of a detained chieftain. After the battle this chieftain, Maja, actually tricked Khaled into an agreement. He had dressed all the women of his clan in warrior armours and asked them to take up positions on the battle stations of their settlement. Then he went to Khaled and told him that his people would not surrender unless Khaled agreed to incorporate certain terms into the surrender agreement. It had been an exhaustive battle and when Khaled observed, from a distance, what appeared to be a mass of warriors he agreed to their terms of surrender. After the surrender, he found that the 'warriors' were, in fact, women and old men. He turned to Maja and said, "You have tricked me!"

Maja said, "I did what I had to do in order to safeguard my people." Khaled had wanted the hand of his daughter in marriage, probably, as compensation and an alliance with the tribe.

The Caliph was relieved at the removal of the threat to Madinah from Central Arabia but was saddened by the deaths of so many people. When he heard of Khaled's marriage he was much angered. The Caliph wrote him a letter:

O' son of Khaled's mother,
What has become of you? You vault to wedlock while the desert around you is still wet with the blood of a thousand martyrs?.....

The indirect reference to Khaled in the letter was significant. It was a censure in itself and also a reminder to Khaled that he was the son of a woman. In the same letter the Caliph also wanted an explanation as to how Khaled could let Maja trick him. Khaled replied everything in a detailed letter but still the Caliph was disapproving.

Some Companions in Madinah then approached the Caliph and said that Khaled was not just the best General in the whole world but also the best warrior. He did not just command his warriors from a tent, he also led the charge. Every day in the course of the battle and every time he charged through the enemy lines he faced death a hundred times. Every time he came out of a battle it was almost as if he was given a new lease of life. His marriage, in a way, was a celebration of the new lease. They said that every time Khaled went into battle he sought martyrdom. It was not his fault that martydom avoided him while others around him fell. The Caliph was finally pacified and decided not to take any action against him.

With the victory of Yamama, Madinah emerged as the undisputed power in Arabia. When a delegation from Musailama's tribe visited the Caliph, he asked about Musailama's teachings. A member of the delegation recited a verse, which Musailama had claimed to have been revealed to him,

O' Frog, you are holy.
Neither you dirty the water
Nor you prevent the drinker.
The world is half ours and half Quraish's
Though the Quraish are a cruel people.

On hearing this verse the Caliph's remark was, "All praise to God. But is this divinity? There is nothing inspirational about it. What great depths had he dragged you to?"

The Mushaf

An important issue arose after Yamama. The Quran had been memorized verbatim by a large group of people known as the Huffaz. Others, like Zaid bin Thabit, had written down the same under the guidance of the Prophet. But a complete serialised compilation had not been authorised in written form. In the Yamama battle many of the Huffaz died. Umar raised the point that if all of the Huffaz were to die, the Book of God, at least a significant part of it, would be lost. He told Abu Bakr that there was a need for an official compilation of the Quran. But Abu Bakr, considering that both oral and written forms were available, negated this proposal stating that the Prophet had not asked for a compilation of the Quran, so he would not either.

But Umar differed and continued to press the point that as revelations of the Quran was an on going process during the lifetime of the Prophet the question of compiling it then had not arisen. Now that the Quran was complete and revelations have ceased, it was imperative that it be collected and compiled into a single volume.

This reasoning appealed to Abu Bakr. He called Zaid bin Thabit, who had been the principle scribe of the Prophet, and entrusted the work of compilation to him. Zaid was overwhelmed by the importance and significance of the work. The Quran had to be correct not just verse by verse but word by word and alphabet by alphabet. The Prophet had also cautioned that the words of God, or the revelations, should not be mixed up with his own words of counsel. Zaid, recognising the ramifications involved, said, "It would be easier to displace a mountain from one place to another." But he had been the chief secretary and scribe of the Prophet and undertook the commission.

Under Umar's direction he collected all the material of the Quran. Zaid did not have the authority to write down anything just by himself, even though he knew it in full being the chief scribe of the Prophet. He had to collect all the information of the Quran from all the known sources. He worked with the Companions who had written down the Quran and with the group of Huffaz who had memorised it during the lifetime of the Prophet. He had to verify that the written pieces given to him had, in fact, been written in front of the Prophet and for each such piece two witnesses were needed to give evidence. After much hard work and deliberation he produced the first compiled manuscript of the Quran known as the *Mushaf*. Abu Bakr, himself a Hafez, checked the Mushaf thoroughly and finally approved it. He took it into his personal custody. Upon his death, this copy was passed on to the next Caliph, Umar.

Meanwhile, in the war efforts, while Khaled had won Central Arabia other corps were engaged in various other regions. Ikrama after leaving Yamama in Central Arabia carried out successful campaigns in Yemen, Hadramaut and Oman subduing the apostate tribes in those regions. Bahrain had apostatised and had supported Musailama in Yamama. Thus a campaign was undertaken under the leadership of another commander named Al-Hadrami. Bahrain lay on the far eastern side of Arabia near Persia and the campaign was expected to be difficult. But it became a cause of great concern when Imperial Persia sided with the apostates and gave them considerable assistance. Irrespective of that, in the battle of Bahrain the Muslims prevailed. Finally, all of Arabia was free of apostasy.

But in the campaign for Bahrain, Abu Bakr was upset by the Persian involvement and realised that the Empires, Persian and Roman Byzantine, would never rest neutral to the rise of the Muslims of Arabia even if the Muslims were to remain within the bounds of the desert. The empires had always claimed the northern Arab lands which were under their occupation. A united and strong Arabia would not be acceptable to them as their occupation would come under challenge.

The War on Imperialism

By virtue of its very anti-imperialist nature, Islam became a target for the empires. On the one hand, Islam was asking the established powers to submit to universalism, on the other, it was fashioning the weak, ignorant and oppressed into a cohesive force. This was against the interests of the established powers whose institution relied on the schisms, weaknesses and inequalities of humanity. It was quite clear that the imperialist forces would attempt to defame, de-stabilise and destroy the power of Islam. Abu Bakr knew that in the past the empires, to protect their interest, had employed direct intervention using armies as well as indirect manipulations using agent provocateurs.

With Persia's interference in Bahrain and the continuing Byzantines threat to execute Syriaics who had converted to Islam, it became a military exigency to look into the Persian and Byzantine affairs thoroughly. The Romans had occupied the Syrian Levantine, Jerusalem and Egypt. The Persians had fought the Romans for the control of these regions and in fact extended their rule up to Yemen. Madinah and Makkah had not been in their targets because one was an oasis and the other a market city in the middle of the desert. But now Madinah has become very significant politically. The distant discerning eyes of the two Empires were watching Madinah very carefully. It was imperative that some action had to be taken before the empires struck seizing a time of weakness of the new Caliphate. For Abu Bakr the right path for the Muslims lay not in 'conquering' any of these regions and become a substitute imperial power, but the *fatah* or opening of the regions to human universality and knowledge.

Abu Bakr took a three point approach to deal with the imperial powers. First, the inimical ruling powers be invited to accept the ideas of human universality. If they agreed to accept Islam they were no longer imperial and the existing ruling establishment would continue to rule. The second option was that they would be asked to pay the *Jizya* tax to Madinah. If that proposal failed then last step would be that the establish power would have to be removed by force. After that the state would remove all the pre-existing taxes that the people paid to the empires and implement the Zakaat in its place. This would ensure that the people would no longer be subject to another human being but only to God. People of those regions would not be harmed or coerced. If they remained firm in their own religion, they had the right to do so but would have to pay the Jizya tax instead of Zakaat. They would still be allowed to lead their own lives and follow their own religion in safety and harmony.

Abu Bakr understood that the vital acceptance of Islam by non-Muslims had to be due to its progressive ideas not due to its swords. Islam did not allow forcing people to convert. A very important aspect was that the economic and social conditions of the people 'opened' must improve and be better than it was before the opening by Islam. The Muslims were not to be a subjugating force but a liberating one. Thus Abu Bakr sent his army to the old and unequal world with the Quran, the book of guidance, knowledge and universality, in one hand and the sword in the other.

The Persian Front

In February 633, Muthanna, chief of the Bani Bakr tribe from north-eastern Iraq, came to see the Caliph. Taking a band from his tribe he had made raids on Persian held 'Iraqi' territories. A number of times they had struck and vanished back into the desert. Muthanna informed Abu Bakr that the state of affairs of the Persian region was in disarray. And due to persecution significant number of people there would welcome freedom from the Persian yoke.

Abu Bakr called forth the Council of the Companions. The situation with regards to the two Empires, Persia and Byzantine, were discussed. After deliberations, it was decided that a military campaign be carried against Persian occupation of Arab lands. This was a colossal decision. There already had been skirmishes with the Romans in the past and now this meant taking on both the empires by the fledgling Muslim power coming from the resource-less desert, where there weren't even shadows to hide behind in case the campaign was unsuccessful. But this mission had one powerful and indomitable idea – Universalism. All were equal under one omnipotent God, and this very idea was absent in the material based structure of the empires. Muthanna left for the Iraqi front with necessary aid and provision and the promise that a Muslim army would soon follow. Khaled, encamped in Yamama, received orders from the Caliph to begin the war against the Persians in Uballa, a Persian district headquarter near the confluence of the Euphrates and Tigris.

This region was strategically very important. Uballa was the gateway of Iraq being the main port as well as a junction of many land routes. The Persian governor was an arrogant and haughty man named Hormuz. He was skilful in his imperial administration and a veteran General. He was a 'Lakh Dirham' official and wore a bejewelled coronet that was worth 100,000 (Lakh) dirham.

Khaled reached the Iraqi front with his army and was joined by four other corps arriving from various regions including the one led by Muthanna. Khaled issued a letter to Hormuz.

Submit to Islam and be safe.
Or pay Jizya and be protected.
Else you can blame only yourself
for I come with a people who desire death
as ardently as you desire life.

Hormuz did not take much notice of the letter. He marshalled his large army and marched for Kazima, which was on the route between Yamama and Uballa. His tactic was to move the battle away from Uballa. But Khaled, the master tactician, made his first move. He took his army off route and went to Hufair, a place nearer to Uballa.

When Hormuz received intelligence he hurried to Hufair. On reaching Hufair, he found Khaled had already moved his army to Kazima. Hormuz again returned to Kazima. By this time his army was totally confused and exhausted. Khaled did not give them time to recover and engaged them. As the armies faced each other, Khaled killed Hormuz in a duel and in the battle that followed the demoralised Persian army was demolished. Uballa fell without any resistance.

Muthanna with his corp seized *Hisn ul Mar'at* – The Fort of the Lady. This fort was held by a Persian Princess Qamarzad, who was related to the Emperor. Muthanna offered her the standard options, the same as Khaled had offered to Hormuz. She preferred the first one and became a Muslim. Muthanna proposed to her and she accepted his proposal.

The next battle was with another Lakh Dirham General named Qarin bin Quryana in a place called Mazar, which was also in eastern 'Iraq'. Qarin deployed his army with the river behind it, so that Khaled's outflanking manoeuvre would become ineffective. Khaled deployed his army in three groups, the centre and two flanks. Duels were fought in front of each group. Three of the main Persian commander died including Qarin. In the subsequent battle the Muslims won over the leaderless Persians. These battles were bigger then those fought before and the Persian army carried a lot of wealth, and thus more *Ghanima*, war booty, were falling into Muslim hands.

After these defeats, the Emperor Ardhasheer ordered two huge Persian armies to be deployed against the Muslims. One was under Bahman the Commander-in-chief of Persia and the other under General Andarzaghar. The second army was joined by Arab auxiliaries of Iraq and the remnants of Qarin's army totalling about thirty thousand.

Khaled force-marched to reach the second army before it could meet with the main army of Bahman. With a force of ten thousand he won this battle in a place called Walaja. The duel before this battle was amazing. The Persian champion was a giant known as 'Hazaar Mard' i.e. a man having the strength of a thousand men. When the Hazaar Mard sent out his challenge Khaled himself stepped forward. He looked puny in front of the giant. But he started off with amazing dexterity and with one heavy blow fell the giant to the ground within the first few moments of the duel.

In another nearby region called *Ulleis* Khaled fought a very fierce battle. Here the Persians and their Christian Arab allies gave a very good account of themselves. But at the end seventy thousand of them died. Khaled said, "At Mauta, nine swords broke in my hand as I fought. But I have never seen an army like the Persians and no army as tough as the Persians of Ulleis."

The Caliph had set a place called Hirah as the final target for the Persian expedition, which meant Eastern and Central 'Iraq' would be under Muslim rule. Hirah fell without any contest. By the time Khaled reached Hirah the Persian Emperor Ardhasheer had died. Due to the succession dispute there was no army to stop him. The city was taken but four citadels of Arab Christians remained locked up and they refused to surrender. After a siege they were ready to talk terms. A peculiar dialogue is said to have taken place between Khaled and Abdul Maseeh, one of the Christian chiefs, on the occasion of surrender. Before starting to discuss the terms of surrender, Khaled asked him a series of questions.

Khaled, "How many years have you seen?"
Abdul Maseeh, "Two hundred."
Khaled, "What is the most wonderful thing you have witnessed?"
Abdul Maseeh, "A village between Damascus and Hirah. A woman goes from Hirah to the village with only a single loaf of bread."
Khaled, "Have you gained anything from your old age? You do not even know where you come from."
Abdul Maseeh, "I definitely know where I come from."
Khaled, "Where from are you?"
Abdul Maseeh, "From the spin of my father."
Khaled, "Then where are you going to."
Abdul Maseeh, "To the front."
Khaled, "Where does that lead to?"
Abdul Maseeh, "To the end."
Khaled, "Where do you stand?"
Abdul Maseeh, "On the earth."
Khaled, "In what are you?"
Abdul Maseeh, "In my clothes."
Khaled, "Do you at all understand me?"
Abdul Maseeh, "Yes."
Khaled, "The earth destroys its fools. But the intelligent defeats earth. I suppose your people know you better than me."
Abdul Maseeh, "It is the ant, not the camel that knows what is in the hole."
Khaled, "Tell me something you recall."
Abdul Maseeh, "I recall the time Chinese ships sailed behind these citadels."
Khaled, "I give you the options to accept Islam or pay Jizya."
Abdul Maseeh, "We do not wish to fight you. We will pay the Jizya and follow our own religion."
As the old sage got ready to depart after the signing of the pact, Khaled noticed a pouch, "What's in the pouch?"
"Poison."
"Why do you have poison?"
"I feared this meeting would not turn out the way it has. I could not bear to see horrors befall my people."

After Hirah, Khaled decided to press for western 'Iraq', which was still under Persian rule. In June, 633 he reached Anbar, the headquarters of the western Sabat District. It was located on high grounds and was very well fortified, protected by walls and a large, deep moat. Even as the Muslims laid a siege around it, the height of the fortification made the Persians within feel non-vulnerable. From on top of the fort walls they stood looking down, without any show of concern, at the Muslim army far below.

Khaled asked the archers to let loose a huge volley of arrows at the Persians. As the Persians tried to see what was happening, many of them lost their eyes. Thus, this battle came to be known as the 'Battle of the Eye.'

Khaled chose a location where the moat was shallowest. He asked all the weak and old camels with the army be killed and dumped there. Soon, to the horrors of the Persian, a bridge of animal flesh and bone was formed. The army, under the cover of the archers, charged the fort itself. The Persians were seized with panic, all that was now left for the Muslims to do was shatter the gates and take Anbar and claim its movable properties as *Ghanima.*

But the Persians offered surrender and was accepted by Khaled. Under the terms the Persians were given safe passage and left only their weapons behind. While the Persian auxiliaries, who were Christian Arabs, decided to pay Jizya and were allowed to settle down with all their rights and properties intact.

Battle after battle, Khaled progressed at a breathtaking speed through Persian dominions - Always at numerical disadvantage, always a brave warrior, always a superb General unfolding strategies upon strategies, and always achieving victories. The Caliph called him the 'Lion' of the Muslims saying, "Mothers are yet to give birth to men like Khaled."

The Byzantine Front

A Muslim garrison was established on the Syriac borders of the Byzantine Empire. This garrison was commanded by a commander called Khaled bin Sayeed. Madinah had permitted him to reconnoitre into the Syriac regions, but not to get involved in any conflict with the Byzantines. In January 634, Khaled ventured into Byzantine-Syria. As he progressed the Byzantine army that was in the region retreated tactically setting a trap. Khaled pushed in further to understand what was happening. But once, he had penetrated far enough so that he was no longer in touch with his base camp, the Byzantines attacked furiously surrounding the Muslim contingent. The Muslim contingent was on the verge of obliteration and to make things worse Khaled's son died in the battle. This deflated him totally and he fled from the battle field. Ikrama took up the command and somehow retreated with the contingent.

The Caliph, after performing a pilgrimage in Makkah, raised an army for the Byzantine Front. Twenty one thousand men were divided equally into four corps under the commands of Amr bin Al-Aas, Abu Ubaidah, Shurabil bin Hasanah and Yazeed bin Abu Sufiyan. (This Yazeed was the paternal uncle of another Yazeed, son of Muawiah, who would trigger one of the greatest tragedies in history.) The overall commander was Abu Ubaidah, but these corps could act independently if required.

Before the corps marched for the Byzantine front, the Caliph instructed the commanders, "In your march, do not be hard to yourself or your men. Do not be insensitive to your men and officers, consult all matters with them. Be just and renounce all evil and tyranny. Unjust people cannot truly prosper or be victories over their enemies. When you meet the enemy, face them. Do not turn your backs to them except for strategic movements. One who turns and flees earns the wrath of God, and hell will be his abode. Do not kill the women, children or the aged. Do not kill any beasts, except for sustenance. And do not break any pacts that you make with other people. You will come upon Christian hermits in monasteries. Let them be as they are and do not harm their monasteries. In all your actions fear God. Invoke his aid in difficult times. Now, in the name of God, advance! May God protect you."

On the other side of the frontier, Heraclius the Emperor of Byzantium decided to smother the four corps which were significantly small by Byzantine standards. He marshalled an army well exceeding a hundred thousand soldiers. Abu Ubaidah, realising Heraclius' plan, wrote a letter to Abu Bakr requesting re-enforcement. Summing up the situation, the Caliph commanded Khaled bin Waleed the 'Sword of Islam' to leave Iraq for the Byzantine-Syria front as soon as possible. In Hirah, Persia, the army of Khaled was divided into two corps. One half of the army remained in Iraq under the command of Muthanna. The other half marched with Khaled for Syria.

Instead of taking the usual known route, Khaled plunged through the dangerous, barren and unfrequented desert to reach Syria quickly. This path was expected to save them time if they could cross it. In the sandy shade-less desert under the constant heat of the burning sun the army's water supply finished on the third day. On the fourth day the old camels were slaughter and the water stored in their stomachs were given to the horses. By the end of the fourth day the men reached the limit of human endurance. On the fifth day, the army arrived at a place where the guide had predicted the presence of a spring. But no spring was to be found. As desperation mounted among the men, Khaled ordered exploratory diggings in the region. Finally, the spring was found. Taking their fill of water, the army gathered food from an oasis that lay further ahead on their way and then marched on taking over a number of Byzantine garrisons and Syrian towns. Twenty miles from Damascus the army halted at a pass. This pass came to be known as '*Saniyat Ul-Uqab*' or the Pass of the Eagle for here Khaled unfurled and fluttered his standard – the black eagle. Khaled has arrived in Byzantium.

Meanwhile, Abu Ubaidah and Shurabil had occupied the Hauran district in the Byzantine front. The town of Busra was in such a location that an army from it could potentially surprise the Muslim army from behind. Shurabil with four thousand warriors moved to lay siege on Busra to diffuse that threat. During his march to Damascus, Khaled was informed about Shurahbil's campaign. He took stock of the situation and changed his plan. He sent a message to Abu Ubaidah that instead of going to Damascus he was setting off for Busra.

Meantime Shurahbil had reached Busra and immediately faced disaster. On seeing that the Muslim army was greatly out numbered, the Byzantines instead of waiting for a siege launched a spirited attack on them. The sheer intensity of the attack plus the numerical superiority made the Muslims army dither and reel back. The situation grew from bad to worse till it became critical and Shurahbil was reduced to praying for help. When the end seemed near, out of nowhere Khaled's army materialised. The sight of his fluttering standard was enough for the Byzantine to hurriedly return to the fort and close the gates.

The next day was to be even more amazing. Eventually, the two armies again came to face each other. The call for the duel was given. Romanus the Byzantine commander and Khaled stepped forward. But instead of fighting, Romanus went to Khaled and submitted to Islam and joined the Muslims flanks. Again the demoralized Byzantines returned to the fort. But during the night a small band of Muslims along with Romanus and Abdur Rahman, the son of Abu Bakr, penetrated the fort through a subterranean route. Dashing to the main gate they opened it. The Muslim army entered the fort. There was some futile resistance, but soon most put down their swords and were spared.

Abu Ubaidah, a senior and respected companion, came to know that Khaled had been made the commander in chief of the Syrian campaign and he was the second in command. He approached Khaled and said, "Father of Sulaiman, I have gladly received the command of the Caliph appointing you the Commander-in-Chief. I bear no resentment as I am well informed about your expertise in matters of warfare."

Khaled said, "If it were not the command of the Caliph I would not have accepted commission over you. I declare you are much higher than me in Islam. I am one of the Companions of the prophet. But it was you that the Prophet called 'The trusted one of the nation.'"

Heraclius was furious due to the defeat in Busra. He ordered all the contingents from the garrisoned forts of Syria to assemble in a place west of Jerusalem called Ajnadeen. Khaled had laid siege on Damascus, but when he learned that a huge Byzantine force was gathering in Ajnadeen, the siege was lifted and the army moved away in formation for Ajnadeen. Taking advantage of this the force of few thousand horseman and infantry from Damascus fell on the rearguard of the Muslim army. The sudden attack from the back caused the rearguard, which was lagging behind the main army, to falter and retreat loosing many men. The Byzantines were able to capture a number of women and forced them into tents. They started to gather booty and at the end of which were expecting to take the women to Damascus. But the women rallied against the soldiers. Led by Khaula, a very pretty woman and sister of the Muslim commander Zarrar, they tore the tent poles and decided to face the Byzantines. As the soldiers tried to get hold of them, the women fought back and attacked the soldiers. Peter the commander addressed Khaula, maintaining a distance, "Surrender, and I will ensure your safety and I shall marry you myself."

Khaula retorted, "You Byzantine dog, how dare you! I will die before I marry you."

Peter asked his men to disarm the women. But as the women kept on defying them, Peter finally ordered his men to draw swords. Then suddenly the Muslims were on them. When the information about the attack on the rearguard reached Khaled, he was on the vanguard. He took some of his men and went to the rear as fast as they could and soon they were upon the Byzantines. In the confusion the Byzantine tried to flee. As Peter ran he found a Muslim warrior blocking his way. When he was told that this was Zarrar the brother of Khaula, he pretended to be chivalrous, "She is your sister. I present her to you." But the act was in vain as Zarrar impaled him with his lance. Khaled's army for the first time struck the Byzantines with vengeance. Only a hundred or so returned to the safety of the city.

Under Khaled's command, all the Muslim forces operating in Syria assembled and camped in Ajnadeen. Forty thousand camped some distance away from the gigantic camp of more than 100,000 Byzantines. During the last inspection of his army Khaled said, "Comrades, you face the biggest army that the Byzantines could amass. If you win this fight all victory is yours. Fight fearlessly and remain resolute in the principles of Islam. Don't turn your back for God sees you. Close your ranks, think clear and be valiant."

Addressing the female contingent he said, "Sisters, ensure your deeds be sanctioned by God. Today your actions will go down in history. I have no doubt you will give splendid account of yourself. If the Byzantines attack you, show them your mettle and the heroic stuff you are made of. Should you find a Muslim deserter, reproach him and will him on to his duty to face the enemy. Infuse into the men a spirit so that they stand steadfast on the face of greatest of adversity."

The commander Zarrar was sent on reconnoitring duties around the enemy camp to gather intelligence. He took off his uniform and bare to his waist went into the Byzantine camp and reached the very centre unnoticed. On his way back he was detected and a group of horsemen chased him. But he escaped after clashing with some of the horsemen.

The Muslim army was deployed in three groups, the centre and two wings, each with a commander. Khaled kept a special action reserve force with himself. This group included Amr bin Al-Aas, Zarrar bin Al-Azwar and Abdullah bin Umar.

The recounts of Khaled's triumphs had preceeded him and he was a larger than life figure. His presence had changed the psychology of the war. At the last moment before the battle begun, an old man dressed in black emerged from the Byzantine ranks and offered Khaled and his army money and gifts if the Muslims withdrew. Khaled declined. Then Zarrar stepped forward and gave a battle cry:

I am the death to the pale ones
I am the killer of Byzantines
I am scourge sent for you
I am Zarrar bin Al-Azwar.

He then fought and defeated, one by one, the Byzantine champions. Then Khaled ordered the charge, and the battle rang out. The whole day the battle raged furiously. In the evening the armies disengaged.

A large number of Byzantines had died during the day's battle and Werdan, their Commander-in- Chief, was distraught. He knew that Khaled's name struck terror in all armies. Khaled's very presence had changed the morale of the armies. Therefore, he decided, the way to win this war would be to take Khaled out of the equation.

Werdan sent an emissary to Khaled proposing peace parley the next morning. In the appointed place, he planted a hidden group that would suddenly come out and dispose Khaled during the parley. The emissary went to Khaled with offer of the peace parley. But as he stood under the gaze of the imposing Khaled he was so overwhelmed that he divulged the truth. Zarrar was given the responsibility of taking care of the hidden group.

The next morning, at the appointed place, Werdan came to meet the Muslims and again offered some money to Khaled to withdraw. As Khaled ridiculed that offer Werdan gave a signal and from behind a hillock ten Byzantine warriors appeared and moved towards them. But amazingly they fell upon Werdan. It was Zarrar and his men who had disposed the hidden Byzantines soldiers and appeared in their uniforms.

The battle soon begun and the Muslims charged furiously driving wedges into the Byzantine ranks. The demoralised Byzantines started to fell in large numbers. Soon Qubuqlar, the new commander in place of Werdan, also fell. Ultimately, with nearly half of their soldiers dead the Byzantines surrendered. Khaled sent the message of victory to the Caliph. Then he marched on to Damascus to complete the unfinished siege.

A graphic picture is painted of the approach of the Muslim army in Damascus by the eighteen century historian, Edward Gibbon, in *The decline and fall of the Roman Empire.*

> 'The sad tidings of the fall of Ajnadeen were carried to Damascus by the speed of grief and terror, and the inhabitants beheld from the walls of the city the return of the Muslim heroes of Ajnadeen. Amr bin Al-Aas led the vanguard at the head of nine thousand horsemen; the bands of the Muslims followed each other in formidable review; and the rear was closed by Khaled in person, with the standard of the black eagle. To the activity of Zarrar, he entrusted the commission of patrolling round the city with two thousand horses, of scouring the plain and of intercepting all succour or intelligence. The rest of the Arabian chiefs fixed in their respective stations before the seven gates of Damascus and the siege was renewed with vigour and confidence'.

The siege of Damascus began on the August 21, 634 CE. The Caliph Abu Bakr died two days later on the August 23. The siege continued till fall of Damascus in September 634 during the Caliphate of Umar.

During the final night of the siege Khaled and a select band scaled the walls and opened a gate in the city wall. He had conquered the city. But Thomas, the son-in-law of the Emperor and commander of the Byzantine forces in Damascus, was alerted that Khaled's army had breeched the eastern gate and broken their defence. He immediately went out of the western gate and surrendered to an unsuspecting Abu Ubaidah on the usual terms that is accepted when the city had not fallen. Abu Ubaidah agreed and proclaimed a general amnesty to the Byzantines.

But when Khaled came to know of this he realised that he had been cheated of the Ghanimah which was now rightfully his possession. He refused to maintain amnesty as he had won the fort. The Muslim commanders met to discuss the issue. But in a council much to the chagrin of Khaled all agreed to overrun Khaled's objection and decided that the amnesty must be upheld.

Thomas, his wife and the Byzantine nobility left immediately along with their convoy and much of their valuables. According to the terms they were given three days of truce and leeway. Khaled accepted the term. But after the third and final day of the leeway and the term of truce was over he went after the convoy with some of his horsemen and soon caught up with them. Khaled attacked the convoy and Thomas was killed in a duel with him. But Khaled let go of the widow to the Byzantines without any ransom.

In Madinah, at the beginning of the siege of Damascus a vital decision had been taken. Umar, on becoming the Caliph, had disposed of Khaled as the Commander in Chief and put Abu Ubaidah in charge of the Byzantine front. The letter of commission was received by Abu Ubaidah in early September. But he had kept silent about it as he wanted to break the news later so as not to disrupt the siege.

Previously in Persia, after Khaled had left Iraq for the Byzantine front, Shahr Iran became the Kisra of Persia. The situation in Persia stabilized and Shahr Iran decided to drive away the now depleted Muslim army. He deployed his army to face the Muslims and sent an insulting letter which stated that the Muslims were so despicable that the Persian army was not needed to defeat them but an army of fowl and swine herdsmen would suffice.

The two armies confronted each other in Babylon. As the battle began, the Persian charge was led by a fierce war elephant. It smashed through the Muslim ranks leaving everything in disarray. Muthanna persevered and ordered the archers to shoot at the elephant. Arrows after arrows started to hit the elephant until it fell. That was followed by the charge of the Muslim army which proved to be decisive.

Even though the battle was won, Muthanna knew that this was not the end of the Persian war. The Persians had enormous resources and would soon raise another huge army and he may not be able to deal with that. He let the Caliph know of his concerns by a letter. But no reply was forthcoming. So, he rushed off to Madinah himself to discover the Caliph terminally sick. Even from his death bed Abu Bakr listened to Muthanna patiently. He summoned Umar and said, "If I die this day wait not till the night. If I yet live till tonight wait not till the morning. Let not sadness for me divert you from the service of God."

Administration

The demarcation of the provinces and setup of new local administration was started by Abu Bakr and continued and augmented by the subsequent Caliphs. Initially, Arabia proper, Iraq and Syria were divided into sub-provinces.

Each of the provinces had a Governor who was the executive administrator and the commander-in-chief of the army. He was also the Imam of the Mosque who led the prayers and was the supervisor of public moral. He administered law and order and was supported by a *Qadi*, a Judge, who imparted justice. He collected tax and revenue with the help of an *Amil*, the revenue collector. While the Muslims paid the Zakaat, the Non Muslims paid the Jizya tax. The Jizya was not imposed on children, women, old or disabled men and worked out to be lesser than Zakaat. Christian Monks were exempted from paying Jizya. Those who paid Jizya were relieved of military duty in which the Muslims, having paid the Zakaat, still partook. If the non-Muslims voluntarily undertook military duty, their Jizya was exempted. The minorities enjoyed cultural autonomy and managed their social affairs themselves.

Besides the Zakaat and Jizya the state had other sources of revenue. *Ushr* and *Kharaz* were taxes on the produce of land. This was one tenth or a little more of the produce. *Fay* was the revenue from state land. *Ghanima* was the moveable properties collected from a battle field after the battle was won. One fifth of the Ghanima was taken by the state as tax.

The government of Abu Bakr consisted of non salaried staffs. All worked by virtue of honorary positions. Abu Bakr himself had continued to be a trader after becoming the Caliph to meet his family expenses. But the Companions requested him to take a salary. They argued that if he gave up his trade he would be able to give more time to the demanding work required by the Caliphate. Thus Abu Bakr started to draw a small amount of money as salary from the treasury, the *Baitul Mal*.

Initially, there was no standing army in the Caliphate. Islam was more an idea to be proffered to the world rather than a nation which would need constant warfare. But the best ideas were not accepted by the established rulers to whom the status quo, however degenerated, was profitable. Strategically, for the Muslims a purely defensive policy proved inadequate in the face of offensive policies formulated by all including the Romans and

Persians. Regular expeditions for defence were required and for each expedition an army was conscripted. This, at a later stage, would ultimately lead to the formation of a paid and standing army. But during Abu Bakr's Caliphate the army remained unpaid and were entitled to four-fifth of the Ghanima. The conscripted army consisted of several contingents including a female one. Some women fought along with the army while most were nurses, water suppliers, cooks, and provided many other services. During battles they also invoked the warriors on to the battle fields.

Portions of revenue that the state received from the Ghanima went to the Baitul Mal under the Caliph's authority who spent it for state expense or social welfare. It was proposed that the Ghanima be distributed among the citizens according to the rank of the recipient. But, Abu Bakr distributed it equally initiating an egalitarian society. The distribution of wealth to the general Muslims increased their buying capacity which facilitated increased trading. The Zakaat was given mainly to the needy. As the state prospered and there remained no destitute or poor people, the Zakaat was distributed among all the Muslims in the form of annuity. This was the first social welfare state in the world.

The Portrait of Abu Bakr

Abu Bakr belonged to the *Taim* clan of the Quraish. He had a multifaceted personality. Aspects like being the closest and most loyal friend of the Prophet, the incredibly successful first Caliph of Islam, and a military and political genius have foreshadowed his other great qualities.

With the death of the Prophet the revelations had ceased. There was no divine source of information for resolving social issues and disputes anymore. Abu Bakr guided his Governors, as the Prophet had guided his, with a definitive method that gave a guideline which would provide a growing framework for legal jurisprudence. On a very high level, to resolve any issue the method he initiated was:

- Analyse the Quran to find an instance of the issue, or a similar issue.
- If that particular issue was non-determinate in the Quran then analyse the Traditions of the Prophet.
- If the issue still remained non-determinate apply individual reasoning or judgement to it and resolve it.

The Prophet had taught Ijtehad or research and its application to the Companions. Abu Bakr initiated the systemisation of *Ijtehad* that would lead Muslim civilisation to the forefront of world jurisprudence, philosophy and science.

He was a philosopher par excellence. His philosophical teachings encompassed many aspects of life. Some of his views are listed below:

On Knowledge:

- "Without knowledge action is futile, without action knowledge is useless."
- "Knowledge is the life of the mind."

On greatness, good actions and kindness:

- "Run away from greatness and greatness will follow you."
- "There is greatness in the abstract fear of God, contentment in the belief of God and honour in humility."
- "To be blessed by God, be kind to God's people (creation)."
- "Good actions are a guard against the blows of adversity."
- "A person who aspires for paradise should learn to deal with humanity with kindness."

On socio-political aspects:

- "If you want to control people, control yourself first."
- "In the matter of justice, all should be equal in your eyes."
- "Solitude is better then the companionship of evil men."
- "To fight against infidels is Jihad. But to fight against the self is the greater Jihad."

Various other subjects:

- "Have earnestness for death and you will have life."
- "He who boasts lowers himself."
- "An evil man is cursed, for his evil lives after him."
- "It is a matter of shame that in the morning a bird rises (and is active) before you do."
- "Do not follow vain desires for God prospers those who are preserved from lust, greed and anger."

Dr. Weil, in his book *A history of the Islamic Peoples*, comments, "Abu Bakr's private life was as irreproachable as was his public life...... As the first collector of the Quran, to him belonged the credit of its complete preservation. As a law giver he set an excellent example for his successor, for in cases not provided for in the Quran and the traditions of the Prophet, he gave decisions in consultation with the jurists, decisions which with few exceptions became binding authorities."

Sir William Muir in his book *The Caliphate, its Rise, Decline and fall*, states, "Abu Bakr had no thought of personal aggrandisement. Endowed with the sovereign and *irresponsible* power, he used it simply for the interests of Islam, and the people's good. But the grand secret of his strength was faith in Mohammad, "Call me not the Caliph of Allah", he would say, "I am the Caliph of the Prophet of Allah." The question with him ever was what did Mohammad command, or what now would he have done? From this he never swerved a hair's breadth. And so it was that he crushed apostasy and laid secure the foundations of Islam. His reign was short, but there is no one to who the faith is more beholden."

He was a man of action. For him life was too short to accommodate any form of languor or laziness. He said, "Our abode in this world is transitory. Our life herein is but a loan. Our breaths are numbered, and our indolence is, but, manifest."

He was not ascetic but preferred simplicity. After he became the Caliph his wife saved a certain amount of money from his income. He had his daily allowance reduced by that same amount saying the amount that was saved was in excess to their need. His prayer to God was, "May my poverty be intentional, not unavoidable."

In 622, in the first year after Hijra, the Prophet had sent an expedition around Madinah consisting of a small group of Muslims led by Ubaidah bin Al-Harith. They confronted a Quraish group led by Ikrama bin Abu Jahl. But the Quraish chose to turn their backs and flee. Ibn Harith let them go. Abu Bakr was a member of the Muslim group and wrote a poem signifying that occasion.

"Could you not sleep because of the spectre of Salma in the sandy valleys,
And the important event that affected the tribe?
You see neither admonition nor a Prophet's call can save
Some of the tribe Lu'ayy from falseness.

A truthful Prophet came to them
And they presented him deception
And said, "You shall not live among us."

When we called them to the truth they turned their backs,
They howled like bitches driven back panting to their lairs.

With so many of them we are kindred in kinship
Yet it had not weighed on them to abandon piety
They should turn back from disbelief and disobedience
If they continue with their idolatrous error
Divine discipline shall not tarry
We are people of Ghalib's highest stock
From which nobility runs into many branches

I swear by the lord of camels, urged on to chant
Their feet bounded by old leather thongs,
Like the red-backed deer that haunts Makkah
Going down to the well's slimy cistern
I swear I am no pretender.

If they do not repent rapidly their error
A valiant band will descend on them.
It will leave women husbandless,
It will leave men dead with vulture wheeling around.
It will not spare the infidels as Ibn Harith did.

Take a message with you for the tribe Sahm
And every infidel with evil intentions:
Though you assail my honour
I shall not assail yours."

Thirteen years after the Hijra, on the 8th August, 634 CE Abu Bakr fell sick. He developed high fever. Some of the concerned companions asked him, "Caliph, may we ask the physician to examine you."

Abu Bakr said that the physician had already seen him. The surprised Companions asked as to what the diagnosis was and what the physician wanted to do about it.

Abu Bakr replied, "The Physician will do what the Physician wills to do."

He repaid the treasury of the amount of allowance that he availed during his Caliphate by selling a piece of land. Earlier he had bequeathed a property to Ayesha, now he wished her to share it with her sisters. His remaining fortune consisted of a slave, a camel, a worn out garment and five dirham. He directed that these be handed over to the new Caliph. When the handover took place, the stern Umar, broke down in tears and said, "O Abu Bakr, may God bless you. You have set a precedence so difficult to follow."

When Ayesha in preparation for the coffin wanted to buy three pieces of clothes needed to wrap the body, Abu Bakr asked her to buy only one as he already had two old pieces. He wanted these two old pieces to be washed and used in his coffin as "The new material would be of more use to the living than the dead."

Such was the Caliph who ruled an emerging empire and who had the two of the greatest empires of the world on their knees.

Umar bin Khattab

586-644

If you desire to see the most noble of mankind, look at the king in beggar's clothing; it is he whose sanctity is great among men. — Abdul Atahiya, Arab Poet.

Umar was selected as Caliph by general consensus just before Abu Bakr's death. Abu Bakr had wished Umar to be his successor but would not impose it on others, as the Prophet had not imposed a successor. Instead he asked Abdur Rahman bin Auf whether he approved the candidacy of Umar for the post. Adbur Rahman favoured the proposal. He then put the nomination in front of other Companions and all were in favour. Usman bin Affan's comment was, "The interior of Umar is much superior to his stern exterior. There is no one equal to him amongst us."

There was a single objection over Umar's candidacy, which was of Talha, who was concerned about the fiery and irascible temper of Umar. But Ali bin Abu Talib overturned Talha saying that he wanted Umar to be the next Caliph. Then Abu Bakr said that Umar's severity was a balancing act to his leniency, "From personal experience I can say that when I had lost my temper Umar had cooled me down. When I have been too lenient he had been severe. With time Umar will achieve the moderation that you desire."

Abu Bakr summoned Umar only after a general consensus was achieved. But as Umar had rejected the proposal to become Caliph two years ago at the death of the Prophet, now he rejected the offer again. Abu Bakr persisted, "The office needs you. I have prayed to God to direct me to the right candidate. And this choice is essential for the unity and concordance of the Muslims.

Finally, Umar relented and Abu Bakr dictated his testament to Usman, "In the name of God, the most merciful. This is the last testament of Abu Bakr bin Abu Qahafa, in his last hour of this world and first of the next.... I nominate Umar bin Khattab as my successor. Thus, hear him and obey him. Approve of his actions if he is right. I nominate him with all good intentions but with the inability of foreseeing the future. However, the doer of ill will be severely accounted for in the hereafter. Fare you well. May Divine blessing be upon you forever."

Umar bin Khattab became the second Caliph of Islam in 634. Umar was the first to be called *Amir al Momineen,* the 'Commander of the Faithful'. He did not take this title as a glamorising sobriquet but as the result of an issue that rose from the question of what his title should be. Caliph means 'representative'. Abu Bakr was the Caliph of the Messenger of God. Similarly, Umar considered himself the representative of Abu Bakr, thus technically he was the Caliph of the Caliph of the Messenger of God. This would be cumbersome and when one of the visiting Muslims dignitaries asked to see the Commander of the Faithful, the sobriquet stuck.

Umar was very tall and well built. He possessed a very powerful personality and imposing presence. He was decisive in his words and actions and his intuition was always so correct that it appeared as if it was inspired. In all, he could be intimidating without deliberately trying to be so. But remarkably, he was humble and could be very soft hearted. Once, as Caliph, he had asked people to gather in the Mosque. When they assembled he stood on the pulpit and declared, "When I was young, I was a shepherd for my aunts. I would work throughout the day for which they would give me only a handful of dates or raisin. That made the day miserable for me."

After saying that he got off the pulpit and walked away. Abdur Rahman bin Auf could not make sense of this speech as it served no point. He went to Umar and said, "Why did you do that for? All you did was belittle yourself."

Umar replied, "My *self* was telling me that I am the Commander of faithful and who could be better than me. So I decided to teach myself a lesson."

Long years ago in Makkah, Umar was a very tall, fiery tempered, strong Quraish youth belonging to the minor *Adi* clan. He was among the foremost of those opposed to Islam.

He was one of the most active in prosecution of Muslims. Once a servant girl had converted to Islam and Umar beat her. When he stopped he said, "Don't think I have stopped due to compassion. I have stopped because I am tired."

The servant girl had replied, "You have stopped because God has willed so."

During the Abassynian migration, he came across one of the Muslim women on her way. Umar asked her, "Are you leaving?"

"Yes," replied the woman, "You have tortured us, prosecuted us. So we are embarking on a journey on God's world to find a place where we can practice our religion in peace."

To the surprise of the woman, Umar said, "May God be with you."

She told this to one of the Muslims, Nuaim ibn Abdullah. Nuaim said, "So now you think he will become a Muslim."

"Yes"

Nuaim replied, "Let me tell you. The donkey of his father will become a Muslim before he does."

In 616, in one of the counsel of the Quraish in Kaba, it was decided that the only way of getting rid of the new religion was by killing the Prophet. Umar volunteered to do the job. In due course, he buckled up his sword and started on his mission for the house of Arqam at the foot of Mount Safa where the Prophet was with his followers. On the way he met Nuaim. Umar was unaware that Nuaim has converted to Islam. Seeing Umar in such an agitated state, Nuaim asked, "Where are you going?"

Umar replied, "To slay the Prophet."

Nuaim was alarmed, and tried to stop him, "Beware, the tribe of Hashim will have their revenge if you hurt him."

An argument started and finally Umar said, "What! Have you too become a Muslim?"

Nuaim replied, "Take care of your own house first. Your sister is a Muslim as well."

That stopped Umar on his tracks. He turned around and headed for his sister's house, where his sister Fatima and her husband, Saeed, were reciting verses of Quran written on a scroll. As he approached, Fatima hid the scroll and stood up to welcome him. Umar thundered, "What were you reading?"

"Nothing," Fatima replied.

Umar caught hold of Saeed's throat and said, "So you have apostatised from your father's religion."

Saeed replied, "We have rejected falsehood and accepted truth."

As Umar was about to strike Saeed, Fatima intervened, "Take your hands off him! Deal with me and say whatever you want to, but do not touch him."

As Fatima tried to protect her husband Umar pushed her away so that she fell and cut her temple. Seeing the cut on her temple softened his stance, "Is it true that you have become Muslims?"

Fatima replied, "Yes, we have. You may do as you wish but we shall not falter from our faith."

Umar arrested his emotions and asked to be shown what they were reading. Fatima produced the scroll but before giving it to him asked him to clean his hands first. After Umar washed his hands and Fatima handed it to him. Umar read the verses of the chapter 'Ta Ha'.

"Ta Ha,
We have not sent the Quran to you
To be an occasion for your distress,
But only as an admonition to those who fear God.
A revelation from God,
Who created the earth and the heavens on high.
God most gracious,
Is firmly established on the throne of authority......"

As he read, he felt his conscience chastise him. He was totally overcome with a different set of emotion and instantly decided to convert to Islam. Leaving his sister's house, he again proceeded for the house of Arqam, but this time with a totally different intention.

When Umar knocked at the door, the guard asked, "Who comes?"

"Umar bin Khattab."

Through the peephole the guard noticed Umar was armed, so he hesitated. Then Hamza said, "Open the door. If he comes in peace, we will welcome him, if he wants mischief, there are enough of us to overpower him."

As Umar entered the Muslims surrounded him and Hamza grabbed hold of his cloak by the hem and asked, "Why are you here, Umar?"

The Prophet approached them and said, "Leave him. Let him come." He then turned to Umar and said, "Umar, how long are you going to stray from the path. Do you not see the truth yet?"

"It is indeed time for me to accept the truth." Umar said, " I have come to profess my faith."

Then Umar held the hand of the Prophet with reverence and said, "I declare there is no god but Allah, and Mohammad is his messenger."

There followed shouts of 'God is great!' among the Muslims.

Unlike others, Umar went about Makkah telling everyone that he had converted to Islam. He knocked at the door of Abu Jehal, the Quraish leader, and said, " I have become a Muslim."

"What?" said Abu Jehal, "Don't!"

"Well, I have." Replied Umar.

"Curse you." Said Abu Jehal and shut the door on his face.

As he walked through Makkah, Umar mentioned his conversion to all he met. This news spread like wildfire. The Quraish were afraid to tackle him, but a crowd grew and started to follow him. Soon, some from the crowd launched attacks on him whenever they could gather some courage. Umar fought back, he attacked whoever led the attack and repulsed them. At one time he grabbed Utba and threw him to the ground. Then pinning him down he poked his eyes with his fingers. As Utba screamed the crowd backed off. Eventually, exhausted, he could fight no more and sat down while the people hit him and ran away. Still he shrugged them off and said, "If we were 300 strong, we would fight you. Either you would leave or we would leave."

This statement would prove to be prophetic. In Badr, the first battle, the number of the Muslims was just over 300. Umar had joined Islam three days after Hamza.

Soon, on an appointed day, the Muslims declared themselves openly in the Kaba. On that day, the Muslims approached Kaba in two ranks, one led by Umar and the other by Hamza with the Prophet in the middle. That was the day the Prophet gave Umar the title of 'Al Farooque' – The Criterion. He was the criterion between the truth and falsehood.

After assuming the Caliph's office Umar brought changes to the Byzantine battle front. He appointed Abu Ubaidah bin Jarrah as the Commander in Chief in place of Khaled bin Waleed.

Khaled had proved to be an extraordinary General and an exceptional person. He had the towering stature of Umar that dwarfed others. In battles he not only ordered the charge but also led the charge and would be in the thick of the battle totally ignoring personal safety, in fact, courted martyrdom. As in battles, he was also assertive in personal and social life and, on a few occasions, is known to have indulged in extravagance. He married beautiful women most of whom were from the opposing tribes he had vanquished, he is known to have taken bath in water mixed with relaxing potions to soothe his wounds, on another occasion he rewarded a poet 10,000 Dirham who wrote a panegyric as a tribute to Khaled. When Umar learned of these he was very aggrieved. He knew that Khaled had become a great role model for the Muslims. But while only a few young Muslims would be able to emulate his leadership at the battlefield, most would be more attracted to a lifestyle that could lead to indulgence. Umar was totally against luxuries, indulgence, eulogising and flattery. He lived an exemplary simple life and made his Generals and Governors do the same. One important factor that affected Umar's thinking was the fact that the repute and awe of Khaled had become so great that it affected not only the moral of the enemies but also affected the attitude of the Muslims as well. Islam was to be represented not by any military force but by its divine knowledge and progressive ideas. Thus the great Khaled had to go and Umar dismissed him. It was neither due to any personal ill-will nor any insincerity on Khaled's behalf that Umar removed him from his position. While Islam teaches dependence only on God the Muslims were becoming dependant on Khaled. Umar, at a later stage, would comment, "Khaled was dismissed because people were being misled and were glorifying him when all glory belongs to God".

Sir William Muir mentions this incident in his assessment of Umar "In early life, of a fiery and impatient temper, he was known, even in the later days of the Prophet, as the stern advocate of vengeance. Ever ready to unsheathe the sword, it was he who at Badr advised that the prisoners be put to death. But age, as well as office, had now mellowed this asperity. His sense of justice was strong. And except it be the treatment of Khaled, whom according to some accounts, he pursued with an ungenerous resentment, no act of tyranny or injustice is recorded against him; and even in this matter his enmity took its rise in Khaled's unscrupulous treatment of fallen foe."

The surprising aspect in the Umar and Khaled state of affair was that it did not affect their personal relationship. Khaled was a cousin of Umar and when Khaled died he made Umar the executor of his will. A veteran of over a hundred battles Khaled had never lost a single one – he *was* the Sword of God. But he had been wounded in every spot on his body. He died after a short sickness in 642. When the news of Khaled's death reached the people, the women of Madinah came out in the streets in tears. Muslims are not expected to exhibit excessive grief or wailing over any death, but in this case Umar said, "Let the women of the *Banu Makhdum* say what they will about Khaled. They do not lie. Over the likes of Khaled weep those who weep."

Earlier, in the Iraqi front, after Khaled had left for Byzantine-Syria with half of the army, the remaining half under Muthanna manoeuvred to a strategic retreat, moving back towards the desert. Muthanna won another battle against the Persians but he knew he did not have sufficient resources to fight a protracted war. Muthanna went to Madinah and acquainted Umar with the need to reinforce the army in Iraq. Umar conscripted and sent another army to boost the one there.

Soon after that the Muslims won two major and decisive battles. One in Yermuk in Syria against the Byzantines and the other at Qadisiyah in Iraq against the Persians. Both, the battles lasted for several days, the fortune of the battle swayed from one side to another, till finally the Muslims won. These two major battles opened up Iraq and Syria to the Muslims. Heraclius, the Byzantine Emperor, who was residing in Antioch, in Syriac region, was no longer safe there and withdrew to Constantinople. His departing words were, "Farewell Syria. It is with great pain that I part from you. Salute, beautiful land."

The battles of Yermuk and Qadisiyah were so important that Umar himself had wanted to lead in Qadisiyah. Some of the Companions concurred but Abdur Rahman bin Auf disagreed, "If you are killed in the battle the Muslims will not have anywhere to go. Send someone else to command and even if we loose, you will still be here to raise another army and lead."

Saad bin Abi Waqqas was appointed Commander of the Persain front. Before the battle of Qadisiyah, General Rustom, commander-in-chief of the Persian army asked for a dialogue. Rabai ibn Amr, a Muslim commander, was sent as the emissary to talk with him. The Persians prepared for the summit with splendour as was the established protocol among the Romans and Persians. Splendid Persian carpets were laid down and a gold pleated tent with a throne was raised for Rustom. All wore expensive clothes and uniforms. Rabai came to the camp riding a short hairy horse, his sword wrapped in a piece of rough cloth as he did not have a proper scabbard, his spear point tied with a string to the staff. He rode his horse straight on to the carpet. He was stopped after which he started to walk on the carpet with his spear point pointing down. And as he walked, with every step the spear-point would poke a small hole in the carpet. He was stopped again in front of the tent by the guards, "You cannot go in with your weapons."

Rabai said, "I come here not on my choice. It is you who asked for a meeting. I continue with my weapons or I go back. It's up to you."

Rustom was informed and he ordered the guards to let Rabai proceed. Rustom watched him approach, then asked, "Why have you come to this land?"

Rabai was not impressed by all the splendour and said, "God has sent us to deliver you from worshipping the creation to worshipping the Creator, to deliver you from the constriction of material worldliness to the vastness of this world and the afterlife, and from the oppression of religions to the justice of Islam".

The point presented was that Islam was not just a 'religion' but a code of universal life. After the dialogue Rabai presented the usual three options: Accept Islam and we go away or pay Jizya and live as you wish or let the sword decide. Rabai represented an army 30,000 strong which was facing the Persian army of 120,000. The dialogue, not surprisingly, was not a success and the decision was left to be determined by the sword. After four days of fierce battle the Muslims prevailed.

Soon after Yermuk, the southern contingents on the Syraic front under Amr bin Al-Aas laid a siege on Jerusalem. As victory had already been won on the northern front, so Abu Ubaidah sent re-enforcement to the south. Vastly outnumbered, the Patriarch of Jerusalem sued for peace saying he was ready to submit to the Caliph personally. This was communicated to Umar in Madinah.

Umar called a meeting of his Council of Companions to discuss the proposal. In the meeting Usman was against the idea saying that surrender of the Byzantines in Jerusalem was inevitable. But Ali said that due to the sanctity of the place to the three religions Islam, Judaism and Christianity, it was preferable that the Caliph receive the surrender himself. Umar agreed with Ali, and leaving him in charge of Madina left for Jerusalem.

Umar, who had never sought grandeur nor cared about personal safety, left Madina with a camel and a slave. Throughout the journey, at times Umar rode the camel while the slave led it on foot and at other times Umar led it while the slave rode it.

In a place called Jabiya near Jerusalem all the Muslim commanders and a deputation from Jerusalem awaited Umar's arrival. They were all astonished to witness the incredible sight of the Caliph leading the camel on foot while the slave rode on its back. After meeting the Muslim commanders, Umar met the deputation from Jerusalem. A treaty was drawn up whereby security of life and property of all citizens of Jerusalem was assured. The safety of churches and all other religious buildings were upheld. The populace were to pay Jizya and those who wanted to leave were allowed to leave in peace.

From Jabiya Umar went to Jerusalem, where he was greeted at the Gate by the Patriarch and the splendidly dressed elite of the city and Muslim commanders. The patriarch handed over the keys of Jerusalem to a plainly dressed Umar. As Umar entered the city, an incredulous and gradually enthusiastic throng greeted him. The general people had been apprehensive and had expected some kind of grand display and probable violence but just saw a simple man on a camel followed by a shining retinue. Umar desired to lead a prayer of thanksgiving. The Muslims wanted to pray in Church of the Holy Sepulchre and the Patriarch accepted. But Umar declined to pray there, "I shall not lead a congregation here, lest this be used as precedence by Muslims to forcibly change Churches into Mosques."

Soon after the 'opening' of Jerusalem, Amr bin Al-Aas started a campaign in Egypt with only 4000 soldiers. After winning a few small battles his campaign gathered momentum and his army grew in size. He laid siege on the port of Alexandria. This siege lasted for a few months. After which the Byzantines forces defending Alexandria left via the sea. The remaining Coptic Egyptians sued for and got the usual terms. From there Amr bin Al-Aas marched to Egyptian Memphis. He laid the foundation of a city called Fustat outside Memphis, which would, in a few years, became the next capital of Egypt. Amr wanted to progress further west into Africa but Umar ordered him to hold and consolidate Egypt.

The State under Umar

Much can be said about the 634 to 644 ten years of rule by Umar. He was a Ruler, Statesman extraordinaire. He was of excellent moral character, a literate person who ruled with iron discipline, impartial justice and incorruptible administration. He was also a great builder and administrator.

Under Umar, the government acquired the formal administrative structure that Abu Bakr had initiated. The Caliphate consisted of eight provinces which included the regions of Arabia proper, Syria, Iraq, Persia, Palestine and Egypt. A Governor was in charge of each province and was served by a retinue of officials including chief secretary, military secretary, judge, police chief, and revenue collector. The provinces were again subdivided into about

100 districts for local administration. Departments of treasury, army and public revenues were established and regular salaries were set up. Population census and land surveys were conducted to assess equitable taxation.

In 636, Umar introduced the Hijri Calendar that starts from the year of Hijra of the Prophet from Makkah to Madinah. In 639, a famine broke out in Arabia and plague appeared in Syria and Iraq. Umar initiated relief operations and managed both regions very successfully. Social welfare provisions were initiated to support the poor and the needy from state funds. The Dhimmis or non-Muslims were officially recognised as full citizens with full legal status.

Umar would nightly patrol the streets of Madinah to find out the condition of the ordinary citizens. One night, he accidentally heard a woman complain that she was lonely because her husband was at the battle front for over a year. After consulting with his wife Umar declared that if a man was with the army without his wife, the man would be given short leave every four months. Temporary marriages lasting for a short agreed period which was a common practice of the time was banned.

In land administration, reforms started due to the demand by the army that like the moveable properties which they gained from the battle fields, four-fifth of the land conquered should also go to the army in the same model as Ghanimah. Umar assembled the Council of Companions in Madina to debate the issue. He proposed that the conquered land belonged to the state. Among those who were in favour of Umar were Usman, Ali and Talha. But Belal and Abdur Rahman bin Auf along with few others were in support of the army. Belal was so vociferous and fervent in his support that at one stage Umar turned and exclaimed, "May God save me from Belal."

There ensued a deadlock until Umar recalled some verses of the chapter 'Al Hashar' from the Quran which dealt with similar circumstances. Upon analysis of the verses it was concluded that the land did belong to the state. And based on it there was consensus that:

- Conquered land was the property of the state.
- The original occupants of lands would not be evicted.
- The original occupants would continue to occupy such lands on payment of taxes to the state.

In the conquered regions, records and accounting were kept in the existing system and language of the country. The rules and taxation were made easier and milder for the general masses. For example, in Egypt under the Romans there were taxes and additional levies. Umar cancelled the additional levies and continued just with the taxes.

In Judicial administration, he probably was the first ruler in history to separate the Judiciary from the executive governance. He appointed independent Judges, Qadis, at all administrative level. People of high status and integrity with sound proficiency and education in Islamic law were appointed to this position and given a substantial salary.

Umar extended the Kaba and the Prophet's Mosque. Before the start of the extension work of the Prophet's Mosque in Madinah he ordered the acquisition and demolition of all the houses around the Mosque to create space. Abbas, uncle of the Prophet and by whose name the much later Abbasid Dynasty would be known, was the owner of one of the houses and refused to sell. He decided to proceed with a legal suit against the state in the court judged by *Qadi* Ubay bin Kab. The Judge, after hearing both sides gave verdict against the state.

Abbas was not motivated by the property but by his rights as an individual. He, having won the case and his rights, announced that he would now donate the house for the extension of the Mosque. Umar was grateful and ordered that Abbas be provided with dwelling elsewhere.

Umar established a state controlled model of governance and economy. It was centrally ruled via provincial Governors who had nominal powers. All the revenue that was collected for the state and the manner in which it was spent was under full control of the Caliph. Though his rule appeared autocratic it was accompanied with diligent accountability. He declared, "Without consultation, the Caliphate is unlawful."

On one occasion the treasury had allotted each individual with a piece of cloth. One day in the mosque, Umar stood up to deliver his speech with two such pieces wrapped around him. Before he could speak, a man stood up and declared, "We refuse to listen to you. What right does the Caliph has to two pieces of cloth while we have been given only one."

At that point Abdullah, son of Umar, rose and said, "I have given him my piece. My father is so tall that one piece was not enough for him."
The man satisfied turned to Umar, "You may proceed, we will listen."

His sense of responsibility made the fear of God extreme. He knew that for every action he took he would be accountable to God. He was very busy with the affairs of the Caliphate, but he would still give time to the people to listen to their concern.

Sir William Muir in *The Caliphate, its Rise, Decline and Fall* states, "Simplicity and duty were his guiding principles; impartiality and devotion the leading features of his administration. Responsibility so weighed upon him that he was heard to exclaim 'O that my mother had not borne me; would that I have been this stalk of grass instead!"

But on one occasion, when he was very busy with urgent work, a Bedouin came and started to pester and complain about a personal matter. Umar butted him with his whip in anger saying, "When I allocate my time to hear your misgivings you don't show up, when I am busy with the affairs of the state you come and disturb the on-going work."

Professor Hitti relates to that incident, “Having in a fit of anger inflicted a number of stripes on a Bedouin who came seeking his succour against an oppressor, the Caliph soon repented and asked the Bedouin to inflict the same number on him. But the later refused. So Umar retired home with the following soliloquy: “O son of Al Khattab, humble thou wert and Allah has elevated thee; thou went astray, and Allah hath guided thee; thou were weak and Allah had strengthened thee. Then He caused thee to rule over the necks of thy people, and when one of them came seeking thy aid thou didst strike him! What wilt thou have to say to thy Lord when thou present thyself before Him?”

Abu Musa Al Ashari, a Governor, came from Iraq and gave a gift to Umar’s wife. The gift was complementary out of goodwill and no favour was asked. But Umar had Abu Musa brought over and returned the gifts along with some vitriolic discourse on what he thought of such gifts. He would say, “Hold yourself accountable before you are held accountable.”

His son Abdullah Ibn Umar once bought some skinny camels and took them to the *Hima* – a guarded state pasture. The camels grew fat over time and Abdullah took them to the market. Umar in one of his regular inspection of the market saw the camels and said, “Who is the owner of these camels?”

The people said that those belonged to his son. He had his son brought to him and inquired about the camels. After listening to Abdullah, he said, “You took the camels to the state pastures where people moved their camels away to give space to the camels that belonged to the son of the Commander of the Faithful. They took good care of the camels because they belonged to the son of the Commander of the Faithful till the camels became fat. So, sell them and make sure that all the profit goes to the treasury.”

On another occasion, after disciplining some men and women who were socialising in the ablution (washing) area of the Prophet’s Mosque, Umar feared that he may have overdone it and may be held accountable by God. Seeing the fear in him, Ali said, “You are a shepherd. If a shepherd disciplines his flock that is justice, if the shepherd disciplines without justice that is oppression.”

One night, Umar went to the house of Ubay Ibn Kaab, a companion and Hafez of the Quran. He wanted to clarify a verse of the Quran that condemns a person who harms righteous men and women. He said, “Ubay, I fear that I may be one of those who are harming righteous men and women.”

Ubay replied, “Umar, you cannot but discipline the people and tell them what is right and what is wrong.”

Umar was austere. It was quite common to see him giving sermons wearing clothes which had patches. When Hafsa, his daughter, said, “Why don’t you have your salary increased a little so that you can have decent food and clothes?”

Umar’s response was that his personal interest did not lie in this world. He was just doing his duty till such a time when he will have the pleasure of joining his two companions – the Prophet and Abu Bakr.

Umar was strict in his dealings with the provincial Governors. He had set up stringent selection criteria for choosing Governors. He set down rules for administration as well as code of conduct. He believed that if the Governors failed to live up to the people's expectation the failure was his own. They were not allowed to have gates in their houses because that may hinder the people from approaching them. He made surprise visits to their houses to check if all the rules were being followed.

He was very much against any ostentation. Once he went to the outskirts of Madinah to receive Muawiah bin Abu Sufian who was at that time the Governor of Syria. Umar and a few companions were riding on simple camels. Muawiah appeared with a well attired entourage on horses and surrounded by body guards. Seeing the Caliph approach, Muawiah dismounted and approached the Caliph. But Umar totally disregarded him and kept on riding. Muawiah sensing something wrong started to follow the Caliph on foot. Soon he was running and breathless, and still Umar ignored him. Abdur Rahman bin Auf felt pity for the Governor and requested, "O Caliph, he is exhausted, talk to him."

Umar stopped and said, "Whose entourage is that?"

Muawiah said, "Mine."

Umar questioned Muawiah about the entourage and the bodyguards and finished saying, "I have also heard that you now have a secretary. People now have to go to your secretary first before they are allowed to reach you. Why?"

Muawiah said, "Caliph, the enemy has dispersed many spies through out our land. Given the opportunity these agents will attack. That is why I have bodyguards. As for the secretary, he makes sure that the people do not take advantage of us. If you disapprove, Caliph, I will do without the bodyguards and secretary."

Umar said, "You always have justifications to whatever question I ask of you. I neither approve nor disapprove of this."

Umar improved the social welfare system that had been established by Abu Bakr. He continued the periodic payment to the general citizens and added child benefit to it. Initially, the benefit was given at the time of weaning and later at the birth of every child. Umar also cared about animals. He ordered that the camels not be burdened with excessive weight and that enough food is given to them.

Umar further emancipated slaves, who had progressed, under Islam, from slavery to bondsmen who were allowed to work in any profession they wanted to. They would have to pay a part of their earning to the family or person to whom they were bonded to. Slave-wives who bore children were freed and became full wives.

Mughira Shubah, the governor of Basra, had a Persian bondsman, named Feroz, who had been captured after the battle of Nihawand in 641. Feroz was a skilled craftsman with various qualities. He was carpenter, iron smith, a painter and could build windmills as well. Because of his skills he was sent to Madinah. He was very pained to see Persians, especially children, in bond-hood. One day, he complained to the Caliph that the tax that was exacted from him by Mughira was excessive. The Caliph asked Firoj to 'obey his master' and went away thinking of making inquiries later. Firoj, on the other hand, thought that by 'obey his master' the Caliph meant that he would have to continue with whatever his master decided. This infuriated the already severely unstable Feroj. At dawn of November 1, 644 CE he took a dagger and hid in a recess of the mosque. As Umar stood to lead the morning prayer, Feroz rushed at him and stabbed him six times. In a frenzy he also lashed out at one and all who came in his way. Thirteen of those who tried to stop him were injured, some fatally. When he was finally cornered, Feroj turned the dagger on himself.

Umar was carried bleeding to his house where he regained consciousness. He realised that he did not have long to live. Abu Bakr had been buried next to the Prophet in the house of Ayesha. Umar asked his son Abdullah to go to Ayesha and request her to let him be buried with his two companions, the Prophet and Abu Bakr. When Ayesha heard of Umar's request she broke down in tears, "I had reserved this place for my own burial. But let Umar's wish be fulfilled. Let him be buried here."

When the news was conveyed to Umar he said, "God bless Ayesha. She has granted my greatest wish. Now I can die in peace."

He instructed his son to be moderate in arranging the burial. Then the question of who the next Caliph would be was raised. One of the persons present said, "I propose Abdullah, the son of Umar."

But Umar rejected the proposal, "...The caliphate belongs to the entire community. I would not like to make it hereditary within my family...". He did not want to nominate anyone, but when asked to leave some instructions, he nominated a committee who would decide on the candidature. The committee of six consisted of Ali bin Abu Talib, Usman bin Affan, Abdul Rahman bin Auf, Saad bin Abi Waqas, Zubayr bin Awam and Abu Talha. He asked them to deliberate the issue after his death, but to come to a decision within three days.

Umar and Jurisprudence

The Prophet during his lifetime would give decisions on numerous issues. These decisions and sayings form part of the Traditions of the Prophet and not part of the Quran. The Traditions, known as the Hadiths, along with the Quran forms the base of Islamic Jurisprudence.

After the death of the Prophet, there were numerous sources of Traditions. Many of the companions who had witnessed the Prophet and had been taught by him, in turn, had taught the Traditions to the next generation causing it to spread significantly. To judge whether a Tradition was authentic or not Umar evolved the initial reference system. The basic procedure was:

- The report of the Hadith should be factually faithful.
- With every Hadith should be attached the name of its narrator or the names of the chain of narrator.
- These narrators should be all men of proven faith and integrity.
- The Hadith or report should be judged taking into consideration the occasion and the circumstances involved, i.e., the context should be taken into consideration to get the true meaning of the Traditions.
- The report must agree with the Quran
- The report must be rational.

Over a thousand juristic rulings of Umar are in record and are used in all the four Sunni schools of jurisprudence that evolved later. His definition of logical deduction or *Qiyas* for the Judiciary was, "When a judgement cannot be found on any issue in the Quran or Hadith and if there is any doubt, contemplate on it and contemplate again. Then research for dicta on similar issue and decide in concurrence."

Umar's rational concept would later be inherited by the school of *Israr Ilmuddin*. He held that Islam was a rational religion and all of its injunction could be tested and justified on the basis of reason and intellect. His theories and principal became the basis of *Ijtihad* which specifically means the use of analysis to extrapolate laws where such laws are not specifically covered by the Quran and Hadith. In addition to the above principles, he also expressed a number of other generalisations that would also be included as the basis of Islamic Jurisprudence. As the Quran had not yet been compiled for the general mass he wanted to ensure that the Traditions of the Prophet were not mistaken for or mixed up with the Quran by the people. He would ask for a witness if someone would relate a tradition of the Prophet. He said, "Relate as few traditions as possible, lest people overlook the Quran."

When asked, if it was appropriate to perform *wadu* or ablution for cleansing before prayer with water given by a non-Muslim, Umar found no objection there. When asked what a person should do if meal was ready and it was also the time for prayer. Umar advised to take the meal first but he also requested the people not to eat anything that gave bitter odour, like garlic before coming to the mosque.

Public Works and Umar

A large number of public works and development took place under Umar. During his rule three new towns were built - Kufa and Basra in Iraq and Fustat in Egypt. Proper town planning was carried out with a square and mosque in the centre of the towns and markets in appropriate places. The housing quarters were established with each houses complying with specified dimensions. Due to his egalitarian bent he ordered that all houses, irrespective to whom it belonged, were to be one story so that all would be equal in status. Administrative buildings for housing official records, treasury, government offices and residences, rest houses, and the first prison houses were constructed. Wells were dug, shelters and meal houses were built along the road between Makkah and Madina. New roads were laid and wayside accommodations were built.

Canals were dug for irrigation as well as for supply of water for drinking. A canal brought water from Euphrates to Anbar. A nine mile canal was dug from the Tigris river to Basra. Another canal between the Red Sea and the Nile that had been dug in earlier ages was re-excavated. The Egyptian Governor, Amr bin Al-Aas proposed a canal to join the Mediterranean with the Nile. This proposal did not materialise at that time, but 1200 hundred years later a canal was dug in a similar plan and is now known as the Suez Canal.

Washington Irving in his book *Lives of the Successors of Muhammad* pays glowing tribute to Umar, "... a man of great powers of mind, inflexible integrity and rigid justice. He was more than anyone else the founder of the Islamic empire; confirming and carrying out the inspirations of the Prophet; aiding Abu Bakr with his counsels during his brief Caliphate; and establishing wise regulations for the strict administration of law throughout the rapidly-extending bounds of the Muslim conquest. The rigid hand that he kept on his popular generals in the midst of their armies, and in the most distant scenes of their triumphs, gives signal evidence of the extra-ordinary capacity to rule."

Gibbon states that "... the abstinence and humility of Umar were not inferior to the virtues of Abu Bakr: his food consisted of barley bread or dates; his drink was water; he preached in a gown that was torn or tattered in twelve places; and a Persian Satrap, who paid his homage as to the conqueror, found him asleep among the beggars on the steps of the mosque of Muslims."

Sayings of Umar

- "Scholarship cannot co-exist with arrogance."
- "If any scholar loves this world, his scholarship is doubtful."

- "All injunctions of Islam are based on reason."
- "Comprehend the teachings of the Quran, for that is knowledge."
- "Don't forget what you preach to others."
- "The less of this world, the freer you are."
- "The criterion for trust is that a person does what he says and says what he thinks."
- "A man will have critics even if he is as straight as an arrow."
- "If your ruler is just, praise God. If he is unjust, pray to God for his removal."
- "Do not be misled by a person's prayer and fasting. Take into account his sincerity and wisdom."
- "Do not be misled by anyone's reputation."
- "If a person has nine good habits and one bad one, the bad one will destroy all the good ones."
- "Do not eat in access. That causes disease."
- "Be neither over zealous nor indifferent in your duties."
- "I am not afraid of the poverty of Muslims. I am afraid of pride that they may develop in becoming rich and thus invite destruction."

Usman bin Affan

579 - 656

Both Usman and Ali wanted to lead Umar's funeral prayer. But this was disallowed as both of them were candidates for the Caliphate. The prayer was led by a person named Suhaib who in the past had been commissioned by Umar to lead prayers.

Talha was away from Madinah and, therefore, the other five sat down to work out the candidacy. But after two days of wrangling and debate, the selection was nowhere in sight. Finally, on the third day Abdur Rahman bin Auf withdrew his candidature. Since, by doing this he proved his impartiality the other four asked him to select the candidate. Abdur Rahman initiated his process of selection by interviewing the other four individually. He asked Ali, "If I do not nominate you, who should I nominate?"

Ali replied, "Then the obvious choice is Usman."

Abdur Rahman put the same question to Usman.

Usman replied, "In that case the obvious choice is Ali."

Abdur Rahman asked Zubayr who replied, "It should be Usman or Ali."

Finally, when Saad was approached, he said "I want you to be the Caliph."

Abdur Rahman said, "But I have withdrawn my candidacy."

"In that case, let it be Usman," said Saad.

In the committee all had wanted Usman or Ali as the Caliph except for Saad who wanted Abdur Rahman or Usman. From this Abdur Rahman concluded that the committee was slightly inclined towards Usman.

In Madinah, it soon became apparent that Usman was the choice. Two factors that influenced the public opinion were, first Ali was younger, less than fifty years old while Usman was almost seventy. In the Arab culture there is always veneration for the older. Besides that there was still time for Ali to become Caliph after Usman. Secondly, Usman was a kind person who had divulged in social welfare and charity throughout his life. The public opinion was moved by the humane aspect of his personality as well.

There may have been a third factor. Usman belonged to the Umayyad clan of the Quraish. Before Islam, the Umayyads had been dominant in Makkah and its commerce. It was the most powerful clan and thus had a powerful sway on public will. Abu Bakr and Umar, both belonging to other clans, had kept the Umayyads in line with all others in concordance with the principle of universality. But the Umayyads were natural leaders, well practiced in management and had moved to important positions by virtue of merit. They may have helped sway the public opinion in favour of Usman.

Finally, on the fourth day after Umar's death, the people gathered in the Prophet's Mosque. Abdur Rahman addressed them, explaining the process he had followed. Then he declared Usman the candidate and gave him allegiance. All who were present gave Usman their allegiance. Ali, though discontent, also gave his allegiance. Thus, in the year 644 Usman became the third Caliph.

When the debate over the next Caliph was taking place, a Persian connection was uncovered in the stabbing of Umar. Abdur Rahman bin Abu Bakr reported that the day before the assassination he had seen the Persians - Feroz, Hormuzan and Jafina - in conference. Hormuzan was a Persian general who had been captured a few years back. He was brought to Madinah to Umar where he accepted Islam. He had lived freely since. As Abdur Rahman had passed them, accidentally a double-edged dagger had fallen from the hand of one of them. It was alleged that this was the same dagger used in the assassination.

When Ubaidullah, a son of Umar, heard about this plot he totally lost his sanity. He drew his sword and went to Feroz's house and killed his wife and daughter. Then after killing the second Persian named Jafina he went to Hormuzan, challenged him and slew him as well. He was still on the rampage trying to figure who else was involve when he was apprehended and locked up.

After assuming office this was the first case that Usman had to judge. The jury consisted of Ali, Amr bin Al-Aas and few other Companions. Ali's view was that law was no respecter of any individual. Ubaidullah had committed the crime and could not be protected just because he was the son of a Caliph. Amr bin Al-Aas and few others took a more lenient view arguing that the recent murder of Umar and its effect on the mental condition of Ubaidullah need to be taken into account as well. After pondering over it Usman decided that compensation should be paid and, in fact, he paid the compensation to the family of Hormuzan on behalf of Ubaidullah. According to historian At-Tabari, Qamazban, the son of Hormuzan, was present in the trail. In his statement he said that his father was not involved and, in fact, had cautioned Feroz to stay away from trouble. Upon this Usman had handed over the fate of Ubaidullah to Qamazban's hands. Qamazban initially wanted to have Ubaidullah executed but later forgave him for the 'sake of God'.

Usman belonged to the aristocracy of Makkah and was born in a rich family of the Umayyad clan of the Quraish. As a young man he was one of the first few people to accept Islam. His family was appalled and his uncle tied him up and tried to force him to renounce. He remained steadfast against all persuasion. His mother decided to boycott him. He had two wives and both of them left him. Usman was much pained at his family's rejection of him.

The Prophet was very impressed by all the sacrifices of Usman. He proposed that Usman be married to his daughter Ruqayya. Usman was an extremely handsome man and Ruqayya was very beautiful. And they became the most handsome couple of Makkah such that a poet mentioned them in poetry as "the sun has met the moon." They were a very happy couple but felt that the Makkah was not congenial for them. Usman and Ruqayya migrated to Abyssinia where Usman had trading contacts. He settled down there and started his trade and was followed by other Muslims. After two years they returned to Makkah. In 622 they again migrated to Madinah and started a new life there. In 624 as the battle of Badr approached Ruqayyah fell sick. The Prophet on his way to the battle field left Usman in charge of Madinah. Ruqayya died while the battle raged. Usman received the news of the victory of Badr while she was being buried.

About a year after that Usman married Umme Kulthum, the third daughter of the Prophet. But barely six years after the marriage she also died. Usman became very depressed and disconsolate. The Prophet seeing his despair asked other people to get Usman married, "If I had another daughter I would have given her in marriage to him."

Usman was soft hearted and generous. He supported poor families and was one of the main financiers of expeditions led by the Prophet. Immediately, after the Hijra, there was a shortage of water for the Muslims in Madinah. Usman bought a well with his personal funds for the use of all Muslims.

The Frontiers

The death of Umar gave the Persians and the Byzantines an opportunity to flex their muscle. The Byzantine Navy moved in and captured Alexandria. Their army also moved into Syria. Through out Persia there were revolts of secession against the Caliphate.

In Egypt, Usman had deposed Amr bin Al-Aas, and placed Abdullah bin Saad as the Governor. The main reason was that Amr was incapable of handling the finance and exacting taxes properly, under him the revenue from Egypt decreased. When asked about the low revenue, Amr had metaphorically replied "The she-camel cannot be further milked." When Abdullah became Governor the revenue increased. On this Amr rejoined, "The she-camel had been milked but the calves had been deprived."

After the loss of Alexandria to the Byzantines, there was a general call for Amr to be reinstated and to recover Egypt as no one knew it better than him. Amr on being requested by Usman agreed to take up the commission. After becoming Governor again, he organized an attack and drove the Byzantines from Alexandria. Soon, as a compromise, Usman proposed that Amr would remain the Governor of Egypt, but Abdullah would manage the finance independently. This was rejected by Amr on the grounds that "while I hold the cow by the horns, someone else would be milking it." In the disagreement that followed Usman once again sacked Amr and made Abdullah bin Saad the Governor.

Under Usman, the Muslims carried out the first naval expedition. Muawiah, the Governor of Syria, had previously requested permission from Umar for a naval expedition. But at that time the Muslims had no naval experience. When Umar asked Amr of it, he said the sea 'twisted the mind', probably speaking of sea sickness. Umar did not agree with the naval expedition and in fact asked the generals not to place their army on the other side of any big stretch of water because that would probably isolate the army and hamper rapid re-deployment. Usman on the other hand gave permission for the naval expedition to go ahead.

Muawiah sent an expeditions and captured Rhodes and Cyprus. This encouraged Abdullah bin Saad to develop a Navy in Egypt. In 652, the Byzantines attacked again with a large navy led by Emperor Constance II himself. A great sea-battle took place which is known as the 'Battle of Masts." Initially, as the two navies engaged, volleys of arrows were exchanged causing death and injuries on both sides. Then the ships moved among each other so close that the masts almost collided. The Muslims boarded the Byzantine ships and gradually fought to an advantage. The Byzantines lost the battle with hundreds of ships destroyed. The Emperor barely managed to escape.

In the Syriac region, two land contingents were sent by Usman which repulsed the Byzantine army and entered further into Asia Minor. On the eastern front, a series of Persian revolts was thwarted. Muslims crossed the Oxus River into Transoxania (Central Asia: Uzbekistan, Tajikistan and southwest Kazakhstan). But the most important event in this front was the death of the last Sassanian emperor Yazdajurd. During Umar's rule, Yazdajurd had taken refuge across the Oxus in the domain of the Khaqan of Farghana in Central Asia. When Umar died, the Persians revolted and Yazdajurd with the support of a Turkic army crossed the Oxus and captured Merv, a city in Persia. He tried to win over Neizak Tarkhan, the most powerful chieftain in the Khorasan region of Persia. Tarkhan proposed a marriage of alliance between himself and one of the daughters of Yazdajurd. Yazdajurd considered this derogatory and sent a rude reply to Tarkhan. This reply enraged Tarkhan who decided now to lead a force against Yazdajurd. The two armies faced each other and initially Yazdajurd had the upper hand. But the Governor of Merv betrayed Yazdajurd and moved his large detachment over to the side of Tarkhan. The outnumbered Yazdajurd was defeated and when he retreated to Merv, he found the gates of the city closed to him. Basically, the Persians were no longer interested in fighting Tarkhan or the Muslims.

Yazdajurd fled to the countryside and asked for shelter in a miller's hut. The miller did not recognise his self-imposed guest. But when he went to the market to get food for his guests, he told the people that he had a noble in his home. This information was carried over to the Governor of Merv. He sent a small detachment to check out the rumour and they found the Emperor. The commander of the force ordered Yazdajurd's head to be cut off. The order was carried out and the head was taken to the Governor while headless body was thrown into the river Murghab. His body was found by some Christian monks, who took it and buried it in a graveyard in Merv. Thus, in the year 651, the lineage of the Sassanian Emperors came to an end.

During Usman's caliphate the Muslims moved further west into North Africa up to Morocco, and they reached the Indian and Chinese borders in the east and on the north took over northern Armenia and Azerbaijan.

Usman the Economist

Usman ruled for 12 years, the first half of the rule being excellent in all respects. But in the second half discontent grew from within the Caliphate leading to a tragic climax. The main impetus of the conflict was due to the rise of a capitalist middle class led by the Umayyad. The nation of the Muslims had grown big and powerful. The economy had become vast and was no more manageable from a single headquarter in Madinah. There was an imminent need for privatisation and decentralisation. Though political decentralisation had been practiced in the large empires, true economic decentralisation was not yet known or understood anywhere in the world. The visionary Usman, coming from an aristocratic merchant environment became aware of this and soon after becoming the Caliph took steps to emancipate the economy. He supported local enterprises in various districts and gave state funds to private enterprises.

Usman changed Madinah from Umar's 'state controlled' state to a compassionate 'free enterprise' state. He decentralised the rule, and the Governors of each province became more autonomous with more executive power. Usman disposed many restrictions that were in place during Umar's time. The Muslims were allowed to buy properties in the conquered regions. The local restriction to all houses to be of equal size and one-storied was lifted. This resulted in buildings and palatial houses to rise in Madinah and elsewhere. Previously, the wealth of the treasury was distributed to all and sundry. Now that the general people had enough wealth, Usman restricted the distribution of wealth from the treasury and gave the money for economic and political reforms. Usman's 'free enterprise' was not unbridled. There were moral checks and balances. But, as is the case of free economy, in due time many individuals and enterprises, including the Umayyads, benefited from the new system which led to discontent among others.

Unfortunately, Usman was way ahead of his time. The 'state control' minded Companions started to fear that the reformations would undermine the egalitarian values of Islam. They did not take into consideration that the Muslim society had risen above the poverty level to a well to do class and at this stage of economic development forcefully imposing injudicious state control would threaten the norms of freedom in Islam. The institutions and processes required to support a modern liberal free economy state were being built up very slowly as the existing technology and economic instruments were not sufficient for rapid support of the endeavours. As each province gained autonomy, along with the rise of a rich capitalist class there also arose a disgruntled class. Initially, there were simple rumbling and rumours. But dissatisfaction gained momentum and a number of political lobbies emerged, some of which were anti-establishment. In the last year of Usman's rule the movement took on enormous proportions.

During Usman's tenure, many of the Companions of the Prophet died of old age. A new generation rose in a new socio-economic environment with new social values. Usman was aware of all this and tried to minimise all defects in the social order and maximize the new economic order. Like in the days before Islam, fashion based on superstition threatened to subvert the society again. In Madinah flying pigeons and shooting divining arrows to predict the future became the vogue. Usman ordered that the wings of such pigeons to be cut and the divining bows to be broken. Orders like these decreased Usman's popularity to some degree among those who were involved in such a culture.

Toward the end of his Caliphate, Usman himself was approaching eighty years of age. The strain of a huge, at times, violently changing empire and its myriad of external and internal issues was tremendous. To run the huge empire he had appointed or retained some of his relatives, on whom he could rely, in key positions including the governorships of four provinces. Two of them had been appointed by Umar before him. As the movement against him gathered more pace, the more he had to depend on the Umayyads to run the Caliphate. This angered the opposition even more and the movement gathered further momentum aggravating the situation. This was the start of the end of political universality. Phillip Hitti observes, "Othman who committed the words of Allah to an unalterable form and whose reign saw the complete conquest of Iran, Azerbaijan and Armenia was a pious well meaning old man but too weak to resist the importunities of his greedy kinsfolk."

The army units were in the far-away frontiers. Besides, Usman himself never called on the army to control internal issues, "Keep in mind that you are to guard the frontiers of the Muslim dominions. You are to protect the life and property of the Muslims."

One of his opponents was Abu Dhar Giffari. He was a prominent Companion of the Prophet and had ultra egalitarian views. He maintained that the wealth of the state belonged to the people and thus should be distributed amongst them. Usman on the other hand argued that the wealth of the state did not belong to the people, rather was under God's jurisdiction. This lead to an altercation between them and Giffari went on exile to a place called Rabza about three miles from Madina. Disagreements on political and social issues rose between Usman and other prominent Companions including Ali, Talha, Abdur Rahman bin Auf and Abdullah bin Masud.

Another source of incitement to the anti-Usman movement came through the agent provocateurs. Some were placed by the Byzantines while others were local disgruntled individuals. Abdullah bin Saba, originally a Yemenite Jew, feigned submission to Islam to carry out subversion from within. He concocted a justification that robbing the rich was not illegal. This was supposedly permissible because the rich people supported tyrants and also because it narrowed the difference between the upper and lower classes. The Governor expelled him from Basra and Abdullah went to Kufa. There he claimed to be a supporter of Ali and accused Usman of religious innovation. When he was asked by the Governor to leave Kufa he went to Syria. Here he pretended to be a devout follower of Abu Dhar Giffari giving voice to anti-Usman propaganda. From there he went to Egypt where he mixed with the dissenters inciting a major uprising.

Usman's concept of the Caliphate was that it was selected on the basis of Divine will. Thus the Caliph had to look after the people and was accountable to God. Put in simpler words, the Caliph had to take decisions, economic or political, for the benefit of the state which may not be agreed upon by all. His decisions would have to abide by the Quran and Hadith, the intrinsic law and constitution. If the Caliph did indeed make any mistake he would be punished by God. For Usman, the office of the Caliphate was a contract with God and giving it up would be breaking of that contract. This concept was not a political gambit on his part, it was a real belief that he upheld. At the end, when all had forsaken him, he still held on to that belief and had to die for it.

The Start of the Fitna

In Madina, the movement was fuelled by Amr bin Al-Aas and Companions Amir bin Yasir and Mohammad bin Abu Bakr. A vilification campaign against Usman had been going on over the last years of his rule. The final revolt against him originated from three regions - Egypt, Basra and Kufa. In Basra and Kufa, due to on-going political instability there, Usman had to change their Governors a number of times which resulted in dissent against him to gather pace. But the main revolt was spearheaded from Egypt. After the deposition of Amr the political environment of Egypt had never really settled due to the presence of a strong pro-Amr group there. When the pro-Usman Governor, Ibn Saad, won the naval battle against the Byzantines, it was belittled by the interested parties saying that the real Jihad was against Usman who had fabricated new values against Islam. Two young men both named Mohammad joined the Egyptian revolt against Usman. One was the son of Abu Bakr, while the other was the son of a prominent companion Hudaifah. Both had personal grievances against Usman. The case of Mohammad bin Hudaifah is ironic. He was an Umayyad and after the death of Hudaifah, Usman took his guardianship. Mohammad wanted to be a Governor when he grew up. But Usman declined on the grounds that he was not yet ready for so high an office. Mohammad said that under the circumstances he wanted to seek his fortune. Usman agreed and gave him some money to start him off. Mohammad ultimately ended up in Egypt and joined the campaign against Usman.

In 656, in the lunar month of Shawal, pilgrims from all over the Muslim regions converged in Madinah on way to Makkah to perform the Hajj. About a thousand men started their journey from Egypt for Madinah. They travelled in four separate groups with the stated intention of performing the Hajj. Unlike other pilgrims, all these men were fully armed. Similar groups started from Basra and Kufa. They camped on the outskirt of Madinah and sent an emissary to Ali. They stated that their objective was to remove Usman and place Ali as the Caliph. Ali rejected the proposal. Then they sent emissaries to Zubayr and Talha, but they too refused.

Even though the rebel's proposal was refused, the act of offering the Caliphate to various Companions was a diplomatic success for them. Ali, Talha, Zubayr and other prominent persons in Madinah now had to take a neutral stance as this did not appear to be a rebellion at that stage. Taking advantage of this the rebels demanded the abdication of Usman. Ali went to talk to Usman and during their discourse said, "I have been sent by the people to talk to you. They have said many things against you. But I cannot think of any way to advise you. Caliph, invoke God's help in solving these problems. I need offer you no advice. All things are clear to you. Right and wrong are far apart...."

Usman replied, "I am grateful that you have come to talk to me. You are a keen judge of men and matter and have the perception for truth. I had hoped that from what you see you would realise the poisonous propaganda that is being spread. But your tone is the same as that of the malcontents..... I have thought about what the people are saying and I will deliberate on this in my address in the Prophet's mosque."

There are a number of historical versions of what transpired next. The standard version relates that Usman asked Ali to use his influence with the rebels to resolve the issue. He also agreed to meet all the political demands including appointing the Governors the rebels wanted. Ali deliberated with the rebels and convinced them to return to their homes on the basis that their basic demands have been met.

The rebels were satisfied and turned back towards their own cities. But when they had gone a little distance from Madinah a person going toward Egypt was apprehended. This person was a bondsman of Usman, and after a search a letter was found on him. The letter bore the Caliph's seal and was addressed to the Governor of Egypt ordering him to rescind any previous directives, arrest the rebels when they return to Egypt and put them to the sword.

This incensed the rebels and they went back to Madinah. By this time all the pilgrims had left for Makkah and Madinah was empty. The rebels laid a siege around Usman's house and accused Usman of betrayal. Usman accepted that the impression of the seal was from his ring but he denied any knowledge of the letter. It was pointed out that the handwriting may have been Marwan's, who was the private secretary of the Caliph as well as an Umayyad. It was assumed that he may have tampered with the political situation behind the back of the Caliph. The rebels then demanded that Marwan be handed over to them, which Usman rejected. He had no wish to hand over anyone to an unruly mob. Ali was totally dismayed at what he thought of as double standards on the part of the Umayyads and parted company and retired to his house. But, even then, he posted his two sons Hasan and Husain at the Caliph's door as guards.

Initially, the siege of Usman's house by the rebels was quite passive. But as the events precipitated, the scene gradually became ugly. The mob denied anyone to move to and fro from the house, disallowing even water to be carried there. Soon, skirmishes broke out and arrows were shot in which people died or became wounded on both sides. Zubayr and Talha were seen moving among the rebels. It was not known why they were there. On being informed Usman went to the front of his house and said loudly, "Talha! Are you there?"

There was silence.

After some time Usman repeated, "Talha! Are you there?"

This time Talha stepped into view.

Usman said, "I did not expect you to be among the rioters. Nor did I expect you not to respond to my call."

At this Talha withdrew to his home. But the rioting continued and soon the mob became violent. Usman had sent a letter to the pilgrims in Makkah explaining the situation to them. The rebels were apprehensive that the pilgrims may return to support the Caliph. That caused them to accelerate the movement to precipitate an outcome. The gate to the house of the Caliph was set on fire. Hasan bin Ali was wounded while defending the house of the Caliph and taken away. This, probably, made the rebels even more apprehensive on account that the Hashemite may now take up arms against them. In the confusion some of the rebels led by Mohammad bin Abu Bakr scaled the wall of the Caliph's house. They entered the house and Mohammad bin Abu Bakr gripped the beard of the Caliph. Usman was not perturbed nor did he ask for mercy. All he said was, "If your father was here today, he would be distressed."

That shook Mohammad bin Abu Bakr and he released the Caliph and stepped back and left. But the other rebels in the room stuck at Usman. His wife Naila tried to protect him using her own body as a shield. But all was in vain. In the tussle she received some injuries including the loss of a finger.

Usman died.

Some of the people in the Caliph's house arrived and fell upon the rebels. The person who had killed the Caliph was also killed in the violence. The rebels left when the women of the house raised a hue and cry.

Previously, the Governor of Syria Muawiah and Mughira bin Shuba had sent Usman messages with three options. They said that he should order a fight back, or go to Makkah or go to Syria for personal safety. But Usman would neither order a fight back against the Muslims nor flee. He stuck to his principles and refused to leave the city of the Prophet. The man of eighty stood for what he believed and faced the rebellion, alone, come what may.

According to Tabari, in his last sermon Usman was more worried about the disunity in the Caliphate rather than his own safety, "...This world will not last, so be not proud of anything in it. ... remain united and do not be divided into factions. Remember, you were enemies of each other. But under Islam, God made you like brothers. See that this unity is maintained at all cost."

The rebels had raised a number of allegations against Usman to justify their actions. The major allegations against Usman were that he had appointed his kinsfolk to powerful position and given them money. But his economic decentralisation was totally misunderstood and misrepresented. What Usman did was never for personal benefit. The total commitment of Usman to Islam is self evident. He became a Muslim in a very difficult time when only a handful had dared to do so and had to face a lot of persecution. He had to leave his comfortable and elite life, his rich family, his wives and migrate to face hardships in foreign lands. He had from the onset been a very generous and charitable man and supported poor families and donated large amounts to noble causes. As a Caliph, he never took any financial benefit for himself. When the agitation had reached the climax his personal wealth had diminished to that of an ordinary person. Sir William Muir in the *Caliphate* observes that much of the history books were written more than a century later during the reign of the Abbasids. They were anti-Umayyad and may have coloured the history against Usman and the Umayyads.

Usman was a reformer. Unlike Umar he was a liberal reformer. He understood the economic necessities of the time that the Muslims had improved buying power and needed commercial enterprises and institutions to carry the society to the next stage of economic development. It was not possible for the Caliphate, any longer, to oversee all the entrepreneurship that was needed and micromanage. So he had diverted the funds from the treasury towards the building of the commercial institutes and ventures. His liberal values were not confined to just economics. Even when facing death he refrained from the use of violence. He was the Caliph and even though the rebellion had gained ground, had he given a call, people would have acknowledged it and come to protect him. This would have led to factional fighting leading to a greater violence and tragedy. His failing, if at all, was the inability to arrest the speed of change.

Before the emergence of the political chaos, most of the Governors who officiated under Usman were very successful. His foster brother, Abdullah bin Saad was very apt in financial matters and also carried on successful conquests into North Africa and crushed the Byzantine navy. Muawiah was exceptionally brilliant in developing Syria and would eventually become the founder of the Umayyad dynasty.

The changing socio-economic environment caused debates, disagreements, and discordance amongst the people. Still, except for the rebels, all adhered to the Caliph and the laws of the state. But the killing of Usman changed the whole scenario. In the complexity of the situation even companions of the calibre of Ali, Muawiah, Talha, Zubayr and Amr bin Al Aas, at one stage or another, were unsure of what was the right stance and what was not and which side was the right one and which one was not. The Prophet was no longer there to guide them. They simply had to take up principled stands as their conscience dictated. This would place them on opposite sides of battlefields with tragic consequences resulting in historical schisms among the Muslims.

Due to this killing there was a return of tribalism that had existed before Islam. There had been rivalry between tribes and clans like the Hashemites and the Umayyads. The advent of Islam had suppressed such attitudes and tribal politics. But the death of Usman caused polarisation among the tribes like Umayyads, who had their base in Damascus, and the Hashemites, who were growing in Kufa (Hasan, 2004). The Hashemites would now fall into two groups the Alids and the Abbasids.

Usman's Greatest Achievement

The historically unique and momentous achievement during Usman's Caliphate was the official compilation of the Quran. At that time in history, various tribes spoke in various Arabic dialects (readings) like Quraish, Hudhyal, etc. When people had come to the Prophet to ask which 'reading' was correct, he is known to have accepted seven of these readings as correct as long as the meaning remained exact.

By the time of Usman, Islam had spread far and wide. Some of the Companions noted that people in distant lands such as Armenia and Azerbaijan were reciting the Quran, though same in overall meaning, slightly differently from one another. This was brought to the notice of Usman. He decided this should not be allowed to happen. To resolve this issue Usman ordered that the *Mushaf*, that is, the compilation which was done by Zaid bin Thabit under Abu Bakr be brought to him. The Mushaf had passed from Abu Bakr to Umar and at the death of Umar to his daughter, Hafsa. Usman wanted a standard copy to be produced according to the Mushaf and copies sent to all the Muslim lands. But instead of just copying the Mushaf, he wanted an expert committee to check it first.

A committee was formed with Zaid, the original compiler of the Mushaf, as the supervisor with members including scholars and authorities like the Companions Abdullah bin Zubayr, Saeed bin Al'Aas and Abdur Rahman bin Al Harith. The Arabic spoken by the Quraish was considered the correct as the Prophet was a Quraish and had uttered the Quran in it. Zaid bin Thabit was told to retain Quraish Arabic as that was the 'reading' in which the Quran was revealed to the Prophet. After corroboration all the working copies and private copies were burnt so that no confusion could arise in future.

Companions like Ubay bin Kaab and Ibn Masud had privately collected the Quran. Ubay's manuscript needed some correction as it had a slightly different ordering of the chapters. The only objection to have come was from Ibn Masud who said that a few verses in which the Quraish were admonished had been suppressed. It is probable that the verses he referred to were actually the Prophet's own admonitions rather then revelations. As this compilation was an open-to-all corroborative research and synthesis, all the companions were allowed to challenge the compilation if they wanted, and all conceded to its exactitude as was much later commented by Ali.

Copies of the Quran were prepared and sent to the provinces. Over time, throughout the vast empire the demand for the Quran grew. To meet the demand it became a practice and an art to make precise copies of the Quran. The compiled Quran facilitated in maintaining its original form.

In later centuries, when the art of paper making became popular, books became very inexpensive. From that stage developed the art of large scale writing and publishing. In the past, Sumerians, Egyptians, Persians, Greeks, Hebrews and Christians had written books on parchments and papyrus. But the sheer scale in which the Quran was copied was unparallel. This revolution contributed extensively to initiate the Age of Books.

Ali bin Abu Talib

599 - 661

The next Caliph, Ali bin Abu Talib, was the cousin of the Prophet and belonged to the Hashemite clan of the Quraish. When he was about five years old the Prophet became his guardian. Ali grew up as a member of the Prophet's household and became a very scholarly, intelligent, enterprising and brave young man. Earlier in Makkah, the Prophet had invited the leaders of his clan, the Hashemite, to a feast to declare his mission. There were about forty of them present on the occasion. After the feast, the Prophet explained his call and prophethood to them. Then he asked, "Who among you will support me in this endeavour?"

All the Hashimites remained quiet. In fact Abu Jahl, the rich step uncle of the Prophet, took on a very hostile attitude. But little Ali stood up and said, "I will support you."

The Prophet though sad at his clan's rejection, was very touched by his young cousin's support. Ali also played an important role during the Hijra by sleeping in the bed of the Prophet while the Prophet went to Madinah with Abu Bakr. This confused the band of the Quraish who wanted to kill the Prophet and thought the Prophet was still in bed, sleeping. In the battle of Badr, Ali was one of the three duellists who fought the Quraish champions before the onset of the main battle. After that his name grew in fame as a great warrior and an incredibly strong person. Starting from Badr, he showed phenomenal valour in all the battles he fought. In Uhud he was one of the few people who kept on fighting when the Muslims were dispersed and thought they had lost the battle. In the battle of the trench he defeated a famous Quraish champion demoralising the Quraish warriors. He always led the army from the front and showed incredible feat of bravery and strength.

In Madinah, the Prophet married him to his daughter Fatima. At that time a large number of people from all over Arabia and further away had gathered and accepted Islam. The Prophet betook on himself to look after them. He gave them whatever provision he could afford to give. Ali and Fatima were living a bare-essential life. Both of them undertook manual labour for subsistence. They used to draw water from wells and supply water to houses and got paid for it. Their hands would become blistered from drawing the water and their shoulders became swollen from carrying the filled pitchers.

Ali was a soldier, a General as well as a scholar and an intellectual. After the conquest of Makkah, the Prophet had sent Khaled to Yemen to invite the people to Islam. As people of Yemen were Jews and Christians the invite was to be a deliberation. The tradition was that individual opponents would face each other in a scholastic debate known as the Mubahila. These debates or intellectual duels could go on for days till one side accepted the superiority of the other.

Once, the Prophet himself had been challenged to a Mubahila by Christian priests in Madinah. The debate had commenced for some time till the priests had asked, "As the

Muslims believe that Jesus was a prophet but not the son of God, how would they explain that Jesus was born of a virgin and did not have a father." This was the key question of the Mubahila and the Prophet had not answered it that day. The next day he had replied, "The Muslims would explain it the same way they would explain the birth of Adam, who did not have a father or a mother."

Having reached Yemen to give the call Khaled was at a total loss. He was a man of action, not a man of words. The Prophet recalled him and sent Ali in his stead. Here Ali proved his scholarship and intellectual genius. For days he debated in the Mubahila with one opponent after another, referring not only from Muslim scripture but from all forms of knowledge including Christian and Jewish scriptures as well. Finally, all accepted his superiority in the Mubahila.

Doctor Henry Stubbe in *An Account of the Rise and Progress of Muhammadanism* stated about Ali, "He feared God much, gave many alms, was just in all his actions, humble and affable, of an exceeding quick wit and of an ingenuity that was not common. He was exceedingly learned not only in those sciences that terminate in speculation, but those which extend to practice."

Once a Jew tested Ali's wisdom by asking a couple of questions that had always been debatable and unanswered. The first question was, "When did God come to exist?"

Ali replied, "God is above considerations of time and space. Creation is not but God is. God was when there was no being. God existed without cause and with no beginning and no end. God is subjected to no limitations, is infinite and the end of all souls."

The Jew asked the next question, "What is fate?"

Predestination has always been another debated issue. Ali tried to avoid the question, "It is a gloomy road, tread it not."

But the Jew persisted, "What is fate?"

"It is a deep sea, avoid it."

"What is fate?"

"It is a mystery of God which is hidden from you, probe it not."

"What is fate?"

Finally, Ali said, "Has God created you for what God has willed, or for what you have willed."

"Indeed, for what God has willed."

"Then God will do to you as God sees fit and that is fate."

Ali was not only scholarly but very noble in every aspect of life as well. An example of his everyday actions expresses his great qualities: One day, after purchasing two pieces of clothes from the market Ali gave the expensive one to his bondsman and kept the cheaper one for himself.

When Abu Bakr became the Caliph, apparently, some problem arose between Ali and the Caliph. There was a piece of land in a place called Fadak that had belonged to the

Prophet. The revenue from the land was used for the maintenance of the Prophet's household and to support wayfarers and poor people. Ali and Fatima laid claim on the land on the basis of inheritance. Abu Bakr had rejected the claim on the grounds that the Prophet himself had given the directive which stated that Prophets do not leave any inheritance. Fatima stopped talking to Abu Bakr and Ali is said to have deferred his allegiance to Abu Bakr for some time.

The Shia Muslims claim that the Prophet had indicated that Ali should be his successor or the Caliph after him. After the 'farewell pilgrimage' the Prophet, on his way back to Madinah, had given a speech with instructions in a place called Ghadir Khum. At one stage he had said, "Ali is the *Mawla* of those of whom I am the *Mawla.*"

Mawla in Arabic has a variety of related meanings but in this context it meant 'Master'. Nothing precipitated from the speach at that time and all went their way. But during the Fitna, civil war that erupted after Usman's death, people on Ali's side said that the statement meant Ali was to be the successor of the Prophet, i.e., the first Caliph. As a reaction, some of the non-Alid scholars would totally reject that anything like that was said. This speech or the supposed meaning of the speech was to become one of the most contentious issues between the scholars of Shia and Sunni sects that would form later.

During the reign of Abu Bakr and Umar the movement of the Companions was mostly limited and they resided in Madinah. They were the 'Parliament' supporting the Caliph in promulgating laws and policies and involving themselves in scholarship. Ali was one of the foremost among them and had become an expert on judicial matters. He was the first to formulate the 'Plea for insanity' in the court. A woman with mental aberration was found guilty of adultery and was to be punished. But Ali interceded that a person not in control of her faculties cannot be considered guilty. She was relinquished of the charge of adultery. Umar held Ali as the best of the judges and had proclaimed, "But without Ali, Umar would be lost."

Once Ali and a Jew came to the court of Caliph Umar to resolve a dispute that had arisen between them. Umar asked them both to sit and said to Ali, "Abul Hasan, tell me your side of the story."

Abul Hasan was Ali's *Kunya*, meaning 'father of Hasan'. People are addressed by their Kunya as a mark of respect. After hearing Ali, Umar turned to the Jew and, "Now you tell me your side of the story."

As the Jew started to speak, Ali's countenance changed and he looked upset. Umar turned to Ali said, "Are you upset because I have placed you in the same footing as this man?"

"No, I am upset for just the opposite reason," said Ali, "you addressed me with respect using my Kunya. But you did not use this man's Kunya when you addressed him."

Umar said, "I pray to God that He let me not live in a land where Abul Hasan is not."

Ali was mainly involved in judicial and scholastic pursuits and policy making during the reigns of the previous three Caliphs. He was forced to the forefront of politics at the end of Usman's rule when the rebel leaders approached him to take up the Caliphate.

Events of the Fitna

Ali's refusal to accept the position of Caliph from the rebels resulted in anarchy in the state with no ruling authority. There was complete lawlessness with the locals shutting their doors and the rebels aimlessly wandering the streets. The common motive of the rebels from Egypt, Basra and Kufa was the removal of Usman. Once that had been achieved, they did not have commonality anymore. And most had wanted the removal of Usman not his death. After events precipitated in murder most of the rebels did not know how to tackle the situation. They even differed on who the next Caliph should be. Four days went by and the rebel leaders realised that their comrades would soon have to return to their homes. But they were unsure what would happen next and had no inkling as to what the attitude of the next government would be towards them. As the heat of the moment cooled, the great impact of the murder of Usman started to sink in the psyche of Madinah and Arabia. The rebels realised that their actions did not have any mass support and there was a good probability that soon they would be treated as criminals and punished accordingly. Thus, it was important for them that they lodge a new Caliph and establish a new government, thus giving the whole episode a sense of legality. They gave an ultimatum that unless a Caliph is chosen by the people of Madinah within the next day, they would be forced to take drastic action.

The people of Madinah and the rebels assembled in the Mosque of the Prophet. The prevailing situation was discussed with the focus on who should be the next Caliph. The discussion went on for several hours and soon slogans were raised in favour of Ali. As the vast majority of people wanted Ali to become the Caliph the rebel leaders approached Ali and asked for his hand to declare their allegiance.

Two aspects became abundantly clear at this stage. First, had Usman's death been natural Ali would have been the next Caliph, there was no doubt about that. Second, the state of anarchy was not affecting the town of Madinah alone but also the governance, control and unity of the greatest Empire of the time that spread from the borders of China in the east to Byzantine and North Africa on the west. The government-less disorder had to come to an end very soon.

Ali put forward his hand and allegiance was given to him by the rebels as well as the vast majority of the people of Madinah. Thus Ali became the fourth Caliph in the year 656. Perhaps the most able person took the mantle of the Caliph in the most inopportune of times. The battle between the egalitarian and commercial forces that was waging during the time of Usman was now to be resolved. Most of the older and influential companions, those of egalitarian bent, those who would have supported Ali, including people like Abu Dhar Giffari and Abdurrahman bin Auf were by now dead. The new generation of entrepreneurs led by the Umayyads had gained economic and institutional power in most of the provinces with Syria being their stronghold under the very able governorship of Muawiah.

Ali's acceptance of the Caliphate had broken the prevailing deadlock and anarchy but it also entailed the tacit forgiveness, on his part, of the rebels. This would prove to be a great political vulnerability for him in the future, when dissident forces would ask for the punishement of the rebels, but he would be unable to comply. Edward Gibbon in *Rise and fall of the Roman Empire*, states "A tumultous anarchy of five days after the martyrdom of Otheman was appeased by the inauguration of Ali, his refusal would have provoked a general massacre."

Uncertainty prevailed immediately after Ali assumed office. Though he had been nominated Caliph by a great majority in Madinah, some of the prominent people had been absent, as Talha had been absent during Usman's nomination. Many of the Umayyads had gone to Syria during the fray or after the burial of Usman. Those who remained did not participate in the selection. The men of *Ahle Safa*, those of austere and scholastic order, did not participate as they generally shunned politics. Abdullah bin Umar abstained as he was neither for nor against this turn of events involving Ali. About Talha and Zubayr there are contradictory reports, but generally accepted one states that they gave allegiance to Ali but later went to Makkah and renounced it. Whatever the case might have been, the environment became ambiguous as at one hand Usman, who had done so much for Islam, had been so cruelly murdered, on the other hand now no less a person but Ali was in charge. Ali found that many were in a dilemma as to what to do and the rebels, to save themselves, were openly supporting him. Taking advantage of the prevailing situation a propaganda was started by the Umayyads against Ali. The pre-Islamic tribal rivalry between the Umayyad and the Hashemite re-ignited.

Ali's son Hasan and cousin Abdullah bin Abbas advised Ali to leave Madinah and withdraw to some safe place in the desert. After things had settled down, the people would realise the reality and come to him themselves to declare their loyalty. But the state of affairs in the Caliphate and its responsibilities weighed heavily on Ali. He was not a person to run away from adversity. He decided to appoint new Governors to the provinces who would be loyal to him. Abdullah bin Abbas was against such changes so soon after Usman's death while the central government had lost much of its credibility and power. He proposed that they wait giving people the time needed to recover. But Ali knew that the Umayyads were consolidating. As time passed they would grow from strength to strength. It may already be too late to stop them. So, he sent his appointees to take over the Governors offices in the provinces. Egypt, Yemen and Basra complied and Ali's Governor's took office. Kufa paid allegiance to Ali but wanted the incumbent Governor to retain office. Syria outright rejected the change. The Governor Muawiah declared that he would pay allegiance to Ali only after the killers of Usman had been punished. Ali sent an emissary to Muawiah explaining that he would do his utmost to ferret out and punish the killers from among the rebels but in the meantime, Muawiah should cooperate with the central government and step aside.

With Ali's consolidation in office, Muawiah feared that the rebels may go unpunished. Ali, though not outright like Umar or Abu Dhar Giffari, had an egalitarian leaning ideology, which caused the Umayyads and the new generation entrepreneurs see in Ali a 'classless' threat looming which may cause them to loose much of the considerable wealth and power they had accumulated over the last decade. At this stage Ali had been more or less accepted as the Caliph over much of the Muslim world except in Syria. Muawiah realised he needed more time to put his case to the people before he could make any move.

Muawiah, among other things to his credit, was a master diplomat and had for twenty years built up a strong and successful administration in Syria. The anger that he felt due to the recent events is entirely justifiable. He detained the emissary that Ali had sent for three months. In the meantime, the bloodied shirt of Usman and the amputated finger of his wife, Naila, were displayed in the central mosque in Damascus causing great indignation and emotions to mushroom. He sent a number of emissaries to different provinces including Makkah to propagate the pathetic and cruel tale of Usman's killing and Ali's assumption of power soon after that. This estranged the people from the central government, which started to become isolated. He also established a network of informers and agents all over the Caliphate for covert activities and intelligence acquisition. After three months Muawiah allowed Ali's emissary to return with the message that Muawiah would send a reply soon in the hand's of his own emissary.

When he was ready, Muawiah sent as emissary with a letter for Ali. When Ali opened the envelop he found in it a blank page. Ali enquired what that meant. Then the emissary delivered Muawiah's message, "Be it known to you that more than 60,000 people have wet their face with tears and are rallying to avenge the death of Usman. The battle standard for them is the bloodied shirt of Usman."

Thus Muawiah formally declared a revolt after consolidating his position both militarily and politically. His emissaries had neutralised the political environment so that many now believed that Muawiah's stand was justified and no one would be in the mood to get involved in any religious fratricide leaving Ali alone to face a very well organised Syria. And Muwaiah, himself, believed he was totally and completely justified in what he was doing.

Ali was furious and decided to raise an army and attack Syria. He called for contribution from Madinah and the provinces. But Muawiah had used his time well. The people were unsure and reluctant. Ali was very perturbed and frustrated. Much later in a sermon in the Prophet's mosque he would say, "...When I ask you to march in summer you request the expedition be delayed till the hot season is over. Then in winter you want it delayed till the cold season is over. These are lame excuses. If you are afraid of the heat and cold you would surely run away from a sword. You do not deserve to be called men."

In Makkah, a different drama of its own was enacting. At the selection of Ali the people of Makkah were left in a passive quandary. Ali had not deposed its Governor. But soon, people with grievance against Ali began to arrive there. The deposed Governor of Basra went there, as did the deposed Governor of Yemen. Talha and Zubayr managed to leave Madinah without informing Ali and arrived there as well. Though, they were non-Umayyad, both were very influential. Makkah, itself, for long had been a mercantile hub and had been ruled by Abu Sufian the father of Muawiah till its conquest by the Prophet.

There was justified indignation against the killing of Usman but the added elements now changed the environment, and it became charged with anti-Ali emotions. Talha and Zubayr renounced any allegiance to Ali. They were related to Ayesha, the wife of the Prophet, and subsequently all of them rallied round her.

Though Ali and Ayesha both belonged to the household of the Prophet, there were times when they had not seen eye to eye. When, years ago, the calumny was spread against Ayesha the Prophet had conferred with his companions about it. Umar straightway declared that it was calumny being spread by hypocrites. Other Companions asked the Prophet to keep his mind in peace. But Ali, then a young warrior, had declared that though he thought she was innocent, Ayesha could be divorced irrespective as there was no dearth of women if the Prophet wanted another wife.

During the rebellion, Ayesha had gone to Makkah to perform the Hajj. When she was returning to Madinah she learnt of Usman's death and Ali's acceptance of the Caliphate. Instead of going to Madinah she retraced her steps to Makkah. Here she raised her voice for the punishment of those responsible for Usman's death. She, the Mother of the Faithful, was the only person who could lead an army from Makkah against the Commander of the Faithful.

Soon an army was raised for this purpose. The ex-Governor of Yemen had come to Makkah with the wealth of the treasury of provincial Yemen. He handed over the wealth for the army. It was decided that Ayesha would lead the army with Talha and Zubayr as her commanders. They would first go to Basra, punish the killers among the rebels there and make Basra their base for further action. As the army of about 3000 started their movement a quarrel broke out among the supporters of Talha and Zubayr regarding who would be the next Caliph if the expedition was successful. Ayesha averted any further escalation saying the issue was premature. But the quarrel had a negative effect on those who had joined the army on the grounds that they were going to rectify an injustice. They now felt that they were in fact going to fight for political ambitions. Thus some of them returned to Makkah. Nonetheless, the army marched on and reached the outskirt of Basra where they were met by the representative from Basra enquiring the reason of their approach. Ayesha after decrying the events in Madina iterated, "...we do not seek war, we seek peace. Such peace can only be established with the full confidence of the people. There is much chaos in the affairs of the Muslims. We want your support in setting it right."

Basra became divided into two camps. The Governor was pro Ali and wanted to defend Basra and mitigate the issue somehow without using violence. But the deputy Governor Hakim bin Jabala regarded Ayesha's army as a rebellion against the Caliphate and wanted to take drastic actions. The events led to the Basran army to be deployed. When the two armies faced each other instead of shooting arrows they started to shout accusations and counter accusations. There was no will to actually fight and Ayesha ordered her forces to be on the defensive. From the Basra side, some people taunted Zubayr and Talha for leaving their wives at home while dragging the Mother of the Faithful to the battleground. They were also criticised for breaking the oath of allegiance to the Caliph Ali. One soldier said, "Mother, if you have come here on your own free will, go back on your own will. If you have been forced to come here, we can guarantee you a safe and honourable conduct back."

Hakim hurled some insulting remarks at Ayesha, Talha and Zubayr and led an assault on Ayesha's army. Ayesha still tried to maintain a defensive position but in the face of the assault she finally gave the order to counter attack. An 'unwilling and partial' battle ensued in which there were fatalities on both sides. After nightfall the forces retired. But the battle intensified on the following days and Ayesha with support from a faction in Basra emerged victorious. Hakim bin Jabala kept on fighting bravely, even though wounded, to his death. The pro Ali faction vacated the city and the remaining people accepted Ayesha as the authority and Talha and Zubayr became her ministers.

Battle of the Camel

Meanwhile in Madinah, Ali realised that if things were to be brought under control he would have to act fast. With great difficulty he managed to raise a small army numbering fewer than 900 fighters. These included people who had participated in the revolt against Usman, but also included others who were dedicated to Ali. Abu Qatada, a veteran Ansar leader, and Umme Salama, another widow of the Prophet, were among those who joined this army. Though much consternation and doubt were raised from many quarters, Ali still set off with this army to establish his authority on the huge Caliphate.

When he reached Rabda, the crossroad between Makkah, Madinah, Basra and Kufa, he found that Ayesha had already taken Basra. Though a few tribes joined him here, he knew that his army was inadequate to take on a hostile army defending Basra. Ali turned to Kufa and decided to tackle it first.

Abu Musa Ashari, the Governor of Kufa, had decided to remain neutral in the situation. On reaching Kufa Ali sent emissaries to Ashari for support. But Ashari received them coldly and refused to change his position. Ali sent another emissary, but with the same end result. Ali realised that Ashari had on both occasions confronted the emissaries himself without letting them approach the people of Kufa. Another mission, led by Hasan bin Ali, was sent by Ali and included people who were from Kufa and yielded influence there. The mission members mingled with the people of Kufa and were able to boost a large support for Ali.

Hasan entered the main mosque when many people had gathered for for the Friday noon prayer. He was given an ovation by the supporters of Ali who had gathered there. Ashari welcomed him and Hasan took the pulpit. He exhorted the people of Kufa to support the Caliph in his endeavours. At that stage Zaid bin Sehwan, a prominent Kufan stood up and said that he had received a letter from Ayesha advising people of Kufa not to get involved in any fighting and stay home. Hasan countered saying, "Isn't it strange that Ayesha should advise the people of Kufa not to fight while she has raised an army for exactly that objective."

Then Ashari took the stage and said, "This is a fight between two group of Muslims. The best that we, the people of Kufa, can do is stay out of it."

Hasan asked, "Did Talha and Zubayr give allegiance to Ali."

"They did," said Ashari.

"Did the Caliph do any wrong to them?" Hasan wanted to know.

"I am unaware of any such wrong." Ashari replied.

"If someone revolts against rightful authority, doesn't the authority have the right to take action against them."

"Yes, it does." Ashari said.

"Then on what grounds do you justify not supporting the Caliph against these rebels?"

This time Ashari did not have any answer. Hasan now went on the offensive, "You own your office to the Caliph Ali?"

"Yes."

"So you are under the Caliph's command and cannot take any action which directly or indirectly supports anyone who rebels against him."

"Yes."

Then Hasan declared, "Your Caliph has asked for help in fighting against his enemies. His enemies have asked the people to abstain. You ask the people to abstain as well. Your action supports the enemy. This is sedition."

At this moment people raised slogans against Ashari. A scuffle broke out between the supporters of the two groups which spread outside the mosque. But the supporters of Ali prevailed and Ashari was deposed. A pro-Ali government was declared. After the situation had settled down, Hasan gave a speech to the people, "...Beware of the rebels when they say they want to avenge the death of Usman. This is merely a pretext. All they want is to remove Ali from the Caliphate and take power themselves...."

In a few short days a 10,000 strong army was raised. This included many warriors who had actively campaigned and won Persia. As Ali led the army to Basra the Bedouin tribes who had declared neutrality now joined him and soon the force was 20,000 strong. The Governor of Basra who had been deposed by Ayesha's force also joined the army. He had been mistreated after loosing Basra, but when Ayesha came to know of that she had ordered him to be released.

Ali, upon reaching Basra, now expected that the large force he commanded would compel his opponents to seek amity. He sent a peace mission led by Qa'aqa, a famous veteran of the Persian war. He ordered his emissaries not to be threatening or condescending with the opponents. When the mission entered Basra they were well received by Ayesha, Talha and Zubayr. When the parley began Ayesha declared that her objective was to punish the killers of Usman and to unify the Muslims.

Qa'aqa asked, "Mother, do you accuse Ali of being a criminal who murdered Usman or do you accuse him of being an accomplice?"

"I do not accuse him of any such thing. The only thing of which I accuse him of is that he did not punish the killers of Usman." Ayesha stated.

"Was the murder of Usman the act of a single person or that of a mob?" Qa'aqa asked.

"Obviously, it was a mob"

"Have things settled down since then?"

"No, things are still in disarray."

"Under such circumstances, how could you expect Ali to punish the killers when those very killers are in control and could cause another rebellion if they wished?"

Neither Ayesha nor Talha or Zubayr had any satisfactory answer to this question. Having successfully explained the quandary Ali was in, Qa'aqa stated, "Do you realise that your action against Ali has forced him not to take action against the killers of Usman?"

"How is that?" Ayesha inquired.

"Instead of dealing with the killers Ali now has to deal with the revolt against him. The rebels are the people who now give him the much needed support. Your action has forced him into their hands."

As Ayesha contemplated on this, he added, "You have raised a Muslim army to fight against Muslims. How do you expect this to bring unity? You have rightly or wrongly killed people in Basra on the charge of killing Usman. You have drawn blood, you should now be satisfied."

Then he turned towards Talha and Zubayr and said, "You had given allegiance to Ali in Madinah. If it was under compulsion, declare *now* the name of a person more worthy of the Caliphate than Ali."

The manner and logic with which Qa'aqa put forward his argument had its desired effect. Finally Ayesha said, "So what do you propose we do now?"

"Strengthen the hand of Ali. When things have settled the killers of Usman will be brought to account."

"If that is Ali's view, then we are prepared for peace under honourable terms." Ayesha said.

Ali was delighted with the success of the peace mission. The following morning he placed a man in the centre of his army holding the Quran over his head signifying that the negotiations would be peaceful under the injunctions of the Quran. The two armies camped outside Basra heaved a sign of relief. Then Ali met Talha and Zubayr in the middle of the field under amicable circumstances and it was agreed that the peace treaty would be agreed upon the next day.

As peace appeared to prevail, one small group from Kufa became worried. This group included those who were responsible for the killing of Usman. They realised that once peace was formalised they may have to face the same fate as their cohorts of Basra. Their leaders met secretly that night to find a solution. The first proposal was that they kill Ali, Talha and Zubayr. But it was rejected on the ground that it would only unite all the parties and they would be hunted down for the killing of not only Usman but all four of them. After turning down a number of proposals they came to the conclusion that peace could not be allowed to be established. They decided to act that very night. Before dawn, they silently gather their men and attacked the sleeping army of Basra. When Ayesha, Talha and Zubayr came to know of the attack, the most obvious conclusion was that Ali had reneged. They commanded a counter attack. The plotters were waiting for that and immediately informed Ali that Ayesha had reneged and attacked them. In the darkness before dawn, the battle began. This battle comes down in history known as the 'Battle of the Camel' as Ayesha led it sitting in the litter of her camel. This battle initiated much greater chaos in later days.

Both the sides clashed with great ferocity. Talha fought bravely, leading from the front. But soon died of the wounds he received one after another. Zubayr left for Makkah as the tide turned against the smaller army. Ayesha was the only commander left on the field. At one stage, seeing people falling all around her, she made a last attempt for peace. She placed Kaab bin Sure, the judge of Basra, in the centre of the battle field holding the Quran over his head asking for peace. But the plotters shouted, "Kaab is the one who declared Talha and Zubayr had not given allegiance to Ali. Slaughter him."

A rain of arrows hit Kaab and he fell down. Ayesha was in the thick of the battle with her litter pierced by arrows. As the battle raged on, Ali realised that unless Ayesha was stopped this senseless killing would continue. He ordered that the Ayesha's camel be brought down. The warriors around Ayesha desperately fought on, but finally some of Ali's men slipped in and struck at the leg of the camel. The camel fell. With no more commanders left on Ayesha's side the fighting subsided. Ali himself approached the camel litter and inquired, "Mother, are you all right?"

Thousands of people had died. Zubayr on his way to Makkah was killed by Ahnaf, the chief of the Qais tribe. When Ali inspected the battlefield and saw some eminent companions of Prophet he felt incredibly sad and bitter. Later when Ahnaf brought the information of Zubayr's death Ali cursed Ahnaf. Instead of celebrating victory, he declared three days of mourning and ordered that except for weapons no property be taken as spoil of war.

Ayesha was borne with much respect to a house in Basra. The stress of leading the army, the physical and mental strain of the battle, the humiliation of defeat, and the death of eminent persons lay heavily on her. She fell ill and stayed in Basra for some time. When she recovered she wished to go to Madinah. Ali, who visited her often, made elaborate preparations for her journey. A number of women from Basra accompanied her. Muhammad bin Abu Bakr, Ayesha's step brother, led the entourage. Ali himself accompanied them to some distance.

Ayesha, upon reaching Madinah, retired from political life and took up scholarship. She came to be recognised as an authority on the Traditions of Prophet.

Ali, instead of returning to Madinah, went to Kufa and declared Kufa the capital of the Caliphate. This was probably in response to the non-cooperation he had received from Madinah when he tried to raise an army there. He set up administration with various functionaries including judges and revenue officers. But soon the state of affairs in Kufa started to deteriorate as well. It was a new town originating from a military cantonment established during the reign of Umar. The majority of the people there were Bedouins and Yemenites, late converts to Islam, without any particular political ideology. They were one of the foremost participants in the revolt against Usman. They had wanted Zubayr as the Caliph, but had later provided support to Ali. When Ali became the Caliph, they tried to change to a 'neutral' status. After Kufa became the capital, they became recalcitrant again. After the victory in Basra, Ali wanted to take action against the sole dissenting province of Syria. But the Kufans did not want to participate in any further battles as so many of them had died in the recent one. When Ali appointed his cousin Abdullah bin Abbas as the governor of Basra, they questioned, "Then why did we revolt when Usman appointed his relatives?"

Although they gave allegiance to Ali, the people of Basra themselves were not a homogenous mass. Few still considered themselves pro Usman while others were neutral. Ali from the very onset was leading a people of a variety of opinion, very susceptible to outside interference. Due to too many opinions the army became very difficult to control. On the other hand, Muawiah's camp was totally homogenous, economy and commerce played an important part in their ideology. Under the new socio-political environment they represented the more practical proposition.

The Syrian Front

Time and events played into Muawiah's hand. He had been conducting a surreptitious diplomatic campaign as he did not want to fight against Muslims. But, unfortunately, the first blood had been drawn in the Battle of the Camel. That had changed the moral grounds and now he could not be charged with initiating the use of the sword for arbitration of issues. Egypt was one of the important provinces with good revenue and its people were still divided. He made a move to take control of the province. There were two tribes in Egypt who were in his favour. He thought of using those tribes to take over Egypt. But the pro-Ali Governor of Egypt Qais bin Saad Ansari was aware of all the political alliances. He made all of Egypt submit allegiance to Ali. He also made a treaty with the two tribes by which they need not give allegiance but were bound to be neutral. This thwarted Muawiah for the time being. So he tried to win Qais over to his side promising him 'perpetual' governorship over Egypt. But Qais refused him.

Muawiah changed his tactic, his agents sowed seeds of doubt in Kufa. Ali was given reports that Qais had secretly changed his allegiance to Muawiah and that was the reason he had been neutral to the two tribes which supported Muawiah. To test him Ali sent an order for Qais to arrest the leaders of the two tribes. But Qais reported that the political situation was still too volatile to make such a move. This made Ali distrust Qais and he deposed him and made Muhammad bin Abu Bakr the Governor. Qais left Egypt and went to Madinah. Later, when Ali had a face to face talk with Qais he realised the loyalty of Qais. He appointed him as his advisor in Kufa.

But the deposition of Qais from Egypt was another small victory for Muawiah. Next he invited Amr bin Al Aas to Damuscus to reach an understanding with him. Amr, who had been politically against Usman, was moved due to the killing of Usman and the Battle of the Camel. Besides the Umayyad entrepreneurs were more disciplined and financially advanced. Muawiah proposed to make him the commander of his army and promised him the governorship of Egypt when conquered. Amr changed his anti-Umayyad stance and joined him. This turned out to be a very significant move in shifting the balance of power from Ali to Muawiah.

There was a revolt in Seestan of Persia that Ali was able to suppress, which enhanced his standing. Then Ali turned his attention to Syria. Envoys were exchanged for a possible peaceful solution, but in vain. Finally Ali raised an army from Iraq, Basra, Kufa and Madinah. This was a large army with 90,000 warriors. He made Ashtar bin Malik the commander of his army. Ashtar was among those who had revolted against Usman. After a long march by the western bank of the Euphrates and than crossing the desert the army approached Siffin near Damascus. There Muawiah was waiting with his army and Ali found that the Syrian army had taken control of the water wells. Ali sent Muawiah an emissary enjoining that according to the rules of war and religious injunction water could not be denied to his force.

Muawiah met with his advisors. Some said Ali was right and water had to be given to Ali's force, even if at certain fixed time of the day. Others said when Usman was under siege, he was refused water and thus they should refuse water to Ali's army. Muawiah was indecisive neither allowing nor refusing Ali's request.

When Ali learnt that Muawiah had not given any clear answer he realised the immediate danger. His men would soon be immobilised by thirst. Ali decided to act fast and a force rapidly attacked, taking the Syrian force by surprise, and captured the wells. The table were abruptly turned. Now Muawiah sent an emissary to Ali for water. And Ali allowed the Syrians water everyday at a fixed time. And thus the two armies came in friendly contact, and there was hope for peace.

For three months the armies faced each other while peace emissaries went back and forth. With two such large enemies in close proximity minor skirmishes took place here and there but there was no serious fighting. But there was no diplomatic progress and soon all peaceful avenues of settlement seemed to come at an end. Out of desperation and impatience the two armies lunged at each other. Ali called for a duel between him and Muawiah to avoid bloodshed. Though, with age, Ali had put on weight and become bald, he had never lost any duel. Muawiah did not take up the challenge. The battle began in earnest and on the first day neither of the sides was able to gain any ground. Ali led his men from the front in the centre of the battlefield. Muawiah directed his battle from a pavilion erected behind his army.

The next day Ali's army gained some upper hand and on the third day Muawiah's army were on the verge of desperation. Seeing defeat imminent the Syrians became disheartened. The next morning they appeared in the battlefield with the pages of the Quran on their lance and cried, "Men of Iraq, if you kill us, what happens to our families? Let's finish this fratricidal war and make peace according to the tenets of the Quran."

The Iraqi contingent of 20,000 men in Ali's army stopped fighting. Ali realised the ruse that the Syrians had employed, so he exhorted his men to fight. But they refused, "You appeal to the sword while they appeal to the Quran."

A very heated argument ensued, threats and counter threats were made. But Ali's army was split and a divided army could never win. On the verge of victory Ali was forced to ask his Commander in Chief Ashtar to stop the fight. An agreement for arbitration was made. Each side would put forward a single arbiter and at an appointed time and place they would decide who the Caliph should be. This decision would be binding.

This was from the on-set an exercise in futility. Ali had only agreed to this because part of his army was no longer under his control and Muawiah had agreed only because he was on the verge of defeat. Both needed time to recoup and regroup. No matter which way the decision of the arbiters went the loosing side would never agree, there was bound to be another battle. The complicated affair of the Caliphate was never to be judged on the whim of two individuals.

Amr bin Al-Aas was chosen to be the arbiter to advocate Muawiah. Ali tried to make Abdullah bin Abbas or Ashtar his arbiter. But his own army argued against this saying one was his relative and the other was not neutral. They suggested that Abu Musa Ashari, the Governor whom Ali had deposed, be made arbiter.

From the very start Ashari was a proponent of neutrality. Ali, despite reservations, accepted this. This made the arbitration team tip in favour of Muawiah as Amr, in all reality, was now a supporter of Muawiah while Ashari was neutral. The team was to meet and deliver a judgement within six months in Daumatul Jandal, half way between Kufa and Damascus.

Ali returned to Kufa with a heavy heart. When final victory was within his grasp, it had slipped because of his own army's vacillation and defiance. But this was just the start of insubordination. A disaffected and disarrayed group emerged within his army. This group included people of various ideals who could no longer support any side. Those who had forced him not to fight in Siffin were now blaming him for accepting the proposal of arbitration. In reality these were the people who were disillusioned and did not want to favour any side anymore. They blamed both Ali and Muawiah for all the troubles. The group lacked good leadership and political direction and took on an fundamentalist ideology. They soon declared that they were the only true Muslims and the others had apostatised and must repent to return to the Muslim folds again. They declared if any Muslim indulged in any wrong doing they held the right to kill that person. Their fundamental tenet was 'La Hukma illa lilla' - no edict but that of God. They called themselves 'Khariji' or the secessionists.

The Kharijites numbered a few thousands and they did not return to Kufa but camped a few miles away in Harura. Ali took some reconciliatory steps but the attempts to negotiate with them failed. The Kharijites army then moved and concentrated in Nahrawan where they were joined by more comrades from Basra and other parts of Iraq. They became violent and Abdullah, son of a prominent Companion named Khabab, and a woman accompanying him were killed by the Kharijites.

At the appointed time the arbiters from both sides met in Daumatul Jandal. Each had a retinue of 400 people. After debating for a long time the two advocates could not come to any conclusion. Finally, Abu Musa Al Ashari proposed to Amr that both Ali and Muawiah should be deposed and the people should select a new Caliph. The exact nature of what transpired next is historically unclear. Apparently, Amr had agreed that first Ashari announce the declaration of deposition of both Ali and Muawiah. Ashari was so keen in his neutrality that he did not foresee the affect of what he was doing. He went to the announcement stage and declared that the arbitration has found that both Ali and Muawiah were no longer fit to be Caliph and thus he was deposing his candidate Ali. Then Amr took the stage and played the master diplomatic card. He declared that since Ashari had deposed his candidate Ali, the remaining candidate Muawiah, thus, was now the Caliph.

Ashari had missed the point that the agreement of the arbitration was to select the Caliph from the two not to vie for any other decision. And Amr had just taken advantage of that, not really gone back on his agreement with Ashari.

After the arbitration, Ashari slipped away to Makkah instead of going back to Kufa. And as the declaration was not a clear decision from both the advocates rather selection of Muawiah based on a diplomatic lapse, Ali refused to abide by it. He gave a call to arms, and soon an army of 65,000 strong was raised. When preparations were being made for the march to Syria, the army raised the issue of the Kharijites. They argued that the Kharijites were now very strong and while the army would be fighting in far off Syria, nothing would be in the way of the Kharijites to take over Basra and Kufa. If they went to Syria without tackling the menace of the Kharijites even their families here would be in danger.

Ali sent a letter to the Kharijites asking them to join him on his march to Syria. The Kharijites replied with insolence. So Ali marched his army to Nahrawan. On reaching the region he fixed his standard on the ground and declared that all those who came under the standard would be shown amnesty. Some of the Kharijites took the shelter of the standard but most remained obstinate. As Ali marshalled his force to launch the attack, the Kharijites rushed and met the army headlong with the battle cry, "Onwards to paradise!"

The small army of the Kharijites were routed and only a fraction escaped. But this small group was to develop a following that would play a big role, in revolts against the Empires that would be established, for some time to come.

After the battle, Ali's army declared that since they were still near Kufa they wanted a few days rest after which they would resume their march to Syria. Ali agreed and marched back to Kufa where the army dispersed. But on the appointed day when the army was to reassemble, a large part of the army did not regroup or return to the camp. Apparently, they were willing to fight the weaker Kharijites but did not care for the arduous expedition against the Syrians.

Ali was left hapless and now misfortune seemed to follow him. In the Egyptian theatre, Muhammad bin Abu Bakr was the Governor. Unlike Qais he was non-diplomatic and his attitude led to the revolt by the pro-Usman tribes. Ali appointed the more experienced Malik Ashtar as the Governor of Egypt to handle this rebellion. As Malik was on his way the chief of the Qaizauma tribe, who were located near the Syrian border, invited him. The chief was a secret ally of Muawiah. He fed and feted Malik and in the process also poisoned him. Malik died within a few hours.

The declaration of the arbiters rejecting Ali's candidacy, the inability to raise a significant army after the battle of Nahrawan and now the death of Malik was politically damaging and detrimental to Ali. His supporters in Egypt waned and faded. When Amr bin Al-Aas attacked Egypt again, under Muawiah's command, Egypt had an army of only four thousand. They were cut down quickly and Muhammad bin Abu Bakr was taken prisoner and killed promptly. Amr on his part had tried to save Muhammad bin Abu Bakr but had been unable to.

Muawiah was already a significant force and the conquest of Egypt now made him very powerful. On the other hand Ali, who still ruled a larger land area, was in lesser control over his people. But still Muawiah did not dare or did not want to lead a full frontal assault on Kufa. Even though there was no one to fight Ali's war, the people held Ali in high esteem.

At the back of their minds both Ali and Muawiah did not want bloodshed among the Muslims. Ali would exhort his people to prepare for battle to uphold their principle but there was no real attempt to raise the army. Evertime the army had rebelled against a decision to fight Ali had grudgingly accepted the contention. He had never forced the point and there was no real zeal in him to fight another Muslim group. Muawiah, as well, restricted his aggression to despatching small military expeditions and diplomatic missions. When Abdullah bin Abbas, the Governor of Basra, went to visit Ali in Kufa, Muawiah sent 2000 horsemen to Basra who spread propaganda about how Ali had broken his promise over the arbitration. Like the Kufans the people of Basra also proved to be fickle. There was a rebellion in Basra which was subdued with difficulty by Ali. There was also a revolt in Bahrain, which was suppressed only after a fight and 500 Bahraini's were imprisoned. They were released on ransom, but the Governor of the city took the ransom money and fled to Muawiah in Syria.

The provinces of Makkah, Madinah and Yemen under Ali' command were more or less unprotected. Muawiah sent a force of 4000 horsemen who first captured Madinah and then Makkah, the pro Ali Governors having escaped. Then they took over Yemen, where there was some resistance. The people who had fought were taken captive and killed. The

Yemeni Governor fled but his young children got killed in the violence. The people of these areas gave allegiance to Muawiah.

Ali sent a force of 4000 to Yemen. The Syrian forces left without fighting, and Ali's government was re-established there. Then Ali's force moved and recaptured Makkah and Madinah. After this, both the sides realised that even small scale fighting would lead to more deaths but no political gains.

The Status Quo

In Arabia a significant middle class had evolved. This was a well-to-do class and the richer among them were 'silent' supporters of Muawiah. They did not agree with days of ignorance of the pre-Islamic days but neither wanted the tribulations and abstinence of a totally egalitarian society. Muawiah, with his economic policy, was able to politically impress this silent class in frustrating Ali.

Ali remained an idealist in a world of crumbling social values. He fought with gallantry in a world that found it more pragmatic to assassinate rather then face the foe. His political philosophy was based on ideology and faith in a world that was now being controlled by economic aspiration and power play. He was invincible in a world of higher laws and values, but unfit in the evolving 'all is fair' political and military environment. He was unaware of and could not understand the economic motivations that made people commit deeds that were outside the sphere of higher values. In a face to face fight he was formidable, but in politics he was mild, unable to punish members of his own army who would show disobedience. Beside this little ineptitude, if ideology is at all that, Ali was a superman. If he had a good economic advisor or a more flexible morality he would have been indomitable. But, unfortunately, people who understood economics were, for very practical reasons, on the side of Muawiah. When things looked stark even Abdullah bin Abbas forsook Ali and went to Makkah. His followers would after more than a century would form the Abbasid Empire.

Muawiah declared himself Caliph. There were now two Caliphs, Muawiah in Syria and Egypt and Ali in the rest of the area which included Iraq, the Arabian Peninsula, Persia and Bahrain. An uneasy status quo prevailed.

But despite all, Ali was not despondent. In the last Friday sermon that he delivered, he warned the people against material enticements of this temporary life. He praised those Muslims who had sacrificed all from the very first days in Makkah and had supported him and finally laid down their lives. He made his son Hussain, Qayes ibn Saad and Abu Ayyub the commander of 10,000 troops each and also declared the names of other commanders with smaller forces. What exactly were his intentions, was he getting ready for another battle, or was he just displaying his prowess for a diplomatic offensive - it will never be known for soon he was to die.

The Assassination

The Kharijites who had survived Nahrawan had gone to hiding. In Makkah, an embittered Kharijite group discussed the changing morality and degradation of the people and their leaders. They decided that the only way left open to check this degradation was to kill the leaders responsible for all the depravity. They did not have the vision or knowledge of socio-economic currents that influenced events. Thus they decided to remove the three main persons involved in the conflicts - Ali, Muawiah and Amr bin Al Aas. They commissioned three young men with poisoned swords to kill them.

In Syria, Muawiah's would be assassin attacked him in the mosque and wounded him but was apprehended and killed. The physicians gave Muawiah a drinking draught which was an antidote. In a few days Muawiah recovered. Amr had led a charmed life. On the night, after which he was to be assassinated, he developed a colic pain and did not go to the mosque. Another person took his place to lead the prayers. The assassin had never seen Amr before and killed this person instead mistaking him for Amr.

The would-be assassin of Ali went to Kufa a few days before the appointed date. There he met and fell in love with a beautiful Kharijite woman. She supplied him with two accomplishes. On the appointed date they waited for Ali in the Mosque Ali came to the mosque early in the morning before any one else and was attacked and injured fatally by the three. The assassin and one of the accomplices were captured and executed. The second accomplice escaped Kufa.

Thus, in the year 661 CE, with the death of Ali an era came to an end. John J Pool in his book *Studies in Muhammadanism* wrote, "The death of Ali was an epoch-making event. We come now to the parting of ways. Henceforward the Commanders of the Faithful ceased to be elected by votes of the people of Madinah or Makkah. Arabia was no longer to be the seat of temporal power. For the future, in Islam, might was to take the place of right."

Doctor Ata Mohyuddin in *Ali, the Superman*, states "Ali has meant many different things to many generations, each of whom has found something to inspire it out of all the diverse wealth of his mind. During his lifetime he was thought of primarily as a warrior fighting first in the battles of God and later for a decade against schismatics. He was also respected for his knowledge and learning and in later years many thought of him as a saint, but it was until after his death the effect which he had exercised over the ethical life of his time began to be appreciated."

Philip Hitti in *History of the Arabs* states, "Valiant in battle, wise in counsel, eloquent in speech, true to his friend, magnanimous to his foes, Ali became both the paragon of Muslim nobility and chivalry and the Solomon of Arabic traditions. Around his name poems, proverbs, sermonettes and anecdotes innumerable have clustered..... He whose worldly career was practically a failure has continued to exert a posthumous influence second only to that of the Holy Prophet himself. The throngs of pilgrims that still stream to his *Mahshad* at Najaf and to that of his son Husain, the Shia ardh-saint and martyr at nearby Karbala and the passionate play enacted annually on the tenth of Moharram throughout the Shia world testify to the possibility that death may avail a Messiah more than life."

Some Sayings of Ali

- The sum total of excellence is Knowledge.
- He who teaches you a letter fetters you with gratitude.
- Wisdom is the paramount friend.
- Knowledge is the ornament of the wealthy and the wealth of the poor.
- The wealth of a miser is as useless as a pebble.
- A wise enemy is better than a foolish friend.
- The right of freedom of speech incorporates the speaking of truth.
- Greed is perpetual enslavement.
- Truth is bitter, but its result is sweet. Mendacity appears sweet, but is poisonous in effect.
- A good disposition is the best companion.
- Good breeding is the greatest inheritance.
- The advice of old men is more valuable then the bravery of young men.
- There is no loss as great as procrastination.
- With the increase of power, decrease desire accordingly.
- The person who listens to a backbiter looses a friend.
- Whatever harm is accumulated due to silence can be undone, whatever harm comes due to speech cannot be remedied.
- The worst tyranny is the oppression of the weak.
- A person who does not take the middle course strays.
- Justice is to give a person what is his due. Mercy goes a step beyond.
- Haste is a kind of madness. One who does things in haste faces embarrassment and if he is not regretful his madness is confirmed.
- Forgiveness is the Zakaat (Tax) of success. If you want to succeed, learn to forgive.
- Learning and good disposition go together and promotes broadmindedness.
- Your three friends are: your friend, your friend's friend and the foe of your enemy.
- Your three enemies are: your enemy, the friend of your enemy and foe of your friend.
- There are two types of people whose hunger is insatiable: the person who seeks knowledge and the person who hungers for the material world.
- There is no distress worse than ignorance, no enemy worse then self adulation

and no companion worse than bad conduct.

- People who run after the material world are like beasts who fall at one another, the strong oppressing the weak.
- Disclose not your secret but to yourself for every sincere confidant has a confidant.
- The world eludes him who seeks it; it runs after him who runs away from it. He who sees it as a place of trail is enlightened. He who is lured by its charm is blinded.
- (When out riding a horse, a retinue of people was following Ali.) He said, "Go back to your work. By following me you will breed inferiority complex in yourself and arrogance in me."
- Do not flatter me. I am not what you say, but I am more than what you really think.
- Cast a glance on this world from a wise man's perspective. She turns out her guests in a short pace of time. She harasses those with whom she fondles and prattles. Whatever part of life is wasted in idle pursuits can never be recalled. Its gratification and enjoyment are soon changed into suffering and pain, its embellishment and decorations are changed into deformation and impoverishment. The days of this life are numbered. Death is inevitable and bound to come soon. After having adorned your person with good deeds, you should not pay any heed whether death catches you or you catch death.

Literary Works of Ali

Ali's poetry was very modern even by today's standards. Dr Ata Mohyuddin wrote, "Ali in his poems is known as a moralist, freely expressing the righteousness of his cause. In these, as in his sermons, he exhorts the pious to be sincere steadfast, to refrain from wrongdoing and stick to faith. The poetry is neither romantic nor lyrical, but reformative. It contains no sensuous feelings or imagery and has nothing about it on which the old school of Arab poets delighted to dwell. There is no praise of women, wine, music, amusement or even of the sword. Ali's eloquence is reserved for the praise of patriotism, humility, modesty, charity, piety and resignation to God's will.... The style of the verses, which like his prose, is racy, lively and unstilted, makes the ethical truths expounded in them much more palatable than they might otherwise have been."

Suyuti in *The History of the Caliphs* gives some examples of Ali's 'instructive' poetry.

When hearts contains despair
And the wide breast is stifled by what's within.
And calamity takes its abode and repose
And sorrow takes up residence in their places
And there appears no avenue for dispelling of distress
And the stratagem of the cunning one avails not
There will come to you, in your despair, a helper
Whom the Near, the Answerer brings
For all misfortune, having reached their limit
Near deliverance is joined with them.

~~~

Do not accompany an ignorant brother;
Beware of him!
How many such have destroyed the forbearing
When they took him as brother.

~~~

A fool attains his world
Through shortcoming imperfection.
Had it been from strength or invasion,
Then hawks would have flown off
With the sparrows' provision.

(From translation by Abdussamad Çlarke in As Suyuti, 1995)

Ali initiated the formalisation of Arabic Grammar. He commissioned Abu Al-Aswad Al-Du'ali, a scholar, to research Arabic Grammar. He gave a note to Abu Al-Aswad on which he had written 'Speech is made of nouns, verbs and particles. Nouns are names of things, verbs provide information, and particles complete the meaning.' Then he said to him, "*Follow this approach* and add to it what comes to your mind." Al-Aswad became the first Arabic Grammarian.

Ali possessed a diverse multidimensional personality that is exceedingly rare or probably absent in history. He was a ruler, an administrator, a general, a warrior, a judge, a teacher, a poet, a scholar, a philosopher and a modern political thinker all in one. He is regarded one of the earliest and greatest expert on Islamic Jurisprudence. Almost all schools of Sufism accept him as the Father of Sufism. Besides being grandly versed in poetry and rhetoric his knowledge also included astronomy, medicine, mathematics and history. Some of his socio-political and ethical thoughts are preserved in a collection of his writings in the book *Nah-jul-Balaga*.

The writing and sayings of Ali is very rich in similes and metaphors. There is a subtle sense of humour in his writing which strikingly brings about the meaning of his statements. After the death of the Prophet some quarters of the Quraish were claiming power because they belonged to the same family tree as the Prophet, Ali said, "It is strange they look at the tree, but neglect the fruit."

Ali's political thoughts are surprisingly modern for his time. He defined the State as "Community in action" where the Government is the instrument of the state to fulfil the purpose of the state. His conception of the *Ummah* or civilisation was that it is an organic entity capable of possessing moral and spiritual qualities. An individual cannot lead isolated life, but must live as a part of the society upholding the '*Haqooq Al Abad*' or *responsibilities of the individual* towards fellow beings. He emphasized the Caliph or ruler should not be ignorant but knowledgeable, pious and not concerned with personal worldly benefits.

~~~

The Political State of the Rashidun

The Prophet had established a modern universal state. Though it was situated in Madinah, anyone in the world could be a member of the state by agreeing to its universality "There is no God but God." An aspect of prime importance in the political setup of the state was that there was no authoritarianism. Though the law of God was supreme the Prophet, himself, is known to have discussed and sought advice on different aspects of political administration from his companions. The economy was free market. The prophet had refused to regulate prices when Madinah was hit by inflation. But to counter exploitation that accompanies the free market, *Riba* (interest, usury and other economic instruments of exploitation) was prohibited.

The two main implements that facilitated governance during the Rashidun Caliphate were the Quran supported by the Sunnah. These two together provided for the constitutional framework of the state and the Council of the Companions was the 'Parliament' of the state. To the Caliph the Companions were representatives of the people and to the people they represented the Caliph. They were advisors of the Caliph in the numerous decisions he had to take thus minimising human fallibilities. They were not afraid to challenge the Caliph or his decisions for the sake of God and people. This representation legalised the Caliphs 'authority to rule'.

A unique balance of rationalism and spiritualism existed in all aspects of the society. There was development and emancipation in social, political and economic sectors of the state: The political setup was modern, the economy was progressing, the people were living
~~~

in a new culture, and education was modern and progressive. In economy, Umar ensured that the state administrators were not allowed to intervene in business affairs. The administration and business classes were kept separate.

But by the end of Usman's rule even as the economy progressed the political administration regressed due to the death of the Companions, which caused the Council of the Companions to weaken and become almost non-existent. Soon the Caliph was ruling the people directly with the aid of his secretariat with no Council of Companions. The succession in the Caliphate also became more and more difficult because of this non-representation. For many people, the non-representative rule lacked adequate political authority and thus the Caliphate lost political control over various regions.

A new committee from the people replacing the Council of Companions would have been able to resolve these issues considerably. Instead the situation deteriorated and it became difficult to even control Governors of the provinces.

That is how it commenced. A volatile design for impending changes vast. The forces were explosive but the forces formative were greater by far. Forces that built Empires.

~~~

Most Gracious!
It is He Who has taught the Quran.
He has created man:
He has taught him speech (and intelligence).
The sun and the moon follow courses computed;
And the herbs and the trees - both bow in adoration.
And the Firmament has He raised high, and He has set up the Balance (of Justice),
In order that you may not transgress (the due) balance.
So establish weight with justice and fall not short in the balance.
It is He Who has spread out the earth for (His) creatures:
In there is fruit and date-palms, producing spathes;
Also corn, with leaves and stalk for fodder, and sweet-smelling plants.
Then which of the favours of your Lord will you deny?
[55:1-13]

~~~

The world in fascination watched
while the empires in splendour spread
and knowledge in excellence bred.

Empires of Faith

The Umayyads

(660-750)

Muawiah was the son of Abu Sufian, the leader in Makkah, and belonged to the Umayyah clan of the Quraish. Abu Sufian and his family embraced Islam when the Prophet conquered Makkah. Muawiah became the secretary of the Prophet. Umme Habiba, the wife of the Prophet, was his sister.

Caliph Umar had made Muawiah's elder brother, Yazid, the Governor of Palestine and Muawiah served under his brother and then became the Governor when Yazid died in the battle of Yermuk. Under Caliph Usman he became the Governor of the whole of Syria. And after the death of Usman he refused to give allegiance to Caliph Ali.

After the death of Ali the people of Kufa gave allegiance to Hasan bin Ali. Just six month had passed when Muawiah commanded his army to invade and capture Kufa. The history of Siffin was repeated; the armies came face to face but refused to fight. Hasan decided to abdicate rather than see any further conflict and death. The condition for the treaty of abdication was that after Muawiah he would be the next Caliph. Hasan went to Madinah and took up residence there.

Hasan was lordly, charismatic, forbearing, possessing tranquillity, gravity and modesty. He was generous, popular and always very proper of speech. But he had married and divorced at a high rate. At one time Ali himself had declared to the people of Kufa, "Do not marry your daughters to Hasan. He is given to divorcing." But the people did not heed as the progeny from such a marriage would belong to the lineage of the Prophet.

After abdication, when Hasan went to live in Madinah, the prayer in the Prophet's Mosque was led by Marwan who had become the Governor. When in his sermons he spoke ill of Ali, Hasan did not complain and bore it all with grace. But soon Hasan was poisoned and died in 671. The hand of Yazid bin Muawiah is implicated by some historians. Suyuti claims that Yazid instigated Jadah, the wife of Hasan, to poison him and had promised to marry her. After Hasan's death when she asked Yazid to carry out his part of the bargain, Yazid simply said, "We were not pleased with you for Hasan, how can we be pleased with you for ourselves."

Though, prominent historian Ibn Khaldun considered the poisoning episode as fabrication. After Hasan's death Husain, Hasan's brother, is said to have found Marwan weeping and said, "You now weep for the one you had abused?"

Marwan had replied, "Indeed, I had done that to one who was more forbearing than a mountain."

Muawiah became the unchallenged Caliph. He was the founder of a dynasty and had remarkable characteristics - astute, suave and diplomatic and an excellent judge of people and events. He was a statesman with a very sophisticated sense of political finesse, "I do not apply my sword where my whip suffices, and I do not apply my whip where my tongue suffices."

Muawiah suppressed a Kharijite revolt in the neighbourhood of Kufa. Then he turned his attention towards the Byzantines. Taking advantage of the civil war between Ali and Muawiah, the Byzantines had reoccupied North Africa. Muawiah wrested it back to the folds of the Caliphate. Uqbah bin Nafi, an Umayyad commander, established the city of Qairowan in North Africa (Hasan, 2004). At about the same time, Muawiah's navy made expeditions to Sicily.

Amr bin Al Aas died in 668 while serving as Governor of Egypt. In the same year, Constans II the Byzantine Emperor died and now Muawiah took the advantage of the situation and attacked Constantinople by land and sea. The siege lasted for seven years but the great walls of Constantinople were impregnable and the siege was lifted when the ships became vulnerable to the incendiary 'Greek Fire' that the Byzantines started to throw at the Muslim ships. The navy had been active in the Mediterranean where part of Crete was occupied and in Rhode a colony was established.

In the east the army conquered Khorasan in Persia and invaded and took control of Afghanistan and penetrated into western India. The Queen Qub of Turkestan was defeated, Samarqand and Tirmiz occupied and Bukhara was rendered to vassalage.

Muawiah decided to make his son Yazid, who had led the land army to Constantinople, his successor probably on the suggestion of his Umayyad advisors. He probably hoped that this would end the irresponsible power struggle that takes place during the selection of a new leader. But the appointment of Yazid was not correct. People were hoping that after Muawiah the adverse feelings and schisms of the *Fitna* would end and be forgotten. But the making of Yazid, not deemed worthy by many, his successor would now ensure the continuity of the same old hostilities. The modern Muslim state was falling back to the old 'Empire' model. Another matter of concern was the fact that the heir was dissolute and known for his preference of the hunt - he had acquired falcons, dogs and lynxes - rather than political astuteness (Khudabakhsh and Margoliouth, 1996). But Muawiah's emissaries managed to get the oath of allegiance from the various quarters of the Empire. Muawiah himself went to Makkah and Madinah and made the people there give allegiance to his son. A few of the people refrained, that included Husain bin Ali, Abdullah bin Umar, Abdur Rahman bin Abu Bakr, and Abdullah bin Zubayr.

But as a whole the Umayyad Empire flourished. The economy grew and commercial enterprises burgeoned. Huge stipends were paid to tribes and individuals in need. The stipends were given according to economic need and not by political expediency or kinship. A large part of the society started to live in an urban environment. A Bedouin poem of the era says (Zaydan, 1994):

Said my consort, 'leave the country,
Come to the forts of Madinah
a new home to build.
Put the name down
to the stipend registry,
For that is what men of intellect do'.

After ruling for 20 years as a governor of Syria and another 20 years as Caliph of a vast Empire the founder of the Umayyad Dynasty died in 680AD.

Though it was ruled by Islam, by the establishment of inheritable rule the political framework of the Caliphate turned into an empire in the complete sense of the word, thus inheriting the charms as well as the imperialist crafts of empires. The issue of succession which should have been resolved after the Fitna, instead, became permanent and would vex the dynasties to come increasingly.

On the other hand, the enterprising Umayyads had many great successes. They made their Empire the greatest in the world. The Caliphate spread over three continents of Asia, Europe and Africa. Large part of Central Asia was captured. In India, an army led by Muhammad bin Qasim captured Sind and a section of Punjab. Eastern regions of Byzantine were occupied. In the Mediterranean naval supremacy was established under Musa bin Nusair. The islands of Ivica, Majorca and Minorca were captured.

Tariq, a lieutenant of Musa, launched an historical attack on Spain in 711 CE. His force of 7000 men landed in Spain and defeated the Gothic king Roderick. Then they occupied Granada, Sidonia, Carmona, Cordova and Toledo. In 712 CE, Musa arrived with a much larger force and conquered Saragossa, Seville, Terragossa and Barcelona thus establishing Muslim rule in Spain and Portugal that would last, in the whole or part of the regions, for about 700 years.

The conquered people were allowed to continue with their local customs and culture and the empire became a benign protectorate rather then an imperial autocracy. Some of the Umayyad rulers established a material way of life for themselves and their religion became rituals. As in the history of other empires, the royal family, nobles, Generals and rich aristocrats deviated away from contact with the general masses.

But, on the other hand, for the first time in history, the will of the general mass also started to assert in all manners of political affairs. The Imams and other scholars were closer to the people and had a great influence on them and were the opposition *per se*. They had the power to mould public views and thus the Caliphs were very cautious of them, either immediately heeding what the Imams said or attempting to suppress their words from reaching the public.

The society was progressive and dynamic and civic emancipation took place at a tremendous rate. The Quran and the Prophet had laid down rules and set examples of cleanliness, behaviour and good manners. During the Umayyad period, thus developed *Adap and Aqeeda* - etiquette, manner and hygiene not just among the royalty and aristocrat but among the ordinary people as well. This was the first time in history that even the poorest of the people were well versed in such behaviour and hygiene.

> Cleanliness and hygiene became paramount in Muslim societies and in the next few centuries amenities and conveniences were available to the Muslims that were unthinkable in the rest of the world. Al Kindi (Alkindus), 9th century philosopher from Kufa, wrote a book on perfumes called *Book of the Chemistry of Perfume and Distillation.* Al Zahrawi (Abulcasis), a physician and surgeon of 10th century Cordoba wrote a volume on cosmetology called *The Medicines of Beauty* which included beautification of hair, skin, teeth, etc., and the use of nasal spray, hand creams, mouthwashes and incense for clothes. At about the same time Muslim culture arrived in Haute Provence of France, via Muslim Spain, where the perfume industry still flourishes after 700 years. (Al Hassani, 2007).
> In the 13th century, a scholar and engineer named Al Jazari created a washing machine which was similar to a tap and sink. The tap appeared as a peacock's head, which when tapped would provide short spurts of water. By this time various types of soaps were also being used. The soaps would go to Europe with the returning crusaders but did not become popular immediately. The improvement in social behaviour also influenced the other contemporary civilisations which came in touch with the Muslims.

A modern administration was organized and regular postal service was established. Arabic was made the state language and coins were issued. The Umayyads were great patrons of learning and established numerous academic institutions. The skills of reading, writing, research, deduction, inference, consensus etc which have been developed mainly by the Ulema scholars and spread all over the Empire by their students would soon be applied to emerging philosophy and rational sciences. Academic methodology that evolved for the general mass was based on learning 'Manners before knowledge'. Thus the primary curriculum for young students would consist of etiquette, manners and religious study and in the secondary stage students would start studying their appropriate subjects like the evolving jurisprudence.

The Umayyads showed a multifaceted pragmatic sense in development of not only scholastic pursuits and culture but also in commerce. Their economic system became the best in the world. Their vast empire was turned into an immense free trade zone which developed an enduring establishment that would last long after the Umayyad reign was over. Their enterprise led to economic upsurge and building of cities and many edifices: Cities like Wasit in Iraq and Tunis in North Africa were built. The famous 'Dome of Rock' mosque was founded in Damascus. The Prophet's mosque in Madinah and the Al Aqsa mosque in Jerusalem were further extended. Buildings, engineering and architecture projects progressed in fervent rate. The water of Barada River was channelled so that the houses in Damascus had running water. Public roads, canals, hospitals, academic and other institutes were built turning this region into the most modern in the world. The Al Waleed mosque remains one of the greatest Mosques in the world. The palace of Al Waleed became the wonder of the age. The palace was made in shining gold and marble, the walls and floors consisted of patterned mosaics while the ceilings were adorned with gold, and fragrant fountains and cascades flowed perpetually conducing a refreshing coolness.

The Tragedy of Karbala

Great tragedies were in store before all the above developments were to transpire. When Madinah gave allegiance to Yazid in 680, Hasan's brother Husain bin Ali and Abdullah bin Zubayr, among few prominent persons of Madinah, refused to do so on the grounds that the Caliphate could not be inherited and Yazid was not competent enough to be a Caliph. The people of Kufa intimated Husain that if he came to Kufa they would give allegiance to him and fight for his Caliphate. On receiving favourable intelligence Husain and his family and some close friends started for Kufa. There were about a hundred members in his entourage including women and children.

A similar journey to Kufa had been undertaken by Ali after the death of Usman, which had frustrated the Umayyads for long. This time they did not intend to let history repeat itself. Yazid displaced the Governor of Kufa with an ardent Umayyad follower named Ubaidullah, who ruthlessly suppressed the Kufans. Leaders and supporters of Husain were hunted and killed. Kufa thus came under the full control of Yazid.

Husain learnt of this change halfway to Kufa. After some initial discussion with his family members Husain decided to plunge ahead. But on reaching Karbala, some distance from the Euphrates (in present day Iraq), the army of Ubaidullah caught up with them. The battlefield was the desert and Ubaidullah placed the army strategically so that Husain and his entourage could not reach any drinking water source.

Two very unequal groups faced each other in October, 680. On the one side a well disciplined army and on the other side a weary, weakened, thirsty and hungry band of men, women and children. Husain proposed three alternatives to avoid bloodshed. That he be allowed to go back to Makkah or Madinah, or that he be allowed to go and talk to Yazid else he be allowed to go somewhere else. But Ubaidullah knew that if they let this opportunity slip they would not find Husain in such a vulnerable situation again. He declined to meet any of the proposals and said that Husain would have to unconditionally surrender and give allegiance to Yazid.

Husain refused to these terms. The army then surrounded the suffering band trying to force it into submission. Husain and his family continued to suffer from thirst, hunger and physical exhaustion but still they declined surrender. The army attacked. Hussein and his family fought bravely. But it was an unequal match from the very onset. One by one they fell some begging for a drop of water as they died, but were refused. Husein's head was cut off. His body trampled about by horses. Some of the children and women were massacred. Only one member of his family in the group, a boy called Zain Al Abedeen, survived. He had fallen ill and was too sick to fight. He and Hasan bin al-Muthanna, who was seriously injured, were among the women and children prisoners taken to Kufa.

This outrageous behaviour shocked the very foundation of the Empire. Gibbon states, "The tragedy of Karbala was so overwhelming that through ages and every clime it has continued to awaken the sympathy of the coldest reader. The day of the martyrdom of Husain is observed throughout the Muslims world with great mourning."

Makkah and Madinah were incensed at the tragedy. The Umayyad Governors were driven away and Abdullah bin Zubayr proclaimed himself Caliph from Makkah. Yazid sent a 12,000 strong army to subdue this revolt. The people of Makkah and Madinah no longer had an army but still they put up a resistance. The people of Madinah put up a fight only to be quickly subdued by Yazid's well disciplined army. Next the army laid a siege around Makkah, positioning themselves on heights. The siege lasted for sixty four days, the city being bombarded by the Syrian mangonels. In November of 683, unexpectedly the news of Yazid's death by natural causes arrived. The army lifted the siege and returned to Syria.

The state of affairs was again chaotic. The events of Karbala and Yazid's unpopularity led to the Umayyad's decrease in popularity and power. The people from various regions gave allegiance to Abdullah bin Zubayr. Even northern Syria, stronghold of the Umayyads, arose in favour of Ibn Zubayr.

Yazid was succeeded by his son Muawiah II. But he developed a dislike for the ensuing political turmoil and abdicated. Under such circumstances, when the house of Umayyad appeared to be crashing, Marwan became the Caliph in 684 and stabilised the political environment. The Umayyad's bestowed him the Caliphate and stipulated that he marry Yazid's widow Fakhita and that after him Yazid's other son Khaled would be the next Caliph.

On assuming power, Marwan launched a military campaign against northern Syria. After subduing the revolt he launched a two pronged attack against the pro-Abdullah Egypt. He himself led one of the armies and soon occupied Egypt. With Syria and Egypt under their fold the Umayyads stabilised.

Post Karbala Umayyad

Entrenched in power Marwan decided to repudiate Khaled bin Yazid's claim to the Caliphate and declared that after him his own son Abdul Malik would succeed as the Caliph. Though the Umayyads submitted to this command, Khaled's mother Fakhita who was now Marwan's wife could not accept this. In an opportune moment she had Marwan smothered to death. Thus the man who had lived through the revolt against Usman and through the uprising in Madinah and Makkah finally died in the hands of his own wife. His son Abdul Malik would say, "The happiest of men is he who has money just sufficient for his wants and an agreeable wife, and who has no acquaintance with our nasty courts." (Zaydan, 1994)

Marwan was a great diplomat and politician. His choice of Abdul Malik was to be vindicated. During Malik's time many reforms took place. Arabic was declared the official language of the Empire and replaced the Persian Pahlavi, Byzantine Greek and other languages of Syria and Coptic Egypt. The first completely new Islamic gold and silver coins were minted. After Muawiah, the Umayyad rulers who achieved greatness included Abdul Malik, Al Waleed, Umar bin Abdul Aziz and Hisham bin Abdul Malik. These were all exceptional rulers and contributed significantly in the development of the Umayyad Empire.

Within a short time the Umayyads became the elite of the world. With Byzantine on the west and China on the east they ruled most of the civilised world. The years 711-713 were momentous with victories in Sind of India, Transoxiana in Central Asia and Spain in Europe. Such a spread of an empire and its development was unprecedented. The Umayyad Arabs developed a sense of superiority, arrogance and ego that was also unprecedented. They ruled by an unwritten chauvinistic superiority policy. As the Arabs had, in fact, become the most learned and progressive people of that period, it became easy for them to assert this chauvinism. Sensitivity against this chauvisnism amongst the non-Arabs, Muslims and Non-Muslims, developed. The Persian, who had a longer legacy of culture and education than the Arabs or the Byzantines, resented it the most.

A few of the Caliphs took measures that were repressive to the Alids, Christains and Jews. The Jizya tax, on a few instances, was used as a tool to discriminate the Non-Muslims. At times, Jizya was even exacted from Muslims who were of non Arab origin and who were expected to pay the Zakaat as well. But all these were exceptions rather then the case except in the case of the Alids and Kharijites. The payment of Jizya still exempted the Non-Muslims from being drafted into the army and participating in battles.

Compared to the rest of the contemporary world, the Umayyads were still the most progressive and just regime. When Umar bin Abdul Aziz became Caliph in 717, he set himself to rectify whatever was inappropriate in the administration. The economy was superb even before him and under two years of his competent rule poverty was totally eradicated. The officials could not find poor people to give alms from the charity fund. Umar's decree was - if poor people could not be found then use the charity to get young men married. When that was done and still money was left he ordered that the money be used to buy slaves and set them free. He removed jizya from non-Arab Muslims.

Though he was Caliph for less then three years only, due to his inviolate character and superb rule, the Islamic scholars agree that if there is a fifth *Rashidun* Caliph it is Umar bin Abdul Aziz. He was the great grandson of the *Rashidun* Caliph Umar bin Khattab from his mother's side and aspired to follow his illustrious namesake.

> Long ago, Caliph Umar bin Khattab used to go out on night walks through the roads of Madinah to see the condition of the general people. He would take a companion or two with him. One particular night, after a tiring day, he was doing his rounds. He felt so tired that he went and leaned against a wall. This was the house of a woman and her daughter. He heard the voice of the mother saying, "Go and add water to the milk."
>
> Adding water to the milk increased its volume and would earn them more money when sold. A younger woman replied, "But that is banned! The Commander of the Faithful has banned the practice of diluting milk."
> The mother said, "Well, the Commander is not here now, go and add water."
> The daughter persisted, "I am not a person who obeys in public and disobeys in private."
>
> As he left, Umar asked his companion to mark the door. Umar would have his son Asm marry this young woman. Umar bin Abdul Aziz was the grandson of this woman and Asm.

Umar bin Abdul Aziz led a simple and austere life and had one wife. His wife was the daughter and sister of past Caliphs and had been given numerous jewelries as gifts. He was very conscientious about the treasury and even requested his wife to surrender her ornaments to the state. He looked after the interest of the minorities. To protect the properties of the minorities he ordered that the Muslims could not buy from the non-Muslims. He handed over the land properties owned by him to the state. He wanted all the princes to do the same. He cut down all the extravagance including the huge salaries and privileges that the royal princes enjoyed.

At the time of his accession Constantinople was besieged by Muslims. He lifted the siege and withdrew the army from there. When the Kharijites resorted to terrorist activities he summoned a delegation from them. He asked them not to cause violence and be at peace. He wanted to know of their grievances and promised to remove those. This led to an understanding and the Kharijites gave no further trouble during his rule.

But his altruistic and specifically egalitarian measures made him the enemy of the nobility who now were deprived of all the extravagance they had become accustomed to. A conspiracy was hatched and he was poisoned to death in 720. He ruled for less than three years, but in the annals of history he is considered a legend and one of the most just rulers.

His short rule stands over all the Umayyads and many Islamic scholars consider Umar bin Abdul Aziz as the reformer of the century (Hasan, 2004).

Disintegration of the Umayyad

In spite of its greatness, the Umayyad dynasty would fall relatively unexpectedly. After Umar bin Abdul Aziz came the short rule of Yazid bin Abdul Malik known as the debauched Umayyad. He was more devoted to two slave girls, Salamah and Hababah, than to the administration of the Empire (Zaydan, 1994). He would be enthralled by their songs. Hababah is supposed to have sung a song that turned out to be prophetic. He was riveted when she sang:

"There is a heat in the curve of the neck.
It can't be cooled, nor softened nor swallowed."

When she asked him, "To whom will you leave your people?"
Kissing her hand he said, "To you."

A few days later on a pleasure excursion, while eating and drinking, he playfully threw a grape stone at Hababah, which flew into her mouth and lodged into her throat. She choked on it and was unable to swallow it and died. For three day, he moaned over her body and refused to let her be buried. He died seven days after her death.

The life of pleasure, hunting and profligacy of the Umayyad Princes caused dismay among the people. An epigram by poet Abdullah Ibn Hisham expresses the feeling:

Wrath satiates us, were we to drain
The blood of Umayyah, our thirst would still pain.
While wasting the people, and without care,
You sons of Umayyah, go hunt the hare!

Ali's assassination, the tragedy of Karbala and subsequent similar tragic episodes of suppression against the Alids were instrumental in the formation of the Shia opposition. This started off as a political opposition but with on going oppression this opposition hardened into a movement which became very bitter against the establishment. The extravagance of some later Umayyad rulers, there imperialist attitude, the lack of adherence to the system of inheritance of the Caliphate, power-play and the lack of discipline soon reduced them to bitter infightings. Matters of personal gratification became more important then matters of the state. In general, there was disillusionment with the Umayyads through out the empire. Thus weakening the Umayyad influence on the general masses.

Minor revolts broke out in various places including Iraq, Bahrain, Oman, Yemen, Makkah, Madinah, Fars and Khuzestan. The Umayyads were able to suppress these. But a serious revolt took place in Khorasan of Persia by the Yemenite Arabs residing there.

The Hashemite Abbasid, descendants of the Prophet's uncle Abbas, had set up an intelligence network in the Caliphate. They sent agents all over the Caliphate to carry out propaganda in the name of the family of the Prophet. They claimed that the house of the Prophet would come to power to set things right. The leader of the Abbasids was Ibrahim who lived in what is now Jordan. The Abbasids mustered support and alliances with the Yemenite Arabs, the Alids, the Kharijites as well as factions of non Arab Muslims.

The Alids had participated in open confrontation with the Umayyad and thus had to suffer much of the Umayyad retribution. Karbala was the first of those revolts. Zaid, a great grandson of Husain bin Ali, again raised a revolt from Kufa in 740 and faced the same fate. After he was killed his son Yahya escaped to Khorasan and from there started another revolt. But his revolt was also crushed and he was killed. There was strategic error in the Alid plans leading to these failures (Hasan, 2004).

During the final revolt, led by the Abbasid, there was a tactical understanding between the Alid and the Abbasid as both were Hashemite. The Alid had chosen Muhammad, a great grandson of Hasan bin Ali, to be the Caliph. But the Abbasid would deny them the opportunity.

The Abbasids had kept a low profile and with superior planning and intelligence network they became the ultimate victor. The Abbasid agent in Khorasan was Abu Muslim, a very able administrator and a General. He developed a loyal following in Khorasan. He supported the Yemenite Arabs revolt against the Umayyad in 748. In the confrontation that ensued the Umayyad Governor fled, but the Yemenite leader was also killed. Abu Muslim, thus, declared himself the Governor of Khorasan with allegiance towards the Abbasids.

Marwan II, the Umayyad Caliph, arrested Ibrahim, leader of the house of Abbasid, and lodged him into prison. This resulted in an outrage in Khorasan and a force from there went on an offensive rampage fighting and capturing the cities Ray, Isfahan, Nihawand, and Kufa. Marwan had Ibrahim killed and Abul Abbas became the head of the Abbasids. In October 749, the people of the liberated region gave allegiance to Abul Abbas and again there were two Caliphs.

Marwan marched to Kufa at the head of a large Syrian force. The Abbasid army was led by Abdullah, the uncle of the new Abbasid Caliph. The two armies met near the Zab River and in a historic battle the Umayyads were defeated. Marwan escaped to Egypt, but he was apprehended and killed. After nearly a century's rule by 13 Caliphs the Umayyad Dynasty came to an end. Marwan II was a professional soldier and a good leader. But by the time he came to power, the forces of disintegration had progressed too far for him to arrest it.

~~~
~~~

Muawiah, the founder of the Umayyad dynasty, was a visionary. Even though he opposed one of the Rashidun Caliphs, he understood their superhuman mental and moral strength. He knew that lesser beings would find it almost impossible to run the new model state as had the Rashiduns. Muawiah was also a pragmatist and understood that such strength was rare. Thus, for state administration, he did the next best thing. He adopted the older Byzantine and Persian state model and subjected it to the modern Islam. The hereditary Islamic Empire was born.

Though, the hereditary Empire portrayed a narrower vision of Islamic universality, it demonstrated political entities such as Empires and Kingdoms could adopt themselves and exist under the shade of Islam. The pristine form, obviously, would be the Caliphate that was ruled by the Rashiduns. The Rashidun Caliphs were both spiritual and temporal leaders of the Muslims. The Umayyads, in their turn, become more temporal and less spiritual leaders.

By the time of the Umayyads, all the Companions had gradually died and the Council of Companions became non-existent. Due to disagreements with the royal family and nobility, many of the great religious scholars (Ulema) left Damascus. This was the distancing of the spiritual from the ruling political apparatus. In absence of the Companions and the Ulema, the Umayyads gradually resorted to a tribal 'group feeling' to administer the empire's political apparatus. The Umayyad princes held the most powerful positions in the political hierarchy and chauvinist attitudes increased. On the long run, this led to the undoing of the Umayyad as the non-Umayyad and non-Arab forces were never content under this arrangement.

Due to their non-representative form of governance two main issues that would continue to vex the empire were the non-adherence to the process of succession of the Caliphate and the absence of accountability of the nobility. The non-accountability meant that the princes and the nobility could lead hedonist and reckless lives. It also meant, like in all empires, the issue of succession required their support and evoked dirty politics, assassinations and murders.

Apart from the political chauvinism, the Umayyads were economically, culturally and militarily modern and very successful. They turned the Muslim domain into the most advanced one in the world.

It was also during the rule of the Umayyads that, after the initial conquests, all major Muslim military expansion came to an end. Obviously, the empires would at one time loose some regions and cities and at other time gain others. But Islam had settled as a dominion and philosophy, imperialism had been checked and the defensive needs of the Muslim people had been taken care of. There was no religious edict in Islam to fight or conquer senselessly. Rather, the beliefs and values of Islam started being propagated by peaceful means.

The Shia clergy also first started to develop at this time. As the ruling apparatus was totally Sunni, the Alids did not have any representation in the political set up. Without any organisation to hold then together, there was a chance that they may disperse and dissipate. They started to adhere to their Imams whose legal rulings would ultimate form the Shia legal sect of Islam.

The Umayyads would face revolts from primarily four groups – The Kharijites, the Alids, A group of companions under Abdullah Ibn Zubair and the Abbasids. The revolts of the first three would be crushed but the Abbasids would succeed in violently eliminating the Umayyads in Damascus.

The Abbasids

(750-1258)

The prime aspect in the proper understanding of these Muslim Empires is to differentiate between the political history and social history. While there were wars, revolts, invasions, royal intrigues and assassinations on the political level the general society was mostly far removed from it all and kept on developing, educating and improving. Socially, culturally, economically and academically the general mass had kept on emancipating despite the political storms.

The character of the Abbasid governance was different from the Umayyad. They were no longer chauvinistic and a variety of people, aside Arabs, gained political ascendancy in the royal administration. The Persians got important positions in administrations and became the Wazir (Vizier or Prime Minister). The money testers and bankers were Jews. They also served as physicians, interpreters and scribes. The Christians got appointed as head of the War Office which caused powerful leaders and chiefs to pay homage to them. Caliph Al Muttaki had Abul Ala Said, a Christian, as his deputy Wazir (Zaydan, 1994). These positions became dynastic with sons succeeding the fathers. Along with them all others enjoyed complete security and earned their keep from the treasury stipend. Justice and tolerance were also found in the Egyptian Fatimid (Shia) dynasty of the same time, where Christians and Jews became Wazirs.

In 751, an Abbasid army under commander Ziyad ibn Salih faced the mighty army of the Chinese Tang dynasty. In the battle near River Talas of present day Khirgiztan, he defeated the Chinese comprehensively and established permanent Muslim authority in Central Asia region. This was one of the very rare fight between Muslims and the Chinese. By the 10th century, in this region, the Muslims would establish a large number of vibrant and modern cities with advanced academic and artisan culture. Some of these cities are Balk, Samarqand, Kashgar, Taskent and Merv.

The Chinese had kept the art of paper making a secret and produced a limited quantity. But it came into the Muslim hands and soon, due to demands as a replacement for parchment and papyrus in book-making, Muslims started producing paper in vast commercial quantity. By the beginning of the 9th century, paper was produced in mills of Baghdad. Books were now very inexpensive and for the first time in history left the palace libraries and made its way to the general household – the Age of Books had started in earnest. By the end of the 10th century the Fatimids and the 11th century the Spanish Muslims were large producers of paper and books as well. By the 13th century, the art of making paper spread to Europe from the Muslim provinces.

By the river Tigris, Al Mansur founded the city of Baghdad. Surveyors, engineers, and art constructionists from around the world were assembled to draw the plans for the city. Over 100,000 construction workers reviewed the plans and started the survey works. The city was circular with the Mosque in the centre. The central part also contained the Headquarter of the Gaurds, the central square and the Golden Gate Palace. Along with the surrounding residential area with villas there were also many parks, gardens, markets, and promenades.

Soon after the Capital of the Abbasid was moved to Baghdad it became the political, commercial and academic centre of the world. A high degree of personal freedom and autonomy was provisioned for and enjoyed by the general mass. This free environment helped further develop the global commerce and trade network that saw merchants from all over the world participate.

The upliftment and development of the Muslim world was accompanied by unprecedented research and advancement into all branches of knowledge and commerce. Similar to Baghdad, renowned throughout the world for academic excellence were the beautiful cities of Cordova in Muslim Spain, Bukhara and Samarqand in (Uzbekistan) Central Asia, Tus and Nishapur in Persia, Al Qahira (Cairo) and Qairowan in North Africa. Universities, academic institutions, libraries, laboratories and observatories were established in those cities. The Al Azhar University established by the Fatimid Dynasty still remain famous to this day. But the most acclaimed was Dar ul Hikma or the Hall of Wisdom established in Baghdad during the reign of Caliph Al Mamun. It was the centre of world knowledge and visited by scholars from far away lands

Prior to the Abbasids, knowledge was mainly divided into religion and philosophy. Some civilizations had worked with science but their science was more a philosophical study of nature and humans. No scientific method existed and everything was theoretical with no empiricism and experimentation. There were no distinctive science or social science subjects. Astronomy was still mixed with superstitious Astrology, medicine still religious with mythical aspects, and mathematics was looked more as a philosophical entity. It was the Muslims who first grasped the totality of science and its distinct subdivision into various subjects and disciplines. During the Abbasid era science took a discrete and concrete shape and for the first time each specific subject as we know today – chemistry, maths, algebra, astronomy, medicine, and many other areas of human learning - were understood and given an identity, nomenclature and taxonomy of its own. The Muslim 'Thought' largely fell into three categories – the Ulema, Sufi and Rational. The Caliphs would patronise one or the other at various times. The rationalist Mutazilite became influential after being patronised by a number of them.

The flourishing scholarly and academic, trade and commercial, agricultural and engineering, political and diplomatic activities attracted scholars, merchants, emissaries and a diverse range of people from all over the world to the Muslim cities. Baghdad became a sprawling cosmopolitan. When the Arab poet Abu Nakhilah visited Al Mansur in Baghdad, he was amazed at what he saw and summed up his amazement in a poem (Khudabaksh and Margoliouth, 1996):

Of the multitudes thronging this place
Don't know the nation and can't tell the race.
Their robes they open and presently fold
And the hoods purchased for riches untold
For the freedman of a freedman or the slave of a slave,
Makes one wonder how much can the Treasury hold?

Political issues were openly discussed and debated in the court. Persian fashion became the vogue in Baghdad. Long roads like the one from Makkah to Baghdad were built with Inns on the side. There was a regular postal service and people travelled the entire length of the Caliphate without fear of bandits or robbers. If the Umayyad had turned the Muslim domain into the most advanced, the Abbasids turned it into the wonder of the world. To all people of different civilisations of the era, Muslims were an object of awe and respect due to their erudition and modern outlook.

The Abbasid dynasty ruled from 750 to 1258. Their rule can be divided into two distinct stages. The first stage comprised of the initial two centuries when the Caliphs were absolute rulers, temporal and spiritual. During this time they spawned great rulers like Al Mansur, Al Mahdi, Harun ar Rasheed (mentioned in the 'Arabian Nights') and Al Mamun. In the second stage disintegration caused the break up of the Empire forming multiple kingdoms and dynasties which existed along with the much diminished Abbasid domain. The Caliph remained the spiritual head of the new kingdoms and empires but his temporal power was restricted and upheld only within his own borders and, at times, nominally so.

Some of the Abbasid rulers had to be relentless and ruthless in one arena – statecraft. Whenever and whoever they deemed a threat to the state or the Caliphal power they would pursue, suppress and destroy with unfeeling cruelty. This they believed was needed as there were constant conspiracies to remove them from power.

Abul Abbas

In 750, three months after the occupation of Kufa, the Abbasid dynasty was founded by Abul Abbas, the first Abbasid Caliph. From the pulpit of the Great Mosque of Kufa the new Caliph first declared the virtues of the descendants of the Prophet and justified their claim over the Caliphate. He then denounced the usurpation and crimes of the Umayyads. After thanking the Kufans for their support he declared that his mission was to destroy all corruptions and opposition saying, "I am the Great Avenger, and my name is *As-Saffah*, the Shedder of Blood."

He came to power after a period of anarchy and knew that to consolidate his authority he would have to deal with iron and blood. Thousands of Umayyad supporter were imprisoned and many lost their lives. His rule started in Kufa but as Kufa had a large Alid following he moved the capital to Anbar.

There is an account that he invited the Umayyad princes for talks to his capital. About eighty attended the summit. At the banquet suddenly a bard started to sing about all the bad deeds the Umayyad princes had committed and on a signal a band of executioners descendent on the Princes and massacred them all. Only one prince called Abdul Rahman managed to break out. He escaped to Spain where he set up an Umayyad state.

As-Saffah subdued various revolts of the Umayyad, Alid, and Kharijite partisans. In the Far East, when a Chinese army appeared and attacked Shash in Central Asia, the ruler of Shash asked for help from Abu Muslim, the Abbasid governor of Khorasan. An army was sent in support of Shash and the Chinese were driven back.

The two most powerful nobles in the Abbasid court were Abu Muslim and Abu Salama. Both had contributed significantly in the overthrow of the Umayyad and both were extremely powerful figures. There was mutual resentment between the two. Political enmity between the two developed to such an extent that one night when Abu Salama was returning home from the Palace a band of Abu Muslim's men accosted and killed him. As-Saffah was wary of Abu Muslim and suspected that he had Caliphal aspirations.

As-Saffah, if the streak of political ruthlessness is put aside, emerges as a very different person. He was generous and had pleasant and cultured manners. He had only one wife and abstained from frivolity and privately led a pious life. After a rule of four years he died of small pox.

Al Mansur

In 754, As-Saffah was succeeded by his brother Abu Jafar who took on the sobriquet of Al Mansur, the Victorious. Al Mansur consolidated the rule of the Abbasids by defeating his enemies within and outside the empire. The opposition by Abdullah, the uncle of the Caliph and Governor of Syria, and Muhammad, the great grandson of Hasan bin Ali and the Alid leader from Madinah, were crushed.

After having Abu Salama killed Abu Muslim had become immensely powerful and was invincible in his strong base of Khorasan. Al Mansur had never fully trusted Abu Muslim's ultimate intensions and presumed that he harboured Caliphal aspirations. Once he had said to his brother, As-Saffah, referring to Abu Muslim and Abu Salama, "If you don't lunch them today, they will dine you tomorrow" (Khudabakhsh and Margoliouth 1996).

He decided the best way to resolve this threat was to remove Abu Muslims from his root stronghold - Khorasan. While Abu Muslim was still in Syria, the Caliph offered him the Governorship of Syria and its dependencies. This was a more prestigious position than the governorship of Khorasan. Abu Muslim refused the governorship of Syria and declared that he had decided to march directly to Khorasan. He also passed derogatory remarks about the Berber mother of Al Mansur (Hasan, 2004).

The doubt that Al Mansur harboured about Abu Muslim's secret aspiration for the Caliphate now consolidated into a belief. He invited Abu Muslim to come to the Court before going to Khorasan. Abu Muslim was received grandly at the court and soon assassinated. There was a revolt in Khorasan, Al Mansur sent a force and the revolt was suppressed with considerable loss of life on both sides. But Khurasan, specially, with strong local Alid group, would continue to be a menace to the Abbasids for a long time.

On the frontiers, the Byzantine took advantage of the revolts and encroached on Abbasid territory. Al Mansur fell upon the Byzantines and drove them back till their Emperor was forced to request for a peace treaty. The Byzantines were defeated twice and on both occasion agreed to pay tribute. Similar fate fell on the revolting Khazars of Armenia in Central Asia. The Abbasid army also annexed Tabaristan, north of the Caspian Sea, and Qandahar in Afghanistan and mounted raids into India. In 756, During the *An Shi* rebellion in China, Al-Mansur sent a force of 4,000 Muslims to assist the Chinese Tang Dynasty. Afterwards, the Muslims were requested to stay and many chose to remain in China.

Al Mansur came to power a few years after the death of his eldest brother Ibrahim, who was killed during the revolt against the Umayyads. As Saffa ruled just over four years before he died. The Abbassid rule was still very weak and there were a large number of internal and external enemies vying to remove him. Thus Al Mansur had to make a number of difficult political and military choices. But he was not a vengeful or brutal person. A blind poet had recited two poems praising the Umayyad, arch-enemy of the Abbassid, unaware that Al Mansur was present in the audience. Al Mansur had rewarded him for his verses.

He was a man of immense energy, intellect and talent, and ruled for 21 years. He was well disciplined and an excellent administrator, builder and statesman. By his time the Muslims had already started to study the sciences and literature with diligence. He initiated an international effort to purchase and collect manuscripts on various fields of sciences, like mathematic, astronomy and medicine, to support the effort of the scholars. His agents scoured the foreign lands of the East and the West and returned with many valuable books. These were promptly translated to Arabic and placed into libraries. Mathematics was already in vogue and books like the Indian *Brahmasupta Siddhanta* were translated to Arabic during his reign. Another book, that was written in Arabic during his reign and would influence the East and the West for centuries to come, was *The Construction and Usage of the Astrolab.*

Trade and commerce had enhanced greatly during his rule. When he died, Al Mansur left behind a stable, powerful, enlightened and a very rich empire.

The next Caliph Mahdi was lenient and generous. He freed the Alids and the Umayyads and returned their properties. He gave huge amounts in charity. On the occasion of the first Hajj after his accession to the Caliphate he distributed millions of dirhams. He was very popular and during his reign the country prospered and society became cosmopolitan. His wife Khaizuran became famous for her beauty and intelligence and whose understanding of state administration was immense. He died in a hunting accident after ten years of rule (775-785). His son Caliph Hadi ruled for less then two years.

During the reigns of Mahdi and Hadi, scholars of various types were patronised and encouraged by the Abbassid. Non-Muslims were also encouraged to partake in scholarly pursuits. Religious scholars of the major religions visited the court where multifaith debates were held. Hadi quite often invited the Bishop Timothenus to his court to discuss religious topics with him. Many of the issues discussed by the two were compiled into a book by the Bishop.

But Hadi undertook some repressive measures against the Alid and they revolted in Makkah. This revolt was suppressed although, Idris, one of the Alid leaders, fled to North Africa and set up an independent Shia state in Morocco with the aid of the Berbers. Hadi also attempted to make his son the heir instead of his brother Harun ar Rasheed who was the designated heir. But Raheed refused to accept that and escaped to Raqqa, an Abbasid provincial area. The renowned administrator Yahya Barmakid, who was the tutor of Rahseed, was imprisoned. Yahya talked with Hadi and convinced him not to take any immediate drastic action against Rasheed.

During this period, some exotic cults with large following developed in the Caliphate. In Khorasan, a self styled prophet named Moqanna declared he was the incarnation of God. He taught a mixture of Zoroastrianism and Islam. His followers dressed themselves in white. In Jurjan, near the east of the Caspian, a sect called Muhammire rose. Their follower dressed in red and preached revolutionary dogmas. The Zindigs were an atheist sect that supported incestuous marriage. All these cults and movement were suppressed or kept under controll by the Abbasids.

Princess Khaizuran

The Abbasid Princesses were erudite and wielded a lot of political clout. One of the most powerful was Khaizuran wife of Caliph Al Mahdi. She was very influential in the governance of the Caliphate and held regular court by herself. When her son Al Hadi became the Caliph in 785, the court of Khaizuran became even more crowded being visited by nobles and Generals every day. Hadi resented his mother's power and asked her not to meddle in the affairs of state. But she continued her court as usual. Once, she was approached by Abdallah ibn Malik, a nobleman, who informed her that the Caliph had denied him permission on a certain official matter (Khudabaksh and Margoliouth, 1996). In due time, she went to Hadi and said, "You must assent. I have promised Abdallah."

"I knew he would go to you, and I shall not grant his wishes just for you." Hadi replied.

"In that case, I will never ask anything of you ever again!"

"That's perfectly all right!"

As she rose to depart in anger, Hadi exclaimed, "Stop! If any General or Councillor of my court goes to your court, I will deprive him of his head and his property. What is the meaning of the cavalcades that comes to you day and night? Don't you have anything else to do? Anything to spin, or read the Quran or have a chamber for privacy? I have repeatedly warned you not to open your doors to Muslims, Jews or Christians."

Khairuzan went away and never spoke to him again. Hadi also took his courtiers to task.

"Who is better, I or you, my mother or your mother?" He asked them.

"You and your mother."

"Who amongst you would like to hear of your mother being talked about?" He asked again.

The reply was none.

"Then why do you go to my mother. And why do you talk of her?"

The courtiers understood what the Caliph was implying and stopped going to Khaizuran.

The next Caliph Harun ar Rasheed recognised the abilities of his mother Khaizuran. She again rose to prominence after Hadi and was allowed to hold her own court (Hasan, 2004). Rasheed delegated her and his tutor the Wazir (Prime Minister) Yahya Barmakid with significant executive power. When Khairuzan died in 789, a state mourning was officially declared.

The Barmakid family of Yahya were great and famous administrators and had served the Abbasids from the time of As-Saffah. Yahya had played an important part in protecting Rasheed from Hadi.

Harun ar Rasheed

Harun ar Rasheed, who became Caliph in 763, achieved legendary fame and his name became outstandingly significant in history and is mentioned in literature as well. By the time of his rule Baghdad was famous for its cultural, intellectual and religious traditions. Rasheed embraced the enlightenment and raised it further to dazzling heights. The scholars researching in the *Bayt Al Hikmah* (House of Wisdom) were sponsored by the state. The library *Kanz Al Hikmah* (Treasures of Wisdom) now had thousands of new books and translations of old ones. To provided the scholars with the best reference Rasheed continued the tradition of collecting a variety of manuscripts and having those translated to Arabic. Translators, Muslims and non-Muslims, were awarded the manuscripts weight in gold.

A prosperous lifestyle evolved throughout the empire with its pinnacle in Baghdad. The court became famous for its culture and grandeur. Baghdad was a splendid city and the royal court was so luminously grand and renowned that it became the subject of many tales and fictions. Rasheed, himself, was a scholar, a poet, an intellectual, a politician and a successful General. He encouraged learning, poetry and music. His name became known throughout the world. He had good diplomatic relations with China and the Frank kingdom of Charlemagne.

During Rasheed's reign, Yahya Barmakid retired from his office after years of service and the Prime Ministership (Wazirate) was conferred to his son Jaafar Barmakid. Jaafar took complete control of the Empire and placed many of the Barmakids in powerful positions. The Barmakids became executives of the Caliphate and became so famous that Rasheed was overshadowed to some extent. He became wary of the situation but had little manoeuvrability as the Barmakids were well entrenched, well respected and very popular due to their efficiency and charity.

The Alids were politically influential in many regions of the Empire including Khorasan. Like before, they also revolted against the Abbasids during Hadi and Rasheed's rule. The Barmakids were Shia, and local Alid meetings were held in Jaafar's residence. Ismail, a Hashemite friend of Jaafar, was concerned about the situation and advised Jaafar to present some of his estate to the Caliphs sons as a gift, which would appease the Caliph. But Jaafar interpreted the suggestion negatively and said that he had done a lot for the Caliph and boasted that he could start a rebellion in Khorasan if the Caliph tried to take any of his properties. This was reported to Rasheed by spies. And when he discovered that Jaafar had also started a secret liaison with his sister Abbasa, Rasheed was incensed and assumed a design behind all this and decided to take care of the situation. Jaafar was executed and the Barmakids were removed from high office (Zaydan, 1994). According to Ibn Khaldun the fall of the Barmakids was due to "the manner in which they seized upon all authority, and assumed absolute control over public revenue" (Ahmad, 1984). Jaafar remains immortalised as the Wazir in the Arabian Nights.

Meanwhile, the Byzantines under Empress Irene were paying tribute to Baghdad. The next Byzantine emperor Nicephorus decided not to pay tribute and sent Rasheed an insolent letter demanding a tribute from him instead. Rasheed declared that the reply will be given in the field of battle. The Abbasid army routed the Byzantine and Nicephorus agreed to pay tribute. It was a cold winter, and as the Abbasid army were on their return journey Nicephorus went back on his word and refused to pay tribute. Rasheed and his army braved the winter and went back and attacked the Byzantines and defeated them again. Peace was concluded with the tribute becoming double the previous amount. During the Byzantine campaigns Rasheed captured many cities including Thebase, Ephasus, Konia, Heraclea, Nicaea,

Andrasus, Skallya, and Malecopea. Cyprus and Rhodes was captured in expeditions by the Navy (Hasan, 2004).

The Christians on the Abbasid frontier with the Byzantines had collaborated with the Byzantines army and used their churches as centres for spying. During the battle with the Byzantine, few of those churches were destroyed and the Christians of the frontier regions were given a dress code. They had to wear a yellow ribbon or yellow cowl so that they would not be able to disguise themselves as Muslims and spy for the Byzantine. On the other hand, he ordered the rebuilding of churches that had been destroyed near Egypt.

Harun ar Rasheed suppressed a number of uprisings. Shia rebellions took place in Azerbaijan and Armenia which were contained. A Kharijite revolt was led by a brave and beautiful woman called Laila in Persia. Under her leadership the Kharijite movement gathered momentum and they won initial successes. She is considered as the historic precursor to 'Joan of Arc' (Hasan, 2004). But finally, Rasheed brought the revolt under control and forced Laila to retire to her home.

In 809, after ruling for 23 years Rasheed died of natural causes while on march to Transoxiana. Before his death he had drawn up a covenant of succession. He was to be succeeded sequentially by his sons Amin, Mamun and Mutasim.

Rasheed and Baghdad were brilliant, legendary and epitomes of enlightenment. Ameer Ali in *History of Saracens* wrote, "Weigh him as you like in the scale of historical criticism, Harun ar Rasheed will always take rank with the greatest sovereigns and rulers of the world."

According to Professor Phillip Hitti in *History of the Arabs*, the ninth century opened with two important names standing supreme in world affairs – Harun ar Rasheed in the East and Charlemagne in the West, and out of these two, Harun ar Rasheed was the most powerful and represented the higher culture.

Al Mamun

Al Mamun became the Caliph in 813 and ruled for twenty years. He was a great patron of learning and knowledge. He established the *Dar Al Hikma,* - The Hall of Wisdom. This was a renowned University with large number of institutes, research centers and observatories. It was unrivalled in the study of sciences and humanities - medicine, mathematics, astronomy, chemistry, zoology, geography, philosophy, and other disciplines. Caliph Mamun also sent scholars to different countries to gather existing knowledge. The knowledge of the Greeks, Indians and Persians was accumulated and added to the works of the local scholars. This formed the greatest collection of knowledge in the world on which the best scholars of the world worked and soon added more and more of their own researches and discoveries. The main library was the *Khizant Al Hikma,* the Library of Wisdom, which contained an unrivalled collection for the study of science and humanities and also had a huge collection of scientific manuscripts in many languages.

By the reign of Rasheed, Baghdad was already known as the world's richest city and greatest centre for intellectual development. By the time of Mamun the number of higher institutes reached 332 packed with students studying various subjects (Al Hassani, 2007).

> Hunayn bin Ishaq (809 – 873) was a director of Dar Al Hikma. His contribution was both original writing and translation. His translation included the Greek 'Hippocratic Oath' and his own writings included medical books, one of which was a book on Ophthalmology (knowledge of eye). His books would become text in the Muslim and later European universities.

Al Amin, who ruled before Al Mamun from 809 to 813, is said to have had a fascination for handsome slave girls dressed in boyish attire with hair cut short (Khudabakhsh and Margoliouth, 1996). This is construed by some, mainly oriental, historians as a depravity for boys. It is most likely that the royal slave girls were dressed in a 'Page' uniform and had nothing to do with depravity. It became a fashion and people started to dress up their slave girls similarly. Soon after becoming the Caliph Al Amin tried to make his son the heir apparent in place of his brother Mamun. But Mamun wrested the power from him and Al Amin died trying to escape.

Mutasim became the Caliph after Al Mamun died of a malignant fever in 833. The Byzantines attacked the town of Capodocipa, killed all the men and took the women and children as slaves. Their army also ravaged Zebetra where Mutasim was born. The Caliph was incensed and personally led the army against the Byzantines. He defeated the Byzantine army and marched on to Ankara and Amoriam. In vengeful mood Mutasim razed Amoriam to the ground killing all the men and took the women and children as slaves. His navy captured Messina in Sicily and then took the Southern tip of Italy.

In the internal politics of the Abbasid Empire, a tension developed between the general Arabs and Persians. Instead of removing this 'clannishness' by applying Islam's universalism via judicial and social equity processes Mustasim tried to force the issue by introducing another 'clan' element. As the tension started to surface, he conscripted Turks into the army in order to keep both these groups at bay. He created an excellent personal army of 10,000 Turks, fully armed, splendidly uniformed and mounted. Though this appeared to solve the existing issues, on the long run it would prove fateful. The Turkic army would soon develop a 'will' of its own.

The next Caliph Wasiq who ruled from 842 to 847 was the son of a Greek 'slave' woman called Karatis. He continued to prevail on rationalism, patronizing science and literature. Trade and commerce grew further during his reign. He was an expert musician and was the author of many musical compositions. He could play the lyre with great expertise. But he was reluctant to take adequate interest in administration, which led to the weakening of the Abbasid rule. Mutawakkil who succeeded Wasiq tried to assert himself by changing some of the current policies. He re-introduced orthodoxy at the expense of the rational Mutazilites and released the orthodox Imam Hanbal, who had been earlier placed in prison. He was authoritarian and dealt strongly with the Turks, Jews, Christian and the Shias.

The Disintegration

Originally Caliph Mutawakkil had nominated his eldest son Muntasir as his heir. But his wife Qabiha, stepmother to Muntasir, nominated her own son Mutaaz to be the heir apparent. She was a very influential lady and Mutawakkil renounced the succession of Muntasir. He also took punitive action against Turk Generals who had become arrogant and irresponsible.

On being removed from the line of succession, an infuriated and indignant Muntasir entered into a plot with the Turk Generals. In a palace coup Mutawakkil was killed and Muntasir became the Caliph. This was the first time the Turk army of the Abbasid had tasted Caliphal blood and real power. From then on the army kept on acquiring more and more strength till they virtually took over all the executive powers of the Caliphs who remained in charge all but in name. During the period of 862 to 870 five successive Caliphs were removed or killed by the Turk Generals. This led to anarchy through out the Empire. There were also a number of revolts by the Shias, the Qarmatians and the Kharijites.

Previously, whenever the frontiers had been attacked by external forces, the Abbasids had repulsed those attacks vehemently and carried out counter attacks into the invader's land. However, in 926, when the Byzantines invaded and captured the city of Maltiyah defeating the Abbasid force stationed there, no action was taken. In the following year the emboldened Byzantines captured Damietta in Egypt and the next year Khalat in Armenia. The Abbasid army had become too engrossed in palatial politics and a royal way of life to really take effective measures against revolts and invasions.

The difference between the latter Umayyads and Abbasids was that the latter Umayyads were Arab chauvinist. Abbasids were relatively more universalists. They came to power with a cause of universal progress for the entire *Ummah,* the universal civilisation that included all Arabs and non-Arabs, and were resoundingly successful in the implementation of the cause. All the facets of the society developed extensively. But once the cause had been fulfilled there was no further motivation left in the governance of the state. In the absence of ideals, self serving interest soon raised its head. Instead of Arab tribalism cultural groupings rose their heads. Some of the later Caliphs became more interested in self preservation, family preservation, wealth preservation, and indulgence rather than serving humanity.

Self-interest soon proved to be the anathema of Abbasid leadership. Moral corruption in the leadership led to an abject corruption of the administration. Most of the later Wazirs would lasted only for a year or two but by that relatively short span of time they would amass millions of Dinar by bribery and extortion. Wazirs would appoint Governors who paid their 'perquisite' to the Wazirs. The Governor would then reclaim what he had given to the Wazir, plus much extra, from the taxes. Down the line the tax-collector would be taking bribe or extortion payment from the merchants and farmers. The army did not need to go to so much trouble, it would simply demand a pay increase. The corrupt administration would not be able to deny the armies and would have to pay the amount which, ultimately, came from the taxes on the ordinary people. Facing raised taxes, corruption and hardships the general masses would become unhappy. The oppressed people would then support dissenting forces leading towards revolts and disintegration.

This self serving attitude also began to permeate into other ethnic components of the Caliphate. The Persians and Turks, among others, who had represented universality in the earlier stages of the Caliphate, now became a motley of self interested groups. They acquired a nationalistic character of nations within the Empire. Thus, the application of a non-universalist policy to a heterogeneous people resulted in self-centric conflicts within the social components of the Empire. As long as the self-interested environment remained the conflicts also remained and could only be suppressed by force and only up to a time.

These were all preamble to the political fragmentation of the empire. One by one many new states formed as the empire become weaker. Besides the already established Spanish Umayyads, these included the independent Shia state established in Morocco, the states of the Aglabids in Tunisia, the Tahirids in Khorasan, Saffarids in Seestan, Kerman and Fars, the Tulunids in Egypt, Samanids in Transoxiana and the Qarmatians in Bahrain and others. Some paid token allegiance to the Caliphate, the more powerful ones controlled it furtively while paying spiritual allegiance openly.

These 'states' lasted for various periods. Some just flickered and diffused while others lasted for a long time producing great rulers and advancement in knowledge. The most famous among them were the Umayyads of Spain, the Fatimids of Egypt, the Buhawids of Fars and the Seljuk Turks of Pesia who built a huge empire.

~~~

The Political State under the Abbasid

The Umayyad's hereditary rule was different from the selected-elected style of rule of the four Rashidun Caliphs. This was one of the prime reasons that many of the religious scholars forsook and left the court of the Umayyads. The intellectual gap was slowly filled up by a more rationalist group of scholars. By the time of the Abbasids this group had entrenched itself with the rise of the Mutazila.
~~~

Rationalism was a natural philosophical progression during the Abbasid. The rationalists were influenced by various pre-existing knowledge base of the Greeks, Egyptians, Persians, Babylonians, Indians and the Chinese. The Mutazilite concept of rationalism was employed by the Abbasid as the philosophy guiding the ruling political apparatus. Under them, rational sciences flourished as never before.

The Mutazilites were not secular but rather religious rationalists. Though still under the tenet of Islam, some of their philosophical views, in details and at times, would vary from the Ulema's view. That led to the conflict between the rationalists (Mutazilites) and the religious (Ulema) scholars. The rational movement also produced, on the periphery, some agnostic or heretical elements. The Ulema were always wary of the political ascendancy of the Mutazilites and this further intensified the clash with them. The Ulema ultimately prevailed and the Abbasid removed the Mutazilites during the time of Mutawakkil from the political office. The Ulema were appeased, but neither they nor the rationalists had any political clout anymore. In fact, the removal of rationalism would become very harmful on the long term as investigation into the scientific universe would come to an end. With the self-exile of the Ulema from the ruling politics during the Umayyad period and the retiring of rationalism during the Abbasid, there remained no guiding philosophy for the Empire, which began to float on imperial whim.

In the 11th Century, Imam Ghazzali would take up the same conflict as a personal quest and set out to discover the 'truth'. Though, ultimately, acknowledging the superiority of the religious view he would attempt to contain all the known intellectual banks – Ulemaic, Rationalist and Philosophical – within the framework of Islam while removing or discrediting some of the theories he considered blameworthy. Much later, the conflict between rationalism and religion would rise again in the renaissance Europe.

The Abbasids, like the Umayyads, were the most progressive rulers of their time. Their academe was by far the most brilliant and economy the most advanced. They had discarded the Arab chauvinism of the Umayyad but still ruled a hereditary empire where the Caliphate passed within the royal family, sometimes with bloody succession strifes. The rule was inherently non-representative of the general mass, sometimes wonderfully great when the Caliph was a person of wisdom and at times discreditable when the Caliph was ordinary as was the case among some later Abbasids. The Abbasid power groups were no longer Quraish but various groups of Arabs, Persians and Turks. Politically, they still fell short of the universal modern state that the Prophet had envisaged.

The Rashidun Caliphs had been both the temporal and spiritual leaders. Both the political and religious authorities were vested in their hand. They and the Muslims had thrived under their rule. The early Abbasids Caliphs were mainly temporal leaders. Though they tried to influence the spiritual leadership, it was the Great Imams and their schools from which the main spiritual and legal guidance emanated. The later Abbasids, as their domain diminished, became more spiritual leaders with little or no temporal influence.

By the time of the Abbasid all military expansions had come to an end and military campaigns took place in imperial self-defence. One that was more of an empire vs empire contest. Religious propagation to various regions of China, India, and South East Asia was achieved by peaceful means.

There are parallels in the history of the 7th - 8th century Arabs and the Ancient Greeks. Before the advent of Islam Makkah was populated by multiple tribes and ruled by a coalition representing the tribes. Similarly, before Alexander's conquest of Persia and Egypt, Athens was populated by different tribes or communes and ruled by a coalition representing the communes.

The Prophet preached in Makkah amid a hostile leadership and he did not accept the existing state gods but just one God. Similarly in Ancient Greece, Socrates preached in Athens amid a hostile state and did not accept the existing state gods but introduced a new one or new ones. The Prophet's immediate successor, Abu Bakr, was totally dedicated to him. Every decision Abu Bakr took, he ensured that it would be the decision the Prophet would have taken. Socrates' immediate student, Plato, was totally dedicated to him. Every dialogue he wrote contained Socrates. He ensured that in his writings all the aspects of his philosophy were represented by Socrates. The main flowering of Islamic knowledge started after the peace of Hudaibiah. The main flowering of Greek knowledge started during the peace treaty with the Persians.

Regionally, Arabia was situated besides two great empires, Roman Byzantium and Sassanid Persia. The Arabs tribes, united under Islam, subdued both the empires and establish new ones which were harbingers of knowledge. Greece also lay by two great empires Achaemenid Persia and the Egyptians. The Greek tribes, united under Alexander, as a Greek nation would take over Egypt and crush Persia. They were also harbingers of knowledge. Comparatively though, after Alexander, the domains that the Greeks established were of temporary duration and restricted size.

Muslims in Europe

Al Andalus: Muslim Spain and Portugal

In the beginning of the eighth century Musa bin Nusair was the Governor of North Africa under the Umayyad Caliphate. He resided in Cueta, a small seaport, located in current Morocco. He deputed one of his lieutenants to take reconnoitring mission across the sea into the Iberian Peninsula (modern day Spain and Portugal).

Tariq bin Ziyad, a man of tremendous energy, embarked on this mission with 7,000 Berber men from North Africa on April 28, 711 CE. After he sailed across the straits he landed on the base of a rocky region. The region came to be named after him as 'Jabal-e-Tariq' or the 'Mount of Tariq'. In contemporary geography 'Jabal-e-Tariq' is known as Gibraltar. Al-Makkari, the 17th Century Algerian historian wrote that upon landing in coast of Spain Tariq had all his ships burnt. To the astonished soldiers he said, "We conquer and establish or we perish." (Ahmad, 1984)

He defeated, first, Governor Theodomir of the south-eastern Spanish provinces, and after two months he faced Roderick, the Gothic king of Spain. The army of Roderick was significantly larger, but the Umayyads were empire builders and more advanced in strategy and weaponry. After a week-long battle, Roderick was defeated and drowned in the River Guadalete (From Arabic: Wadi Laqqa) and Tariq occupied Toledo without further resistance. In spite of reservations from Musa bin Nusair, Tariq thrust his devastating cavalcade further north capturing one town after another. By the end of the year he had conquered half of Spain.

Musa bin Nusair arrived in 712 with a further force of 18,000 and within 2 years almost the whole of Spain and Portugal was conquered (Hasan, 2004). Musa bin Nusair's aim was to conquer the south of Europe and return to Syria via land. The Caliph Waleed did not agree with him and instead summoned them to Damascus.

Tragedy was in store for these two Generals, ironically, in the hands of the Caliph. They were very loyal to Caliph Waleed and when they reached Damascus the political scene had changed. Waleed was dead and his brother Sulaiman had become the Caliph. Waleed had tried to make his son the successor by revoking the succession of Sulaiman. Sulaiman on becoming the Caliph decided to consolidate his rule. Anyone who was loyal to Waleed was removed from power. Musa and Tariq were disgraced and not allowed to continue with their services.

Abdul Aziz, the son of Musa, married Egolina, the widow of Roderick, and became the Governor of Andalus. He was an efficient administrator and diplomat. But Sulaiman had him assassinated. After that, Andalus was ruled by a succession of Umayyad Governors till 756. During this time many families from Syria and North Africa migrated to Spain.

Caliph Sulaiman would also remove another famous Umayyad General, Mohammad bin Qasim, who had conquered vast areas on the east up to India. These actions would breed silent discontent for which the Umayyad would later pay.

~~~

The first social revolution that took place in Spain under the Muslims was the empowerment of the local people. Before the Umayyad Muslims established their state, the serfs – be they Christians, Jews or Visigoths – had to face much persecution and intolerance. The Muslims on the other hand legalised property rights and respected other religions. The increased security and establishment of a more ordered and harmonious way of life for all the different people living in the South Iberian Peninsula led to an agricultural revolution.

~~~

The Umayyad Prince Abdur Rahman who had escaped death from the hands of the Abbasids arrived in Morocco and took shelter with the Berber tribe to which his mother belonged. At that time, among the rulers of Andalus were two main factions, Yemenite and Qaisite Arabs, who were at odds with each other. Abdur Rahman, with support of his Berber force and the Yemenite faction, won power and became the Amir of Andalus in 756. Thus he became the founder of the Umayyad Dynasty in Al Andalus.

Abdur Rahman, experienced with the advanced Umayyad developments in Damascus, started a mission for modernising the region. He set up educational institutes throughout the state, with hostels for free lodging of students. He organised a modern administration. He provided public baths in all the cities and a mint for coins in Cordova. He rebuilt the walls of Cordova with seven access gates. He constructed a palace with gardens called '*Muawiyat-ul-Rusufa*', a replica of the palace which was owned by his grandfather Hisham in Damascus.

He built a Grand Mosque which was extended by his son Hisham. It had 193 pillars of pure white marble with 19 arches and 19 gates with a gold lamp giving light day and night. He built canals and an aqueduct to supply water to Cordova, and started construction of a bridge on the river Guadelquiver (From Arabic: Wadi al-Kabir, 'The Great River'). He improved agriculture introducing exotic plants like the date tree.

Hisham, his son, ruled from 788 to 796 and continued the modernising trend including that of the administration. He sent scholars to train in Jurisprudence to Makkah. After their return they took up professional position in the administration. He completed the bridge over Guadelquiver and established a number of schools and public buildings. Despite administering great state undertakings, in personal life he was simple and avoided ostentation.

~~~

After all of Spain and Portugal came under Muslim rule, the first attack on France was launched in 719, and the Province of Septamania was overrun and its capital Narbonne captured. At one stage the Muslims occupied Bordeaux and Burgundy including the cities of
~~~

Lyons, Besancon and Sens. But they were defeated by a coalition of German and Frank forces in the battle in Toures in 732. The Muslims were driven out of France in 759 (Hasan, 2004). After that the Franks would invade Spain and hold regions on the north for some time, then the Muslim armies would drive them and invade into Toulouse, Narbonne or Lyon in southern France in an 'on and off' manner till 975.

When Hisham was ruling Spain at the end of the 8th century, Empress Irene of Byzantium offered marriage to Charlemagne as an alliance against Baghdad. The King of the Franks put this off diplomatically. He had his own problems, namely, the Spanish Umayyad to deal with. Instead of making enemies of the mighty Abbasid he preferred to ally with them and sent a delegation to the Caliph with many gifts. The gesture worked and Harun ar Rasheed sent him many gifts including an elephant. This was an interesting political alliance between the Muslim Abbasids and Christian Franks with the Franks pitted against the Muslim Spain and the Abbasids against the Christian Byzantium. Some Historians claim that the Abbasids fomented revolts in Umayyad Spain allowing Charlemagne to attack and capture Barcelona. But the Iberian Ummayads recovered and in a few years defeated the Franks and took Gascony from them. The war between Andalus and the Franks was not conclusive but Charlemagne defeated the Umayyads and stopped any further Muslim advance into France.

~~~

Among the great rulers of Al Andalus three were named 'Abdur Rahman'. The first was the Umayyad Prince and founder of the dynasty. The next was the thirty year rule (822 – 852 CE) of Abdur Rahman the Second. He had to contend with the usual revolts and conduct military campaigns against the Franks. During his time arose a movement of fanaticism among the Spanish Christian monks. They came out in the open to revile Islam and the Prophet and actively courted death as a form of martyrdom. Some of these fanatics were executed, but Abdur Rahman spared the life of its leader Euologius. The phase passed and gradually the fanaticism subsided.

During his reign, Abdur Rahman constructed many fine buildings including mosques and educational establishment in the cities. In Cordova, extending over miles along the Guadelquiver, were excellent buildings and beautiful gardens. Water was supplied via pipelines from the Sierra Moreno Mountain. The reputation of the Spanish University spread all over the civilised world. Spain's art and science became one of the most advanced in the world. Jews, Muslims and Christian worked and researched together. By the end of his rule in 852, Spain was the most progressive country of Europe.

Abdur Rahman the third ascended to power in 912 CE and ruled for half a century. He was the ablest of all the Spanish Umayyads and by the end of his reign Cordova had became 'Jewel of the World', second only to Baghdad. On one side of the Sierra Morena hills he built a new town called Al Zahra, naming it after the Queen Zahra. The town, a wonder of its
~~~

time, took forty years to build. The Zahra Palace, at the centre of the town, had 750 gates. He was the first Iberian ruler to claim the title of Caliph.

Under his rule the Umayyads had beaten back the Franks and the Fatimids in North Africa and thus ruled not only all of Spain and Portugal but outposts in North Africa as well. The whole country enjoyed unprecedented economic, academic and social prosperity. His court was attended by eminent scholars, philosophers, poets and ambassadors of many countries.

Irrigation techniques brought large wastelands under cultivation. Trade and industry developed with textiles becoming a huge industry. Cordova alone boasted 30,000 weavers. Leather industry also flourished in Cordova while pottery and weaponry industries flourished in Calatayud and Toledo respectfully.

~~~

Al Hakam II became caliph after Abdur Rahman III in 961. He continued to be patron of knowledge and building edifices that his father had started. The disintegration forces that had initiated in the previous century during the reign of Amir Muhammad I started to gather force. The administration was run by the Wazir and the army by its General thus curbing the Caliph's authority.

Hisham II, son of Al Hakam II, became Caliph at the age of only eleven years in 976. He ruled up to 1009 with the help of his Prime Minister, Ibn Amir. As Hisham was young and inexperienced, Ibn Amir became all powerful and declared the Prime Minister-ship hereditary within his family. He was a man of vigour, a good general and administrator. He undertook more than fifty campaigns including those against Leon and Navarre and also drove back the Franks from Catalonia and Barcelona. Once again the Muslim rule extended across the Pyrenees into France. After Ibn Amir's death his sons, Abdul Malik and then Sanchol, proved to be less effective.

Hisham II was not of an assertive bent and let Sanchol rule the state. When Sanchol went on a campaign to the north a local Umayyad Prince named Muhammad revolted. Sanchol abandoned his campaign and returned only to be defeated and killed by Muhammad in 1009. Hisham was still considered a potential threat by Muhammad but he did not want to kill the harmless recluse. Instead he had a person similar in appearance to Hisham buried with regalia and it was let known that Hisham was dead. At the same time Hisham was secretly put in a prison. After that Muhammad started to live an immoral and lax life. When he was short of finance, he retrenched a large part of the army.

Events took place in rapid succession. The Berbers gathered around another Umayyad prince Sulaiman. Soon a civil war ensued between Sulaiman and Muhammad. Both sides asked for help from the Christians and in the process the Christian rulers of Leon, Castile and Catalonia gained about two hundred fortresses as a bargain. Muhammad prevailed in
~~~

the civil war but was soon killed by the Slavs. Hisham II was amazingly released and reinstated as the Caliph in 1010. But in 1013 when Sulaiman returned after recouping with the help of the Berbers, Hisham left Spain and went to Makkah. Sulaiman became the Caliph and gave many important state positions to the loyal Berbers. This led to dissatisfaction in the other components of Cordovan society. Ali bin Hamud, the governor of Cueta, on being invited by the Cordovan people marched on to Cordova. In the confrontation that ensued Sulaiman was killed.

In 1031, the people of Cordova revolted against the leveraging of extra taxes and killed the Prime Minister and deposed the then Caliph Hisham III. That was the end of the Umayyad rule. Spain fragmented into numerous independent principalities and petty states. Squabbling and infighting became common among them.

~~~

Towards the end of the 11th century, the Iberian Christians decided to rally together and drive away the squabbling Muslims. But with the support of the Al Moravid and then the Al Mohad rulers of Africa the Muslims retained Spain. For about a century a status quo prevailed. But Muslim Spain never really unified against the *Reconquista* of the allied Christians and saw their territories increasingly eroded. Gradually, the Muslims first lost Northern Spain and then the southern regions and by 1236 only Granada remained under Muslim rule but mostly as a vassal state. It still maintained its ideal as a centre of learning with scholars writing books on various subjects, beautiful poetry being written and exquisite monuments being developed. The Nasrid Princes lived in the famous Al-Hambra palace on a hilltop overlooking beautiful gardens. In 1492 the rule of Granada was finally surrendered to the joint forces of Catholic monarchs King Ferdinand and Queen Isabella, monarchs of Leon and Castille. The condition of surrender was that the Muslims would be allowed to pursue their culture and religion without persecution. But within two years the King went back on his word. Muslims and Jews were forcefully converted to Christianity. Islamic culture was prohibited, graves desecrated and libraries burnt. The Spanish Inquisition that was commissioned by Ferdinand and Isabella brought back the religious intolerance of the Pre-Islamic days.

A major portion of the Muslim population left. Those who had any skills which could be utilised in foreign lands departed. Those who stayed and converted were still discriminated against and not given any important office. In 1609, Phillip II finally expelled all the remaining Muslims.

> 1992 was the 500th year of the Christian reconquest of Spain. On the occasion the King Juan Carlos, the monarch of Spain and descendent of Ferdinand, has publicly apologised for the inhumanity and intolerance shown to the Muslims in those times.
~~~

The Muslims left Spain leaving behind an enduring legacy. The 'Jewel' that they created in the Iberian Peninsula was not only of the material kind but was a superb example of harmonious co-existence and illuminating knowledge as well. Muslim Spain was richer and more progressive than the Franks and the Byzantines, the two other contemporary powers of Europe. Like Muslims the world over, the Muslims of Spain patronised scholars and their thirst for knowledge. Philosophers and scientists had produced a huge amount of the most advanced works which were recorded in books. As the Christians took over the disintegrated Muslims states and principalities the scholars, their knowledge and their books that survived the ravages of the battles were transferred to the new rulers. From the 11th century onwards these works were translated to Latin. And the enlightened knowledge spread from Spain to the rest of Renaissance Europe. It was the knowledge and advanced economic system that Spain inherited from the Muslims made it the great global power of the colonial world till the 17th century after which newer powers were to rise.

S. P. Scott, the 19th century American historian, wrote of the Spanish Muslim agriculture and irrigation system as "the most complex, the most scientific, the most perfect, ever devised by the ingenuity of man." The French scholar Robert Briffault is more encompassing when he wrote in his book the *Making of Humanity*, "Muslim Spain wrote one of the brightest chapters in the intellectual history of medieval Europe. Between the middle of the eighth and the beginning of the thirteenth centuries the Arabic speaking people were the main bearers of the torch of culture and civilisation throughout the world. They were the medium through which ancient science and philosophy were recovered, supplemented and transmitted in such a way as to make possible the Renaissance of Western Europe."

Sicily and Italy

The Muslim rule in Sicily started in 827 and lasted for 264 years. West Sicily was under the Aglabids of North Africa and then the Fatimids after they overthrew the Aglabids. The Byzantines ruled the eastern part of Sicily, but were forced away in 966 leaving the entire island to the Fatimids. And soon the island became a centre of culture and education. From the end of the 10th century up to the first half of the 11th is considered the golden age in the history of Sicily. Modernisation of agriculture, promotion of industry and commerce made the island prosperous. About 300 schools and a similar number of Mosques were established in the city of Palermo.

According to Professor Francesco Gabrieli in *Muhammad and the Conquest of Islam,* during this period the Muslims had established at least three Principalities in southern most regions of mainland Italy as well (Hasan, 2004). By the beginning of the tenth century these principalities were annexed by the Italians.

During the second half of the eleventh century the Amirs of Sicily lost their political control leading to anarchy and the final capture of the island by the (French) Normans. The Normans did not bring about any drastic change in the administration but just replaced the Amirs. In fact the general Muslims still occupied the highest positions under them. Two of the monarchs who were responsible for the propagation of knowledge into pre-Renaissance Italy were the Norman King Roger II and his grandson Frederick II, Emperor of Italy and King of Sicily.

Roger II and Al Idrisi

King Roger II (1097-1154) consolidated all the Norman conquests into one Kingdom which he ruled from Palermo. He was an enlightened person whose palatial court welcomed Muslim scholars and professionals. The Englishman Thomas Brun was the *Quad* (Arabic: leader) of his royal *Diwan* (Arabic/Persian: Governing body of the state). The title of his Prime Minister George, also in charge of the fleet, was 'Amir of Amirs' (*ammiratus ammiratorum* from which the word Admiral was derived). George was formerly under the employment of a Muslim Prince of Mahdia (now Tunisia).

Abdallah Al Sharif Al Idrisi Al Qurtubi, one of the greatest geographers and cartographer of the Middle Ages, was born in Cueta in 1099. He was educated in Cordova, after which he embarked on a journey of the world. He visited many regions including the Central Asia, Middle East, Constantinople, France and England. King Roger invited him to his court and sponsored a project to record all the known places of the world. For fifteen years, Al Idrisi and other scholars under him worked to produce the book which he named *Al Kitab Al Rujiri* (The book of Rogers). Roger, not after any personal fame, wanted to name the book

Nuzhat Al Mushtaq fee Ikhtiraq al Afaq (Delights of him who desires to journey through the climes). However, Al Idrisi retained the name of *Al Kitab Al Rujiri* as a respect to his sponsor.

Al Idrisi's book was the best geography book of his age showing details never known previously (Hasan, 2004). He postulated that the earth was spherical and that the water body remained undisturbed in this spherical surface due to 'an equilibrium of no variation'. Muslim geographers had recognised that the earth was spherical and Al Idrisi was the first to construct a spherical globe of the world. Due to accuracy his maps would be copied for three centuries by geographers without alterations (Al Hassani, 2007).

Roger's love for knowledge would retain Muslim knowledge in Sicily and propagate it to Italy. Al Idrisi's maps would find its place in European libraries and navigation centres, including Spain and Portugal, and be retained for centuries. Roger ran an Islamised system of government and could speak Arabic. For this some later European historian would call him 'The Pagan', probably meaning 'The Muslim'.

The Mediterranean Islands

From the ninth to the thirteenth century various Mediterranean Islands came under Muslim rule. These islands include Crete, Cyprus, Rhodes, Malta, Corsica, Sardinia and the Balearic Islands. The Muslims rule over the Islands generally extended around a century.

The Shia Dynasties

The Fatimid (909 - 1171)

The Shia doctrines support the precept of leadership of the community by a divine Imam. According to the Twelvers, the biggest Shia sect, historically there are twelve 'infallible' Imams of whom Ali, Hasan and Husain are the first three. The twelfth Imam Mohammad Al Mahdi is supposed to be in a spiritually hidden state. They believe that Ali should have been the first Caliph and Abu Bakr, Umar and Usman were usurpers. The later Shias divided into a number of subgroups some making very tainted and unsubstantiated observations about the first three Caliphs. Other small deviant groups made a deity of Ali. Such assertions are not found among the earlier Alids and their Imams.

The sixth Imam Jaafar Al Sadiq had initially nominated his eldest son Ismail as the successor. But the son predeceased the father and the nomination went in favour of the younger son Musa Kazim. On the death of Al Sadiq in 765 this led to a schism within the Shia. A group believed that since Imamate was divine it could not be revoked and as such Ismail remained the Imam for them. This gave rise to the Ismaili sub-sect. The Ismailis settled in Syria and sent out missionaries on a large scale particularly during the Imamate of Al Habib in the 9th century. Soon they got significant converts in Egypt, Yemen, Bahrain and India.

In the 10th century one of the missionaries Abu Abdullah Hussain converted and mustered a force of 200,000 Berbers in North Africa. He promised them that the Mahdi, the promised Messiah, would soon appear to them. He then informed the Ismaili Imam Ubaidullah to proceed to North Africa as the ground work had been done for him to lead the Shia movement there. Ubaidullah founded the first Ismaili Shia state. He had to face the challenge of the Abbasids, the Spanish Umayyads, and fight the Berbers who revolted against him and even had to fight the Idrisid Shia of North Africa. But he managed to establish the Fatimid Empire that was to last for three centuries and rule over North Africa including Egypt, Syria and adjoining area of Sicily and Malta. By the time of Caliph Al Muizz, who died in 975, the Fatimids ruled an area greater than the contemporary Abbasids. The famous Al Azhar University which continues today was established by the Fatimids. They were great promoters of learning.

In general, the Fatimid Caliphs were well disposed towards the minorities specially the Christian and Jews. Similar to those living in the Abbasid domain, the minorities worked in high positions within the administration. The established Islamic principles allowed better Synagogues and Churches to be built. The Caliph Al Aziz had a Christian wife and he made her two brothers Patriarchs of Jerusalem and Alexandria.

Caliph Al Hakim was an exception. There are two opposing historical reports about him. On the one hand, he is the establisher of an academy called *Dar Al Ilm*, The House of Knowledge, in the lines of *Dar Al Hikma,* which lasted for 165 years. On the other hand he is said to be suffering from mental aberration and homicidal tendency and was cruel to the minorities. Much of this may have been political propaganda by his opponents which finally resulted in his death.

He was only eleven years old when he succeeded to power in 996. His regent Burgawan, whose interest was in hedonism rather than state administration, publicly denounced Al Hakim and said that he was a lizard. When Al Hakim was a bit older he had Burgawan assassinated. During his rule people are said to have suffered much. Some source record that he had a passion for darkness and ordered that all administrative work should be done during the night. Further, all shops were to remain open throughout the night. He prohibited women from going outside and ordered the shoemakers not to make shoes for them. He also ordered dogs to be killed (Hasan, 2004).

During a war the Byzantines had destroyed a number of Mosques. Al Hakim reacted by having the two Christian Ministers executed and Churches destroyed. He discriminated against the Christians and ordered the Church property seized. (Zaydan, 1994). If all these are facts, he was an exception in Islamic history in his attitude towards Christians.

Towards the end of his rule he declared that he was the incarnation of God. When people protested against his misrule Al Hakim had a whole bazaar in Fustat burnt. One night Al Hakim went to the Mukattam hill and never returned. His clothes were found with dagger marks on it. After him, his sister Sittul Mulk became the regent in favour of the sixteen year old son Az Zahir. Sittul Mulk rescinded all the eccentric ordinances of Al Hakim. The minorities were given back their rights and Churches rebuilt.

~~~

The 10th century CE was the age of the Alids. The Fatimids ruled North Africa, Sicily, Egypt, Makkah, Madinah, Jerusalem and Syria. The Shia Buwahid ruled over the dominions of the Abbasid including Iraq and Persia. The Qarmatians ruled in Bahrain. Thus a large part of the Muslim regions were under the rule of the Shia rulers.

Buwahids (945 - 1055)

The Buwahids were Persian Daylamites from the south west of the Caspian Sea. Starting as rulers of an independent principality they expanded southward occupying Isfahan, Shiraz and the provinces of Ahwaz and Khujistan in Persia. By that time the Abbasid Caliphate had disintegrated considerably and the Caliphs exercised power over only part of what is modern
~~~

day Iraq. The other territories and regions were autonomous or independent monarchies. The Abbasids Caliphs had nominal and ceremonial powers and conferred titles on the rulers and other powerful individuals.

In 945, the helm of power behind the Abbasid Caliphate was held by the Turk General Shirzad who was known by the title of '*Amir-ul-Umara*'. To keep the army happy Shirzad increased the pay of the soldiers. But as there wasn't sufficient money in the treasury, the taxation on the people had to be increased. This led to a revolt by the people providing the Buwahid with an opportunity to intervene. They marched into Baghdad in 'aid' of the people. Upon the defeat of Shirzad the Caliph Mustakfi conferred the office of Amir-ul-Umara on the Buwahid leader Ahmad bin Buwahid.

The Buwahids were Shia and on assuming power had thought of giving allegiance to the Fatimid Caliph. But on reflection they realised that if they gave allegiance to the Fatimids then they would become subjects to the powerful Fatimid Caliphs and thus would lose some of their executive autonomy. Besides, their own rule was in a Sunni majority area and the Fatimids were in distant lands. Even though politically nominal the Abbasid Caliphs, as spiritual leaders, did have great influence throughout the Sunni Muslim world. These political considerations led them to give allegiance to the Sunni Abbasid Caliphate. They went to the extent of repudiating the descent of the Fatimids from Ali and Fatima.

The Buwahids were to dominate the political scene for 110 years. They established a strong administration and military. They became great promoters of science and learning. The renowned scientist Ibn Sina (Avicenna) and poet Ferdowsi were visitors to their court. The Buwahids sponsored a large number of scholars including mathematician Nasawi, historian Miskawaih and geographer Istakhri.

An observatory was established in Baghdad and libraries were built in Ray, Shiraz and Isfahan. Hospitals, administrative and public buildings were developed in Baghdad and Shiraz. There was economic prosperity and peace in the region.

The army of the Buwahids consisted of Shia Daylamites. But at a later stage they came to depend more on the Turks who were Sunnis. There always was some tension between the Turks and the Daylamites. When Shia-Sunni riots broke out the Daylamites would take the side of the Shia and the Turks would support the Sunni. Around the year 1000 the sea trade route changed from the Persian Gulf to the Red Sea. This led to a decline in economic activity in the whole region. Payment for the army had to be decreased or delayed leading to revolts. Infighting between the Buwahids also broke out. These events considerably weakened their administration and in 1055 the Seljuks finally overpowered them.

The Qarmatians (899 ~ 1067)

During the Abbasid rule, groups of Shias organised themselves as secret groups against the Abbasid. One of these groups, the Qarmatians, a splinter Ismaili sub-sect, established a republic in Bahrain in the 10th century and became very powerful with a strong army. They were named after their leader Qarmat. They deviated from Islam and apparently did not believe in the Hajj pilgrimage. They launched raids along the routes of pilgrimage and plundered and killed the pilgrims. Finally, they attacked Makkah, killed a large number of pilgrims and carried away the symbolic black stone of Kaba. This caused a shock through out the Muslim world and the Fatimid Caliph condemned them. The black stone marks the centre of focus in the Kaba. The Qarmatians had probably expected that once they took the stone away, they would become the focus of the Islamic world. But that never materialised and the stone was finally returned after some years.

The Qarmatian religion became esoteric and at one stage they appeared to have been influenced by Zoroastrianism. Their 'terrorist' activities and religious experiments weakened their influence on the general people. In 976 they faced a military defeat by the Abbasid, after which they stopped their misadventures and became introverted. In 1067, Abu Abdullah Uyuni with the help of the Seljuks defeated the Qarmatians and started the Uyunid dynasty.

There is confusion about the Qarmatian history. Though much negativity has been attributed to them, initially, they also had good philosophers and scholars in their folds. The Fatimid Ismaili Caliph al-Muizz had endorsed the Neo-Platonised cosmology that was first propounded by the Qarmatian Dai (Missionary) Muhammad Al Nasafi in his *Kitab Al Mahsul (Book of the Yeld),* written at the beginning of the 10th century, in preference over the 'Kuni Qadar' mytho-Islamic cosmology of the early Ismailis. Because of this the Sunni polemicists blamed the Ismaili sect and accuse them of *Ilhad* (deviation in religion) for adopting a doctrine of the Qarmatians.

The Seljuks

(1037-1197)

The Turks were originally the inhabitants of eastern Central Asia who would migrate to the west and form great empires. The Seljuks, originally, a tribe of Ghuzz (Oguz) Turks from Turkestan, were the builders of one of the largest empire in history. In the 10th century under their leader Seljuk they migrated to Transoxiana where they accepted Sunni Islam. This led to their emancipation from a tribal culture to an advanced one.

During the time of Tugril Beg, a grandson of Seljuk, the Ghaznavids were the rulers in Khorasan in Persia. After the death of Ghaznavid Sultan Mahmud, Tugril took possession of Merv and Nishapur and declared himself king in 1037. They defeated the Ghaznavids and became the dominant power in Khorasan. The domain of the Ghaznavids was then restricted to North India and Afghanistan.

After consolidating his position Tugril embarked on an incredible campaign of conquest. By the year 1055, he had conquered, Khawarizm, Tabaristan, Balkh, Jurjan, Hamdan, Ray, Isfahan, Azerbaijan, Mosul and Armenia in Central Asia and Persia. From where Tugril stood now his shadow fell on Baghdad. He almost completely encircled the Buwahid dominion. The Caliph Al Qaim was at odd with the oppressive Turk Generals of the Buwahid and appealed for help to the Seljuks. Tugril responded to his call and after a power struggle defeated the Buwahids. The indebted Al Qaim conferred the title of 'Sultan' to Tugril Beg. Thus the political and military power of the Caliphate came in the hands of the Seljuks. Successively, the Seljuks produced five great Sultans who extended their rule from the border of China in the East to the Mediterranean on the West, from Georgia on the North to Yemen in the South.

The Seljuks were patrons of science, art and literature. Seljuk Sultan Malik Shah established the observatory of which the illustrious Umar Khayyam of *Rubayyat* fame was the Director. Two other very famous and fascinating individuals who worked for the Sultanate of Malik Shah were Nizam Al Mulk the Wazir (Prime Minister) and Hasan bin Sabbah a court official. The Wazir Nizam Al Mulk was a great administrator and ran the government agencies with infallible dexterity. He was a scholar extraordinaire and an expert in political science. He wrote a famous book *Siyasat Nama* meaning the *The Art of Politics*. He established the Nizamia University in Baghdad, which became famous for its learning and scholarship. The other individual, Hasan bin Sabah was the architect of a revolutionary government with no borders named the *Assassins*. The English word 'Assassin' comes from the name of this group.

The Seljuk disintegration started with the rise of internal strife among the Seljuk Princes, which led to civil war. As they lost control and grew weak Abbasid Caliph Muktafi was able to undo the subjugation to the Seljuks and finally become independent. Some of the Seljuk

Amirs, like Khawarizm Shah, also declared their independence. This left a patchwork of small Turk states in Anatolia. One of these principalities was destined to become the Ottoman Empire in a few centuries.

The Abbasids regained their complete independence in 1152, but their dominion was restricted to a part of Iraq only. In 1171 the reign of the rival Fatimid Caliph came to an end in Cairo. Thus Egypt, Syria and North Africa came to be under the spiritual mandate of the Abbasid Caliph. This was the time when Saladin was fighting the Crusaders.

The Assassins of Alamaut

Hasan bin Sabbah (~1050 -1124) was a master theologian, a revolutionary genius and organiser who devised and put into practice the 'Dawa' (Mission) of the Nizari, a subsect of the Ismailis, replacing the Dawa of the Egyptian Fatimid Ismailis. He was born to the main Twelver Shia sect but adopted the Ismaili sect after studying it considerably. The Ismaili missionary organ had a three layered hierarchy:

The Fidayeen – The foot soldier in the lowest rung
The Rafik – The Comrade who commanded a group of Fidayeen
The Dai - The Missionary who carried out the 'Dawa'

He was introduced to the Ismaili mission by a Rafik named Amira Darrab. Hasan worked for Seljuk Sultan Malik Shah, and probably due to his involvement with the Ismaili faction and court conspiracies led to problems with the Wazir Nizam ul Mulk. Hasan bin Sabah left the Seljuk court and went back to his home town in Qum in Persia. After considerable travelling he went to Egypt where he was well received by the Fatimid Caliph Mustansir. He was commissioned by him to propagate the Ismaili sect in Persia. With characteristic devotion Hasan studied the 'Dawa' and established himself as a Dai.

On the death of the Fatimid Caliph Al Mustansir of Egypt in 1094, the designated heir Nizar was by-passed and Al Mustali became the Caliph with the support of the army. The dissenting group, in favour of Nizar, came to known as the Nizari Ismaili. On his return to Persia Hasan opted to represent the Nizari group instead of Caliph Mustali. He returned to Isfahan and became the Chief Dai designated to the mountainous Alborz region. Hasan gathered a good following and soon, in 1080, managed to acquire the Fort of Alamaut located in an inaccessible area in the Alborz Mountains (about 100 Km from present day Tehran). After moving to Alamaut he and his followers set up a revolutionary government without any political region or domain.

To defend Alamaut he built a 'Fidayeen' corp which was totally dedicated to him and ready to die instantaneously at his command (Hasan, 2004). Then he turned his attention to studying and sending out his missionaries to preach. Alamaut became famous for its gardens and libraries. He became well versed in mathematics and astronomy. He knew the Quran by heart and lived an austere and pious life.

He acquired some more forts and soon his followers spread out to different areas of Persia and Syria. Sultan Malik Shah sent out a number of expeditions against the Assassins. But the expeditions were fruitless due to the inaccessibility of the mountainous strongholds and were defended by the Fidayeens who fought with a fearless fury. A cold war ensued and Hasan started to send the Fidayeens to secretly assassinate his enemies. They were masters of disguise and spoke many languages and dialects. They infiltrated into the services of all the surrounding rulers and struck at them when the order came from Alamaut. They came to be feared by all including the Crusaders, Kings, Princes, Sheikhs, and Sultans. Stories and tales, some fancy and remarkable, about Hasan and the Fidayeens spread all around and they came to be known as the Assassins, which was probably derived from the name of their leader 'Hasan'. It may, as well, have been derived from the word 'Al Assas' meaning the foundation - Alamaut was the base or foundation of their mission. There is a claim that the name was derived from 'Hashish' but that probably was an attempt to discredit the group. Though Hasan was politically radical, personally he was an austere, devout and pious person and would have nothing to do with intoxicants.

As they became more powerful the Assassins entered into pacts with or against a number of states including those in Europe. After the death of Hasan bin Sabah in 1124 the Assassins continued their activities under subsequent leaders up to 1256 when the Mongols attacked them. The victims of the Assassins included, among others, the Abbasid Caliphs Mustarshid, the Fatimid Caliph Amr Billah, the Fatimid Wazir al-Afdal, ibn al-Khashshab of Aleppo, il-Bursuqi of Mosul, Raymond II of Tripoli and Conrad of Montferrat. Saladin was attacked by the Assassins and Prince Edward, who later became Edward I of England, was wounded by them. Political assassinations were sometimes carried out by the Assassins for their allies. For example, the Knight Hospitallers contracted them to kill the Patriarch of Jerusalem, while the assassination of Conrad of Montferrat by the Assassins may have had the approval of Richard the Lionheart. This happened during the Third Crusade.

The Development of Thought

The spread of the Islamic civilisation was accompanied by the development of knowledge. The initiation of this development took place from the Quran. The revelation of the first verse of the Quran was the defining moment at which the essence of the modern era was born.

Read in the name of your Lord and Cherisher, Who created -
Created man out of a clot that clings.
Read! And your Lord is most bountiful
He Who taught the use of Pen.
Taught Man what he knew not.

This revelation initiated the quest for knowledge that would start the Muslim scholarship first into religion, theology and jurisprudence and then into philosophy, science, social science and literature.

The Prophet, through his revelations, was the fundamental source of knowledge. When he died Abu Bakr, under Umar's request, initiated the first corroborative research by his commissioning of Zaid bin Thabit for the compilation of the Quran, and by his establishment of the methodology by which Jurisprudence was initiated.

In the past knowledge had been practiced by all civilisations, Mesopotamians, Egyptians, Hittites, Chinese, Greeks, Indians and Persians. But the quest for knowledge that the Muslims took on transcended all boundaries – imperial, political or philosophical. It would be impossible to categorise and comprehend Muslim practices of knowledge as a single subject or entity. The best way to understand this enormous system is to understand:

1. The chronological derivative construct, that is, the succeeding derivation of knowledge – Jurisprudence, then Sufi-Philosophy, and then Sciences - that took place from the initial knowledge of the Quran and Hadith, and later incorporation of knowledge from previous civilisations.
2. The knowledge spheres or universalities created by the various types of scholars – Alims (Ulema), Sufis and Rationalists - and their practice of knowledge.

Chronological Derivation

The initial basis of thought was the Quran from which and based on which all the subsequent thoughts were derived and constructed. In the very start, when the people were unable to comprehend any particular part of the Quran, the Prophet would explain it and supplement it. The range of his thought was unbelievably vast and was applicable to all aspects of life from very small individual issues, like how to wash or how to eat in a proper manner, to big issues, like how to manage warfare or run a government. His thought level could easily shift from local issues to global issues. He showed how to tackle the rational-physical world as well as how to pursue the spiritual world and how to enrich the philosophical world. After his death, the Muslims were forced to start thinking for themselves. The Prophet was no longer there to supplement the Quran for its application to daily life. This led to the research on *Sunnah* or the 'The Way of the Prophet' that included his sayings and habits, the book form of which is called the Hadith or 'Tradition'. This compilation and research for Jurisprudence led to the scholarships of the Imams and the establishment of their Schools of Jurisprudence. Chronologically, Muslim Thought developed in the following three stages.

Stage 1:
The revelation of the Quran.
The compilation of the Quran

Stage 2:
The research and development of schools of Jurisprudence based on Quran and Sunnah
The research and development of the schools of Hadith

Stage 3:
The development of Sufi and Philosophical schools
The development of Rational Sciences.

The above stages provide an ideal view of development of 'thought' in time. After the first stage there were various overlappings. In the third stage knowledge from pre-existing civilisations, like those of the Greeks and Indians, was also incorporated.

Universal Spheres

The second way to comprehend the development of Muslim 'thought' is by the division of knowledge into spheres or categories. There are three universes of knowledge developed by the Muslims:

1. The Ulemaic Universe: This was formed from the traditional study of the Quran and the Sunnah, and Jurisprudence.
2. The Sufi Universe: The unorthodox beyond rational philosophical and sometimes termed as mystical or mental universe.
3. The Rational Universe: The three dimensional logical universe.

The Ulemaic Universe is the overarching Truth. Rationalism and Sufism are two different methods or processes investigating into this Truth. Ulemaic thoughts are concerned with Divine guidance required for the progression of life as we know it. Rationalism is concerned with laws, processes and forces that govern the balance in and the evolution of the physical universe. Sufism had been the human endeavours into understanding metaphysics and bringing this understanding to human domain. During the first four Caliphs a clear cut difference between these universalities had not developed. They had the capability to give rational injunctions from within the Ulemaic world. The later Caliphs would alternate mainly between Ulemaic and Rational thought, a few being influenced by Sufi thought as well.

There have been conflicts between the three Thoughts. While, in general, the Rational and Sufi thoughts have accepted their evolution from the Ulemaic thought, the Ulema have distanced themselves from them. The Ulema are not against any form of knowledge or investigation of knowledge itself. The main reason for distancing was to stay in a pure and pristine form away from any innovation in religion for all generations to come.

In the course of history, the Sufi movement had divided into two types. One consisted of the mainstream Sufis who were brilliant scholars investigating into theology, philosophy, literature and culture in creative new ways. The other group was more mystical and sometimes heretical claiming the ability to intercede with God on behalf of people and similar superstition. These two groups are analogous to astronomy and astrology – one a science and other superstition. Even few learned Sufis of the past like Al Hallaj had declared themselves part of Godhead. Such occurrences forced the Ulema to maintain a distance from the Sufis.

Similarly, Rationalist at times developed condescending attitude towards religion and philosophy. While investigating into part or subset of creation, some rationalists, in various ages, develop an anti-religious attitude. Such demeanour made the Ulema maintain a certain distance from the rationalist as well.

As the infinite creation unfolds, more and more knowledge comes within the realm of human understanding. As the human mind probes into newer and unknown areas it would be very easy to be lost in this vast cauldron of knowledge. It is impossible for the individual to comprehend the entirety of knowledge. But it becomes easy to make judgements and presumptions based on the understanding of a significantly small part of reality, which would be erroneous under the bigger picture. To keep civilisation from getting lost in this vast cauldron, it is the Ulemaic universe that acts as the absolute centre of the confusingly relative universe. It is the anchor to the Right Path – *Siratul Mustakim*.

The Universe of the Ulema

The Quran

This is the Book of which there is no doubt,
a guidance for those who are conscious of God. [2,2]

According to Professor Masudul Hasan, the Quran provides a set of doctrines which expound knowledge of the structure of reality. It contains a set of injunctions which form the basis of the Muslim sacred law. It also contains metaphysics about the nature of God, the structure of the universe, and human destiny. It contains all the injunctions necessary for an individual to know who they are and know their obligations. The Quran recounts the stories of various peoples through out the course of history. The message is couched in historical terms, but it is addressed to the human soul, and depicts the vicissitudes of human soul in terms of the accounts of the bygone people.

J. Davenport writes in *Apology for Muhammad*, "The Quran is the general code of the Muhammadans; a religious, social, civil, commercial, military, judicial, criminal, penal code; It regulates everything from the ceremonies of religion to those of daily life, from the salvation of the soul to the health of the body, from the rights of all to those of each individual, from the interests of man to those of society, from punishment here to that in the life to come."

S.P. Scott in *History of the Moorish Empire in Europe* states that, "The Quran commands relief of the oppressed, protection of the defenseless, mercy to the orphans and kindness to animals. It enjoins the strict performance of agreements, even though entered into with members of hostile creed, … It pronounces awful penalties against the murderer. In its pages the proud deference that usually attaches to aristocratic birth and distinguished station is ignored; titled insolence in not permitted to assert superiority over the unpretentious worshipper, and the monarch and the beggar meet as brethren before the throne of Almighty Allah."

In *Iqbal Nama* a conversation between Johann Wolfgang Von Goethe, German writer of the *Faust*, and his biographer Johann Peter Eckermann is mentioned. The text states, "It is in view of this essential aspect of the Quranic teaching that Goethe, while making a general review of Islam as an educational force, said to Eckermann: 'You see this teaching never fails; with all our systems, we cannot go, and generally speaking no man can go, farther than that'." (Ahmad, 1984).

The Quran is a miracle that can be held in one's hand. It is the collection of all the revelations to the Prophet over a period of twenty two years. The name of Quran is derived from the word 'Qara' which means collection as well as to read or recite. It is divided into

114 chapters known as *Surahs* of unequal lengths. Ninety of the Surah were revealed in Makkah and are relatively short, fervent, doctrinal and prescriptive in form. Twenty of the Surahs were revealed in Madinah and are much larger, regulative and legal in manner.

Another system of dividing it is into thirty, more or less, equal parts known as *Siparah*. Half a Siparah is the *Nisf*, the third is the *Thulth* and the quarter is the *Ruba*. Depending on the structural methodology applied the numerating of paragraphs (ruku) verses, etc., can vary. As an approximation there are more than 500 ruku, 6000 verses, 75000 words and 300,000 letters.

Both the meaning of its verses and the Arabic phonetic rendition of the Quran is so unique in its beauty, profundity and applicability that it is unworldly. Thus, the meanings of its verses as well as its Arabic recitation by itself are both held sublime. In his book *Islam*, A. Guillaumme writes 'The Quran is one of the world's classic that cannot be translated without grave loss. It has a rhythm of peculiar beauty and a cadence that charms the ears. When it is read aloud or recited it has an almost hypnotic effect.'

As the verses of the Quran were revealed, the Prophet would recite it to his companions many of whom would memorise it or write it down on various objects like papyrus, parchment or animal skins. The written verses would be reread to the Prophet as a way for him to check and correct it if needed. The memorisation of the Quran led to the establishment of the school of the *Huffaz*. Each member the Huffaz, known as *Hafez,* would memorise the entire Quran. This school started from the time of the Prophet continues to exist today. There are thousands of Hafez today who can reproduce the Quran verbatim from memory. If all the copies of the Quran are destroyed, they can produce an exact replica from memory.

Zaid bin Thabit was the principal secretary to the Prophet. He, along with others, used to record the verses.

It is in Books held greatly in honour
Exalted in dignity kept pure and holy
Written by the hands of scribes
Honourable and pious and just. [80, 13]

Like the one above, other verses - [85,21] [56,77] [25,5] - from the Makkah period and another one [98,2] from the Madinah period also attest to the verses being written down during the period of revelation. Abu Daud (b. 817), the renowned expert on Prophet's traditions has written how the Prophet explained to the scribes where and in which chapter of the Quran the verses should belong.

During the Caliphate of Abu Bakr, Zaid bin Thabit working with members of the Huffaz and Companions including Umar bin Al Khattab engaged in a phenomenal corroborative work of compilation. His main objective was that not a single verse, not a single word be altered from the way the Quran had been revealed to the Prophet and from the way the Prophet had recited it to the Companions. He went to all the people who had written down the verses in parchment or papyrus and acquired these from them. In his thoroughness he also collected all other materials on which the verses were written on – which included pieces of leather, leaves and flat stones. He painstakingly corroborated with all to produce the *Mushaf*. This was the first major corroborative research work undertaken by the Muslims.

Vaglieri comments on the Quran in *Apology for Islam*, 'The proof of divinity of the Quran is the fact that it has been preserved intact through the ages since the time of its revelation till the present day.'

Similarly R.V.C. Bodley states in *The Messenger*, 'What is important is that the Quran is the only work which has survived for 1400 years with an unadulterated text. Neither in the Jewish religion nor in the Christian is there anything which faintly compares to this.'

J. Leonard states in his book *Islam*, 'As Allah's word, there is sanctity in the Quran for every Muslim that exceeds the reverence of the Christians for the Bible, as much as the fiery splendour of the sun surpasses the cold pale glamour of the moon.'

Another property of the Quran is that it is for all types of people. It gives meaning to life and a way to live it from the very young to the very old, from the very simple to the very sophisticated. Any individual can read it and derive a way of life appropriate to the understanding level of that individual. And that way of life would fit harmoniously within the bigger scheme that unifies all the individuals. The Caliph Ali once commented on the Quran, 'Allah has made the Quran a drink to quench the thirst of the learned, a spring for the hearts of the jurists, a guide for the pious, a proof for those who *discourse* it, an evidence for its adversaries, and a convincing proof for those who pass judgement.'

Centuries later, in the modern age, Vaglieri echoes the same notion, 'On the whole we find in the Quran, a collection of wisdom which can be adopted by the most intelligent of men, the greatest of the philosophers, and the most skilful of politicians.'

The Quran initiated a mass quest for knowledge which led, over historical time, to the assimilation and improvement of pre-existing knowledge, the development of the scientific methods and discoveries of new fields of knowledge and its dissemination to all the societies of the world.

Tafsir: Exegesis of the Quran

The first discipline that rose out of the study of the Quran was the schools of Interpretation and Commentary of the Quran. The science of Tafsir started with the Prophet. He gave commentary of the verses to the Companions.

And We have sent down unto you (also) the Message
That you may explain clearly to men what is sent for them,
And that they may give thought. [16,44]

After the death of the Prophet the Companions took up the interpretation of the Quran. Besides the Rashidun Caliphs the most famous of the commentators of the Quran were: Abdullah bin Abbas, Abdullah bin Masud, Ubay bin Kaab, Zaid bin Thabit, Abu Musa al Ashari and Abdullah bin Zubayr. They belonged to the group who had seen the revelations coming down to the Prophet in person and had been taught by the Prophet himself. They passed on this knowledge to their own followers, the Tabiun, the next generation that had not seen the Prophet but seen the Companions. Then the Tabiun set to the task of developing the science of Tafsir. After that, through generations, the Tafsir of the Quran continued as the Quran came to be viewed from new perspectives with passing time.

The Quran has a historical dimension but does not claim to be a book of history, rather it uses historical parables to teach morality and humanity. In relating historical events the Quran does not place stress on dates or details of events. More significance and importance is placed on the rationale and lessons learned from those events. Many of the verses of the Quran are held to have duel meanings, the literal and the esoteric.

The Quran also employs a variety of techniques, like analogy and parables, to explain situations and ideas. For example, the Quran mentions 'Jinns', which in one place may appear to be a 'hidden' sentient life form other than humans, while in other places it may be interpreted as a metaphor for foreigners or the representation of some alien aspect. Surah Al Naml [27:17] mentions Solomon marching with his great army towards Sheba. The army consists of battalions of men, jinns and birds. They go through the valley of ants where one ant warns the other ants of the approaching army and Solomon is aware of what it says. Based on the period of history and the composition of his army, it is quite easy to interpret the men as Hebrews, Jinns as foreigners or mercenaries in the army, the birds as advanced scouts and spies and the ants as non-aligned simple folk living in the open country.

Depending on the type of interpretation of the Quran two schools of thought developed:

1. The *Zahiris* who favoured a literal and the obvious interpretation of the Quran.
2. The *Batinis* who favoured interpretation by seeking the hidden or esoteric meaning.

In time this led to the two different manner of interpretation of the Quran.

1. The orthodox interpretation which favoured the literal meaning. This was endorsed by the scholars and Imams of the Ulemaic Universe.

2. The rational interpretation that used reason to interpret rather than tradition. The skills developed from this school would lead to the experimentation in and development of the Rational Universe.

Though different in principle both the schools led to similar methodology in interpreting the verses. First, the context or the circumstance of the revelation was taken into account and, second, maximum use of lexicography and grammar would be applied to the verse to ascertain the true meaning as it would pertain in the time of the Prophet.

Later, a majority of Quranic scholars decided not to dwell on such type of debate as, first of all, it in not the parables or analogies themselves that are important rather the lessons portrayed and conveyed via these techniques, and secondly, if a variety of interpretations continued to flourish no two interpretation would be same leading to a confused proliferation of meaning of the verses.

In a few decades following the death of the Prophet the schools of Tafsir developed. The mains ones with the largest student followings developed in:

1. Makkah under the authority of Abdullah bin Abbas.
2. Kufa under Abdullah bin Masud.
3. Madinah under Ubay bin Kaab.

The first complete and famous commentary of the Quran was done by At-Tabari (d. 923). He collected abundant exegesis to produce his Tafsir which was to become the foundation for later Tafsir works.

> Abu Ja'far Muhammad bin Jarir at-Tabari was from Tabaristan in Persia. He was an exceptional scholar who wrote voluminously. His two most important works are the *Jami al-bayan fi ta'wil al-Qur'an*, also know as Tafsir At-Tabari, and *Tarikh al-Rusul wa al-Muluk*, History of the Prophets and Kings. The current English translation of his Tafsir consist of 40 volumes each consisting of a few hundred pages. His History is an even larger piece of work and consists of history from the beginning of the world to 10th century CE. This book was one of the primary sources of history. Such massive works did not exist before his time and are still rare.

The next great classical work on Tafsir was done by Al –Qurtubi (1273), another great scholar from Muslim Spain. His Tafsir has a legal basis, i.e., used to derive legal rulings. In later years, commentators formulated various types of rules that enabled Arabs and non Arabs to interpret the Quran. One such book of rules is that by Abul Qasim Mahmud Al Zamakshari (d. 1144) known as *Al Kashshaf*. In his Tafsir he also quoted from Arabic poetry and dwelled on the rhetorical beauty of the Quran. He was a Mutazilite, i.e., a rationalist scholar and also supported the doctrine of 'Ijaz' (The inimitability of Quran).

The Abbasid era saw the weaving of foreign ideas into the Islamic philosophical fabric. One result was the rise of scholastic Theology, *Ilm al Kalam*, which led to philosophical discourses on articles of Islamic faith, the attributes and unity of God, and similar topics. Fakr-Uddin Razi (d. 1209), a renowned participant of this movement, named his commentary *Al Tafsir Al Kabir*. He was an Asharite scholar who represented a compromise between the rationalist and the traditional Ulema. His commentary was an Asharite response to Al Zamakshari's Tafsir. Abdullah bin Umar Al Baidawi (d. 1282) made improvements on the Al Zamakshari commentary and named it *Anwar Al Tanzil wa Asrar Al ta'wil*. Some Sunnis consider this as one of the best commentaries. Among the popular commentaries to date is the ten volumes abridged *Tafsir* of Ibn Kathir (d. 1343). His method is to explain the verses of the Quran by other verses of the Quran or by Hadith.

In some of the Tafsirs, the commentators included information from the Jewish exegesis. This was generally used to elaborate stories mentioned in the Quran and was considered acceptable as the Jews (and Christians) are the people of the Book. Muslim scholars considered that the Israelite or biblical exegeses were to be accepted as may or may not be completely correct. So, they would ensure that only those accounts were included in their Tafsirs which had some basis in the Quran.

Tafsirs are still being written. Among the recent Tafsirs, *Maarif ul Quran* by Mufti Shafi Uthman and *Fi Dilal Al Quran* – in the shade of the Quran- by Sayyid Qutb are popular. After the initial study of the Tafsir had begun, towards the end of the 1st century after the Hijra, Muslims took up the task of promulgating jurisprudence. Known as *Fiqh*, the Islamic Jurisprudence would be derived from the Quran and the Sunnah by the great scholars commonly called Imams.

The Sunnah of the Prophet is the best Tafsir as the Prophet was the living embodiment of the Quran. The Rashidun Caliphs promulgated laws from the Quran and the Sunnah with the support of the Council of the Companions. During that time period those who distinguished themselves as jurist were Umar bin Khattab, Ali bin Abu Talib, Abdullah Ibn Umar, Abdullah Ibn Abbas and Abdullah Ibn Masud. They developed two fundamental rules, Consensus of Opinion and Analytical Deduction, to support the deduction of law. These were impressive and novel concepts in the days when the lands were ruled by kings and emperors who were dictators at best and tyrants at worst and anyone asking for the right of consensus could be subject to condemnation and death.

Within a very few decades after the death of the Prophet the Muslims had carved an empire. There was a great need for the development of laws and social norms for the state to be governed by, and for the individuals to adhere to. It was not possible for every individual to sift through the Quran and the vast Sunnah and interpret these uniquely and follow an ordered life. The interpretation of the Quran alone would be a huge task due to the simple fact that it required the detailed knowledge of the revelations as well as application of the vast and complex Arabic vocabulary. While the collection and interpretation of the Sunnah, passed orally by the Companions, could only be achieved through an enterprise that would cover the entire lifetime of individuals. And that is exactly how it was done. Schools of law developed during the Umayyad time and matured in carly Abbasid era. The first schools were established in Madinah, Makkah, Kufa and Basra.

Coulson in *History of Islamic Law* states, 'Islamic Jurisprudence had in fact been essentially idealistic from the outset. Law had not formed out of the practice of the courts or the remedies therein available as the Roman law had developed .... or the English common law from the writ, but had originated as the academic formulation of a scheme, alternative to that practice; its authority did not lie in the fact that it was observed but in the theoretical arguments of the scholars as to why it ought to be observed.' (Hasan, 2004).

In fact, the scholars who formulated the principles used multiple resources. They were brilliant jurists, experts in the legal deduction from the Quran and the Sunnah, and authorities on the verdicts that had been pronounced by the Rashidun Caliphs. The traditional legal schools used various systems, tools and techniques in the development of Fiqh or Islamic Jurisprudence. The techniques included *Shurah* – consultation, generally in an assembly, *Ijtihad* – analysis or research, *Qiyas* – analogical deduction, *Ijma* - consensus, and a host other legal tools.

Using this conglomerate of legal knowledge they developed a massive legal system. A significant number of schools of law developed but only a few would persist over time. The founders of these schools called the Imams were totally independent in their thoughts and bowed to no political authority. Their only allegiance was to God and for their piety, hard work and non-compromising attitude to any type of corruptions they were highly respected and exerted profound influence on the general mass. They were the people who dared to criticise the Caliphs. Thus clashes between them and the ruling political entities were inevitable. They were offered high positions in the bureaucracy, which they refused considering it enticement for allegiance. This would bring the wrath of the Caliphal office on them. All four Great Imams at one stage or another would clash with the state. Among them, Abu Hanifa and Hanbal directly and fervently confronted the state.

Calling these men great and brilliant scholars would be an understatement. They were institutions and the real architects of empires. They formulated legal systems on which empires would be run. Abu Hanifa and Malik would see the Fall of the Ummayyad and the Rise of the Abbasids.

School of Imam Abu Hanifa (b. 699 CE, 80 AH)

Imam Numan bin Thabit is more popularly known by his *kunya*, Abu Hanifa. He was born in Kufa which had been the capital during Ali's caliphate. A number of the Prophet's companion had lived there of which twenty four had participated in Badr (Ahmad, 1984) and had thus become a centre of great learning. Abu Hanifa lived in the age of Tabiun. Few of the Companions like Anas bin Malik and Sahl bin Saad were still alive during the youth of Abu Hanifa. Aini, the commentator of *Hidayah*, claims that Abu Hanifa had been fortunate enough to hear hadith directly from the Companions.

Imam Abu Hanifa, with his disciples Abu Yusuf, Al Shaibani, Yahya bin Abi Zaid, Hafs bin Ghias, Daud At-Tai, Habban, Zafar, Mandal, and others, worked for thirty years to produce a comprehensive code of law. Shorter versions of this code are still extant.

Imam Hanifa's school was in Kufa and was the legacy of Abdullah bin Masud. His school was unique in the sense that the best of his disciples were extremely knowledgeable and had the authority to submit their ruling in matters of legal promulgation. After his death they grew in fame to the level of the Imams. Abu Hanifa gave importance to analogical deduction (Qiyas) and also used consensus (Ijma). Many scholars were of the opinion that consensus should be limited to the Council of Companions. But Hanifa argued that consensus was valid for people of all ages. He also introduced the concept of Juristic Equity or fairness and impartiality of law in his formulations. Local social conditions affected both the Abu Hanifa and Maliki schools. Abu Hanifa lived in a cosmopolitan city with large number of ethnic groups along with Arabs. He faced a wider political and cultural state of affairs and, consequently, a great variety of legal issues. Thus his jurisprudence was more rational and universally applicable (Ahmad, 1984). Malik thrived more on a dominantly Arab culture.

Abu Hanifa, of Persian origin, inherited the business of a clothe merchant and was a social and charitable person. He was handsome and had a empathetic demeanour. When he was quite young an accidental meeting with Imam Shabi changed his life. As Abu Hanifa was going past the Imam said, "Where are you going, youngman?"

Imam Shabi possessed *Farasa* or insight. He could look at a face and talk a few words and would understand the person's personality. This quality of insight was possessed by all four of the Great Imams. Abu Hanifa mentioned the house of a merchant as his destination and the Imam continued to talk to him and said, "Whose classes do you attend?"

Abu Hanifa replied, "Nobodies, Sir."

Imam Shabi said, "I see signs of intelligence in you. You should sit in the company of learned men."

That changed Abu Hanifa's life. His thirst for learning grew. He sat in a number of schools and learned from many scholars and Imams. Shubah of Basra, a great Tabiun scholar and authority on Hadith, commented on Abu Hanifa, "As I know the sun is bright, so I know that learning and Abu Hanifa are doubles of each other."

Yahya bin Muin, one of the teachers of Imam Bukhari, commenting on the merits of Abu Hanifa said, "It is enough for me that Shubah had permitted Abu Hanifa to teach Hadith and its narration. After all, Shubah was Shubah."

His main teacher was Imam Hammad, head of one of the legal schools. Hammad was the student of Ibrahim An Nakhi and Imam Shabi. These two had three teachers Al Masrookh ibn Azda, Suraeeh and Alkam Ibn Qayes. These three had received their Fiqh from Ali bin Abu Talib and Abdullah bin Masud.

Ata bin Abi Rabah, whose school was in Madinah, was another of Abu Hanifa's famous teachers. Ata had the distinction, by a government declaration, that only he could give Juristic Decisions, *Fatwa*, during the period of Hajj. Abdullah bin Umar, son of the Caliph, had once commented on the knowledge of Ata, "Why do people come to me when they have Ata to go to?"

When Abu Hanifa sat for interview to be admitted to Ata's school, Ata asked him to explain his beliefs. Abu Hanifa said, "Sir, I do not speak ill of our previous generation, I do not call the unbelievers sinners and I believe in Freewill and Predestination."

That had pleased Ata and he admitted Abu Hanifa in his class.

In Makkah, Abu Hanifa became the student of Ikramah who was the disciple of the Companion Abdullah bin Abbas, forefather of the Abbasids. Imam Hanifa visited the schools of Imam Malik when he visited Madinah. It was not beneath him to attend the classes of Imam Malik who was thirteen years his junior. And Imam Malik would have him sit besides him during lectures in his class. This was a major summit meeting between two great Imams. Abu Hanifa is said to have gone for Hajj every year and during his sojourns met scholars like Imam Jafaar Sadiq. He went to Basra 20 times and would have powerful debates with the Kharijites and the Mutajilites.

Through his visits and interaction with all major schools of Islam Abu Hanifa developed a very comprehensive understanding of the Sunnah, the legal deductive methods of the

Companions and prevailing legal environment. This would help him develop the first great school of Jurisprudence in the Muslim world. He is credited to be the greatest authority on Muslim canon law.

In 737 CE, after Imam Hammad died, his chair was offered to Imam Abu Hanifa. He accepted it and initially was somewhat apprehensive by the enormity of the responsibility but soon devoted himself to the job. His fame grew and students from all over the world came to attend his classes. Among his students were people of various political alignment and the discourses in the classes would take on political hues.

Yazid Bin Umar Bin Hubaira, Governor of Kufa, during the Caliphate of Marwan II wanted the Imam to accept certain respectable position in the government which he refused. The Governor then tried to force the Imam to do his bidding. He was put behind bars and flogged everyday under orders of the Governor. But he still refused the position. He was released after a few days, and left Kufa for Hejaz where he stayed for more than 2 years.

In 749 CE, the Abbasids overthrew the Umayyads and Abu Hanifa returned to Kufa. But the Abbasids were going through political turmoil and their relation with different groups was at a low. For Abu Hanifa matters did not improve. The Alid revolt during the time of Al Mansur was suppressed by the arrest of many Alids. Abu Hanifa had never supported the excesses of the Umayyads nor liked the suppression of the Alids by the Abbasids. But that would also turn the Abbasid ire on him. Even though he was not an Alid he too was arrested. When he was brought to Baghdad the courtiers recognised him and presented him as the greatest Alim (singular for Ulema) scholar alive to the Caliph. Imam Hanifa was offered the position of the Chief Justice but he rejected it, "I cannot accept it as I am not fit for the job."

The Caliph became angry, "You are lying!"

Abu Hanifa replied, "That vindicates my claim. A liar cannot be a Chief Justice." (Ahmad, 1984)

Imam Hanifa was imprisoned. But his disciples and the general people were allowed to visit him. Abu Hanifa died in prison while praying. Some sources claim that there was a royal conspiracy and attribute his death to poisoning. The number of people that thronged for his funeral was huge. His *Janaza* prayer was held six times with thousands of people praying in each. People kept on arriving for twenty days. One estimate says that more than 300,000 attended his funeral in those few days.

Imam Abu Hanifa and his students wrote a large number of books. Some of his books are as follows:

- *Kitaab-ul-Aathar* – A compilation made after the study of 70,000 Hadiths
- *Aalim wa'l-muta'allim*
- *Fiqh al-Akbar*

- *Jaami'ul Masaneed*
- *Kitaabul Rad alal Qaadiriyah*

The students of Imam Abu Hanifa also became famous Imams. Abu Yusuf and Mohammad bin Al Hasan Al Shaibani were the foremost among them.

Abu Yusuf became the Chief Justice under Caliph Harun ar Rasheed. He was a versatile scholar, apart from Fiqh and Hadith he also wrote a book named *Al Kharaj* which contained topics on economics such as classification of land depending on productivity, tax and tribute. He would admonish the Caliph without any fear or concern for himself when he thought that was necessary.

Mohammad bin Al Hasan went to Madinah after the death of Imam Abu Hanifa. He further studied Hadith in the school of Imam Malik. Later, he became one of the tutors of the Great Imam Shafii. Imam Shafii said about him, "When Imam Mohammad expounds a point, it seemed as if an angel of revelation has descended on him."

Even later, When the Great Imam Hanbal was asked where he had learned all the subtle points of law, he had replied "From the books of Imam Mohammad". Mohammad's famous work is *Mabsut* which he co-authored with Abu Yusuf. His other books are *Siyar Sagir Wa Kabir, Jami Al Saghir, Jami Al Kabir, Al Hujaj, Ziyadat, etc.*

School of Imam Malik (b. 711 CE, 93 AH)

Madinah was the extraordinary seat of learning. The influence of Zaid Bin Thabit and Abdullah ibn Umar was dominant. In that environment, Malik bin Anas was born in a family of scholars who also owned a business of arrow making. Malik's grandfather, father, uncles and brother were all highly learned persons. His grandfather was one of the participants in the Zaid bin Thabit's project of writing down of the Quran. Malik was striking with an aura of elegance and majesty. His students would remain quite during his lectures. There was no contradicting or debating with him. Politically, while Abu Hanifa and Hanbal would directly confront the state, Malik engaged the state from within.

But, as a child, he had started his life on a different note. He liked to play with pigeons and wanted to be a singer. His parents brought the turning point in his life similar to what Imam Shabi had done for Abu Hanifa. One day the father asked a question regarding Fiqh. Malik could not answer but his brother did. His father commented, "Playing with pigeons has distracted you from acquiring knowledge."

This comment affected Malik and he felt angry. Soon he went to his mother and said, "I want to become a singer."

Probably the mother and father were concerned and had discussed about him in private. The mother replied, "To be a singer you have to have the looks but you dont."

Instead of saying 'No' she just finished off that particular aspiration in him diplomatically. Then she said "Go to Imam Rabiah Ar Ray to study Fiqh."

Imam Rabiah, Malik's first teacher, was an elegant and learned scholar. His title Ray means Qiyas and like Abu Hanifa he favoured analogical deduction. Soon after that Malik joined the school of Abd Al-Rahman ibn Hurmuz. Ibn Hurmuz was a non Arab, lame and became blind at a later stage of life. But he was a great scholar who had learned from Abu Hurayrah and Saeed Al Khudri, two great companion of the Prophet. Malik studied under Hurmuz for seven years. He proved to be an exceptionally devoted student. Once in his classroom a snake was found. All the students ran out except for Malik. He was too engrossed in his studies to notice or care about the snake. He avoided the market and shopping and idle chatting. Every day in the early morning Malik would go to the house of Ibn Hurmuz and took him to the Mosque or wherever he wanted to go. Abu Hanifa used to do the same for Hammad.

Imam Malik had another great teacher named Nafi. He was a non Arab and servant of Abudullah ibn Umar and learned from him. He also had the opportunity to serve and learn from Ayesha, Umme Salamah, Abu Huraira and others. He became a great scholar by virtue of his association with the Companions. He was selected as the 'Master Scholar' by Caliph Umar bin Abdul Aziz. Nafi was a very busy person and disliked people bothering him. So Malik used to wait at his door for Nafi to come out to talk to him.

Imam Malik became very famous and was called the *Imam Dar Al Hijra* or the Imam of the House of Migration. He had a large number of Arab and non Arab students to whom he taught in a system that he devised himself. He scrutinised all kinds of narrations and sermons of the Prophet, expiations from the Quran, sayings and biographies of the Companions. Based on this detailed knowledge he then compiled his famous work the *Muwatta* which comprises of nearly a thousand Hadiths. He was very strict in choosing fully authentic Hadiths and is known to have not included even those narrated by his father or uncles.

Malik's school was centred in Madinah. The Quran, Hadith, Consensus and, to a lesser extent, Analogical eduction were the standard sources of law. To this Imam Malik added a fifth source, that of Juristic Deduction (*Istidlal*). He propounded the concept of public welfare (*Maslihat*) as the basis of deduction. The emphasis on the Prophet's Traditions, the precedents of his Companions and customs prevailing in Madinah had relatively more weight in this school.

Imam Malik accepted funds and financial aids from the state. But that never made him pro-establishment. His juristic decisions once contradicted the existing political policy. He was asked by the Governor (Amir) of Madinah that if a man was forced to divorce would that divorce be legally binding. Imam Malik replied that in Islam anything that is done under coercion is not legally binding. This had political ramifications as at that time Mohammad, the Alid leader, had revolted and the Calliphate needed to force his followers to submit allegiance. But Imam Malik's *fatwa* meant that their allegiance would not be binding. The Imam was asked to retract but he refused. He was imprisoned and flogged for his non-compliance. When the people of Madinah were on the verge of rebellion due to this treatment he was released.

Much later, when Caliph Harun ar Rasheed visited Madinah, he wanted to listen to the *Muwatta* and sent for the Imam. The Imam sent a message, "Rasheed, learning Tradition was patronised by your forefathers. They had utmost regard for it. If you do not respect it as a Caliph no one else will. People come to seek knowledge, knowledge doesn't seek people."

That resulted in Harun ar Rasheed, the Caliph of the greatest empire in the world, to go and sit down among the students of Imam Malik and listen to the *Muwatta*.

A great contribution of the Imam was the codification of the *Fiqh* of Madinah. He died at the age of nearly 90 and was buried in the *Jannat al Baqi,* The Garden of Heaven cemetery near the mosque of the Prophet. He wrote a number of books of which the famous works are:

- *Al-Muwatta*
- *Al-Mudawwana al-Kubra*

School of Imam Shafii (b. 767 CE, 150 AH)

In Principles of Jurisprudence, Usul al Fiqh, Imam Shafii stipulated that Jurisprudence has four sources: the Quran, the Hadith, Ijma (consensus), and Qiyas (analogy). The methodology of Shafii's school sought a balance between the previous two schools. Shafii agreed with Malik's adoption of Juristic Deduction as the fifth source of law but, like Hanifa, extended the scope of consensus by establishing a literal interpretation of the Prophets dictum, "My people will never agree on error," indicating that consensus was a necessity. His school only accepted those traditions or Hadiths that could be projected back to the Prophet.

Mohammad Idris as-Shafii was born in the Gaza region the same year Imam Abu Hanifa died. He belonged to the Hashemite Arab. His father died when he was very young and was brought up by his mother. She was a learned and intelligent woman in her early twenties. She decided not to take pleasure in her own life but made her son's acquisition of knowledge her priority. She moved to Makkah, the city of learning and Islamic fellowship. Besides the Hashemites were influential in Makkah which would provide Malik support. His mother took him to one of the schools but he could not get admitted as they were unable to pay the fee required by the school. That did not deter him. The *Muallem* accepted him in the school but not as a full fledged student. He had to work for the school to be there. He was very sharp, intelligent and had an excellent memory. He would learn what the others were taught and after the classes he would help the other students with their studies. When the Kuttub heard of this he invited him to join the class saying, "It will be a sin to charge money from you".

As-Shafii memorised the entire Quran and started learning Hadith. His thirst for knowledge grew and he decided to go to Madinah and become a student of the famous Imam Malik. He memorised the *Muwatta* in nine days and went to Madinah.

He took a letter of reference from the Governor of Makkah. But Imam Malik just threw it away. Shafii decided to stand his own ground and said, "I am a student who loves knowledge. I have memorised the Muwatta and have travelled from Makkah. I will be honoured if you accept me as a student." The *Farasa* of Imam Malik immediately realised the potential of this young man. He said, "Fear Allah and avoid sins. One day you will prevail. Let not the light in your heart be extinguished. Come tomorrow, I will teach you."

Shafii went to Madinah before the age of 20 to study under Imam Malik and remained his student till the death of the Imam. Besides his *forte*, Jurisprudence, he grew up eloquent in speech, well versed in poetry, had considerable knowledge of medicine, and was a good archer, horseman and spear-thrower. He was of dark complexion, slim and had very handsome facial feature. His poetry was of high quality and would be collected into a book at a later age.

It is 'time' that we blame
On us is the shame
If tongue it did not lack
Time would blame us back

The Governor of Yemen offered him the position of the Administrator of Najran which As-Shafii accepted. But he would last only for a short while in that position. He was a man of principle and censured the people in authority for their wrong doings. This earned him the ire of the elite. At that time some political tension aroused between Caliph Harun ar Rasheed and the Alids. When some nine revolutionary Alids were arrested Imam Shafii was also arrested as 'this man could achieve with his tongue which others would fail to with their swords'. He was taken to Baghdad and produced in the court of Harun ar Rasheed. The nine Alids were executed. But when his time came Imam Muhammad bin Hasan Al Shaibani was present in the court of the Caliph. He interposed strongly declaring Shafii a famous scholar. Harun ar Rasheed then held discussions with Shafii and was much impressed with his knowledge and released him under the patronship of Al Shaibani who took him to live in his house. Harun ar Rasheed gave Shafii a large amount of money in gold coins. Shafii gave it all away to the poor.

Imam Shafii then turned his attention to the further study of Jurisprudence. He was already a master of the Maliki system, this time he studied the Hanafi system with Hanafi

Jurists and spent his time debating with Al Shaibani. Imam Shafii like Imam Hanifa, incorported a variety of Fiqh - Makkah, Madinah, Kufa - and produced jurisprudence for the variety to people of the Muslim empire. He wrote the first edition or the draft edition of his famous work *Ar Risala* during this period of time. Two years later, he moved to Egypt after visiting Syria and Makkah. His lectures there were much appreciated, though a small group of people in Makkah were disappointed to see him shift from the Maliki system not comprehending that a great legal system was being born. On a short return to Baghdad he was offered the position of Judge in Baghdad which he declined. Imam Hanbal, who had attended his study circles in Makkah, would say, "The Jurists are children compared to Imam Shafii."

At the age of 50 he went to Egypt permanently and started writing earnestly. He told his students, "If you want knowledge learn to love times of seclusion, eating less and avoiding foolish people devoid of knowledge." He produced the final version of *Ar Risala* while suffering from intestinal disorder and died six years later. Nearly 400 years later, in 1212 CE, the Ayyubid Sultan Malik Al Kamil built a big domed Mausoleum over his grave. Before the advent of the Ottomans the Shafii School held absolute pre-eminence in much of the Muslim lands (Ahmad, 1984).

The best known works of Al Shafii are:

- *Ar Risala* Jurisprudence coming down from the Companion.
- *usul al-fiqh,* the study of origin, sources - consisting of the Quran, the Sunnah, qiyas, and ijma – and principles on which Islamic Jurisprudence is based on.

School of Imam Hanbal (b. 780, 163 AH)

Abu Abdullah Ahmad bin Muhammad bin Hanbal was either born in Baghdad or in Merv of Khorasan and moved to Baghdad soon after. His grandfather was a revolutionary taking active part in the Abbasid campaign against the Ummayad and later held important position under the Abbasid. His father was a reputed warrior (*Mujaheed*) and he died in a battlefield at the age of thirty. Since then he was brought up by his mother Safiyah bint Maimunah. He was a Shaibani Arab, the same as the famous Muthanna who attacked Persia during the time of Caliph Abu Bakr. Like Imam Shafii he was tall and dark and at a later age would dye his hair red with henna. He was a very intelligent and inquisitive student and by the age of sixteen had memorised the Quran and became a scholar of Hadith. He was a person of complete self control living a very modest life. He was immaculately mannered and did not like to be obligated to anyone. If someone gave him a gift, he would soon give that person a return gift. Throughout his life he was a man of piety and righteousness. He travelled a lot and had attended the study circles of Abu Yusuf, Imam Shafii and others.

His uncle was an Abbasid functionary and would send secret reports to the Governor about the people of the city. Once he asked Hanbal to deliver the report to the Governor. After sometime the Governor demanded the reports from his uncle. His uncle said, "But I have sent you reports on a regular basis!"

Hanbal was summoned and the uncle asked, "What happened to the reports I gave you?"

Hanbal countered, "Did you really expect me to deliver those reports?"

The uncle asked, "Then what did you do with them?"

"I threw them into the river."

At that the Governor said, "From God we come and to him is our return! This young man had got very strong views."

Imam Hanbal went to Hajj five time, three of which were on foot. During a Hajj he met Imam Shafii, who was not famous yet but, all the same, Hanbal was fascinated by him. Once he was in Makkah with friend Yahya Ibn Mayeen and decided to go to Yemen to learn from Sheikh Abdur Razzak of Yemen.

He earned money carrying luggage for people and then went to Yemen. When the Caliph Mamun was distributing gold to the scholars most scholars accepted the donation, but not Imam Ahmad.

He was very dedicated to his mother and got married at the age of 40 only after his mother died. Imam Hanbal said to his students, "I lived with Ayesha for 30 years and we never raised our voices at each other or complained against each other."

After the death of his first wife he would remarry. He was a virile person and a son was born at the age of 70. His elder sons Abdullah and Saleh were very close to him and became great Jurists of their time.

He spent 40 years of his life in the pursuit of knowledge, and only after that he accepted the position of a *Mufti*. As his fame grew due to his piety, learning and absolute faithfulness to Traditions many disciples and admirer gathered around him. He worked on the Fiqh of previous schools, suggesting improvements and in the process became the founder of a new independent school of Jurisprudence - the Hanbali School.

During his time rational philosophy was being espoused by a group of Theologian Mutazilites. They were supported by the Caliphs Mamun, Mutasim and Wasiq. Even from the time of the Umayyads some basic concepts of religion, like the attributes of God and the nature of the Quran, were being debated upon. The Mutazila view was that it was 'created by God' and the orthodox view was that it was God's speech as an indescribable pre-existent Word of God. This debate became a great political issue in Baghdad. This conflict attained immense proportions due to Caliph Mamun's support for it and his command that everybody else believe in it. Why such an abstract concept took such immense proportions is not clear. He probably also used it to place the expanding and influential legal institutions under his political control. Maybe he took on rationalism as the tool to run the government. The issue was religious, but the actual conflict was between the political and the legal institutions. The Ulema had to undergo a public acceptance of the Mutazilite view and those who refused to accept this hypothesis were punished or removed from office. This inquisition came to be known as the *Mihna*. Many of the Ulema sided with the hypothesis of the Mutazila. Imam Ahmad bin Hanbal and Imam Muhammad bin Nuh openly declared their opposition. They were imprisoned and Imam Muhammad died shortly. Imam Ahmad bin Hanbal had to undergo persecution for a long time.

Mamun was an intellectual but his brother Mutasim was more a military man. Under him Imam Hanbal was tortured for a considerable period. He was flogged, his flesh would be torn and bits of the whip would embed in it. He would bleed and faint but he did not accept the theory because it was not to be found in the Quran.

For Imam Hanbal, Islam and its judiciary had to be free from political interference and could only be accountable to God. A well wisher visited him in prison and after seeing the condition of the great man said, "You have been tortured, you are being coerced. Under such condition it is not a sin to say what you must say for your freedom."

He asked the Imam to superficially accept the 'Createdness of the Quran' theory of the Mutazila and simply walk out of the prison - a free man. But to the Imam it was not as simple as that, for to him it meant the surrender of the legal institution. The Imam took his guest to the window of his cell and pointing outside said, "Do you see all the people who live out there?"

"Yes," replied the friend.

"If I say that I accept then those people will also accept the theory. And even though I know it is not true they will think it to be so."

Incredible as it may sound, Imam Hanbal openly forgave Caliph Mutasim when he fought and defeated the Byzantines in retaliation for the killing of Muslims in Capodocipa and Zebetra. During the time of Wasik, he was not tortured but kept under house arrest. Finally, it was Caliph Al Mutawakkil who changed the stance of the Caliphate declaring all discussion on the Quran to be stopped, the Mihna to be ended and the prisoners to be released. He treated Imam Ahmad with respect and dignity.

Caliph Mutawakkil offered him funds but he refused. When his sons, who now were Jurists *(Fuqaha)*, accepted state funds, he severed relationship with them. Imam Ahmad became ill at the age of 77 and died. When a coffin from the royal house was prepared for him, his sons objected. They said that he had refused state wealth in life they could not use state wealth in his death. Hundreds of thousand of men and women poured into the city from all over at the news of his death. The *Encyclopedia of Islam* states that his tomb was the scene of demonstrations of such ardent devotion that the cemetery had to be guarded by civil authorities (Ahmad, 1984). His funeral prayer was attended by his son and many members of the royal family.

Hanbal's assertion was that human reason alone was not sufficient as a source of law. His school favoured the literal interpretations of Hadith where consensus and deduction took a minor position. The *Musnad* is his most famous work and is extant and for which Hanbal researched and collated thousands of Hadiths. Ibn Nadim's *Fihrist*, an index of books from the 10th century CE, lists a large number of books written by Imam Hanbal which are no longer extant.

It was his non-compromise through out the Mihna ordeal, him alone standing against three successive Caliphs that made Hanbal great. Imam Ahmad ibn Hanbal had influence on later reformers like Ibn Taimiyyah and Ibn Abdul Wahab. He also inspired the Salafis whose belief is that path of the first three generations of the Muslims, before the division of the Muslims and formation of all the sects, is the accurate one.

The Shia Fiqh

The Shia Muslims share the same core belief as the Sunni, but they believe that the descendants of the Prophet through his daughter Fatimah and his son-in-law Ali are the Imams or *Khalifa Ilahi* of Muslims. They believe that divine guidance of the Imams comes not from any revelation but through inspiration. And this inspired knowledge makes the Imams the guide for the people. This concept of Imamat is a fundamental belief of Shia Islam and is based on the concept that God would not leave humanity without access to divine guidance.

The Twelvers sect, the *Athna Asharis*, are the dominant group among the Shia. Ali was the first Imam with the following eleven being his descendents. The twelfth Imam Mohammad Ibn Hasan was placed in a *spiritual hidden state* by God but is living and will return to redeem the Muslims and be the ultimate Saviour, the Mahdi, when the world will need one most. The Shia Muslim disagrees with the Caliphate of Abu Bakr, Umar and Usman and believe that Ali should have been the first Caliph.

The other Shia sects - Ismaili, Zaidi and Bohra - have a different number of Imams and a different path of succession, and similar to the Sunni do not consider Mohammad Ibn Hasan as the Mahdi. The Zaidis are close to the Mutazila School in certain aspects of rationalism.

The School of Jaafar As Sadiq (b. 702 CE, 83 AH)

The 6th Shia Imam, Jaafar Ibn Muhammad As Sadiq was born in Madinah in 702 CE. He lived for 65 years and was the Shia Imam for 34 years. He was a highly learned individual with knowledge of multiple disciplines: astronomy, chemistry, Islamic theology, philosophy, medicine and physics.

As a child, he was a very intelligent student. In early childhood, he was taught by his grandfather Ali ibn Hussain (Zain al Abedin) the great grandson of the Prophet and survivor of Karbala. In school he used to discuss complex matters of Fiqh and Jurisprudence with much older students. While still a student he concluded that the orbital way the sun rises in the east and sets in the west implies that the world was not flat but spherical.

Imam Jaafar Sadiq was one of the greatest intellectuals of Islam and dedicated his life to the spiritual and intellectual development of the community. In fact, at one time or another, his school had been visited by world renowned personalities like Imam Abu Hanifa, Imam Malik, Wasil bin Ata and the famous chemist Jabir ibn Hayyan (Geber). Twelve Hadiths from Imam Jaafar Sadiq has been quoted in the Muwatta. He is highly respected by the Naqshabandi Sufi chains as well.

At this stage of history the Shia and Sunnis had not crystallised into two distinct sects. The term Sunni had not yet been coined and the Shia were still considered a political group, the Alids, who harboured the view that Ali should have been the first Caliph. But the development of different Jurisprudences and the establishment of the political nomenclature 'Sunni' and the 'Shia', would finally consolidate the division.

During the Imamate of Jaafar As Sadiq came the end of the Umayyad Dynasty and the start of the Abbasid Dynasty. He viewed the political upheavals with great sadness, specially the suppression of the Alids. Politically, the Abbasids were probably more apprehensive of Imam Jaafar then they were of the other Imams. One of the main points which the Abbasids had used to take over the empire was that they belonged to the house of the Prophet. From that perspective, Imam Jaafar had a better claim to the Caliphate. The Imam was placed on watch by security personal of the Caliphate and was occasionally summoned to Baghdad by the Caliph Al Mansur. When on one such occasion the Imam was about to leave the Caliph asked if he could be of any service to him. Jaafar Sadiq replied, "The only service I seek from you is that I should not be given the trouble to attend your court again" (Ahmad, 1984).

Imam Jaafar died in 765 CE at the age of 65. Shia scholars attribute his death to poisoning and royal implication in the plot. Whatever the case may be, Al Mansur recognised the fact that, "The real leader of Muslims, the most learned man and theologian has left this world." He was buried in Madinah, in the famous Jannatul Baqi cemetery.

The Jaafari school of Jurisprudence differs from the four Sunni schools in the greater use of Ijtihad (research). There are also secondary differences in issues of religious taxes, commerce, inheritance and the allowance of temporary marriage *Nikah al Muta*. As these differences were deemed as superficial and not core, there have been numerous fatwas regarding the acceptance of Jaafari *fiqh* as an acceptable Muslim School by Sunni religious bodies.

The 1959 Al Azhar fatwa states that a Muslim does not need to follow any particular school and can change schools. In 2007, the *Amman Message* was issued calling for tolerance and unity in the Muslim world. Subsequently, a three-point ruling was issued by 200 Islamic scholars from over 50 countries which recognised eight legal schools – Hanafi, Maliki, Shafi'I, Hanbali, Athna Ashari, Zaidi, Ibadi, Zahiri.

All the schools of Jurisprudence carried out massive work in their legal formulations. At the same time, another set of scholars or Imams were carrying out a different but extraordinary work and research to consolidate and compile the great books of Hadith. These consisted of the Prophet's sayings and traditions. Eventually, skills thus acquired were applied to other disciplines of knowledge such as in the research of the Sufis and the Rational Sciences.

The Hadith

Pray as you see me pray
-The Prophet

The Prophet epitomises the unique role model for all humans. His Tradition represents his sayings and actions. It also includes a very important aspect of religion. When his Companions needed any of the verses of the Quran to be clarified, he would interpret and explain it to them. For example, the verses of the Quran ask to establish prayer in one's life. But it was the Prophet who clarified that it meant praying five times a day and the prescribed manner in which one should pray.

He had enjoined on his followers to emulate him. But he had also warned them not to confuse between the revelations and the Traditions. Thus the first research that the Muslims engaged in was on the Quran, which consisted of the revelations. After the Quran had been compiled, scrutinised, its precision sanctioned, and its copies had spread all over the Muslim world, it was time to codify the Prophet's interpretation of the Quran and his Sunnah. There was a need to collate all these so that people could apply the Prophet's Sunnah in their everyday life and legislations could be promulgated from them.

The Great Imams had done significant work in the field of Sunnah by compiling their Musnad. They collated his Traditions with the main aim of using it in formulation of laws. Besides these work on jurisprudence, there also developed schools and scholars who specialised purely on the subject of *collection, verification and compilation* of Sunnah without any direct relation to jurisprudence.

By the time methodical research on Sunnah had started there had been a wide verbal proliferation of the Prophet's sayings due to parallel and multiple channels of oral propagation. It took stupendous effort and toil by scholars, working their entire life with just this one purpose, to collect all these traditional 'sayings and actions' of the Prophet from various regions of the empire, apply processes to sift through all the sayings and match various sources and to introduce methodologies that could discriminate between the authentic and unauthentic sayings.

Each one of the sayings or actions of the Prophet, which had been put through the above criteria, was noted down and individually considered a Hadith. The word 'Hadith' means a news or communication, and in this respect is a news or communication about the Prophet. Each Hadith was divided into two segments, the 'Matan' and the 'Isnad'. The Matan consisted of the actual text of the Hadith, while the Isnad, a reference system, was the chain of narrators who had propagated the Hadith. It detailed how an individual Hadith was transmitted from the time of the Prophet up to the time the Hadith was being written down. An example of Isnad and Matan is given below from the Hadith book of Imam Bukhari.

Isnad: Al-Bukhari narrated on the authority of *Al-Humaidi Abdullah bin al-Zubair* on the authority of *Sufyan* on the authority of *Yahya bin Sa'id al-Ansari* on the authority of *Muhammad bin Ibrahim al-Taymi* on the authority of Alqamah *bin Waqqas al-Laithi*, who said I heard Umar bin al- Khattab saying from the pulpit:

Matan: "I heard Allah's Messenger (may Allah bless him and grant him peace) saying: *The reward of deeds depends on the intentions, and every person will get the reward according to what he has intended; so whoever emigrated for worldly benefits or for a woman to marry, his emigration was for what he migrated.*"

This means that the compiler of the Hadith Bukhari heard it from *Al-Humaidi Abdullah bin al-Zubair* who heard it from *Sufyan* and who received it from *Yahya bin Sa'id al-Ansari* and so on with the chain ending with Umar bin Khattab who was present when the Prophet uttered the Hadith. The compiler would have to check the list of narrators (in this case *Al-Humaidi Abdullah bin al-Zubair*, *Sufyan* and *Yahya bin Sa'id al-Ansari* and so on) of the Hadith to judge its authenticity. It was essential for each person in the chain to be a reputed individual known for their knowledge, upright character and sanity. The process of judging through the chain starts with the last name in the chain. If that person is found acceptable according to the established criteria then the next person up in the chain would be judged. If the second person up in the chain passed the test then the third one up in the chain would be judged and this would go on till the Prophet is reached. If all the people in the line were judged as an authority only then the Hadith was deemed correct or *Sahih*. In many contemporary books the full Isnad are not mentioned, only the name of the narrating companion is mentioned to make it less cumbersome. But understanding the Isnad is an art in itself and there are scholars who specialise in it.

Based on its authenticity Hadiths were divided into three categories.

1. Sahih Hadith – There was no doubt about the content, Matan, and the authority of the Isnad.
2. Hasan Hadith – These are the Hadiths which have a correct Isnad but there may be some reservation about the content. This condition would arise from anyone in the Isnad line who may have 'misheard' part of the Hadith.
3. Zaeef Hadith – These are weak hadiths that have an imperfect Isnad, such that, the character or reliability of any single person mentioned in the Isnad is doubtful.

There are further classifications of Hadith into Mutawatir, Ahad, Mashur, etc. These classifications and their sub-classifications are based on various criteria like the number of chain of narrators. For example, if the same Matan or text came down via multiple Isnads, thus corroborating each other, it was deemed as 'Mutawatir'.

There are two types or systems of Hadith books based on the arrangement known as Musnad and Musannaf.

- Musnad- arranged by the names of the first transmitter (Companion) in the Isnad of the Hadith. The Musnad of Ahmad bin Hanbal is of this category.
- Musannaf- Hadiths categorised by the subject matter of the Matan such as marriage, divorce, sales, trade, prayer, etc. The most famous Sahih Musannaf Hadiths are the works of:

1. Al Bukhari (b. 810)
2. Muslim (b. 817)
3. Abu Daud (b. 817)
4. Al Tirmidhi (b. 824)
5. Ibn Maja (b. 824)
6. Al Nasai (b. 830)

The Shiite work of Hadith includes not only the Prophet's traditions but those of their Imams, of subsequent ages, as well. The famous Shiite works are those of:

1. Muhammad bin Yakub Al Kulluni (b. 864)
2. Muhammad Al Hummi (d. 991)
3. Tahir Al Sharif Al Murtaja (b. 965)
4. Muhammad Al Tusi (b. 995)

The Imams travelled widely through out the Islamic world meeting with a host of scholars, collecting, corroborating and putting the Hadith and its source to the standard methods of testing. Once satisfied they would collate the Hadiths into a book. Thus, each book consisted of work spreading over the entirety of a very enterprising lifetime. These Imams were pure scholars neither politically nor legally inclined and thus did not get into major crisis with the rulers and royalties. The classification of Hadith by subject matter had assisted in the development of Jurisprudence. Muslims scholars consider Hadith to be essential supplements to and the interpretation of the Quranic verses.

The Isnad of the Hadith would develop into the modern reference system or bibliography. Before the Muslims, scholars were not systematic about referencing the source of their knowledge. The Muslims scholars were the first to systematically refer and acknowledge their sources whether Muslim, Greek or Indian.

The Sufi Universe

Everywhere I look, I see Your winning face
Everywhere I go, I arrive at Your dwelling-place

To be precise Sufism is not mere mysticism. Sufism is a knowledge sphere, which includes a great degree of creative intellectualism that has developed significant philosophy, literature, and sciences. It is a process of deep thinking and self purification that, in its time, had led civilisation to the forefront of human thought. It is not religion but has derived passionate and motivating spiritual energy from religion. What Sufism is, is actually unclear to even many of its adherents. One way to understand it is to realise that sufism is *a quest for God, not to comprehend God as that is humanly impossible but to experience or 'feel' God. As Mutazilite Rationality led to the study of Science, Sufi Mysticism led to the study of Arts.*

In the spectrum of knowledge, Sufism lies between the Ulemaic and Rational universes. It is a mental universe that experiments with phenomena beyond the known realms of physical laws and established metaphysics. Thus, like philosophy, Sufism can also be considered as the fountainhead of innovative and creative thinking. It has started with thinking into metaphysical aspects but had soon revealed aspects of human desires and behaviour which then led to development of profound poetry, literature and culture on the one hand and a understanding of human psychology on the other. Later Sufis have aspects of subtle psychology ingrained in their poetry such as in verses of Jami, a 15th century Sufi poet-philosopher:

Brother, you are 'thought' wholly
Rest is bone and muscle solely
If your thought is a rose, a rose bouquet you are
If your thought is a thorn, fuel for fire you are

By the 10th century, the schools of the Great Imams gradually turned into dogmatic sects and Ijtihad (research and analysis) was banned. The Caliphate had also become highly politicised. Confined by these two powerful and rigid forces the scope for the free thinking people become highly restricted. Sufism became an intellectual rebellion against the religious and political dogmas. At one stage, the Sufis clashed with the orthodox Ulema, but would subdue themselves after the death of Hallaj in the 10th century, then re-invent themselves as the architect of 'popular culture' that would influence the world, such as the works by poet Jalaluddin Rumi, author Nizami and the legendary humour of Nasruddin Hodja. Their ecstasy would be diversified as stated by Rumi:

Think not all ecstasy are the same.

In attempts to understand God, at times, Sufism had strayed away from the fundamental precepts of Ulemaic thought, as was the case of Al Hallaj, and had precipitated into chaos. While at other times, it had been a bridge between the Ulemaic and Rational thoughts. Thus Sufism can be a double edged sword depending on the learning and calibre of the person wielding it. When Sufi innovation has led to culture and rational science it has been brilliant and when it had tried to affect or alter the Ulemaic concepts it had become dangerous.

The start of Sufism took place in the hands great scholars. Hasan Al Basri (642 - 728), a *Tabii* (generation after the Prophet's Companions) Imam, though he predates the Sufi movement, attracted the respect of later Sufis due to his great scholarship and asceticism. He was also a believer of *Qadriya* or free will concept as against the *Jabriya* or predestination concept and disagreed with the notion that God could predestine man to do evil. His rebel student Wasil Ibn Ata became the proponent of rationalism which started the school of the Mutazilites. This school would also absorb the Aristotelian and Platonic philosophies within their realm. The great Philosopher-Scientist-Sufi Imam Ghazzali did not create any Sufi order but systematised the Sufi System and contained it under the fold of orthodox Islam.

People like Hasan Basri and Al Ghazzali who are highly respected by Sufi scholars, and the original Sufi like Ibn Arabi, Abdul Quader Jillani, Jalaluddin Rumi, Nizami (some of whom established the still existing Sufi orders) were all men of highest literacy and foremost in knowledge of their time in science, philosophy, psychology, theology, literature and linguistics. The vast amount of knowledge that they absorbed, assimilated and the incredible thought process by which they produced books upon books of 'new' knowledge did not give them time to partake enterprise in the material world. They were too dedicated in perfecting their chosen fields of knowledge to care much about this world – and thus their asceticism. Sufi asceticism was not a vogue or escapism but a practical measure and a well laid methodology. Sufis also assisted in the spread of Islam in various regions where they took different appellations like Dervish or Pir. A list of the renowned Sufis is given below.

Age	**Sufis**
9th Century	Al Fuzail, Shafiq Falkhi, Maruf al Karkhi, Bashr bin al Harith, Abu Bakr Al Shibli, Ahmad bin Harb, Al Harith bin Asad Al Muhasibs, Hatm Al Assam, Dhun Nun Misri, Ahamd bin Khuzriya, Abu Yazid Bustami, Sahl bin Abdullah Tustari, Abu Abdullah Al Tirmidhi
10th Century	Ibrahim al Khawas, Abu Hasan Al Nuri, Abul Qasim Al Junaid, Amr bin Usman, Al Hallaj, Samnun, Al Rudhbari, Ibn Khafif, Abu Nasr Al Sarraj, Abu Bakr al Kalabadi, Abu Talib al Makki
11th Century	Abu Abdul Rahman Sulami, Abul Hasan Al Kharqani, Abu Nuaim al Isahahani, Abu Said bin Abi Al Khair, Abul Qaidm Al Qushayri, Abul Qasim Al Gurgani, Abul Ali Al Farmadhi Al Tus, Abdullah Al Ansari, Abi Al Hajweri (Data Ganj Baksh), Abu Bakr An Nassaj.

12th Century	Abdul Hameed Al Ghazzali, Abdul Qadir Jilani, Yusuf Al Hamdani, Ahmad Al Yasavi, Abu Madyan Shuabi, Ibn ul Kizani, Abu Najib as Suhrawardi, Amad bin Arrafi
13th Century	Ibn Al Farabi, Ibn Al Farid, Jalaluddin Rumi, Hafiz

In the eight century, Kufa, Basra and Khorasan became the initial areas of Sufi thought. In Kufa, Abu Hisham was probably the first person to be called a Sufi. In the same century Rabia Basri was a prominent Sufi. She established the divine 'Doctrine of Love' which played an important role in progression through the Sufi meditation stages.

O Lord,
If tomorrow on Judgment Day
You send me to Hell,
I will tell such a secret
That Hell will race from me
Until it is a thousand years away.

O Lord,
Whatever share of this world
You could give to me,
Give it to Your enemies;
Whatever share of the next world
You want to give to me,
Give it to Your friends.
You are enough for me.

O Lord,
If I worship You
From fear of Hell, burn me in Hell.
O Lord,
If I worship You
From hope of Paradise, bar me from its gates.

But if I worship You for Yourself alone
Then grace me forever the splendor of Your Face.

O Lord by Rabia - translation by Andrew Harvey and Eryk Hanut - 'Perfume of the Desert'

In the ninth century, elaborate Sufi theories were developed and started to attract the attention of the general mass. As they became popular they started to have more conflicts with the rulers due to their difference in political views, and with the Ulema due to the divergence in religious views. Dhun Nun Misri developed his theory of Gnosis, the knowledge of God. The Ulema disputed with him and he was charged and brought before the Caliph

Mutawakkil. But on hearing the details of his views the Caliph did not find anything religiously or politically unconventional and he was released.

Abu Yazid Bustami established the concept of *Fanaa* - the 'Theory of Ecstatic Annihilation in God' (Ahmad, 1984). His school carried forward Rabia Basri's 'Doctrine of Love' a step further by postulating that an individual in the Sufi quest for the love of God could reach a stage where the humanity in the individual ceased to exist and union with God took place. Al Harith bin Asad Al Muhasib established the school of speculative Sufism. He laid the foundation of science of Sufism in his two books *Al Riya li Huqquq Allah (The observance of Allah's right),* and *Kitab ul Nasiha (Book of Counsels).*

Sufi thoughts were innovative and thus also had the propensity of misleading the mind. As the Ulema were becoming concerned about Sufi practices and its nonconformist views, Al Muhasib and Sahl bin Abdullah Tustari postulated that true Sufism had nothing unorthodox. Tustari wrote a commentary on the Quran from the Sufi perspective to establish his point of view.

In the tenth century, the Mutazila rationalists were patronised by the Abbasid court. The intellectual conflict became triangular between the Ulema, the Sufi and the Mutazila. The Mutazila tried to explain everything by reason. The Ulema and the Sufi did not agree that everything could be explained by reason. But Ulema and the Sufi also disagreed with each other. The Ulema were prescriptive and within the binds of Sharia while the Sufis were non-prescriptive while still giving importance to faith and Gnosis. The Ulema considered that the innovative Rational and the unorthodox Sufi thoughts had the ability to mislead people.

The friction between the Sufi and Ulema developed into a great clash when a Sufi named Al Hallaj tried to break down the boundary between the Sufi and the Ulemaic thought. In the state of *fanaa* or self-annihilating ecstasy a Sufi is said to go through mental experiences that cannot be explicable to the rational mind and are not acceptable in the Ulemaic world. Al Hallaj, in his ecstasy, declared "*Ana Al-Huq*", i.e., I am *Al Huq*. The literary meaning of *Al Huq* is the Truth but *Al Huq* is also a recognised name of God. In his book *Kitab ul Tawasin* Hallaj wrote that he was Whom he loved and Whom he loved was he, thus two spirits in the same body:

If you see me, then you see Him,
And if you see Him, you see us both.

Whatever Hallaj had experienced or meant was beyond the understanding of the common masses. He did not practice in private but proclaimed his concepts in public. The implication of the statement 'Ana Al-Huq' was enough to rupture the fabric of the contemporary society. Its acceptance could lead him to be idolised or worshipped by people. This was heresy at the highest level and had the potential of fragmenting the society. He was executed in 922.

It was becoming clear that the doctrine of ecstasy was leading the Sufis to an uncontrolled situation where not only 'reason' did not exist but faith itself was becoming distorted. To them nothing existed aside the Individual and God and that too was becoming fused. The execution of Hallaj made the Sufis circumspect. To refrain from public expression of this 'state of mind' Sufi Al Junaid propounded the doctrine of Sobriety or Silence. The Sufis would remain silent about their experiences or mask these, in speech or writing, by the use of metaphors or esoteric symbolism. Later Sufis would make statements similar to Hallaj but from a poetical realm, not from a prescriptive religious base.

A number of books were written during the tenth century by Sufis. Aside the main content matter many of those books also advised that the Sufis to remain within the constraint of Sharia. Some of these books are:

Book	Author
The Food for the Hearts (Qoot al Quloob)	Abu Talib Makki
Book of Flashes (Kitab al Lama)	Abu Nasr Al Sarraj
The Doctrine of the Sufis (Kitab al Taarruf li Madhab ahl al Tasawwuf)	Abu Bakr Kalabadi

In the eleventh century, Sufism started to develop into an organised discipline. Along with the Sufi conceptual clarifications there also developed systematic methodologies needed to attain the Sufi status. Biographies of Sufis also appeared in this century. Al Isfahani wrote a biographical compendium of ten large volumes. These biographies showed that the genuine Sufis were devoted to Islam and lived within its sanction. A wide ranging account of the Sufis, *Tabaqat ul Sufia*, was also written by Abu Abdul Rahman Al Sulami claiming that the endeavour of the Sufis was the same as the Ulema. He wrote an interpretation of the Quran from the Sufi point of view as well.

The *Risala* written by Abul Qasim Al Qushayri is an exposition of orthodox Sufism. He also wrote a commentary of the Quran from the Sufi point of view. Data Ganj Baksh wrote the comprehensive classic manual of Sufism, *Kashf al Mahjub (Lifting of the Veil).* While another manual for the Sufis, *Manzil al Saairin (Stages of the Traveller)*, was written by Abdullah Al Ansari. The Sufis were able to convince the people that their movement was not a separatist movement but a reformist one. All along, this notion is corroborated by many Sufis who wrote against the atheistic or pluralist philosophers and maintained accord with the Ulema. Much later, Jami would write in his *Lawaih* (*Flashes of Light*):

Philosophers devoid of reason find
This world a mere idea of the mind;
It is an idea – but they fail to see
The great Idealist who looms behind.

Many of the great Sufis had established their own schools or 'Orders'. The Sufi schools developed methods of indoctrination for its disciple-students. Each school developed a methodology by which human faults - emotions like animal instincts, material attachments, desire and hatred - were removed leaving the Sufi-initiate liberated so that their full mental capacity could be applied in the pursuit of knowledge and the union with God.

In Sufi training methodology, a Sufi 'travels' or rises through a number of mental stages each having a Station and a State. The 'Stations' are the positions like renunciation, abstinence, striving, silence, fear, sorrow, hope, awe of God, etc., that one reaches through one's own efforts. The associated 'States' like the state of desire in the self, the state of yearning for knowledge, the state of love for God etc., are conditions of the individual bestowed by God. The number of stages that the methodology has varies between Sufi Orders but can be generalised into three:

The first stage is of contemplation and meditation in which the individual realigns ones mental faculties. The individual detaches from worldly desires and attractions and initiates a love for God alone. Regularised prayer with meditational 'Dhikr' or remembrance of God is invoked. The individual takes food but is not attracted by the taste. The individual controls desires and stops hating, lying, ill speaking or craving vengeance. Slowly the individual achieves total control of one's own mental faculty.

Once the first stage or 'Station' is achieved, the individual is in a 'State' that is at peace with the self and in love with God. Now the individual starts to absorb all the knowledge that is required for the field the individual seeks to master. In the past various Sufi's have worked on various field. It was gnosis in case of Dhun Nun and poetry in case of Rumi. It can be any branch of knowledge that opens up to a new thought process. Along with this still continues the constant devotion to God via prayers and meditational 'Dhikr'.

The third stage arises when the individual is totally annihilated by the love of God. This leads to a state of total ecstasy and 'intoxication' as the will merges with knowledge and the self with the love of God. This stage, in which the Sufi is purified and becomes oblivious of worldly desires, is known as 'Fanaa'. By this stage the mental faculty is so strong that worldly desires and fears are no longer existent in the self.

The fundamental root of self purification, inherent in Sufi methodologies, comes from the Quran and the Ulemaic injunctions that consider worship to be aimed at the purification of the soul.

But those will prosper who purify themselves
And glorify the name of their Guardian- Lord
And lift their hearts in prayer. [87:14-15]
Gardens of Eternity, beneath which flow rivers
They will dwell there forever
Such is the reward of those who purify themselves [20:76]

With time, the Sufi methodologies became refined and came to be known as *Tariqa* (Sufi spiritual methods) at variance from *Sharia* (tenets of Islam). Any Tariqa that contradicts the Sharia came to be considered innovative and erroneous by the Ulema. This was because Sufism borrowed from, as well as influenced other cultures. The stages of some, not all, Sufi orders are reminiscent of the Persian Amesha Spentas and the 'Fanaa' state is analogous to the 'Khod Ah' or self realisation of Zoroaster and the 'Know Thyself' of Socrates or Buddhist 'Nirvana.' Sufi adherents, on the other hands considered Sufism to be subservient and complimentary to Sharia (Khawaja, A.A, 2002). At later periods, Sufism became very popular producing large volumes of 'thoughts' in verses over different regions of the world. People of various cultures became attracted to it and started to practice Sufi methodologies which caused an intermingling of Islamic and Non-Islamic cultures and thoughts.

The twelfth century saw the establishment of the following Sufi orders:

Sufi Order	**Established by**
Naqshabandi	Yusuf Al Hamdani
Qadiriya	Abdul Qadir Jilani
Yasaviya	Ahmad Al Yasavi
Kinziya	Ibn ul Kizani
Suhrawardi	Abu Najib as Suhrawardi
Rifaiya	Amad bin Arrafi
Shadhiliya	Abu Madyan Shuabi

Al Ghazzali, who lived in this century and experimented with Sufism, did not establish any Sufi order or methodology and remained totally within the bounds of religious orthodoxy. Besides Al Ghazzali, the other great thinker of this time period was Abdul Qadir Jilani, a Theologian per excellence. His compendium *Al Ghuniya tut Talibin Tariq ul Haq (Sufficiency for the Seekers of the Path of Truth)* is considered a prototype of theological studies. This book contains an exposition of the Sufi way of life. Jilani became the founder of one of the Orders of Sufisın. His *Fatuh Al Gheyb* is a remarkable book on Mysticism (Ahmad, 1984).

The 13th century produced three great Sufi luminaries:

1. Ibn al Arabi
2. Ibn al Farid
3. Jalaluddin Rumi.

Ibn al Arabi, a great scholar, proposed the theory 'God is the only reality and existence.' This is based on the Sufi statement, 'To whatever side I turn, I see nought but Allah,' and also has relevance to the concept of emanation of creation from God. Ibn al Arabi wrote a number of books including *Fatuhad al Makkiya (Makkah Revelations)* and *Fusus al Hikma (Bezels of Wisdom)*. There are 800 works attributed to him.

Ibn al Farid postulated the theory of the 'Perfect Man'. According to him a perfect man is the miniature of reality. He is the microcosm in who is reflected all the perfect attributes of the cosmos. The Prophet was the Perfect Man. A similar, but non-religious, concept was put forward half a millennium later in Nietzsche's postulation of the 'Superman'. Ibn al Farid was a mystic poet. His *Nazm ul Suluk (Poem of the Way)* is the longest Arabic poem written in praise of the Prophet.

The fame of the poet and mystic Jalaluddin Rumi has remained legendary over the centuries. He still remains one of the most widely read poet in the world. UNESCO issued a UNESCO Medal in his name in 2007. His epoch making work is the *Masnavi*, a literary masterpiece presenting a panoramic view of the Sufi Gnosis and attainment of Communion with God.

Quietness.

You've no idea how hard I've looked for a gift to bring You.
Nothing seemed right.
What's the point of bringing gold to the gold mine, or water to the Ocean.
Everything I came up with was like taking spices to the Orient.
It's no good giving my heart and my soul because you already have these.
So- I've brought you a mirror.
Look at yourself and remember me.

~~~

The Gift of Water.

Someone who doesn't know the Tigris exists
brings the caliph who lives near the river
a jar of fresh water. The caliph accepts, thanks him,
and gives in return a jar filled with gold coins.

"Since this man has come through the desert,
he should return by water." Taken out by another door,
the man steps into a waiting boat
and sees the freshwater of the Tigris.
He bows his head, "What wonderful kindness
that he took my gift."

Every object and being in the universe is
a jar overfilled with wisdom and beauty,
~~~

a drop of the Tigris that cannot be contained
by any skin. Every jarful spills and makes the earth
more shining, as though covered in satin.
If the man had seen even a tributary
of the great river, he wouldn't have brought
the innocence of his gift.

Those that stay and live by the Tigris
grow so ecstatic that they throw rocks at the jugs,
and the jugs become perfect!
They shatter.
The pieces dance, and water....
Do you see?
Neither jar, nor water, nor stone,
nothing.
You knock at the door of reality,
shake your thought-wings, loosen
your shoulders,
and open.

Poems from The Essential Rumi - Coleman Barks

The general direction that Sufism took would lead to the development of imaginative/ creative fields of learning like psychology and literature. The Sufis, generally, did not propound scientific theories but created the environment that helped evolve rational thought. Jami even when writing metaphysics digresses into the rational:

The essential modes in earth and heavens
Are facets of Him who is a veiled Immanence
Hence, inquirer, learn what is essence
What is attribute, cause, and consequence.

Many Sufis had a common vehicle, poetry, which they used to portray their thoughts. Before the Sufis, mostly an epic form of poetry existed. It was the Sufis who innovated numerous different forms that metamorphosed to modern poetry. Over time, from this bud of poetry arose a culture of new genres of song, music, dances and literature. In these endeavours the Sufis generally refrained from animalist-anthropomorphic art form which tends toward the sensual arousing of base desires rather then the higher aesthetic qualities of the human mind.

The Rational Universe

Rational thought first made its impression on Muslim scholars in the debate between predestination and free will in late 7th century. The school of *Jabriya* held that all things and actions are predetermined by God. While the school of *Qadriya* postulated that action was contingent on free will. This debate raged during the Umayyad period and moved away from its true meaning taking on a political hue. A large section of people were still critical of the Umayyad 'usurpation' of power and their harsh treatment of the Alids. The Jabriya hypothesis supported the Umayyads since if all things were predetermined then the Umayyads were not responsible for their actions. The Qadriya opposed this hypothesis on the basis that humans possessed free will and were thus responsible for their actions.

This ability to think independently, starting from the above predestiny-freewill dialectical form, led to the development of multiple schools of thought like the Kharijite, Murjite, the Mutazilite and the Asharite. All these groups would endeavour on some combination of Reason and Theology until Reason became an autonomous and independent subject. The Mutazilites would call it *Ilm Ul Kalam* (Scholastic Theology). All these school arose trying to resolve some socio-political issue or debate within the theological-philosophical context. Some of these schools lasted for centuries, improving or changing over time. Through out this milieu, the school of the Traditional Ulema under the shade of the Sharia acted as the peg to which all these free-roaming ideas were tethered to, so that none got 'lost' in the vast unknown universe of 'thought' and so that once the idea had been 'spent' or found no longer applicable, its adherents would have a path and a point to come back to. Without the Ulemaic Thought, the other schools would no longer have an absolute point of reference. The changes in the Traditional Ulemaic schools have been in its tools rather then in itself. For example, in promulgation of laws, it has sometimes applied Ijtihad (research) and at other time Taqlid (emulate). But in itself it remained unaltered. Thus in the divine framework it never changed but was the guide to any change.

The massive philosophical-theological debates that took place in the first century of Islam had opened the gates of academic rational faculty. Already huge research had taken place during the research of the Traditions, in the 9th century the scholars turned their acquired research skills and thought processes in the rational direction. The rationalists approached their work with the same religious zeal that had been applied to the previous works on Jurisprudence and Traditions.

By the Abbasid time there was an academic upsurge and an unprecedented amount of scientific work was done. In the past civilisations what had been vague thoughts within the envelope of philosophy, in the hands of Abbasid Muslims turn into defined sciences. New disciplines of science, arts and commerce were developed. In effect, they would perfect the sciences and arts as is understood today.

The Schools of Mutazila

The Mutazilite schools of rational thought were established by prominent scholars like:

Wasil bin Ata (d. 753),
Huzail bin Hallaf (d. 851)
Nazzam bin Siyyar (d. 845)
Mamar bin Abbad (d. 842)
Bashr bin Mutamir (d. 848)
Jahiz bin Bahr (d. 877).
Abu Ali Al Jubai (d. 915)
Abd Al Jabbar (d.1025)

The Mutazila schools dealt with the doctrines of synthesis of revelation and reason. Of the above list, Wasil bin Ata was a student of Hasan Basri. He left the school of Hasan due to theological differences with him and founded the School of the Mutazila. After him the prominent Mutazilite Huzail wrote a book named *Five Fundamentals – Divine Speech, Freedom of Will, Predestination, Reason and Justice*. He argued that reason should be favoured and that it was possible to achieve virtue by rational argument. In the 10th century, Abu Ali Al Jubbai wrote down the Principles of Rational Argument in a book named *Usul*. The Mutazilites put forward five principals, which are:

1. Divine Unity – The absolute unity of God. There is not any degree of anthropomorphism in their concept.
2. Divine Justice – Life is a test for beings that possess free will. Only because they have free will they can be held accountable for their mistakes.
3. Promise and Threat – On the day of Judgement, God will carry out both His promise to reward the good and His threat to punish the evil.
4. The Transitional position – Those Muslims who committed great sins and die without repentance are neither believers nor unbelievers. They occupy a transitional position between the two. (The Kharijites claimed that any Muslim who committed great sin was not a Muslim anymore. The Murjites, another theological group in early Islam, held that only God has the authority to judge who is a true Muslim and who is not. Whether a person was a great sinner or not, all Muslims should consider all other Muslims as part of the community. The Mutazilite position was intermediate between the Kharijite and the Murjite.)
5. Good and Evil – Good should be promoted and evil suppressed.

By the end of the 9th century the Mutazilites were under attack from the Traditionalists on one side and the philosophers, atheist, and deist on the other side. In the great conflict between the Mutazilites and the Traditionalist Ulema, it would be a mistake to consider the Traditionalists as irrational. They harboured aspects of rationalism as well, only the perspective was different.

School of the Asharites

Starting from the end of the ninth century and throughout the tenth century, the Intellectual scene became dominated by the philosophy of Abul Hasan Ashari. He proposed a mix from both the Traditional Ulema and the Mutazila views. He noted that Gnosis could not be comprehended by reason alone, i.e., religion was not a set of doctrines that could be explained by logical concepts alone. But, he gave reason a more significant part in religion then the orthodox Ulema. He believed in free will, elaborating the thoughts of scholars and theologians like Abu Hanifa, Dirar ibn Amr and Ibn Kullab.

Al Ashari established the doctrine of *Iktisab* (acquisition) which states that God creates actions which are acquired by humans and thus by this acquisition humans become responsible for them. He taught that the universe consisted of minute indivisible particles and moments of time created by God. Created substance, by themselves, are not sufficient to cause events. Causality, two events that are cause and effect, is illusory in the sense that the world is sustained and governed through the direct intervention of a primary causation which is Divine. He upheld the Ulemaic view that God is the ultimate cause of things and rejected the Aristotelian notion of causality as believed by the Mutazila. What is discerned as the 'law of nature' is really the will of God or the laws of God. This doctrine later came to be known as 'Occasionalism' and would be reflected in the works of Ghazzali. Later philosophers like Johannes Clauberg, Louis de La Forge, François Lamy, Nicolas Malebranche, David Hume, George Berkeley and G.W.Liebniz would also research into occasionalism.

Al Ashari also developed the Ashari Islamic *Aqidah* (System of Belief / Creed) denoting and explaining subject-matters over which Muslims hold conviction, i.e., belief in God, prophets, angels, books of God, judgement day and destiny. A prolific writer, his writing took a scientific turn. At the start of the 11th century, his work was expounded by Al Baqillani and Al Baghdadi. Al Ghazzali belongs to this school and outshines even Ashari in his works.

While high profile theological and political debates were occurring a different type of revolution was taking place among the general mass. They had got acquainted with a variety of academic disciplines, new and old, and were silently pursuing a massive amount of work that would change the shape of knowledge like never before.

Upsurge of Literacy and Knowledge

"God, help with your grace. The soul craves for facts and not for theories. And for that reason the preface is restricted to these very words. God willing, the book will demonstrate the aim of its publication. We seek God's help and blessing."

- Ibn Nadim, a book seller, in the preface of the Fihrist, an index of books, composed in 987

Following the Prophet's injunctions to read and follow the Quran, all men and women were induced to read. Initially, young people were taught in the Mosques. Next, small schools developed adjacent to Mosques. The first systematic style of schooling for the young people developed for the study of Quran and Arabic. A large number of schools were established for all in the empire. For the first time in the history of the world, literacy came to all of the common mass in a society. By the 9th century a significant proportion of the population were literate. Among them were the litterateurs (*Adeeb*) who were distinct from the Ulema. In the *Mikhlat*, Amuli states that, "He who wants to be an Alim should cultivate a practical branch of learning. But he who would be a litterateur, let him delve into the entire range of learning" (Khudabaksh and Margoliouth, 1996).

The Prophet's injunctions to seek out knowledge influenced the masses to dedicate themselves to the pursuit of knowledge. The litterateur soon developed a hunger for the practical and the systematic. Soon there would be four types of schools: the primary schools, the reader's school which mainly taught Arabic language and Quran recitation, the Hadith schools and medical schools (Al Hassani, 2007). Gradually, the curricula of the schools evolved to include philosophy, history and geography that came out of 'litterateur's science' and became independent subjects, and unlike the past, this time these subjects also developed their own method of enquiry and style. In the 8th century the Umayyad Khalid son of Yazid bin Muawiah gave up the throne to study chemistry (Al Hassani, 2007).

With academic progress, Jurisprudence was separated from Religious Studies. This new science attracted a large number of students who wanted to earn their livelihood as a jurist, judge or teacher. Bright students could master enough of Jurisprudence in two years to get a job. On the other hand studying the Traditions or the exegesis of the Quran was long and onerous job and took an entire lifetime. Tradition and Tafsir was more attractive to the students who wanted a life of dedication and research.

The other product of the literature's learning was the clerk who, one day, would become supreme in the royal courts. The Umayyads did not have any Wazir or Prime Minister. They had powerful 'clerks' who carried out the executive orders. Under the Abbasids the 'Chief Clerk' emerged as the Prime Minister (Wazir) and became more powerful then the Generals and other nobilities.

As schools developed out of mosques so did universities and libraries. In fact, *Jamiah*, meaning university, is linguistically the feminine of *Jami*, which means a large mosque. In the Arabic/Muslim context the place of high learning is tied to religion. Three examples of such mosque-universities is the Al Azhar University of Cairo, Al Qarawiyin of Fez in Morocco and University of Sankore in Timbuktu in Africa. Al Azhar which is still existing as a full fledged university had the famed Physicist of the 10th century Ibn Haitham as one of the Alumni and the great sociologist and historian of the 14th century Ibn Khaldun as a teacher. Al Qarawiyin, one of the first natural science universities in history was established by a rich lady of Fez named Fatima Al Fahri. The Sankore University was also funded by a wealthy Mandika lady and constituted of a number of institutes. By the 12th century it had 25 thousand students and taught diverse subjects like Islamic studies, medicine and surgery, law, literature, astronomy, physics, chemistry, philosophy, geography, history, etc. It became the intellectual centre of Mali, Ghana and Songhay. The universities also offered oratorical and poetical competitions and apprentice classes in farming, fishing, construction, tailoring, shoemaking, navigation, etc. (Al Hassani, 2007).

With the huge development of schools and universities, the demand for books was correspondingly high. Besides libraries in the universities there were mosque libraries and private libraries. Libraries cropped up in every mosque of any importance and were called *Dar Al Kutub* or the House of Books. The general public were allowed to borrow books from these libraries.

Besides the Mosques, the nobilities and general public also took pride in private collections. Stories of book lovers of the 9th century are still quite famous. Among the well known book lovers are the philosopher and scholar of 8th century named Al Jahiz, a court aristocrat named Fath ibn Khaqan, and a *Qadi* named Ismail ibn Ishaq. Al Jahiz studied in Baghdad and wrote 200 books in fifty years including the seven volume *Book on Animals* which included discussion of social organisation of ants and communications between animals. He loved books and read every book that came his way. At the age of 92, a pile of books in his library fell on him and he died a bibliophile's death. His quote on books became very famous: "The book is silent as long as you need silence, eloquent whenever you want discourse. He never interrupts you if you are engaged, but if you feel lonely he will be a good companion. He is a friend who never deceives or flatters you, and he is a companion who does not grow tired of you."

Ibn Khaqan had special sleeves made in his robes to carry books, so that he could read them whenever he had free time. Ismail ibn Ishaq was famous as an avid reader of all kinds of book – theological, philosophical or literature. Historian Edward Gibbon tells the tale of a book lover who refused the invitation of the Sultan of Bukhara as he could not leave his books behind. It would take 400 camels to carry his books (Al Hassani, 2007). Even a Court Marshall in Baghdad left behind, in 924, books worth 2000 dirham. Sultan Adud-ud-Dawlah had a separate building for his library with books from every branch of learning, categorised in shelves.

By the 10th century, all the three great rulers of the Islamic world – Spain, Egypt and Baghdad – were lover of books. Al Hakam of Spain had his agents scoure the East for any new books they could acquire. There were 200,000 volumes in his library (Khudabaksh and Margoliouth, 1996).

The Verdant Verses

As science and philosophy developed in the hands of Muslims, poetry also found succour in all Muslims domains. The Rashidun Caliphs, especially Ali and Abu Bakr, were poets of very high calibre. As the Umayyads established their empire, Arabic became the international language and soon Arabic poetry was being written from Spain to India in sweeping verses of great emotions and beauty about the rulers and warriors as well as about nature and landscape. Various types of poetry were written and new genres like the Ghazal were introduced. Umar bin Abi Rabia and the female poet Al Khansa spun their verses in this era. In the early Abbassid period, poetry further diversified under the influence of the Sufis. Many poets like Al Mutannabi and Abul Ala Al Maari flourished. During the Middle Ages the Muslims poets were writing in Persian verses as well. Historical stalwarts like Ferdowsi, Omar Khayyam, Rumi, Hafiz and Nizami penned their emotions during this era. And after that Muslim poets were writing poetry in many different languages and forms. The variety of poetry that the Muslims wrote and established had not been encountered before and would influence the Renaissance which led to the poetic brilliance of the European Romantic age. This influence would initiate from Andalusia. As early as the 10th century, Muslim Spain was a poetic seat of variegated verdant verses (WR2, 2009).

My Beloved Comes *Ibn Hazm, 11th century, Cordova*

You came to me just before the Christians rang their bells.
The half-moon was rising looking
    like an old man's eyebrow or a delicate instep.
And although it was still night, when you came,
A rainbow gleamed on the horizon,
Showing as many colours as a peacock's tail.

The Garden *Abd Allah ibn al-Simak 12th century, Granada*

The garden of green hillocks dresses up for visitors in the most beautiful colours
As if a young woman's dowry was spread out glittering with gold necklaces
Or as if someone had poured out censers of mush powder
    mixed with the purest aromatic oils.
    Birds trill on the branches like singing girls bending over their lutes

And water falls continuously like neck-chains of silver and pearls
These are splendours of such perfection
        they call to mind the beauty of absolute certainty
                the radiance of faith

Reading *Ibn 'Ammar, 11th century, Silves*

My eye frees what the page imprisons:
the white the white and the black the black.

White Skin *Ibn 'Abd Rabbihi, 10th century, Cordova*

I have never seen nor heard of such a thing
Her modesty turns pearl into carnelian
Her face is so clear that when you gaze on its perfections
You see your own face reflected

Grainfield *Ibn 'Iyad, 12th century, Central Andalusia*

Look at the ripe wheat bending before the wind
like squadrons of horsemen fleeing in defeat,
bleeding from the wounds of the poppies.

Blue River *Muhammad ibn Ghalib al-Rusafi 12th century, Ruzafa, Valencia*

The river of diaphanous waters
murmuring between its banks
would have you believe
it is a stream of pearls.
At midday tall trees
cover it with shadows
turning it the colour of metal.
So now you see it, blue,
wrapped in brocade,
like a warrior in armour
resting in the shade of his banner.

Apology *Ibrahim ibn Uthman, 12th Century, Cordova*

Don't cross me off as fickle
because a singing voice
has captured my heart.

One must be serious sometimes
and light-hearted at other times:

like wood from which come
both the singer's lute
and the warrior's bow.

Tide In The Guadalquivir *Ibn Safr al-Marini, 12th Century, Almera*

When the West Wind ripped the river's tunic
the river overflowed its banks
to pursue and take revenge;

but the doves laughed, and made fun
from a sheltering thicket,
and the river, shame-faced,
crawled back into his bed
to hide under its veil.

Written from Al-Zahra *Ibn Zaydun, 11th century Codova*

From al-Zahra I remember you with passion.
The horizon is clear, the earth's face serene

The breeze grows faint with the coming of dawn.
It seems to pity me and lingers, full of tenderness.

The meandering waterway with its silvery waters shows a sparkling smile.
It resembles a necklace unclasped and thrown aside.

A day like those delicious ones now gone by
when seizing the dream of destiny we were thieves of pleasure.

Today, alone, I distract myself with flowers that attract my eyes like magnets.
The wind roughhouses with them bending them over.

The blossoms are eyes.
They see my sleeplessness and weep for me;
their iridescent tears overflow staining the calyx.

In the bright sun, red buds light up the rose bushes
making the morning brighter still.

Fragrant breaths come from the pome of the waterlilies,
Sleepyheads with eyes half-opened by dawn.

Everything stirs up the memory of my passion for you
Still intact in my chest
Although my chest might seem too narrow to contain it.

Would God grant calm to my heart if it could cease to remember you
And refrain from flying to your side on wings trembling with desire?

If this passing breeze would consent to carry me along,
It would put down at your feet a man worn out by grief.

Oh, my most precious jewel, the most sublime,
The one preferred by my soul, as if lovers dealt in jewels!

In times gone by we demanded of each other payments of pure love
And were happy as colts running free in a pasture.

But now I am the only one who can boast of being loyal.
You left me
          and I stay here,
                    still sad, still loving you.

The Couplets of Jajals (Ghazals) and Jarchas of Muwashshahs written by the Spanish Muslims would directly influence the formation of Spanish genres. One of earliest example is the *Cantigas de Santa Maria* which are religious songs depicting Virgin Mary composed upon the order of Alfonso X, King of Castile and Aragon (Al Hassani, 2007). This was followed by the *Cantigas De Amigos* and *Villancicos* and would lead to the emergence of amazing dramatic plays of the 16th century.

Masters of the World

There have been two great nexuses of knowledge in history of the world. The first was the regional syncretisation of knowledge by the ancient Greeks. The other was the international syncretisation by the Umayyad and Abbasid Muslims. The Greek syncratised the knowledge of the Egyptians, Babylonians, and Persians. The Muslims did the same in a global scale and included knowledge from Greeks, Egyptians, Persians, Chinese and Indians.

Copies volumes would be needed to hold the names of the great masters of the centuries when the Muslims ushered in the golden era of the world. And for each one of these names a thousand names have been lost in the erosion of time. But an introduction to some of the masters would give an understanding to the quality of work done, width of the fields engaged in and the dedication behind it.

Abu Musa Jabir

The latinised name of Abu Musa Jabir Ibn Hayyan (721– 815) is Geber. He was also known as Al Harrani. His father, Hayyan Al Azdi, belonged to the Yemeni Azd tribe and was a pharmacist as well as a political activist. Though at one stage Jabir is said to have studied under the Umayyad prince Khaled Ibn Yazid, his father was a pro-Abbasid activist. Hayyan was sent to Khorasan to gather support for the Abbasid revolt. But, eventually, he was caught and executed. The family fled to Yemen, where Jabir studied the Quran, Mathematics and other subjects under Harbi Al Himyari, an Arab scholar. After the Abbasids took over power, Jabir went to Kufa where he passed most of his life. He practiced medicine and chemistry there and became the student of the celebrated Imam Jaafar Sadiq.

His patron was the Barmakid Wazir of Harun ar Rasheed. After the fall of the Barmakids he was placed under house arrest in Kufa. But he was allowed to spend his time in scholastic pursuit till he died in early 9th century. He studied astronomy, engineering, philosophy, pharmacy, medicine, physics but his main fame lies in Chemistry. Of the over a hundred important treatises he had written 22 were on chemistry. He introduced experimental methods to Alchemy, the word being derived from the Arab word 'Al Kimya', and changed it from a speculative science to modern chemistry. He is known as the Father of Chemistry.

He perfected the chemical processes and techniques of crystallisation, distillation, calcination, sublimation and evaporation. He developed the alembic, an apparatus used for distillation. Using the alembic and other apparatus he discovered new minerals, acids (nitric, hydrochloric, citric and tartaric) and compounds. His also worked on applied chemistry which includes development of steel, dyes, leather tanning, working with varnishes, paints and greases, lettering in gold, use of manganese dioxide in glass making, development of aqua regia to dissolve gold, etc.

He categorised substance into three types: metal substance, substance that can be ground to powder (non metals) and spirits (volatile). About sixty of his books were translated to Latin and a few to other European languages. The translations included *Kitab al-Zohra (The Book of Venus)*, Kitab *Al-Ahjar (*The *Book of Stones) and* Kitab *Al Kimya (The Book of Chemistry), Kitab Al Rahmah (The book of Mercy), Kitab Al Tajmi, (Book of Concentration),* etc.

Commenting on his works, George Sarton says, "We find in them remarkably sound views on method of chemical research. A theory on geological formation of metals". According to Max Mayerhof, "His influence may be traced throughout the whole historic course of European alchemy and chemistry." The Geber crater on the moon is named after him.

Al-Khawarizmi

Muhammad ibn Musa Al Khawarizmi was a mathematician, astronomer, geographer and astrologer. Not much is known of his early life except that he was born around 780 and his name suggests that his birthplace was Khawarizm which is now Khiva in Uzbekistan. He passed his life as a scholar in Caliph Mamun's Darul Hikmah (House of Wisdom), Baghdad. The scholars of the Dar had developed the basic mathematical foundation on which Al Khawarizmi developed his work.

Al Khawarizmi is known as the father of algebra. The term 'Algebra' was derived from the name of his book *Al kitab Al muktasar fi hisab* ***Al jabr*** *wal mugabal (The compendious book of calculation by completion and balancing).* This was the first book on the systematic solution of linear and quadratic equations. His next major work was on arithmetic. His book on this subject is named *Kitab fi isti'mal al-'adad al-hind (On the calculation with Hindu Numerals).* Both of these books were translated to Latin in 12th Century. *Frattati d'Arithmetica,* the Latin translation of *Kitab Al Jamawat Tafriq* edited by Bon Compagni in 1157 is still extant (Ahmad, 1984). Al Khawarizmi's Latinised name isAlgorithmi and from it came the term Algorithm.

His third major work was on Geography. Al Khawarizmi became a supervisor in the Caliph Mamun's project to draft a map of the world. He supervised the work of 70 geographers and also assisted in determining the circumference of the world. His book on this subject was *Kitab Surat al Ard* (*Book on the face of the earth).* It contained longitude and latitude coordinates of cities and geographical features like mountains, seas, islands and rivers. It also consisted of weather zones formed by longitudes and latitudes. One of the resources used in this project was Ptolemy's Geography.

His work on astronomy is the *Zij Al sidhind* or *Astronomical tables* that comprises of 37 chapters of astronomical and calendar calculations. His other works includes books on mechanical devices such as the astrolabe and the sundial. In the *Legacy of Islam*, Carra De Vaux writes, "In the 18th century Leonardo Fibonacci of Pisa, an algebraist of considerable importance says that he owes a great deal to the Arabs. He travelled to Egypt, Syria, Greece and Sicily and learned the Arabic method there, recognised it to be superior to the method of Pythagoras, and composed a *Liber Abaci,* in 15 chapters, the rest of which deals with algebraic calculations. Leonardo enumerates the six cases of quadratic equations just as Al Khawarizmi."

The importance of the translation of Khawarizmi's Algebra by Robert Chester can "hardly be exaggerated, because it marked the beginning of European Algebra" (Ahmad, 1984). A crater on the far side of the moon is named after Al Khawarizmi.

Al Kindi

Abu Yusuf Yaqub ibn Ishaq known as Al Kindi was born in Basra in the 801. He is known as Alkindus in the West. Of his time, he was the dominant philosopher, scientist, and encyclopedist – a versatile genius.

As a natural philosopher one of his focuses was on intelligence and soul. His doctrine states that an externally active cause, the Divine Intelligence, is the cause of the existence of the world. Both immortality and freedom could only be acquired in the world of intelligence. Attainment of these two leads to the development of intellect to such an extent that one can acquire true knowledge of God and Universe. The Latin translation of his philosophical work *De Intellectu* contains what is known as the first doctrine of Intellect.

He translated and wrote commentaries on a number of philosophical works of Aristotle. His theory on the Universe was similar to that of Aristotle (Ahmad, 1984).
Al Kindi was the earliest physicist contributing in specific gravity, refection of light, optics, etc. Two of his great works are *De Aspectibus* – a treatise on geometrical and physiological optics which influenced Roger Bacon and Wirelo, and *De Medicinarum Compositarun Gradibus* in which posology was attempted to be established mathematically.

Phillip Hitti comments, "His principal work on geometrical and physiological optics based on the optics of Euclid and Theon, was widely used both in the East and West until superseded by the greater work of Ibn Haitham."

He was the first to explain the real cause of the blue colour of the sky by light refraction. He applied mathematics to physics and optics. He also endeavoured to ascertain the laws that govern the fall of bodies.

Al Kindi was a great original musical theorist. According to George Sarton, he is the earliest writer of music whose work has come down to us. His works contain notation for the determination of the pitch. Out of his seven treatises on music, three have been preserved up to the present time, namely, "*The Essential of Knowledge in Music*," "*On the Melodies*" and "*The Essential Book on the Composition of Melodies*." Al Kindi described rhythm (iqa) as constituent part of Arabian music. "Measured song or mensural music must, therefore, have been known to the Muslims centuries before it was introduced in Europe," Phillip Hitti states.

Al Kindi also contributed in meteorology, astronomy, astrology, mathematics and medicine. Only a few of his contributions in original Arabic have survived. But, a larger number of Latin translations by Gerard of Cremona are still extant. Gerolamo Cardano (d 1575), the famous renaissance physician, mathematician and inquirer of truth from Pisa, includes Al Kindi in the twelve most eminent philosophers for subtlety and wisdom (Ahmad, 1984)

Al Razi

Abu Bakr Muhammad ibn Zakariya Razi (Latinised to Rhazes) was born in Rayy, Persia (865 – 925). He was a physician, chemist and philosopher. He has made lasting contributions to these branches of science and philosophy recorded in over 184 books and articles.

There are various reports that as a young man Razi was a Jeweller, a money changer or a lute player. He may have been all three. He studied Alchemy, but around the age of thirty the experiments started to affect his eyes. He gave up Alchemy and went in search for physicians for a cure. They appeared to have treated him and also led him to the study of medicine and philosophy. He studied day and night and soon surpassed his masters. He became famous and was appointed Director of the hospital of Rayy. During the reign of Caliph Muktafi he moved to Baghdad and was the Chief Director of a hospital. After Muktafi's death he returned to Rayy and taught students.

When he was not with patients or students he was writing most of the time. He did not charge the poor patients for treatment. He was very ethical in his practice and wrote, "The doctor's aim is to do good to enemies and friends. My profession forbids harm as it is for the benefit and welfare of humanity. God requires that physicians do not practice shameful remedies."

He became blind at old age. There is an anecdote that he refused to be treated for cataract as he "had seen so much and was tired of the world," and the treatment would be useless as the "hour of death was approaching."

He is considered to be the Father of Paediatrics and wrote *The Diseases of Children* (Ahmad, 1984), the first book to deal with paediatrics as an independent field of medicine. He was a pioneer of experimental medicine, neurosurgery and ophthalmology. Razi wrote the first 'home' medical manual for the general public. On general health his advice was, "Your first thought should be to enhance your natural vitality."

He was the first physician ever to write articles on allergy and immunology. He also discussed seasonal 'rhinitis' (allergic asthma or hay fever). Razi was the first to understand that fever or temperature is a natural defence mechanism of the body in fighting a disease. He was also the first to work with and describe smallpox. "His writings on smallpox and measles show originality and accuracy, and his essay on infectious diseases was the first scientific treatise on the subject." – Quoted from the Bulletin of the World Health Organization (May 1970)

In Chemistry, Razi made an in-depth study of sulphuric acid. Razi, Al Kindi and Jabir were among the first to distil ethanol and refine its use in medicine. He developed several chemical instruments that are still used. At an early stage he had studied the transmutation of metal in Alchemy. As his fame increased people started to believe that he had found the secret of the Philosopher's Stone and was able to turn base metals like iron to gold. A General asked him whether that was the reason why he treated poor patients without a fee. Razi's reply was, "I understand Alchemy and have worked on it for some time. But still don't know how to transmute copper to gold. Despite ancient research there is yet no answer. I very much doubt if it is at all possible."

Razi was trying to understand if elements could be transformed to other elements. It could not be in the domain of chemical synthesis. But it was queries like this by the Muslim scientists that would finally lead into investigation, in the modern age, of how elements are formed by nucleo-synthesis in the stars.

He was a rationalist and dismissed the idea of potions and symbols in medical science. He refuted some of Galen's work including the theory that the body consists of four humours (fluids) and diseases were caused by imbalance of these fluids. He dismissed Aristotle's theory that all substances are compounds of the four elements – earth, fire, water and air. At some stage of his life he, like some rationalists of all ages, was also a critic of dogmatic religion and is said to have stated "How can one think philosophically while attending to old wives' tales based on contradictions, which contains inflexibility, ignorance, and dogmatism?"

His monumental work was the *Al Hawi* or *the Virtuous life*. It contains observations of diseases and therapies as well as references from Arabic, Greek, Indian and Persian sources and at the end is his own interpretation and comments. For this work alone many consider him one of the greatest medical scientists of all times. It was translated to Latin in the 13th century by the Sicilian Jewish physician Faraj Ibn Salim under the orders of Charles I, King of Sicily, and was named the *Continents*. "Its influence on European medicine was very considerable." Says Max Mayerhof. His outstanding work on small pox and measles is *Al Judar Wal Hasba* is the earliest, authentic and original work on the subject. It was translated into Latin and other European languages and printed in Venice in 1489, in Brussels in 1549, in London in 1747 and in Gottingen in 1781 being published more then forty times (Ahmad, 1984). Razi along with Ibn Sina remained up to the 17th century the indisputable authority on medicine. Michael E. Flannery's comment on Razi was "Indeed, Pharmacy can trace much of its historical foundations to the singular achievements of this ninth-century Persian scholar."

Ferdowsi

Ferdowsi's full name was Hakim Abul Quasem Ferdowsi Tusi (935–1020). He was a great Persian poet and the author of the *Shahnama* (Epic of the Kings) which is one of the greatest epic ever written, if not the greatest, and is the national epic of Iran. He devoted 35 years of his life to this masterpiece. The *Shahnama* narrates the mythical and historical past of Persia (Aeran Veage of the Gathas) from the creation of the world up till the Islamic conquest of Persia in the 7th century.

The *Shahnama* is a superb and poetical recast of the massive Persian prose historiography. The work is divided into three successive parts: the mythical, heroic, and historical ages. It also has praise for his patron and the references to the source materials. The mythical part is the shortest, with about 2100 verses. It gives an account of formation of the world and creation of the first man as was believed by the Sassanians. The age of the heroes consists of about two third of the Shahnama. The rest comprises the historical age. Ferdowsi mentions the Achaemenids, Sekander (Alexander) and the Sassanids in resplendent poetry – rich, lavish and moving.

Ferdowsi revived and regenerated the Persian language and cultural traditions. Though written a thousand years ago, Ferdowsi had produced such a profound language that there has not been any significant change in the language over this period. Many modern Iranians see him as the father of the modern Persian language.

He started his work under the patronship of the Samanid Dynasty. But before he finished the epic the Samanid Dynasty fell to the Ghaznavids. He continued to work under the new patrons. The final edition of the Shahnama contained some sixty thousand distiches (couplets). Wrapped in seven massive volumes he took it to the court of Sultan Mahmud of Ghazni. But, it is said, the Sultan not finding himself included as a protagonist in the book's acknowledgment was irate. Instead of giving Ferdowsi the agreed 60,000 gold dinar, he offered 20,000 silver dirham.

The poet, angry and sad, rejected the offer and returned to Tus. Finally the Sultan, coming to understand the greatness of the work, sent the money to Ferdowsi. But Ferdowsi died just before the money reached him. His daughter, in respect to her esteemed father, refused to accept the money. The money was used to build a beautiful stone caravanserai nearby, on the road from Merv to Tus, for travellers to rest and trade and tell stories. Ferdowsi was buried at the yard of his own home, where his mausoleum now lies. Ferdowsi was aware of the greatness of his work and thus wrote:

I've journeyed to the end of this great epic
All the lands will talk of me.
I shall not die, for the seeds I've sown
Will keep my name from the grave,
All men of sense and wisdom will acclaim
When I am gone, my praise and my fame.

Regarding the Shahnama Saint-Beuve said "If we could realise that great works such as the Shahnama exists in the world, we would not become so much proud of our own works in such a silly manner"

Several copies of the great work remain intact. Though two of the most famous, the *Houghton Shahnama* and the *Great Mongol Shahnama*, were broken up into sheets to be sold separately in the 20th century. A single sheet of the *Houghton Shahnama* was bought by the Aga Khan Museum for Euros 904,000 in 2006. The *Bayasanghori Shahnama* is included in UNESCO's *Memory of the World Register* of cultural heritage items.

Abul Wafa Busjani

Abul Wafa (940-998) was the first recognised applied scientist. He was brought up during the period when a new dynasty was being established over Persia. The high point of the Buwahid dynasty was the reign of Adud Ad Dawlah from 949 to 983. Adud was a great patron of science and the arts and supported a number of scientists. Abul Wafa moved to his court in Baghdad in 959 and joined other distinguished scientist in Baghdad like Al Quhi and Al Sijzi who worked there as well.

Some time between 961 and 976 he wrote *Kitab fi ma yahtaj ilayh al-kuttab wa'l-ummal min 'ilm al-hisab* (*Applied mathematics for scribes and businessmen*). This was an applied mathematics book, the first of its kind. Abul Wafa, though an expert mathematician, did not use the numerals. All the numbers were written in words and all calculations had already been worked out to make it easy for professionals who did not have mathematical background. In the preface to this book Abul Wafa wrote that it "... comprises all that an experienced or novice, subordinate or supervisor in arithmetic needs to know," and was for "the art of civil servants, the employment of land taxes and all kinds of business needed in administrations, proportions, multiplication, division, measurements, land taxes, distribution, exchange and all other practices used by various categories of men for doing business and which are useful to them in their daily life."

The work was divided into seven parts, each part containing seven chapters with topics on:

- Ratio and fractions
- Multiplication and division and negative number
- Area of figures, volume of solids and distances calculation
- Different taxes and calculations
- Exchange and shares between types of crops, and problems relating to their value and exchange
- Miscellaneous topics like the granting and withholding of permits for ships on the river, merchants on the roads, payment of soldiers, units of money
- Miscellaneous business topics

Another text written by Abul Wafa for applied use was on applied geometric constructions for a craftsman. The book was in thirteen chapters and delved into the design and testing of drafting instruments and various geometric solutions. He solved many of the problems, using ruler and compass constructions where possible, which was in itself an innovation.

He investigated into the orbit of the Moon and wrote the *Theories of the Moon*. Tycho Brahe, the Danish Renaissance astronomer, is credited with rediscovering the variations of the moon that was initially discovered by Abul Wafa (Al Hassani, 2007). In the calculations of the book he became the first to use the Tan trigonometry function. He devised a new method of calculating sine tables and compiled tables of Sines and Tangents at 15' intervals. He also introduced the Sec and Cosec in trigonometry and studied the interrelations between the six trigonometric lines associated with an arc. Among his other works is the *Kitab al-Kamil* (Complete book), a simplified version of Ptolemy's *Almagest.* His trigonometric tables were accurate to 8 decimal places while Ptolemy's were only accurate to 3 places. The observational data in it have been used by many later astronomers. Abul Wafa translated and wrote commentaries on the works of Euclid, Diophantus and Al Khawarizmi. These commentaries have since been lost. A crater in the Moon has been named after him.

Ibn Al Haitham

Abu Ali Hasan ibn Al Haitham is one of the most outstanding optician, mathematician and physiologist. He was born in Basra in 965. He was commissioned by Fatimid Caliph Al Hakim to determine a method to control the annual flooding of the Nile. Al Haitham, realising the task was insurmountable, feigned madness till the death of Al Hakim.

Like many of the old masters, Al Haitham was a versatile genius but his main contribution lies in Optics. He made monumental discoveries like the one which positions the retina as the seat of vision. Contrarily, the Greeks Ptolemy and Euclid had assumed that to see something the eye sends out visual rays to the object of vision. John William Draper in *History of the Intellectual Development of Europe* observes that, "He was the first to correct the Greek misconception as to the nature of the vision showing that the rays of light come from the external objects to the eyes." Haitham also determined the height of the atmosphere, its lessening density with height, and the reflection and curvilinear refraction of light through it.

His *Kitab Al Manazir* (Book on Optics) became very influential. Max Meyerhof admits, "Roger Bacon and all mediaeval writers on optics – notably the Pol Witelo or Vitello, base their optical works largely on Alhazens's *Opticae Thesaurus*. His work also influenced Leonardo da Vinci and John Kepler. The latter modestly entitle his fundamental work on dioptics *Ad Vitellionem Paralipomena* (Frankfurt 1604)" (Ahmad, 2007). A crater in the moon has been named after Al Haitham (Alhazen).

Abu Raihan Al Biruni

Al Biruni (973 – 1048) was born in Khawarizm (Khiva, Uzbekistan) and was a devout Muslim and follower of the Sunni Asharite School. He first worked with Abu Nasr Mansur who was a Prince of the ruling family of Khawarizm. Mansur was a student of Abul Wafa and the discoverer of the 'law of sine' in trigonometry. When the ruling family was overthrown Al Biruni fled at the outbreak of the civil war. But, apparently, returned and wrote, "After I had barely settled down for a few years, I was permitted by the Lord of Time to go back home. I was compelled to participate in worldly affairs, which excited the envy of fools, but which made the wise pity me."

He never had a pen out of his hand, nor were his eyes off a book and his thoughts were always directed towards his studies (Ahmad, 1984). He finally ended up working for the Ghaznavid (Afghanistani) rulers who had won over Khawarizm. He accompanied Sultan Mahmud of Ghazni, a patron of learning, in his campaigns to India. There he studied the

Indian civilisation and their religions for years and wrote the *Tarikh Al Hind (The Chronicles of India)* which a few centuries later was translated to Latin and came to be known as the *Indica*. In this book he discussed the theories of scientists Aryabhata, Brahmagupta and Varahamihira. He critically studied contemporary Indian sciences and philosophies and accepted or refused those based on reason. Al Biruni believed that Hinduism was ultimately a monotheistic faith like Islam. He wrote that the Hindus also believe God to be one, eternal, without beginning and end and acting on free-will and that "the Hindus, no less than the Greeks, have philosophers who are believers in monotheism."

Biruni wrote nearly 150 books on various subjects:

- Astronomy
- Earth Sciences: meteorology, mineralogy, gems, geography, geology, geodesy and mapping theory,
- Mathematics: arithmetic, geometry and trigonometry
- Physics: mechanics, static, dynamic and time measurement
- Medicine and pharmacology
- Social science: History and chronology, comparative religion, anthropology
- Other miscellaneous topics.

His extensive astronomical encyclopedia *Kitab al-Qanun al-Masudi* (Latinized as *Canon Masudicus*) was named after his mentor Sultan Masud son of Sultan Mahmud. He drew a line between Astronomy and Astrology and rejected Astrology as a science. He introduced a number of theories and techniques in Astronomy.

Abu Said Al Sijzi, a contemporary of Biruni, proposed the heliocentric movement of the Earth around the Sun. Al Biruni's calculation agreed with the rotation of the earth on its own axis. In the 13th century, Qutb al-Din discussed heliocentrism in his *The Limit of Accomplishment concerning Knowledge of the Heavens.* In the 16th century, Copernicus presented a fully predictive mathematical model of a heliocentric system. It was later elaborated by Kepler and defended by Galileo.

Al Biruni proposed that our galaxy comprised of numerous nebulous stars. He corrected Ptolemy's calculation of the distance between earth and moon. He invented a number of astronomical instruments and wrote the first treatise on the planisphere and the orthographical astrolabe. Other instruments he invented were the hodometer, and the first mechanical lunisolar calendar computer which employed a gear train and eight gear-wheels.

On his contribution to geodesy and geography, John J. O'Connor and Edmund F. Robertson wrote in the *MacTutor History of Mathematics archive*: "He introduced techniques to measure the earth and distances on it using triangulation. He found the radius of the earth to be 6339.6 km, a value not obtained in the West until the 16th century. His *Masudic canon* contains a table giving the coordinates of six hundred places, almost all of which he had direct knowledge."

In Physics, he defined gravity as "The attraction of all things towards the centre of the earth." According to him, gravity was present within the heavenly bodies and celestial spheres. He criticised Aristotle's views of the bodies not having any levity or gravity and of circular motion being an innate property of the heavenly bodies. He was the first to apply experimental scientific methods to mechanics particularly for the determination of specific weights. He worked in fields of statics and dynamics and was the first to realise that acceleration is connected with non-uniform motion, which in the 17th century became part of Newton's second law of motion.

Al Biruni was active in social sciences as well. He wrote detailed comparative studies on the anthropology of peoples, religions and cultures in the Middle East, Mediterranean and South Asia. He is considered the first anthropologist and was also a pioneer of experimental psychology. He discovered the concept of 'reaction time', "Not only is every sensation attended by a corresponding change localised in the sense-organ, which demands a certain time, but also, between the stimulation of the organ and consciousness of the perception an interval of time must elapse, corresponding to the transmission of stimulus for some distance along the nerves."

In his books *Kitab fi Tahqiq ma li'l-Hind* (*Researches on India*) and *The Chronology of the Ancient Nations*, he was the first to distinguish between the historical method and the scientific method. Al Biruni was also the pioneer of Comparative Religion. Arthur Jeffery, Protestant Australian professor of Semitic languages, states, "It is rare until modern times to find so fair and unprejudiced a statement of the views of other religions, so earnest an attempt to study them in the best sources, and such care to find a method which for this branch of study would be both rigorous and just."

Many consider *Asrar Al Baqiya* as his most brilliant work. It is a chronology of ancient nations containing minute and accurate information of geographical and historical information. It contained accurate longitude and latitude and information of calendars and eras of ancient civilisation. He also discussed the rotation of the earth on its axis and geologic explanation of spring formation. Al Biruni was the first to suggest that the Indus Valley was a basin filled with alluvial soil (Ahmad, 1984).

Ibn Sina

Abu Ali Al Husain ibn Abd Allah ibn Sina or Avicenna (980-1037) was another great multifaceted talent. He was a renowned physician, Islamic philosopher, encyclopedists, mathematician and astronomer. Born in Bukhara in 981 he was the son of a mid-level government official of the Samanid Dynasty. The society to which he belonged was academically enlightened and his home was a meeting place for learned men, his father being his first teacher.

By the age of ten, Ibn Sina had memorized the Quran and studied Arabic poetry. He studied Islamic and Greek philosophy, metaphysics and learned logic from a renowned philosopher Abu Abdallah Natili. He had also begun to study medicine at a relatively young age from various teachers and by the age of sixteen he had mastered medicine.

The Samanid ruler Nuh Ibn Mansur had been ill for some time and despite the attempts by his physicians his conditions did not improve. Ibn Sina was able to successfully treat him. This earned him great admiration and the favour of the Samanids. He was given free access to the royal library. Access to such a uniquely stocked library immensely facilitated his development in a wide range of subjects. Henceforth, Ibn Sina was self-educated.

By the age of twenty-one, he mastered formal learning in a formidable array of subjects. Ibn Sina, being contemporary to Al Biruni, lived through the same tumultuous periods when Persian dynasties were trying to gain political ascendency over the Abbasid Caliphate in Baghdad while new Turk blood was replacing Persian domination in Central Asia. Due to this political instability and fall of dynasties he had to wander from town to town working as a physician, teacher or administrator. But at night he would hold scientific and philosophical discourses with students that would gather round him.

Next he served, taught and carried out research in the court of Khawarizm Shah in Jurjan where the famous meeting between him and his great contemporary Raihan Al Biruni took place. Then he went to Hamadan to serve as the court physician of the Buwahid. There he completed two of his most famous books, the *Kitab Al Shifa (The Book of healing)* and *Al-Qanun fi al-Tibb (The Canon of Medicine)*. Ibn Sina spent the last 14 years of his life in relative peace in the court of the ruler Ala Ad-Daulah in Isfahan. He died in June 1037 while on a military campaign with Ala Ad-Daulah, leaving behind his vast findings and knowledge. Of the 450 treatises he wrote 240 are still extant.

The Kitab al-Shifa consists of a monumental encyclopedia embodying a vast field of knowledge containing philosophy, science and metaphysics. The science section of the *Shifa* also contains a very important chapter on Earth Sciences / Geology. This chapter contains six sections: on the origin of mountains, the affect of mountains in cloud formation, sources of water, physical geography / geology of earth terrain, and the origin of earthquakes. In his well known treatise *De Conglutiatione Lapidum* he discusses the formation of mountains and earth crust. He also forwards the scientific cause of earthquakes. Jamil Ahmad (1984) considers him the Father of Geology. Many of such discoveries are now attributed to James Hutton, the 18th century earth scientist, and other later scientists.

The Mathematics volume of the *Shifa* was divided into four branches -arithmetic, geometry, astronomy and music. Each of these branches had their own subdivisions: arithmetic - algebra, Indian addition, and subtraction. Geometry - geodesy, kinematics, statistics, hydrostatics, and optics. Astronomy - subdivided into astronomical and geographical tables and included the calendar. In the 12th century *Shifa* was translated to Latin and was named *Sanatio*.

Besides *Shifa* his well-known philosophical treatises are *al-Najat* and *Isharat.* The *Kitab al-Isharat wa at-Tanbihat* (*Book of Directions and Remarks*) is his book on the mystic's spiritual journey starting from the development of faith to the reaching of the final stage that is the vision of God. Ibn Sina completed many works on philosophy, on the Arabic language and on the military campaigns that he participated in. He was a great rational Philosopher and tried to harmonise the abstract philosophical form with the Islamic religious faith. He reorganised and modified Aristotelian and Neo-Platonic concepts within the context of Islamic theology.

He also studied other disciplines of science. While conducting astronomical research, Ibn Sina observed Venus as a spot against the surface of the sun. He deduced that it was relatively closer to the earth than to the sun. In physics, his contribution comprised to the study of energy in different forms like heat, light, and mechanical, and such concepts as force, vacuum and infinity. He made the important observation that if the perception of light is due to the emission of some sort of particles by the luminous source, the speed of light must be finite. He propounded an interconnection between time and motion, and also made investigations on specific gravity and used an air thermometer. In the field of music and sound, his contribution was an improvement over Farabi's previous work and was far ahead of knowledge prevailing elsewhere on the subject. He concluded that there were consonances that the human ear is unable to distinguish. In the field of chemistry, he did not believe in the possibility of chemical transmutation as, in his opinion, the metals differed in a fundamental sense. These views were radically opposed to those prevailing previous to his time. He wrote treatises on minerals which became one of the main sources of mineralogy for the 13th century European encyclopedists.

His most famous book is the huge medical encyclopedia of medicine, *Al-Qanun fi al-Tibb* (The Canon of Medicine). It consisted of the entire medical knowledge available from ancient time to his own. Added to the historical knowledge was the vast, very modern and practical contribution of Ibn Sina himself. For example, he was the first scientist to graphically describe, in minute detail, the different parts of the eye. He was the first to describe meningitis, and the first to suggest the treatment for lachrymal fistula by the use of a medical probe into the throat canal. He set up the basic standard of how to test new medicines which remains more of less the same today. In addition to the pharmacological methods, *Al-Qanun* described 760 drugs and became the most authentic medical text of the era.

Its systematic approach and its intrinsic value superseded the works of Razi, Ali ibn Abbas Maliki and Galen. It was translated into Latin by Gerard of Cremona in the 12th century and became the textbook in European medical schools. From then until the 17th century, *Al-Qanun* served as the chief guide and text for medical science in the West. Dr. W. Osler, in *Evolution of Modern Science,* wrote, "The Qanun has remained a medical bible for a longer period than any other work". From 1470 to 1500 it was reissued 16 times with 15 editions in Latin and one in Hebrew. It was reissued more than 20 times during the 16th century in various European languages (Ahmad, 1984). It is the most studied medical book ever written. In 1930, Cameron Gruner partly translated *Al-Qanun* into English under the title *A Treatise on the Canons of Avicenna*. Sir Jadu Nath Sircar, prominent Indian historian, paying eloquent tribute to Ibn Sina stated that, "Avicenna was the greatest intellectual giant of the middle ages."

Portraits of Ibn Sina and Al Razi still adorn the Grand Hall of the Faculty of Medicine in the University of Paris. A crater in the moon has been named after him.

Nizam Al Mulk

Nizam al Mulk was the title of the Seljuk Wazir (Prime Minister) Abu Ali Al Hasan Al Tusi (1018 - 1092). He was the chief administrator of Khorasan under the Ghaznavids before becoming the Wazir for the Seljuk Sultans Alp Arsalan and Malik Shah.

Gibbon regarded him as 'one of the most illustrious ministers of the East.' Besides being an administrator extraordinaire he also was a great scholar and social scientist. He wrote the extensive treaties *Siyasat Nama* which means 'The book of Politics'. He also wrote a book titled *Dastur al-Wuzara*, written for his son Abolfath Fakhr-ul-Mulk which outlines princely education, manners and conduct.

Nizam Al Mulk established a large number of colleges of higher education and libraries throughout the country. The most famous were the Schools of Nizamia University which gained world renown. These schools, in many aspects, were to be the models of universities that were established in Europe.

After administering the affairs of Malik Shah for some thirty years Nizam Al Mulk was overthrown by his enemy the Chamberlain Taj Al Mulk due to the instigation of the Sultana (Queen) Turkhan Khatun. He was impeached after he had impetuously declared that his cap and ink-horn, the badges of his office, were connected by divine decree with the throne and diadem of the Sultan. In 1092 he is said to have been assassinated at an old age, near Nahavand of Persia, by a member of the Assassin sect who had approached him disguised as a dervish.

Nizam Al Mulk was buried in Isfahan in the grounds of a theological school, in the north of Ahmad Abad, which he had built. The mausoleum contains a number of other graves which are said to include those of Malik Shah and Turkhan Khatun.

There is legend in which Nizam Al Mulk was a contemporary student with young Omar Khayyam and Hasan bin Sabah in a Madrassa school. The three of them made a pact that if one should rise to prominence, he would help the other two to do likewise. Nizam Al Mulk became a Wazir and offered both of them positions of rank within the court. Omar refused the position but instead asked for the means to continue his studies indefinitely. Hasan accepted the appointment and became a royal official. But at a later stage he rebelled and was forced to flee after plotting to dispose Nizam. Then he went to Alamaut and established the sect of the Assassins.

Omar Khayyam

Omar Khayyam (1048 - 1131) was a poet, mathematician, philosopher, astronomer and physician who lived in Persia. Today he is best known for his poetry, the quatrains (*rubaiyaas*) in *Rubaiyat of Omar Khayyam.*

He was educated in Nishapur and then in Samarqand where he lived for most of his life. He refused opportunities proffered by the Nizam Al Mulk and led a calm life devoted to the quest of knowledge. He travelled to the great centres of learning of Samarqand, Bukhara, Balkh and Isfahan in order to further study and exchange views with the scholars there. He continued the mathematical work of his predecessors and ranks among the foremost in contributions to major fields of Algebra and Geometry. His book *Maqalat fial-Jabr wa al-Muqabila* (*Treatise on Demonstration of Problems of Algebra*) is a masterpiece in the development of Algebra. He also contributed immensely in the development of analytical geometry. His mathematical discoveries remained unmatched for centuries, up to the time of Descartes (1596-1650).

Sultan Malik Shah assigned him the task of determining an accurate solar calendar in a new observatory at Ray that was required for the annual revenue collections and other administrative purposes. Khayyam introduced the calendar which was named Al Tarikh al Jalali.

Khayyam's contributions to other fields of science included development of methods for the accurate determination of specific gravity. He also proposed a heliocentric theory well before Copernicus. Ten books and thirty monographs written by him have been identified, four are on mathematics, three on physics, three on metaphysics, one on algebra and one on geometry. But since the translation of Rubayyat of Omar Khayyam by Edward Fitzgerald in 1839 his fame as a mathematician has been eclipsed by his popularity as a poet. The book has become one of the most popular classics of world literature. It is a poem on love, mystery, and freedom of thought in 150 quatrains. The last three quatrains of Fitzgerald's fifth edition are as follows:

Ah Love! could you and I with Him conspire
To grasp this sorry Scheme of Things entire,
Would not we shatter it to bits—and then
Re-mould it nearer to the Heart's Desire!

Yon rising Moon that looks for us again—
How oft hereafter will she wax and wane;
How oft hereafter rising look for us
Through this same Garden—and for one in vain!

And when like her, oh Saki, you shall pass
Among the Guests Star-scatter'd on the Grass,
And in your joyous errand reach the spot
Where I made One—turn down an empty Glass!

Al Ghazzali

Abu Hamid Al Ghazzali (1058-1111) was one of the greatest minds of all times. He was one of the rare individuals who was absolutely versed in all forms of knowledge - Rational, Ulemaic and Sufi. He was contemporary to the celebrated Omar Khayyam and the renowned administrator and political scientist Nizam Al Mulk. He belonged to an enlightened family coming from, according to the most reliable sources, the village of Ghazala near Tus. At a very early age he studied the Quran, the Traditions and Jurisprudence and also came in contact with Sufi thoughts. He would become a foremost scholar in Islamic theology, philosophy, jurisprudence, cosmology, epistemology and psychology.

After studying Jurisprudence in Mazardaran in Persia he, a young man, was returning to Tus with his notes with a party. They were attacked by robbers who carried away all their property. Al Ghazzali, aghast at the thought of loosing his precious notes, went to the robbers and requested the leader for those to be returned.

The robber asked, "What are these notes?"
Al Ghazzali replied, "These are notes of lectures. These represent knowledge."
The robber returned his notes, laughed at him and said, "What kind of knowledge you claim this to be when it can be taken away from you?"

Back in Tus, Al Ghazzali memorised all his notes. During 1077 -78, he went to Nishapur to study in the school of Imam Al Haramain. There he studied theology, philosophy, logic, dialectics and natural science. He would engage in debate and successfully refute the arguments of fellow students. Soon he started to lecture and began to write. He realised that true knowledge was attained through self-seeking and soul-searching, not from parents or teachers. Al Ghazzali applied himself to the quest of knowledge and to understand the world and creation. Due to over application to his studies his health suffered. Inspite of that, Al Ghazzali remained a searcher of absolute truth and nothing less:

'Accept what you see and let hearsay alone.
The sun has risen, what need of Saturn?'

But observation was just the start of his contemplation. He is considered a pioneer in the philosophical methods of 'doubt and skepticism', He justified scepticism on the ground that, "One who does not doubt does not investigate. One who does not investigate does not perceive, and one who does not perceive remains in blind error." It would be only in the 17th century that Rene Descartes, a key figure in western epistemology, would deal with skepticism. Ghazzali wrote on occasionalism, which sought to understand the connection between the brain and actions of the body, that became very popular in 17 century Europe. He also worked with the causal theory and, according to him, cause-and-effect were two separate events one following the other like fire and burning. One caused the other, or was related to the other, only because God or God appointed intermediary, the angels, made it so happen or made it a law. The causal theory would later be studied by philosophical greats like David Hume of 18th century England.

Ghazzali maintained that scholars should pursue all form of knowledge, "For men are hostile to that of which they are ignorant."

He was moved by the Prophet's saying, "All child are born with the natural religious disposition. It is the parent that, then, makes it a Jew, a Christian or a Magian."

After the death of Imam Al Haramain, Al Ghazzali joined the scholar's circle of the great Wazir Nizam Al Mulk. He was appointed to the Chair of Theology in the Nizamia University. He soon became renowned for his knowledge and lectures. This was also the time that he wrote his early books. His fame spread not just in Baghdad but to distant lands. Chiefs and Potentates would ask for his legal decisions, based on Canon law, for governance. As his fame grew the students of his class increased. Three hundred of the most brilliant from all over the world attended his classes with the addition of one hundred more who were from the royal families.

But all this was not sufficient to extinguish the thirsting brilliant flame of his intellect. He had to investigate the ultimate truth. He found that all the knowledge – theology, philosophy and science - that he had acquired was not sufficient to answer the questions that kept on rising within him, what to accept and what not to. Soon he started to suffer from a crisis of epistemological skepticism. At the height of reputation and adoration he had a physical breakdown. After recovering he declared he was going on pilgrimage. His real aim was to go away from the busy world and understand knowledge through the gnosis of the Sufis and scholars. He had learned about divinity from scholarly Sufis but he now wanted in some form to 'experience' it. He was in practice an empiricist. He left money for the maintenance of his family and gave away the rest. He appointed his brother to the chair of the University and then left on the pure intellectual quest unrestrained by any wants, needs, or ego.

He went to Damascus in Syria and lived an ascetic life with his identity initially concealed. He went around cleaning the ablution area of the Mosque and lived in retreat and solitude, in his words, 'Practicing discipline and mortification, the cleansing of the soul, purification of the heart in recollection of God.'

Once he settled down to the new life he engaged his intellect to transfer his thoughts into tangible knowledge – books. At least eighty of his books are still extant and most of these were written during his wanderings and his fraternising with great scholars and learned Sufis. He would come out of the quest after deciding that Gnosis is superior to other philosophies.

Few students went to meet him after he was accidentally discovered. As they talked they found in him, in their words, an 'ocean inexhaustible'. He later wrote, 'After your ship has been wrecked, true happiness and things of real significance remains with you. And these consist of two things, the mind filled with peace and the heart, thus freed, filled with the knowledge of God.'

During this period he wrote the huge and famous multivolume compendium *Yahya Al Ulum Al Din* (*Revival of the Science of Religion*). It is a discourse that covers a variety of Islamic religious sciences which includes Jurisprudence, Theology and Sufism. It is one of the most widely read book over the last thousand years. The opus is divided into four volumes each containing ten parts.

The first volume *Rub Al-ibadat (Acts of worship)* deals with the knowledge and the requisites of religion: prayer, charity, purity, fasting, pilgrimage, recitation of the Quran, etc. The second volume *Rub Al-adatat (Norms of Daily Life)* concentrates mostly on man and society: the manners relating to eating, marriage, earning a living, friendship, etc. The third *Rub Al-muhlikat (The ways to Perdition*) and fourth *Rub Al-munjiyat (The ways to Salvation)* volumes deal with the inner life of the soul and discusses first the vices that must be overcome and the virtues that has to be achieved.

In the very beginning of the *Yahya*, Al Ghazzali places knowledge and learning at the top of all human pursuits. Al Ghazzali quotes from the Prophet that the superior rank held by pious learned man in relation to the simple worshipper is like the superior rank that the Prophet holds in relation to the best of men. He states verses from the Quran and numerous sayings of the Prophet exhorting knowledge.

He mentions that the Caliph Ali had said to a Companion "O you perfect of knowledge! Knowledge is better than wealth, for knowledge guards you whereas you guard wealth. Knowledge governs while wealth is governed. Wealth diminishes with spending but knowledge increases therewith."

"Learning is mankind's glory
The learned - beacons on the road to truth
The worth of a Man is his knowledge, nothing more
The fool is his incurable foe,
Knowledge is the prospect of immortality,
For man dies but wisdom lives forever."

Quote by Ali in *Yahya* of Al Ghazzali

By the time of Ghazzali, the Islamic Empire had spread vastly and it contained numerous people, cultures, philosophies, ideologies and sciences. The empires had then disintegrated and the people were at a loss as to which of the philosophies, ideologies and sciences to accept as Islamic and which one to be discarded. The brilliant mind of Ghazzali set to work, he experimented with all the above, one after another, purged the non-Islamic notions out of these, and brought them all – philosophy, Sufism, science, arts and commerce – under the standard of Islam. He came to be known as the *Proof of Islam*.

In *The Incoherence of the Philosophers*, Ghazzali challenged philosophical notions, many of which were Greek and Hellenistic, and brought in a divine element. He categorised the sciences like medicine into a praiseworthy group and those like astrology into a blameworthy group. His support for the study of anatomy and dissection was influential in the rise of anatomical science and dissections carried by the 12th century physician, parasitologist, pharmacist, surgeon and Islamic scholar Ibn Zuhur (Avenzoar) and 13th century polymath Ibn al-Nafis. (Ibn al-Nafis had mastered a incredibly wide range of subjects and was a physician, anatomist, physiologist, surgeon, psychologist, and ophthalmologist and is most famous for being the first physician to describe the circulatory system. He was Hafiz of Quran and Hadith scholar, a Shafii jurist, lawyer, theologian and Islamic philosopher. He was also a logician, novelist, science fiction writer, grammarian, and linguist).

One day, after two years in Damascus, Ghazzali went to a college and chanced to attend a lecture. The lecturer, without knowing of his presence, was quoting Ghazzali's works to the students. Ghazzali left without saying anything as he was afraid that this would breed pride in him which would hinder the path he had chosen. He started wandering and went to Jerusalem, the Hijaz, Hebron then to Cairo and Alexandria. In his wandering he met and held long discussions with different scholars. For some time, he settled in Egypt and taught there. Finally he returned to Baghdad. Hearing of his return the new Wazir Fakr Al Mulk Shuhada requested him to teach at the University again.

In his quest for knowledge Ghazzali had tried to understand the universe, the creation and its relation to the Creator – The Ulemaic universe. In its investigation he had employed rational knowledge, metaphysics and gnosis. He had rejected the Greek influenced metaphysics outright. He accepted the methods of Aristotelian natural sciences and logic but found it limited in scope. It was unable to answer all the epistemological questions. He thus placed it below Sufi gnosis which gave some answer to his quest.

While teaching, this time, he had to face much criticism and calumny from other scholars aimed at him and his ideas. The criticisms came from the rationalist who thought he had rejected them and the Ulema who thought that he had placed Sufism above Ulemaic rules. But, in fact, to Ghazzali Sufism was only a method of investigation into the Ulemaic Universe.

When Fakr Al Mulk was assassinated, Ghazzali retired to his home in Tus. At this time he wrote his autobiography *Al Munqidh min al-Dalal* (*Apologia pro vita sua / The deliverer from Error*). In it, Ghazzali recounts how his epistemological crisis was resolved by 'a flash of enlightenment that God cast into his breast'. He recognised the superiority of Gnosis to all other philosophies in this respect. He mentioned that the learnt knowledge to the way of God was not the same as its experience. And thus he had forsaken all to experience it. He had cut off all impediments that afflict the soul, "The strongest ties that fetter the soul are those of the creatures and love of position. The joy of exercising authority and control and of being superior to others, and of being their leader is the joy which in this world most prevail over the souls of the intellect."

He rejected any further invitations to teach rather he was very happy and content with his disciples in Tus, teaching them and propagating his ideas and knowledge till the time of his death. Ghazzali was buried besides the grave of Ferdowsi. When Ghazzali realised he was dying, he wrote some verses which are as follows:

Say to my friends, when they look upon me, dead
Weeping for me and mourning me in sorrow
Don't believe that the corpse you see is myself.
In the name of God, I tell you, it is not I.

I am a spirit, and this is nothing but flesh....
Until today I was dead, though living amongst you
Now I live in truth with the grave clothe discarded....

I give you now a message of good cheer
May God's peace and joy be yours for evermore.

He wrote and taught not only about philosophy and religion but also about psychology and science. In his works he deals with the concept of the self, concept of normalcy and localisation of functions in human brains. He also wrote down his observations of animals.

Regarding the resurfacing of the old pantheistic notions Ghazzali interceded that the apparent multiplicity represented the same Divine Unity. In his book *Mishkat Al Anwar*, he redefined and brought to culmination the hypothesis of Emanation of the Universe from God that the Neo-Platonic philosophers were trying to achieve. The whole book was based on a single verse, the 'Ayat an Nur' or 'Verse of Light' of the Quran renowned for its beauty and imagery:

'God is the Light of the heavens and the earth
The similitude of His Light is as if there were a niche
And within it a Lamp: the Lamp enclosed in Glass
The glass as it were a glittering star
Lit from a Blessed Tree
An Olive, neither of the East nor of the West
Whose oil is nigh luminous, though no fire has touched it
Light upon Light; God guides to His Light whom He will
And God strikes similitudes for men, and God has knowledge of everything.
[24,35]

Ghazzali had critics and detractors, some as famous as him. One of them was Abul Walid Ibn Rushd (Averroes) who was a great rationalist philosopher and the Qadi of Seville in Spain. He commented that Ghazzali's teachings were at times detrimental to the Sharia and other times to philosophy. Ibn Rushd accused Al Ghazzali of inconsistency in advocating the doctrine of emanation in the Mishkat al-Anwar. Abul Faraj Al Jawji, a traditionalist and preacher, commented that the Traditions Ghazzali used were not free from fault, "Very cheaply has Ghazzali traded Theology for Sufism."

As he had detractors so Ghazzali had followers. The Spanish philosopher Abu Bakr Ibn Tufayl said that Ibn Rushd had misinterpreted Ghazzali's *Mishkat* as it consisted of allusions and symbolic utterances. Abdul Quader Jilani who inspired the Quaderia Order of Sufis was influenced by him. Jilani maintained a balance between the *Sharia* of the Ulema and the *Tariqa* of the Sufi. The mystical psychology of Ibn Al Arabi, a Spanish mystic, and his theory of knowledge compounded with an 'inner eye' follows the theories of Ghazzali.

Many such luminaries were influenced by Ghazzali. The sphere of his influence did not remain restricted to the Muslim world. Mediaeval Jewish scholars read and discussed his books to a great extent. Many of his books were translated to Latin and Hebrew. Christians both in the East and the West came under his influence. Among them was Gregorius - Bishop of Guba, Lakaba and Aleppo - who, in the 13th century, quoted freely from Ghazzali in his books.

In the 12th century, with active support from Muslim scholars, Archbishop Raymond of Toledo established an entire school for translating the Muslim Arabic books to Latin. Among the books were those by Ghazzali. Christian scholasticism and mysticism derived significant conceptions from the Muslim writers. The Dominican friar Raymond Martin expressed under the authority of the Muslim writers including Ghazzali that the joy of the next world is spiritual and above sensual.

Saint Thomas Aquinas, who is considered the Catholic churches greatest theologian, in the 13th century, studied the books of Muslim writers and admitted his indebtedness. In his works St Thomas uses the arguments from Ghazzali's *Kimia Al Saada*, the theme from *Hikmat fi Makhliqat Allah* and *Yahya*. He incorporates Ghazzali's notion of vision, Divine grace, light of glory or *Nur Allah*, and even uses Ghazzali's very words 'The sun, though superlatively visible, cannot be seen by the bat, due to excessive light.'

Another renowned person who has admitted his indebtedness to Muslim thinkers and has quoted Ghazzali as one of his source is Dante Alighieri. He is considered the 'Father of the Italian language' and referred to as "the Supreme Poet" (*il Sommo Poeta*) of Italy and forms "the three crowns" along with Petrarch and Boccaccio. In his *Divine Comedy* the ascent through the seven heavens 'where the Blessed dwells' was influenced by literature about the Prophet's ascent to Heaven. even though he viewed the Prophet in a negative light. It was also Dante who introduced the word 'Assassin' into Latin in the same epic:

'Io stava come il frate che confessa
Lo perfido assassin...'

'like a friar who is confessing
the wicked assassin...'

A much later writer who had been influenced by Al Ghazzali was the French mystic Blaise Pascal (1623-1662). His knowledge of Al Ghazzali's teachings came to him through his study of the French edition of Raymond Martin's *Pugio Fidei*. Pascal's famous wager for and against belief in God contains teaching and arguments which are also to be found in

Al Ghazzali. Pascal held that to wager for the existence of God resulted, if it were true, in infinite gain, and if untrue, in no loss. Al Ghazzali had proposed the very same alternatives.

Fakruddin Razi

Fakruddin Razi, often confused with Al Razi, was born in the 12th century. Fakruddin was the first to define 'Physics' and was among the first physicist in the modern sense. He wrote many books of which *Sharh Uyun al-hikmah* (Commentary on Uyun al Hikmah) became very famous. It is divided into three parts – logic, physics and metaphysics. The physics (tabiiyyat) section includes topics like space, bodies, time, motion and meteorology. Another book *Mabahith al mashriqiyya fi ilm alilahiyyat wal tabiiyyat* (Eastern Studies in Metaphysics and Physics) also deals with physics. Eight hundred years ago, he proposed the notion of multiple Universes beyond the known Universe based on his Tafsir of the Quran. This theory has been reiterated by prominent Theoritical Physicists only recently.

Ibn Rushd

Abul Walid Muhammad Ibn Ahmad Ibn Rushd, known as Averroes in the West, was born in Cordoba, Spain in 1126. He was a master of philosophy, theology, law and jurisprudence, astronomy, mathematics, medicine, physics and geography.

He comes from a family of legal scholars belonging to Imam Malik's school. His father and grandfather were both chief judges (Qadi) of Cordoba under the Al Moravids. He was contemporary and a friend of Ibn Zohr (Avenzoar), a great physician. He became the Qadi of Seville in 1160 after which he served in the courts of Cordoba and Morocco. He held strict rationalistic views that conflicted with the orthodoxy.

He is considered one of the greatest philosophers of all time. According to his school of thought, Averroism, there is no conflict between Islam and philosophy. In *Fasal Al Maqal (The Decisive Treatise)* he claims analytical thinking as a prerequisite to the interpretation of the Quran. He was the proponent of reason and rationalism which would spread and influence all of West. He wrote the *Tahafut Al Tahafut* (Incoherence of the Incoherence) which was a critical refutation of Ghazzali's *Tahafut Al Falasifa* (Incoherence of the Philosophers). Ernest Renan in his work *Averoes et j'averroisme*, published in Paris in 1852, states, "There is nothing to prevent our supposing that ibn Rushd was a sincere believer in Islamism, especially when we consider how little irrational the supernatural element in the essential dogmas of this religion is, and how closely this religion approaches the purest Deism." (Ahmad, 1984).

Ibn Rushd toiled extensively with most of Aristotle's works and produced critical advanced commentaries in a Muslim context. He considered the rule of the Rashidun Caliphs as the model for the Republic in which the dreams of Plato was realised. He stated that intellect and human soul did not involve any intermediate state. This was a refutation of the Neo-Platonic and Ghazzalian emanation hypothesis.

He was a great scientist as well. In physics, he was among the first to define force and also worked with the theory of motion that was proposed by Ibn Bajjah (Also known as Avempace, whose musical theories would be very influential in the West). In Medicine, he wrote a medical encyclopedia *Kulliyat* (General Medicine). The Latin translation is known as *Colliget*. He wrote a commentary on Ibn Sina's *Canon* and supported the human dissection work that was being carried out by Ibn Zohr (Avenzoar). In Psychology, he divided intellect into Active intellect, Material intellect and Passive intellect. In astronomy, he criticised the Ptolemaic model of planetary motion and proposed an alternate model and was the first to study and describe sunspots.

From the 12th century Ibn Rushd's works were translated into Latin and his rationalistic thoughts were introduced to Europe which influenced the European thought to a great extent. Ibn Rushd's ideas were assimilated by many Christian scholars including Siger of Brabant and Thomas Aquinas. In the classic work *An Introduction to the Study of Science* George Sarton states that Ibn Rushd "deeply influenced Jewish philosophy through many translations and disciples. Jewish Averroism reached its zenith under Levi Ben Gershon in the first half of the fourteenth century, and it continues to prosper until the end of the fifteenth century. The Christian schoolmen were influenced as the Jewish, and in various ways."

The philosophy that most fashioned European thought and transformed it to the modern age was Averroism. From the end of the 12th century to the end of the 16th century Averroism remained the dominant school of thought in spite of negative reactions that it created first among the orthodox Muslims of Spain, then the Jewish Talmudist and finally among the Christian clergy. His writing ultimately became the prescribed studies of the University of Paris and other institution of higher learning and was translated into Latin, Hebrew, German and English. The Latin '*Editio Princeps*' of Averroes' commentaries were published 50 times in Venice alone. Ibn Rushd as 'Averroes' is mentioned in the Divine Comedy by Dante. He also appears in a short story by Jorge Luis Borges and in the novel Ulysses by James Joyce. The Asteroid 8318 in named 'Averroes' in his honour.

~~~

It can be summed that knowledge, as understood today, was fashioned by the Muslims. The Greeks had shone like brilliant supernovas but soon their works were lost and forgotten. The Greeks themselves had killed Socrates and caused the Master, Aristotle, to go into exile. It was the Muslims who rediscovered their works, and who were the first to really understand the works of Aristotle and others. It was the likes of Ghazzali, Ibn Rushd and Ibn Sinna who resurrected their works, expanded those works by books and commentaries and then presented those to the world who had forgotten them. The Muslims also gathered
~~~

knowledge from other regions, like India and China, and then produced new branches of science, social science and literature.

Books on a variety of distinct scientific and social science were pioneered and published by the Muslims. For example, the first books on politics, independent of religion, were written in the 8th century by Ibn Al Muqaffa. Over the centuries many political science books were written by luminaries like Abu Yusuf, Al Jahiz, Abu Nasr Farabi, Al Mawardi, Nizam ul Mulk, Fakr ud Din Razi, and others.

Some further examples in the scientific world are the works of Al Kindi who wrote 265 books and treatises on Physics. He wrote on matter, space, time, and motion. Al Khazini wrote *The Book of Balance and Wisdom* and discovered that the density of water increased nearer to the centre of the world. *The Book of Artifices* was written by three sons of Musa bin Shakir and contained over a hundred mechanical processes. A book on mechanics, *The Book on Knowledge and Mechanical Contrivances*, was written by Abul Faiz al Zazari. The *Historian's History* states that Newton owns more to Muslim scholars for his laws of gravity than to an apple falling from a tree.

Music and songs were patronised by the royal houses including the Umayyad, Abbasid, Ottomans and Moghuls. From the 9th century, the Muslims were researching and propounding books on theories of music. Some of these books are *The Essential of Knowledge on Music* and *On the Melodies* by Al Kindi, *Kitab al Musail* and *Kitab al Mausiq* by Hunayn bin Ishaq (9th Century), and *Kitab Mausiqal Kabir* by Al Farabi (10th Century). In *Kitab al Shifa* Ibn Sina deals with the healing properties of music (11th Century). Nasir ud Din Tusi wrote *Kitab fi Ilmi Mausiqi* and *Kanzul Tuhaf*. An encyclopedia of oriental music, *Kitab al Afghani* was written by Abul Faraj Al Afghani (12th Century). Various theories on music were expounded in the books *Book of Musical Modes* by Safi ud-Din Abdul Mumin and *The Extra Need* by Al Nuweri (13th Century).

There were numerous astronomers and observatories in the Muslim domains. The work in Darul Hikma alone is phenomenal. They worked on the obliquity of the ecliptic, the precession of the equinoxes and length of the solar year and compiled the most precise astronomical table known as 'Tables of Mamun' after the Caliph.

Architecture developed in all Muslims domains from the time of the Umayyad, who built the grand Al Waleed Umayyad Mosque of Damascus and Al Hambra in Spain, to the Moghul who built the Taj Mahal.

Reports of the contributions of Muslim scholars, their researches and inventions are re-emerging from the opaque political clouds of the past. Remarks being made by modern scholars and intellectuals attest to the great works carried out by the Muslims. Some of the examples are as follows:

In the 1927 book *Studies: Indian and Islamic* by Khuda Buksh the following comment of the French scholar Sedillot can be found, "What characterised this school of Baghdad from its inception was its scientific spirit. Proceeding from the known to the unknown, taking precise account of the heavenly phenomena; accepting nothing as true which was not confirmed by experience or established by experiment – such were the fundamental principles taught by the masters of the sciences."

Franz Rosenthal in *History of Muslim Historiography* states that it was the Muslims who achieved a definite advance beyond previous historical writing in the sociological understanding and systematisation of history. The development of modern historical writing gained speed and substance by utilising Muslim literature, from the 17th century onwards, this enabled the western historian to see a large section of the world through foreign eyes. The Muslim historiography shaped the present day historical thinking.

Gibbon in *Decline and Fall of Roman Empire* wrote that Chemistry owes its origin and improvement to the Muslim Saracens. They first invented and named the alembic for the purpose of distillation, analysed the substance of three kingdoms of nature, defined the distinction and affinities of alkalis and acids and converted the poisonous minerals into soft and salutary medicines.

According to A. H. Christie in *Legacy of Islam* not only did Muslim scholars transmit to posterity a large fund of ancient learning, but Muslim artisans also preserved, developed and spread abroad the traditional workshop practice of arts in the orient. Such arts had not previously penetrated Europe, or, if were known there in former times had perished during the Middle Ages.

George Sarton in *An Introduction to the History of Science* discusses the advancement of Muslims in Botany. From the numerous books written by the Muslims on botany, agriculture, types of plants and herbs with description properties, types of soil and manure, he states "Horticulture improvements constituted the finest legacies of Islam, and the gardens of Spain proclaim to this day one of the noblest virtues of her Muslim conquerors. The development of agriculture and horticulture were some of the glories of Muslim Spain."

Professor Phillips Hitti in *History of the Arabs* recognises that in creative use of drugs, the Muslim made remarkable advance. They established the first apothecary shop, they founded the earliest school of pharmacy and they produced the first pharmacopoeia.

Professor Alfred Guillaume - scholar of Oxford University, Professor of University of London and visiting professor in Princeton University in New Jersey – states that, "We may be sure that those who accuse the Muslim scholars of lack of originality and of intellectual decadence have never read Averroes or looked into Algazel but have adopted second hand judgments. The presence of doctrines of Islamic origin in the very citadel of Western Christianity, the *Summa* of Aquinas, is a sufficient refutation of the charge of lack of originality and sterility."

Modern day scholars are now rediscovering the great contributions of Muslims and Muslim culture to the world. These contributions were not limited just to the empiricism of science and the profundity of philosophy but also stimulated the world of popular culture, poetry and romance.

The Epic of Romance

It is impossible to conceive of men and women without thinking of romance. Writers of all the ages have written stories of love and passion. But pure romance - the all annihilating human love - took its form in the hands of the Sufis. They invoked a love so ardently human that it pushed animal lust to the sidelines but burned more powerful like an unquenchable flame. Thus was born the epic of pure romance. One of the greatest of such writers was Nizam Ad-Din Abu Muhammad Ilyas known as Nizami (1141-1209) of Azerbaijan.

Johann Wolfgang von Goethe, the 18th century German poet, novelist and playwright, stated that Nizami was "A gentle, highly gifted spirit who, after Ferdowsi, had collected the heroic traditions, chose for the material of his poems the sweetest encounters of the deepest love. He presented lovers, *Majnun and Layli*, *Khusraw and Shirin*, who were meant for one another by premonition, fate, nature, habit, inclination, passion and staunchly devoted to each other. But becomes divided by mad ideas, stubbornness, chance, necessity, and force, then miraculously reunited, yet in the end again in one way or another torn apart and separated from each other."

One of the most famous of Nizami's work is the story of Laila and her *Majnun*, which means a person, passionately in this case, mad. This story is an original and not based on any heroic tradition but on the love of an 8th century Bedouin poet, Qayes ibn Al Mullawah, for a girl of his tribe Laila Al Aamiriya. His love was reciprocated by her, but it only led them to a great tragedy. A star-crossed fortune separated them and, finally, both died unable to bear the separation.

Laila and Majnu is also a psychological study into the effect of unrequited desire and self inflicted depression. Nearly a century after Nizami, Ibn Taimiyyah, in his psychological work the *Disease of Desires and Passionate Love*, would point out the relationship between desire and depression. Later Muslim scholars provided a religio-psychological methodology that cures individuals of mental afflictions like depression and egotism, which came to be known as 'Purification of the Heart/Soul'. But such a cure was not available for Nizami's protagonists.

Laila Majnun

Qayes is born to a Sayeed of a noble house who had long implored God for a son. From his very childhood the beauty of love becomes perceptible in Qayes.

'As light penetrates water
The jewel of love glowed
Through the veil of his body.'

And Laila is the beautiful Night, as her name means, obdurate and mysterious like the flow of her dark hair. She belongs to a clan related to Qayes. The two young ones have a tryst with their kismet in a local school. Both fell in love and soon their affection becomes evident. Qayes is totally besotted and starts to write of his feelings for her in verses reciting to the passer-bys of his love for her. People talk about it, while some complain and hurt them.

As time goes by, the father of Qayes asks for her hand in marriage with Qayes, but is refused. Her father thinks that Qayes is a complete madman spreading rapacious scandal about her at every street corner and destroying her reputation. Having been refused, Qayes tries to restrain himself from seeing her. But the agony of unfulfillment proves too much, it breaks his heart. Laila's family restricts her from going out or seeing him as people in the street talks of them. Qayes, forlorn, slips away from reality becoming an outcast. Lost in his longing he is only able to think of her and write poems about her. His father, in an attempt to cure him of this malady, takes him to pilgrimage. But Qayes does not want to be cured. He beats the wall of the Kaba and cries out:

"Let me love! Oh, my Lord,
I beseech, let my love grow more
Even if I perish, let it endure"

He becomes mad in love, a Majnun, and soon leaves everything behind and goes out to live in the wilderness. He wanders the desert like a drunken lion, spontaneously chanting exquisite verses describing the beauty of Laila and the depth of his love for her. Soon, the fame of his verses spreads and people starts to come to see him and to hear his words. Some write down the beautiful verses that he utters.

Meanwhile, Laila lives in silent agony. While Majnu's love is sweeping, consuming, daring, disregarding, damning and annihilating, Laila's is veiled, subsuming, gnawing, stabbing and no less ecstatic. She grows graceful, even more beautiful and wise.

On the outside she blossoms,
The inside sheds tears of blood

Her life oscillates from *'The tears of her eyes to the fire of her heart.'* And nothing can keep the voice of her love, the poet, from reaching her. Every child in the bazaar sings his song. Every passer-by hums his verses. And all brings to her the message of love that his voice had spoken. She refuses suitors and starts to write poetry herself on small pieces of paper and then throws those to the winds. And passer-bys pick those up and knows who it is for. They deliver those to him hoping to hear some more of his poems in reward.

'Thus many a melody passed
between the nightingales
drunk in passion.'

No one can console Majnu or bring him back to his people, to his home. The Prince Nawfel, a lion at war and a gazelle at love, takes up the cause of the lovers. First, he advises Majnu to give up the desolate life. Then, as Majnu's love and grief bears heavily with him, he goes to war against Laila's clan and defeats them. But even in defeat Laila's father remains obstinate, too much has happened and too much has become public; ego makes him deny logic. To him it becomes a matter of self-prestige and the prestige of his clan. He declares that Qayes has totally razed Laila's reputation and *'not even a wind passes without mentioning her name.'* He will kill her first rather then give her hand in marriage to such a madman. This ultimatum binds the hands of Nawfel and he knows that he cannot do anything more. With a sad heart he leaves.

Eventually, Laila is married to another man who takes her away. But she cannot bring herself to bear a conjugal life. Her husband, being in love with her, accepts the arrangement of a marriage without passion. When Majnu learns of her marriage from a taunting stranger he is unaware of her sacrifice of passion for him. He is devastated by her 'disloyalty' and sinks further within himself in the wilderness.

Tormented I endure, resigned, your blows
Your, if I die, will be the blood that flows

His father dies of grief for his only son. Misfortune after misfortune tends to strike Majnu down. Even the animals in the wilderness starts to feel his anguish and instead of shying away they gather round him protectively.

Zayd, an old man, takes a letter from Laila to Majnu in which she consoles him on his father's death. She also mentions that her husband knows of her disposition and her faithfulness towards Majnu.

Our bodies are separated, but the soul is not divided
I know what suffering is yours.

An incredible change overcomes him, he is ecstatic with joy. Majnu thanks God for making him a pure soul and prays for His grace. That night in a wonderful dream he sees a miraculous tree that grows in the desert. From it falls a jewel on his head forming a diadem.

But shortly afterwards his mother also dies. Laila decides to meet him. Finally, on the appointed date and time, they meet. In the meeting, Laila keeps a distance of ten paces of propriety from Majnu.

So far I am allowed, no more
If I approach the fire, I shall be consumed.
Nearness brings disaster, lovers must shun.
Better to be ill, then ashamed of the cure.
Why ask for more.

He is oblivious of everything, the joy of seeing his love is enough for him to be in ecstasy and he gifts her with sublime poetry. As the day breaks, they go their way.

Fate, undone by the depth of feelings, cannot keep aloof and speaks in the voice of Nizami, the narrator himself:

'For how long are you going to deceive yourselves?
And for how long you refrain from seeing yourselves
as you are and will remain?
Each grain of sand takes its own length and breadth
as the measure of the world
Yet besides a mountain range it is nothing.
You are the grain of sand, a prisoner of your own will.
Break the cage
break free from yourselves
and free from this world

What you thought was real is not reality

Follow Nizami
burn your own treasure
like a candle

Then the world
your sovereign
will become your slave.

Her husband, realising that he will never get her love, dies of a broken heart. This removes the chain of propriety that had bound Laila. She is free but local tradition forces her to mourn for her husband for two long years before she can be with Majnu. After all that had passed, this taboo of tradition finally proves too much for her, she openly mourns for the love of Majnu. And gradually:

Of the full moon only half remains
Of the Cyprus on the shadow
The tulip sheds petals.

She can no longer bear the overwhelming pain and dies. When Majnu hears of her death he is numb and overwrought with grief. Over the following days he goes to her grave, repeatedly, and finally dies there. After their death there are no more impediments, the world finally recognises their love, and he is buried next to her.

Zayd, the old man, tends the joint grave. One night, he sees a vision of the two of them in Paradise, and is told that:

'These two friends are one and eternal companions
He is Majnu, king of the world in righteousness
She is Laila, the moon of idols in compassion
In the world, like rubies uncut, they treasured their fidelity
They found no rest and no fulfilment for their heart's desire
But here they suffer grief no more
And thus it will be till eternity
Whoever endures suffering in the world
will be joyous and exalted in the next.

~~~

Nizami's love epic was to endure through the changing world. Over centuries from the original Persian hundreds of versions were written in various languages including Arabic, Latin, Turkish, Urdu, Hindi, English and Bengali. Different versions of the story still continue to be written. Hundreds of songs in different languages have been sung crowning the love of *Laila and Majnu* mesmerising millions. The story was adapted for opera while many dozens of movies had been made. It became the inspiration of a new genre of creative arts.

There are many parallels between *Romeo and Juliet* and *Laila Majnun.* To start with, the names of both the stories are the names of the two lovers. There is a quarrel between the two houses of the lovers. Both the lovers die at the end. The story mentions both Majnun
~~~

and Romeo as 'madman' in love. The heroine is loved by a second person, the husband of Laila and the fiancée of Juliet. Both are victims of circumstances and both die towards the end. There is a benevolent Prince in both the story who sadly is unable to save the lovers.

Nizami ends his tale with the following words:

O you, who thoughtlessly repose
On what the flattering world bestows

Reflect how transient is your stay!
How soon even sorrow fades away!

The pangs of grief the heart may wring
In life, but heavens removes the sting.

The world to come makes bliss secure
The world to come eternal pure

What other solace for the human soul
*But everlasting rest virtues universal goal.**

* (adapted from James Atkinson, 1856)

Character of Humour

The Great Seljuk Empire disintegrated at the end of the 12th century. One of their direct offshoots was the Seljuk Sultanate of Rum (also called Konya or Iconium). This dynasty (1077 – 1307) ruled in the Anatolian Turkey with capital in Iznik and later in Konya. In the 13th century during the rule of this prosperous dynasty a man by the name of Nasruddin Khodja is believed to have been born in the village of Hortu in Sivrihisa, Eskisehir. He would live most his mature life in Aksehir and then in Konya. This man, who was a Sufi-philosopher and would become a judge, possessed a tremendous sense of humour for which he became very famous. His witty and satirical sayings came to be celebrated far and wide.

Based on this character, Muslim literature presented the first international comedian to the world. There developed a large number of popular tales about him. The tales presents Nasruddin as a simpleton but in many cases there is a wisdom, philosophy and morale behind the obvious humour. Some contain amusing ingredients against despotic rulers or dull judges while others are purely humorous:

Once, the people of a village, infamous for their taunts, invited Nasruddin to deliver a lecture. So he went to the pulpit and asked, "Do you know what I am going to talk about?"

"No." said the villagers.

Nasruddin was annoyed, "Well, I won't speak to a people who don't even know what I want to talk about!"

The people were embarrassed and called him back the next day. On the pulpit Nasruddin again asked, "Do you know what I am going to talk about?"

"Yes," chorused the villagers.

"Well, since you already know, I don't have to say anything," said Nasruddin and went away.

The confounded people again invited him the next day. Nasruddin asked the same question. This time the people were ready, half of them said "Yes" and the other half said "No".

Nasruddin smiled and said, "Well, in that case, the half who knows tell it to the other half who doesn't."

A man asked "How old are you?"

Nasruddin replied, "I am forty."

The man said, "But you said the same two years ago."

"I never change my word. I still stand by what I said," replied Nasruddin.

Returning from the desert, Nasruddin said, "In the desert I caused a whole tribe of dangerous bloodthirsty Bedouins to run."

"Wow!" said the listener, "how did you manage that?"

"Easy. When I saw them I just ran and they ran after me."

One evening, Nasruddin returned home to find nothing to eat. He asked his wife, "What happened to the meat I brought in the morning?"

His wife, who had fed the meat to visiting relatives, said, "The cat ate the meat."

Nasruddin took the scrawny cat and weighed it. The weight was the same as that of the meat that he had earlier bought. He turned to his wife and said, "If this is the cat where is the meat and if this is the meat where is the cat!?"

A neighbour who was always borrowing things came over and wanted to borrow Nasruddin's donkey. Nasruddin didn't particularly like the man and said, "Sorry, but the donkey is not here."

Just then the donkey let out a bray. The man turned and said, "I just heard your donkey."

"Well, are you going to believe me or a donkey," said Nasruddin.

Nasruddin started a consultancy. His sign read – 'All questions answered. 100 dirhams for two questions'. A trickster trying to upset Nasruddin went to him and said, "Isn't a 100 dinar too much for just two questions?"

"Yes," replied Nasruddin, "what is the next question?"

One day, in the market place, Nasruddin declared that he was a fool. To prove the point he stood by the market place and said if anyone offered him two coins he would take the smaller one. Some people offered him two coins and he took the smaller coin. Soon, people were laughing at him for taking coins of very small denominations in place of gold dinars. When he was alone, a decent man asked him, "Why are you making a fool of yourself?"

Nasruddin smiled and said, "This way they give me a lot of money for nothing just to prove that its not them but I am the fool."

Once Nasruddin invited an arrogant scholar over to his house for a debate. When the scholar arrived at the appointed time he found Nasruddin away and his door locked. He was furious and in his anger wrote 'Stupid fool' on Nasruddin's door and went away without discerning why Nasruddin was not in. When Nasruddin returned he saw the writing on his door and immediately realised what had happened. So he sent back a message to the scholar, "I am very sorry I was not home to receive you. I realised you had come when I say your name on my door.'

Wife asks, "Nasruddin, Why do you always answer a question with another question?"
Nasruddin says, "Do I?"

During Ottoman time, his fame and anecdotal tales had spread to distant lands of Asia and Europe. Over time, thousands of such tales were attributed or added to his repertoire. His tales are known to have circulated in a large number of languages - Albanian, Arabic, Armenian, Azeri, Bengali, Bosnian, Bulgarian, Greek, Chinese, Hindi, Italian, Pashto, Persian, Romanian, Russian, Serbian, Turkish and Urdu. As the tales about Nasruddin spread, he came to be called by different names in different cultures – Nasruddin Hoca in Turkey, Hoja Nasreddin in Greece, Juha in North Africa, Molla Nasruddin or Nasruddin Hodja in Azebaijan, Aghanistan, Iran, India, Pakistan and Bangladesh, Nasir Al Din in Arabic countries, and many such variations.

Besides the variation in name due to linguistic differences, local cultures fashioned local characters in the lines of Nasruddin. Sly Peter of Bulgaria and Macedonia, Birbal and Gopal Bhar of India, Giufa of Sicily, Djoha of Sephardi Jews and many such characters are based on Nasruddin or were associated with him in tales.

In later periods, numerous books and whole novels were written about Nasruddin. In 1943, Yakov Protazanov of the Soviet Union made a film 'Nasreddin in Bukhara'. In Bukhara of Uzbekistan there is bronze statue of the smiling Hodja riding on his famous donkey. In Aksehir of Turkey the 'International Nasreddin Hoca Festival' is held every year between July 5–10. UNESCO proclaimed the year 1996 the 'Nasreddin Hoca Year'.

Nasiruddin lived at a time when the Crusades had started. During his lifetime Saladin and Richard the Lionheart were fighting for domination in Jerusalem and the Levant.

Europe and the Crusades

'There are two lordships, that of the Saracens and that of the Romans, which stand above all lordships on earth, and shine out like two mighty beacons in the firmament.'

- Patriarch Nicholas I of Constantinople in 914

The two lordships that the Patriarch Nicholas mentioned were the empires of the Romans Byzantines and the Abbasids under Caliph Al Muqtadir. Up to start of the 10th century, the land west of Rome was beyond the civilised fringe inhabited by barbarians, and historical events of consequence that had taken place there were the occupation by the Romans, the slow spread of Christianity from 450, the occupation of Spain and Portugal by the Muslims and the rule of the Frank King Charlemagne.

The first great political impact that the barbarians from the west made was the sacking of the Western Roman Empire in 476. They forced themselves to be considered very significantly, albeit dangerously so, by Byzantium - the Eastern Roman Empire. At that time Byzantium was an empire comprising of the Eastern part of Roman Empire and the provinces of Syria, Asia Minor and Egypt. But the 7th century loss of all these provinces to the Muslims in the east would make Byzantium look westward for the need for resources, manpower and ultimately a new identity.

The arrangement in 800 between the Church and Charlemagne was the first political expression of this shift of political gravity towards the west, which consist of much of present day Europe. With the loss of the East, the West was now needed to be acquired and civilised. Full scale proselytising began with state backing and force. After that the crusades would bond together what the Church had initiated. Even though superficial political divides and schisms would remain in Europe a common religious identity was found and forged.

Italy

The fall of Greco-Roman civilisation had caused the regression of Mediterranean Europe. Before Christianity could gain grounds development was hampered due to the absence of any widespread social, moral and commercial networks. Infrastructures needed for large scale commerce had not yet been built. A merchant adventuring far would more likely be robbed or relieved of his goods. Long distance movement of goods was only possible by the powerful landlords with support of their forces. Even the lords themselves were mostly restricted to trading and commercial ventures just within their own domain and depended on the limited output of their manual labour. The economic activity available for the general mass was mostly agrarian labour work.

In Italy, after the 9th century, first Venice and Amalfi and later other cities including Naples became commercial centres trading with the Muslim east. By the tenth century the Tari, a Muslim coin, was in use in the Italian Peninsula. Works of Muslim geographers also show detailed descriptions of South Italian commercial ports (Holmes 1988). These indicate the large extent of European contact with the Muslims. In fact, in 971, when Venice started to manufacture weaponry and sell it to the Muslims they invoked the indignant disapproval of Emperor John Tzimisces. Ibn Hawqal's *Book of Routes and Kingdoms* written in 977 stated that Amalfi was the most prosperous, the most noble, the most illustrious, and most affluent and splendid town in Southern Italy. In 996, a few hundred Venetian and Amalfitan merchants, including Jews, were present in Muslim Alexandria. Such commercial ventures in addition to the revenue from agriculture led to the emergence of the rich merchants of Italy and formation of aristocratic Houses. These Houses and their Princes in the cities started to take interest in culture and arts.

Slaves brought by the Germans and the Vikings and goods, including Flemish clothes and woollens made primarily from English wool were sold via Italy to the Muslim Spain and other Muslim domains. The main trade routes to the Far East existed via the Muslim lands, and probably a minor one through Russia, where silver from Saxony was exchanged for silk and spice.

Kingdom of the Franks

The first biography written in North Europe was that of Charlemagne (747-814) by one of his cleric administrators named Einhard. Charlemagne was a strong, tall man who liked to exercise and ate moderately. He was multilingual speaking Frankish, Latin and Greek. He learned arithmetic, rhetoric and astronomy but was not able to write. But, in an age when most of European rulers, except for the Byzantines and Spanish Muslims, were not literate he promoted scholarship.

He was more than the traditional Frankish Warrior-King who led his army to war. The striking aspect about him was the seriousness with which he embraced the Christian zeal and the sponsoring of art and learning (Robert 1997).

Charlemagne extended his Frankish kingdom by capturing Saxony. He defeated the Danes and the Bretons and subdued the Hungarian Avars and the Slavs. He contained the Umayyad Muslims and pushed them back to Spain. He conquered Lombard Italy in 774 at the behest of the Pope Hadrian. In 785 Charlemagne declared that anyone who refused baptism or insulted Christianity would be beheaded.

In 799, the Romans revolted against Pope Leo III, who was ambushed by some Roman nobles on the street. They tried to gouge his eyes and cut out his tongue. The Pope escaped and went to Charlemagne who had him re-installed. In 800, Charlemagne went to Italy where he was crowned Emperor by the Pope. This was the first indication of the ultimate movement of political power from the southeast of Europe to the northwest. And this was also the first major instance that the Church and State cooperated in spreading Christianity into West Europe.

Charlemagne died in 814 and within 30 years his Empire was divided into three kingdoms. As further disintegration occurred the Vikings plundered the regions and burned monasteries. Even though Charlemagne's Empire crumbled, his Christian legacy endured. In 1000, Otto III of Germany visited his tomb and in 1165 he was canonized by Holy Roman Emperor Frederick Barbossa. Much later Phillip II of France claimed descent from him though it was well known that the ancestors of Phillip II had in fact wrested the kingdom from the descendents of Charlemagne.

By 900, Christianity had been enforced by the state in Gaul (region of present day Italy and France), Germany, Britain and Ireland. New ideas of law and commerce, arts, writing and literature began to spread in Northern Europe.

The Crusades

Christianity set a uniform moral ground and laws all over Europe. Around 1000, when the Muslim Empire began to disintegrate, the barbarians in Europe, such as the Vikings and Magyars, had been converted and a large portion of the Europe population now could unite under the common identity of Christianity. At the end of this century, the Byzantines, having experienced the brunt and impact of the Muslim Empires, now appealed to the Pope for moral and political support. There had been Christian successes in Spain and the Mediterranean Islands, which finally were causes for encouragement to go on the military offensive. At the same time the Pope realised that a common cause would help assuage the disputes between the Church and the feudal states of Europe on the one hand and distract the constant squabbling among the states themselves. In 1905 Pope Urban II proclaimed a call to arms for Christian Europe – a crusade to remove the Muslims from the holy land of Jerusalem. The cry rose from every pulpit declaring that anyone who participates in the crusade would earn the blessing of the Church and full remission of all sins. About 150, 000 people responded to the call. They included significant numbers of Franks and Normans who already had a taste of success in Spain and Sicily.

This highly motivated army started its march and in the first encounter defeated the Seljuk Sultan Qilij and annexed his Capital Nicaoa. The Sultan retreated to Anatolia. Then the army marched again taking Armenia and Syria. The Fatimid Caliph of Egypt was quite content to see the discomfiture of the rival Abbasid-Seljuks, but was devastated when the Crusaders moved towards Egypt's direction annexing Tripoli, Jerusalem and Galilee. The disunited Muslims were unable to offer any resistance. The Assassins of Alamuat openly supported the Crusaders.

After the fall of Jerusalem the Crusaders massacred a large portion of the Muslim population. The Crusaders boasted that 'their blood rose to ankle depth'.

After their victory, the Crusaders formed four independent Principalities in the occupied region, the Kingdom of Jerusalem, the Principality of Antioch, the State of Edessa and the State of Tripoli and set up a fifty mile wide corridor along the Mediterranean littoral up to Jerusalem.

For fifty years this stalemate continued. Then Imad ad Deen Jangi, the ruler of Mosul (modern day Northern Iraq), launched a Jihad against the Crusaders. In 1144 he marched through Armenia and captured Edessa, the first Crusader State. But he died in 1146 and Edessa was lost for some time till his son Nur ad Deen Jangi recaptured it.

~~~

The fall of Edessa, not once but twice, was distressing to Europe, and Pope Eugene III proclaimed the Second Crusade (1144 -1155). Two armies were led by Louis VII of France
~~~

and Conrad III of Germany. But this time the Crusaders faced problems from the very onset. Both of these armies were defeated and cut down by the Seljuk Turks in separate battles. The remnant went to Jerusalem and after getting reinforcement there, instead of going to Edessa, they lay a siege around Damascus which was ruled by a Seljuk Chieftain. Damascus appealed to Nur ad Deen and he responded. Upon his arrival, the Crusaders fell into dispute and ultimately lifted the siege and returned unsuccessful. With Damascus under his rule Nur ad Deen established a strong state that inhibited the movement of the Crusaders.

~~~

A man called Salah ad Deen Ayyubi, known as Saladin, was born in Tikrit and moved to Mosul (present day Iraq) and then to Damascus (present day Syria) working under his uncle, Asad ad Din Shirkuh, a Kurdish military commander from Armenia. Taking over the mantle after the death of his uncle Saladin removed the Fatimids, ending their Caliphate in 1171, then captured Damascus and eventually would became the Sultan of Egypt, Syria, Hijaz and North Yemen. He was a very able General and administrator, a highly educated man well read in mathematics, geography and medicine, imbued with Islamic knowledge, and was courteous and chivalrous.

The Christian rulers of Jerusalem had become oppressive and disunited having squabbled over inheritance of the kingdom. Guy of Lusignon was the King by virtue of having married Sybilla, the Queen of Jerusalem. In a battle fought in Hattin the Christian force was defeated by Saladin and King Guy was captured. Soon the city of Jerusalem capitulated. After ruling for 88 years the Christian rule of Jerusalem ended.

When the Crusaders had conquered Jerusalem they had carried out a massive slaughter of the Muslims. Thus as the Muslim army won there was a great fear of retribution in Jerusalem. But the Muslims under Saladin adhered to the principles of Islam. There was to be no vengeance and Saladin declared a general amnesty. Those who wanted to stay could stay in peace and those who wanted to leave could leave with all their property in safety. Europe was astonished at this magnanimity and many poems and stories of Saladin's chivalry became popular.

Saladin's declaration of the Abbasid as the undisputed and sole Caliph was also very significant, not because it unseated the Fatimids but because it was a great unifying movement in an environment of disintegration. In a world of political fragmentation it was a moral unification.

Saladin's forces spread north and captured the whole region including Acre, Sidon and Beirut from the Crusaders. When Saladin's army besieged Tyre, Conrad, the Marquis of Montferrat, was able to defend Tyre from within its strong walls. Saladin lifted the siege of Tyre and his army moved to the south taking Caesarea, Arsuf, and Jaffa. This finally resulted in the call for the Third Crusade in Europe. Richard of England, Phillip of France and Leopold
~~~

V of Austria arrived to take up the cause. The Holy Roman Emperor Frederick Barbossa led a huge army but died of drowning in a river before reaching the holy land.

Saladin in the meantime had released King Guy on the promise that Guy would never take up arms against him. But Guy found a priest to annul the pledge. He went to Tyre and demanded the Key of Tyre from Conrad on royal authority. Conrad refused saying that Guy had lost the right to be a king after loosing the battle in Hattin. In this fiasco, Richard supported his vassal Guy while Philip and Leopold supported their cousin Conrad. When Guy's wife Queen Sybilla died her half sister Isabella became the heiress of Jerusalem. She was hastily divorced from her current husband and married to Conrad who thus became the de-facto king of Jerusalem. This was a political loss for Richard.

Soon the religious zeal evaporated out of the Third Crusade and it became a power-play with multiple sides looking after its own interest. There were no outright military successes, battles being won by Saladin's army and the crusader intermittently. Whenever the Crusaders won they argued over the spoils of war. Each of the Crusader fraction opened confidential parleys with Saladin in attempts to work out political advantages. But Richard proved to be the strongest among them. Unable to coup with Richard's politics, Leopold and Philip returned to their lands in 1191.

Richard lost a political battle when the Barons of Jerusalem elected Conrad as the King. But soon after that Conrad was killed by the Assassins. Immediately after the murder, Isabella, the heiress of Jerusalem while pregnant with Conrad's child, was married to Richard's nephew - Henry of Champagne, and Richard thus remained the undisputed leader of the Crusaders. At the end of 1192, Saladin and Richard finalised a treaty by which Jerusalem was submitted to Saladin's control. Saladin agreed to allow unarmed Christian pilgrims to visit the city.

Soon Richard departed but on his way back he was imprisoned by Leopold and charged with the murder of Conrad. A captured Assassin, upon torture, had admitted Richard's complicity in the murder. Richard requested that the Assassins be produced to witness the charge against him. Soon, a letter from the Assassin leader Rashid Al Din Sinan was produced in which it was claimed that Conrad had captured an Assassin ship and was thus condemned to die and it had nothing to do with Richard. Later, it would be found that Sinan was already dead and it was unlikely that he was the author of the letter. But, meanwhile, Richard was ransomed at 150,000 marks and returned to England in 1194. He died five years later of an arrow wound in his early forties.

When Saladin died in 1193 all his wealth had been distributed among his subjects. He left behind only one piece of gold and few pieces of silver. After the death of Saladin the Crusaders launched another attack. While the Crusaders besieged Beirut and Tibnim, Malik Al Aadil, Saladin's successor, took Jaffa by a storm cutting off the crusaders from their base on the sea coast. The demoralized Crusaders negotiated for peace and finally returned to Europe.

~~~
~~~

The call for a Fourth Crusade, which took place in 1204, was given just six years after the third one. But the Fourth Crusade turned out to be a greater farce. It was abandoned by the Pope as the Crusaders, instead of fighting to recover the Holy Land, sacked the Christian capital of Constantinople. The Latins and the Greeks had harboured resentment towards each other since the Great Schism of 1054 - the conflict that had taken place between the Western Roman Catholic and the Eastern Greek Orthodox Christians of Byzantium. The ruler of Byzantium at the time of the Fourth Crusade was of the Greek Angelus Dynasty while the Franks and the Venetian Crusaders were Catholics. Besides the existing resentment the Venetian had other scores to settle. In 1182, the Venetian merchant community were expelled from Constantinople by the local Greeks. This event was still fresh in the Venetian memory. And more recently they had been contracted to build ships and train its crew to take part in the Crusade. It took them a full year while they put aside their normal commerce. But when the time to sail came, they were underpaid significantly which caused more resentment.

The Byzantine Emperor Isaac II Angelus had recently been deposed. His son Alexius Angelus promised to pay the Crusaders enormous sum of money if they would install him as the Emperor of Byzantine. This led to the siege of Constantinople by the Frankish and Venetian crusaders. Soon things got out of control and Constantinople was sacked and murder, loot, rape and destruction progressed in an enormous scale for three days. A lot of the art work preserved there was destroyed. Hagia Sophia, the Orthodox Christian Basilica, was desecrated, and the silver iconostasis and holy books in it were destroyed. The Fourth Crusade led to the weakening of Byzantium from which it never recovered.

~~~

In the Fifth Crusade (1216-1221) the Crusaders were led by the King of Hungary, the Austrian and Bavarian Dukes and Potentates of Germany. A force of about 100,000 was mustered. Initially the Crusaders marched to Jerusalem but could not break its defences. They turned towards Egypt with the plan that if Egypt was subdued Jerusalem would fall on its own. An alliance was worked out with the Seljuk Sultan of Rum who attacked the Ayyubids in Syria so that when the Crusaders attacked Damietta, an Egyptian port, it would open up two fronts to the disadvantage of Egypt. After a siege of eighteen months Damietta was captured. This was a strategic victory that demoralized the Ayyubid king Al Kamil of Egypt. He offered peace on the basis that if the Crusaders returned Damietta to them then the Egyptian would hand over Jerusalem.

But the Crusaders scented victory and wanted both Egypt and Jerusalem. They rejected the offer and started for Cairo. The Egyptians, realising the military superiority of the Crusaders, changed their battle tactics. They opened the dykes of the Nile and inundated the country side through which the Crusaders were marching. The flood stranded the Crusaders and they were cut off from their base unable to go forth or back. As the Crusaders faced
~~~

famine and disease the Egyptian attacked them. The Crusaders were forced to sue for peace. They gave up Damietta and in return the Egyptians agreed to continue to give access to Christian pilgrims going to Jerusalem. A peace treaty of eight years was agreed to.

~~~

The Sixth Crusade (1227 – 1229) under Emperor Frederick of Germany proved very fruitful. Initially when the Pope commissioned him for the Crusade he was indecisive in taking up the cause and the frustrated Pope had excommunicated him. Frederick married Isabella Yolande, grand daughter of Isabella and Conrad Montferrat and the heiress to the throne of Jerusalem, and declared himself its King. He then marched with his force for Palestine. The Patriarch of Jerusalem did not recognize his mission as he had been excommunicated and some European quarters refused to support him. But Frederick still marched on the political basis that he was the consort of the Queen of Jerusalem.

Al Kamil, at that time, was in quarrel with other Ayyubid nobles and busy suppressing rebellions in Syria. Frederick opened a negotiation with Al Kamil and arrived at a ten year peace treaty. In the treaty Frederick was to help Al Kamil retain his position in Egypt while Jerusalem, Nazareth, Bethlehem and all the cities between Jafaa and Accra were handed over to him. This was a great victory for the Frederick and the Pope reconcilcd with him.

~~~

Before the Seventh Crusade another element was introduced in the fray – the Mongols. Back in 1194, the Khawarizm Shah was able to capture whatever was left of the dominion of the Seljuks ending their reign. After 1200 the Khawarizm Shah Alauddin Muhammad conquered most of Persia and extended his empire from the border of China to Anatolia. The Khawarizms, in turn, were defeated and ousted by the Mongols. They retreated to their allies, the Mamluks of Egypt, and on the way took Jerusalem in 1244 and thus the region again came under Muslim rule.

The Seventh Crusade (1248 – 1254) was led by King Louis IX of France and was a disaster. Louise was captured by the Egyptians and kept as prisoner for a number of years until he was released on ransom the sum of which was equivalent to France's one year's revenue.

Aftermaths of the Crusades

Few more half hearted crusades were fought but all failed to attain the military objective. But politically the success of the whole episode was stupendous - the fusion of a European identity under the common cause of Christianity.

The contact with the Muslim Empires, likewise, was also very important for Europe. The porous activity of the merchants brought about a lot of information about development in various sectors of Muslim dominions. When the Crusaders and pilgrims returned from the Muslim lands they brought back tales of incredible cities and progress that awakened the interest of Europe. Large scale translation of Muslim science, arts and philosophy was done in Spain, Portugal, France and Sicily. These contacts with Muslim culture, modern outlook and high quality urban life would influence Europe and initiate the break down of the rigid society and establish the foundation of progressive social groups and communities, and durable modern institutions.

Once the foundation of society had been laid down by Christianity, morality alone was no longer capable of enacting social progress. The need for pragmatic and rationalistic views and policies became apparent. But the incoming seepage of the alien Muslim culture and knowledge was not deemed well by the Church. While the Church was agreeable in incorporating arts into their domains they stood firmly against the admission of science and changes in commerce. Advent of rationalism was likely to make ritualistic religion unacceptable to the general mass. The clergy establishment, somewhat corrupt at times, was a beneficiary of the existing commercial system and thus the status quo was more profitable. But this stance caused disillusionment among the people regarding the Church as it failed to come in grips with the new environment. A need developed to find an alternate system of progress.

These dynamic changes imparted on Europe a readiness for the next stage of socio-cultural development that would lead to the Renaissance of Italy and subsequent cultural and industrial evolution of Europe.

The Scourge of God

To God we belong and to Him is our return [2:156]

In 1206 CE, in far off Mongolia, Taimujin was elected the chief of the Mongols. He united the many nomadic Mongol tribes of northeast Asia. He took on the title of Chengiz Khan and from his capital in Karakorum, he embarked in one of the most spectacular career of conquest that the world has ever seen. During his life, the Mongol Empire would eventually occupy a large part of Asia. His descendants would make the Mongol Empire the largest contiguous Empire in history by conquering China, Russia, Eastern Europe and a significant part of Asia and the Middle East.

After establishing Mongol rule in China, Chengiz moved west. Obliterating the Kara Khitayas of Transoxiana (Central Asia) he reached Khawarizm (modern day Uzbekistan) in 1218. There he sent a Mongol trade delegation. In the border town of Utrar the Khawarizm Governor suspected the delegation of spying and had them executed. When Chengiz Khan demanded compensation the Khawarizm Shah refused. The Mongols then unleashed a ferocious multi pronged attack on Khawarizm. One of their legions decimated Utrar and massacred all of its population. Molten gold was poured down the throat of the Governor who had executed the trade delegation. Another legion led by Chengiz himself captured Bukhara where he assembled the vanquished people to the main Mosque. From the pulpit he declared, "I am the Scourge of God, come to punish you for your sins."

All the assembled people were executed and then the Mongols proceeded to Samarqand. The city fell after a weak resistance. A large portion of the population was gathered in an open field outside the city where they were butchered. A tower of severed human heads, the symbol of Mongol victory, rose in the field. Two more legions destroyed Khojend and Gurganj. After the fall of Gurganj, the Mongols breached its dam and flooded the town. The people drowned and those who escaped were massacred. The Khawarizm King Mohammad Shah fied on the face of the brutal onslaught.

The Mongols crossed the Oxus and reached Khorasan in 1221. Whatever came in their path was destroyed and devastated leaving in their wake a hallmark trail of destruction. City after city were turned into rubble and hundred of thousands of people slaughtered in each of them. Tirmiz, Merv, and Sanjar the Seljuk capital were all reduced to dust and blood. In Nishapur a son-in-law of Chengiz was killed. Extra Mongol troops were dispatched there and the city was turned into a carnival of blood, bones and butchery presided over by the widow. But Herat, where the populace surrendered without fighting, was spared.

Khawarizm King Mohammad Shah died within a year of his escape. His son Jalaluddin Mangbarni raised an army. He confronted and defeated a Mongol army near Kabul. After this defeat Chengiz himself led an army against Jalaluddin. The two faced each other near the bank of the Indus River. Jalaluddin fought heroically being forced back step by step by the Mongol onslaught. When there was no more room to fight he dived into the river and swam to the other side. Chengiz Khan saw all this from a vantage point and was very impressed by the bravery of the young prince. He refused to send his warriors after him.

The civilian and military code to rule the Mongol Empire was established by Chengiz Khan which was named Yassa. Unlike its savage warfare, the Mongol administration, with time, turned out to be very progressive. As the empire became huge its population, initially dominated by Mongols and Turks, became ethnically and culturally diverse. These diverse groups considered themselves culturally Mongols. In administration and professional fields merit was the basis of advancement. Religions were tolerated and there was tax exemption or reduction for religious leaders, doctors and teachers.

After the death of Chengiz in 1227 the Mongol domain was divided among his four sons. Ogadai inherited western Mongolia and was declared the Great Khan, Toulai inherited eastern Mongolia, Chagtai inherited Turkestan and Transoxiana while Jochi inherited the Russian and surrounding regions.

Ogadai was a large man with an imposing personality. He was very intelligent and charismatic but humble as well. He was a Buddhist and his mother and his chief consort were Christians. During his rule the Mongols turned Korea, Georgia and Armenia into vassals and completed the annexation of Persia and China except for the territories of the Song Dynasty. Next, they moved towards Europe and captured almost all the regions from Russia to Hungary and Poland. The Mongols were unstoppable and Europe was unprotected and ready to fall. As they started the winter campaign for the rest of Europe, Ogadai died.

Ogadai's son Kuyuk became the Great Khan. There arose dissension among the Mongols and Kuyuk pulled out of Poland and Hungary, which caused the cessation of invasion in this region and Europe was spared. Soon an independent Mongol state, with capital in Saria by the Volga, was formed. This state withdrew allegiance to Kuyuk. Thereupon Kuyuk started to consolidate his position in Khorasan. The Seljuk Sultan Kai Khusro was turned into a vassal of the Mongols.

After a succession conflict Kuyuk died in 1248 and Mongke became the Great Khan. Under him Kublai was the ruler of China while Halaku was charged with the conquest of the Middle East. From Samarqand the forces of Halaku Khan crossed the River Oxus in 1256. Halaku set his sights on the Assassins of Alamaut. He sent an ultimatum to the Assassins to demolish their fortress and surrender. The Assassins were under the impression that their mountainous fortresses were impregnable and evaded any reply. But under the Mongol onslaught the Assassins finally fell and their fortresses were destroyed.

Some years ago in 1242 the last Abbasid Caliph in Baghdad Al Mustasim came to power. By that time, the population of Baghdad was gradually dwindling with people migrating to more enterprising cities, the most populous of which was the capital of Egypt.

During his reign riots broke out between the followers of Hanafi and Hanbali schools and also between the Shia and Sunni. At one stage, Kark, the main Shia suburb was totally destroyed and many Shia killed. The Minister to the Caliph was a Shia named Muwayyid ud Din. Seeing the plight of the Shias he was very pained and ultimately turned to treachery. He secretly contacted the Mongols and invited them to take over Baghdad.

While attacking the Assassins, Halaku had asked the Caliph to send a contingent against the Assassins as well. But Mustasim had refrained hoping that the two devils, Mongols and Assassins, would undo each other. Now Halaku using the non co-operation as a pretext sent an ultimatum to the Caliph. In 1258 the Mongols besieged Baghdad and after a token resistance Baghdad fell. The palace of the Caliph was plundered and the Caliph made a captive. Under Halaku's order the Caliph was given, instead of food, a plate full of jewels.

Mustasim said, "This is not edible."

Halaku said, "Then why did you hoard this! Why didn't you use this to make real soldiers?" Pointing at the iron door, he continued, "Why didn't you make arrow heads out of this? Why did you not stand at the bank of the river so that I could not cross it?"

Mustasim finally replied, "This is the will of God."

Halaku said, "Then what happens next is also the will of God."

The Caliph was put into a sack and trampled to death under horse's hooves. After plundering of the city was over it was put to the torch. Thus burnt the universities, libraries and all the institutions of learning and knowledge built up through ages. A large number of books and scrolls were thrown into the river before the city was put to the torch. A significant portion of the population of Baghdad was marched to a field outside the city. Here, they were slaughtered and a mountain of skulls was piled.

The unstoppable Mongol wake of destruction continued to progress through the Muslim domains. In two years time they conquered Aleppo, Hims and Damascus in Syria. Then they turned towards the last Muslim bastion – The Mamluk Egypt.

The Mamluks in history are defined as slaves. But it would be wrong to attach the usual connotation of 'slaves' to such people under true Islamic rule. Though the Prophet and the Caliphs had preferred freeing slaves and set many examples, it was not possible to abolish slavery at one go due to various social factors. A large number of prisoners were available chiefly due to wars and needed to be re-integrated to the society. Slavery provided the method of this integration. If all were to be suddenly set free they would have no place to go and, mostly, no support to survive. Thus in Islam slavery had emancipated to a stage where the slave men and women were bonded to a house and become a recognised profession. They had the rights of any other people and could rise to any level in the society according to their merit. Female slaves had given birth to Emperors, while males had become Generals and Sultans.

The Mamluks 'slaves' were bonded to the house of the Sultan. They were very well trained, cultured and sophisticated people. Mostly serving in the military some had risen in administration as well. In India and Egypt they had risen to become Sultans. In India the Mamluk Sultan Nasir-ud-Din Mahmud, Gias-ud-Din Balban and his successors had ruled from 1206 to 1290. In Egypt, the Bahri Mamluks ruled from 1250 to 1517.

In 1260, on reaching Gaza, Halaku sent an ultimatum to the Egyptian Mamluk king Kutuz. It was an insolent, threatening and humiliating message that enraged Kutuz to extreme. He had the Mongol ambassadors executed and their bodies hung at the gates of the city. Then he marched the Egyptian army to measure swords with the Mongols. Baybras, The ablest and the bravest of the Mamluk Generals, lead the vanguard. In the meantime Mongke, the Great Khan, had died and Halaku returned leaving command in the hands of his step brother Ketgugha.

The two armies clashed in a titanic and historical battle at Ayn Jalut in Palestine. In this battle the Crusaders were in favour of the Mongols, but the Assassins now turned against them. The Mamluks rose to the occasion and comprehensively defeated the Mongols, shattering the myth of Mongol invincibility. Ketgugha died fighting on the battle field and much of the Mongol army was routed.

The Mongols finally met their match in the Mamluks. In 1280 the Mamluks delivered another crushing defeat to the Mongols in Syria. The Mamluks of India did not languish behind. Under Sultan Gias-ud-Din Balban the Mamluks of India defeated two Mongol attacks in Multan in 1279 and 1286. These were Chagtai Mongols from Transoxiana who had been in northwest India for some time. In the last battle Muhammad the son of Sultan Balban died while chasing the Mongols.

The Mongols returned to India thrice in the beginning of the fourteenth century. But thrice they were beaten back by the Khilji Sultans. Thousands including their leader were captured and Alauddin Khilji ordered them to be trampled to death under the royal horses. But the female and children were not harmed. These defeats plugged any further Mongol advance into India.

Sultan Baybras

The person who is credited with breaking the invincibility of the Mongols and striking the final blows to the Crusaders was named Baybras.

For a century after the fall of the Abbasid, the Mamluks remained the main power in the Muslim domain. General Baybras, after defeating the Mongols in 1260, had wanted the governorship of Aleppo as a reward. But King Kutuz denied him even though he had promised the governorship to him before the battle. Baybras and other nobles then staged a coup in which Kutuz was killed and Baybras became the Sultan (Hasan, 2005).

Baybras proved to be a great administrator as he had proven to be a great General. He built roads, bridges and dug canals in various part of Egypt. He established a fast postal service and founded funds for the welfare of the poor. He modernised the army and the navy and built fortresses in strategic areas.

He embarked on annual expeditions against the Crusaders and won back the fortified cities of Caesarea, Arsuf, Safed, Cilicai, Derbesek and other regions from the Knight Templars. His conquest was crowned by the capture of Antioch, the Syrian capital of the Crusaders. He raided Tyre and Accra and captured the great fort Crac Des Chevaliers also known as Hisn-al-Akra from the Knight Hospitallers and induced the Crusaders to pay tribute. Then he took action against the Assassins who had again formed strongholds in some mountainous forts. The fortresses capitulated in front of his forces. He displaced and settled the Assassins in Egypt, where they lost their fanatic trait and were assimilated.

He turned Sudan into a vassal state and later took successful campaigns against the Mongols in Cilicia and Asia Minor (Turkey). He invited an Abbasid representative who was living a life of exile and declared him the next nominal Caliph with title of Al Mustansir. He cultivated alliances and friendships with other nations including Byzantium, Sicily, Aragon, Seville and Anjou. The Mongols of the Golden Horde ruling over Russia, Ukraine, Moldova, Kazakhstan and the Caucasus, who were descendents of the Jochi Mongols and had converted to Islam, became his great ally. He married a daughter of Berek Khan, the Golden Horde ruler.

The extraordinary deeds and achievement of Baybras made him famous. Legends were fashioned about him and storytellers for ages told numerous stories of his exploits.

Mongol Assimilation

After Chengiz, the Mongol empire was divided into four domains among his sons. With time these subdivisions transformed into three major domains, those of the Il-Khans of Persia, The Chagtais of Transoxiana and the Golden Horde Khanate of Russia and Eastern Europe.

The changes in the Mongol's culture and attitude came from within. While their sword had broken the back of the Muslims, the intellectual and spiritual superiority of the Muslims defeated the Mongols. The first of the Mongols to accept Islam were the Golden Horde. Gradually, all the Mongols who settled down in the Muslim domains were assimilated. And at one stage, amazingly, they became the torch bearer of Islam. Among their descendants were the Great Moghuls of India and the mighty Taimur (Tamerlane) of Samarqand.

When the Mongols were fighting the Muslims, a loose alliance was formed between the Mongols and European rulers. After their second humiliating defeat in 1280 at the hands of the Mamluk the Mongols tried to incite their European allies to launch another Crusade, promising them a huge cavalry support and restoration of the Holy Lands. But they were snubbed by France and England and also by the Pope. The main difference was that the Mongols wanted to undo Islam completely, but Christian Europe wanted the mastery of the region without the undoing. In 1291, Sultan Al Ashraf Khalil of Egypt occupied Acre, the last stronghold of the Crusaders, which closed the chapter of the Crusades in the Muslim lands.

Gradually, as the Mongols converted to Islam the state of affairs in the Muslim domains showed a return to normalcy. But the ease with which the initial Mongol onslaught had demolished the Muslims, destroyed the Abbasid Caliphate and the subsequent horrifying experiences left its mark on the Muslim psyche. As a reaction the Muslims began to rethink and realign their politics and philosophy.

Philosophical Realignment

The study of History of the Umayyad and Abbasid period provides a picture that the Muslim societies were going through a roller coaster ride. The wars, the eccentricities and intrigue of royalties, and the high profile debates on philosophy and religion apparently seemed to dominate the social life. But the general society and the average Muslims were far removed from all these calamities. Once the empire had been formed and political administration had settled down, the wars only affected the border regions. The revolts, to the mass, were political opponents trying to out do each other. The general public would get involved only under exceptional cases. The average Muslims viewed the intrigues and the debates from a 'long distance' perspective. All this was 'news' to them and when they would hear of it, it did not matter much to their daily life. Their daily life consisted of education, commerce and culture and a progressive social style typical to the Muslim world.

During the mediaeval ages most of the world - Middle East, Central Asia, Spain, North Africa and China - saw a tremendous upsurge in knowledge, learning and improvement of human social condition. The development of thought influenced, as expected, the development of society in the empires and kingdoms. Irrespective of the governing political entity, wherever the Muslim travelled in that vast central tract of civilised regions between China and Byzantium, the Muslim was always under the shadow of the faith – the same God, the same prayers, the same laws and the same custom. For the common Muslim a practical code of citizenship guaranteed her or him freedom throughout most of the civilised world. There was no need for passports or visas.

The average Muslims led a stable life throughout this period. They were the most advanced demographic group in the entire world and involved in a modern way of life, civic sense and education. Their commerce was the best as they controlled a huge free trade zone in the centre of the civilised world.

But a 'Tri-Military-Event', which directly affected the people, would change the psyche of the Muslims. The first two events were the loss of Spain and the Crusades that had dented the Muslim empire from the west. The last and the greatest shock was the destruction, humiliation and suffering inflicted by the Scourge. Except for Egypt and India, much of the Muslim world was at throes for their very survival. At that instance of history, the futility of science and scholarship appeared pronounced. When survival in the face of the sword was the main issue, the scientists and scholars - debating with perishable books over minute germs, algebra, chemical reactions and physical laws – had proved themselves, seemingly, to be most worthless.

The immensity of the Mongol tragedy, including the cruel death of the Caliph, sent shock waves all over the Muslim world. A stormy reassessment of the Muslim culture and history took place. The Scourge had obliterated centuries of advancement. So it appeared that the pursuit of knowledge and learning were all too futile and ephemeral. This pursuit had not been able to save a single life, it had not sharpened a single sword against the onslaught of the enemies, it had not emboldened a single person to stand and face this scourge. To survive and rebuild the empire, warriors were needed.

Apparently, the only thing that could conquer and save empires were men of metal, men who feared nothing not even death, men who could forge ahead irrespective of what lay in front - a sword, an army, a storm, a mountain or a sea. Thus a cultural change appeared in the psychological outlook of the Muslims. Up to this juncture there existed a factious balance between rationalism and orthodoxy. Now social science, martial orthodoxy and mysticism prevailed over pure science.

By this time Christianity had established a moral framework throughout Europe. It was waiting for an impetus to take the next step towards rationalism. Thus the Christian West was moving toward rationalism and the Muslim East away from it. The philosophies of Ibn Rushd and Al Ghazzali had become well known in both Europe and the Muslim world. Ibn Rushd's rationalism triumphed in Europe and Al Ghazzali's Gnostic philosophy in the East.

These were temporal regional socio-political exigencies that were necessary for the next stage of development. Al Ghazzali's philosophy gave Muslims the instant spiritual and psychological strength and unity to fight back the many disintegrational forces and chaos that they had been subjected to and, again, build mighty and grand empires the likes of which the world had not seen before. Ibn Rushd's rationalism led Europe to the Renaissance in its fight against laid-back institutions, socio-cultural backwardness and dogmatic way of life. The new European philosophical organisation would, on the long run, take them to great new heights of empire building and further into modern statehood.

A parting of ways took place between 'rational sciences' from Muslim thought. Rational studies no longer existed in the schools where, from then on, mainly Ulemaic and Sufi thoughts were to prevail. Besides, most of the books and libraries of important learning centres of the Middle East and Central Asia had been destroyed by the Scourge. After the fall of Baghdad the Mongols had emptied its libraries in the Euphrates. The millions of volumes caused a bridge across the river and for days the river water was stained black from the ink washed out of the books. Over the next few centuries research and development in the Muslim domain would slow down and grind to a halt.

Under the circumstances, rationally thinking, that was the right direction *for that time*. The change in focus from the scholastic to the military led the Ottomans to build one of the finest army the world had ever seen, the Janissary, and re-conquer what the Muslims had lost and even more. The Muslims did not feel the pinch of the loss of rational science immediately because they had already advanced so far that even without further development they were still ahead of all the other nations up to the seventeenth century. Their technological advantage allowed the Ottomans to build huge cannons while the Europeans could only muster very small ones. The lack of knowledge in metallurgy would cause the bigger ones the Europeans manufactured to blow up. Such disadvantages made them embark on research to improve their condition.

The acceptance of Ghazzali's philosophy motivated the Ulema and the Sufis. They took up the standards of Islam with a new zeal and progressed far into India and to South East Asia. Though Islam was not totally new in some of these areas, this movement was instrumental in the peaceful mass conversion of the populations there.

The aftermath of all these changes saw the rise and fall of many Muslims dynasties in the 13th to 15th centuries. They included the Zayanid of Algeria, the Marinid of Morocco, the Khiljis of India, the Ilyas Shahis of Bengal, the Muslim legacy of Mongol Persia - Sarbadarans, Jalayars and Muzaffarids, the Malay Sultanate of Malacca, the Indonesian Samudra Darussalam, Sultanate of Demak, Aceh Sultanate and many more.

But among all these two men were set to make their mark in history - Taimur, for burning bright as a Supernova and Othman of the Turks, for establishing an empire that would become the superpower of the world. This was also the time that would see the rise of Europe.

The Rise of Europe

Frederick II

The man greatly responsible for the rejuvenation of knowledge in Italy was Frederick II (1194-1250), who was a German of the Hohenstaufen dynasty. He was King of Germany, Sicily, Burgundy, and Italy. He was also King of Cyprus and Jerusalem and the Holy Roman Emperor. Frederick is among the great European Emperors and definitely the greatest in the thirteenth century who strove independently to bring enlightenment to Europe. He was one of the rulers who had been involved in the struggle with the Papacy known as the Investiture Contest.

His father was Henry VI, Holy Roman Emperor and his mother Constance was the Sicilian heiress and daughter of King Roger II. Sicily was the largest and most powerful political entity in all of Italy and its domain included the Island as well as southern Italy. Constance, according to chroniclers, gave birth to Frederick in a public square to eliminate any doubt of his royal heritage. When the one year old infant was declared future King of the Germans, it was opposed by his two uncles Phillip and Otto. He was two years old and travelling from Italy to Germany when news of his father's death reached them. He was hurried back to his mother in Palermo, Sicily. She crowned him King of Sicily and became the Regent. When she died in about a year, Pope Innocent III became his guardian and recognised him as King of Sicily.

But there was never meant to be a good relationship between the Papacy and the young king. There had always been political tension between the Papacy and European imperial powers. Emperor Frederick Barbarossa, the grandfather of Frederick II, was the greatest German Emperor of the twelfth century. He had ensured that the field of conflict between the Papacy and Imperial power be established in Italy deliberately overshadowing the centre of the Pope's power. The marriage of his son Henry VI to the Sicilian Heiress Constance was alarming to the Papacy as this meant being encircled by a united imperial force. The birth of Frederick II, who would forge that unification, was utterly threatening to the Papal power and Frederick became their enemy the day he was born.

After the death of Henry VI, Pope Innocent III had initially supported Otto then turned to favour Philip. When Philip died he crowned Otto the Emperor in 1209 on receiving a guarantee of papal independence. But Otto soon showed complete disregard for the guarantee and launched attacks on Italy and was excommunicated in 1211. With no options left and to counter Otto, the Pope crowned Frederick II King of the Germans in1215. Otto was defeated by the French and withdrew to Saxony where he died in 1218. The next Pope Honorius after much negotiations and a promise from Frederick to go on Crusade finally crowned Frederick the Holy Roman Emperor in 1220.

Frederick was brought up in Sicily where he came in contact with the Muslims and was very attracted by the depth of their knowledge and devotion to science, literature and arts. Instead of killing or repulsing the Muslims he let them settle on the mainland and build mosques. He also enlisted Muslims in the army and used them as his personal bodyguards. Gradually, He developed an unquenchable thirst for knowledge. In a time when many European monarchs and nobles were illiterates he could speak in seven languages including Arabic. He was instrumental in getting translated many Arabic books including those by Ibn Rushd (Averroes) and on account of being a patron of Muslim culture he was accused of being a Muslim by the bishops (Ahmad, 1984). He became an enthusiastic patron of science and arts and established the University of Naples in 1224 which is now known as Universita Federico II.

He promulgated the 'liber Augustalis' also known as the Constitution of Melfi probably in 1231. This was a collection of laws for the rule of his land by virtue of which Sicily evolved from feudalism to the first central-governed state of Europe. This was quite extraordinary considering the timeframe and many later philosophers and nobles had drawn inspiration from it. The constitution remained the basis of Sicilian law, with small changes, till the beginning of the nineteenth century. He also became the patron of the Sicilian School of Poetry. The poetry from this school had influenced Dante and his peers. The school started the use of Tuscan Idioms as the preferred language of Italy and thus influenced the literary form that was to become the modern Italian language. Frederick loved Falconry and had a treatise on Falconry by Arab scholar Moamin translated to Latin and named *De arte venandi cumn avibus* (The Art of Hunting with Birds).

He prohibited duels in which two individual at odds with each would fight to the death. The duels did not bring victory to the righteous, as was believed, rather to the stronger. He prohibited so-called physicians from practicing pharmacy. This stopped quacks from diagnosing imaginary diseases in persons so that they could sell phoney medicines. Contradictory to his contemporaries, he was a proponent of reason. A man much ahead of his time his brilliance was recognised and he came to be known as *Stupor Mundi* - the 'Astonishment of the World.'

In 1226, the trepidation that the Papacy had felt since he was born started to materialise. Frederick declared that he wanted to extend his imperial powers to the north Italian cities. Opposition to this proposal was fomented in those cities. Because of these troubles and his cordial understanding of Muslims and their progressive scholarship he delayed his departure for the Crusade. In 1227 Pope Gregory IX excommunicated him for the delay.

Earlier in 1225, Frederick had by proxy married the heiress of Jerusalem, Isabella Yolande, and assumed the title of King of Jerusalem. In 1228, he finally set out for the Crusade despite the excommunication. Frederick was excommunicated a second time, this time for going on to crusade under excommunication. Frederick still commenced on his mission but the excommunication had had its effect and he reached Palestine with a smaller army than anticipated.

Al Kamil, the Egyptian ruler, in control of Palestine was facing problems from rebellious relatives and a possible revolt from within. He was in no situation to take on a third antagonist under the circumstances. Frederick became a guest of Kamil and the two negotiated a solution. Frederick gave assistance to Kamil to hold on to his throne while Jerusalem, Nazareth and Bethlehem were handed over to Frederick.

Both Frederick and Kamil had enemies who criticised them for the way by which they arrived at their agreement. But when Frederick returned from the Crusade, there was a resurgence of his popularity. This was the only successful Crusade after the first one and Europe was grateful to the man who had reinstituted Jerusalem without spilling blood. In 1231 the Pope lifted the excommunication of Frederick.

On his return Frederick again dominated north and central Italy. He was by now hostile to the Papacy, and sacked some of the northern cities. He seized Rome and imprisoned the clerics. Innocent IV, who had become the Pope, fled from Rome to Lyons. This conflict continued even after Frederick's death in 1250. A few years after his death, his empire began to disintegrate. There was a systematic assassination of his character which was already precocious in life and now was maligned in death. Added to his imperial threat to Papal authority, his lifelong interest in Islam, his then-not-understood rationalism rated him with Dante's heretics. Fantastic claims of his blasphemy against religions and medical experimentation on humans were made. Pope Gregory IX called him the Antichrist. But the Joachimite preachers and many Franciscans took his side. The Preachers absolved him, while condemning the Pope and said that Frederick, according to Joachimite eschatology, was the good Antichrist and had come to cleanse the Church of riches and corruption.

Despite the break-up of his empire and his character assassination, his thoughts and ideas prevailed over politics and spread all over Italy and Germany. His red porphyry sarcophagus lies besides his parents in the Cathedral of Palermo. Ludwig I of Bavaria build a bust of Frederick in the Walhalla Temple. His coronation robe can be found in the Kunsthistorisches Museum in Vienna. On it is written the Islamic Hijri year 528 and a benediction in Arabic.

After the Hohenstaufen dynasty, for about three generation, there was cooperation between the Anjou French and the Papacy by which the Angevin ruled Palermo and Naples. The Sicilian revolt against the Angevin paved the way for Sicilian Island occupation by Peter III of Aragon from North East Spain. For nearly a century, the Angevin and the Argonese were in conflict with each other which led to public disorder, decline of authority and fall of economy. The land and people of Sicily became impoverished and the interest in art and culture waned.

The Italian Renaissance

The term renaissance or 'rebirth' can strictly be applied only to the Greco-Italians, while for the rest of Europe this was the advancement from the non-rational and barbarian roots towards a cultured rationalistic civilisation. Just preceding the Renaissance the Italians were suffering from an identity crisis. After being conquered and ravaged by the barbarians on the west and the loss of Egypt, Syria and most of Asia Minor on the east to the Muslims, the once mighty Empire felt incredibly small and insecure.

In the study of the stupendous amount of scholastic work done by the Muslims, the Italians found a link to their own Greco-Italian legacy and culture – Aristotle, Plato, Socrates and innumerable others whose pagan names and thoughts had been erased from history by the Holy See. This was the identity they were searching for and they grasped at it with a passion. They, the Italians and their Princes, could again feel proud to be Italians. There arose a wild surge for the Roman culture – art flourished, philosophy flourished, rationalism flourished, schools and universities were established.

From this time hence there was a re-alignment of the Greco-Italian identity. The Ancient Greeks and Romans had considered themselves not Europeans but part of the Mediterranean-Asian identity. Their civilisation, friends and foes all belonged to that region. Now that identity was lost and a new European identity was forged. There was a shift in the cultural and psychological makeup away from the Mediterranean (Roberts 1997). Emerging Europe also needed a past to be proud of, so they inherited it from the Greeks and Italians. This was a marriage of convenience between the aristocratic Greco-Romans to the nouveau rich Europe.

The time of the Renaissance was not a stable period in Europe. Since the Mongol calamity in Eastern Europe, one after another disasters ravaged Europe till the middle of the fifteenth century, the win over the Muslims in Spain being the only relief. Conflicts were endemic in Europe during the end of the middle ages. The conflicts varied form feuds between nobles with private armies to those between states. The most protracted one was the 'Hundred Years War' between England and France raging from 1337 to 1453. After the Crusades had ended the Black Death appeared. By mid fourteenth century the Plague swept through Europe with devastating speed killing at least thirty percent of the populace.

> Agnolo di Tura del Grasso of Sienna wrote, "In Sienna a horrible and cruel event the plague began in May. I cannot start to describe its relentless maliciousness. Anyone who witnessed it is stunned by grief and those who did not see it are blessed. They died instantly, with swellings developing in armpits and groins, they fell while talking. Fathers forsook their children, wives deserted husbands, brothers abandoned each other, all ran away from each other as the contagion seemed to spread by breath and sight."

At the start of the Renaissance, the independent cities of North and Central Italy were small with narrow and unhygienic streets. Walking across Florence end to end would take 20 minutes (Roberts, 1997). There were five main cities Naples, Milan, Florence, Venice and the Papal States. The rulers of the cities were the rich merchant families who were referred to as 'Princes'. One of the most famous was the Medici family who ruled Florence in the fifteenth century. Cosimo Medici was one of the first patrons of arts and science. He promoted the scholar Ficino, sculptors Ghiberti and Donatello and architect Brunelleschi. Besides the mercantile families, the other important category of people was the Condottieri mercenaries who did the fighting for the cities and were paid by the Princes. In Milan, after the Visconti family the mercenary family of Sforza became the rulers. The first ruler was the powerful captain Francesco Sforza followed by Ludovico Sforza 'The Moor'.

The commercial cities also had, though disapproved by Church, money exchangers and lenders. Many of the wealthiest families were merchants as well as 'bankers'. In Florence there was a dowry bank in which a sum of money was paid at the time of the birth of a female infant. When she grew up to marriage age this would increase and form her dowry. Girls were considered marriageable at the age of twelve and by fifteen most were married.

The rich indulged in fashion and entertainment such as hunting parties, falconry and music. The significant part of the population in Italy, and Europe, were country peasants working in the fields. They were considered lowly by those who worked in the towns, the town folk earning twice that of the country peasant. Medicine was not well developed and the hospitals in Italy were more a place of rest for the sick than that of cure. Some of the 'doctors' practiced in the dangerous blood-letting of the sick people by cutting their veins to let out 'bad' blood and 'cure' them. Though the rich families had political differences with the Church the general people were still very religious. This was all to change soon.

In the 12th and 13th centuries religious studies became organised and great interest developed in theology and philosophy and mass translation of Muslim works began. In the 14th century Petrach sowed the seeds of the intellectual humanist movement. By the end of 15th century the rest of Europe caught up with Italy in literate manpower and had overtaken it in demand for books due to establishment of numerous Universities. Paris, having influenced by the proximity of Umayyad Spain, had started the book revolution in the 13th century. The subsequent establishment of Universities in Prague, Vienna, Caen, Bordeaux, Dole, and Louvain increased the demand for different types of books. Printing started in second half of the 14th century. Gutenberg's invention of types in the mid 15th century gave a tremendous boost to printing and book publishing.

From the myriad confusion of the past emerged a new kind of civilisation with its power based on freedom of thought and its wealth based on emergence of industry and improvement of agriculture. European national demarcation became culturally defined by the rise of various modern languages - French, Italian, English, Flemish, Catalonian and Czech.

Mining, metallurgy and shipbuilding also became very important. Most large European town would have a public clock by the 16th century. Europe was forging ahead, but it was England that started to accelerate ahead of all. By the first half of the 17th century the first fire engines were made and the first postal service between London and Edinburgh was established.

During this period, the Papal office had degenerated to some extent. The greatness of the true Christian spirit had been suppressed and was replaced by worldly aspirations. When Martin Luther (1483–1546), an Augustinian Friar, came to Rome he was appalled by the wealth and hypocrisy of the Church. The Church raised money by selling 'pardons' to people who had committed or intended to commit a sin. The pardons were pieces of paper bearing pardons from the Pope sold by Church agents. Luther was provoked enough to quarrel with the Pope. He was excommunicated in 1521 but his 'Reformation' movement continued in Switzerland, France, Scotland and Germany and gave rise to the Protestants.

Stalwarts of the Renaissance

The Renaissance would spawn a huge number of stalwarts in different fields of arts and science. Few important ones, along with some reference to relevant previous Muslim works, are listed below.

Bacon

Roger Bacon (1214-1292), an English philosopher and Franciscan Friar, is the originator of the experimental method in Europe. Bacon had studied Muslim works from Cordoba and was influenced by Muslim scholars like Ibn Haitham, Al Kindi, Ibn Firnas and Ibn Sina. He quotes Ibn Haitham extensively in his work on optics in *Opus Maius*. A great impact on him was the work of Al Razi *The Book of the Secret of the Secrets* translated into Latin *Secretum Secretorum*. He could speak Arabic and would publicly praise the works of Arabs/Muslims (Al Hassani, 2007).

Petrarch

Francesco Petrarca (1304 –1374), known as Petrarch, is considered by many to be the 'father of the Renaissance Humanism.' An Italian scholar, he is best known for his Italian poetry, the *Canzoniere* and the *Trionfi* and his translation of ancient works. He was very concerned with the accuracy of previously translated manuscripts. He checked all the translations himself, 'I prefer to observe with my own eyes than those of others." His *Secretum* *meum (the Secret Book)* is a self examination of his Christian faith in dialogue. It was found after his death and was probably not meant for circulation. In the dialogue his secularism and secular achievements didn't preclude God. According to him God had given intellect and creative potential to humans to be utilised to their fullest.

Petrarch was the model for the Humanist Movement, an eclectic search into knowledge. The intellectual movement began in Florence at the end of the 14th century. Initially, the Humanists were simply teachers of Latin literature but over time, their knowledge improved. They came in contact with knowledge that had been translated to Latin and translation works were considered so important that they markedly improved modern philology. By the mid-15th century humanists were teaching moral philosophy, grammar, rhetoric, poetry and history.

Petrach was initially a priest, but gave up the vocation. In the Church he saw a lovely woman named 'Laura' and fell in love. She was already married and there was little or no contact with her. But he wrote of her in his poems and harboured her in his heart forever.

Da Vinci

Leonardo Da Vinci (1452 – 1519) was an Italian polymath. He is considered a mathematician, engineer, inventor, anatomist, painter, sculptor, botanist, writer and musician. He lived in Florence when Lorenzo Medici governed it. Michelangelo, Raphael and Niccolo Machiavelli flourished at the same time as Da Vinci. He learnt painting in the studio of artist Verrochio. He painted one of the angels in 'Baptism of Christ' by Verrochio. When Verrochio saw his student's work has surpassed his, he decided it was time to retire. Of the twelve of Da Vinci paintings that has survived the most famous is 'Mona Lisa'. Much has been written about the painting and the mysterious smile of the lady in the painting, but the real genius of the painting is in the subtle play with the shades of colours that makes the face look lifelike, almost a photograph rather than a painting. His other famous painting is the 'Last Supper' which shows Jesus and his apostle on the table eating their last supper together.

Da Vinci's fame also lies in his notebooks with 5000 pages of notes and sketches. These notebooks are filled with various types of sketches: fossils, skeletons, plants, muscles, embryos and eye structures. There are designs for irrigation and notes on the strength of material. There are highly imaginative sketches of flying machines and military weaponry These also included sketches of pumps, lathes, cranes and steam engines. He made cleve devices for the King Francis I of France and died still in his employment. Some of his work are reminiscent of the Banu Musa brothers of the Abbasid era and Al Jazari, engineer of th 13th century.

Da Vinci also drew the vitruvian man, a man of perfect proportion from the Roma Canon of Vitruvious. Da Vinci's illustration was considered innovative because it showe that the centre of the man was not the navel but lower. The same conclusion had bee reached by Muslim scholars of the *Ikhwan Al Safa* five centuries earlier (Al Hassani, 2007 Da Vinci completed the work on the camera obscura invented by Ibn Haitham and develope a full design.

Machiavelli

Niccolo di Bernardo dei Machiavelli (1469 – 1527) was a diplomat, political philosopher, musician, poet and playwright. He was a Florentine diplomat and visited the French court on several missions. He became the right hand man to the Borgia ruler of Florence and had led a band of soldiers against Pisa. His famous work 'The Prince' proposes that a ruler should do all within his means, morality not withstanding, to govern and control the state and people. The departure from moral was opposite to that of the 11th century *'Dastur al-Wuzara'* and *'Siyasat Nama'* of Nizam Al Mulk. These two books advised the rulers to rule on the basis of morality. On the other hand, the stupendous 14th century work of Ibn Khaldun *'The Proglemena'* was more an objective study into statecraft rather than advice to rulers.

Michelangelo

Michelangelo di Lodovico Buonarroti Simoni (1475 – 1564), was the greatest sculptor and one of the great painters of the Renaissance. His best known works are the *David* and the *Pieta* sculpted early in his professional life. He painted the famous Frescos, *The Last Judgment,* on the altar wall and the scenes from Genesis on the ceiling of the Sistine Chapel in Rome. He also designed the dome of St. Peter's Basilica. His use of the large pilaster columns revolutionised classical architecture.

Copernicus

Nicolaus Copernicus (1473 – 1543) is considered the first astronomer to postulate the scientifically based heliocentric theory that put the sun in the centre of the solar system. For thirty years, he read and re-read the translations of Arab books and Greek works and carefully studied the stars. Then in the middle of the sixteenth century he declared that the earth was not the centre of the Universe as held by the Church but, in fact, the earth moved round the sun. Seventy years after the publication of his famous book *'On the Revolutions of the Celestial Spheres'* the Church declare him a heretic.

His theories were based on Nasir Al Din Tusi and Ibn Al Shatir's works and was also influenced by Al Zarqali's Toledan Astronomical Tables and Al Battani's comprehensive astronomical treatise that included star catalogues and planetary tables. His planetary model and theories were mathematically identical to that of Ibn Al Shatir, prepared a century earlier (Al Hassani, 2007).

Kepler

Johannes Kepler (1571-1630) the German astronomer, mathematician and astrologer is famous for the eponymous laws of planetary motion. In optics, Ibn Haitham's six century older work influenced him. He improved the camera obscura further enlarging the projected image. He also relied on Ibn Haitham's study on refraction of light (Al Hassani, 2007).

~~~

Da Vinci died in 1519 and in 1520 Suleiman the Magnificent became the Sultan of the great Ottoman Empire. He ruled an Empire much bigger then the biggest European countries put together and from a splendid capital, with beautiful and artistic palaces and gardens, which alone was larger than the most famous of the Italian cities put together. But the Europeans had already chosen to stride on a path that in a few centuries would make them surpass all other empires including that of the Ottomans.
~~~

Return of the Empires

The 13th century Mongol onslaught was a cataclysmic crisis the likes of which the Muslims had never faced. Much of the Muslim lands had been devastated, cities burnt, uncountable numbers killed, their knowledge base destroyed and they were left without an effective Caliph. It would take a few centuries for the Muslims to recover and come out of this desolation.

The same 13th century Mongols onslaught had driven a band of Turks from Khorasan to Armenia. When the Mongolian fury had abated the band decided to return to Khorasan. On their way back, while crossing a river, their leader was drowned. That made the band change directions and instead they went to Asia Minor which was under the rule of the waning Seljuks. They successfully negotiated employment under the Seljuks and were awarded a fief. In 1288, Othman the founder of the Ottoman dynasty became the chief of this fiefdom.

After the Mongols left Asia Minor, in the ensuing political vacuum Othman made his move. He declared himself an 'Amir' or the ruler of an independent Principality. He ruled for thirty eight years changing his fief to a Kingdom mainly by conquering Byzantine areas. He was courageous, sagacious and unostentatious and also a person who acquired what he wanted. A couple of anecdotes highlight this trait.

> Before Othman began his conquests a council was held among the Turks to enunciate their future policy. Othman suggested a policy of regional expansion. But his uncle Dundar opposed this policy. Othman removed the opposition by having his uncle executed.
>
> Sheik Ebadali was a religious scholar who had a very beautiful and cultured daughter called Mal Khatun. She was affectionately known as 'Kamuya' – the brightness of the moon. Othman proposed marriage but Ebadali did not agree. One night Othman was the guest of Ebadali. The next morning he narrated a dream to the Sheikh. In the dream, a moon had risen from the chest of Ebadali and when it had become full, it hid in the chest of Othman. Then a tree had burst forth from his loins that covered the whole world. Ebadali, thus, interpreted the tree to be the global dynasty that was yet to come. He agreed to marry Mal Khatun to Othman. (Hasan, 2005)

His first son Alauddin had studied under the grandfather, Sheikh Ebadali, and become a scholar passing most of his time in studies and religious practices. His second son Orkhan became a seasoned soldier of many campaigns and was asked to become the ruler after Othman. But he hesitated to take power in place of his elder brother only accepting when

Alauddin, himself, asked him to take power promising to be his minister. From then on the two, the scholar and the soldier, would decide the future of the Turks. This was a good example set by them but not followed by many future Turk royals.

Orkhan expanded his conquest and took on the title of 'Sultan'. As he grew powerful, the Byzantines were at times forced to seek his support. In 1338 Byzantine Emperor Andronicus III died leaving a four year old son John Palaeologus as the heir. The administration was managed by co-regents Anna, the mother, and Grand Chancellor Cantacuzene. But conflict soon broke out between the two co-regents and both sides sought Orkhan's assistance. Cantacuzene offered Orkhan the hand of his daughter Theodora. Orkhan married her and sent his troops to the aid of his father-in-law. With the aid of the troops Cantacuzene besieged Constantinople. In a year's time a treaty was signed. Under the treaty another daughter of Cantacuzene was to be married to the young John. Thus Cantacuzene became the father-in-law of the Turk Sultan and the Byzantine Emperor. (Hasan, 2005)

When the Serbians attacked Byzantium, the Turkish troops drove them away. For the loan of Turkish troops Byzantium gave Orkhan the Tzympa fortress in European Hellespont. But relationships did not always stay so accommodating. At other times the two domains would come head to head as well. Though, ultimately, Orkhan became the owner of the whole of Asian domain of the Byzantines.

Orkhan died at the age of seventy two when his son Murad (Murat) became the Sultan. He ruled for thirty years and vastly enlarged his empire both in Asia and Europe. He led campaigns in Bulgaria, Macedonia, Serbia, Thrace and some states of Asia Minor. Upon the annexation of southern Bulgaria the border of the Ottoman Empire extended over the Danube. Murad's death took place in a dramatic way. A Balkan coalition under king Lazar sent a challenge to Murad. The Turkish force marched west from Bulgaria and engaged the coalition. It was a hotly contested battle with loses on both side. A Serbian noble, Milos Obilic, rode to Murad's camp declaring that he was a deserter and had intelligence that he wanted to pass on to Murad. The plan was to kill Murad by stratagem and demoralize the Turks. The noble knelt before Murad paying homage then suddenly stabbed him inflicting a fatal wound. The noble was instantly executed.

The wounded Murad declared to his men that his death was imminent but as a last wish he wanted to hear the news of victory before he died. This made the Turk army charge into battle with unprecedented fury and ferocity and soon victory came their way. King Lazarus was brought before Murad and executed upon his command. Soon Murad breathed his last as Serbia was reduced to vassalage.

His son Bayazid the 'Thunderbolt' (Beyazit), given the title due to his dashing bravery in fields of battle, became the Sultan. He agreed to a peace treaty with Serbia under which Serbia became a vassal to the Ottomans and was bound to provide five thousand troops whenever asked. To consolidate the deal he was married to Princess Despina of Serbia.

He expanded his conquest in Asia Minor and also annexed Bulgaria and Greece. Constantinople was placed under siege and significant. Byzantine land was under his command. The Byzantine emperor Manuel II Palaeologusa orgnaised a large coalition of European powers for a new crusade against the Ottomans. The battle took place in 1396 in which the Crusadors were led by the King of Hungary and future Holy Roman Emperor Sigismund, They were comprehensively defeated in the Battle of Nicopolis.

While Bayazid was on the pinnacle of his power in the west, another Conqueror was rising on the east. The Amirs (Beylics) of Asia Minor whom Bayazid had displaced appealed for help to Taimur the Conqueror.

Taimur the Conqueror

After Chengiz, his son Chagtai ruled Transoxiana. Gradually the Chagtais also converted to Islam. Later Transoxiana came to be divided into Turkestan and Transoxiana proper.

Born in Kish of Central Asia in 1336, Taimur belonged to the Gurkhan section of the Birlas Turks. From his maternal side he was a descendent of Chagtai and was an office holder of the Turkestan ruler. But discrepancies developed between him and the ruler and he had to leave his country. He wandered around in various lands till the ruler of Seestan engaged him to suppress a local revolt. Taimur suppressed the revolt and in the process captured some forts. The Seestan ruler now feared that Taimur would become too powerful and decided to attack and dispossess him. In the battle that followed Taimur was dislodged and one of his legs was wounded giving him a permanent limp. Thus he came to be known as 'Taimur Lang' or Taimur the Lame (Tamerlane).

But in a few years time, Taimur was back in Central Asia and riding on the crest of rapid campaigns became the ruler of Turkestan and Transoxiana. Then he captured Khawarizm and Kashgar and consolidated his rule in Central Asia with his capital in Samarqand. That was just the beginning for soon after that he launched himself into a staggering career of conquest that is rare in history. Taimur was a Muslim but the ferocity and cruelty of his conquest was more in line with the Mongols.

He captured Khorasan bringing the ruling Kart dynasty to an end. His campaign in Persia gathered pace with him attacking and converting states of Shiraj and Mazandaran into vassal states. Then he turned towards Seestan with a vengeance for giving him the limp. The capital, Sabzwar, was demolished after a fierce battle and a mountain of heads was built in the Mongolian style to signify the victory. Then after capturing large part of Persia he turned towards the west and occupied Azerbaijan and Georgia. He engaged the Golden Horde Khanate and sacked their capital Sarai on the Volga. He then marched to Moscow and defeated the Duke. Where Alexander had refrained and the Mongols had failed he tore into India and sacked Delhi, at that time, the capital of the Tughluk Sultans. The Sultan escaped but Taimur left a wake of devastation and mountains of heads behind. Taimur invaded India using the pretext of taking Islam to India, when Delhi itself was being ruled by Muslim Tughluk Sultans. After his conquest of India was over he left with significant wealth. Next he took Syria from the Mamluks and occupied Baghdad.

Meanwhile, Ottoman Sultan Bayazid had dethroned the Amirs of Asia Minor. These Amirs invoked the help of Taimur. The two biggest army of the world, 1.8 million with Taimur and 1.2 million with Bayazid clashed in Ankara on the 21st of July 1402. After the titanic upheaval the Ottomans were defeated and Bayazid and one of his sons, Musa, were captured. Bayazid died after about a year in prison. There were rumours that Bayazid had been ill-treated, work of Oriental fictions, but the scribes of Taimur's court writes in their chronicles that Bayazid was well treated and Taimur mourned his death. Taimur released Prince Musa, the captured son of Bayazid, to take and bury the body of Bayazid.

Among the prisoners was a delicate looking officer who had taken part in the battle and fought very bravely. On being produced to Taimur, he was amazed to see that the officer was, in fact, a beautiful woman in soldier's uniform. Seeing bravery and beauty personified in a single person, Taimur fell in love. He proposed marriage and was accepted. The name of the lady was Hamida Banu. (Hasan, 2005)

Finally, when Taimur returned to his home in Samarqand the lands from the Ganges in the east up to the Volga and the Mediterranean in the west lay at his feet. The conquests of Taimur exceeded those of other Generals known in History. In his conquests he had destroyed the Muslim powers in the Volga valley which opened up the doors for the rise of Russia (Hasan, 2005).

He developed Samarqand so that it became one of the best cities in the world. To improve his city he had assembled skilled artisans, engineers and designer from all over the world. Then he built a tomb for himself, the 'Gur-i-Mir', bearing in golden inscriptions the history of his exploits.

In 1405, he started a campaign to conquer China. But the conqueror, fittingly, died while leading a campaign of conquest. His body was brought back and buried. His tomb is one of the main attractions of Samarqand.

Harold Lamb writes in *Tamerlane – the Earth Shaker*, "Five hundred and fifty years ago a man tried to make himself master of the world. In everything he undertook he was successful. We call him Tamerlane." He further states, "In the beginning he was a gentleman of little consequence – master of some cattle and land in that breeding ground of conquerors of Central Asia. Not the son of a king as Alexander was, or the heir of a chieftain like Chengiz Khan. The victorious Alexander had at the outset his people, the Macedonians, and Chengiz Khan had his Mongols. But Tamerlane gathered a people." Further comparing Taimur, Lamb states, "Taimur, in common with Chengiz Khan, had the strange genius of war that made them appear superhuman. Much as we admire the campaigns of Caesar, the exploits of Hannibal, or the inspired strategy of Napoleon, upon reflection, it is becoming clear, that the two conquerors from Asia are, with Alexander, the masters of war upon the stage of the world. Their feats of arms may have been duplicated by other in miniature, but never on the earth as a whole."

The defeat of the Ottomans by Taimur gave the beleaguered Byznatines the much needed respite. Similarly, the death of Taimur and the consequent break-up of his empire would give the Ottomans the respite they needed to rebuild their empire. Thus, the achievements of Taimur though earth-shattering were not historically binding. He did not incorporate the Islamic philosophy of governance nor adhered to it's morality in battles which would have given his empire more permanency. He was an Alexander with no Aristotle.

The Ottomans

In the 15th and 16th centuries the Ottomans ruled over the greatest empire in the world. They conquered Constantinople in 1453 and Athens in 1456. Serbia was assimilated into the empire in 1459, Bosnia in 1462, Albania in 1468, and Herzegovina in 1481. The Ottomans accomplished everything in a grand manner, be it building palaces and roads or be it going to war. They were the first in Europe to have a permanent military music corp called the *Mehterhane*.

All through these centuries their successes, their domains, their cities all appeared otherworldly which dumbfounded both friends and foes. Their ceremonies were more lavish than the Romans, their dignity higher than the Persians, and wealth greater then all. More than thirty nations were incorporated into this empire. As in other Muslim empires there was no great missionary impulse and rule was collaborative. Its dignitaries, officers and troops were largely Balkan Slavs. Its merchants were Armenian and sailors were Greeks.

In 1402, the defeat at Ankara to Taimur and the death of Bayazid put the Ottomans suddenly on the brink of extinction. All the states in Asia Minor gave tutelage to Taimur. But the death of Taimur gave the Ottomans a respite of sorts. Five of Bayazid's sons had been involved in the battle of Ankara. The division led by the eldest son Mustafa was utterly routed. After the battle Mustafa was not found, nor his body discovered. The other brothers got embroiled in an eleven year conflict of succession. There was stress and chaos in the empire. Finally, the youngest brother Muhammad (Mehmet) emerged victorious. Muhammad turned out to be a superb administrator. He established good ties with the Europeans and, without any campaigns, managed to coax the Asia Minor states back to Turkish tutelage. He set up an era of consolidation and prosperity. For his personality he became renowned as 'The Great Gentleman.'

After him, his son, Murad (Murat) II succeeded the throne and reigned from 1421 to 1451. At the very start of his rule the Byzantine ruler Manual II resorted to stratagem. He produced from his prison a person called Mustafa and acknowledged him as the son legitimate heir to the throne of Bayazid. Manuel had first secured a stipulation that Mustafa would repay him for his liberation by giving up a large number of important cities. The pretender was landed by the Byzantine galleys in the European dominion of the Sultan where he gathered an army. For the Ottomans that was the end of fragile peace with Byzantium. Murad defeated and executed Mustafa and lay siege on Constantinople and bombarded it with his cannons. Manuel's successor sued for peace and agreed to pay a heavy tribute.

But further campaigns by Murad proved unsuccessful and the Turks were defeated twice by a coalition led by Hungary along with Poland, Walachia, Bosnia and Serbia. On the call for crusade by the Pope Eugenius, contingents from France and Germany had joined the coalition while Venice and Genoa gave naval support. In the peace negotiations Hungary ceded Walachia while Serbia and Szegaddin became free from Turkish tutelage.

Annoyed at the failure at these campaigns Murad abdicated in favour of his fourteen year old son Mohammad (Mehmet) II and retired to the Magnesia Palace. Europe, on the other hand, was not satisfied with the peace treaty. The Pope made Hungary abrogate the treaty and a large army moved towards the Ottomans. The young Muhammad was at a loss and Murad was forced to emerge from his retreat and take command. He marched to Europe and after a fluctuating battle at Varna in 1445 finally decimated most of the European army which re-established Ottoman supremacy in Europe.

Murad abdicated again putting Muhammad back on the throne. But the next year a revolt by the Turk army occurred in the capital Adrionople. Murad was once again forced to emerge from his retirement. When he arrived in Adrionople, he was received with joy and ovation and the revolt sputtered to an end. This time he decided to stay at the helm of power. The same year he defeated another coalition of Bosnia, Hungary and Serbia. After the victory, the Turks reclaimed the lands they had lost and annexed Serbia while Bosnia again became a vassal. Murad built a large number of colleges, hospitals, caravanserais (inns), public building and mosques throughout his realm. He became the only ruler to be recalled to power after twice abdicating.

Conquest of Constantinople

On his death Muhammad II became the Sultan. Emerging from his father's shadow Muhammad proved to be a brilliant ruler. His first and foremost aim was to remove the ever present challenge of Byzantium. He decided to take the double walled and forted Constantinople itself. He made a fortress 'Anadolu Hissar' on the Asian side of the Bosporus and trained his cannons from there on Constantinople. Constantine XI the Byzantine Emperor objected to the erection of the fortress and threatened to release Orkhan, a grandson of Bayazid, and support his claim to the throne.

This, instead of stopping the construction, caused Muhammad to build the fortress at a hectic pace. On the 6th of April, 1453 the siege of Constantinople began with bombardment from land and the sea. Gradually the thick double walls were reduced to ruins. The final assault took place on 29th May, 1453. In desperation Constantine called out, "Isn't there any Christian who can cut off my head!" He died fighting bravely and Constantinople fell marking the end of the Empire that rose with the Caesars of Rome.

This victory became an historic landmark and Muhammad took on a number of titles, including 'Muhammad the Conqueror' and 'Emperor of the Holy See'. He made

Constantinople his Capital. Over the past, a sizable population had emigrated from Constantinople due to the decline of Byzantium Empire. Now Muslims from all over the realm came and settled there. Dwellings, mosques and public buildings were developed and the city again became one of the grandest in the world.

The Turks defeated an alliance of Persians and Venetians. As a result, they gained the Aegean Island of Euboea from the Venetians. They also annexed Crimea and occupied the fort of Oranto in Southern Italy.

After Muhammad, Bayazid II led a lacklustre rule for thirty one years. He had to fight Jamshed, his brother, who demanded that the Empire be divided. Bayazid had replied that the Empire was a bride whose favours could not be shared. Jamshed also known as Jem in history was defeated by Bayazid. Salim (1465 – 1520), the son of Bayazid, had great influence over the army and forced the abdication of his father. Salim's brothers revolted and in the consequent battle were defeated and killed. Then under the incitation of the Saffavid Persia a number of Shia revolts occurred. Ruthlessly, Salim had a large number of Shias killed and suppressed the revolt. Then, with his army, he marched against the Saffavid and defeated them in 1515 capturing Tabriz the capital. In the peace treaty Kurdistan and Diyarbakir provinces were ceded to the Ottomans.

In the next two years he fought the Mamluks of Egypt and defeated them. Thus Egypt, Makkah and Madinah fell under the Turk domain. He returned to Istanbul (Constantinople) with the nominal Abbasid Caliph who had resided in Cairo. In Istanbul the Abbasid handed over the title of Caliph to Salim. Thus Caliph Salim took on the spiritual leadership of the Muslims.

Like many of the rulers, he had a dual characteristic, ruthless politically but very cultured socially. He was man of high literary tastes and could also engage in ethical and religious discourses. He patronized trade, commerce, and learning and also strengthened the navy by building 100 galleys and 150 new battle ships.

Sulaiman the Magnificent

Next to come to power was Salim's only son Sulaiman (Suleyman), known in world history as Sulaiman the Magnificent (1494 – 1566). He was not only the greatest Ottoman but one of the greatest rulers of all time. He had a dignified bearing and was a striking figure in a brilliant court that was visited by very large numbers of foreign monarchs, nobles, Generals and great merchants.

The time of Sulaiman had produced famous rulers like Akbar the Great of India, Henry VIII and Elisabeth of Britain, Chares V of Germany, Francis of France and Shah Ismail of Persia. But in comparison to 'Sulaiman, the Lord of the Age' all turned pale. His empire extended over three continents Asia, Europe and Africa inhabited by a number of different 'races'.

He was very educated, cultured and was a distinguished poet and goldsmith. He was multilingual and spoke four languages: Turkish Chagatay, Persian, Arabic and Serbian. Suleiman instituted legislative amendments relating to society, education, taxation, and criminal law and came to be known as *Kanuni,* 'The Law Giver.' His canonical law, the *Kanuns*, established the mode of the empire for centuries after his death. He was a great patron of culture, and the designer of the golden age of the Ottoman Empire's artistic, literary and architectural development. He constructed the city of Seven Hill on the Bosporus and a number of bridges and aqueducts in various regions. He built many grand mosques and mausoleum as well. The architect genius Sinan was patronized by him. In spare time he would write copies of the Quran. Some of the copies are still extant in Istanbul.

Militarily, Sulaiman had two frontiers to contend to. On the eastern frontier were the inimical Saffavids and the rising Portuguese naval power in the Indian Ocean that had set up bases in west coast of India and east coast of Africa. On the western frontier was Europe with the vast powerful Austrian-Habsburg realm. The Austrian-Hapsburgs were also the rulers of the Holy Roman Empire after the fall of Constantinople. Sulaiman personally led 13 military campaigns and entrusted his senior officers to others. He gave more priority to his campaigns in the west.

In his first campaign in Europe he captured the vital Fortress city of Belgrade that had remained independent even after the Ottomans had taken Serbia and Bosnia. Francis I of France formed an alliance with Sulaiman after suffering a major defeat at the hands of the Hapsburg. The Ottomans then attacked Hungary and won a great victory in which Louis II of Hungary was killed. The capital Buda fell to the Ottomans. Sulaiman also annexed most of the Middle East and large stripes of North Africa reaching Algeria. Under his rule, the Ottoman fleet dominated the seas from the Mediterranean to the Red Sea and the Persian Gulf.

Sulaiman's court could hold up to six thousand courtiers. While the court was in session, he did not like people speaking pointlessly, thus when he was present all were silent. The very silence of six thousand nobles in front of their Sultan was intimidating and overpowering. At one time, recalling his namesake Prophet and King Solomon, he had declared "Truly, I have surpassed you".

~~~

Ottoman glory reached its height under Sultan Sulaiman the Magnificent. The Ottomans excelled in a number of disciplines. The Ottoman architecture was grand producing buildings such as the Topkapi Palace, ordered to be built by Sultan Mohammad the conqueror of Constantinople. This was a complex of courtyards and gates that housed 4,000 people. By the 15th century the Ottomans had revolutionised schooling by setting up the schools in
~~~

complexes of fantastic architecture, known as *Kulliye*, which included hospitals, dining areas, and mosques with delicate minarets and large domes.

In the 16th century, Sulaiman ordered the construction of massive new complex of religious, educational, public and commercial buildings and built with a mosque, madrassa school, hospital and hospice. The cities were subject to strict building regulation far in advance of most European cities (Nicolle, 2008). Awe inspiring architecture and creative literature were in fashion. Turk textiles, carpets and ceramics became vogue in Ottoman Turkey and Europe. The world maps and mariners manuals produced by the Ottomans, such as those by Piri Re'is and Ali Macar, were one of the best of their times.

In the 17th century it was a Turk named Lagari Hasan Celebi who invented the first manned rocket. He launched himself in a rocket using three thousand pounds of gun powder as the firing fuel. Willen E. Burrows in his book *This New Ocean, The Story of the First Space Age* mentions, "The rocket then carried Celebi high into the air, where he opened several 'wings', and then glided to a safe landing in front of the royal palace (Al Hassani, 2007). Another Turk, Hararfen Ahmed Celebi experimented flying with wings. Evliya Celebi records this in his book *A Book of Travel* stating the he used Al Juhuri's calculations derived from the study of the eagle in flight. After nine flight experiments he modified the shape of the wings on which were stitched eagle feathers.

During the 18th century the Turkish military *Mehter* Band music influenced the rest of Europe. Composers like Mozart, Beethoven, Haydn and Gluck imitated the "Janissary Music" used by the fearsome Ottoman *Janissary* infantry (Nicolle, 2008). Turkish musical instruments like the Turkish Crescent, also known as the Jingling Johnnie, were eventually adapted by the Europeans.

The Saffavids

The sixteenth century saw the rise of two other magnificent empires, the Saffavids of Persia and the Moghuls of India. The rise and fall of these two empires were amazingly interwoven in time and space.

The Saffavids started off as a dynastic religious order with Safi-ud-Din as the Sheikh or head of the order. The charismatic Sheikh was a great Shia scholar with a Sufi propensity. He had a large following in Persia and Asia Minor. Over time as the Dynasty progressed their fame spread out. The third Sheikh of the Dynasty was Khawaja Ali. Taimur, on defeating the Ottomans, decided to pay his respect to the court of Khawaja (Hasan, 2005). He was very impressed by the spiritual eminence of the Sheikh and asked, "How can I serve?"

The Sheikh responded, "If you truly want to be of service then release the Turks you have imprisoned."

Taimur ordered the release of the Turks and left. The released prisoners were much indebted to the Sheikh and most of them became his followers. The Saffavids gained a lot of power and prestige for being the 'Order' which a person of Taimur's status had served.

With the passage of time the Order became more influential. When a later Sheikh named Haidar was killed by the ruler of Shirwan, Haidar's young son Ismail became the new Sheikh. The Order had a group of warrior-followers called the Qizilbash (Red Heads) because of their red headgear. The Qizilbash gathered round Ismail and when he was sufficiently strong he attacked and executed the ruler of Shirwan. Then he marched to Tabriz and occupied it and declared himself *Shah* Ismail in 1501.

Shah Ismail was a handsome man, an outstanding General and a poet. After consolidating his position he launched a campaign of conquest. By 1510, showing extraordinary valour, he overran the whole of Persia and adjoining areas included Hamadan, Shiraz, Kerman, Najaf, Karbala, Van, Baghdad, and Herat, as well as other parts of Khorasan. He then had to contend with two big Sunni powers the Uzbeks of Central Asia on the north and the Ottomans on the west. The first challenge came from the Uzbeks, the Muslim decedents of Chengiz Khan's son Jochi. The ruler of the Uzbeks, Shaibani Khan, sent him two symbolic gifts, a beggars bowl and a sceptre signifying that the Saffavids were beggars and not worthy of wielding the authority of the sceptre. Shah Ismail replied with two gifts of his own, a spindle and some yarn, signifying that Shaibani was a female indulging in idle chatter and was no match to him in the battle field.

The two armies confronted each other near Merv in 1510 where Shaibani Khan was defeated and killed. Shah Ismail then invaded the Uzbek territories and further captured Balk and Herat. One of his prisoners turned out to be the sister of Babar, the Sunni ruler of Kabul and the future founder of the Moghul Dynasty of India. Shah Ismail returned her to him with due respect. He also helped Babar to capture Samarqand.

After being victorious against the Uzbeks, Shah Ismail lost a battle with the Ottomans and had to cede some territory. His son became ruler in 1524 and ruled for 53 years. But most of the time he had to spend fighting the Ottoman and the Uzbek invaders. In 1577, Mohammad Shah Khudabanda became the king of the Saffavids. He was partially blind and thus the control of power was in the hands of his Queen Madh-i-Ulya. She was very beautiful and intelligent but could be ruthless as well. Her father had been killed by a local chief. By the time she assumed power the local chief was dead. Hence she summoned his son to the capital and had him assassinated.

To secure the succession of her son, Hamza Mirza, she plotted to kill off all the other rival Princes. According to her plan, one by one the Princes, her stepsons, were being killed off. Soon Prince Abbas, one of her stepsons and also the Governor of Khorasan, was summoned by her to the court. He delayed going there on one pretext or another.

In the meantime, Sultan Murad III of Turkey launched an attack against Persia through Georgia and Shirwan. Crimea, an ally of Turkey, took part in this battle with Adil Giray, the brother of the Crimean King, as commander of the Shirwan front. The Persians lost in the Georgian front but won in Shirwan. Adil was taken prisoner and was presented to the royal court in Qazvin. Adil was a very handsome man and when he was produced in front of the Queen she lost her heart. Lovelorn and spellbound she abandoned her state objectivity and ultimately plotted the flight of Adil from prison. But the plot was leaked and some of the nobles, who were opposed to her rule, took rapid action. Both Madh and Adil were executed. (Hasan, 2005)

The blind Khudabanda vested power on Prince Hamza Mirza. He was a capable General and in the battle front thrashed the Turks on a number of occasions. But, unfortunately, he was assassinated following a conspiracy, most likely by those who had the Queen executed. Khudbanda now vested power on another son Abu Talib. But Abbas revolted at this decision and marched with a strong force to Qazvin. Instead of seeing any further carnage within the family Khudbanda abdicated in favour of Abbas.

Abbas ruled for forty two years and history records him as 'Abbas the Great'. On assumption of power Abbas reorganised the administration and the army. Then he launched himself against the Turks and Uzbeks. Initially, he lost ground against the Turks. But in 1597 he routed the Uzbeks and thus gained his first victory. He had set about modernising his army and employed British military experts for the job. When his army was sufficiently equipped and included an artillery brigade, the most modern unit of an army at the time, he decided to confront the Turks. This time the Persian emerged victorious and regained all the lands that the Turks had occupied earlier.

Hormuz was a strategically important port on the Gulf of Persia. The Portuguese had occupied it about a century ago and held it since. Shah Abbas drove the Portuguese from Hormuz and allowed the British and Dutch to set up factories in the port. He changed his capital to Isfahan which became a grand city with the population of more than half a million.

The city included around 2000 inns, 200 public baths, 50 seminaries and 150 mosques. Large number of public building were constructed which were grand but also masterpieces of intricate and exquisite design. This walled city came to be known as 'Half of the world' for its beautiful edifices. Meshhed, situated near Isfahan, was turned into a centre of religious development and pilgrimage area for the Shia where Shah Abbas would visit annually, sometime walking all the way from Isfahan.

While he grew up, due to Madh's plotting and blindness of Khudabanda, Shah Abbas did not know any parental or filial affection. He grew up as a protagonist in a grandiose, imperial but very impersonal world and inherited a cruel insensitive spot. When he was informed that his sons were plotting against him he had them killed or blinded. Thus his empire was inherited by his grandson Shah Safi.

The Saffavid dynasty ruled up to 1730 when the military genius Nadir Shah crowned himself the King of Persia. The Saffavids were very cultural minded. Shah Tahmasp was a painter and Shah Ismail was a great poet using themes and images in original lyric and didactic religious poetry. They were builders of exquisite palaces, mosques and other edifices with fine workmanship on beautiful tiles. If the Ottomans had a streak of grandiose, the Saffavid creations had the sense of intricate beauty.

The Moghuls

The majority of historical edifices of India, most of them grand in global scale, are of Moghul origin. The Moghuls established the greatest empire that India had ever seen. They were great builder of cities, palaces of unique architecture, and beautiful artistic gardens with fountains and flowing streams which still exist today. The most famous of their edifices is one of the wonders of the world, the Taj Mahal. The Moghuls were very literate and cultured, and patrons of fine arts delving deeply in poetry, painting, perfumery, classical songs and choreography. The illustrious Nau Ratan (The Nine Jewels) of Akbar's court are historically famous as nine intellectually and artistically talented personalities. Such court patronization of talents in social science, astronomy, music, poetry and fine arts continued throughout the dynasty.

Besides enduring architecture and arts, the Moghuls have left behind a unified 'Indian' political identity. Before them the subcontinent was a milieu of culturally and religiously diverse states. It was the Moghuls, starting with Akbar, who had consolidated the concept of an Indian political entity representing the whole of India.

The Moghuls were great romantics. Their emperors are known to have fallen in love with women whom they have cherished throughout their life and to their death.

Babar

Zahiruddin Mohammad Babar (1483 – 1530) was the son of the ruler of Farghana, a Principality in what is now Russian Turkmenistan. He was the descendent of Taimur from his father's side and of Chengiz Khan from his mother's side.

Taimur had divided his empire into three kingdoms. His sons Shahrukh ruled the eastern domain from Herat, and Miran Shah ruled the western domain from Tabriz while Central Asia and Transoxiana was given to Pir Muhammad, who was Taimur's grandson. With the passage of time the dynasty disintegrated and only Khorasan, Transoxiana and Afghanistan were left to the Taimurid. Finally, these also splintered into principalities. Farghana was one of the Principalities.

After the death of his father Babar became the ruler at the age of eleven years only. From thereon, he had to face a titanic struggle to assert himself as a ruler. He had to contend with seasoned rulers such as the Uzbek Shaibani. At fourteen years of age he captured Samarqand in 1497, but while he was there the Uzbeks occupied Farghana itself. He marched back and recovered Farghana but in the process lost Samarqand. He marched for Samarqand again and thus vacillated till Shaibani Khan dispossessed him totally. That made him move south and capture Kabul in 1504 and from there with the help of the Saffavid forces recaptured Samarqand. But ultimately, the Uzbeks again drove him out of Central Asia back to Kabul.

In this struggle, Babar gained experience as an administrator and general. Even in the midst of the struggle he did not overlook his studies and became a scholar and a very cultured person. He became a poet, an artist and a naturalist. He, in later life, wrote an autobiography *Tuzuk-i-Babari* which is valued as a literary masterpiece.

In India, after the Mamluks (13th century), Delhi was ruled by the Khilji dynasty (early 14th century) then the Tughluq dynasty (14th – 15th Century), who were originally Turks who had migrated to India, and finally by the Afghan Lodhi dynasty (15th – 16th Century). When Babar was in Kabul Ibrahim Lodhi was the Sultan of Delhi. Acrimonious factions had grown within the Lodhi family and one of the factions invited Babar to India. Fortune had not favoured Babar in Central Asia and so he responded to the invitation and turned his attention to India. In 1526 Babar met the significantly larger army of Ibrahim Lodhi at the Panipat battlefield about 90 km from Delhi. The field of Panipat was to become famous in history as great battles were to be fought there in later ages.

By the time of this battle, Babar was an experienced and hardened General. His battle strategy led to victory and he occupied Delhi and Agra. Then in a short period of four years Babar had to fight three major and stressful battles from disadvantageous positions in which he humbled the pride of the brave Hindu Rajputs and captured the remnants of Afghanistan. The meaning of his name Babar is 'Lion' and like a majestic lion he fought and carved out a kingdom.

Humayun

After Babar's death his son Naseeruddin Humayun (1530–1556) succeeded to the Moghul throne. He was a sociable and peace loving person. But fate did not allow him any peace at all. At his deathbed Babar, a warrior but also a scholar who was aware of history of kingdoms and successions, advised Humayun not to be cruel or harsh with his brothers. Humayun promised to his father and kept true to his word. When his brother Kamran, the ruler of Kabul, annexed Punjab he remained quiet. But the loss of Punjab made the Moghuls considerably weaker and this made the Afghan group in India revolt under a very able General named Sher Khan. While Humayun was engaged in the campaign to suppress the Afghans, the ruler of Gujarat, Bahadur Shah, revolted. Humayun marched away from the Afghans and went to Gujarat and suppressed the revolt there. Bahadur Shah fled and took refuge with the Portuguese in the Island of Diu.

But by then Sher Khan had captured Bengal and consolidated his powers. When Humayun, in pursuit, reached Bengal the heavy monsoon downpour started and the rivers swelled making large scale army movement impossible. An epidemic struck down his force which made Humayun retreat to Agra. But Sher Khan took the opportunity to harass the Moghul force and finally engaged them in battle of Chausa in 1539. The weakened and demoralized Moghuls suffered a decisive defeat. Humayun escaped with the assistance of a water carrier. The Moghul treasures fell into the hands of the Afghans and Sher Khan declared himself the Emperor of India with the title of Sher Shah.

The next year the Afghans again defeated the Moghuls comprehensively, and this time Humayun lost all his wealth and support. With a close band of followers he wandered about in the deserts of Sindh for three years. Frustrated and friendless, he was on the verge of loosing all hope. Then one night, when he was trying to sleep, he noticed a spider trying to spin a cobweb. The spider would reach a certain point and then fall down. It would turn around, reach the place again and would fall down again. This kept on happening over and over again through out the night until finally the large cobweb was completed. Humayun was amazed at the tenacity and the perseverance of the spider and its final success. That night changed Humayun and he came to believe that 'if you cannot achieve your objective in the first time then try a hundred times.'

He went to the Saffavids and with their help won back Delhi fifteen years after loosing it. Even though fate had denied him, he was more a scholar than a warrior. He built a library-observatory in Delhi and while coming down the stairs he slipped and fell injuring himself. He died of the injury a year after securing Delhi.

Akbar the Great

Jalaluddin Akbar (1556-1605) was the next emperor. When Humayun died the thirteen year old Akbar was with General Bairam Khan leading an expedition against the Afghans in Punjab. He was declared King immediately but that was a fragile claim as forces loyal to him only controlled Kabul, Kandahar, part of Punjab and Delhi. His first challenge was from King Shah Muhammad Adil of the Afghan Sher Shah Dynasty. Adil's force had 1500 war elephants and was led by a Hindu General named Hemu. The Moghul advisors asked Akbar to leave India and go to Kabul for safety. But Akbar took the decision to stay and fight. He met the Afghans in the second battle of Panipat and defeated them in 1556. That was followed by an amazing sequence of conquest that converted almost the whole of India into the Moghul Empire. His crowning conquest was the defeat of the Rajputs who were an indomitable warrior people of India. Renowned for their bravery the Rajputs fought Akbar bitterly, and at times, to the last man. But finally, the superiority of the Moghuls prevailed. By the age of fifteen Akbar had established himself as Emperor.

Over the last decades, there had been many battles and wars - Afghan versus Moghul, Rajput versus Moghuls, Muslims versus Muslims and Hindus versus Muslims. As a result great bitterness and hatred had been fomented. There was a hardening of religious and ethnic attitudes. Some Muslims had, contradictory to the Quranic injunction, forced Hindus to convert. While some religious scholars had incorporated many non Islamic concepts like the biblical doctrine that considered the origin of the earth to be about 7000 years old. These were all schismatics further dividing a perpetually fractious region. Akbar decided to eradicate hatred, ignorance and superstition from the environment and establish an enlightened Indian creed of governance. Like the Multi-faith debates sponsored by the Abbasids and the Fatimids he formed groups of Hindus, Christians, Muslims, Jains, Zoroastrians and Buddhist and held weekly meeting with them to discuss the basic premise of religion and establish a creed of rule. His biographer Abul Fazal wrote, 'The Emperor was aware of the hatred between the Hindus and the Muslims. But he was convinced this arose from out of mutual ignorance. So this enlightened ruler sought to dispose of this ignorance by making the book of each religion accessible to the other. In this way he wished to show Hindus that some of their customs and superstitions had no basis with their sacred books, and also convince Muslims that it was absurd to ascribe a mere 7000 years of existence of the world.'

He married Rajput Princesses and allowed them to follow their own religion in the royal palace. This brought him the alliance of the Rajputs. The 'Sati' was a religious practice of the Hindus whereby a dead man's widow was burnt alive along with the dead body of the husband. The wife did not have the right to live beyond the husband. Akbar banned the custom, saying that Sati could not be forced on an individual. The Jizya tax was cancelled which caused the Hindus to view him with favour.

In the new empire Akbar faced numerous conflict and issues – political and social – due to the heterogeneous demography that needed to be reconciled. As *Ijtihad* had been closed down for centuries there was no way to promulgate new laws to face these new situations. Akbar decided to create a creed from the existing religo-cultures of his empire called 'Deen-i-Elahi' (religion of God) that would facilitate his rule. His syncretic creed had its opponents. The Muslims religious leaders considered it heresy fearing that this may spawn a new religion as even among the Muslim nobles Islam was being compromised. Non-Muslims had their own reservations. Bhagwan Das, a Hindu Rajput chief, commented that if the Emperor asked him to accept Islam that would be much easier to consider rather than subscribe to a caricature of religions. The European Jesuit Antonio Monserrate commented. "He cared little in that allowing everyone to follow his own religion he was in reality violating all religion!"

But even as 'Deen-i-Elahi' created its controversies, it also created a political success. All the different people of the empire learned to co-exist and an *Indian* empire was established. There was an influx of scholars and artists mainly from Persia whose works would influence Indian literature and philosophy creating unique architecture, art and manuscript paintings.

Akbar's rule of forty nine years was very prosperous. He built a new city, vitalised the administration and reorganised land reforms. To support the administration, his royal astronomer and renowned scholar, Amir Fatehullah Shirazi, developed a solar calendar based on the lunar Hijri. This calendar is still utilised in Bangladesh and the eastern states of India.

When Akbar came to power Moghul rule covered a precarious kingdom. When he died the Moghul's were the rulers of one of the mighty Empires of the world. The German expert on India, Heinrich von Stietencron states in his book *Hindu Myth, Hindu History: Religion, Art, and Politics, 'Akbar's eclecticism brought about a pluralist ambiance that history associates with his governance. He got Todar Mal from Gujarat to set up the revenue system of the kingdom. It was like England and the rest of the world taking Adam Smith from Scotland and making him the father of modern economics. It is Todar Mal that we owe variation in taxation on the basis of fluctuations in rainfall and nature of the soil which he achieved through resurvey of the land in India. Akbar's rule was a patch of effulgence in a general darkness on earth. Poets and artists gravitated to it; faiths rejected in other lands escaped to India to find tolerance.'* (Wood, 2007).

In 1585, Ralf Fitch, ambassador of Queen Elisabeth I visited the court of Akbar carrying a letter from the Queen. The letter stated:

'From Elisabeth by the Grace of God Defender of the Faith, to the Most Invincible and Most Mighty Prince Zelebdin Echebar King of Cambaya.'

The letter stated, *'The singular report of your imperial majesty's humanity has reached the uttermost part of the world...'* and that the ambassador was at the door of Akbar's court *'with courteous and honest boldness...'* hoping for *' mutual and friendly traffic of merchandise on both sides.'*

A military expedition was being prepared and Akbar was busy. He did not have the time to personally see the Ambassador. He was the Emperor of a 100 million people. Elisabeth ruled 3 million people something like one of his Principalities (Wood, 2007).

Jahangir

Akbar's son Nuruddin Salim Jahangir (1605–1627), the next Emperor, consolidated the empire further. His reign of twenty two years was marked with prosperity and relative peace. He gave the British some concessions to carry business in India.

During Akbar's reign, the Ulema had become divided into two groups. One group supporting the royal court and the other group that was against edicts like 'Deen-i-Elahi'. Sheikh Ahmad of Sirhindi, an orthodox reformer, launched a very strong campaign against the creed. He was brought to the royal court where he refused to bow in front of the Emperor as that was against Islam. He refuted charges of public instigation brought against him. But the Ulema in favour of the royal court still condemned him. He was imprisoned in the Fort of Gwalior. But even in prison Sheikh Ahmad influenced many of the inmates. As his popularity surged Jahangir released him and made him an advisor. Under his advice 'Deen-i-Elahi' was abrogated. By then the concept of a multi-ethnic and multi-religious Indian empire had already crystallised and thus 'Deen-i-Elahi', which was always religiously unacceptable, had also become politically redundant.

Two very romantic legends are ascribed to Jahangir: While a young Prince, he is said to have fallen in love with a very beautiful and provocative court dancer named Anarkali. Akbar's royal will had come in between the two lovers. When it became clear that the two were inseparable, even at the threat of death, Akbar ordered that Anarkali be walled alive in the dungeons of one of the Palaces. This was carried out and Jahangir, though forlorn, returned to his normal life. Some romantics further express that later, in secrecy, Akbar had the wall breached and Anarkali was transported to a distant land. Historians disagree with this story and some maintain that Anarkali was, in fact, a wife of Jahangir and mother of his son Parwez.

The other popular story of the young Prince is that he fell in love and wanted to marry a girl of a noble family named Nur Jahan. But Akbar did not approve of the match and Nur Jahan was married to a Persian noble Sher Afghan. They moved to Burdawan where Sher Afghan was a Faujdar or Commander of the Moghuls. When Jahangir became the emperor Sher Afghan died. The rest of the story is historically reliable. One day Jahangir came face to face with the beautiful widow in a fair - 'Meena Bazaar' - and immediately proposed. They were married and she became his Empress.

Both Queen Nur Jahan and Emperor Jahangir were erudite and scholarly. Jahangir wrote his autobiography *Tuzk-i-Jahangiri*. Nur Jahan was an intelligent lady who in the later part of Jahangir's reign dominated the politics of the Moghul Court. She gave audiences at her palace and the ministers consulted with her on most matters. Jahangir even permitted coinage to be struck in her name. In 1626, Jahangir was captured by rebels while on his way to Kashmir. Nur Jahan negotiated the release of her husband.

Nur Jahan married her daughter, Ladli, from Sher Afghan to Shahriyar one of the sons of Jahangir. She then employed her political clout to build Shahriyar as the heir apparent. Another Prince, Khurram, objected to this and a family discord ensued. When Jahangir died in 1627 he was buried, according to his wish, in Lahore, after which started the final struggle for succession. After some bloodshed Khurram emerged victorious and Nur Jahan retired from politics and lived the rest of her life in comfort in Lahore. She had a tomb built over her father's grave and devoted time in the art of perfume making.

Shah Jahan

Shahabuddin Mohammad Khurram took the title of Shah Jahan –Emperor of the World (1628–58). Shah Jahan's rule was another golden era for the Moghuls. After suppressing the usual post-succession revolts he undertook campaigns against the Persians and the Uzbeks of Central Asia. The Moghuls captured Qandahar from the Persian and Balk from the Uzbeks. But these victories were short lived, as the Moghuls gave up further conquest and the regions reverted back to previous ownership in a few years. The Portuguese had erected a fort in

Hugli in Bengal without any permission, and were supporting piracy. An expedition was sent by Shah Jahan which drove the Portuguese away.

The living standard of India continued to prosper during Shah Jahan's rule. His reign is famous throughout the world for its splendour and magnificence. Like his predecessors he was also a great builder. When his greatest love, his wife Mumtaj Mahal, died he built an enduring edifice over her tomb – the Taj Mahal. This dream in marble and gems, one of the wonders of the world, took seventeen years to be erected – a lasting memento of an Emperor's love for his Queen. In the early 1630s, social scientist Muhammad Qazwini Padshanama wrote, 'The eye of the Age has seen nothing like it under the nine vaults of the enamel blue sky, the ears of Time has heard of nothing like it in any past age… It will be a masterpiece for ages to come, increasing the amazement of all humanity.'

This monument also bears the largest inscription of the Islamic text on edifices. Twenty five Surahs from the Quran are inscribed on the great gate, mausoleum and mosque of the Taj. The inscriptions are in elegant black inlay on rectangular marble plaques with ornate floral patterns above the gate arches. All the Surahs speak of the Day of Judgement, Divine Mercy and Paradise promised for the faithful. The Emperor's love was not restricted to this life, he wanted the same Queen in the hereafter.

When Shah Jahan became sick his sons began the fight for succession to the throne. In 1658, Aurangzeb became the Emperor and retired Shah Jahan to a castle near the Taj. The old Emperor would sit by a window and stare towards the Taj for hours remembering his love. He died eight years later.

Aurangzeb

Muhiuddin Muhammad Aurangzeb Bahadur (1618- 1707) ruled the largest Indian empire in history. To establish his rule he first had to battle with his brothers whom he defeated and had two of them executed. He then had to contend with revolts throughout the empire. He suppressed revolts of the Assamese in the East and the Pathans in the West. The ninth Sikh Guru, Tej Bahadur, who had served in the Moghul Army in Assam settled down in East Punjab and took on the title of 'Sachcha Badshah' or 'The True King'. He started to exact tax from the people there. This became a kingdom within the empire and was deemed seditious by the Moghuls and he was captured and ordered to accept the Moghuls as his sovereign. When he refused he was executed. His son Gobind Singh became the tenth Guru and turned his follower into a paramilitary and exhorted them to wage war against the Moghuls. When the Moghul army seized them, Guru Gobind managed to escape but his two sons were captured and executed. While living a fugitive life and hunted by the Moghul forces the Guru sent an epistle of appeal called 'Zafar Nama' to Aurangzeb. This letter also contained information of the atrocities committed by the Moghul forces on the Sikhs. This made Aurangzeb become remorseful and he issued an order that Guru Gobind should not be harassed anymore.

In the South, the Marathas revolted under a very capable leader named Shivaji. He declared himself Maharaja and remained undefeated by the Moghuls. On his death his son Sambaji became the leader who was captured and executed.

Under Aurangzeb, the Moghul Empire was huge, covering almost the whole of India. Aurangzeb had to send expeditions constantly against revolts that cost the treasury much. After the expeditions his army was not allowed any plunder so the treasury remained unfilled. He re-imposed the Jizya Tax on the Non-Muslims to get much needed revenue. This was deemed discriminatory by the Non-Muslims and added fire for subsequent revolts.

Unlike his predecessors he was devout, orthodox and unostentatious. He did not allow music and dancing girls in his court. He was the last great Moghul and when he died his sons started the predictable succession struggle. But none of his progeny proved to be of great calibre. Aurangzeb had aroused much fervour during his rule. People either adored him or abhored him and, thus, after his death there were two distinct types of assessment of him. One group of historians considered him the greatest of Moghul Emperor, while the other group attribute his orthodox policies for the reason for the disintegration of the Empire.

The Nadir Nemesis

In the third decade of the 18th century both the Moghul and Saffavid empires were being rocked by forces of disintegration. The nemesis of the two dynasties rose in the person of a Persian General named Nadir Quli, who created an Iranian empire that stretched from the Indus River to the Caucasus Mountains.

At first he appeared as the saviour of the Saffavid Empire which was being encroached upon by the Ottomans on the west and the Russians of the north. The Arabs of Oman and Afghans also revolted, and finally the Afghans defeated the Saffavid Persians and captured the capital Isfahan and declared themselves the master of Persia. Nadir Quli, a General of Saffavid Shah Tahmasp II, led expeditions after expeditions till he drove the Afghans from Persia. When Tahmasp died he became the regent for the infant heir Abbas III.

He then embarked on a military campaign in which he drove the Turks away and forced the Russians to handover Baku and Derbend. When Shah Abbas III died Nadir ascended the throne taking the title of Nadir Shah. He, similar to Taimur, led a series of successful campaigns in Central Asia and against the Afghans in Qandahar. During the fight against the Afghans, he had requested Moghul Emperor Mohammad Shah to close the Moghul border and not let the Afghan refugees in. Mohammad did not entertain his request and in fact detained the emissary. After winning Qandahar, Nadir Shah attacked India.

Defeating the Moghuls in a series of encounters he progressed to its capital Delhi. The Moghuls capitulated after being defeated in the final battle near Delhi. A huge tribute was settled upon and Nadir Shah entered Delhi as a victor with Muhammad Shah following him in the procession.

But when his officers went to gather the tribute they were fired upon and some of them were killed. Nadir Shah was enraged and he ordered a massacre. For three days the residents of Delhi were indiscriminately massacred. Muhammad Shah appealed to him to stop. Nadir finally ordered the Persians to stop but the indemnity was increased by a huge amount. The Moghuls were helpless and agreed to pay.

After a few months Nadir Shah left. He crowned Muhammad the Emperor of India but went away with all the treasures of India. This included the famous Peacock throne of Shah Jahan made of gold and encrusted with valuable gems, and the famous Kohinoor Diamond, which would end up in the crown of the British monarchs. This plunder of wealth totally broke the backbone of the Moghuls from which they were never to recover.

Nadir Shah next stormed Central Asia and captured Bukhara and Khiva. He fought and defeated the Turks again in 1745. He returned to Persia to suppress internal revolts. During the revolts, Nadir had not felt safe from his own family and had sent all his sons to his ancestral home fort Kalat-i-Nadiri. His suspicion was vindicated as he was assassinated by the Commandant of his own security guard at the behest of his nephew Ali Quli. After Nadir's death his Empire disintegrated.

Advent of the British

Britain's rationalism and the consequent industrial revolution placed it in the forefront of nations. It progressed far in industry, communication, weaponry and policy. Since early 17th century the British East India Company had set up business enterprises and factories along the sea coast of India in Mumbai (Bombay), Kolkata (Calcutta) and Madras. These were all established with Indian permission and partnership. But when India fragmented these enterprises together had enough resources to become a powerful chain, first economic then military. By the mid 18th century, the British East India Company had become engaged in trade and commerce in Bengal and had established some factories. Bengal in eastern India was ruled by independent Nawabs. Without the permission of the Nawab of Bengal they started to build fortifications and an army to 'protect' their people and interest there. The Nawab Siraj-ud-Daulah forbade them to continue with the fortifications. Ultimately, the British conspired with Mir Jafar, the uncle of the Nawab. They also brought in a charge of breaking a treaty against the Nawab and marched their forces against him. The Nawab marched to the battlefield of Plassey with all his nobles including Mir Jafar. When the two forces met, at a critical juncture, the forces of Mir Jafar and his allies turned and joined the British. The Nawab somehow escaped but was hunted and killed by Mir Jafar's son Miran. The British proclaimed Mir Jafar the new Nawab. But the real power came to be held by the British and ultimately they became the ruler of Bengal.

Meanwhile in North and Central India, after 1782, a famine broke out which caused immense distress. The Moghuls who already were plundered of everything by Nadir Shah were now in dire straits. After the death of their incumbent Prime Minister, the Moghul Emperor Shah Alam II invoked the Hindu Maratha General to take up the helm of his government. Thus the military power of the empire went into the hands of the Maratha. After 1785, real power of India was held by the Sikhs in Punjab, the British in Bengal and the Maratha in the central region 'for' the Moghuls.

In 1803, the British had consolidated enough strength in Bengal to challenge the might of the Marathas. After defeating the Marathas they occupied the Moghul capital Delhi. Shah Alam II was forced to make the British his vice-regent. In effect the power was handed over from the Marathas to the British. The Moghul dynasty continued their ceremonial power till 1857 when, after an unsuccessful revolt by the Indian soldiers against the British, Emperor Bahadur Shah Jafar was exiled to Burma by the British ending the Moghul dynasty.

~~~

The Political State of the later Muslims

Like the Umayyads and the Abbasids the succession of rule in all the subsequent Muslim Empires and States were inherited and passed down the royal family. The demographic representation in the state apparatus had widened considerably. For example, the Ottomans had numerous ethnic groups working in their politico-economic structure while the Moghuls had incorporated the Rajputs in their power structure.

The Muslims produced great rulers, administrators, and Generals. Some of them were conquerors in the imperial sense. Most of them sponsored fine arts, architecture, commerce and social sciences. Good schooling systems were mostly available in all Muslim domains. But pure scientific research and development remained negligible or absent.

The Europians would discover that, on the long run, constant technological progress along with adequate investment (which can be equated to high national savings) were paramount for economic growth. Other economic factors like natural resources, demand and supply, population growth, etc., though very important in the short run increased growth rate only temporarily. Without technological advancement a time arrives when the economy cannot grow any further. This is known as the 'steady-state' in which there may be significant production of goods in the economy but the rate of economic growth, over time, is zero. This was one of the main factors due to which countries that engaged in research and development eventually overtook the Muslims countries in worldly might. And that was the root of the Muslim's ultimate weakness in later history.
~~~

Development of Language and Culture

Today, the term 'civilisation' is applied to different groups of people – archaic and contemporary. But in the past the concept of civilisation was absent and people thought themselves as belonging to an empire or kingdom or state-nation or a religion. It was the Muslims who first explicitly brought in the concept of 'The Ummah', the universal civilisation, from which developed the modern concept of 'civilisations'.

The influence on the world civilisations by Muslim culture and science is very aptly and beautifully represented in Al Hassani's work *1001 Inventions*. He mentions of Al Jazari, an engineer of Diyarbakir in today's South East Turkey, who gave birth to the concept of automatic machines and manufactured a large number of these machines at the start of the 13th century. Al Jazari studied the simple old contraptions from the past, such as Egyptian, Archimedean and Indian water bowl which had holes in them through which water would run out and give time periods, and based on those principles he developed complex mechanical clocks of all shapes and sizes. The most famous of his clocks was the nearly two metre high state-of-the-art automatic Elephant Clock. To depict universality he added an Indian elephant, an Egyptian phoenix, a Chinese dragon, Persian carpets and Arabian figures in the design of the clock.

King Nasir Al Din, son of the great Saladin, told him, "You have made peerless devices, and through strength have brought them forth as works; so do not lose what you have wearied yourself with. I wish you to compose for me a book which assembles what you have created separately, and brings together a selection of individual items and pictures.'

Al Jazari wrote an outstanding book on engineering *The Book of Knowledge of Ingenious Mechanical Devices*. This book described fifty mechanical devices in six categories which would prove as important resource for future engineers.

Muhammad, Ahmad and Hasan, the three Banu Musa brother of the 9th century developed toys and trick devices. Their toys included fake mechanical animals with water and sound mechanisms. Trick devices in the past were developed by famous 'engineers'. In later period, the likes of Leonardo da Vinci had been employed to create trick devices.

Al Hassani traces the history of 'Coffee' back to an Ethiopian Arab named Khalid who noticed that his goats became lively and excited after eating a certain kind of berry. This berry was boiled in water thus making a drink named *Al Qahwa*. The Sufis of Yemen started to drink it to remain awake in order to meditate (*Dhikr*) through out the night. In the 15th and 16th century *Al Qahwa* spread to Makkah, Cairo and to Turkey. The first *Al Qahwa* house, or as later called Coffee house, appeared in Venice in 1645 through European trade with North Africa and Egypt and would soon find its way into England.

It was also the Muslims who first wrote copious books on the game of chess, its history and game strategies including openings, endings and game-moves that made the game interesting and popular. Abul Hasan, commonly known as Ziryab, was a musician and celebrity trendsetter from modern Baghdad. In early 9th century he migrated to Spain and introduced chess at the time of Abdul Rahman II. From there chess went to Europe across the Pyrenees. Cardinal Damiani wrote to Pope Gregory VII to ban the game of the infidel from spreading among the clergy. Chess was a favourite of the Abbasids and produced great masters like Al Suli, Al Razi and Al Aadani. Written around 1370 the *Book of the Examples of Warfare in the Game of Chess* first introduced 'Blind Abbess and Her Nuns' game-plan. In one of the recent championship a Russian grandmaster won a game by playing an amazing move. This move had actually been crafted by Al Suli, a thousand year ago.

Baghdad was the centre of fashion and Ziryab came to Spain with more then just chess. He brought all the fashion of Baghdad like formalised 'three course' fine dining and luxurious dresses that included winter and summer wear along with the dates for the seasonal change of the dresses. Ziryab became a fashion icon and the first fashion brand in Spain. Hair fashion, toothpaste, deodorant and leather shoes with light cork soles supported by him were in vogue.

In the musical arena, Al Kindi provided a detailed fretting of *Al Ud,* which was the ancestor of instruments like lute. Al Farabi wrote five books on music, the masterpiece being *The Great Book of Music*. He invented the *rababah,* the older version of rebec of the violin family, and *qanun*, a table zither. The guitar came from the Muslim *quitara* and the naker drum from the *naqqara*.

Muslims were master story tellers. Stories like Sinbad, Ali Baba and forty thieves have seen many re-enactments. There are many others stories like *Laila Majnu* which have influenced world culture. Another good example is the *The Story of Hayy ibn Yaqzan* written in the 12th century by Abu Bakr ibn Abd Al Malik of Andalusia also known as Abubacer. This is a story of a child shipwrecked on an Island. For year he endured a lonely struggle and psychological anguish till a spiritual person by the name of Asal arrives in the Island. Defoe's *Life and Strange Adventure of Robinson Crusoe*, said to be inspired by Alexander Selkirk's four year solitary dwelling on an Island, has striking parallels with Abubacer's work. The first English translation of *Hayy Ibn Yaqzan* was published in 1709 and *Robinson Crusoe* appeared eleven years later.

The Islamic empires have seen the development of not only literature but languages as well. Persian, an ancient language, was brought to its modern form by the ink of Muslim poets like Ferdowsi. Another great example of such cultural development is India. Islam gave it the greatest empire, the Moghuls, and a unique political identity. Before the Muslims, India used to be a region with a large number of independent kingdoms or nations divided on the basis of languages, cultures and ethno-religious identities – Dravidians, Aryans,

Buddhist, Jains, and others. Despite that, Al Biruni promoted the concept of these different people within the region extending from the Himalayas to Cape Comorin as one civilisation. Amir Khasru lovingly articulated about India as one nation where people spoke Sindhi, Bengali, Punjabi, Telegu, Tamil and Kannada (Wood, 2007). It was, of course, the Moghuls starting from Akbar that cemented India into one political entity or nation.

All through the rule of the first Muslim Sultans and then the Moghuls and even through the British period a silent and peaceful cultural evolution had taken place due to Islamic proximity. To understand the effect of this cultural evolution it is necessary to go further back in time.

The Sanskrit language was introduced to India by the ancient Indo-Iranian Aryans who had moved into Northern India mainly after the collapse of the Indus Valley Civilisation. Over the millennia, after mixing with the existing local languages many new local languages were derived from Sanskrit, for example Pali, Prakit, Brujoboli and Mithila. From these languages, in turn, were derived the modern languages of the northern regions of the subcontinent like Hindi, Bengali and Urdu. On the other hand, in the southern regions of the subcontinent, modern languages like Tamil, Malayalam and others were derived from the extinct Dravidian languages that had existed all over the subcontinent before the arrival of Aryan Sanskrit. The arrival of Muslims would affect the Indian culture starting from the North.

North India

When the Muslims came to India, like the previous introduction of Sanskrit by the Aryans, they also introduced a number of languages – Arabic, Turkish and Persian. During this period a local vernacular language derived from Prakit was spoken by the general mass in and around Delhi. The Muslims named it 'Hindustani' referring it as the language belonging to people living east of Indus River. Propinquity caused the absorption of various words and linguistic styles from Muslim languages into Hindustani.

The first person to intellectually advance this language was Amir Khasru, a Muslim poet extraordinaire of Turkish descent. This legendary person was born in Patiyala, India, in the 13th century. His contribution to Indian literature and music is immense. He categorised North Indian classical music into genres and modes. He created genres like 'Khayal' and 'Qawali' and modified the modes such as Drupad which has achieved timeless popularity. His poetry was in Persian and in a mixture between the native language and Persian which he called Hindvi – a form of Hindustani. From his work evolved a language of wide spectrum, i.e., spoken by various groups with nominal differences. One side of this spectrum used more Persian derivatives while the other side used more Sanskrit vocabulary. The part of the spectrum that used relatively more Persian and Arabic would become known as Urdu and an

Arabic script would be applied to it while the part that used relatively more Sanskrit would be called Hindi and the local Devanagri script would be applied to it.

The Sultans, especially Quli Qutub Shah, liked the Persian dominated language very much. His army was multilingual and needed a unifying language, thus he made Urdu the official language for the army. The word 'Urdu' in old usage means army or camp. 'Rikhta' is the other term used to denote the language and means 'mixed'.

The popularity of Urdu increased in the hands of powerful poets over centuries like Mir Taqi Mir, Mirza Ghalib and Mohammad Iqbal, finally, taking a very elegant form. Mir and Ghalib gave Urdu poetry its beauty, plucking the thousand year's refined sweetness of the Persian literature. The main subject matter of their poetry being love – both the love for God and that for woman. While Iqbal gave it the depth of philosophy, the strength of conviction and pragmatism of politics.

Mir Taqi Mir

Mir composed love, an exquisite love. At one side is the pleading, obsessed, tempestuous lover and on the other side is the totally oblivious, deliberately so, and teasing beloved. He expresses tantalising coquetry in differing subtlety:

It is the start of love, and you weep?
Patience, so much is yet to follow.

'They say goddesses had hearts.
God, of what age they talk of?'

And he expresses the feeling of the lover's helplessness:

'And I thought the ways of love was child-play
How naïve could I have been.'

He presents a humour that can only be found in the tragedy of love:

'As tears dropped off my eyes she says "say no more,
I like not tales of tragic sufferers."
Finally, when I said "what do I do, kill myself!?"

She replied, "Yes, you should do something."

'Gaze at the mirror, such a beautiful face
Such cruel words appear so unseemly.'

And the sensuous feeling:

The touch of her, so exquisite
Is this life? Is this body mine?

But in real life Mir was not all helpless love. Born in 1723 he saw the destruction of Delhi by Nadir Shah. The killing of his patron Shams ud Daulah left him penniless. He had to migrate to Lukhnow in North India to get a new patron, Nawab Asaf ud Daulah. The vagaries of time made him write:

'I do not understand those who like to worship,
I wouldn't be god if I could, I would be ashamed.'

But his philosophy remains unperturbed:

Even Mir is a beggar, but he begs for one thing only
This world and the hereafter together.'

Mir composed couplets of Ghazal, a genre of Arabian legacy, which is of a deceptively simple, delicate and veiled metrical style. But his life he unveiled in a difficult style. He was arrogant, whimsical and ill-tempered. In this respect Abu Sayeed Ayyub, a 20th century Indian writer, compares him with Baudelaire. Charles Baudelaire's verdict about the world was:

'An oasis of horror surrounded by a desert of boredom.'

And his comment on human incapacity and irk was:

'Any where!
Anywhere as long as it is out of this world
....
This country bores, O Death!
To drive to the Gulf, Hell or Heaven – what matter!'

While Mir stresses the same horror and incapacity as:

'This all around Apocalypse is His handiwork
It is the work of this Chaos-Creator that afflicts all.'

Mirza Ghalib

Ghalib was fourteen when Mir died in 1810. Ghalib remains the most popular Urdu poet and has a cult following to this day that is poetically fanatic. Even though he wrote in the same Ghazal style as Mir, there are times when he did not follow the poetic grammar but created his own.

His time was the age of the famous courtesans of North India. They were ladies who were chosen for their beauty and were highly trained in etiquette, manners, songs, dance, poetry, humour, coquetry and romantic rhetoric from their very childhood and were able to spellbind any male person. They were so amply sophisticated that the aristocratic families would send their young men to their 'courts' to learn etiquette and manners. Ghalib, non-materialistic as poets can be, was infamous for having a scandalous affair with a courtesan. He was quite aware of his non-too-savoury reputation.

A poet delightful, you are Ghalib
But suffer from infamy, you do.

Like Mir he too is frustrated by the beloved:

' I, a thousand thundering wail
And you, an amazing non-response!'

But if Mir was totally lost in his love, Ghalib was more manipulative:

'Allure of the garden, plucking of petals
Beauteous spring, sin in my heart.'

He too brings out satire from the torments of love:

'After killing me she renounces cruelty
Alas, the repentance of the nippy repenter.'

'Life and death becomes indifferent in love
I live for the same traitor for whom I die.'

And he asks questions that do not need answers.

'I long and she exasperates.
Lord, what is it!?'

And his questions become more philosophical:

Where is it, my Lord, the second step of desire?
In the quagmire of existence I find only one footprint.

His *Diwan* still remains very popular. Dr Abdul Rahman Bijnori says of the *Diwan e Galib* "O Ghalib, if the art of poetry were a religion, then this book would form the divine gospel of that religion." (Ahmad, 1984)

Mir and Ghalib have enormously influenced the high and popular Indian culture. One good contemporary example is the Indian film industry. From the very onset this industry has consistently relied on the verses of Mir and Ghalib to beautify and elate the lyrics and dialogues of the movies.

Mohammad Iqbal

In Mir and Ghalib, melodrama is supreme. But Iqbal is a different quality entirely. Mohammad Iqbal, the poet philosopher is endowed with a number of appellations – Allama Iqbal (where Allama means scholar), Sir Mohammad Iqbal, Dr. Mohammad Iqbal and a string of other titles. His poetry in Persian and Urdu was mainly political and philosophical thus thematically opposite to Mir and Ghalib. He was influenced by poems of Muslims like Rumi and the philosophy of Europeans like Neitzsche, Bergson and Goethe. Among his most famous works are *Asrar-e-Khudi (Secrets of the Self), Rumuz-e-Bekhudi (Mysteries of Selflessness), Shikwa (Complaint), Jawab-e-Shikwa (Reposte), and the Bang-e-Dara (Call of the Caravan).*

In *Asrar*, Iqbal envisages that the aim of life is attaining self-realisation and self-knowledge. It is a doctrine of self development. His verses resonates the stages through which the "Self" has to pass before finally arriving at its point of perfection, enabling the knower of the "Self" to become the vicegerent of God on Earth. He vehemently attacks the so-called mysticism that preaches a sterile life, as those of Great Sufi Poet Hafiz of the 14th century. On the other hand, he is much 'influenced' by the dynamic mysticism of Rumi which is full of vitality and activity. Iqbal is indomitable in the face of adversity and accepts any socio-political disadvantage as a challenge and, in fact, dislikes tranquillity:

'May God give you storms
Your ocean lacks current.'

One of his famous poems *Shikwa* is a 'Complaint' to God regarding the fate of the Muslims and the levels of depredation to which they have sunk to from the peak they had reached in the past. If Mir had made a delight of love's treachery, Iqbal, referring to the fall of Muslims and Europe's rise, dared to assign infidelity to God:

'Sometime it is them sometimes it's us
That you favour with intimacy.
It is blasphemous to say thus,
But You too are promiscuous.'

And God's riposte in the *Jawab-e-Shikwa*, another poem by Iqbal, is:

The Creator's law is justice
Through all eternal fate,
Unbelievers who live like Muslims
Merit rewards of faith.

He considered Europe the most advanced in philosophy but felt that it needed to be complimented by a theistic underpinning to make its quest whole. Conversely, he disliked conservatism in religion, or any where else, and considered that a reconstruction of Muslims thought was needed to be aligned with the modern world. His *Javed Nama,* a long Persian Poem, is lesser known but contains a profound humanitarian message. The model of the poem was a counter to Dante's Divine Comedy, which in turn, had been inspired by Abu Al-Ala Al-Ma'arri's *Risalat Al-Ghufran*, all inspired by the Journey of Prophet *Miraj* to the heavens. In *Javed Nama*, Iqbal and Rumi travel through the Heavens talking to historical personalities who give their views on the diverse problems that the contemporary world faces. It is the Hindu sage Viswamitra who utters the root issue:

The East saw God but failed to see the world of matter
The West got embroiled in the world and neglect God.

(Translation by S. A. Valid, in Ahmad, 1984)

Iqbal's poetry and philosophy can be categorised into two stages. When he was young, he was an ardent Indian nationalist writing poems of Hindu-Muslim amity. When he studied in Europe, he developed an antipathy towards nationalism and became an internationalist and developed a philosophical maturity. After obtaining his Master of Philosophy he returned to India where he became disillusioned at the plight of the Muslims and their gradual political isolation in the national arena. He started to believe that in India the Muslims were likely to loose their universal identity and thus he, even though an internationalist, was among the first to envisage a separate nation for the Muslims of India. His notion would influence the formation of the state of Pakistan.

Iqbal's fame transcended national borders and during his lifetime it reached the distant corners of the civilised world. Features were written about him, and his poems were translated in many of the modern world languages – English, Bengali, Latin, Arabic, French, German and Russian by famous literary scholars (Ahmad, 1984)

North East India

Along with Urdu and Hindi, the other most common language of Northern regions of the subcontinent is Bengali. It is among the richer and scientific languages of Indo-European origin. The oldest known text similar to modern Bengali can be found in the *Charjapad*, a book of lyrical poems by Buddhist monks. The language of *Charjapad* is vernacular and is the mother language of Bengali, Assamese, Oriya and Bishnupriya Manipuri. The book was written in the beginning of the 10th century when the Buddhist Pal dynasty ruled. In 1095, the Sen (Sena) dynasty usurped power from the Buddhists and ruled Bengal. The Sens were Hindu Brahman-Satriyas and, for political reasons, passed the decree that only Sanskrit was to be practiced in their domains and all local languages were banned. A religious injunction was declared that anyone who practiced any local language would go to the vilest hell. This hindered emancipation of local languages.

But in 1204, the Muslims occupied Bengal. The Muslims ruled first as Governors for the Sultan of Delhi and later as independent Sultans of Bengal. Their arrival nullified the Sen decree against the local languages. It was during the Muslim rule that the Bengali language started to take form.

The original language of the Muslim rulers was Turkic, Persian and Arabic but the people of Bengal spoke local languages. There was a disconnect between the rulers and the general masses. To overcome this divide the Muslims started to sponsor the local language that would develop into modern Bengali. The Sultans had a taste for culture. Ghiyas-ud-din Azam Shah (r.1393–1410) of the Ilyas Shahi Dynasty (1338 ~ 1487) tried to attract the great Persian poet Hafiz to his court.

Ala-ud-din Husain Shah (r.1493–1519) and his son Nusrat Shah (r.1519–1532) of the Hussain Shahi dynasty (1493–1539) became patrons of Bengali literature and language, and many Sanskrit works were translated into Bengali at their court. Paragal Khan, Wazir to the

Sultan, commissioned poet Parameswar to translate the epic *Mahabharta* to Bengali. This was the first rendition of the epic to the Bengali language. Similarly, other great literary works and epics, like *Laila Majnu* of Nizami, were translated and *Sri-Krishna-Keertan*, the Indian love poem by Boro Chondidas, was written in Bengali during Muslim sponsorship and rule.

After the fall of the dynasties of Bengal Sultans, the Bengali language continued to develop, on its own, through the Moghul and British Period till 1800 when, during the time of Governor General Lord Wellesley, Fort William College was established in Kolkata. This was a centre for the study of Asian languages including Bengali and Hindi. Many Hindu Bengali intellectuals like Ram Mohan Roy, Iswarchandra, and Bankimchandra were affiliated to the college and furthered Bengali literature and language.

But at this stage the Muslims abstained themselves from western culture and education and, thus, stayed away from this college as well. Politically, they were the aggrieved party as the British had taken India from the Muslim rulers, and thus were not keen about the foreign British 'culture' and, indeed, some preferred to return to religious orthodoxy. Many preferred the Aliya Madrassa, set up with the assistance of Governor General Warren Hastings in 1781. In the Madrassa Arabic, Persian and Islamic Fiqh were taught. This narrowing down of curriculum was against the past trend when Madrassas were centres of religious as well as general learning. The British interest was in the graduates from the Madrassa who would assist in translation and the running of the administration.

The Bengali script, like other north Indian scripts, originated from Brahmi alphabet of the Asokan inscriptions. It was first typecasted in 1778 by the Englishman Charles Wilkins who commissioned a Muslim Maulana and a Hindu Pundit to develop and finalise it.

Towards the end of the British rule, in the first half of the 20th century, when Bengali poet Rabindranath Tagore got the noble prize, Muslims started to return to participate in the creativity of Bengali literature. The most famous was the prolific writer and poet Nazrul Islam who infused the body of Bengali literature with a fire, a conscience and a soul. He introduced universalism and defiance to an otherwise ornate and supple language.

Kazi Nazrul Islam

Nazrul was the most versatile of the Bengali litterateurs. His versatility was not only in the genres of literature - poems, songs, ballads, short stories, novels, and essays - that he had produced in abundance but also the variety of thought - religious, rational, political, and romantic - that he had communicated, which to a lesser poet would be philosophically conflicting. He introduced the genre of Bengali Ghazal and composed 3000 songs. He enriched the language by introducing and intermingling Persian and Arabic vocabulary into Bengali. His philosophy was as widely encompassing as was his work. He was first and foremost a

Bengali poet but his writing also exhibits the profound influence of Islam. He was a proponent of Muslim reformation:

Beats the drums, tie the turbans,
Muslims, raise your heads!
Rises the call for a new age;
In the ruins of the fort
The standard flutters again.

Which made it easy for him to be a humanitarian:

'Who asks about the religion of a drowning man!?
Say, it is a human that drowns
Child of my mother.'

He married a Hindu lady and named his children with the combination of Bengali and Arabic names. His writings included Hindu religious *Keertans*. He was an extraordinary proponent of female rights when the world still looked at women with a conservative eye, he wrote:

'Of all the greatness and goodness
Achieved in this world
Half has been achieved by men
The other half by women.'

He was a romantic. Romance and nature abounds in his poems, songs, and stories.

'With anklet of dry leaves
the whirlwind dances
Music of shimmering currents
In swells of waves she goes'

The poet who penned with the ink of flame was, true to the nature of all great artists, callous to the material world. There was a time he possessed a chauffer driven Chrysler and other times he was pawning personal stuff to meet expenses. He wrote the 'Ode to Poverty'

'Poverty! You made me great
Honoured me the honour of Christ
Conferred me the crown of thorns'

But the most outstanding feature in him was non-acceptance of anything oppressive. He had a soul of rebellious nature, fierce against all repression. In 1922 he wrote the '*Vidhrohi*' *(The Rebel)*, a poem which immediately captured rapturous attention of the mass.

~~~

The Rebel

Say, O Valiant!
Say, my head is towering high!
    Bows the Himalayan peaks at such visage!
Say, O Valiant!
Say, tearing through the Firmament
    vaulting the sun, moon, planet and stars
Piercing the heavens and the earth
    through the throne of God
have risen, I, the eternal wonder
of the Universal Creator
The storm-god fury blazes on my forehead
the shinning mark of victory
Say, O Valiant!
Say, My head is ever towering high!
I'm indomitable, impudent and brutal
I'm the Dance Lord of the Doomsday
I'm cyclone, the devastation
I'm the monstrous terror, curse of the world
I'm irresistible
I smash all to smithereens
I'm lawless and wild
I squash all bonds, rules and disciplines
I defy all laws
I sink laden boats
I'm torpedo, the dreaded floating mines
I'm Dhurjati the destroyer
    the abrupt tornado Nor'wester
I'm the Rebel, the Rebel Regent
    of the Universal Creator
Say, O Valiant!
Say, My head is ever towering high!

From the few starting verses above, it dawns that 'The Rebel' is a rebellion based on human universalism. But there is an esoteric underpinning to the literal in it – and that is the source from which Nazrul had his inspiration. The style that starts sentences with the word
~~~

'Say' is Quranic. In the Quran there are numerous verses that start with '*Qul*' by which God is asking the Prophet to proclaim something and thus '*Qul*' is rendered as 'Say O Prophet'.

Say O Prophet, "Truth has arrived, and Falsehood perished: for Falsehood is (by nature) bound to perish"[17:81].

That is where the 'Say O Valiant' of Nazrul comes from. The opening verses of 'The Rebel' that refers to the piercing through the heavens and the earth and the Throne of God is a reference to the ascension of the Prophet through the heavens to the 'Throne' of God in his journey of '*Miraj*'. This same journey of the Prophet has also influenced poets like Abu Al-Ala, Dante Alighieri and Iqbal. In fact, Nazrul's rebel is a *rebellious essence* of the Prophet.

In the next verses of the poem, Nazrul personifies all the uncontrollable and terrifying powers of nature, mythical gods and men in his Rebel. Then, further on, he gives romance a berth:

I'm the braid of the unbridled maiden
the flame in her eyes
I'm the intense romance of sixteen
I'm bliss
I'm the forlorn heart of the recluse
I'm the sigh of a widow
I'm the hysteria of the hopeless
I'm the agony of all homeless
I'm the burning venom of the humiliated
I'm the affliction of the jilted
I'm the trembling heart of a stolen kiss
 the first maiden touch
The fleeting glance of a secret love
 And the ploy for the glance
I'm the love of a restless girl
 the jingling of her bangles
I'm the eternal child, the eternal youth
I'm the modesty of the coy country lass
I'm the North-wind, the mountain breeze
 the lost East-wind
I'm serenade of the Balladeer
 the music of his lyre
I'm the hot stirring thirst
 the scorching sunray
I'm the flow of the desert spring
 the verdure azure shades
I prance in delight
 Insanity! I am insane
I've found myself
 and crumbled all confines

Further down the poem he declares his mission:

I'm Parashuram's adamant axe
I'll rid the world of warriors
        and bring peace just and fair
I'm the plough on Balaram's shoulder
I'll uproot the exploited world without care
        a great joy for the new beginning
Weary of battles, I, the Great Rebel,
        shall rest in peace
when the anguished cry of the oppressed
        shall reverberate nowhere, no more,
and the saber of the tyrant
        will clash no more in battlefields
only then shall I, the Rebel,
        will rest.

A clinical aspect of the poem is that Nazrul attributes all the powers of the created – including those of demigods and mythical characters - to the human rebel but he carefully avoids ascribing any power of the Creator, God capital G, to the rebel. He uses the parable of the mythological sage Bhrigu stamping on the bosom of god Vishnu to represent the destruction of injudicious ideals.

I'm the Rebel Bhrigu
        I leave my footprint on the chest of god
I am the destroyer of such creator
        The curtailer of unfeeling callous destiny
I'm the Rebel Bhrigu
I'll stamp my footprint on the chest of god
        and tear apart the bosom of whimsical destiny
I'm the eternal Valiant Rebel
Alone I have risen above the world
        my head held towering ever high!

At the culmination of the poem, Nazrul's Rebel takes the mettle of the sage Bhrigu who had the audacity to kick the Indian god of creation, Vishnu. The sage was angered for as he had approached Vishnu, the god has been too preoccupied with his consort to percieve the arrival of the sage. It is the callous and whimsical destiny that the Rebel is going to severe and in that resolve he has risen towering in a valiant manner.

~~~
~~~

In another of his universal-humanist poems 'The Egalitarian' (*Shammyobadi*) he refers positively to various religions and philosophies. But when it comes to the Prophet he uniquely links him to the main theme of the poem – equality.

'At this altar the desert's Prince
Used to hear the divine call,
From this throne, he also sang
Quran's message of equality for all.'

In another poem he states:

'Martyrs for religion
We are that nation
Equality fraternity we brought
And the planet enlightened
We are that nation.'

At a young age, Nazrul had received religious education and studied the Quran and for a short time worked as a *Muazzin* (One who give the call to prayers- the Adhan) at a local mosque. When he grew up he joined the Indian British Army. But he was, as expected of a rebel, against the British rule of India. He left the army and started writing against the British rule but was soon imprisoned for his anti British publications. He worded his defiance:

'We nave to shed all fear, weakness and cowardice. We have to live *demanding* the right of justice, not *begging* for it. We won't bow our head before anyone – if need be, we will mend shoes at street sides, we will live modest lives based on our own earnings, but we won't turn to others for pity or charity. This awakening spirit of freedom and dignity is what I want to see in the Muslim youth.... This is the essence of Islam's teachings. I invite all to embrace this teaching. In my life I have embraced this very teaching. I have suffered pain, I have embraced all the hurt with smile, but I have never bowed before humiliation of my spirit. I have never surrendered my freedom.' (WR8, Mohammad Umar Farooq, 2010.)

His works, due to the prevailing imperial political expediency, did not receive the international recognition, evaluation and acclaim it deserved. When he became very sick due to the incurable 'Pick's disease' he had expected financial support from various quarters which did not materialise. His mental faculties becoming stifled and physically racked by paralysis and pain, he with great difficulty wrote a letter to a friend: '…And probably the money will arrive, like Ferdowsi's, at the time of my funeral. I have instructed my family not to accept it.'

Finally his mental faculties succumbed to the disease. Maybe he had tried to accommodate too many contradictions in his philosophy. He turned into a docile mute with no comprehension of the social issues he had contemplated, culture that he had inspired, political battles he had waged or the religion that had inspired him. In 1947, he received the news of the departure of the British from the subcontinent without any understanding. When his wife died of prolonged illness he just sat in the background without any concern.

But the fiery words that had poured out of his pen endured. In 1972, he was declared the National Poet of Bangladesh. The last few years of his life, financially supported by the government, he lived in comfort and peace. In one of his poems he had written – *When I die bury me there where I can hear the Adhan.* His wish was granted, he lies buried near the Dhaka University Mosque and from his grave the five time calls to prayer (Adhan) is clearly audible.

Begum Rokeya Sakhawat

Born in 1880 in Rangpur, Bengal (now Bangladesh) Rokeya Khatun was a writer and social worker. She belonged to a highly literate Muslim family. Her elder sister, Karimunnesa, had also earned renown as a poet. Rokeya was married, at the age of sixteen, to Khan Bahadur Sakhawat Hussain, who was the Deputy Magistrate of Bhagalpur, Bihar. She was encouraged by her husband to carry on her education. She launched her writing career by writing an essay in Bengali titled *Pipasa* which means 'Thirst'. She wrote poetry, short stories, essays, and novels. She also took up the cause of female education and female emancipation but, tragically, her supportive husband died in 1909. In memory of her loving husband she set up a school for Muslim girls and named it 'Sakhawat Memorial Girls High School'. But due to a property dispute with her in-laws she had to move to Calcutta (now Kolkata).

The death of her husband and the move to Kolkata caused her to temporarily suspend her writings. She found a great sponsor in Kolkata in Nawab Badruddin Haider who was a prominent Muslim elite and philanthropist of the society. He was the first to give financial and moral support to her projects (Bhowmik, 2002). Once she settled down, she started to write again and was published in the magazines *Al Islam*, *Bongio Mussulman Sahitya Patrika* (Bengali Muslim Literary Magazine), *Sawgat, Nowroz, Masik Mohammadi* (Monthly Mohammaden) and *The Mussulman* (The Muslim). She re-established the school and set up social welfare organisations such as *Anjuman e Khawateen e Islam* (Association for Islamic Women). Her work for women's emancipation took place at a time when all over the world women were considered unequal. During her time women had not yet been given voting rights. In USA and Britain, woman voting rights materialised in the 1920s.

For the rest of her life, Begum Rokeya remained busy with the school, the association, her writings and campaigning for female emancipation. She believed women equal to men. In her short story *Naristan* or 'Land of Ladies', she writes of the heroine who in a dream visits a fantasy land where men have gone indoors and women run everything in the state. It was her assertion that women, in their own segregated way, were equal to men. But her vision of emancipation was not aimed at any type of feminine outlandishness, it envisaged women being progressive, educated, dignified and contributory to the society.

Rokeya died of heart complicacy on December 9, 1932. But her works would historically influence the region. In Bangladesh, December 9 is celebrated as Rokeya Day.

Like the Indian subcontinent, the influence of Muslim culture on all the other continents is significant but, mostly, unrealised. Today all these cultural advances are taken for granted by people, like a cup of coffee, unaware of its origins. This is mainly because, some time in the past, the progressive contributions of Muslims to the world slowly came to a stop. The Muslim 'thought' was founded on a *balance* of Ulemaic and Rational conceptions and even Sufi inputs. When people began to disregard one or the other, this balance became disrupted.

We sent our messengers with clear signs and sent down with them the Book and the Balance (of Right and Wrong), that men may stand forth in justice; and We sent down Iron, in which is (material for) mighty war, as well as many benefits for mankind, that God, Unseen, may test who it is that will help Him and His messengers. For God is Full of Strength, Exalted in Might. [57:25]

And the firmament He has raised high, and He has set up the Balance,
In order that you may not transgress (due) balance. [55:7]

It is God Who has sent down the Book in Truth, and the Balance (by which to weigh conduct). And what will make you realise that perhaps the Hour is close at hand?[42:17]

Did you think that We created you in play (without any purpose), and that you would not be brought back to Us? So Exalted is Allah, the True King: there is no God but He, the Lord of the Supreme Throne! [23:115-116]

If you turn back (from the Path), He will substitute in your stead another people; then they would not be like you! [47:38]

Part 3 - Dawn of the Modern Era

The European Age

Upto the 17th century, the Church was not only a religious institution but very rich and powerful with influence on all the European states. The monarchs were averse to this and wanted a separation from this influence. The reverse example of the contemporary Ottomans was very glaring. At that time, the Ottomans were in their magnificent peak ruling without any interference from religious institutions. If fact, the Sultan was also the religious head of the Empire.

In 1618, a war broke out between the Catholics and the Protestants and was fought for thirty years, which later took on various political hues. The war was fought in what is now Germany at the end of which the Church had exhausted it powers. The 'Peace of Westphalia' that was established in 1638 would see the influence of the Church decline. This and some other events would take place in Europe leading to the formation of the modern nation-states.

Two of the main events that led to the modern era were the Industrial Revolution and the French Revolutiɩ n. The industrial revolution, starting from Britain, enabled the making of machines that worked and produced goods in mass scale for human consumption while the French revolution gave a new concept of state governance, in place of the hereditary monarchy, that represented the general mass. These two put together produced the model for a new state which was efficient and advanced.

These changes did not just happen by themselves. The West over the last few centuries had produced a profusion of brilliant academics, scholars, scientists, social scientists and innovators. They were the thinkers who shaped this new world.

The foundation of the European age was laid when the Europeans had taken on the mantle of knowledge where the Muslims had left off. In *Making of Humanity*, Robert Briffault avers:

> "It is highly probable that but for the Arabs modern Europeans civilisation would never had risen at all. It is absolutely certain that but for them it would not have assumed that character which has enabled it to transcend all pervious phases of evolutions. For although there is not a single aspect of European growth in which the decisive influence of Islamic culture in not traceable, nowhere is it so clear and momentous as in genesis of that power which constitutes the permanent distinctive force of the modern world and supreme source of its victory – natural science and scientific spirit."

The development of European knowledge started from Spain during the Muslim rule. After that came the Italian Renaissance and next the illumination moved to France, a country with borders with both the above mentioned countries. And finally it moved to West and North Europe. It was not just academic knowledge that was transferred across to Europe but a whole culture - poetry, architecture, etc – a whole way of life and a new manner of thinking. Robert Briffault further states,

> "It was under the influence of Moorish revival of culture and not in the fifteenth century that the real renaissance took place. Spain and not Italy was the cradle of the rebirth of Europe. After sinking lower and lower in barbarism, it had reached the darkest depths of ignorance and degradation when the cities of Saracenic world, Baghdad, Cairo, Cordova, Toledo, etc were growing centres of civilisation and intellectual activity. It was there that the new life arose which was to grow into a new phase of human evolution. From the time when the influence of their culture made itself felt began the stirring of new life."

A few centuries ago, in the Muslim domain, the tidal wave of research that had originated from the Quran, the promulgation of Jurisprudence (Fiqh) and the collection and systematisation of the Hadith ultimately led to philosophy and rational sciences. The huge mass of people reading, writing and doing research came upon various branches of knowledge. Innovations started to take place, while old knowledge like Indian and Greek were understood and improved. Soon, from this incredible mass of scholars rose a plethora of the greatest minds, scientists, philosophers, physicians, geographers, historians, etc. The great contributions of thc Muslim scientists have not escaped the notice of great scholars of recent times. George Sarton, a science historian, comments,

> "The most valuable of all, the most original and the most pregnant works were written in Arabic.... From the second half of the eighth to the end of the eleventh century, Arabic was the scientific and most progressive language of mankind. During that period any one wishing to be well informed and up-to-date had to study Arabic. It will suffice here to evoke a few glorious names without contemporary equivalents in the West: Jabir b Hayyan, Al Kindi, Al Khawarizmi, Al Farghani, Al Razi, Thabit b Qurrah, Al Battani, Husain b Ishaq, Al Farabi, Abul Qasim, Ibn Al Jazzar, Al Beruni, Ibne Sina, Ibne Yunus, Al Karkhi, Ibn Al Haytam, Ali b Isa, Al Ghazzali, Al Zarqali, Umar Khayyam – a magnificent array of names which it would not be difficult to extend. If any one tells you that the Middle Ages were scientifically sterile, just quote these names to him. All these scientists flourished between 750 and 1100 AD."

When the Muslims, after the scourge, regressed from rational science, its seeds had already been transported and were waiting for the roots to germinate in Europe. There were three stages in the transfer and assimilation of knowledge from Muslims lands to the West. There were, obviously, overlaps in the three stages.

1. Translation of Muslim works to European languages.
2. Assimilation of the translated knowledge all over Europe and into various languages.
3. Research and works by the initial group of western scholars based on Muslim knowledge.

1. Translation of Muslim Works

A large scale translation of Muslim Arabic text to Latin started in the 11th century and continued through the Renaissance. The main centres of translation were in Spain and Sicily. Professor Hasan presents a list of these translations in his *History of Islam*.

Gerard of Cremona alone had more then 80 books translated from Arabic which included the scientific, philosophical and various other works of Thabit ibn Qurra, Hunayn ibn Ishaq, Al-Zarkali, Bani Musa, Abu Kamil, Abu al-Qasim, Al Kindi, Al Farabi, and Ibn Al Haitham. He also translated Al Razi's medical and chemical works, Jabir ibn Aflah's *Elementa astronomica*, the *Almagest*, Al Khawarizmi's *On Algebra* and *Almucabala*, the Arabic texts of Archimedes' *On the Measurement of the Circle*, Aristotle's *On the Heavens*, Euclid's *Elements of Geometry.*

Gerard edited the *Tables of Toledo*, the most accurate compilation of astronomical data of the time. These tables were completed by Al-Zarqali, known to the West as Arzachel, the 11th century mathematician and astronomer of Cordoba. Al Farabi, who is acclaimed as the "second teacher" after Aristotle, wrote hundreds of treatises. Gerard's Latin translation of Al Farabi's book on the sciences, *Kitab al-lhsa al Ulum,* which discussed classification and fundamental principles of science was named *De scientiis* (*On the Sciences*). He also translated Ahmad ibn Muhammad ibn Kathir al-Farghani's (Alfraganus) *Elements of Astronomy.* Gerard also wrote original treatises on arithmetic, algebra and astrology.

Michael Scott, a Scottish scholar, and his successor Herman the German translated Ibn Rushd's summaries and commentaries on Aristotle in late 12th century. Constantine, an African Monk, translated the medical treaties including *Al Kitab Al Maliki* by Ali bin Abbas in the 11th century. Many of the books he translated were from the Al Qawrawan Mosque

University complex (Al Hassani, 2007). Faraj bin Salim, a Jew from Sicily, translated Razi's *Al Hawi* and *Tawwim Al Baldan* of Ibn Jazlah. Astronomical tables of Majriti and works of Khawarizmi and Abu Ma'sher Jafar were translated in the 12th century by Adelard of Bath in England. Robert of Chester translated Al Khawarzimi's *Algebra* while Abraham bin Ezra translated Al Biruni's *Commentary on Khawarizmi's Tables*. John of Seville translated the medical and philosophical works of Al Farghani, Al Kindi and Al Ghazzali. Tivolo of Spain translated the astronomical works of Al Battani while Stephen of Sicily translated the medical works of Al Majusi. According to *Historian's History* the theories of Kepler on atmospheric refraction were derived from Ibn Al Haitham's *Twilight*.

In Italy, Burgundio of Pisa translated the works of Ibn Rushd in the twelfth century. Paravisius translated *Taysir* of Ibn Johral. *Qabus Nama*, a major Persian work from the 11th century, was written by Amir Ansar Al Moali Keikavus, the Ziyarid ruler of Persia. This work contains 44 chapters and outlines princely education, manners, and conduct set in ethical didactic prose in original style and tone. This book influenced the *Dastur al-Wuzara* of Nizam ul Mulk. The German translation of the Qabus Nama was the source of inspiration for Goethe's *West-ostlicher Divan*. It has been translated to Turkish, English, French, Japanese, Russian and Arabic.

These centuries of translation not only vastly improved the knowledge of Europe but also gave it a brand new lexicon. Words like alchemy, alcohol, amulet, cipher, cheque, elixir, tariff and many others have direct Arabic and some Persian origin. In Europe, renaissance took place due to a number of factors. But if a single enabling factor is to be stated, it would be 'Renaissance is the transliteration of Muslim works and thoughts to European languages'.

2. Assimilation of the translated knowledge:

Along with the translation of Arabic texts by the Europeans came the assimilation of this knowledge. Up to the fifteenth century a major part of scientific activity of Europe consisted of assimilation of the Muslim sciences and systematisation of it. Among the great western scholars and luminaries who played a major role in assimilation of Muslim knowledge include Alexander of Halle, St. Thomas Aquinas, Albertus Magnus, Robert Grosseteste, Roger Bacon, Arnold of Villanove and Peter of Abano.

During these first two periods, in some instances, the works of Muslims would be attributed to the translators themselves or to the scholars who had actually provisioned it from Muslim works. This was not an act of gleeful plagiarism but happened due to the existing anti Muslim political environment that is reflected in the Crusades.

In the 11th century, learning in Europe was restricted within the monasteries, within the clergy, to the study of the Holy Bible and related books. With the appropriation of Muslim knowledge the scope of learning rapidly expanded. The works of Ibn Rushd and other Muslim scholars' were instrumental in new institutions to appear in France. The learning centres moved from the monasteries to the cathedral schools. Two of the most famous schools were those of Chartres and Notre Dame. The monk-philosopher-intellectual Theirry of Chartres taught that science was compatible with religion. By the end of the 12th century these schools started to develop into universities. And before the end of 13th century these universities were granted royal charters.

The arrival of Constantine the African monk in southern Italy with huge number of translations gave the impetus to the blossoming of knowledge in the University in Salerno, which became famous for its medical schools. Muslim knowledge also stimulated the universities in Padua and Bologna in Italy. The University of Bologna, which was famous for legal studies, was given its charter by Emperor Frederick Barbarossa in 1158. The University of Naples was established in 1224 and is one of the oldest continuous functioning academic institutions of the world. It was established by Emperor Frederick II, who is known for his great respect for Muslim knowledge.

From Italy and France Muslim knowledge would spread to England.

3. Research and works by the initial group of western scholars based on Muslim knowledge:

In the European universities the translated works of Muslims remained the main teaching text, some till the eighteenth century. Based on the knowledge acquired the Europeans then started to write original works which are those well recognised today.

One of the earliest such text was written by Fibonacci, who was born in 1170. Also known as Leonardo of Pisa, he went to Bougie in Algeria to learn mathematics from a master called Sidi Omar. His study included algebraic and simultaneous equations. He also visited the libraries of Alexandria, Cairo and Damascus, after which he wrote his famous *Liber Abaci* (Al Hassani, 2007).

Roger Bacon, (1220 – 1292) considered the Father of the European Renaissance, exhibited knowledge clearly centuries ahead of European thought. He is credited as the originator of the 'Experimental Method' in science. Before Islam, knowledge was mostly theoretical, scientific experimentation was negligible, and scientific inventions harboured more on accidents. The Greeks were empiricists and theoretical geniuses but as noted by H G Wells in *An Outline of History* they lacked scientific experimentation. It was the Muslims who really started protracted scientific experimentations and developed a scientific methodology. Robert Briffault admits that Roger Bacon was an apostle of Islamic sciences and from there he transmitted the Experimental Method. Because of his passion of Islamic sciences he was imprisoned by the Franciscans and his writings were censored and purged before these could reach the public.

As the number of books by European authors increased, later scholars could now base their research on the European books alone. After this point, arbitrarily the 1600s, Europe saw a remarkable rise in learning and development of knowledge.

Gradually, the contributions of the Muslims were forgotten and erased. In the political fields of Europe, from time to time, there has been a feeling of enmity towards the Muslims. As Europe rose and the Muslims stagnated, the lack of knowledge of Muslim contribution led the anti Muslim feeling to change its hue from enmity to one of condescension. Thus politics masked Europe's intellectual debt to Islam. Finally, the greatest harm to the history of knowledge was committed when a cruel fable was invented that Muslims had been just 'keepers' of knowledge from past civilisations and had simply passed them on to Europe without themselves doing any work.

During the compilation of the Hadith the Muslim scholars had started a reference system, the Isnad, to determine the original source. These were written down with each Hadith. In rational science as well they started to credit previous works, like those of Socrates, Aristotle, Ptolemy, etc. Thus the old names were passed on and the old masters got their due credit. But when their turn came, the European scholars overlooked the Muslim names in the reference system except for a tiny minority. The Muslim contributions were either erased or remained Latinised, like Geber for Al Jabir, in overlooked historical-academic records only. In the *Intellectual Development of Europe*, John William Draper laments,

> "I have to deplore the systematic manner in which the literature of Europe has continued to put out to sight our obligations to the Mohammedans. Surely they cannot be much longer hidden. Injustice founded on religious rancour and national conceit cannot be perpetrated forever. The Arab has left his intellectual impress on Europe. He has indelibly written it on the heavens as any one may see who reads the names of the stars on a common celestial globe."

In a similar manner, great Muslim rulers and majestic dynasties have been much maligned by oriental historians. Much focus have been paid on their negative aspects, taken out of context, and attempts made to make their great achievements appear mediocre.

The Vatican, in 1970, had tried to rectify the prejudice against Muslims. A document, *Orientations pour un dialogue entre chretiens et musulmans* (Orientations for a Dialogue between Christians and Muslims) by Father Maurice Borrman, produced by the Non-Christian Affairs at the Vatican stated that they must stay away from the out-dated image of Muslims that has been inherited from the past, or distorted by prejudice and slander. The document notes with regret that far too many Christians, brought up in an atmosphere of open hostility, are against any reflection on Islam. The text under the title of *Nous liberer de nos prejuges les plus notables* (Emancipating ourselves from our worst prejudices) asserts that there is a need for deep purification of attitude, particularly, from certain 'set judgement' that are all too often and too lightly made about Islam. It says that such views that are too easily or arbitrarily arrived at, which the sincere Muslim finds confusing, should not be cultivated in the heart (WR9, 2011).

Taste of a Colony

European colonial expansion is synonymous with its intellectual and rational development on the one hand and sea faring and naval development on the other. It was not by luck or pure chance that the Iberians (Spain and Portugal) were the first Europeans to take to the seas and establish colonies on other continents. It was the influence of the Spanish Muslims that had enabled them to do so.

The only land connection that the Iberian Peninsula has to the rest of Europe is through the Pyrenees Mountains bordering France, the other three sides being bordered by the sea. The Muslims of Spain and Portugal, being barricaded by the Franks on the north, did not have any land connection to other regions of the world. The only way to survive was via the seas, and survive they did in an enlightened and grand manner. They developed enterprising naval and commercial connections with distant lands. With the unfriendly Abbasid on the east, the sea faring was also directed towards North West Africa. They improved cartography, maps, naval instruments and ship design. They had become experts in the geography of the great seas and used mathematics and astronomy to guide them across. The shape of the Earth, the African coast and some Atlantic Islands were already known to the Muslims. The geographer Al Idrisi's had produced maps in Roger of Sicily's court in the 12th century that would be used in various regions including Europe without alterations for three centuries. The Muslims had highly refined the use of astrolabe by the 9th century and introduced it to Spain. It would remain the most popular astronomical device in Europe till the mid 17th century.

All this seafaring knowledge of the Spanish Muslims was automatically inherited by the later Portuguese and the Spaniards. Thus it was they who made the first European naval expeditions. Ceuta, the small but strategic North African port across the southern coast of the Strait of Gibraltar, was occupied by the Portuguese Prince Henry the Navigator in 1415. This capture opened up the door of Saharan trade routes. It was the first little step that was to start the process of colonization.

In Europe, the translated tales of Muslim travellers from Al Masudi (9th century) to Ibn Batuta (14th century) were read with great interest. Along with these travelogues the translated geography books also whet the taste for exploration by western intelligentsia. This, ultimately, led to the epoch-changing voyages and journeys of Magellan, Vasco da Gama, Marco Polo, Christopher Columbus, James Cook and Ferdinand Magellan.

As the Spanish Muslims had been land-locked by the Franks, so the Europeans were also hedged in by the Ottomans. During hostilities between Byzantium and the Ottomans, Europe would become completely landlocked. Land travel to India and China became difficult, so an alternate sea route was always sought after. When Constantinople fell to the Ottomans the Portuguese discovered the sea route to India around Africa. At about the same time the

Italian Christopher Columbus decided to investigate another route to India across the Atlantic. The world was unaware of the existence of the Americas that lay between India and Europe. Al Idrisi's maps and the '*Elements of astronomy on the celestial motions*' by Al-Farghani (Alfraganus – a lunar crater is named after him), the famous Muslim astronomer of the ninth century, were contributory in working out the circumference of the world at that time.

Columbus' proposal for funding to sail west was rejected by Portugal, while England was hesitant. Spain having just defeated Muslim Granada agreed to sponsor the trip hoping to find a more competitive trade route. Even though it appeared remote at that time, Columbus did offer a new alternative. In the contract between Columbus and Spain, Columbus on discovery of the lands would be given high rewards including being made 'Admiral of the Seas', given 10 percent of all revenues from the new lands, be able to buy one eighth of any commercial ventures into the new land, as well as other benefits. Ultimately, Columbus discovered West Indies and reported that the 'Indians' were non violent and friendly people. He made a number of trips to the Indies. He had a stint at Governorship of Hispaniola but he fell out of favour of the Spanish settlers. They complained that he had ruled his domain as a tyrant. The Spanish Crown relinquished him of all his contracts and arrested him in 1500. He was later freed and died in 1506. Columbus had discovered America in the first voyage in 1492. In this voyage he led three small ships named Santa Maria, Pinta and Nina. Santa Maria, nicknamed Gallega, was the flagship commanded by Columbus. Two brothers Martin Alonso Pinzon and Vincente Yanez Pinzon captained the Pinta and Nina.These two brothers were Muslims and related to *Abuzayan Muhammad III*, the Moroccan Sultan of the Marinid Dynasty (1196-1465). They, most likely, were not practicing Muslims as in 1480 the Spanish Inquisation had started and by 1502 all the Muslims of Spain would be forced to convert to Christianity or leave Spain under threat of death.

> By this time sea-faring had progressed in other areas of the world as well. In the first half of the 15th century, China with 3,500 ships became the biggest navy in the world. Its ships, miracles of marine engineering, were the largest of their time. The admiral Zheng He, a devout Muslim, belonged to the retinue of Prince Zhu Di. The Prince later became the Emperor Yong Le.
>
> Zheng He, a towering figure, was the real Sinbad. He made seven epic voyages, each two years long, sailing through the Indian Ocean, the Persian Gulf and visited thirty seven countries including East Africa and Arabia. His journeys took place before the voyages of Christopher Columbus or Vasco da Gama. About his fleet he wrote that sixty two of the largest ships were 449 feet long and 180 feet wide, that is, four times the size of Columbus' ship 'Nina'. The fleet contained fresh water tanker ships, poultry ships and even farm ships that would supply the sailors on their long journeys in the days when food preservation technology did not exist. Many trading and diplomatic breakthrough were made due to these journeys. By the end of the seven journeys China became the topmost in naval power and technology.

But after Zheng He's death and the onset of Confucianism the Chinese became political introverts. Ultimately, many of the ocean going vessels were destroyed in 1525 by imperial decree. Zheng He remains the most famous Chinese sailor in history.

Colonial Expansion

In Europe, after the initial adventure-expeditions for short term trade and economic gains, the impetus for exploration became colonisation. First the indigenous South American tribes were subjugated which brought in much wealth in particular gold and other precious metals. The new found wealth was used to modernise and develop, among other thing, the navies. The first navies that developed, as expected, were the Portuguese and Spanish, while England's alliance treaty with Portugal which favoured trade led to knowledge transfer and enabled the development of a very strong English Navy.

First hand knowledge of distant lands coupled with the emancipation of rational thought made the Europeans a formidable force. They slowly spread out across the world setting up colonies that would last up to the mid 20th century. In their conquering episode the Europeans at times showed remarkable bravery and dexterity and at others times great treachery and exploitative brutality.

Though colonialism had started in the 16th century, it was mostly restricted to the Americas, as regions of less cultural and technological advancement were colonized in the first phase. Eventually, the Swedes, Dutch, English and the French arrived in the Americas. In North America, in the final tussle, the British defeated the French and established themselves as the colonial power there.

The Europeans established business presence in various regions like India, Iran, Macao, etc. They overtook the Muslims in trade and commerce. By the start of the eighteenth century the Europeans had accumulated enough experience, knowledge, wealth and power to take bolder steps. In the second phase of colonisation the more advanced lands were brought under colonial rule. On the further side of the world Spain conquered the Philippines, while the Dutch became the dominant power in the Indonesian archipelago. Macao, where the Portuguese had established business since the 17th century, was gifted to the Portuguese by the Qing government in 1887 after the Opium War.

The British were involved in a lucrative business of supplying opium to China from British India. When the Chinese ruling apparatus declared this illegal, the Opium War erupted. The British Indian army arrived in 1840 and engaged in a number of battles with the Chinese. By 1860, China was forced to ratify the Treaty of Nanjing and then the Treaty of Tientsin which gave Britain many business as well as political and territorial concessions in China. This ratification also granted a number of privileges to France and Russia who had supported the British.

This period was also the time when institutionalised racism was introduced. Artwork from ancient Egypt, Persia, Greece and Rome clearly depicts awareness of racial features and skin colour. But nowhere is any evidence of any discrimination or divisiveness solely based on race. It was only in the 19th century, after Europe's colonisation of Africa, that their scholars became racist towards the dark skin. A political exigency for racism was that the individuals running the colonial administration would have to stay overseas in the colonies for long periods. In the colonial regions these individuals were at a risk of being assimilated by the native people. Thus racism was used to make them feel superior and keep them segregated from the natives. It also provided the justification, to themselves and to the people back home, why they should rule and exploit other people and their resources. In moral philosophy, though, this was a huge step backwards. For racism was nothing more than the age old tribalism with a new appellation. Irrespective, the white tribes were on the colonial rampage.

Fall of the Ottomans

After the ethnic cleansing of Muslims from the Iberian Peninsula, the only European-Muslim entity that remained was the Ottomans. By the time of Sulaiman the Magnificent, the Ottomans had established very modern legal, civil and military administrative systems. The logical progression should have been towards scientific enquiry, as the Muslims had done in the past. This would have required political vision.

As few of the later Ottoman Sultans were incompetent the Empire, gradually, came to be run by a competent administration led by talented Grand Wazirs and sometimes influenced by the royal ladies of the Harem. This was a makeshift arrangement and not a solution to the governance of the state, and led to decadence in both civil and military administration. By the end of the 18th century the empire still huge, lost its momentum. As the Europeans rose rapidly in terms of social, scientific, material and military progress, the Ottomans stagnated. The 19th century saw the Ottomans start to decline in earnest with a loss of much of their European lands.

The final destruction of the empire took place at the hands of European imperialism. But that was just the surgical tool that took the Ottomans apart. The real disease was the lack of modernisation and progress. The backward agricultural system was unable to feed the huge Ottoman population. The Ottoman industry was of a pre-mechanised craft-based stage. The military had to buy equipments from Europe to modernise itself. The need for food and equipments would cause budget deficits.

Several Sultans had attempted important reforms. Selim III (1761-1808), for instance, initiated reforms in taxation, commerce, and the military. But internal resistance, including that from the now-decadent Janissaries, made administrative changes almost impossible. He was finally assassinated. The biggest of these attempted reformations was the *Tanzimat* meaning 'Regulation' that started in 1839 following the accession of the reformist Sultan

Abdul Mazid (Abdul Mecid). It was aimed at remodelling the economy, administration, armed forces, and the legal and educational systems so that the Ottomans could compete with the Europeans. But opposition to the reformation cropped up from within the Sultanate by segments whose personal interests would be affected by the changes.

The reformers tried to adapt the state model more along the European line. Turkish students were sent to London, Paris and Vienna to receive higher education. A medical school with French doctors was set up in Istanbul. But the root issue - scientific research and development that would have given the Ottomans ability to progressively improve their agriculture, industry and military, instead of depending on Europe - was not incorporated. Industries set up by borrowing or buying European technology eventually lagged behind due to an absence of local scientific 'research and development' that was required for progressive improvement with time. In a short time such industries would become outdated compared to European ones. To meet their budget deficit the Sultans borrowed money from Europe but had to pay huge interest that further drained their economy. The Muslim economy opened up to the economic exploitation of *Riba* and that would be a major factor to its economic ruin and downfall.

In 1861, Abdul Mazid abdicated and his successor, Abul Aziz, was less interested in or incapable of carrying out the reformations. The European economic and financial penetration into the Ottoman system began on a massive scale. Soon many of the local craft-based industry were destroyed. In 1874 the Ottoman's state debt, largely to foreign banks, increased to an extent that there was a financial collapse. In 1876, Sultan Abdul Aziz ended the *Tanzimat* with the cancellation of the Ottoman constitution. The reformation mostly failed to achieve its goals. The main beneficiary of the reformation was the military, which was modernised not by local development of military wares but mostly by buying from Europe at huge expense.

Up to the 19th century, Albania, Bosnia, Crete, Herzegovina, parts of Bulgaria, and most of the cities in Ottoman Europe had Muslim majority populations. Ottoman defeats resulted in the killing and expulsion of Muslims from the lost territories. These ethnic-cleansing European-Balkan nationalist movements would continue up to the end of 20th century when the Bosnian Muslims would face genocide.

Unlike the Ottomans, the Russian Czar Peter the Great (1682-1725) had been able to combine new western technological advances with traditional autocratic power. The result was that by the 19th century, a strong Russia was able encroach on Ottoman territories even though Britain, fearful of Russia's advances, at times supported the Ottomans in the Ottoman-Russian conflicts. The oppressive behaviour of the new Russian authorities in Crimea, western Caucasus and eastern Black Sea coastal regions forced massive emigration of Muslims into safer regions of Ottoman cities and country areas.

The *Tanzimat* also had provisions for further improvement of the non-Islamic *Millet* or religious groups of the empire. The Europeans considered those only as cosmetic even though there was substantial benefit in it. Some of the local *Millet* also took a negative stand on many issues. They did not want to stand up and fight the Sultanate's foes but still wanted all the rights of a full Ottoman citizenship to remain intact. Previously, a rule of collaboration and the best economic conditions had kept all the ethnic groups within the Empire happy. But in the 19th century, due to a falling economy and consequent misrule made nationalism attractive to the ethnic groups.

During this period, Egypt became very powerful under the leadership of a Turco-Albanian named Mohammad Ali. He modernised and westernised Egypt and its army. Initially, he was nominated *Pasha* (Governor) of Egypt by the Ottomans. When the Arabs revolted against Turkish rule and captured the Hijaj, the Turkish government asked the Pasha to contain the rebellion. Egypt fought the Arabs for seven years and defeated them. Mohammad Ali next conquered Sudan and became the Governor of Egypt, Arabia and Sudan. When the Greeks revolted the Egyptian forces virtually crushed the Greek rebellion in 1821 after the Turkish forces were unable to defeat the Greeks. Though, the Greeks would ultimately gain independence in about a decade.

In return for his services Mohammad Ali now wanted the governorship of Syria and Palestine, which the Sultan refused. Egypt attacked and conquered Syria. When the very capital of the Ottomans was threatened the European came out in favour of Turkey. They preferred a weak European Turkey to a strong Egypt. At the Sultan's request Russia, Britain and Austria-Hungary invaded and seized the Lebanese coast from Egypt. Subsequently, at a treaty in London in 1841, Mohammad Ali was forced to reduce his army to only 18,000 men and all conquered regions under him were returned to the Ottomans. Mohammad Ali died in 1848.

In 1830, a combination of English, French and Russian invasion forced the Ottomans to recognise the independence of Greece. This fomented further interest for independence among European, Arab and other subjects of the Ottomans. Ultimately, the end of the Ottomans came in the First World War at the start of the 20th Century.

Power Struggle in Europe

The French revolution gave France a modern people's state. After the revolution, the European monarchies and empires were all concerned about the revolution spilling over from France to their domains. Various coalitions of Britain, Prussia, Russia and Austria attacked the republic of France. Napoleon Bonaparte, a French General, fought these coalitions successfully. In 1804 he declared himself Emperor of France and fought with every major European power and gained control of most of Continental Europe. But a disastrous invasion into Russia in 1812 left his army depleted from which it and he never recovered. His final defeat came in 1815 in the Battle of Waterloo in Belgium against an army jointly commanded by Duke of Wellington of United Kingdom and Gebhard von Blucher of Prussia. Besides his battle tactics, Napoleon's greatest legacy is the Napoleonic Code which is the bureaucratic foundation of modern France.

By the close of the nineteenth century, it had become 'clear' to the western nations that it was not possible to amass and sustain sufficient wealth and power, and feed its hungry industries, by using internal resources only. It was a 'necessity' to have overseas colonies. Russia had colonised its adjoining lands on the east. Now Japan, United States and Germany joined the fray. After Napoleon's France, Germany became the prime military power of continental Europe. The attempt by Germany to become a regional colonial power eventually led to the two world wars in the 20th century.

Germany in 1870, unlike Britain and France, was a well ordered but still mainly agrarian economy. Then its industrialisation gathered pace and it became highly industrialised with two thirds of its working population involved in manufacturing. It replaced France as the great European continental power west of Russia (Roberts 1997). The meteoric rise was a cause of apprehension to its neighbours. This apprehension of their neighbours bred a counter fear in Germany itself that the other powers would do their best to stop Germany from taking its place in the world. It needed to do something to protect its new found place and prestige. The fundamental German policy was that to protect itself Germany needed a strong armed force, and to sustain its economy further inroads were needed into colonies.

But by then lucrative regions had already been distributed among others and carved into colonies. North America was independent and a rising power on its own, South America was already divided amongst the colonial powers, India and Australia were British, the Indonesian Archipelago was Dutch, China was within British and French influence. This ultimately meant that for any new power to rise there had to be a redistribution of the existing colonies, and that was what the established colonial powers could not allow. Military conflict was inevitable and such conflicts were already taking place on a smaller scale. The United States, after overthrowing the Monarch of Hawaii, annexed the Republic of Hawaii in July 4, 1894 turning it into an American territory. That led to the Spanish - American war in 1898 by which Spain was forced to cede Philippines, Cuba, Puerto Rico and Guam to the United States. Japan attacked and defeated the Chinese (in 1895) and the Russians (in 1905) and in the process occupied Korea, Taiwan and Southern Sakhalin.

Germany was the strongest power among those flexing their muscles at this time but their military prowess was not enough to engage in both of its fronts, the east with Russia and the west with France, at the same time. Russia had become weak since its defeat in the hands of the Japanese in 1905. Thus the German strategy was to conquer France before Russia could recover and mobilise. Once they had achieved that then they would be able engage the Russians in the eastern front as needed. But as the second decade of the 20th century rolled in, Russia started to make recovery faster than anticipated. It became a concern for the Germans as a resurgent Russia could attack them while they were still engaged in France.

Originally, the Germans had calculated a possible war in around 1920 (Grenville, 1994). By then their Navy would be strong enough to challenge the British. But rapid recovery by Russia forced them to engage in war much earlier. The First World War started in 1914.

The two warring alliances were the Entente Powers and the Central Powers. The Entente Powers comprised of the United Kingdom, France, Russia and their associated colonies. Other nations that joined them later were Italy in April, 1915, and the United States in April, 1917. The Central Powers consisted of Germany, Austria-Hungary and the Ottoman Empire. Bulgaria joined them in 1914.

For the first time in history, a war was not determined on the battlefields, but became a war of attrition. The main factors leading to victory were which countries could produce and supply more weaponry and more young men who would die at the battle fields. It was a war fought from factories and homes. The war ended in 1918 and the victorious Entente Powers redrew the map of Europe and their colonies. The Central Powers lost territories and colonies from which many new nations were created. The German Empire lost its colonies, were blamed for the war and had to pay huge punitive reparations. The Austro-Hungarian and Ottoman Empires were completely dissolved. The Anatolian part of the Ottoman became the Republic of Turkey while the rest of the Empire was awarded protectorates which would lead to the formation of nations, Kingdoms and Emirates. Austria-Hungary was divided into several successor states including Austria, Yugoslavia, Hungary and Czechoslovakia. The Russians had withdrawn from the war in 1917 and lost much of its western front with the formation of independent nations of Finland, Estonia, Latvia, Lithuania, and Poland.

After the First World War, the international political philosophy had changed. Death, destruction and pain that the imperial and colonial politics had caused made the world leaders realise that a change in thinking was needed. This did not completely eradicate violence but led to a belief that a more benign world was needed and, more importantly, that such a world could be achieved. The dominant view of the political scientists of that time was idealist. They believed that wars were taking place because the world institutions were set up in such a way and with such policies that war became inevitable. They believed such institutions had to be changed and new pro-peace institutions - such as permanent international courts of justice, binding arms control and investment in social improvement and outlawing war as national policy - had to be established.

World War I led to the end of the post Napoleon world order. The League of Nations, the precursor of the United Nations, was formed for the states to work out the differences between them. One of the prime objectives of the league was to stop wars by a process of collective security. If one nation was attacked all other nations were to act against the transgressor in concert. But the great powers deemed this a threat, that the collective might of the League may be used against them. The United States, despite the support of President Wilson, failed to join the league due to the opposition by the Republicans.

After World War I Germany was suffering from super inflation and had fallen to economic throes due to the reparations it was paying for the First World War. That led to a super-nationalistic upsurge in Germany with the Nazi's leading the country to war. The league failed to maintain peace, which resulted in the World War II in which Germany along with Japan and Italy would, ultimately, fight the rest of the world. The war started before any significant pro-peace institutional changes that had been envisioned could take root in the international arena. There was an added element in WWII. The fight for energy, oil, gathered a critical momentum. Germany even attacked Russia to lay their hands on Russian oil fields, but in vain.

Though the British-French and their allies 'won' the war, this marked the end of the colonial age.Gradually, countries like India, Pakistan, Malaysia and Algeria became independent. The capitalist United States and the socialist Soviet Union became the two super powers. Most of the neo-independent states would align with one or the other of the two camps. Later, a few countries including Indonesia, India and Egypt would try to form a third non-aligned group.

The views of the 'realist' political scientists, that became dominant in the West at this stage, took the opportunity to blame the World War II on the 'Utopian' view of the idealist. The 'realists' envisioned that there will be wars, so it is better not to let others gain supremacy. Pre-emptive aggression was preferred over defensive actions. But even with declining state sponsor the idealist view prevailed as an undercurrent. This led to a variety of outcome – support to grant independence to colonies (though the inability of the colonial powers to further extend their resource needed for colonial control was one of the prime factors), hippy movement and 'flower power' flourished. Objective reporting in the media was encouraged and for sometime a culture of platonic love and romance developed in recreational industries such as movies and story books. While the developed world was becoming more 'realistic' in political philosophy, the new emerging Third World countries, in spite of being the battleground of short wars, were to remain idealistic for some more time, probably clinging to hope rather then to conviction.

The United Nation was formed in place of the League of Nations. But this time the big powers were guaranteed protection by including them in the Security Council and giving them the power of 'Veto'. Any one of them could veto one and all of the UN's resolutions or actions. So, the United Nations, in effect, could only be used against those countries which did not have the power of veto. But, it was accepted by all as it was the only place where all could, at least, get together and raise their issues. It also formed forums that were beneficial to all. For example, the United Nation Council for Trade and Development, a forum which served as the spokesperson of the world poor, was formed.

The overall environment was still optimistic, especially in the developing nations. Despite battles and small wars being fought, the world populace up to the 1970s still believed in an idealistic and happy world. The G-77 which formed the group of developing nations stoutly asked for the introduction of the New International Economic Order (NIEO) that would make structural change in the world political economy - international trade and commerce - so that the hindrances to the development of poor countries would be removed. But at the end of the 1970s these values would come to an end and materialism rather then humane ideals would become more and more the ruling standard of world political leadership.

In the 18th century, Europe had started to surge ahead of the rest of the world. It was the dawn of the Industrial age which had started from Britain. Healthy population growth, increased agricultural output and technological innovation were the key factors driving the Industrial revolution. Over the ages, science had kept on advancing and in the 18th century it had developed where man could create all manner of machinery to assist in processes of mass production. Colonial expansion provided both wealth for the development of the industries and infrastructure and external markets for the end products.

The technological advance started slowly in the second half of the 18th century and gradually accelerated. By the late 19th century the effect of industrialisation was marked by major shift in socio-economic and cultural life. The manual labour based economy was slowly replaced by a machine based economy. First the textile and iron making industries were mechanised. Energy usage, from refined coal, increased. To facilitate trade, the communication infrastructure had to be developed. The road and canal networks were improved and developed, then railway and steam ships eventually took over the job of mass transport of people and goods. In the 19th century, industrialisation spread all across Western Europe and North America.

Innovations improved textile manufacture, Mining, Metallurgy, Steam power, Chemicals, and Gas lighting. Improved roads, navigable rivers and artificial canals made transport far more efficient. Machine tools were improved so that newer and more efficient and better machines could be made. Improved diet, longevity and cheap labour, which included the use of children, were available for the industries. Factories leapt up and the process of urbanization and housing developed. This would lead to a better organisation of labour.

Research and Development (RAD), the root of the innovations that developed the machineries for the factories, became the mainstay of staying ahead in industrial competition. In continental Europe, factories started to develop in various nations. Soon these nations would start their own RAD and become self dependent. The Ottomans set up factories but failed to setup their RAD.

In the United States, industrialisation started in north-eastern region where rivers with fast currents were located and water power was used to run factories. In the 1860s with the application of steam-power industry began to spread across the nation.

The second stage of the Industrial Revolution started in late 19th century and included the development of chemical, petroleum, electrical industries, and in the 20th century the automotive industries. It was marked by a transition of technological leadership from Britain to the United States and later also to Japan and Germany. By the 1890s, industrialisation had created the first giant industrial corporations with burgeoning global interests, when companies like U.S. Steel, General Electric, and Bayer AG joined the railroad companies on the stock markets.

The industrialisation of Japan started when a group of Japanese politicians known as the Iwakura Mission toured Europe and the United States in 1871. On the advice of this mission the Japanese government started a state-led industrialisation scheme and plans for colonisation. Modern education was expanded and Japanese students were sent to study in the west to develop skills. In the 20th , Japanese RAD would improve until they became second only to the US. In the later half of the 20th century, China and India joined in the industrial age. Thus, under European enlightenment, all the empires of antiquity had turned into developed nations except for the Muslims.

Political and Economic Theories

With industrialisation and colonisation the western countries accumulated more wealth at a rate faster than ever before. The consequent changes in the society required new economic processes for the management of the modern state. In 1776 Adam Smith published his work *The Wealth of Nations* which is considered the start of classical economics. It was the time in which the modern state was emerging from the legacy of feudalism and the classical economists perceived economy in the light of a national income rather than a ruler's treasury.

The vital suggestion of Adam Smith was that the free market that appeared chaotic was actually self regulating. The basis of the Smith's work was class-based and described a system in which individuals sought to improve their own conditions in a competitive environment. The national income was divided up between labourers, landlords, and capitalists in the form of wages, rent and interest. One of the main arguments in favour of capitalism was, and still is, that it made some very rich but also increased wealth for all, as evidenced by raising life expectancy, reduced working hours, and no work required of children and the elderly.

Despite those improvements, many found capitalism as biased towards the rich. Marxism rose essentially as a working class reaction to the Industrial Revolution and the inequalities in the distribution of wealth created by capitalism. According to Karl Marx, industrialisation polarised society into the few but very rich bourgeoisie and the much larger in numbers and much poorer proletariat. He believed that the industrialisation process was the logical dialectical progression of the feudal economy. And the full development of capitalism would produce the foundation that would lead to the development of socialism and eventually communism. Socialism asserted economic equality among people and the abolition of private property, either wholly or partially.

Karl Heinrich Marx was a philosopher, political economist and revolutionary of the 19th century. He is most famous for his historical analysis which is stated in the opening line of the Communist Manifesto: "The history of all hitherto existing society is the history of class struggles". Called the Father of Communism he argued that his analysis of capitalism revealed that the contradictions within capitalism would themselves bring about its end. "Communism is for us not a state of affairs which is to be established but an ideal to which reality will have to adjust itself. We call communism the real movement which abolishes the present state of things. The conditions of this movement result from the premises now in existence."

After the death of Marx his ideas began to exert a major influence on workers' movements. This influence was given added impetus by the victory of the Marxist Bolsheviks in the Russian October Revolution. Many regions of the world including the Soviet Union, Cuba, China, etc, inherited Marxist political system or ideas during the 20th century and Marxism still remains influential or controversial in various regions.

During the Industrial Revolution an intellectual and artistic resentment had also developed towards the capitalist industrialisation processes. This was known as the Romantic Movement. Its major exponents in England included the poets William Blake, William Wordsworth, George Gordon Byron, Samuel Taylor Coleridge, John Keats and Percy Bysshe Shelley. The movement stressed the importance of 'nature' in art and language, in contrast to 'monstrous' machines and factories. The mention of 'Dark satanic mills' in Blake's poem *Jerusalem* and Mary Shelley's novel *Frankenstein* reflected concerns that scientific progress may also have a negative effect on humanity. Later this theme is continued in J.R.R. Tolkien's *Lord of the Rings* where the antagonists are shown as anti-environmental 'industrialist'.

~~~

The Political State of Europe

The people's representative modern state came out of Europe. It is representative because its government is chosen by the people via elections. All the Institutions that support a modern state were developed. For example, technology and communication developed to where the mass population can arrive to voting stations on the dates of election and the votes could be counted within the required time. Due to mass communication people became aware of what is happening in the country and education apparently made them mature enough to take the correct decision on choosing the government. This solved the issue of who the next ruler should be, an issue which had afflicted the world for so long. All these issues were resolved by centuries of dedication by European scientists, scholars and finally by their politicians.

Long ago, the four Rashidun Caliphs had run a people's representative state as well. Similar to the classical economist they also considered the wealth of the nation belonging to the people. But due to the absence of technology the society was not ready for the development
~~~

of modern institutions. The later Caliphs opted for hereditary rule. But, unlike the Rashidun state, the modern states are not universal and views the world as divided into unequal groups of people, some wealthy and others poor, some strong and some weak. The poor and weak nations do not have much protection against the rich and strong ones aside for some international forums like United Nations and World Bank, which are, again, biased towards the rich and strong.

The American Age.

In the 18th century, while Captain James Cook was claiming New South Wales of Australia and Robert Clive had started his conquest of Bengal in India, the USA was declaring Independence from the British. It declared its independence on the 4th of July, 1776 proclaiming that 'all men are created equal" and have "certain inalienable rights". The constitution of the US was adopted on September 17, 1787. Ten amendments were made to the constitution in 1791 which is known as the US Bill of rights.

The constitution of the United States is of supreme importance to the world and a milestone in modern history. Under its influence slavery was slowly eradicated, first from the northern states and then from the southern states after a civil war. To the southern politician, as their economy was based on a slavery institution, this would have appeared harmful and self defeating. But, in reality, industry had developed to the extent that society needed skilled and semi-skilled labour force rather then slaves. By the 20th century, USA became the most dynamic nation in the world, which even the world conquering Europeans started look up to.

The 20th century saw the start of space exploration, the Internet, and the rise of mega corporations along with media moguls which took control of human society. The US led the world in academic excellence and scholarship. In trade and commerce it developed an international presence and became the largest economy of the world. It geared up its resources to reach out to outer space, overtaking the Soviet Union, in reaching the moon. Its technological advancement developed and sustained the Internet which has moved from the status of a technology to that of an essential global requirement and culture. Development and innovations continued as never before. Telecommunication, rocket science, medical science, nuclear science, genetic engineering, artificial intelligence, outer space research and many other disciplines improved at a breath-taking pace. By the start of 21st century the full DNA of man was deciphered and cloning was better understood.

After the Second World War, when the transition of world power took place from the British Empire to the United States, the two main foreign issues it faced were:

- The power of the rising Union of Soviet Socialist Republics (USSR)
- The assurance that oil, life-blood of the industrialised world, would keep flowing from the Middle East to the industrial hubs of the developed world.

At the start of the 20th century, socialism was not an 'evil' word, not in Europe and not even in the USA. It was, in fact, the pampered philosophy of the most renowned western intellectuals and philosophers. But, mainly after the World War II, as the USSR started to export socialism as a political weapon the United States reacted with a counter policy.

In its global fight against the USSR's 'moral' socialism, the USA unleashed the 'power' of capitalism. The main policy was to surround and contain USSR with a host of capitalist states. It assisted, extensively, war torn Japan and Germany to recover their economy and become world capitalist powers. In Europe it created the North Atlantic Treaty Organisation (NATO). It set up regional cooperation with Muslim countries forming the Central Treaty Organisation (CENTO), which included Great Britain, Iran, Pakistan, and Turkey, and the South East Asian Treaty Organisation (SEATO), which included Australia, Great Britain, France, New Zealand, Pakistan, the Philippines and Thailand. It collaborated with small far Asian regimes like Singapore, Taiwan and Korea. The alliance between the Muslims - Saudi Arabia, Iran, Pakistan, Indonesia - and America against the atheist Soviets grew to great heights. With the assistance of Pakistan the USA made 'friendly' overtures to communist China to further isolate USSR. In the USA itself, in the 1950s, many Americans even though not pro-soviet were persecuted just for their support for socialism or for having a socialist bent of mind in a purge known as McCarthyism.

During this period, the USA and Soviet Union fought a clandestine Cold War in which, under a pall of nuclear threat, only their spies plotted and sometimes killed each other. But it was a very hot war for the countries allied to the two superpowers. They did all the real fighting for the superpowers. At this juncture, the Muslims were one of the most gullible people easily goaded to war and they had the natural resources with which they could pay for the weapons needed.

After Nikita Khrushchev, Premier from 1958 to 1964, the Soviet Union did not have any exceptional leader, and the people's interest to carry on the great socialist march dried up. The driving 'ideal patriotic' force to develop the nation slowly died its death since those who had participated in the revolution died. Once the fundamental economic infrastructure had been built and people had come out of poverty, there was no further incentive for individuals or the market to perform above average. After the Second World War the Soviet Union needed to shift gradually to an open market to keep its economy dynamic. But instead, the Soviet Union retained the socialist policies and their economy stagnated. The Soviets had also tried to build up their own group of allies. But, the Soviet allies were the 'poorer' nations more worried about their own economy rather than to fight for ideology. Cuba was the exception in that it stuck to its ideology due to the great influence of its leader Fidel Castro and the revolutionary figure of Che Guevara.

The socialist doctrine of the USSR enabled a more efficient distribution of capital but less efficient accumulation of it. By the mid 20th century, the Soviet industry and agriculture were both stagnant. The Soviet misadventure into Afghanistan in the 1980s caused it much economic woes and the lowering of petroleum prices by the Arab-led Organisation of Petroleum Exporting Countries (OPEC) disabled it to recoup any revenue. When finally, the economic woes become uncontrollable the USA offered a detente. In the peace talks that took place in the 1980s, the Americans were able to 'talk' the Soviet Union into disintegration in 1991. Overnight, the Soviet Union broke up from a superpower to a number of independent capitalist nations, some falling to third world status while still maintaining nuclear capability. These countries became dependent on USA and Europe for aid or assistance. It would be not before the 21st century that Russia became stable enough to come out of the influence of USA and regain its wealth and some of its old economic and social capabilities. Irrespective of dynamic political and military factors involved, the USA and the outgoing Soviet regime have shown a remarkable dexterity in handling the disintegration of the Soviet Union. This was the first time that an armed and yet virile 'empire' had disintegrated without any violence of significance. Had it been handled incorrectly there was a great probability of extreme divisive violence within the Soviet Union and some possibility of a nuclear war between the USA and Soviet Union.

The year 1979, reflects the typical dynamic politics of the 20th century. In 1979, the de facto leader of China, Deng Xiao-Ping took the second step of economic emancipation by opening China partially to the global market. The first step of Chinese consolidation was done by Chairman Mao, who had taken over a war ravaged, foreign influenced, drug addicted, lethargic, agrarian and divided China and over one short generation had converted this heterogeneity to a homogenous industrial nation. The Chinese became disciplined, hardworking and kept on modernising the industry and developing the nation even when living on a subsistence pay. The people remained poor as the state had only enough to keep the development work going on and not enough to pay the workers. The view from the outside thus made China appear poor, desolate and lacking human rights. But this sacrifice of one generation allowed the development of the foundation of modern China. Once the industrial foundation and basic infrastructure was laid, as the second step, Deng slowly opened up China to more advanced global commerce. Thus was born a super-economy.

In 1979, Margaret Thatcher became the Prime Minister of UK with the sole belief that only an open market economy would develop the world. She did rescue the ailing British national economy and helped in bringing down the Berlin Wall. She and the US President Ronald Reagan were both conservatives and their common vision about the world was that every country should open up its market in the same pattern as the developed countries of Europe and the USA for global development.

In 1979, Ayatollah Ruhollah Khomeni took over power in Iran with a philosophy diametrically opposed to the USA-UK political vision. He believed that the western political practice was oppressive and aimed at world domination, that their attempts to open up the markets of other countries were actually aimed at economically exploiting those countries. He also believed that the deliverance of the world was by adhering to the tenets of the Prophet and Islam.

Many of the Muslim nations had gained their independence as an after-effect of the two world wars and were thus mostly allied with the victors, who had agreed to their independence. One big sore in this smooth relationship was the introduction of Israel. To the Jews, after millennia of wandering, a nation of their own was a wondrous gift and one near

Jerusalem was a gift from God. They immigrated to Israel from various countries. The Jews got a highly deserving home, but, unfortunately, by arrogating the rights of another group of people living there. For the Palestinians, the majority who had been living in those lands with a Jewish minority, this was home invasion and then forced eviction. They were forced to leave their home and live as refugees in the surrounding Arab countries. Those who remained in Israel were relegated to a third class citizenship. Thus, specially in the Muslim world, the very legitimacy of the new nation came into question. The introduction of Jewish Israel would heighten the element of religion in politics in the Middle East.

The Israelis, with American and European support, became the most modern and powerful state in the region. The political environment of the Middle East changed with an ironic twist. For a thousand years when the Europeans had oppressed the Jews, they had found sanctuary, respite and dignity in the Muslim lands, be it in Muslim Spain, Fatimid Egypt or Ottoman Turkey. The office of the Grand Rabbi had been, in fact, located in Ottoman lands. Suddenly, after the formation of Israel, they became the greatest enemies of the Muslims.

The result was the formation of a conflict zone and, as it happens in any conflict zone, this led to cyclic hostility of hatred and more hatred. In the wars that resulted, the Israelis fought with their backs to the wall. Albeit unrecognised by many, this was the only home they had and one they have got after thousands of years. In dealing with the Palestinians, who had become a minority now, some elements in the Israeli government took Pharaoh as a role model rather than Moses. As the Pharoahs had dealt so harshly with the minority Hebrews, the Israelis showed little compassion towards their Palestinian minority. Moses was able to escape with his people away from the Egyptians. The Palestinians had nowhere to go. They fought back with whatever they could lay their hands on. Geo-strategically, the conflict became the destabilising factor that kept the region dependent on superpowers and oil-flow remained under the control of the corporations.

Most Muslims remained American allies in global politics. The USA, on its side, wooed the Muslims for their resources and alliance against the socialist Soviets. The Muslims also preferred the Christian West rather then any godless people. The relationship between Muslims and the USA proved to be a great problem for the Soviet Union. In a number of countries, pro Soviet governments were toppled with the aid of local Muslim powers. In Afghanistan the American-Mujahideen alliance led to Soviet attrition and finally their withdrawal. But this alliance was to change after the collapse of the Soviet Union. After the victory in Afghanistan the USA withdrew, leaving the country in a state of factional civil war and ruined economy. Pakistan was concerned with the continuous and dangerous unrest on its western flank and in an attempt to control it helped in the establishment of a hardliner Islamic government in Afghanistan, the Taliban, which brought the civil war under control.

Muslim discord

By this time the Muslims had undergone multi dimensional fragmentation. Large part of Muslims lands had been colonised and after the First World War its largest entity, the Ottoman Empire, disintegrated. After Second World War the colonies became independent but as a number of small countries. From the very onset the Muslims had been multicultural and multiethnic and over history had fragmented into a large number of religious sects. The introduction of Nationalism caused the Muslims to become nations with diverse character and outlook. Economic resources of these countries also varied remarkably. The only common factor was that most of these countries had a population with low level education.

After the colonial era, Muslims attempted to catch up with the modern age. They flirted with Democracy, Capitalism, Socialism, Islamic Socialism, Monarchism, Socialist institutions like Pan-Arabism, and other political forms but nothing led to development or return of the balance that had previously existed in Muslim society. All attempts were to fail due to internal weaknesses and external political and military interferences as well. The geo-political issues like oil, Jerusalem, and similar regional conflicts, and absence of appropriate guidance and leadership were also against the development of the fledgling Muslim states. This led to the propounding of strict political and religious philosophies like those of Sayid Qutb and Abul Ala Maududi.

The end of the Cold War, ideally, meant less global tension and thus lesser wars. But that was bad news for the armament industries which could not thrive without wars. People would not be induced to shoot at empty air and waste money in buying weapons. The arms manufacturing and associated industries, the intelligence gathering and covert agencies, all of those that had been set up and geared to fight in the Second World War and then the Cold War, no longer had a job. Their jobs could only exist if there was a tangible enemy to fight. Wars in resource rich but prosaic and emotive Muslim nations were always financially beneficial for such agencies and industries. Wars against such nations were also winnable.

From the mid 20th century and onwards, the world armament industries sold a huge quantity of arms to the Muslims. The only result, as far as the Muslim countries were concerned, was that their resources were depleted, their infrastructure destroyed, development hampered and none of their aims achieved. At this juncture of time the Muslims were far behind in rational thought and could be easily manipulated, far behind in economic welfare and thus could be easily led by greed, corruption or promise of aid, and far behind in military prowess and thus easily coerced. The Muslim countries became weak in all aspects of nationhood. In many corruption became rampant. The judiciary being controlled by corrupt politicians. Some such countries were used to harbour torture cells by other countries. War between Muslim nations became historically perennial. The destruction became profitable for international construction industries. In other countries, the voice of political opposition would be silenced by banning opposition media and putting the political leaders in jail. Many activists would get killed by unknown assailants. Political instability caused local industries and finance to stagnate and foreign enterprises to fill this vacuum.

The Muslims did not have the ability to fight any sustained conflicts with any other nations except fight wars between themselves. The natural resources that could be used to educate and enlighten Muslims and set up industries and modern institutions like the media and research centres to uplift the nations were instead used to buy arms and ammunitions. With hatred between the Muslims rising, the priority was always given not to economic but to emotive issues.

After the Second World War the political ideology of the West had shifted from 'Idealism' to 'Realism', which meant that the West viewed any other rising power as a potential threat. Thus, powers like emancipating China, India or the collective Muslims were potential enemies. The case against Islam was exacerbated by an historical fear that Muslims had proven in some occasions to be imperialistic in the past and who had occupied and ruled large chunks of Europe for a thousand years and who had rebounded back from destruction during the Scourge and formed greater empires. Muslims were again a resurgent force and would soon be powerful enough to 'destroy', as the realist tends to suggest, the western way of life. And, of course, the Muslims had natural resources that were crucial for the global industries. China, independently, and India, as a Soviet ally, overcame much of the hurdles and emancipated to become big economies. But most Muslim country economy failed to emancipate.

In 2001, after a multi-pronged terror attack was carried out on US soil there was an upsurge in anti Muslim feeling. Allegedly, this attack was planned by the members of a Mujaheedin unit which had close connection with the Taliban and had initially fought the Soviet occupation in Afghanistan with American support but had become estranged from the USA after the end of the Soviet war. Few conservative American political lobbies cultivated anti-Islamic compulsions sometimes shrouded sometimes openly.

Muslims in the International Media

The mass media, mainly the conservative ones, was applied to 'discredit' Muslims. The TV channels, radios, movies, newspaper, news magazines constantly portrayed Muslims as villains. Over the decades, hundreds of American movies depicted Arabs and Muslims as weird, uncouth, untutored beings even though such scenes were not required in the context of the movies or its storyline. The caricatures and cartoons of the Prophet, some outright offensive, were published in the western media even though it is well known that Muslims find it distasteful in creating images especially of religious figures. The painting or making statues of animal or human forms were discouraged in Muslim culture because it was noted that many such arts evolved over time. When it had become lax it led to nudity, promiscuity and lewdness and when it became reverential it led to idolatry. Not only the Muslims but one of the Commandments of the Old Testament also forbids creation of image.

Besides the above, a large number of websites cropped up with nothing better to do than to deliberately misinterpret the Quran and lay aspersions and innuendo on the Prophet or those whom the Muslims hold dear. Videos and movies were made denigrating Islam and the Prophet and these blatant propaganda and abominations were allowed under the guise of "Freedom of Speech". Verses of the Quran which were only revealed during battle periods or about people who wanted to harm Muslims were generalised in an attempt to paint the Muslims as a belligerent society. An example is given below:

> In the days of the Prophet, when the Muslims lost the Battle of Uhud, many wanted to run away and live among their Christian and Jewish friends for safety. This would have caused a scattering and diffusion of the Muslims of Madinah when unity was of paramount importance for the very existence of the Muslim state depended on this cohesiveness. Then a revelation came to the Prophet (see Ibn Kathir, Al-Tafsir, vol. 2, p. 68):
>
> *O you who believe! Do not take the Jews and the Christians for friends; they are friends of each other; and whoever amongst you takes them for a ruler/ patron, then surely he is one of them; surely God does not guide the unjust people.* [5:51]
>
> The verse asked the Muslims to look after each other and not to seek others as protectors. In recent time, this verse was deliberately taken out of context and construed to mean the Muslims cannot be friends with Jews or Christians, whereas in reality, a Muslim is allowed to have, not just friend, but even practicing Jewish or Christian wife. According to Hadith, Muslims have to take care of and respect parents even if the parents are non-Muslims. The respect that Islam shows to these religions is clear in the following verse.
>
> *Those who believe (in the Quran) and those who follow the Jewish (Scriptures) and the Christians and the Sabians and who believe in God and the last day and work righteousness shall have their reward with their Lord; on them shall be no fear nor shall they grieve. [2:62]*

Unfortunately, dubious research works that attempts to show the Quran and Islam in a negative light easily finds high profile place in the media. Crimes committed by criminal who were by chance Muslims started to get undue media attention but those who worked on social welfare - giving charity opening schools and hospitals – hardly got mentioned. Due to a variety of resistance, building Mosques and even schools for Muslim children became difficult in many western regions. Local cultural traditional crimes such as 'honour' killing and female circumcision were portrayed as Islamic. All these and other similar activities corroborate the impression of a concerted effort to create *Islamophobia* and discredit and confuse Islamic traditions.

Muslim Minorities

The Muslims of the past had spread out in the world taking the torch of knowledge to various regions. They had uplifted societies and built advanced empires in various parts of the world improving the lot of many people. But by modern age, all the great Muslim achievements had been forgotten and Muslims themselves had regressed into a backward society. They became the target of various local powers. The regions which had in the past been beneficiary of Muslims contributions now took onto themselves to suppress or oppress the Muslims.

All over the world, Muslims minorities - for example, Uyghurs in China, Ingushetia-Chechnyans in Russia, Kashmiris in India, Mindanao Muslims in Philippines and others – faced difficulties in one form or another. In many place, the suppression was more implicit, with denial to Muslims of basic rights such as good education, job promotion and migration.

But at other times this oppression took on a barbaric form. In the 1990s the then Serbian government started an ethnic cleansing of Muslims in Bosnia-Herzegovina leading to the systematic killing of thousands of Muslims, raping of Muslim women, burning of their villages and towns. Muslims were forced to move en mass from their ancestral homes. Their only crime was that they were Muslims. At such a time, while all the helpless Muslim countries watched the horrifying events impotently, it was the United States of America that took matters into hand and came out in support of and to the rescue of the Bosnian Muslims. It also was the West that brought international attention to the social plight of the Uyghur Muslims in China and the suppression of Ingushetia-Chechnyans in Russia. The Muslim countries did not have the international media presence needed to bring such atrocities to global light. This inability is reflected in the progressive violent ethnic cleansing of the Rohingyas of Myanmar / Burma.

Thus while the Muslims were lost in a labyrinthine maze other countries were working out of it.

The Asian Renaissance

With the development of huge economies of China, India, Japan, ASEAN, South Korea and the huge energy resources of the Middle East, Asia became the dynamic region of the world. The rise of Asia is in no little measure indebted to the West, to the advancement the great European minds have brought to the technological, political, economic and legal systems. It was Japan that showed the way by first adopting the European colonial model and then, after the Second World War, undergoing a paradigm shift to the American entrepreneurs model. The Asian momentum picked up in the second half of the 20th century with the economies of Singapore, Hong Kong, Taiwan, South Korea, and Malaysia showing wonderful growth. In the next phase countries like China, India and United Arab Emirates started to flourish. Tribal rules of the past became transposed to modern governments in Kingdoms and Emirates. Though the styles of development were different for each country, all their political systems - capitalism, socialism, communism, monarchies or hybrids - were improvisations based on Western ideas.

The desire to emulate the West rose from the highly perceptible reality that the West had become blatantly better developed then the other regions of the world. The West showed remarkable development in all aspects of nationhood - their economy had become dynamic, their science and academe advanced, their society progressive. Their people were more knowledgeable, educated and healthy and their women enjoyed more freedom and rights, their cities larger, more beautiful and more disciplined, their government and politicians more intellectual and less corrupt; their countries and their houses more secure, their food and clothes more abundant and of greater variety; their roads better and traffic system more disciplined. The West had become the builder of the world.

When successes arrived to Asia these were staggering. Asia rose to its huge former self - cultured, philosophical, spiritual and proud. The tallest buildings came to be in Taipei, Kuala Lumpur and Dubai. The world's biggest movie industry and some leading refineries came to be in India, the UAE became the home of investment funds, worlds largest Ferris Wheel in Singapore, Shanghai produced maglev trains that moves in a blur (Legrain, 2010). China was not building just buildings and roads it was building cities after cities.

The Story of Wealth

Money

Long, long ago, when wild tribes roamed the world there was no money, all exchange of goods happened either by barter or by force. As the tribes coalesced and developed into ancient kingdoms and empires such exchange of commodities became impracticable. For example, if there was a seller or supplier of a cow who needed some cloth in exchange, and if a buyer, creator of demand, wanted a cow but only had wheat to offer in exchange, the transaction could not take place. The buyer would have to go to someone else who had cloth and exchange his wheat for the cloth. Then he would take the cloth to the supplier of the cow and exchange it for the cow. The cost of the transaction would be high, very time consuming and complex. A medium for the exchange of commodity was needed – Money.

There must have been some form of exchange media in the older civilisations like Sumeria and Babylon. The Temples and Ziggurats of Egypt, Sumeria and Babylon are known to have acted as a type of Bank involved in transactions and loans. But it is the Chinese and the Persians who are the first known user of coins. The Persians developed an elaborate banking system before the 5th Century BC. Darius the Great introduced the first common coinage, the Daric, on a very large scale revolutionising economic activity. This led, by the 3rd Century AD the time of the Sassanid Persians, to the formation of banking houses and the evolution of a credit system based on letters of credit written on parchments. The ancient Indians, Greeks and Romans all used metallic coins but at a later time in antiquity then the Persians. According to Will Durant (American writer, historian and philosopher) the Greek cities would develop a temple based banking system by the 5th Century BC. The later Byzantine Romans of 5th Century CE are known to have an elaborate interest system as found in the Justinian code.

> The most valuable coin ever minted was by the Mughals in 17th century during the time of Emperor Shah Jahan famed for the Taj Mahal. The Mughals used a Thousand Muhur coins each made from twelve kilos of pure gold and worth today millions of US dollars.

When the Muslims took over Byzantine Syria and Sassanid Persia, the first Muslim Governors kept minting the Roman gold and copper coins and the Persian silver Drachma. By the time of Caliph Usman, Arabic religious inscriptions were added to these coins. During the reign of the fifth Umayyad Caliph Abdul Malik the Islamic coins devoid of images and consisting of inscription from the Quran were minted. The outer edge inscription of one such coin read, 'In the name of Allah, this dirham was minted in Damascus in the year 81 (After Hijri).' The weights for the gold Dinar and the silver Dirham were standardised.

The establishing of a monetory system would entail the study of Economics. From the very start of Muslim history, Muslim scholars involved themselves in economic research. Abu Yusuf, the student of Imam Hanifa was one of them. Imam Ghazzali, Ibn Taimiyyah, Ibn Khaldun and many others would delve into economics and produce important works. For a thousand years, Muslims would build empires and nations from Spain to China, based on a non-interest based economic system.

The Tang Dynasty of China was the first to introduce paper currency in 800 CE, which was kept in circulation by the subsequent dynasties.But it was the Muslims who internationalised the use of the financial paper instrument. By the times of Abbasid Harun ar Rasheed (9th century) an elaborate and widespread Muslim banking system had developed. A Muslim businessman could cash a *Sakk* in China which was drawn on resources in Baghdad. Or they could draw a *Sakk* in India and spend it in Spain. This would ultimately lead to the development of the contemporary paper money and cheques – the term being derived from *Sakk*.

> Economic activities and upliftment of the society have been highly encouraged in Islam. Abject poverty has always been frowned upon. The Prophet had prayed, "God save me from *Shirk* and poverty." Caliph Umar had at one time said, "If poverty was a man, I would have killed him."
>
> Entrepreneurship and self dependence were always promoted by the Prophet. A destitute man had once come to the Prophet seeking help. The Prophet asked, 'What do you have?'
> "Nothing," the man replied.
> "Absolutely nothing?" the Prophet inquired again.
> "I have a blanket," replied the man.
> "Bring it to me," said the Prophet.
> When the man brought the blanket, the Prophet put it on sale. It was sold for two dirham. The Prophet said to the man, "Go and buy a metallic axe with one dirham and feed your family with the other."
>
> When the man came back with the axe the Prophet himself attached a wooden handle to it, "Go and cut wood and sell it. Come back to me after fifteen days."
> When the man returned in fifteen days he had managed to save ten dirham by selling wood. The Prophet said, 'This is better for you than to rise up in the day of judgement with the stigma of a beggar.'

Sakks found in the Cairo Geniza dated from the 12th century shows that the *Sakks* were remarkably similar to contemporary cheques. These displayed a sum to be paid and then the order to pay the bearer followed by the date and name of the issuing source (Bloom and Blair, 2002).

Jewish financiers doing business from the Muslim lands with Europe and the Crusaders took these paper instruments and its concept to Europe. In 13th century, the crusading Knight Templars used the *Sakk* system for pilgrims travelling from Europe to the Holy Land. Towards the end of the 13th century, paper currency the 'Chaw' was introduced in Persia. In the next phase of development, medieval goldsmiths of London started to write paper promises to pay the bearer in gold and silver. The promise to pay the bearer ten pounds of sterling silver led to the development of the British 10 pound note. The past few centuries would see the phenomenal growth of the paper money first in Europe and then throughout the world.

From its initiation and up to the First World War, modern paper money was directly convertible to gold. This fixed the value of money of all countries to each other via gold. If a country owed another country a sum of money, it would give the owner country the equivalent amount in gold that would lessen (contract) its own money supply. The country receiving the gold would expand its money supply by the amount of gold received. In 1944, under the Bretton Woods agreement, all the world currencies were fixed not to gold but to the US dollar. The US dollar in turn was fixed to gold.

> The Bretton Woods Conference of 44 countries, representing the victors of the World War II, also saw the birth of International Monetary Fund and the International Bank for Reconstruction, which would later become the World Bank. The aim was to avoid a financial depression similar to the one that affected USA and Europe after the World War I. The agreement defined the post-war international economic system.

The fixed value of currencies was workable as long as all the countries in the world developed at the same rate. When Japan and Germany developed at a rate faster than the rest of the world the value of their currency increased to an intrinsic dollar value greater than the fixed value. The balance of trade and payment deficits would thus impair those countries whose intrinsic money value was higher.

In the 1970s, in the absence of any further realignment of foreign currency exchange the agreement collapsed. The US dollar was no more convertible to gold. All the currencies were allowed to float, its exchange rate being determined by its demand and supply. The value of money thus represented the economy of the nations and its health. The prime responsibility then fell on the central banks and governments to keep their economy healthy that would instil public confidence in it that would keep the value of its currency up.

In the 20th century a new development occurred: the metallic coin and paper money was partially replaced by the plastic cards. In the 21st century the popularity of the credit and debit cards soared and in the future silicon chips are expected to replace significant use of metallic and paper money.

Market: Economic Systems

In the ancient past, when the world had not yet seen any great civilisation, the size of the market was small due to the geographically restricted range of communication and law situation. A trader would not go beyond the few villages where he was known and beyond which he did not know whether his goods will be sold, seized or robbed. As kingdoms and empires developed so did uniform morality and the authority of the ruler over large areas. The trader could now market his business over a larger geographical area. The free market concept kept on developing in an environment where the kingdom and the wealth of the kingdom belonged to the king.

An exception was the state of Madinah set up by the Prophet. From his time to that of the Rashidun Caliphs the *Bayt Al Maal*, the state treasury, was under God's jurisdiction and all the wealth in it belonged to the people not to the Caliphs. During a period of inflation in Madinah the Prophet had refused to fix the price of goods even when he was approached to do so (reported in Traditions by Ahmad, Abu Daud, Tirmidhi, Ibn Majah, Al Dari and Abu Yala). But his 'free market' was also exploitation free as Interest, manipulative trading and all unfair and unequal commercial activities were stamped out. When the Umayyad converted the Caliphate to hierarchical monarchism the *Bayt Al Maal* became the property of the royal family. Despite this, the Muslims developed an interest free economic system that was the least exploitative and most efficient for its time.

Adam Smith declared in 1776 that the 'Wealth of the Nations' belonged to the people, which would cause the old kingdoms to evolve into nationalist states ruled by governments or nationalistic kingdoms ruled by monarchs with parliaments. He was against mercantilism, i.e., the running of the economy by an alliance of merchants and royalty, and believed in a free market. The 18th -19th century classical economists developed theories about the way the market works with relevance to the dynamics of economic growth. This was a tremendous advancement in economic theory. And from that time onwards the Muslims not only lost their control on economics, they stagnated to a level where they could not even comprehend the mechanics of modern economics.

The West was in supreme control of the world economy and their ideas of economic models developed dynamically. By the beginning of the 20th century the capitalists favoured economic freedom and free competition and the western countries implemented free market policies like *laissez faire*. The free market paradigm was supposed to keep the economy in a self regulating equilibrium of supply, demand, price, income and investment, but in the 1930s, a great depression reduced the economies of the West drastically. Bank after bank folded shutting down a large number of speculatively priced businesses and making millions jobless. The self regulating mechanism had not worked and the equilibrium was shattered, proving a flaw in the classical economic theory.

In 1936, Keynes published his masterpiece, *The General Theory of Employment, Interest and Money* which would tackle this situation. The fundamentals of his theories were based on a model which considered that within a nation the flow of wealth is circular. Money from business firms flow to homestead as salary. The homestead buys and consumes goods which cause the wealth to flow back to the business firms and is reinvested and salary given from the profit. As long as this cycle of flow is maintained the economy keeps on developing. But if there is leakage from this cycle, that is, money leaks out to other countries or avenues or investment decreases, then the economy stagnates or contracts causing recession. Even savings that are not re-invested can be considered as leakage as it is wealth that does not participate in the economy (Though, on the long run, saving plays an important role in economic development).

The economies of most Muslim nations in the 20th century were full of such leakages, with Malaysia, UAE and Turkey being the possible exceptions. Due to huge imports the economy of the Muslim nations never grew, even though many had huge natural resources. The Muslims imported huge quantities of arms and ammunitions, luxury goods and even basic commodities as they had not industrialised themselves to be self reliant in any of these. Some of these countries implemented mega-projects, including infrastructural, which had very high maintenance-revenue ratio. The maintenance cost of these utilities proved to be higher then the revenue earned from these. The countries that had natural resources subsidised these developments. Which, in many instances, meant using up of revenue to maintain a financially non viable project. Those that were devoid of natural resources depended on loans, grants and foreign aid. But interest payments would prove to be a greater leakage for a poor country.

Unlike the Muslim nations' economies the western economies progressed even though they did face great volatilities and crises from time to time. To control market volatility Keynes argued in favour of demand management by Governments. This meant that the Government should interfere to keep the demand of the nation within a healthy range. He felt that a Government should spend more, for instance in infrastructure, schools, etc., when the economy is going down thus causing money injection into the economy. This would cause a ripple effect as the people who make profit from the government injections will spend on items they need or desire, which will benefit another round of people who, in turn, will buy what they need. This will cause an overall cyclic increase in the investments. On the other hand, if inflation is in the offing then the government should stop spending thus lessening demand and causing the economy to cool. After its introduction, the Keynesian school of economics became the predominant one in developed nations. This was also the time when Hitler and Stalin were autocratically running governments that had complete control of economy.

Most Muslim nations at this juncture did not have sufficient data or information of their economy. Basic statistics were unknown or incorrect. While rich Muslim countries did not have correct economic policies, poor ones struggled to meet basic necessity. Models like Keynes' were far from understood or implemented and, at times, not even relevant.

After Keynes, the next economic model was that of the Neo-classical School postulated by the economist Milton Friedman. In mid 20th century, this school put forward the theory that government meddling by injecting money will cause spiral inflation that will go out of control. It did not believe in government feeding the demand of a nation. The government should attempt to manage resources on the supply side as opposed to the demand side. If the labour market, technology, raw materials and energy resources are mangaged then the market and the people will toil to meet their demand by themselves.

When, in the 1970s, the Organisation of Petroleum Exporting Countries (OPEC), which includes Muslim countries, increased the price of oil, it sent shocks throughout the industrialised world. Oil was needed by all the industries and increase of its price caused expenses to increase. When governments tried to protect national economies and jobs by implementing the Keynesian formula of injecting money for demand management, the inflation predicted by Friedman set in.

The Reagan-Thatcher conservative coalition of USA and UK introduced the neo-classical policy. This led to a shift in the economic paradigm from Demand Management of Keynesian policy to that of Supply Management proposed by Friedman, which meant that the governments give up macroeconomic meddling on the demand side and got involved in managing microeconomic supply side features like deregulation, privatisation and overall liberalisation of the economy. It was expected that this would increase efficiency and decrease 'red tape'.

In the early 1980s, as the developed countries faced recession and then inflation they raised their interest rates. The poor developing countries were now expected to pay back loans and interest instalments at this greatly hiked up rate. The developing countries were unable to pay and a credit crisis developed. When the IMF and World Bank were asked to help, they agreed to provide the funds with strings attached. The indebted countries were told that they would have to implement supply side reforms to become eligible for the loans. They had to reduce Tariff and restrictions that protected domestic industry. They had to devalue native currency which would make their produce internationally cheaper and free their markets to foreign investment. Many social welfare programs were also to be cut down. The poor countries protested vehemently but to no avail and had to agree as there was no alternative funding source. After a few years of 'supply side management' the UK and USA saw an increase in total income but the poor countries became poorer. Their living standard dipped lower than what it was a few years previously, and the divide between the rich and poor nations increased. The divide increased not just between nations but also between the people of individual nations. Some African nations even had negative growth at this period. The developing countries which had initiated the New International Economic Order (NIEO) in the previous decade now had more pressing problems. This led to the demise of NIEO as the developing countries tried to come out of their acute short term problems and could not afford to work with long term structural changes. It would be only in the 21st century that with the rise of India, China and Asean that the Asian countries would see a turnaround.

But the economic models so far developed had their failings. One of the main defects that remains unresolved are financial crashes that national economies face time and again causing ripples into the world economy. By the 21st century, economic crises have struck Japan, Argentina and South East Asia. But the biggest one struck the USA leading to recession in the USA and many other countries significantly the developed ones. The two main factors for these financial meltdowns are financial speculation and interest.

Tools of exploitation.

Interest

The Islamic term for Interest on loan is *Riba.* It is considered a tool of exploitation and expressly forbidden. The exploitative nature can be seen in the simple example below:

A transaction in which loan is involved generally has three parties. These three parties comprise the buyer of the product (often a shop, house or business), the producer or supplier of the product being bought (a real estate company or individual owner), and the lender (often a bank) who lends the money to the buyer so that he can buy the product. If the loan arrangement is in fact a partnership, i.e., the bank enters into a partnership with the buyer that they will share profit or loss from the venture, the bank will ensure that the need of the buyer is justifiable and the venture is viable. If it is not viable the bank stands to lose money, as in all partnerships, and will not provide the funding. On the other hand, if the bank loans the money to the buyer on interest there is lot less compulsion, as far as the bank is concerned, to judge if the need of the buyer is justifiable and whether the venture is viable, because in case there is a loss, it will be borne only by the buyer. The bank will simply sell the property/ product and recoup its finance and leave all the losses to the buyer.

The supplier wants to sell at as high a price as possible, the lender wants to lend as much as possible to make as much profit as possible. In such interest-based transactions it is only the buyer who stands to loose, while the supplier and lender only stand to profit.

In an interest associated loan system there is a tendency to lure people toward loans. People start to take a loan for things they do not really need and live beyond their means. In this way the society becomes debt driven and individuals become economic slaves working only to pay off debt. In the UK, loans rose from 30% of national income to 100% from 1963 to 1998. Peter Warburton, a UK financial expert and winner of economic forecasting award warned that an explosion will rock the western financial system to its foundation as the credit and capital markets have grown too rapidly, and with too little transparency and accountability.

In such a situation, it is very important to understand the psychology of human need and want. Human need is limited and justifiable, but human want is insatiable.

The mutual rivalry for accumulating (more and more wealth and worldly gains) diverts you from the real purpose of your life till such time that you reach your graves. [102:1-2]

In Islamic connotation a loan is not to be defined as a profitable transaction but is given on a humanitarian basis. It is different from partnership. It is generally acceptable in serious circumstances. This makes individuals self dependant and enterprising instead of reliant on loans. If money is provided for profit it is no longer a loan.

Under the present systems, loans have become a highly profitable business on the basis of interest it earns. But this loaning system favours the rich capitalist. The financier is sitting on money that needs to be invested or it loses value over time. Thus, when the financier approves a loan it is not a favour to the borrower but an investment. And so, there is no reason why the financier should get only a share of the profit but no share in the loss, in case that happens. People agree to pay interest because all the financiers together have left no better option open.

In the international arena the effect of interest is even more marked. Many developing countries which have taken loans, have to service the loan interest out of their budget. Thus much of their budget is diverted from development projects to loan servicing. Then further loans are required to keep the national economy from collapsing, which in turn increases the interest. Thus a vicious cycle is established where the borrower has to abide by all the demands of the creditor to be in the 'good books' in order to get further assistance. These countries lose their economic independence and thus their self pride and self governance.

If interest is taken out of the loan system then the incurring of debt will decrease. Loans without interest will be given only on true needs and humanitarian grounds, and investments will only be made on genuine ventures.

According to Imam Ghazzali, 'Riba is prohibited because it prevents people from undertaking real economic activities. This is because when a person having money is allowed to earn more money on the basis of *interest*, either in spot or in deferred transactions, it becomes easy for him to earn without bothering himself to take pains in real economic activities. This leads to hampering the real interests of humanity, because the interest of the humanity cannot be safeguarded without real trade skills, industry and construction."

That interest is unfair had been recognised over ages. Aristotle's view was that it is animal that begets, and so money should not beget money. The Book of Deuteronomy [23:20] instructs that an Israelite cannot take interest from another Israelite. Martin Luther, in his Reformation Movement, called on the Christians to return to the original teaching of the Bible by prohibiting usury based transactions. In Islam interest has been banned because it is the instrument of economic exploitation.

The Concept of Money

Justice Usmani in *The text of the historic judgement on Riba* deals in detail on the negative aspects of Interest based economics and also provides supporting views of many philosophers, economists and financial experts. He states that Imam Al Ghazzali was the first person to present a modern theory on money. Al Ghazzali saw money as 'having no intrinsic usufruct or utility, but needed by all humans, because everybody needed a large number of commodities……. Therefore, the transactions of exchange are inevitable. But there must be a measure on the basis of which price can be determined, because the exchanged commodities are neither of the same type, nor of the same measure which can determine how much quantity of one commodity is a just price for another'. He considered money 'as judges and mediators between all commodities so that all objects of wealth are measured through them; and their being the measure of the value of all commodities is based on the fact that they are not an objective in themselves..... They may be circulated between hands and act as a fair judge between different commodities and work as a medium to acquire other things'.

The Ghazzalian analysis that money is a medium of exchange and a measure of value is now universally accepted. But the attribution of interest, which can be considered as the price of money, turns money into a commodity itself. The economists who support interest know that money cannot be qualified as a 'consumption good', as it cannot be consumed like food or used like clothes, and so have placed it into the category of a 'production good'.

This concept was criticised by Ludvig Von Mises, the acknowledged leader of Austrian School of Economics, who agreed that the majority of economists consider money as a production good but, with due respect to them, he found that their position is not thoroughly justified. He contended that arguments from authority do not make a concept valid. The proof of a theory is in its reasoning, not in its sponsorship. He gave support to the theory that money is neither a consumption good nor a production good but a medium of exchange. It is due to predomination of interest in world finances and due to the vested interest of powerful institutions benefiting from this interest that economists have failed to further follow up on such analyses.

The Mechanism of Interest

The rate of interest is leveraged as a control over market dynamics. The general idea is to use it to slow down or speed up the economy as the situation dictates. When the economy is thought to be performing more than it should, or an inflationary bubble is growing, the rate of interest is increased to 'cool' the economy. People have to pay more interest on their loans and stop taking further loans and refrain from further investments. Their profit margin decreases and businesses that are unable to meet this inflated interest payment go bankrupt. When businesses are down and economy is contracting interest rate is decreased to 'heat' the economy. Then people have to pay less interest on loans and can take further loans and invest more.

But such application of interest rate has fundamental defects. To be precise, people save money if their *income increases* and not due to change in interest rates. And they *invest* due to an *expectation of profit* not due to the change in interest rate. It is also not necessary to use Interest rate to control the economy. If the Government injects too much money in the economy, people will be able to take more loans and increase their buying that will cause more demand for goods than the ability to supply. This will cause inflation (Price hike). If there is leakage of money i.e. money is removed from the economy by Government or other means, then people possess lesser money which decreases demand, then there will be recession. Thus, Leakages and Injections of money also work independent of interest rate.

Raising Interest rate hurts all and not only the overheated businesses. Michael Rowbotham, a popular political and economic writer from UK, views the government's method of lowering and raising interest rates as a management device to deter new borrowings also suddenly hits other people and businesses with existing debts with huge extra charges. He asserts that this is an injustice quite lost in the almost religious conviction surrounding this ideology. It appears that this method of controlling banks, inflation and money does seem to work, but as a 'sledge-hammer works at carving up a roast chicken.'

James Robertson, a renowned British financial author, speaker and sustainable monetary reformist, considers that pervasive interest is responsible for the universal systematic transfer of money from the rich to the poor. This transfer of resources from poor to rich is shockingly clear in the Third World debt crisis. He states that those who have more money to lend, get more in interest than those who have less, and those who have less, often have to borrow more.

From this perspective the argument to redesign a money system that would be interest-free, inflation-free, fair and efficient for the twenty-first century is very strong.

Speculation

Money represents some kind of good or service, so for each dollar an equivalent amount of good or service has to exists somewhere in the economy. If not, then the dollar is speculative and it causes a bubble, i.e., a representation of non-existing wealth in the economy. It is, in reality, just a piece of paper. The more such dollars the bigger the bubble. In the capitalist market the tendency to invest such 'baseless' money to make more profit and increase the value of the enterprise is almost impossible to resist. This wealth, which can also be stated as the hiked-up market price of assets and businesses, creates the economic bubble ready to explode just waiting for a trigger. Speculation is intricately related with interest, it is exploitative and similar to large scale gambling and thus discouraged by majority of Islamic scholars.

The first known speculations are the cases of medieval goldsmiths of London issuing gold certificates against gold that they did not possess. At that time this was considered fraudulent. In the current 'fractional reserve lending' system, the same has become a standard legal practice. Banks advance loans in amounts ten times greater than their deposits making money out of nothing. In the UK in 1977 the total money issued by the government was £ 25 billion. But the banks had put into circulation £680 billion. Of the whole money supply more than 96% is nothing but a huge bubble created in computers and other transactions. These can be considered as baseless money. Under the circumstances, in the stock exchange perspective, the shares do not reflect the wealth or real value of the companies but the speculated values that the public is required to pay. But once the public looses confidence on it the share price plummets.

The baseless money created by banks is in turn the subject to further speculative trade in the form of derivatives known as Futures and Options. The original baseless money is in reality not money but claims over money. Then the derivatives, such as Futures and Options, are speculative claims over the claims of baseless money. People make millions even billions by such derivatives causing a huge bubble. In the new millennia while the total combined GDP of 188 countries was $30 trillion, $150 trillion derivative transactions were circulating around the world. And nearly 80% of this trade was controlled by only two dozen huge banks and hedge funds. James Robertson claims that $945 billion transferred around the world on a daily basis are purely financial transaction, unlinked to transactions in the real economy. Thus speculation, in real terms, is the supplying of more money to business owners than the real worth of their business.

During the 1930's western depression, the Southampton Chamber of Commerce set up an 'Economic Crisis Committee'. In 1933, the Committee's recommendation was 'In order to ensure that money performs its true function of operating as a means of exchange and distribution, it is desirable that it should cease to be traded as a commodity.' Nine hundred years ago, Imam Ghazzali had put forward the same view that when money is exchanged for the same denomination, it should never be turned into an instrument for generating profit.

Professor John Gray of Oxford University in *False Dawn*, states that the foreign exchange market had reached, in 1998, the astonishing sum of around $1.2 trillion a day, which was over fifty times the level of world trade. Of these transactions about 95% were speculative in nature. Complex new derivative's financial instruments which were based on Futures and Options were used in such transactions. According to Michael Albert, economist and writer, the daily volume of transactions on the foreign exchange markets of the world holds some $900 billion – equal to France's annual GDP and some $200 million more than the total foreign currency reserves of the world central banks. He forecast that this type of globalisation of free market and speculation was in the process of collapse.

At the beginning of the 21st century, when the housing sector of the USA faced problems with recouping bad loans, everybody realised that they were in an economic bubble situation. Companies and financial institutions could not meet their credit requirements. People trying to cash in their shares and investments as the prices came down further aggravated the situation. This triggered financial chaos and big businesses closed down or were pushed to the verge of collapse. People lost their jobs and could not afford to pay mortgages, neither spend nor invest.

Richard Thomson states, in *Apocalypse Roulette*, that financial derivatives have grown from a start in the early 1970s to a 64 trillion dollar industry by 1996. This figure can be written as 64,000,000,000,000. To further emphasize the incredibly huge sum Thomson asserts that if all those dollar bills were laid end to end, they would stretch from the Earth to the sun sixty six times, or to the moon 25,900 times.

By far, it is the rich corporations who own these speculative 'ability to transact' for which only a fraction of the real wealth is created and created mostly by the labour of poorer nations. This gives the rich the ability to stay rich without engaging in substantial labour.

James Robertson in his work *Transforming Economic Life* iterates that today's monetary and financial systems are not only unfair, but ecologically destructive and economically inefficient as well. The money-must-grow imperative drives production (and thus consumption) to higher than necessary levels. Instead of providing real services and goods it causes world wide economic effort to make money out of money. He observes that of all the dollars transferred daily around the world more then 95% are purely financial transaction in nature and has no links to transactions in the real economy.

Mahathir Mohammad, former Prime Minister of Malaysia, put the whole episode into perspective while giving a special address in Istanbul, Turkey, 2011, on the theme "The Future of Islamic Finance Creating Global Linkages and Connectivity to the Growth of Real Economy to Promote Financial Stability Economic Growth, Employment and Prosperity". Since the second half of the 20th century the developed nations found it difficult to compete with the emerging economies of Asia and Latin America. The decline of manufacturing, construction, trade and service industries in the West led these countries to their switch to the financial markets beginning with investments in the share markets of the world. This switch promised huge capital gains from investments in the share markets of the world. What followed was a spate of financial innovation of products that bear no relation to the real business done by the companies and corporations concerned. These innovations included derivative products such as collateralized debt obligations (CDOs), short selling, hedge funds and currency speculation, which bore no relation to real economic activities. Wealth was made out of no real economic activity, thus huge profits and greed fuelled a boom that in reality was unsustainable. The financial system collapsed more than once, the last one being that which precipitated the financial crisis in 2008.

In the share market, a reliable measure of economic growth is the dividend. But it was not the dividends which attracted their investments in stocks and shares. It was capital gains made from the repeated and sustained purchases of shares that would push up the share prices not the actual growth of the company concerned. Once the share prices appreciated, the shares would be sold and capital gains collected. This would cause the share price to crash but that would not affect those who had already made their profit. First the huge pension funds then the hedge funds got into this business. The huge size of their investments influenced market behaviour. They were not concerned about whether the actual businesses were growning or not. On a dollar share the dividend might be just 10 cents, but if the dollar share is pushed up to 5 dollars, the investment in one share at 1 dollar could yield 4 dollars in capital gains.

The Collapse of 2008

The banks in USA and other western countries began to lend money for housing and other assets even to borrowers who could not possibly repay their loans. If the borrowers failed to pay the loans, their properties could be seized and sold. The banks believed they could never lose on the loans made. To be doubly sure, the loans were bundled and sold to insurance companies or to mortgage companies. For the lenders, their loans have been securitised through insurance and secondary mortgage. They just could not lose even if the loans became non-performing. All this seemed perfect until not just loan defaulters but companies and whole economies started to collapse.

From a larger perspective, in the USA national wealth growth appeared strong, inflation was low and housing price kept on rising. Banks were making profit and were lobbying to maintain the status quo, it was not the time to look at what was behind the growth. Interest was kept low despite the fact that the financial and housing sectors were booming without substantial growth in real terms. Keeping the interest low was also a political decision then an economic one. One of the factors that influenced it was that in 2001 the USA had been devastatingly attacked by only a handful of terrorist. That had undermined its reputation of being an economic, political and military safe haven. And with the rise of Asia and South America, this could lead to undermine the United States status of *The Superpower* of the world. Thus political decisions influenced the financial sector more than rational economic ones: The economy of a Superpower must remain super.

The housing bubble swelled between 2000 and 2004. China possessed undervalued surplus currency which it could afford to invest overseas. From 2005, this money was used to keep the housing bubble and the speculative derivatives business on a high and the interest rate down (Legrain, 2010). This inflow of cash was very suitable for both the US financial and political sector. In the feeling of super confidence nobody believed that housing and financial sectors could fall. It fell big.

Another factor that further influenced the collapse was in the foreign affairs. The war in Afghanistan and Iraq (2003) turned out to be more costly then was anticipated. The previous

1990 Iraqi war was substantially funded by the Saudis, Kuwaitis, Japanese and others. This time no such funds materialised. Revenue from oil deals would be slow or long term forthcoming. This caused weakness in the larger economic infrastructure. The economy was strained, the banks had lent out too much and bidders had put the prices too high. The bubble burst.

But during the same period, the Islamic finance system made steady progress and was least affected by the financial crises. As the Islamic system dealt with real economic growth it did not rise as spectacularly as the interest based speculative system but it evolved on a solid foundation. Thus, it attracted much attention.

Islamic Finance

Islamic Finance is not a new phenomenon. From the 7th century to the beginning of the 20th century many countries and Empires in the world have been run on the basis of Islamic Jurisprudence or Islamic Finance. The economic institutions and financial instruments had included money, coins, cheques, loans, businesses, partnership, etc., all without interest. But by the 19th century, Islamic Finance would stagnate. This was more due to 'scientific' regression rather than a financial one. The Muslims did not industrialise so the finance that was needed to run an industrialised economy also did not materialise.

In recent decades, there had been attempts to establish an Islamic financial system. The Islamic Development Bank was established in Jeddah, Saudi Arabia, in 1975 by the Organisation of Islamic Conference (OIC). It has been financing interest free loans to both governments and private sector. Up to the year 2000 it has provided more than \$21 billion as interest free finance. There are more than 200 Islamic banks and financial institutions in 65 countries which, in 2000, had a total deposit of \$112 billion and assets of \$147 billion with a growth rate of more than 10 % per annum as against the growth rate of 7% by the world financial sector. Dr Ahmad Muhammad Afi, President of the Islamic Development Bank, in a written submission in 1999, stated that, 'Islamic banking is distinctive in two respects: concentrating on the real sector of the economy, it imparts tremendous stability to the economic system by achieving an identity between monetary flows and goods and services, and by operating on a system of profit and loss sharing in its evolved state, it insulates the society from the debt-mountain on the analogy that if the economies enter into recessionary or deflationary phases, the principles of profit and loss sharing protects the states and economic operators from the evils of accumulation of interest and minimizes defaults and bankruptcies.'

The Islamic economic system is yet to mature and it suffers from a number of drawbacks, one of the main ones being the environment it operates in. Even in Muslim countries, the governments support an interest based system, so the new relatively small non-interest based institutions have to co-exist with the interest based institutions or not exist at all. There are also a huge number of financial processes and regulations which need to be changed, developed and implemented for the system to evolve to its pure form. This change cannot be expected to happen overnight and the real benefits that it offers to lenders and borrowers will not come immediately.

John Tomlinson in *Honest Money* writes that changing debt to equity will not cure all economic ills. The benefits it produces will not necessarily follow automatically. There will have to be concerted effort to ensure that it does. But, obviously, without this attempt to conversion these benefits will not be realised at all. The benefits that will occur are that the banking and monetary system will not collapse, nor will there be the threat of collapse again. Shares values considered as liabilities will disappear and will be replaced by assets of a specific values. In the new environment all the depositors will be able to withdraw their total deposits simultaneously.

At the end of the 20th century, Philip Moore in *Islamic Finance* wrote that the global trend to shift from a bond or loan based financial system to an equity or capital-share based one agrees in many respects with Islamic economic principles. He concurs that in the recent times the Western world has indeed been progressing towards Islamic principles of finance without realising it.

Corporation: The Invisible Empire

If the attempt to establish a modern commercial state during the time of Caliph Usman led to the chaos or *Fitna*, then the attempt to establish the European modern state has led to *Fitna al-Akbar*, the Great Fitna, starting from the Spanish global colonisation to the World Wars. In fact, over the centuries this was one long drawn war fought over possession of colonies that would finally lead to millions to be blown to death, atomic weapons used, mass starvation, famine, poverty, disease, and exploitation of the ignorant. More wars were fought in this period of time then any other in history, and civilian death and destruction wrought havoc as never before. As after the Fitna rose the mightiest empires, so after the Fitna al-Akbar rose mightier ones – the Corporations.

The first of the crude corporations were the East India Company and the Dutch East India Company of the 17th century. These were commercial entities as well as imperial tools used to colonise. The corporations took their present form in the USA. In the mid 19th century the corporate laws of the USA were more in favour of the general public rather then the directors and corporate shareholders, their charters being regulated by the states. Thus corporations were not very favoured by the business circle. Soon these laws were changed and the corporations were given a greater degree of autonomy and fund raising capacity. Small shareholder power decreased and the executives and directors got greater control. Under favourable laws the corporations began to flourish. Since the First World War, there has been a huge rise in the armament, automobile and oil industries.

In time, the larger corporations bought smaller corporations, forming conglomerates and spreading their financial base. Multinational corporations became very complex entities consisting of huge networks of overlapping holding companies in different countries. Likewise, their shareholders and directorships organised into multiple chains and branches in different regions of the world where each chain may be 'unaware' of the other chains. The sub units, companies, in the chains themselves became large enough to be called corporations in their own right. A labyrinth of such entities, made more complex by acquisitions or mergers, has made it impossible to understand the structure spanning the globe and the profit flow from the root unit to the top unit in the hierarchy. Thus transparency may be only effective nationally but impossible to follow on a global scale. The issue with today's corporations is that even though they are multinational, the ultimate profit goes to a few individuals while those who provide the manpower and raw materials receive a fraction of their rightful share.

More than two thirds of world trade is carried out by multinational corporations. The absolute reach and size of these corporations are phenomenal. The Swiss based *Nestle SA* in 1997 owned assets worth almost 38 billion US dollars. This was greater than the annual GDP of many countries like Ghana, Guatemala, Nepal, Morocco or Romania.

Imperialism has been transformed to the advanced science of capitalism. And capitalism has metamorphosed the old concept of empires and empire building to corporations and corporate takeovers. Today's corporate empires are a lot more sophisticated, a lot less perceptible, and far more powerful than any empire of the past. These financial behemoths are strong enough to influence governments and control the international mass media, which enables them to mould world public opinion.

This concentration of wealth and power has both advantages and disadvantages. The corporations spend billions in developing countries bringing new jobs and some degree of technology transfer. The new trading opportunity and environment at times also imbues a drive for efficiency and further enterprise to cascade. On the other hand, the investment may cause a long term siphoning of profits out of the host country. There may be no technological transfer or transfer of only an insignificant nature. The local culture may become infected by the materialism of corporations giving rise to social problems like divorce, psychological disorders and unhappiness in general.

The outcome of such ventures depends, to a greater part, on the governments of the host countries. They and their experts have to work out the pros and cons, and the cost and benefits of the ventures. Obviously, the motive of the corporations is to maximise profit. Thus the corporation would prefer to deal with governments who are easier to influence, where personal interests are above national ones or simply with those people who are too ignorant to understand the long term ramifications of a venture.

The corporations, like old colonial empires, still make use of overseas human and natural resources. They pay a 'salary' and 'price' but do not have to take the responsibility for the well being of the overseas people they employ or whose natural resources they use. The well being of these people are left to national governments which are often incompetent. The religious empires of the past, despite failures or success, were responsible for the well being of the people under their domains.

There is an oligopoly of a few Multi National Corporations dominating the world trade. An oligopoly can act like a monopoly if they form a cartel. They can dictate where the profit goes, what the price of commodity should be, and decide who to pick up as partners and who to deny entry in global trade. Within countries, governments ensure that there is no monopoly in business and breaks up oligopoly cartels. In fact, cartels within countries are punishable by the law. But in the global scene there is no such law. And as this oligopoly of corporations is invisible, the collusion of the cartel can be invisible as well.

In the face of global integrations, a very difficult time lies ahead for isolated small nations with small economies. With global rules of trade set in favour of the big integrated economies those failing to integrate into a favourable group will simply become unsustainable, their culture will stagnate, and their resources will fall prey to predatory forces. A very common question that is asked in contemporary times is 'Is globalisation good or bad?' In reality this question lacks sophistication. Globalisation is advancement of human civilisation and will keep on happening unless a cataclysm affects the planet. The real question is 'Is globalisation taking place without exploitation?'

Unbridled capitalism in the myopic short term is causing economic disparity and social unhappiness to increase. Speculative valuation by the rich of their assets, their business entities and their enterprises is widening the divide between the haves and have-nots. Today the world is producing more wealth then any previous time but unhappiness, neurosis, depression, jealousy, hatred and violence are rife in the world.

Among the corporations one of the most profitable concerns in the world is the armament industry. A huge arms industry developed during the two World Wars and persisted through the Cold War. The only way to keep these industries profitable is by 'creating' wars which keeps up the demand for armaments. The corporations are cold and calculating and the human factor is missing and the human individual is expendable in these calculations. Not a single bullet is made without the sole intention that one day it will take a human life and that power will fetch the bullet a good price.

The real issue is not the corporations themselves. These are the most efficient financial machines of the present age. The issue is how they are administered and manipulated. In the long run interest-free and non-exploitative corporations have the potential to reduce wars and violence, and bring benefit to the entire world. One of the brilliant moves in the advanced nations is the integration of their economy. Political and moral agendas alone cannot sustain harmony and peace among people. To overcome the cultural differences economic integration is necessary. Nations with integrated economies will not fight each other as both sides stand to loose. Europe is fast leaving its national identities and forging the continental one – European. They are letting their economic union – same currency, no travel restrictions between countries – to consolidate this identity. Thus, the integration in Europe will do marvels for all Europeans. Of course, development of parallel social and technical institutions with a positive political will is imperative, as is apparent in Europe. Anti-integration issues will come to the fore from time to time. As long as these can be managed the long term benefit will be great. In other regions, local big economies may force integration on smaller ones.

Nonetheless, corporations are the best integrating tools that can form a benevolent universal empire. This empire cannot be created by weapons but will have to be architected by economic forces dedicated to humanity, not to political or racial borders. As in the 19th century laws were made which enabled the corporations to become favourable to the capital providers; it is now time to enact laws that will make the corporations in favour of humanity. It is time to move the emphasis from 'capital' to the 'individual'.

Nations and countries have outlived their utility. Political boundaries are already crumbling and multilateral economic groups are forming. In the near future many of these political entities, nations as we know today, will cease to exist or exist only in name. These will be replaced by regional groups held together by large financial, technical and academic institutions and fused by powerful mass media. A time will come when all the corporations will integrate to form one universal corporation.

Media: The Imperceptible Army

The media is one of the most powerful institutions in the present world. By information, misinformation and disinformation it can win wars, change cultures, and bring down regimes. It can be classified into two types – corporate and government media. The corporate media are part and parcel of the corporate world and are themselves corporations, and thus their alliance is obvious. Most of these are centre rightist in their views. The government-supported media are less influenced by the corporations and harbour politically centrist and nationalist views.

The western media is an international conglomerate that acts within a loosely unified framework. The media of the developing countries are mostly internally focussed and many, including much of the Muslim media, simply feed news from the western media. In the developing countries the media becomes more an instrument of local politics with the ruling political party using it in favour of their government.

With improvement in communication technology the power of media has become greater than the strongest army and more potent than weapons of mass destruction. They can sway international public opinion towards any issue, they can cause the rise of internal divisive and battling forces in a country or they can assuage divisions and cause calm. They can sell economic and political ideas and alter the image of a philosophy or a nation. The best part is that no military intervention is needed to accomplish all this. It is this powerful media and the people involved in it that can become the harbinger of a harmonious 'globalised' world as nationalistic ideas are left behind and universal ones sponsored.

Psyche of the World

In the 14th century, Ibn Khaldun, while postulating a theory, had stated that people come together due to a group feeling. The empires are run by people who belong together due to some adhesive common ground between them. Thus, It can be said that the smaller the group the better knit together it is and the larger the group the more loosely held together. But to run an empire a large number of people of various cultures are required. Thus, there form concentric circles of groups with diminishing importance and belongingness. The Umayyad Empire had started off on a universal note. But the very fact that it was a hereditary empire belonging to the Umayyad changed the complexion of the Empire. Around the core of the royal family formed concentric layers of allegiances. The most important, and belonging to the first inner circle round Umayyad core was that of the Quraish Muslims. The next circle around the Quraish was that of the rest of the Arab Muslims. Further out, the next one was the non-Arab Muslims, and finally, the protected religions – the Christians and Jews. As this was against the universalism of Islam, the whole system existed only implicitly.

In the late 20th century capitalist world, a similar concentric hierarchy was also evident. The core consists of the Americans, the first circle outside it was the group of the Anglo-Saxons – Britain and Australia. The next one consists of the rest of the Europeans. Further outward were the non-European countries which constitute big economies and which can be considered friendly, for example, Japan after the Second World War and India after the fall of the Soviets. The rest of the world including China and Russia did not belong to the system. The position of the Muslims remained that of a beloved enemy or an inimical love.

Following on from Ibn Khaldun's theory, this 'belonging' system also distrusts and alienates those who do not belong. The reason is a remnant mass psychology of fear arising from the historical past that still exists between cultures of the world. Politically, Idealism claims that this can be changed and fights it teaching and using high moral policies while Realism simply accepts it as the reality and reacts to it.

In the ancient past when wild tribes, disassociated from moral guidance and true religion, roamed the world and basic necessities were hard to find, a starving tribe would rob the food, shelter, women and children of another tribe in order to merely survive. Single people were the easiest targets. Belonging to a tribe was thus the best way of survival. In an animal world, it was natural not to trust anyone or any group to which one did not belong.

Following the teachings of the Prophets, civilisations were initiated, humanity progressed beyond wild tribal life and the knowledge they acquired was sufficient to support primitive institutions. As knowledge grew Monarchism became the instrument of rule, a vast improvement over tribal groups. As kingdoms were forged greater violence became a requirement for their expansion and upkeep. An individual with leadership qualities would soon get a significant following, such as a tribal leader. But the leader would also have to provide the means of sustenance and well being of the followers. To expand the group of followers to a small kingdom would require even more wealth. But, in those non-technological days, there was no way to produce a large quantity of wealth rapidly.

There were limits to entrepreneurship and the production of wealth sufficient to run a kingdom in a short time period was impossible. Life was agro-based, and without machinery only small regions could be cultivated after which there would be the wait for an entire season to reap the profit from a crop. Moreover, the cultivated fields would be small so the amount of crop would only be sufficient to feed the producers, their families and a few others. Artisans could not produce large quantities of goods as each individual item was hand crafted. Trade took a long time to complete. With beasts as vehicles of transport only a limited amount of goods could be transported from one place to another and that, too, over a long time. Even with ships, though larger in volume could be carried, it would still take a long time to transport. The easiest way of accumulating wealth in a short span of time was, of course, conquest. And thus the glorification of 'conquest', which in truth was massacre and plunder of goods and resources, but served to justify the acts of violence against humanity.

As time went by, the greatest of the monarchies transformed into empires. Kingdoms rose and fell, empires formed and disintegrated. They fell whenever the animal psyche caused ignorance, greed and desire to increase leading to acts of suppression and oppression. As a natural consequence, this would breed fear, revulsion and revolt among the people who suffered or who competed with each other. The land area of the kingdoms would enlarge or shrink depending on the strength of the kingdom relative to adjacent kingdoms, the stronger one always encroaching and preying on the weaker ones, and always ensuring that the smaller kingdoms remain small and weak by periodically plundering it or forcing it to pay huge tributes. Meanwhile the weaker kingdoms would always be waiting for the stronger to start weakening or disintegrating – giving them the opportunity to strike. The Greeks under Alexander did exactly that to the Persians. Similarly, the Romans and Persian were constantly fighting battles with each other. The Umayyad ensured that the Alid, their arch-rival, were constantly suppressed and unable to rise. When the Abbasid grasped power, the first thing they did was to dispose of all the Umayyad Princes so that they would never be a threat. The Ottomans constantly invaded and occupied large chunks of European states so that they would not rise as a challenging power. When the Europeans became powerful they did the same to the Ottomans. The British policy of divide and rule ensured that the foreign nations remained weak and subjugated.

Throughout human history there have been revolts against ruling establishments and empires. During the Muslim empires there have been revolts mainly based on ideological differences. During the colonial period the revolts were not just ideological but against political and economic subjugation. With industrialisation, developed regions and corporations developed an insatiable hunger for resources. Since the 20th century, as countries became independent and were able to shake off their colonial-political domination they became subject to economic domination. The revolts, as well, started to flare up against economic subjugation. Though, on the face of it, these conflicts appear to be between cultures and religions, the root cause always was economic domination or the fight against it.

Finally, when nationalism arrived and replaced imperialism, humanity was led to the place where it stands today. But self centred unilateral forces still remain very active. The psyche of distrust still prevails leading to conflicts and wars. Corporations, media, intelligence agencies and the military are all geared towards self-centred benefit and advantage. But the progress of knowledge - scientific, economic and moral – is now causing nationalism to become redundant. Now humanity has arrived at the brink of universality.

Universalism is being hindered by the prevailing global disorder and conflicts. The world remains in disorder due to the inability to find common grounds in the precepts of international morality. In the partisan world, while there has always been talk of building bridges, there are very few who actually cross the bridge to find out what actually lies across the bridge. They only have a long distance view. Even cultures living together are subject to distortions by forces like the media. The reason is selfishness in individuals, a refusal to share, which is exploited for political gain. The result is that there remains too much distrust to establish common grounds. The distrust prevalent everywhere builds to dislike and hatred. Under such emotions, that affect the mass, very improper actions appear rational. For example, individuals elected in national elections are not necessarily the best the country has to offer. Fear of other nations or greed for other's resources may cause warmongers to get elected. The country with nuclear weapons tries its utmost that its neighbour doesn't develop any nuclear weapon. The rich countries try to control the economy of the not-so-rich. Institutions like International Monetary Fund and World Trade Organisation are inclined in favour of the rich nations. The strong nations find it necessary to control the UN using vetoes.

Judaism, Christianity and Islam come from the same root and are closest of the religions and, in reality, the closest natural allies. Yet Jews, Christians and Islam have fought with each other not because of their religion, as mistakenly thought, but due to the same tribal psyche of distrust – the call of religion was only used to hide the real reason. Jerusalem is the city where these three religions meet. And this city has been, and is still, the cause of such pain and disgrace to humanity. That is a slap in the ethical face of Jews, Christians and Muslims.

In explaining the disorder among humanity rationalists apply the 'Survival of the fittest' credo. This only reduces humans to an animal level as it implies that the weak definitely *will* be oppressed by the strong. Such a dogma is applicable to animals not to moral sentient beings.

The psyche that leads to disorder and conflict is inculcated into individuals from the institution that teaches divisiveness to the young minds – the primary schools. In most secular schools there is an absence of structured moral teaching and, in fact, many wrong aspects of history are given priorities in the curriculum that are taught to the children. History books, unfortunately, refers to the kings and emperors who have been the greatest conquerors and in the process have murdered and plundered the most as the greatest heroes. The scientists and philosophers who through hard work, tenacity, and insignificant material benefit, have uplifted human civilisation are in the background. The Prophets who have been the fonts of knowledge and moral guidance are completely missing. This gives the child a bad role model to follow. History is geared toward nationalistic pride, with many instances of miscuing and leaving out the genuine achievements of perceived antagonists. Thus the child develops a racial or national bias towards the group to which they belong and a fear and dislike towards others. Where schooling leaves off, the mass media steps in distributing views, not news, that divides the whole world into groups of embattled people.

The Muslim World and its Regression

Socio-Political Aspects

Muslims have belonged to countries and nations and their patriotic zeal has been no less than any other. They obeyed the laws of country of their residence and contributed to its upliftment. But a Muslim has also been an international or, more correctly, a universal citizen – an equal membership to a fraternity for all who claim it. In that respect race, gender, political borders, local cultures are all secondary. In all reality there is no clash between culture and Islam. A person can speak in any language and still be a Muslim. The discordance is between Universal Islam and Nationalism.

In real terms, and contrary to popular perception, Islam is not the acceptance of one religion in place of another but the acceptance of the universality that all humanity is the same. It does not approve or disapprove of culture as long as it does not cross basic moral borders or impinge on the indivisibility of humanity. It sees an Asian as the same as an African as the same as a European. Islam does not differentiate between humanity. The only criterion on which it is willing to classify humanity is that of 'righteousness'.

By extension, Islam also requires equality in the systems and mundane affairs of the world. That the global legal framework be same for all humanity, what applies to one applies to all, unlike the precepts of Nationalism in which some nations enjoy much advantages and benefits over other nations. That the world economic model should be universal and that it should benefit all humankind by the same degree and that the benefits of science and commerce should be accessible to all on equal terms irrespective of nationality, race and other divisions. The conflict that arises between Islam and nationalism is not because Islam harbours a fundamentalist culture but because it contains an inherent anti-exploitative Universalist element.

The perception of religion is different for Muslims. This is due to various factors. There are some religions that had been against science and progress. People of those religions had to fight against their own religion to attain advancement. So they consider religion as regressive taking them backwards into the past. On the other hand Islam gave science and progress to the Muslims. It encouraged and provided for the improvement of all aspects of life. So religion to the Muslim became an universal, progressive and complete code of life.

Islam can be a complete code of life as people of all religions and creed can also live within its domain with equal rights as long as they obey the basic tenets of morality and humanity. This is possible because there is no theocracy and no coercion in Islam that could force anyone to follow any religion. Islam is the only system that has been supremely successful in implementing real multiculturism where all others have failed. The Persians and Romans did become multicultural at a stage of their history. But the Persians, themselves, remained a separate superior tribal 'Aryan' race and the Romans became multicultural only because of the political pressure from different people of the empire had become insurmountable. It was only the Muslims who accepted multiculturalism from the very onset as a process of co-existance of all humanity. Within Islam the political side has always been secular in the sense that all people can co-exist with due rights, respect and dignity. The minorities are treated as covenanted people with the right to exist with their own culture, religion and legal courts. The Quranic verse '*let there be no compulsion in religion*' is fundamental in establishing that. Islam it may sound strange due to a lack of understanding, is not a dogmatic religion.

Similar to its universal perceptions, worship in Islam is different as well. Islam only accepts and submits to a singular God – the only Creator of all creation, of whatever there is, known or unknown. Worship is not praying for boons or uttering praise, it is a absolute submission to the Will that leads humanity to the path away from all animalism through a subliminal evolution to a higher plane fit for the Regent of the Almighty. The five pillars of Islam – faith, daily prayers, fasting, Zakaat (tax) and Hajj (pilgrimage) - are different aspect of worship. These are the pillars on which higher achievement are to be built upon. These are the means by which the ends are to be achieved. But worship in Islam crosses even these boundaries. Every action that a Muslim undertakes – going to work, wearing clothes, eating food, washing the self, meeting friends – becomes a worship if it is done according to Sunnah.

Over historical time, Muslim societies have experimented with various socio-political systems, most times with superb success and some times, as in recent past, with tragic failures. The root Muslim philosophy is not restricted to religious creed but is complemented by practical, this-worldly exigencies as well. *Tawakkul* – faith in God's dispensation – is a core concept in Islam. But *Tawakkul* is not irrational or blind that leads to judgemental impediment.

When a few Bedouins came to Madinah and were entering the Mosque without tying their camels, the Prophet asked, "Why do you not tie the camels?"

The Bedouins replied, "We have *Tawakkul* in God."

The Prophet said, "Tie your camel first and then have *Tawakkul*."

Caliph Umar dealt with the same issue in his characteristic manner. One day, at an odd hour, he found some men in the Mosque. He wondered why they were not at their work and asked them, "What are you doing here?"

One of the man replied, "We have *Tawakkul* in God."

Umar rapped the man with the stick-end of his whip and said, "Know and understand that the sky does not rain gold and silver."

That made the men to hasten to their work.

As Islam does not favour *Tawakkul* with intellectual passivity, at the same time, it does not condone one-sided dominance of rationalism. It establishes a balance. It emphasises a modern, practical, moral, material, workable, beautiful and adaptable way of life.

But seek the abode of the Hereafter in that which God has given you, and do not neglect your portion of worldly life, and be kind as God has been kind to you, and seek not corruption in the earth. Indeed, God likes not the corrupt mischief maker. [28:77]

To check and balance blatant materialism it encourages the necessity to consider and comply with moral standards and the concept of universal humanity. This balancing act has caused Muslim political philosophy to be very dynamic and pragmatic throughout history.

The very initial political system of Madinah, in the 7th century, was a modern state with an elected/selected Caliph supported by a council of companions. The society consisted of a priest-less way of life, the daily prayers being led by the Governors and Generals. The central political decisions were taken by the Caliphs with the consensus (Ijma) of the Companions. Decisions regarding complex and difficult situations were arrived at by analogy (Qiyas), which is one of the tools of *Ijtihad*.

After Caliph Umar's 'state controlled' way of governance, Usman changed over to a decentralised 'commercial' one. Then the Umayyad changed the political system to a chauvinist hereditary empire. The Abbasid took the chauvinism out of the equation but remained a hereditary empire.

The 8th century saw the development of 'falasapha' and 'kalaam', that is, philosophy and rationalism with the rise of the School of Mutazilite. They were influenced by Greek philosophy to an extent. During the Abbasid era, some of the Caliphs sponsored the rationalist

Mutazilite philosophy within their political framework. The Ulema were in conflict with the Mutazilite as their rational influence led to a tendency among the general people to move away from religion or to take up the interpretation of the Quran and Sunnah on themselves leading to harmful innovations. Considering that an exhaustive work had been completed on jurisprudence, the Ulemas decided on ban *Ijtihad* to generate Fiqh and, instead, started the use of Taglid (emulation). Taglid has a subtle variation in meaning, but is generally understood to be that the individual should follow or copy an established scholar or Imam in matters of jurisprudence.

During the conflict between Ulema and Mutazila a third group, the Asharites, followers of Al Ashari, rose to prominence. They accepted the scientific and technological view of the Mutazilites but rejected their metaphysics. In this aspect they were nearer to the Ulema. In fact, they represented a balance between Ulemas and Mutazila. Ghazzali consolidated this view and at the same time gave Gnosticism some span in Muslim philosophy.

The rise of the Mutazilites and Asharites marked the peak of scientific innovation in Muslim civilisation. Ibn Rushd (Averroes), born some years after the death of Ghazzali in the 12th Century, became the most advanced proponent of rationalism. Both his and Ghazzali's ideas were at conflict with each other, but ironically enough, both were very intensely successful - Ghazzali in the East and Ibn Rushd in the West.

When Muslims were handed over a series of losses by the Iberians and had taken a beating from the Crusaders in the West and totally destroyed by the Mongols in the East, it was the spiritual 'strength', preached by the likes of Ghazzali and Ibn Taimiyyah, that kept the mass from becoming totally dispersed, demoralised and divided. The Mongols, who had vanquished the Muslims with the sword, lost the spiritual war and converted to Islam. This led, ultimately, to the formation of the Magnificent Ottomans, the Sophisticated Saffavids and the Great Moghuls.

After the Mongol Scourge in the 13th century, before the rise of the subsequent empires, in the vast and mighty struggle that raged over the shattered Muslim world, scientific rationalism lost its place from Muslim thought. The Islamic scholastic focus changed to Arts and Humanities. Besides grand architecture, non-animalistic painting, poetry and other fine arts the Muslims also produced remarkable works of social science and history. At this juncture of time, the Muslim society still produced great individuals who would act as shapers and reformers of society. Two such individuals were Ibn Khaldun and Ibn Taimiyyah.

Ibn Khaldun

Ibn Khaldun who lived in the 14th century was the Father of Social Science who produced, among his many works, an incredible seven book series known as *Al Kitab Al Ibar (Universal History)*. The first book is known as the *Muqaddima* (*Proglemena*) which contains the scientific method of history - the first of its kind. His work comprised the fundamentals of demography, hectography, philosophy and the psychology of history, modern economics and sociology. He analysed, researched and documented these disciplines centuries before they were actually established elsewhere. Before him the subject of History was a mere chronicle of events, mostly haphazard, with no distinction between the real and unreal. He wrote history in a modern way with a modern methodology that he himself introduced.

In the *Proglemena* he states that to discover historical truth, while guarding against error and mistakes, attentive examination of historical elements and sustained application of its methodology was needed. Self satisfaction can be gained by simple reproduction of historical experience. But if the fundamental principles of the arts of government, the nature and events of particular civilisation or the circumstances which characterise those times are not compared with that occurring at present then it is very likely that the historian will fall into errors and lose the way of Truth. He was the first who actually implied that the present was the key to the historical past.

He was also the first to establish theories on social conflict and the rise and fall of civilisations. He was the first to deal with the aspect of nationalism. He defined nationalism, which he called *Al Ashabiya*, as an advanced form of belongingness. He said 'a group feeling' bring people together and they become powerful eventually developing into a large civilisation. For example, the Umayyad group established the Umayyad Empire.

He wrote about some basic concepts of economics. He propounded the fundamental theory that economics is a value-adding process in which labour, skill and technique come together to enhance the value of a product. He laid down the theory that all profit comes from labour as was later remarked by Marx. Ibn Khaldun also wrote, 'The differences in behaviour between generations are only the expression of the differences which separate them in their economic way of life'. This can be compared with the famous and very similar statement by Marx, 'The method of production in the material matters of life determines in general the social, political and intellectual processes of life'.

He wrote of Royal Authority about a century before Machiavelli wrote his 'The Prince'. Professor Ludwig Gumplowicz, a Polish-Jewish political scientists, states, "At any rate, the priority must be rightly attributed to the Arab sociologist as regards those counsels which Machiavelli, a century later, gave to the rulers in his *Prince*."

The great Florentine, Machiavelli, instructed in the art of governing people, doing so as a far-sighted politician. But Ibn Khaldun was able to penetrate into the social phenomena as a profound economist and philosopher, a fact which shows in his work such far-sightedness and critical art as was totally unknown to his age. (Ahmad, 1984)

Ibn Taimiyyah

While Ibn Khaldun was giving a socio-economic-historical explanation of the society, living at about the same time, Ibn Taimiyyah (1263-1328) was trying to reform it. He was a Hanbalite scholar and a great original thinker. He was born a few years after the Mongol devastation and had to contend with the remnants of the Mongol and the Crusaders. The Caliph had been killed by the Mongols and there was no effective leadership in the Muslim world. In Egypt, a person of Abbasid lineage was setup as Caliph, but this was just a formality as this 'Caliph' did not even have nominal political or religious influence on the Muslims.

Ibn Taimiyyah grew up in a period that was tumultuous for the Muslims. He saw division of Islamic thought due to various social factors into a number of disparate ideologies. The whole of the Muslim world had become a dynamic region with a large variety of philosophies and innovations causing changes and conflicts. The encroachment of pantheistic ideas, moral and ethical degradation, rapt political disintegration, Shia-Sunni conflicts, etc., were threatening to permanently change the universality of the Muslim society.

These factors and principally the absence of a strong and stable leadership among the Muslims made Ibn Taimiyyah propound the philosophy of the *Salaf* – the first three generations of Muslims. He wanted to hold on to the pristine core of Islam that would purge the society of the pervasive disparate ideologies and bring back the universalism of the Prophet till there was appropriate leadership. He rejected not only *Shirk* (taking idols besides God) but was totally against any type of *Bidat* (religious innovations). He always spoke fearlessly in the strongest possible language and did not care for the consequences. Like Imam Hanifa and Imam Hanbal, his mission would inevitably lead to a conflict with the Egyptian and Syrian rulers and the Ulema who supported them.

Before this conflict became serious, his exhortation to fight against the Mongols had a very positive response from the masses. He himself fought valiantly in the battle of *Marj As Safa* in which the Mongols were routed. He was made the Principal of a college and then the Judge (Qadi) of Damascus. But he kept up his mission and spoke against the Ulemas for their frivolity and not understanding the true spirit of Islam. He condemned the Sufis who believed themselves to be above the general law. He pointed out fallacies in Ghazzali and his hostility to the exponents of Greek philosophy was most pronounced. He treated Ibn Arabi's doctrine of the Unity of Being to a most severe criticism (Ahmad, 1984).

He based all his arguments and judgements on the Quran and Sunnah. Soon opposition mounted against him and he was removed from office. He then wrote books which included a strong criticism of the devotional visit to tombs, even that of the Prophet. His actions created a strong reaction and he was imprisoned in Egypt then moved to Damascus. He kept on writing from prison on various subjects till his pen and paper were taken away. He died while in jail and it cast a gloom over Damascus. Like Imam Hanifa, his funeral was attended by over 300,000 people a large number being women. He had been fearless from the start to the end of his life. When he was being threatened he had said, "What can they do to me? My paradise is in my heart. If they imprison me I will contemplate God. If they exile me I will contemplate God's world. If they kill me I will be a martyr."

He wrote a large number of books of which nearly fifty have survived. The *Minhas us Sunnah* and *Siyat us Sharia* give his political insights. Besides religious and political subjects he wrote on various economic concepts such as Just Price, Just wage, Market Mechanism and Regulation. He also worked on behavioural aspects of humans in his discourse on 'Purification of the Soul'. His student Imam ibn al-Qayyim al-Jawziyyah has written articles on behavioural and physiological disorders. Ibn Taimiyyah's brilliant mind was to influence reformers like Ibn Abdul Wahab of later years.

The fall of the Muslim civilisation has not been sudden. The Prophet had died leaving behind a Islam that had all the ingredients of religion, law, politics, economics, rationalism, social welfare, and all that is required for a civilisation to thrive and prosper. But over time these tenets would be modified that, sometimes, instead of emancipation would lead to slow regression. The first major change was when Muawiah changed the political state of Islam to hereditary rule. The other major change was the suppression of rationalism from Islam when the later Abbasid decided to contain and remove the Mutazilite. Cultural Islam was abandoned when the Sufis left the pursuance of literature and arts and started to pursue a pseudo-mystic religion in the name of Islam. The women of Islam, who were the most progressive and unpretentious in the world, went indoors when their nations fell to colonial powers. Over time, not only science but all aspects of progress and emancipation that Islam stood for had weakened or ceased to function.

In later centuries it was Europe, having risen as a collection of colonial powers that formed the modern political framework and started to influence the world. In Muslim realms, there was no follow-through on the works of their many past geniuses. There developed an imbalance due to the departure of rationalism and science. The Saffavids and Moghuls had their independent political theories but those were never translated to a modern context as was needed in the later part of their rule. The later Ottomans had become an old-fashioned empire with their strength based on administration and the military. As the Ottomans fell there was a belated attempt to harness the western political processes and knowledge but in vain.

By the second half of the 19th century, there were very few people left in the Muslim world who were of the calibre that could even comprehend the profundity of the ideas and theories of the likes of Ghazzali, Ibn Rushd, Ibn Taimiyyah or Ibn Khaldun. This was a great regression in the society of Muslims. It was also from this time that the Muslims started to feel helpless but, to a large extent, were unaware of the cause of their helplessness.

Along with socio-politics, regression would also affect legal, economical and others aspects of Muslim society as well.

Legal Aspects

Sharia and Fiqh

I leave two things for you. You will never go astray while holding them firmly: The book of God and the way of His Prophet

- The Prophet

Sharia constitutes of divine knowledge that was revealed to the Prophet, as well as the way of Prophet that is his *Sunnah*. The Quran is the embodiment of the Divine knowledge and the Hadith is the embodiment of the Sunnah. The central notion of Sharia is that Justice is the foundation of everything in the universe. If Justice is denied than the foundation is weakened and, as a reaction, there is chaos. Justice is universal and does not take into account religion, race, nationality, gender, wealth, economic difference, language or anything else. Everything has rights - animals, trees and even inanimate matter. The Sharia asserts that a human being does not serve any other human being whosoever – religious leader, emperor, president, prime-minister – and submits only to God. Sharia does not discriminate between human beings except in one case, *Taqwa*, which is virtue and piety that leads to a reverential understanding of God's will, God's knowledge and God's creation. There is no theocracy under the Sharia, only scholars debating laws that are good for humanity, and thus, Muslim legal system is 'secular' in its application.

Limits have been set in the Sharia that keeps humans humane. It provides the balance so that humans do not become animals led by instinct and desire, that they do not became mechanised in a materialistic world, and also that they do not become vegetative, inanimate and non-productive.

Sharia is the supra-constitutional framework of Islam constituting of the Quran and Sunnah. It is the point of reference for the promulgation of all laws. Sharia provides for the regulation of both the outward and inward aspects of society and individuals. Thus, while it is the source of laws for human actions, it also places emphasis on internal aspects of humans like intention, generosity and sincerity. The Sharia, unlike other legal systems, is universal in its application and not for a particular nation or group of people but, at the same time, not enforceable on non-Muslims.

The Sharia is immutable - what is universally good is good and what is universally harmful is harmful - but it gives humans the derivative right of law making to adjust to changing context and environment, i.e., Fiqh. The Sunnah is used by Fiqh as an intermediary to understand and interpret the divine knowledge of the Quran. The whole corpus of Quran, Sunnah and Fiqh fall under the subject of Islamic Law. The *Fiqh* (Jurisprudence) that the Great Imams promulgated was based on the *Sharia*, which means that the ultimate authority of their Jurisprudence is Divine.

Sharia provides for a lenient legal system. Though in the hereafter the punishment for sins is severe, the Quran is very light handed in prescribing punishments in this world. In most cases, sincere repentance is sufficient penance. The Hadith advises people, who have witnessed or have come to know the wrong doings of others, not to expose them. Except for sins like murder, much of the sins, especially of the personal kind, should be hidden by people and not be spoken of.

Misunderstanding of Sharia

In the contemporary world, some of the injunctions of Sharia appear to be harsh. There are two such injunctions in the criminal law section - Adultery being punishable by death and theft being punishable by the cutting of the wrist of the thief. What needs to be taken under consideration is that the Sharia delivers a balance. It recognises the immense ramification of the crime and places a strong deterrent to such a crime but, at the same time, it also recognises the type of crime and the people involved and makes the verdict almost impossible to deliver. The context of the punishment for adultery and theft can be explained as follows.

The social ramification of adultery is immense. It can cheat an unsuspecting person into bringing up someone else's child. It can arouse emotions leading to violence and murder. It can wreck whole families including the lives of the children of the individuals involved. The Sharia recognises the ramifications and decrees that an adulterer be stoned to death. But the harsh decree is a deterrent and is balanced by prescribing the additional conditions that is required for passing this verdict. There must be four witnesses to the act, each of them of good moral standing, to prove to the court that the act had taken place. It is quite difficult to get a single witness of such an event. Even if people have witnessed such an event they generally shy away and keep quiet. Even so if, in such a case, four witnesses are somehow collected in the court and if one of them have some blemish on his or her character, for the court the act has not taken place. To further complicate it, the witnesses must have witnessed the act in the 'pen in the inkpot' situation.

It is quite difficult to pass the verdict of 'stoning to death' act unless guilt is self declared. A person must plead guilty of such an act in the court for four times. Even if the person retracts on the fourth time the case is dismissed. After four times pleading of guilt the person's sanity needs to be checked before any judgement is passed. It is quite clear that to deliver verdicts against crimes of the above nature are almost impossible.

Theft or what is meant by it also needs to be understood in context. In the past society, when there was no police force to look out for thieves, no jails to hold thieves, no insurance to claim after goods have been stolen, no banks to keep one's valuable, theft was a very serious business. Every thing a family owned was in their home. The adults of the house would have to go out to daily work leaving unprotected young children or women and helpless elders at home. The women and elders of the house also had to leave house for everyday chore. They would leave their whole life's earning at home, which would probably be an unprotected fragile house or even a tent. And if whatever they had was stolen it would ruin the whole family financially. Thus the cutting of wrists was put up not as a threat for mere thievery but to protect the well being of entire families and their life long earned fortunes. On the other hand, when there was a famine, Caliph Umar bin Al Khattab abrogated the cutting of the hands of thieves. This proves instances of dynamism in Islamic Jurisprudence.

Dr. David Nicolle in *Ottomans Empire of Faith* writes, 'The concept of compensation rather than vengeance was central to Sharia law, although the Old Testament Biblical idea of "an eye for an eye" remained. As a result, murder was punishable by death. Alternately, a substantial fine, could be paid to a victim's family as a form of recompense for their loss of a productive member of the community. The ultimate choice remained theirs. As far as amputation for theft was concerned, in practice, physical mutilation as a form of punishment was far less frequent under Islamic Ottoman rule than had been the case in the Byzantine Empire. One of the important Hadith or saying of the Prophet Muhammad states, "Let there be neither injury nor vengeance for that injury." This statement, when taken with the numerous Quranic verses which advocated mercy, ensured that the maximum penalty was exacted only in the case of serious and persistent of cases.'

Another misunderstood aspect of the Sharia is female rights. First of all, Islam provides for female emancipation. The Sharia does not restrict women from any freedom. In the family men have roles to play – son, brother, husband and father, and similarly women have their roles to play – daughter, sister, wife and mother. Thus according to their roles men and women are different but equal as individuals. An example would be that the roles of doctors and engineers are different in the society but as individuals they are equal. Islam does not restrict women to an indoor life, but only that they should maintain modesty when they go out. In fact, sexuality is encouraged between husband and wife.

The concept of not allowing women to study is un-Islamic. When the European colonisation of Muslim societies took place, much of the women went indoors as a reaction. In many places, women stopped partaking education as attempts were made to influence them in foreign cultures in the course of general education. But these were in reaction to prevailing political situation. The Prophet had proclaimed that seeking knowledge is mandatory for ALL Muslims – and that includes both men and women. Under Islam both men and women can study, work, develop careers, join the armed forces, look after children, look after home, be part of social and political enterprises but at the same time they also have to fulfil their due familial roles of mother-father, husband-wife or daughter-son to maintain social harmony.

Three Islamic aspects of female rights have caused debate in recent times. One is that of inheritance, in which a daughter inherits half the amount from father's wealth than the son. That would, simplistically, give the son two third of the wealth and the daughter one third which, apparently, appears discriminatory. But in Islam, even through individuals have rights and responsibilities, the economic unit of the society is the family. When the wife inherits one third from her parents and the husband inherits two thirds from his parents a balanced one whole is inherited by the family. In the extended family institution, as the son receives more from his parents than the daughter, he is also responsible for the wellbeing of the parents at old age rather then the daughter. The daughter is thus set free to look after and be more responsible towards her own family and her own children. And as the wife/mother contributes a lot more at home, the husband/father is fully liable for the financial upkeep of the family.

The second injunction that has caused debate is that in documenting financial transactions, the witness of two women is equal to that of one man.

...and call upon two of your men to act as witnesses; and if two men are not available, then a man and two women from among such as are acceptable to you as witnesses.. [2:282]

This was needed because at that time very few women were literate, specially, in the writing and documenting financial transactions. The verse simply explains the reason and the condition why two women were so required:

...so that if one of them should ***make a mistake****, the other could remind her. [2:28].*

Scholars say that if a woman becomes educated enough not to '*make a mistake*' then the condition itself may imply that she doesn't need another supporting woman. It would be incorrect to consider this as disempowerment of women. If it were so, Ayesha would not have become one of the foremost *Muhaddith* (Tradition) scholars of Islam. It should be remembered that the words of Ayesha about Prophet's Tradition were accepted as legal authority by the Imams of Fiqh and Tradition. Her statements were not simply what she had witnessed; each of her statements was the Law. She was a major contributor to the jurisprudence that ruled a greater part of the world for a thousand years.

The third debated aspect is polygamy in Islam. The general Muslim family is dedicated to its women and takes care of them more than in any other culture. Generally, the ratio of women versus men in the world remains more or less equal. Men and women are paired off equally by nature. Thus, polygamy is the exception rather than the case. But Islamic injunctions are for all time and regions. There has been periods in time when ratio of females to male has increased dramatically due to wars, migrations, diseases, etc. The injunction of polygamy is to accommodate such special cases. If the wife becomes sick and unable to carry out her functions, the husband can marry again without divorcing the first wife. A divorce would render her helpless. It also accommodates the 'other' woman who remains illegitimate in some societies. Popular media honing into the lives of exotic Kings and Emperors of the past have distorted this view. Despite sponsored views, the reality is, that as there are women who have nothing to do with polygamy, there are also women who are quite comfortable with polygamy and who do not mind to share a home.

Islamic law was derived by scholars on the basis of what is 'good' for the people and for their emancipation. The methodology is similar to the Idealists of contemporary world with the additional facet that the ultimate authority came from the Quran and Sunnah. Its success can be judged from the fact that this legal system ruled vast tracts of civilisation for a thousand years. Joseph Shacht in *Pre Islamic Background and Early Development of Jurisprudence* states that the Sharia took the camel drivers of the Arabian Desert to the glorious height of world leadership and turned the illiterate, uncultured and uncivilised Bedouins into teachers and guides of the entire humanity. Professor Nallino in *Influences of Roman Law on Muslim Law* gives an example of how very advanced laws, such as that of 'Contract', had been derived from the Sharia. Before Islam, the purchase-sale was considered a 'real' contract. Whereas all the Muslim schools of law are unanimous, and more correctly so, in considering it a purely 'consensual' contract. The Muslim scholars did not arrive at this conclusion by a return to the Roman conception nor because they always posed the problem of the distinction between 'real' and 'consensual' trade, but simply on the basis of a passage of the Quran [4:33], where it is ordained that the commercial acts should take place by virtue of consensual contracts. Professor Shacht states that the principal that this Quranic injunction introduced could be considered a complete abnormality in the history of old statutes (Ajijola, 1998).

The Development of Fiqh

Fiqh is applied Sharia or a compendium of laws derived by scholars from the *Sharia*. Along with the legal codes, Fiqh also constitutes processes and principles, *Usul e Fiqh*, by which dynamic mundane laws are derived from the immutable divine Sharia. Unlike Sharia, it falls within the domain of human intellect. The derivation of law were not done by factions of an assembly of political parties serving one political agenda or another but by sober jurists and scholars who understood the people, upheld justice and had a vast religious, historical, contextual and contemporary knowledge.

The first two source of legal deduction was the Quran and the Sunnah. Application of consensus (Ijma), analogical deduction and reason were also used in determining laws. Of the Jurist Schools, the Hanafi gave Ijma a wide berth, the Shafii gave it relatively lesser importance. The Maliki gave the Ijma of Madinah more importance over others and the Hanbali accepted the Ijma of the Sahabas only. The other subsidiary criteria that were used in the formulation of law are:

- Removal of difficulty: The enacted law cannot be difficult or a burden on anyone.
- Reduction of religious obligation: In terms of allowed and prohibited, a few things are prohibited in the Sharia and the rest, though not mentioned, by default are all allowed.
- Realisation of public welfare: The law should be for the general good of the people. It cannot be harmful to any.
- Realisation of universal justice: the law should be equitable irrespective of religion, gender, race, etc.

The evolution of Fiqh categorises the development and application of Fiqh into six stages. The following categories are further extension of those stages.

Period of the Prophet.

In early 7th century, the Prophet taught the *Sahabi* (companion of the Prophet) to judge using the edicts in the Quran, and next by those in the Sunnah; and if the edict that was required to judge the specific case was still absent then to use their own reasoning. He taught the Companions *Ijtihad* (research and reasoning) so that they could govern the regions they were sent to. He would also sit with the companions in *Shura* (assembly or parliament) and ask for their opinion, thus teaching them consensus.

The Sahaba Period

This was the age of the four righteous Caliphs in the mid 7th century. The companions practised *Ijma* and at times the Caliph would call on a *Sahabi* to give his individual *Ijtihad* on certain issues. The individual Sahabi in giving the opinion ensured that all understood it was his opinion, which cannot be infallible. Thus the deductive processes of Fiqh principals like *Ijtihad* and Ijma (Qiyas) became established in this age.

At this time there were no religious sects, and only one *Madhab* existed in Islam. Differences in individual opinions were respected, and were considered just that - individual opinions. The Sahaba (Companions) were relatively flexible in opinion and in matters of Jurisprudence compared to the scholars of later periods. They gave importance to, and would very carefully weigh, the opinions of other Sahaba.

The Umayyad Period

During the Umayyad period (661-750) the state treasury, *bayt al mal*, became the property of the Caliph and the royal family. Such acts made many scholars leave the capital of the Caliphate – in a kind of self exile. There was a public demand for such scholars all over the empire which also facilitated this move. As the scholars spread out, rulings based on Ijma (consensus) declined and those on individual *Ijtihad* increased. The Kharijites, who were a seceded group, hardened into a sect. Though a strong bonding developed within the oppressed Alids, they were still part and parcel of the single Muslim *Madhab*.

In this period, the scholars belonged to two main streams, people of Hadith or *ahl al Hadith,* and the people of opinion or *ahl al Rai*. This division occurred due to the expansion of the empire. Damascus and Kufa had become the hub of the international empire with many new people and new cultures encroaching on these cities. To deal with the new environment and situations the Traditions existing there were not sufficient and rulings based on opinion were required. On the other hand, the Hijaz (Makkah and Madinah), no longer the political centre, was spared this influx of people. There the abundant existing Hadiths and rulings of the Companions were sufficient. Hadith fabrication or misrepresentation also took place in this age.

This age saw the first compilations of the Fiqh. The Fiqh of this period included the legal rulings of Ali bin Abu Taleb, Abdullah bin Abbas, Abdullah bin Umar, Ayesha bint Abu Bakr and Abdullah bin Masud. Those compilations are no longer extant but are referenced in the works of later scholars.

Early Abbasid Period

In the Early Abbasid period (750~950), though the Abbasid Caliphs had occasional political confrontations with the legal scholars, by and large, they respected and sponsored the scholars. Their family members and children would be students in the schools of such scholars.

Centres of learning improved, diversified and increased. Great schools were established in North Africa, Spain, Persia, India, Central Asia and Southern Russia. A large number of scholars travelled between these centres of learning. Debates and interactions including multi-faith ones were common. In this environment of cooperation the Great Imams established their schools. Besides the four great Imams other Madhabs like those of Imam Al Auzai, Imam Sufyan At Thawri and others flourished. In the later part of the period, after the death of the Imams and their immediate students, the cooperation between the schools decreased and they took on sectarian or dogmatic views.

Fiqh was initially compiled in books consisting of a mixture of legal rulings, Hadiths, opinions of the Companions and the Tabiun (generation after the Companions), an example of which is the *Muwatta*. The next type of books consisted of the Principles of Fiqh along with Hadiths that corroborated the principle. The *Al Umm* of Imam Shafii is of this type. The third type was books purely of principles and secondary principles. The *Mudawwanah* of Sahnun ibn Said is an example of this type.

In this period the Sunnah was collected in its entirety in the books of Hadith. Books of Tafsir (exegesis of Quran) were also written. This age also saw the flourishing of science, philosophy and social science.

Late Abbasid Period

During this period (~950-1258) all the other Madhabs besides those of the four Great Imams disappeared. The remaining four became highly systemised and organised. The rulings of the founding Imams were analysed and principles behind the ruling codified. This greatly facilitated researching through legal rulings within the Madhabs. But the emphasis on finer details caused a minor segregation to develop between the Madhabs.

Ijtihad was confined within the established Madhabs only and was on the decline. Comparative Fiqh evolved, but was used more to justify the views of each Madhabs rather than arrive at reconciliation. As the controversy between the Schools became bitter, Sufism became a kind of revolt of brilliant minds against this quibbling.

By the 10th century CE, a huge corpus of legislation to run the most powerful empires had been developed. It encompassed all the detailed fields of legislation including family law, criminal law, trade and commerce laws, and laws for wealth, war, peace, international relationship, social obligations, politics, etc. Principles, derived principles, and applied principles of legislation had already been developed. At this time, the Abbasid political unity weakened with local independent or semi-autonomous dynasties being established in Egypt, Persia, and other parts of the realm. Due to this politically uncertain environment Muslim jurists thought that individual *Ijtihad,* promulgation of law based on individual reasoning, could become harmful in inexperienced hands. And since, according to their understanding, *Ijtihad* and *Tafsir* had been exhaustively accomplished by the scholars, so it was time to close the door of *Ijtihad.* Thus formulation of new laws stopped significantly. Legislation took on a rigidity which would not relax up until recent times.

Period of Decline

This period starts at the fall of the Abbasid in 1258 and continues to date. In the 13th century, when the Mongols ransacked the Islamic world and Baghdad was under their control the Jurists were apprehensive that under 'foreign' rule Fiqh could go out of control. In this uncertain environment the Jurists of Iraq again declared that the doors of *Ijtihad* were closed which stopped any further formulation of laws.

The closing of Fiqh was a declaration in duress with the general people under the yoke of the Mongols. There were attempts to close Fiqh previously but this time the declaration was more effective. The scholars who had survived the Mongol onslaught were too busy fighting for their fundamental existence. The people did not have sufficient scholars to go to and were further cornered by the ruling Mongols. Research and analysis died. It became the period of stagnation and decline of dynamic Fiqh. *Taqlid*, in this case blind following, of the Madhabs became the norm and each Madhab, which was a jurisprudence school in reality, took on a religious sectarian form. The absence of *Ijtihad* coupled with *Taqlid* had a bigger legal ramification. Jurisprudence rather then being dynamic became purely based on precedence. Over the centuries this led to an inflexibility in legal regulation and legal processes that has made the implementation of the legal system progressively difficult.

The Ottoman revival

The Ottomans had initially established a marvellous legal system which enabled all the various ethnic and religious groups to co-exist congenially. Though, everyone was subject to the Sultan's *kanun*, each *millet* or local religious group had their own religious governance. The previous dominant School was that of Shafii, under the Ottomans the Hanafi School became predominant. This would continue for a few centuries.

Industrail age

But with the onset of the Industrial age significant legislative gaps became apparent which were supplemented by introducing aspects of European legislation. Finally, as Ottomans succumbed to the Europeans, European legal codes replaced the ailing Muslim laws throughout the Muslim world.

The industrial age had created a new global environment for which the Muslims were not ready. In Europe, on the other hand, the new environment saw the promulgation of new laws as required. One such example, are laws of employment. These laws can be considered having four levels in a hierarchy as shown in the table below:

Table: Legal Hierarchy

Hierarchy	Legal Category	Description
4	Agreement	Agreement between employee and employer, certified by Industrial Commission.
3	Award	Issued by Industrial Commission. Generally, binding to a whole industry rather than particular employer and employee. Has more authority and can nullify a contradicting Agreement.
2	Statute Law	Laws enacted by legislation of the parliamentary bodies
1	Common Law	Foundation of precedents, the verdicts passed by courts from the 12th century. In employment contracts it has precedence of rights and obligations of employees and employers. Where there is no relevant legislation, award or agreement on a specific issue the Common Law may be used to arrive at a verdict.

In the above English law derived hierarchy the foundation is the Common Law, over which lies the Statute law, over which rests the Awards with finer details of employment and on the top are the Agreements with the finest details. In Islamic law the foundation is the Sharia, above which lies the Fiqh, which is vast, but specific laws on industry and the modern economy are missing. These laws are missing in Islamic jurisprudence simply because all legal derivation had stopped long before industrialisation.

Economic Aspects

Islamic economic policy is to ensure that first and foremost the basic needs of all individual are met. But there is no restriction on production, which means that individuals may work for and indulge in luxury items provided that all source of income and all expenditures are *halal* (legal) as well. Islamic Jurisprudence details all goods and services that are *halal*. Islam allows individual ownership and disposal of wealth, but determines the manner of ownership and disposal. Savings is allowed and there is a nominal tax, Zakaat, on it. Keeping the economy in fluid flow is also encouraged:

O, you who believe! Spend of the good things which you have earned, and of that which We bring forth from the earth for you. [2:267]

And let not those who are niggardly, who withhold the gifts God has given them from His Grace, think that it is good for them. Rather it is worse for them. That which they hoard will be their collar on the Day of Judgement [3:180]

Hoarding which is now known to be harmful to economy is disallowed:

And those who hoard gold and silver and do not spend in the way of God, let them know that a severe punishment is awaiting them. [9:34]

During the Caliphate of Abu Bakr and Umar in the mid 7th century, the *Bayt Al Mal* was under the control of the Caliph, but the wealth belonged to the people, the ultimate owner being God. In the Prophet's time just and progressive economic policies dealing with agriculture, trade and commerce had been implemented. By the time of Umar, the Muslims were in charge of a huge economy due to those policies. Usman decentralised the economic system giving a larger share of economic activity and financial decision making to the Governors and the business community. Muawiah brought the *Bayt Al Mal* under the ownership of the Caliph.

Since then, many Muslim scholars have done admirable economic research. Their researches are reflected in a number of concepts and techniques that were applied in early Islamic commerce. These led to the formations of partnership (*mufawada*) and limited partnership (*mudaraba*), trusts (*waqf*) capital (*al mal*) and capital accumulation (*nama al-mal*), organisations and enterprises independent of state, and the use of bills of exchange, cheques, promissory notes, accounts, ledgers and loans. Some of the renowned scholars who divulged into economic thought include Abu Yusuf (student of Imam Abu Hanifa), Ibn Khaldun, Al Maqriji, Al Dulaji, Al Biruni, Ibn Taimiyyah and the indomitable Al Ghazzali. Many of their early concepts were adopted and further advanced in Europe in later centuries.

In the days of the empires – Umayyad, Abbasid, Ottoman, Mughals - the Muslims evolved the best economic system that included a vast free trade zone, and was modern for their time and non-exploitative by all historical standards.

When industrialisation came to Europe it changed the very character of the western economy. The accumulation of wealth grew so rapidly and became so vast that it went beyond all capacities of measure. The classical economist reacted by developing relevant economic theories to appropriately run the emerging economic system. The Muslims, devoid of industrialisation, did not face this situation and thus never developed a modern Islamic economic model.

In the 20th century, the Muslim nations fell in the category of small to medium sized economies. Though all ended up being capitalist in character, some tried to develop a socialist Islamic economy. But these attempts saw setbacks after failures to emancipate the economy and ceased when the Soviet Union collapsed. The change over to capitalism did not bring about any remarkable growth in the Muslim world mainly due to political instability.

The Muslim economic thought have become static and stunted. Most of Muslim state divulged on short term demand management. Mid term supply side factors, such as level of technology, capital stock and labour market, were misunderstood or overlooked. The management of long term factors - such as type of state governance needed for political stability, advanced education system for the populace that can uplift scientific and social science standards to a competitive level, and public saving capacity or capital accumulation-were absent or inefficient.

During this period, a few of the smaller non-Muslims countries like Singapore, Taiwan and South Korea made considerable economic progress. This was due to appropriate state policies, internal political stability and also support from the capitalist world trying to harness capitalist powers during the Cold War between socialist and capitalist ideologies. But it was only the bigger countries like China, India and Brazil that made real inroads as major economic powers on their own accord. As economic development came to larger countries which had big economies, even with low per capita income, endeavours by relatively smaller countries towards formation of regional economic groups took place. Examples of such groups are the European Union and Association of South Asian Economic Nations (ASEAN). Most of the Muslim nations, falling in the small to medium category of countries, were unable to belong to any significant economic zone or to form one themselves.

Scientific Aspects

Science, the investigation and understanding of the inherent laws of the physical universe, is considered as *Baraka* or blessing from God. In the pre-Islamic past, some aspects of science and social science had existed in one single conglomerate of knowledge referred to as philosophy. The Egyptians, Babylonians and Indians schools worked on medicine, mathematics and astronomy, and the Greek schools improved on those and further worked on subjects like history, geography, ethics and logic. But most of the sciences that were studied in those times were still under the wrapping of either religion or philosophy, i.e., those schools were basically religious or philosophical in character. Thus, they were theoretical in nature. It was the Muslims, during the Abbasids, who truly separated all the distinct disciplines and further more developed the sciences into specialised branches like algebra, optics, chemistry, and social science and gave these exact methodology as is understood today.

Ironically, the contemporary Muslims are the hardest hit with the absence of science and scientific research. The rejection of this *Baraka* had gradually led the Muslims to great weaknesses for which they continue to pay.

The Rational Question

Islam has a rational component. It speaks of *Deen* and *Dunya* – the religious world and the rational world – and does not seek to neglect either. This component makes the co-existence of religion and rationalism productive. But a delicate balance has to be maintained.

Dunya or rationalism inherently must ask questions. It sees the world, it sees the universe and starts to question trying to analyse, synthesise and decipher everything. And it is able to get results that caüse advancements, for example, those of scientific nature. The pride of discovery and understanding of universal mysteries develops a self dependency and arrogance that makes rationalism not just ask question about the creation but also, at one time, it challenges *Deen*. That is where the conflict between religion and rationalism arises and that is why Islam advices a balance be applied.

The great conflict between rationalism and religion took place during the Abbasid period between the Mutazilites and the Ulemas. Though, the Mutazilites themselves were balanced, their influence was leading to various groups – some unorthodox and some profane - to rise within the society. Ultimately, the Ulemas won and science, for various reasons as noted earlier, became dormant in the Muslim society. But the balance of Deen and Dunya was not restored.

In a few centuries, this fight between rationalism and religion moved to Europe, this time the Christian Church represented the religion. But by this time science had made great inroads and become exceedingly powerful. The parables and metaphors of religious teachings became ridiculous in the exactness of science. For example, based on the biblical history, religious scholars had calculated the origin of earth to be a few thousand years old. That became laughable to the rationalists whose palaeontology and radio-carbon dating methods started to give dates in millions and billions of years. Christianity lost the state and lost much of its graphic social influence. The balance was not restored. But rational Europe rose in scientific strength becoming the most powerful continent.

Progressively and relative to Europeans, the Muslims became weaker and weaker. Having defeated rationalism, the Muslims felt the pinch then the punch and finally the flat knock-out blow from rationalist Europe. Thus in recent times, the importance of science has returned to the forefront of Muslim considerations. Many scholars have raised the ramification of *Taqlid* (emulation) in a modern society. As far as *Deen* is concerned the *Sunnah* cannot be changed, religion cannot be reinvented, thus *Taqlid* is a requisite. But, as far as *Dunya* is concerned, such as in the modern sciences, innovation is pre-eminent.

The presence of both religion and rationalism is important in Islamic societies. The interdependence is quite astonishing. Today, rational science has given the age of the world, a huge 4.5 billion years. It is easy to forget that it was not the rationalists but the religious scholars who first started to count the number of years the earth has existed for. Science has only corrected the method of calculation, it did not create it. Furthermore, the Quran does not contradict science or even aspects of science like evolution. There are verses in the Quran that can be interpreted in favour of evolution.

The importance of religious morality lies in the fact that without it rationalism can only judge between right and wrong. Pure rationalism lacks the essence of good and bad. It is self centred, and so, according to it there is nothing wrong in endeavouring for more and more and to the make most of life even at the detriment of others. Concepts such as 'Human rights' and 'Freedom' become plain slogans or political intruments. It is only those with moral inclinations can selflessly think of 'good' for others, and 'care' for others. Science, without morality, instead of being a wonderful tool for humanity, can become the newest uncompassionate idol.

Sufi Aspects

In the Sufi universe the intellectual core has disappeared from the various schools. The words of scholars like Ibn Taimiyyah turned out to be true, as much of the scholarship that had been the principal driving force of Sufism disappeared leaving behind a hollow mystical shell. While the real Sufis became a minority, the shallow ones innovated systems which at best became non-productive and at worst misled people to idolatry.

The concept of 'Holy Saints' is not Islamic. Islam has great respect for religious scholars but holy reverence is reserved for God alone. But some later Sufis, mostly self-declared and less educated ones, imported saintly pretences into their orders. Some taught people to seek blessings at the graves of 'Sufi-saints' while others made people believe that mystics could provide boons, could see the future or protect from harms. The minnow Hallajes graduated from *bidat* (innovation) to *shirk* (idolatry).

In the past, the Sufis had played very important roles. They had taken the free-thinking inherent in Islam and opened doors of enquiry in the frontiers of human thought. That had ultimately led to momentous development in social science, literature and culture. The likes of Ghazzali had used it to open queries not only into theology but into behavioural and rational sciences as well. The likes of Rumi and Nizami had dominated the cultural stage of the world.

Today, all of that is lost and foreign culture is undermining Muslim culture and values. The Sufis definitely have their role to play. They have to harness their innovative skills into the frontiers of knowledge and evolve a rich and fascinating culture again in which the young Muslim will take succour, not be misled or controlled by contending foreign cultures. For that they may need to play a significant role in the contemporary media. The Sufis have to make themselves relevant to today's issues, not to what was relevant hundreds of years ago.

Dilemmas of the Faithful

By time (I swear)
Indeed humanity is in loss!
Except such as have faith and do righteous deeds
And join together in the mutual teaching
Of truth, of patience and constancy
[103:1-3]

Today, the Muslim world has lost its centre of gravity. Muslims are full of opinions, counter opinions and ideas that contradict each other and that can become counterproductive. There are contentious issues in every aspect of Muslim life: economical, legal, religious, cultural, technological, political, social, individual, etc.

The uncertainties being faced by the Muslims are multifarious and numerous varying from the very small non-issues to issues of global proportions: The Muslim nations do not know how to deal with the political, economic and military situation they find themselves in. Literacy is lagging far behind among Muslims. There are still regions in Muslim domains where Muslim women face un-Islamic barriers in gaining access to education and emancipation. Universities are again being established in Muslim nations but advanced and productive research that collaborates with local industries to develop technology are absent in most. There is complete dependence on foreign technology. The creation of wealth, especially in urban areas, is causing social ills - a fall in morality and rise in stress, psychological disorder and unhappiness. The Muslim social events and celebrations, based on the lunar calendar, are difficult to organise. The Muslims cannot even agree on the start and end of the lunar months, and celebrate the festival of Eid together, even though it is now possible to workout with precision the lunar calendar.

Political instability in Muslim nations is another great cause of hindering economic development. Too much hatred in the political sphere makes the government and opposition come to violent conflicts, which results in puerile and rash non-issues to overshadow real economic issues. The instability acts as a deterrent to investment, foreign as well as local. Foreign investment, though creating jobs initially, in the long run is siphoning off wealth as profit. To compensate for this the Muslim countries are struggling to invest in other countries. The poorer ones do not have enough resource and expertise to invest overseas, and the ones that do face numerous issues. When, in 2006, an Arab consortium from the Emirates bought the Peninsula and Orients Ports Company, American politicians raised an uproar that the ports would be used by terrorists. The consortium had to sell off the American ports to another 'non-Muslim' company.

Advice and aid from International bodies like the IMF and World Bank have not been conducive to the development of the economy of the Muslim nations. Sometimes, going against these directives have been productive. At the end of the 20th century when the Asian countries faced economic crisis the IMF prescribed a package for Malaysia that included advices like floating of its currency. Malaysia decided that the whole package would be negative for its economy and took steps that were opposite to what the IMF package had prescribed. Contrary to what the IMF predicted, Malaysia was the first among the Asian countries to recover from the crisis.

This kind of ill advice has been faced by non-Muslim developing countries as well. An example is that of Pohang Iron and Steel Company, POSCO, the integrated steel industry of South Korea. In early 1970s, the Korean government applied for a concessionary loan from the World Bank to set up a steel industry. The WB declined on the grounds that there was not sufficient local and international demand for the product. The government still went ahead, finding alternate sources of funding, and implemented the industry. The government also developed infrastructure for the industry by investing in road and rail communications, improvement in port facilities, water supply and power stations. It also created a local market for the steel by subsidising local manufacturing industries like motor companies. POSCO turned out to be a hugely successful and profitable venture which stimulated other supply industries to be developed in the country (Rodrik, 1995). Most Muslims nations have not shown the resolve or vision to plan or face such issues.

Though, the United Nations Organisation, the IMF, the World Bank and the developed countries give prescriptions of economic models, such as free market, for the Muslim nations to follow in order to develop, this type of advice is not foolproof. Ideally, the free market remains the best mechanism for economic growth. But in the real world, opportunist groups of people tend to take control of the market and maximise the profit for themselves. The general populace, supplier of labour or raw material, gets minimal benefit and remains poor. This leads to the difference in wealth among people or nations.

To reverse the above situation some nations have applied corrective measures so that their local markets remain favourable for local development. China and India have applied controlled markets during recent times that have led to the emancipation of their economy. China developed as a closed communist economy and India, while politically democratic, developed its basic industrial foundation and market under a government-controlled economic system which had not allowed foreign corporations to make inroads in their economy. Generally, such corrective controlled markets can not last after the correction has taken place, that is, basic local infrastructure, supportive institutions, technology, and marketing and managerial skills have developed and national industrial foundation have matured sufficiently so that the market can compete with economies of scale and deflect global commercial predation. Once that has happened the market should revert to a free one, which is the most efficient process for economic growth. India has opened up its market to all foreign investments and is investing in other countries as well. The Communist Party of China, representing a much larger economy, is undergoing gradual transition from a controlled market to a semi-free market and ultimately a free market. Unlike India and China, the Muslim nations have not been able to identify their particular method or process to develop.

Ignorance and complacency has led the Muslims to indolence resulting in an inability to resolve problems being faced. This impotency of the Muslims in all the fields of science, economics and social science is the result of a lack of vision, myopic and inflexible policies, and the subsequent subjugation of Muslim people. History reveals that Islam breeds individuals who are builders and shapers of empires. These individuals have been advanced and progressive in their outlook. But in the recent past that culture of advancement has changed. 'Thought' or intellectual development has been stifled.

The Muslim social fabric consists of a very strong disciplinary and motivational system. It consist of the unique unwavering focus of *Tawheed* (unity of God), the Quran, the five times daily prayers; all these are to instil, and over the ages has imbued, Muslim individuals to a quest to attain greatness in one facet of life or another, be it science and rationalism, social science, Sufi philosophy, or Ulemaic jurisprudence. For a long time now all of these have stagnated leaving a great intellectual void in Muslim psychological makeup. To the general mass the five pillars of Islam have became mere rituals. These are no longer an act of sublime prayer or self purification. These are no longer training and disciplining for achievement of greats deeds. These are no longer means to the end but ends by themselves. The Muslim world has become a society of mere indigent dogmas. It is like a grand old school with highly motivated teachers and students attending their five daily periods of classes with great punctuality but learning nothing and studying nothing in the mute classes beyond primary education. The quest and substance for the complete code of life has gone. The future of the Muslims in a rapidly globalising world is not very bright.

Globalisation and the Muslims World

There is a fundamental philosophical conflict the Muslims have faced in recent times. According to Muslim universal philosophy all the Muslim people belong to the whole Muslim world and the whole Muslim world belongs to all the Muslims. Even in the days of empires the Muslims could move from one empire to another or from one kingdom to another at will. It is not just a matter of free movement but a manner of free universal life and culture. But the prevailing European state model is just the opposite; in it people belong and are restricted to a state only (Though the European Union is moving in the opposite direction).

Thus there has always been an implicit and voiceless discord in the psyche of a universal people restricted within artificial borders. This conflict has, in an invisible manner, kept Muslims in a confused state socially, politically and economically.

On the long run, unless any cataclysm causes world regression, globalisation will see global governance. But the world is too complex to form global governance in one single step. First, the nation-states will and are forming regional forums. Then the regional forums will coagulate to form bigger forums and so on.

In the short run globalisation will be defined by three categories of organisations that have already started to erode and undermine the power and self determination of nation-states. These are economic institutions like multinational corporations and banks, inter governmental organisations like the UN, and thousands of non governmental organisations (NGO) that are active in social as well as 'activist' endeavours. These, along with processes like free trade agreements, are the driving forces behind the economic regionalisation of the world.

The large countries – like USA, China, Russia, India, Brazil, etc. - with large population and large economic and defensive capabilities will define the next step in globalisation. The other regions that will have great influence are the regionalised economies like European Union and ASEAN. These are also the regions that constitute world corporate and NGO powers.

The Muslims, though comprising of one fifth of world population, holding large resources and constituting of a number of nation-state-kingdoms, do not possess any of the above globalising forums, entities or processes. They posses insignificant corporate and NGO power and do not have any active economic regional forum.

It is probable that in a near-future regionalised world the Muslim states will join a variety of regional forums. Though prediction is hazardous, it is likely that countries like Indonesia and Malaysia will further unite, is one form or another, with an ASEAN – Chinese grouping. Indonesia has a remnant Indian culture that may cause it to establish some links with India as well. Bangladesh is likely to be absorbed into an India economy with which it has strong cultural ties. It is already dependant on India for commodities and water resources, India being the upper riparian for all Bangladeshi rivers, and soon it is also likely to start sharing energy with India as well. The condition in Pakistan and Afghanistan is too mobile to hazard any guess. Pakistan has ethno-cultural ties with India but in the past had formed regional economic cooperation with Turkey and Iran and political ties with Saudi Arabia and USA. Afghanistan has historical affiliations with Pakistan and Central Asia. The Central Asian Muslim states are likely to form a grouping with Russia and some other previous Soviet States. Turkey will ultimately ally themselves with Europe. Iran may form alliance with a Russian block. Once the Palestine issue is resolved, Israel will emerge as the most advance country in the Middle Eastern region and, with end of animosity, may form economic cooperation with the regional Arab countries. This group will continue its positive relationship with the USA. The African Muslims will become part of emerging African economic entities.

Unlike the Hindus represented by India, Christians represented by USA, Europe and South America, Buddhists represented by China and Japan, the Muslims are not likely to play any important role or have any 'say' in global decision making. None of the Muslim states will become permanent member in the UN or get the power of the Veto. No Muslim state will be able to block any anti-Muslim resolution and will have to depend on the sympathy of non-Muslims for that. Their representation will be limited to the passive voices of small countries in agencies like the General Assembly of the UN. Many of the Muslim countries will exhaust their natural resources in a few decades. These countries have also developed high maintenance infrastructure that will bleed revenue causing hard economic times unless a rapid paradigm shift is made towards industrialisation and manufacturing. As for forming a regional economic forum that will be strong enough to participate in global decision making, the divisions among the Muslims are too great for any such viable regional partnerships. The scenario is represented by the sterile condition of the Organisation of Islamic Conference.

The Muslims, who are a people with universal or global philosophy and should fit into a global world very easily, are not ready for and, can be considered unaware of the unfolding episode of globalisation. One viable group of Muslims that may develop a voice in the future are those living in the West, China and India. Exposure to good academe and higher organisational capacity may assist them to develop good NGO capability and even attain corporate power. But the time to attain global power is passing by. Once, in the near future, when economic regionalisation and corporate formations have stabilised, it will become very difficult to form further new regional forums or new corporation as the competitions will become too high. At such a time, only a miracle can give Muslims any say in global decision making. Though, in the past, Muslims have fashioned miracles.

In the day of *Qiyama* with the single blast of the *Sur* horn all life and all of creation – the mountains, the seas, the planets and the stars - will come to a catatrophic end. It will herald the resurrection and beginning of the judgement day for all humanity. The Prophet has said, "If you have a seed. You see that *Qiyama* has befallen, the world is crumbling, and you have a seed. Plant the seed."

Voice of the reformers

In the past reformers, viewing the decline of the Muslims in general, have spoken time and again. Each one of them had put forward their own philosophy and solution for resolution. Their proposed solutions have differed, as they have spoken from different perspectives, but all were aware that somewhere something has gone wrong that needed to be corrected. Ghazzali, Ibn Rushd and Ibn Taimiah have been such reformers. Some of the foremost of reformers of a later age are:

- Mohammad Ibn Abdul Wahab (1703-1792), a prominent Theologian and reformer influenced by Ibn Taimiyyah. He was from what is now Saudi Arabia and faced the same issues that Ibn Taimiyyah had faced – rapidly changing multiple Islamic societies. To stop innovative cultural influence and the taking of other idols, religious or intellectual, which undermines the universality of Islam he started a movement of unification by going back to the original Islam of the Quran and Sunnah before any divisions were created. 'Wahabism' is mistakenly considered by some as a sect or faction in political Islam.

- Ahmad ibn Abdur Rahim (1703 – 1762) of India also known as Shah Waliallah. He was a great scholar with an in depth understanding of all Islamic Sciences. He proposed that a person be free to choose which ever Madhab or sect he or she wants. He also called for the opening the doors of Ijtihad and a re-unification of all the schools of Fiqh.

- Muhammad Ibn Ali Shawkani (1757 – 1835) of Yemen studied Fiqh under the Zaidi Madhab. After that he studied Hadith in depth and gave up affiliation to any particular Madhab. He started independent Ijtihad and declared Taqlid as *Haram* (Prohibited). He wrote books on the subject and was criticised by the scholars of his time.

- Jamal Al Din Afghani (1838– 1897) belongs to the modern day thinkers who called for reform and free thinking in politics, religious and scientific matters. He travelled throughout the Muslim world – India, Makkah, Istanbul and Cairo – calling for reform, and denounced Taqlid. He and some other scholars argued that the Baghdad Ijma that closed Ijtihad was not infallible as it took place under duress, fear (of Mongol occupation) and intellectual stagnation.

- Mohammad Iqbal (1877-1938) a great modern thinker, poet and philosopher of the Indo-Pakistan subcontinent called for the political and spiritual revival of Islamic civilisation. After studying in England and Germany he established a law practice but primarily involved himself with writing scholarly works on politics, philosophy, economics, history and religion.

Dialogue with God - 1

Since the fall of its later empires, the Muslims have been in a constant search for the reason which had led them to the lamentable situation they found themselves in. Iqbal portrays the psychological bewilderment and the insight of the search by the Muslims in his poem *Sikwa (The Complaint)*. In this poem he questions and, in a veiled manner, indicts God for the Muslim's woeful state.

The Complaint

Why must I forever suffer loss, oblivious to gain,
Why think not upon the morrow, drowned in grief for yesterday?
Why must I attentively heed the nightingale's lament of pain?
Fellow-bard, am I a rose, condemned to silence all the way?

No; the burning power of song bids me to be bold and not to faint,
Dust be in my mouth, but God - He is the theme of my complaint.

~~~

True, we are forever, famous for our habit to submit,
Yet we tell our tale of grief, as by our grief we are constrained.
We are but a muted lyre, yet a lament inhabits it
If a sigh escapes our lips, no more can sorrow be contained.

God give ear to the complaint of us, Your servants tried and true,
You are used to songs of praise, now hear a note of protest too.

~~~

Strange indeed was the spectacle of Your world existing before our days.
Here men bowed down to stones, they paid their reverence to trees.
Only to the visual image was attuned the human gaze -
How could hearts adore a God no eye percipient may seize?

Well You know, was there anywhere to name Your Name?
By the Muslim's strong right arm Your purpose to fulfilment came.

~~~

Though the Seljuks had their empire, the Turanians had their sway,
Though the Chinese ruled in China, the Sassanians in Iran.
Though the Greeks inhabited abroad, fruitful acres in their day,
And the Jews possessed their cubit, and the Christians owned their span.

Who upraised the sword of battle in Your Name's most sacred cause?
Or who strove to right the ruined world by Your most hallowed laws?

~~~

It was we, and we alone, who marched Your soldiers to the fight,
Now upon the land engaging, now embattled upon the sea.
The triumphant call to prayer in Europe's churches to recite,
Through the wastes of Africa to summon men to worship You.

All the glittering splendour of great emperors we reckoned none,
In the shadow of our glinting swords we shouted, "God is One!"

~~~

All of our life we dedicated to the dire distress of war,
When we died, we died exultant for the glory of Your Name.
Not to win a private empire did we draw the swords we bore,
Was it the quest of riches to Earth's frontiers that we came?

Had our people striven for the sake of worldly goods and gold,
Would they then have shattered idols they might have gainfully sold?

~~~

In the press of mortal combat if the hour of worship came,
Then the people of Hejaz, to Makkah turning, bowed in prayer.
King Mahmoud, Ayaz the slave, their rank in service was the same,
Lord and servant - at devotion never difference was there.

Slave and master, rich and needy - all the old distinctions gone,
Unified in the adoration of Your Presence, they were one.

~~~

We erased the smudge of falsehood from the parchment firmament,
We redeemed the human species from the chains of slavery
And we filled the Holy Kaba with our foreheads humbly bent,
Clutching to our fervent bosoms the Qur'an in ecstasy.

Yet the charge is laid against us we have played the faithless part,
If disloyal we have proved, have You deserved to win our heart?

~~~

Hark, the idols in the temples shout "The Muslims are no more."
Jubilant to see the guardians of the Kaba's shrine depart.
The world's inn is emptied of those singing cameleers of yore,
Vanished is their caravan, Qur'an closed pressed to reverent heart.

Disbelief is loud with laughter, are You deaf, indifferent?
Disregard You Your Unity, as if it nothing meant?

~~~

So, is it on others only that the world its love bestows,
We, who walk Your chosen path - to us a phantom world is left.
Be it so, bid us be gone, and the Earth belong to those,
Yet protest not that the Earth, of Unity, is now bereft.
~~~

For no other cause we live but Your remembrance to maintain,
When the Saqi is departed, can the wine-cup yet remain?

~~~

Gone is now the thronged assembly and Your lovers too are gone,
Ended are the midnight sightings, silenced dawn's deep threnody.
They bestowed their hearts upon You and with their reward passed on,
Scarcely were Your faithful seated when they were dismissed from You.

So your lovers came, so with the promise of "Tomorrow" went -
Now come, seek them with the lantern of Your beauty's blandishment.

~~~

Laila's pangs are still the same, Qayes yearns as fiercely as of old,
Still amid the forests and vales of Nejd the fleet deer run.
Beauty rules the same as ever, hearts deep passions still enfold
Still abide the folk of Ahmad, still you are their Lord, the One.

Then what mean Your high displeasure, since its cause is all unknown?
What denotes it, that Your eye is turned in wrath upon Your own?

~~~

Did we ever shun You, or Arabia's Messenger forsake?
Did we tire of idol-breaking, and to idol-making turn?
Did we cry an end to passion, growing weary of love's ache?
Did we quit the path of Salman, cease from Qarni to learn?

Still the fire of "God is Greatest" in our hearts we keep ablaze,
Still Belal the Abyssinian guides us in our daily ways.

~~~

On the summit of Faran, You made Faith complete and whole,
Took captive hearts a thousand with a single simple sign.
You it was that Love's quintessence set afire, a blazing coal,
Flamed the assembly with the ardour of Your loveliness divine.

Why is it, that in our bosoms not a spark remains today?
We are still the same burnt chattels, what, have You forgotten, pray?

~~~

Turns anew the wandering people to the Hejaz their bridle-string,
Skyward lifts the wingless nightingale the lilting love of flight.
In the garden every blossom fragrance-drenched is quivering,
Strike the silent lute, long eager for Your plectrum to alight.

String-imprisoned melodies await Your touch to sing in choir!
Sinai is trembling, trembling to be ravished by Your fire.

~~~

Now the secret of the garden by the rose's scent is spread,
Shame it is, the garden's blossoms should themselves the traitor play!

Now the garden's Lyre is broken, and the rose's bloom-time sped,
And the minstrels of the garden from their twigs have winged away.

Yet one nightingale sings on there, rapt by his own melody,
In his breast the plangent music tosses still tempestuously.

~~~

Life is joyless now, and death no comfort promises to bring,
To remember ancient sorrows is the sole delight I know.
In the mirror of my mind what gems of thought are shimmering,
In the darkness of my breast what shining revelations glow!

Yet no witness in the garden may the miracle attest,
Not a tulip there lies bleeding with a brand upon its breast.

~~~

Break, hard hearts, to hear the carol of this nightingale forlorn,
Wake, dull hearts, to heed the clamour and the clangour of this bell.
Rise, dead hearts, by this new compact of fidelity reborn,
Thirst, dry hearts, for the old vintage whose sweet tang you knew so well.

Though the jar was cast in Persia, in Hejaz the wine first flowed,
And though Indian the song be, from Hejaz derives the mode.

(Parts of *Sikwa* from the translation by A.J. Arberry)

Resolution of Dilemma

The original Muslim society of Madinah was intellectually balanced consisting of spirituality, philosophy and rationalism. Thus, in the past, Muslims had developed the Ulemaic Jurisprudence, the Sufi philosophy and the rational sciences. If Islam is to remain a complete code of life then morality alone, though fundamentally important, cannot suffice. The intellectual balance needs to be regained. On the foundation of morality, Muslims need an efficient and a socially just political system, equitable economic model and an advanced scientific academe.

Since the 20th century there has been a resurgence of Muslim thought. Having become unfit to survive with dignity in the modern environment, ordinary Muslims started to think again. Since the beginning of the 21st century the thought process has intensified and multiplied resulting in polarisations and the formation of multiple groups of thought, with each nascent school advocating its own idea as the solution. These solutions have included ideas such as active self education, blind emulation, or even violent resurgence. There is a possibility that, if a lack of vision continues, these variety of ideas may again fragment the Muslim world but it is expected the most correct ones will sustain.

The Muslims came out of the backward tribal desert and took on reckoning with the most powerful empires of the world not because they had suddenly acquired a superior weapon, a more efficient financial policy or any magical potion. They had acquired something else: they had converted to become the most moral beings in the world. It was not that they just believed that they were morally right, they *were* morally better than all others. And despite all opposition they would not forsake their high standards. That is an indomitable force - the true strength that lies in Justice and Truth. The other factor the made the Muslims powerful for a thousand years was not because of their weapons and wealth but because they were the most knowledgeable people. The indomitable combination of morality and knowledge accepts no defeat.

Dialogue with God - 2

Iqbal's corollary to his *Sikwa* (*Complaint*) is another poem the *Jawab - a – Sikwa* (*The Riposte)*. This is God's reply, to the poets *Sikwa,* in which the Muslims find themselves much to blame for their situation.

The Riposte

The Riposte starts with the 'Complaint' of the poet rising up through the heavens. It causes a commotion and the heavenly bodies are baffled at the complaining voice. The complaining poet says:

> Arrogant and cunning was my love and on such mischief bent
> That the very walls of heaven fell down before its wild lament.

And the Angels are bewildered and perplexed at the unknown voice and are amazed at the Muslims.

> So enormous is their impudence, at God Himself they rail

The voice of God replies with indignation indicating the best part of the complaint was that it was at least beautifully phrased.

> We would fain be bountiful, but no petitioner is there…
> Free to all Our loving kindness, none is worthy of Our care
>
> Were there any to receive it, We would give a royal throne
> A new world We have to offer, were one earnest seeker known.

The Voice condemns the Muslims of becoming nerveless and impotent, of taking strange new idols, of loosing the love of God and way of the Prophet:

> Nations comes to birth by faith, let the faith expire and the nation die
> So, when gravitation ceases, the thronged stars asunder fly.
> You will sell your father's graveyards, nor account such traffic base;
> Not a nation in the world so lightly spurns its native place
>
> Why you are a people bereft of every art,
> You are like a barn where lightning nestle and will not depart.
>
> ~~~
>
> One and common are the profit and the loss the people bear
> One the Holy Sanctuary, one Quran, one God you share
> One and common are your Prophet and your creed
> But to act as one, and Muslims – that would every bound exceed
>
> Here sectarianism triumphs, class and caste there rule the day
> Is it thus you hope to prosper, to regain your ancient sway?
>
> ~~~

You are all intoxicated with the joy of fleshy ease
Ali's poverty you will not, Uthman's wealth your dare not seize
Are your Muslims? Is this the way Islam would have you tread?
What relationship of spirit links you to your glorious dead?

They possessed the realm of China, they ascended Persia's throne
You have not their manly honour, and are great in words alone.

~~~

Every Muslim was a lancet poised to sever falsehood's vein
On his right arm he trusted, by his strength he could attain
On the mirror of his being ceaseless action's lustre shone
And while you are scared of dying, he had fear of God alone

If the child learns not the knowledge that has made his father sage
Then what right has he by merit to his father's heritage?

~~~

Self destruction is your fashion, noble self-esteem was theirs;
Yours the tongue that idly blabs, theirs the hand that greatly dares;
You would flee from brotherhood, a brotherhood for which they died
You are fain to pluck a bud, they mastered all the garden wide.

Nations to this day rehearse the legend of their loyalty
And their truth still stands inscribed upon the scroll of history

~~~

Let the gardener not be downcast to decry the garden's plight
The choking weeds and brambles will vanish out of sight
Soon the starlight of the blossoms shall the naked boughs adorn
And where the martyrs shed their lifeblood crimson roses will be born

Look upon the deep vermilions flooding the eastern skies
It is your horizon, glowing to behold your sun arise.

~~~

Your are like the scent imprisoned in a bud; yourself release!
Load your pack upon your shoulder, fan the meadow with your breeze
To a mighty desert let your insubstantial mote increase
From a murmuring wave become the roaring tempest of the seas.

With the power of love triumphant life the lowly from their shame
Light the world, too long in darkness, with Muhammad's radiant name.

~~~

In the sea's caressing billows, in the savage storm no less
In the cities of far China, Morocco's wilderness
In the Prairie, in the mountains, in the valley, in the field
In the faith of every Muslim is the mystery concealed

Let the eyes of the people till the very end of time
Testify to the great wonder, '*We have made your name sublime*'

~~~

You have Reason for your buckler, and your sword is Love Divine
'God is Greatest' – All but God consume with your bright flame shine
So accoutred, my brave dervish, seize the world beneath your sway
You are a Muslim and Destiny your edict must obey
Be faithful to Muhammad, and We yield Ourself to you
Not this world alone – the Tablet and the Pen shall be your prize too.

(Parts of *Jawab-e-Sikwa* adapted from the translation by A.J. Arberry)

When Iqbal started authoring his masterpieces, the Muslim world had already fallen into turmoil and the last vestige of the Ottomans and the Caliphate was being destroyed. A Pan-Islamic reaction was natural in him. But this reaction in his writings was more a certitude to the Muslim glory, rather then a precipitation into any empire building. He wanted an enlightened Muslim society that belonged to the confederation of the world. His notion was not exclusive of other philosophies; rather he suggested an inclusive model, whereby the Muslims would come to terms with the new and modern world and would be in the forefront to contribute as they had done in the past.

In his *'The Reconstruction of Religious Thought in Islam'* Iqbal deals with philosophic viewpoints based on Islamic traditional philosophy in the light of the contemporary world. He wanders through the ideas of many great philosophers and scientists - Ghazzali, Rumi, Kant, Einstein, Nietzsche, Descartes, Hegel and others - analysing with ease, supporting some and criticising others and applying the Quranic verses and works of true Sufis that points to, defines and corrects these divergences. Sufism to Iqbal was a powerful force in philosophy and not *devoid* of science but was supra-science. 'The more genuine schools of Sufism have, no doubt, done good work in shaping and directing the evolution of religious experience in Islam; but their latter-day representatives, owing to their ignorance of the modern mind, have become absolutely incapable of receiving any fresh inspiration from modern thought and experience.'

In the relationship between religion and philosophy, Iqbal continues, 'Philosophy, no doubt, has jurisdiction to judge religion, but what is to be judged is of such a nature that it will not submit to jurisdiction except on its own term.'

He had common praise and criticism of Ghazzali and Kant. 'It cannot, however, be denied that Ghazzali's mission was almost apostolic like that of Kant in Germany of the 18th century. In Germany, rationalism appeared as an ally of religion, but she soon realised that the dogmatic side of religion was incapable of demonstration. The only course open to her was to eliminate dogma from the sacred record. With the elimination of dogma came the utilitarian view of morality, and thus rationalism completed the reign of unbelief. Such was the state of theological thought in Germany when Kant appeared. His *Critique of Pure Reason* revealed the limitations of human reason and reduced the whole work of the rationalists to a heap of ruins. And justly has he been described as God's greatest gift to his country. Ghazzali's philosophical scepticism which, however, went a little too far, virtually did the same kind of work in the world of Islam in breaking the back of that proud but shallow rationalism which moved in the same direction as pre-Kantian rationalism in Germany. There is, however, one important difference between Ghazzali and Kant. Kant, consistently with his principles, could not affirm the possibility of a knowledge of God. Ghazzali's, finding no hope in analytic thought, moved to mystic experience, and there found an independent content for religion. In this way he succeeded in securing for religion the right to exist independently of science and metaphysics. But the revelation of the total Infinite in mystic experience convinced him of the finitude and inconclusiveness of thought and drove him to draw a line of cleavage between thought and intuition. He failed to see that thought and intuition are organically related and that thought must necessarily simulate finitude and inconclusiveness because of its alliance with serial time. The idea that thought is essentially finite, and for this reason unable to capture the Infinite, is based on a mistaken notion of the movement of thought in knowledge. It is the inadequacy of the logical understanding which finds a multiplicity of mutually repellent individualities with no prospect of their ultimate reduction to a unity that makes us sceptical about the conclusiveness of thought. In fact, the logical understanding is incapable of seeing this multiplicity as a coherent universe. Its only method is generalisation based on resemblances, but its generalisations are only fictitious unities which do not affect the reality of concrete things. In its deeper movement, however, thought is capable of reaching an immanent Infinite in whose self-unfolding movement the various finite concepts are merely moments. In its essential nature, then, thought is not static'.

> Ghazzali and Kant have biographical parallels. Both were brilliant and rose to fame at a relative young age, both gave up their work for a time to pursue epistemic truth and were requested by well wisher's to come back and rejoin their works. After a gestative period both produced master pieces, with Ghazzali writing *Yahya Ulum Al Din* and Kant producing *Critique of Pure Reason,* which in both cases eclipsed, to a great extent, all previous works by other scholars and greatly influence later ones.

To Iqbal, science consists of an incomplete part or sectional view of Reality. 'Natural Science is by nature a sectional view; it cannot, if it is true to its own nature and function, set up its theory as a complete view of Reality.' And thus he finds religion, 'which demands the whole of Reality and for this reason must occupy a central place in any syntheses of all the data of human experiences, has no reason to be afraid of any sectional views of Reality.' Thus religion and science can co-exist as both aim in reaching the most real. He states 'The formulation of the theory of evolution in the world of Islam brought into being Rumi's tremendous enthusiasm for the biological future of man. No cultured Muslim can read such passages as the following without a thrill of joy:

Low in the earth
I lived in realms of ore and stone;
And then I smiled in many-tinted flowers;
Then roving with the wild and wandering hours,
O'er earth and air and ocean's zone,
In a new birth,
I dived and flew,
And crept and ran,
And all the secret of my essence drew
Within a form that brought them all to view -
And lo, a Man!
And then my goal,
Beyond the clouds, beyond the sky,
In realms where none may change or die -
In angel form; and then away
Beyond the bounds of night and day,
And Life and Death, unseen or seen,
Where all that is hath ever been,
As One and Whole.

On the other hand, the formulation of the same view of evolution with far greater precision in Europe has led to the belief that "there now appears to be no scientific basis for the idea that the present rich complexity of human endowment will ever be materially exceeded." That is how the modern man's secret despair hides itself behind the screen of scientific terminology.' Having tackled the issue of evolution, Iqbal next questions reincarnation, 'Nietzsche, although he thought that the idea of evolution did not justify the belief that man was unsurpassable, cannot be regarded as an exception in this respect. His enthusiasm for the future of man ended in the doctrine of eternal recurrence - perhaps the most hopeless idea of immortality ever formed by man. This eternal repetition is not eternal *becoming*; it is the same old idea of *being* masquerading as *becoming*.'

In his last chapter 'Is religion possible' in *'The Reconstruction of Religious Thought in Islam'*, Iqbal reignites Kant's question 'Is Metaphysics possible?' Iqbal was critical of Kant's negative opinion, 'Kant's verdict can be accepted only if we start with the assumption that all experience other than the normal level of experience is impossible. The only question, therefore, is whether the normal level is the only level of knowledge-yielding experience. Kant's view of the thing-in-itself and the thing as it appears to us very much determined the character of his question regarding the possibility of metaphysics. But what if the position, as understood by him, is reversed? The great Muslim Sufi philosopher, Muhyaddin Ibn al-Arabi of Spain, has made the acute observation that God is a percept; the world is a concept. Another Muslim Sufi thinker and poet, Iraqi, insists on the plurality of space-orders and time-orders and speaks of a Divine Time and a Divine Space. It may be that what we call the external world is only an intellectual construction, and that there are other levels of human experience capable of being systematized by other orders of space and time - levels in which concept and analysis do not play the same role as they do in the case of our normal experience.'

In the modern world, as was during the time of Iqbal, there is dominance of rationalism. But many philosophers, and not necessarily Muslims, contend that rational philosophy is not sufficient for the infinite universe. To be rational, Infinity itself is not rational. In 'reality' every thing has a beginning and an end. The acceptance of the supra-rational in Islamic thought gave rise to the third category, the Sufi philosophy which had acted as the early research and development sector of Muslim thought.

But still, the rational philosophy of the West, despite all the criticisms that can be made of its deficiencies, deserves its credits. The glamour, glitz and hegemonic attitude of the West may look anti-Islamic, but the glamour and glitz is just superficial and a by-product of material success which can easily be distanced from, and moral checks and balances applied to the hegemony to improve the model and make it more acceptable. The profundity of the core western values cannot be ignored. As the Muslims took on the thoughts of the Greeks and improved and applied those, the same needs to be done with the current western philosophy. As Muawiah and the Umayyad Muslims took the Persian and Roman monarchic system and applied Islam to it to make a system more modern, one that built a huge empire, so now the Muslims need to accept the workable systems of the West and apply Islam to them and further improve the existing model.

Let there arise out of you a band of people inviting to all that is good,
Enjoining what is right, and forbidding what is wrong
They are the ones to attain felicity. [3:104]

Say, my lord commands justice
And set your whole selves to Him
At every time and place of prayer, and call upon Him
Making your devotion sincere as in His sight
Such as he created you in the beginning
So shall you return [7,29]

For Muslim men and women
for believing men and women,
for devout men and women,
for true men and women,
for men and women who are patient and constant,
for men and women who humble themselves,
for men and women who give in charity,
for men and women who fast (and deny themselves),
for men and women who guard their chastity,
and for men and women who engage much in God's praise,-
for them has God prepared forgiveness and great reward.[33:35]

The Tapestry of Tomorrow

Tomorrow, the differences between humanity will not suddenly disappear. There will remain contending groups. But tomorrow's universality should see the end of the violent conflicts between those groups. All the various groups should live harmoniously and productively. Muslims have a duty to endeavour for such a world. They have done this once before - the peace of Hudaibiah.

To achieve its ends the Muslim world is in crucial need for peace and organisation, even an unjust or one-sided peace like Hudaibiah. It may be psychologically difficult to cultivate such a peace due to the untold sufferance and affront that the Muslims have faced. Even the great Khattab had qualms about the peace treaty of Hudaibiah. But the Muslims used the respite well. They educated themselves turning into very advanced beings of very high morality. Then they went out to the world and explained that the Islam they harboured was not for any select group of people but for the benefit of the entire mankind. The world accepted them.

A Supreme Quest

The quest to improve the self and the world is a duty of all Muslims. When the Prophet set up his borderless state in Madinah, he did not model it on previous old kingdoms, no matter how wealthy or mighty those had been. Madinah appeared humble but it was the most modern and progressive city the world had ever seen. From that enlightened beginning Islam produced the best rulers ruling the best empires. Fighting was still required in those times as the world was still in an 'uncivilised' stage where it was necessary for self defence and so the Muslims also produced the best warriors.

It is time to view and perceive the world from the current perspective. When Makkah fell to the Muslims, the chief act of the Prophet, aside from declaring general amnesty, was to break the idols in the Kaba. What the Prophet was doing was not breaking some statues. He was breaking the inequitable, unfair and incorrect old ideas and systems that the idols represented. Those were the times when mud and stone idols were used to divide people, breed inequalities and oppress people. It was imperative that those be broken. Today idols are no longer pieces of rocks. In the sophisticated world the real idols have also become more sophisticated. These idols are the cause behind racial and gender discriminations, poverty and corruption, illiteracy and ignorance, hedonism and exploitation. It is the duty of Muslims to break these idols now.

Breaking a statue is not a heroic work anymore; any child can do that now. All one needs is to buy a hammer. But to study a thousand books, gather the knowledge therein and harness it into a power that will emancipate the Muslims out of the tribulations of today - that is a hard job, that requires Ijtihad and that is the quest supreme.

Every Muslim, male or female, is a Mujahideen or warrior. They had been the bravest of warriors wielding the sword and as the ages progress they, today have to become the best warriors of knowledge; warriors who fight not with arms and ammunition but with words, deeds and intellect; the academic warrior, the corporate warriors, the media warriors, and all others who are not out to conquer or plunder but to establish truth and a more modern way of life. This war will be tougher than any war ever fought, and will be fought with weapons more potent than weapons of mass destruction. These will be fought and won with weapons of mass construction – knowledge, dedication and humanity. Deliverance of the Muslims is not in violence but is scholarship. The nation that educates its people today, rules tomorrow. And the way to rule a civilised world is by contribution not exploitation.

It is time for every Muslim women and men to take up the *kitab* (book) and the *Qalam* (pen) and start their quest and assist humanity to move forward. The Prophet said, "The ink of the scholar is holier than the blood of a martyr." The warriors of the pen stand, in rank, ahead of the martyrs of the sword. All those who strive in this quest are the *Gazis* or victors. It does not matter when the victory comes or in which generation victory comes, defeat is not an option.

This Quest will change the world like never before. It will seek not to exploit but emancipate humanity. It will establish the true Universal Corporation based on the non-exploitative and anti-riba policies of Islam. Like the Islamic state set up by the Prophet, this corporation will have no borders and no discriminations. Ijtihad or Research and Development will take the Muslim Universities way ahead of all the others as was the case in the past. The quest of the mass media will show that a simple television station propagating truth is more effective than a hundred nuclear bombs. It will establish a media not used as a propaganda machine for brain washing of unsuspecting individuals but only to establish the truth and empower the people. Violence may have been needed for building imperialistic empires of the past, it is not required for building the Empire of Truth.

The Nation of Peace

Islam always is a proponent of constructive powers; destruction is un-Islamic. Islam has come as a blessing and salvation not just for Muslims, but for the entire humanity, in fact, for the entire creation. The role of the Prophet is mentioned in the following verse of the Quran:

And We have not sent you except as a mercy to mankind [21:107]

Islam stands for peace and justice with no prejudice. During the time of the Prophet a debate was going on between the 'People of the Book' and the Muslims. The 'People of the Book' claimed that they were superior as their Prophets had come earlier and their book was the original. The Muslims countered that their book was better as it has superseded all the previous books and their Prophet was in fact the Seal of all Prophets. Then came the revelation:

Neither your desire, nor those of the people of the book can prevail: Whoever does evil will be requited accordingly. Nor will he find, besides God, any protector or helper. If any do deeds of righteousness – be they male or female – and have faith, they will enter Heaven. And not the least injustice will be done to them. [4:123-4]

Muslims are the people, one and all, appointed with the overarching task of unconditionally improving the life of all. Even if others perceive them as 'enemies', Muslims cannot consider anyone as an 'enemy'. No matter how inimical a person or group seems to be, to a Muslim they are all the creation of God Almighty. Now is the time for humanity to take the next step forward where killing of another human being is 'unthought of'. There will remain no enemy, as a human being cannot be an enemy. When Jesus said, 'Love your enemies,' this is precisely what he meant. Violence and conflicts within humanity cannot be resolved by divisive forces but by the application of universality. Islam stands for such universality which is visionary and contends that all people in the world are indifferently good. The Muslim ideal is to build a better world for entire humanity. Islam envisages a pluralistic world and equality in this diversity.

Unto every one of you We have appointed a (different) law and way of life. And if God had so willed, He could surely have made you all one single community; but (He willed it otherwise) in order to test you by means of what He has given you.
Vie, then, with one another in doing good works! Unto God you all must return; and then He will make you truly understand all that on which you were inclined to differ. [5,48]

Does not man see that it is We Who created him from sperm? Yet behold! he stands forth as an open adversary!
And he makes comparisons for Us, and forgets his own origin and creation: He says, "Who can give life to dry bones and decomposed ones at that?"
Say, "He will give them life Who created them in the first place! for He is Well-versed in every kind of creation!
"The same Who produces for you fire out of the green tree, when behold! With that you kindle your own fires!
"Is not He Who created the heavens and the earth able to create the like thereof?"
Yes, indeed! for He is the Creator Supreme, of skill and knowledge infinite!
Indeed, when He intends a thing, His Command is, "be", and it is!
So glory to Him in Whose hands is the dominion of all things:
and to Him will you all be brought back. [36:77-83]

Indeed He will gather you together

on the day of Resurrection,
about which there is no doubt. [4:12]

When the earth is shaken to her utmost convulsion,
And her burdens the earth throws up from within

And man cries distressed: 'What is the matter with her?'
On that day will she declare her tidings,
For that your Lord will have given her inspiration.
On that day will men proceed in companies sorted out,
to be shown the deeds that they had done.
Then shall anyone who has done an atom's weight of good, see it!
And anyone who had done an atom's weight of evil, shall see it. [99:1-8]

A day when men will be like moths scattered about and the mountains like loosened wool
Then he whose balance will be found heavy will be in a life of good pleasure and satisfaction
But he whose balance will be found light will have his home in an abyss
And what will explain to you what that is? - A fire blazing fiercely!

Then, on that day, not a soul will be wronged in the least, and you shall but be repaid the meeds of your past deeds.
Indeed the Companions of the Garden shall that day have joy in all that they do;
They and their associates will be in groves of cool shade,reclining on thrones of dignity;
Every fruit (enjoyment) will be there for them; they shall have whatever they call for;
"Peace!" - a word of salutation from a Lord Most Merciful! [36:54-58]

Epilogue

Is the reward for good other than good? [55:60]

Civilisation has progressed through a dual process. The first process contains aspects of inquiry like rationalism which has led to all scientific research and advancements. This gives humanity the ability to mould and control nature. The second process is behavioural development which includes adaptation of morals and ethics which give the ability to humans to restrict self-centred desires, in other words, it gives humanity the ability to control the self and be an affable part of humanity.

The *control of the forces of nature* gives humanity great powers like nuclear power as an example. The *control over the self* gives humanity the discipline needed to put the power to good use and not to employ it for selfish and destructive reasons that would, ultimately, harm all. If the process of scientific development outstrips the process of moral evolution then humanity is likely to develop powerful weapons and use it against itself. If the process of human moral evolution stays ahead of scientific development then the same forces that were used to develop weapons will be used to develop technology for the benefit of humanity, to remove its pains and to evolve humanity further.

There are many instances of historical times when the cumulative development of human morality has lagged slightly behind scientific development. That is the reason there has been great wars. In the past this moral lagging has caused one human group to inflict great pain on another. But during those periods the weapons had not been powerful enough for it to destroy whole civilisations. Now a scientific threshold has been crossed. The humankind has gained the ability or the explosive power to destroy the whole world, and consequently, destroy humanity. If self-centred desires remain prevalent among the cultures of the world, it *will* cause conflicts. And if conflicts remain, sooner or later the world-destroying forces *will be* employed. Every conflict reaches a stage when the opposing sides do not care anymore of consequences.

The theory of restricting proliferation of weapons without restricting the proliferation of conflicts rising from self-centred desires of the world cultures is but a naïve dream, which may eventually prove to be a nightmare. In the history of humanity no technology could be restricted to any one culture. It will take a nuclear war to stop nuclear proliferation. And even then, it will only temporally delay the proliferation. The world *will* reach a situation, sooner than later, when every nation or even smaller groups will have ability of mass destruction. And every type of conflict has the potential to develop into mutually destructive force once it crosses the *point of moral criticality* when one group starts to think of the other as 'the enemy' and the destruction of whom appears 'justified'. If the hatred and conflict of the present world still remains, the destruction of the world will be inevitable.

In a world of conflicts the weaker will remain 'fanatic' because only irrational fanaticism can give victory from a position of weakness. To remove this trait the more powerful nations will have to lead by example. They will need to stop imposing on smaller nations and let them grow out of their existing fears. The smaller nations will need to develop and feel safe and secure. The current political trend is totally opposite to that. The choice, now, is between the accomplishment of this seemingly difficult task of higher moral development or large scale destruction in a not distant future.

None of the world philosophies, cultures or religions hankers for war. It is the existence of financial greed and selfishness in certain groups that leads to conflicts. It is more *rational* to remove the exploitation prevailing in the world that causes hatred and conflicts. If a scientific threshold has been crossed, then the moral threshold of human harmony also needs to be crossed to maintain the balance. This will evolve humanity to the next higher plane of existence.

Jesus and his Disciples have proven that it is possible to reach a higher plane in one lifetime. In a barbarous, exploitative and imperial world they have waged a war of love, humility and morality. They had reached out to the people and the people of the world had accepted them in spite of vicious and bestial imperial attempts to stop them. It is time to lead a similar movement to fight all the corruption and exploitation besieging the current world. With most of the political and religious institutions now on the side of world economic powers, there is a lack of political will to openly support this endeavour. Thus, it is up to the Muslims to launch this movement of love and humility – The second coming of Jesus.

By the start of the 21st century, except for the Muslims, all the ancient civilisations like China and India have started to assert their international presence, authority and control along with the West. Historically, Muslims have faced international disorder and have relegated from the top of the civilised world. At the end of the Ummayad-Abbasid era the Muslims were totally fragmented, defeated and passed through more than two centuries of chaos. But they recovered, sometimes through a painful process, and re-established themselves as global authorities in the form of the Ottomans, Saffavids, Moghuls, etc. The current period is another stage of rebuilding like the one that had existed between the Abbasid and Ottomans. Despite the condition of Muslim political entities, the Muslim individual and thus the Muslim Ummah is more enlightened today than a few decades ago.

And so, in the Muslim consciousness, there is an incredibly strong desire to re-establish itself among the nations of the world again. There is also a latent anger due to the injustice and humiliation they had to face in recent times. On the other hand, there also remains a degree of fear in the thinking of some non-Muslims regarding the development and resurgence of Muslims. This anger and fear both need to be diffused and discarded. It has to be understood by all sides that the development of Muslims will also benefit and progress the whole world, as it had in the past. The words of Islam are powerful, progressive, just and enterprising enough to negate the necessity of violence. And, as a proof, all contemporary areas of Muslim conflicts have resulted from defence of themselves rather then due to encroachment on others.

As for the Muslims themselves, multifarious ideas have cropped up as to how to re-establish themselves. The arbiter between these ideas can only be the Quran and Sunnah. And the Quran has always advised for a peaceful balanced development. Scientific, economic, and rational growth must be balanced with growth in morality and spirituality. The rational philosophy of Ibn Rushd and the moral spirituality of Al Ghazzali has developed in geographical separate regions. It is time to put the two together in correct context and balance so that one will develop humanity and the other guide it. Both are aspects of knowledge and both need to be constantly developed with the unswerving dedication of Ibn Taimiyyah.

For the individual and the society this means a constant quest for knowledge. Islam envisages that every day every individual - woman or man, young or old - should have more knowledge than the previous day.

There shall be no more prophets. From now on humanity must find its own way. There is no alternative to this quest. Thus, the vision for humanity can be summed up to a single statement:

Read, in the name of your Lord!

Acknowledgement

The wondrous achievements of great Muslim scholars and intellectuals have been hidden behind a veil of ignorance and political intrigue. A few modern scholars, both Muslims and Non-Muslims, continue to strive for that historical truth. Some of them are referred to in this work, and my acknowledgement is to them.

Though this book contains a lot of reference to religious matter, it is not a book of religion. That is in the jurisdiction of the Ulema who spend their lifetime - studying and researching - in pursuit of religion. This is more a look at the flow of knowledge through time and the effect that Islam had on that flow.

This book has also been an attempt to rationalise. Some of the interpretations in it may be unintentionally inaccurate and may contradict with the views of the Ulema. I acknowledge this book does not have the authority to challenge the Ulema, for, if viewed in a dispassionate way, there is nothing rational about life and death. They, the Ulema, bow to no rational or worldly authority. They say *Allahu alam* – God knows best – and they are sound.

References and Bibliography

- Ahmad, Aziz. 1975: A History of Islamic Sicily. Ediburgh university Press. Edinburg.
- Ahmad, K. Jamil, 1984: Hundred Great Muslims. Ferojsons Pvt. Ltd. Lahore.
- Ahmed, M. Mukarram. 2005: Encyclopedia of Islam. Anmor, New Delhi.
- Ajijola, A.D. 1998: What is Sharia. Adam Publishers and Distributers, Dehli. Abu Zahra, Muhammad. 2005: The Four Imams. Translated by Aisha Bewley. Dar Al Taqwa ltd. London.
- Al Alim, 2005: Hadith of Muhammad Ibn Ismail Al Bukari, Multimedia Edition, ISL Corporation, USA.
- Al Ashanti, AbdulHaq and Bowes, Abdur Rahman. 2005: Before Nicea.The early followers of Jesus. JamaihMedia. UK.
- Al Hassani, Salim T S. 2007: 1001 Inventions. Muslim Heritage in Our World. Foundation for Science Technology and Civilasation. Manchester, UK.
- Al- Sharif , Mohammad Mahdi, 2001: Ibn Ishaq – Ibn Hesham 's *Seeratun Nabi*, Dar Al-Kotob Al-ilmiyay, Bierut.
- Atkinson, James. 1836: Laili and Majnun. A.J.Valpy M.A (Publisher to the Oriental Translation Fund &c.) London.
- Azami, Rashad Ahmad. 2003: Stories of the Prophets by Ibn Kathir (1301–1373). 2nd edition. Darrusalam, Riyadh.
- Barks, Coleman. 1997: The Essential Rumi. Castle Books, New Jersey, USA.
- Barnett, Mary. 1996: Gods and Myths of Ancient Greece. Universal International. Australia.
- Bhowmik, Rita. 2002: Chotoder Begum Rokeya. Meera Prokason (Publications), Dhaka Bangladesh.
- Blanchard, O. and Sheen, J, 2009: Macroeconomics.
- Bloom, J. M. and Blair, Sheila. 2002: Islam: A Thousand Years of Faith and Power. Yale University Press, USA
- Briant, P. 2005: The History of the Persian Empire. In: Forgotten Empire – The World of Ancient Persians. Editors: John Curtis and Nigel Tallis. University of California Press with the British Museum. USA.
- Briffault, R. 1928: The Making of Humanity. George Allen, London, UK.
- Bringmann, K. 2007: The History of the Roman Republic. Translated by W.J.Smith. Polity Press, UK.

- Brosius, M. 2006: The Persian - An Introduction. Routledge, USA.
- Brunschwig, J and Lloyd, G.E.R., 2000: Greek Thought. The Belknap Press of Harvard University Press.USA.
- Bucaille, Maurice. 1995: The Bible, the Qur'an and Science. (translated from French 'La Bilble, le Coran et la Science' by A. D. Pannell and author). Millat Book Centre, New Delhi.
- Burket, Walter, 1985: Greek Religion. Harvard University Press, Cambridge.
- Burkert, Walter, 1987. Oriental and Greek Mythology. The meetings of Parallels. In: Interpretations of Greek Mythology by Jan Bremmer. Croom Helm Ltd. Australia
- Clarence-Smith, W.G. 2006: Islam and the abolition of Slavery. Oxford University Press. Oxford.
- Clarke, A. 1995: The History of the Khalifas (original written in 15th Century by Jalal ad Din As Suyuti). Translated by Abdassamad Clarke. Ta Ha Publishers London.
- Clark, Peter. 1998: Zoroastrianism. An Introduction to an Ancient Faith, Sussex Academic Press, UK.
- Cleaver, Tony. 2006: Economics: the basics. Routledge, New York.
- Cohen, Mark. R. 1994: Under Crescent and Cross: The Jews in the Middle Ages. Princenton University Press. Princeton, New Jersey.
- Cottrell, L. 1958: The anvil of civilisation: an outline of the birth development and inter-relationship of the ancient civilisations of Western Asia and the Mediterranean, 4000- 400B.C. Faber, London.
- Curatola, Giovanni. 2007: The art and architecture of Mesopotamia. New York : Abbeville ; Enfield : Publishers Group UK [distributor]
- Curl, J. S. 1999: A dictionary of architecture. Oxford University Press, N.Y.
- Curtis, J. and Tallis, N. 2005: Forgotten Empire – The World of Ancient Persians. University of California Press with the British Museum. USA.
- Doi, A.R.I 2002: Sharia - The Islamic Law. Percetakan Zafar Sdn. Bhd. Kaula Lumpur.
- Donner, Fred McGraw. 1981: The Early Islamic Conquests. Princeton University Press. Princeton, New Jersey.
- Einhard, 1960: The life of Charlemagne. Translated by Samuel Epes Turner. University of Michigan Press. Michigan.
- Eliot, Alexander. 1990: The Universal Myths – Heroes, Gods, Tricksters and Others. Truman Talley Books / Meridian. New York.
- Esposito, John L. 1999: The Oxford History of Islam. Oxford University Press. New York.
- Fagan, M. 1998: People of the Earth. An introduction to Prehistory. 9th Edition. Longman, N.Y.

- Fakry, Majid. 2001: Averroes (Ibn Rushd): His life, Works and influence. Oneworld. Oxford.
- Ferdowsi, Abolqasem: 2006. Shahnameh: Persian Book of kings. Trans. Dick Davies. Viking Penguin. New York.
- Gascoigne, Bamber, 2003: Christianity. Constable and Robinson Ltd, UK.
- Gelpe, R. 1966: The Story of Layla and Majnun. Bruno Cassirer (Publishers) Ltd. UK.
- George, Andrew. 1999: The Epic of Gilgamesh. Penguin Classics. London
- Green, Roger L. 2004: Tales of Ancient Egypt. Puffin Classics. UK.
- Grene, David. 1987: Herodotus The History. The University of Chicago Press, Chicago.
- Grenville, J.A.S. 1994: The Collins History of the World in the Twentieth Century. Harper Collins Publishers. London.
- Grimal, Nicolas 1992: A History of Ancient Egypt. Blackwell Publishing, UK.
- Hall, M.H. 2007: A History of Archaic Greek World. Blackwell Publishing, Australia.
- Hamilton, Edith. 1969: Mythology. NAL Penguin, USA.
- Haq, S.M. 2002: Kitab Al Tabaqat Al Kabir (Original written in 9th century by Ibn Saad). Volume 1. Translated by S. M Haq. Kitab Bhaban, New Delhi.
- Hart, Michael H. 2008: The 100: A Ranking of the Most Influential Persons in History. Golden Books Centre SDN.BHD. Selangor Darul Ehsan, Malaysia.
- Harvey, A and Hanut, E. 1999: Perfume of the Desert. The Theosophical Publishing House. Wheaton, Illinois, USA.
- Hasan, Professor Masudul. 2000: Hadrat Uthman Gani.2nd Edition. Kitab Bhaban, New Delhi.
- Hasan, Masudul: 1997: Hadrat Abu Bakr Sidique, Kitab Bhavan, New Delhi.
- Hasan, Masudul. 1998: Hadrat Ali Murtada, Kitab Bhavan, New Delhi.
- Hasan, Masudul. 2001: Hadrat Umar Farooq. 2nd Edition, Kitab Bhavan, New Delhi.
- Hasan, Masudul. 2004: History of Islam. Vol I. Revised edition. Adam Publishers, New Delhi
- Hasan, Masudul, 2005: History of Islam. Vol II. Revised edition. Adam Publishers, New Delhi.
- Hawkins, T.D. 1982: The Neo-Hittite States in Syria and Anatolia. In: The Cambridge Ancient History III, Part I. Ed. Boardman, John et al. Cambridge University Press. Cambridge.
- Hitti, P K, 1970: History of the Arabs. 10th Edition, Macmillan and St Martin's Press, London, UK.
- Holmes, George. 1988: The Oxford illustrated History of Medieval Europe, The Oxford University press. Oxford.

- Humbert, J-M and Price, Clifford. 2003: Imhotep Today – Egyptinizing Architecture. Cavendish Publishing, Australia.
- Ibn Hashem. 2001: The Prophets Biography. (original written in the 9th century). Translated by Mohammad Mahdi Al Sharif. Dar Al Kotob Al Ilmiyah, Bierut.
- Ibn Khaldun. 1969: The Muqaddimah:An Introduction to History. Trans. Franz Rosenthal. Princeton University Press. New Jersey
- Ibn Saad. 2002: Kitab Al Tabaqat Al Kabir (Original written in 9th century). Volume 1. Translated by S. M Haq. Kitab Bhaban, New Delhi.
- Ibn Al Arabi, Qadi Abu. 1995: Bakr Defense Against Disaster (original written in 12th century. Edition by Al Murabit, Shykh Abdalqadir) Madinah Press Cape Town
- Imdadullah, M.N.M. 2006: Yahya Ulum Al Din of Iman Ghazzali (6th Bengali Edition). Vol 1 – V. Bangladesh Taj Co. Ltd. Dhaka
- Imdadullah, M.N.M. 1995: Kasasul Ambiya (Story of the Prophets, 4th Bengali Edition) Vol 1-2. Bangladesh Taj Co. Ltd. Dhaka.
- Iqbal, Mohammad. 2003: The Reconstructin of religious thought in Islam. 8th edition. Kitab Bhavan, New Delhi.
- Jami, Nuruddin Abdurrahman. 1906: Lawaih. Translated by E. H. Whinfield and Mirza Muhammad Kazvini. Royal Asiatic Society, London.
- Jeffery, L.H. 1982: The Cambridge Ancient History III, Part I. Ed. Boardman, John et al. Cambridge University Press. Cambridge.
- Kegley, C. W. and Wittkopf, W.R. 1993: World Politics Trend and Transformation. Fourth Edition. St. Martin's Press, New York.
- Khudabakhsh, S and Margoliouth, D.S. 1996 : The Renaissance of Islam. (Translation of *Renaissance des Islam,* 1922 by Adam Nez) Bangladesh co-operative book society. Chittagong.
- Khuda Buksh, S. (Khudabakhsh, S) 1927 Studies: Indian and Islamic. Trubner's Oriental Series. Kegan Paul, Trench , Trubner & Co Ltd. Reprinted 2001 by Routledge, London.
- Ebrahim, M. 2005: Shamaa –il Tirmizi. (By Shayk Al Hadith M. Z Kandhlawi, 14th century) Translated by Muhammad bin Adburrahmaan Ebrahim. Adam Publishers and Distributors, New Delhi.
- Qadwa, M.M. 2004: The Differences of the Imams. (By Shayk Al Hadith M.Z. Kandhlawi. 14th century). Translated by Mawlana Muhammad Qadwa. White Thread Press. California.
- Kemp, Barry J. 2006: Ancient Egypt – Anatomy of a Civilisation.2nd Edition. Routledge, USA.
- King, P. J. 2004: One Hundred Philosophers. ABC Books, Australia.
- Khawaja, A.A. 2002: Maulana Ashraf Ali Thanvi – His views on Moral Philosophy and Tasawwuf. Adam Publishers and Distributors, Delhi.

- Lapidus, I. M. 2002: A History of Islamic Societies. 2nd Edition. Cambridge University Press. Cambridge.
- Legrain, P. 2010: Reshaping the Economy after the Crisis Aftershock. Little, Brown. London.
- Littleton, C.S. 2002: Mythology. Duncan Baird Publishers, California.
- Longford, Lord. 1974: The life of Jesus Christ. Sidgwick & Jackson. UK.
- Luqman, Nagy. 2008: Islamic History. Goodward Books Pvt. Ltd, New Delhi.
- Michaelson, Carol, 1996. Ancient China. Allen & Unwin Pty Ltd. Australia.
- Monk, Ray and Raphael, Frederic. 2001: The Great Philosophers. Phoenix. UK.
- Morenz, Ludwig D. 2003: Literature as a reconstruction of the past in the Middle Kingdom. In: Never had the like Occurred, Egyptian view of its past. Ed. John Tait. Cavendish Publishing, UK.
- Murray, T, 1999: Encyclopedia of Archaeology. The Great Archaeologists. ABC-CLIO Inc, California.
- Newton, Isaac. 1728: The Chronology of Ancient Kingdoms Amended. J. Tonson and J.Osborne and T. Longman, London.
- Nicolle, David. 2008: The Ottomans Empire of Faith. Alto Books Pty. Ltd. Victoria, Australia.
- Nicholson, R. A. 2002: The Mystics of Islam. World Vision Inc. Bloomington, Indiana, USA.
- Lings, Martin, 2005: Muhammad, his life based on earliest sources, Millat Book Centre, India
- Philips, A.A. Bilal. 1990: The evolution of Fiqh. Tawheed Publications, Riyadh.
- Pollock, S. 1999: Ancient Mesopotamia. Cambridge University Press. UK.
- Pomeroy, S.B. et al. 1999: Ancient Greece. Oxford University Press. UK.
- Purvis, Andrea. 2007: The Landmark of Herodotus. Pantheon Books, New York.
- Qureshi, Sultan Ahmed. 1997: Letters of the Holy Prophet. Islamic Book Services, New Delhi
- Raheem, M.R.M.Abdur. 1988: Muhammad the Prophet, Pustaka Nasional PTE LTD, Singapore
- Roberts, J.M. 1997: A History of Europe. Allen Lane The Penguin Press, USA.
- Rodrik, D. 1995: Getting Interventions Right: How South Korea and Taiwan grew rich. Journal of Economic Policy 20.
- Sarton, G. 1927: Introduction to the History of Science. Vol 1-3.The Carnegie Institution, Washington. USA.
- Schacht, Joseph. 1950: The Origins of Muhammadan Jurisprudence. Oxford:Clarendon Pr. UK

- Scott, S. P. 1904: History of the Moorish Empire in Europe. Vols 1-3. J. B. Lippincott Company. London, UK.
- Sharif, M.M. 2001: A History of Muslim Philosophy. Vol I & II. Adam Publishers and distributors, Delhi.
- Shaw, Ian and Nicholson, P. T. 1995: British Museum Dictionary of Ancient Egypt, British Museum Press, London.
- Smith, Margaret. 1944: Al Ghazzali the Mystic. Kazi Publication, Lahore.
- Suter, Keith. 2005: 50 Things You Wanted to Know about world Issues... Bantam, Sydney.
- Tait, John. 2003: Never had the like Occurred, Egyptian view of its past. Cavendish Publishing, UK.
- Tingay, G.I.F. and Badcock, J. 1989: These were the Romans. 2nd Ed. Dufour Ediftions Inc., Penn. USA.
- Usmani, M. T. 2001: The text of the historic judgement on Riba, 23 Dec. 1999. The Other Press, Malaysia.
- Walker, P. 1992: The Political Implications of al-Razi's Philosophy", in The Political Aspects of Islamic Philosophy. Edited by C. Butterworth. Cambridge, MA: Harvard University Press, 61-94.
- Williams, H.S.901904, The Historians History of the World. The Outlook Company.UK.
- Wood, Michael. 2007: India. Basic Books, New York.
- Yahya, Harun. 2008. Atlas of Creation. Translated by: Carl Nino Rossini / Ronald Evans Edited by: Timothy Mossman. Global Publishing, Ankara.
- Zaydan, Jurji. 1994: History of the Islamic Civilisation. Translated by: Margoliouth, D.S. and Litt, D. Third Edition, Kitab Bhavan, New Delhi.

Web Resources:

- WR1, July 2009. Origin of the Greek Gods: http://www.argyrosargyrou.fsnet.co.uk/Myths4.htm,
- WR2, Sept 2009. Andalusian poetry: http://www.islamicspain.tv/Arts-and-Science/andalusi_poetry.htm **Unity Productions Foundation,** Potomac Falls, VA , USA
- WR3, Sept 2009. Sufi Poetry,http://wahiduddin.net/sufi/sufi_poetry.htm
- WR4, Sept 2009. Muslim Heritage http://muslimheritage.com/
- WR5, Sept 2009 http://www.newworldencyclopedia.org/entry/Gilgamesh,_Epic_of
- WR6, Nov 2009 UNESCO: http://whc.unesco.org/en/tentativelists/5325/
- WR7, Dec 2009 Watt, Montgomery 2004. Biruni and the study of non-Islamic Religions: http://www.fravahr.org/spip.php?article31
- WR8, May 2010. Towards Understanding Nazrul. http://www.nazrul.org works_on_nazrul/articles/farooq_rebel.htm
- WR9, March 2011. Witness-Pioneer. http://www.witness-pioneer.org/vil/Books MB_BQS/14quran.htm